Lecture Notes in Artificial Intelligence 8916

Subseries of Lecture Notes in Computer Science

LNAI Series Editors

Randy Goebel
University of Alberta, Edmonton, Canada
Yuzuru Tanaka
Hokkaido University, Sapporo, Japan
Wolfgang Wahlster
DFKI and Saarland University, Saarbrücken, (

LNAI Founding Series Editor

Joerg Siekmann
DFKI and Saarland University, Saarbrücken, Germany

Shin-Ming Cheng   Min-Yuh Day (Eds.)

Technologies and Applications of Artificial Intelligence

19th International Conference, TAAI 2014
Taipei, Taiwan, November 21-23, 2014
Proceedings

Springer

Volume Editors

Shin-Ming Cheng
National Taiwan University of Science and Technology
Department of Computer Science and Information Engineering
No. 43, Sec. 4, Keelung Rd., Da'an Dist. Taipei City, 106, Taiwan
E-mail: smcheng@mail.ntust.edu.tw

Min-Yuh Day
Tamkang University
Department of Information Management
No. 151, Yingzhuan Rd., Danshui Dist., New Taipei City 25137, Taiwan
E-mail: myday@mail.tku.edu.tw

ISSN 0302-9743   e-ISSN 1611-3349
ISBN 978-3-319-13986-9   e-ISBN 978-3-319-13987-6
DOI 10.1007/978-3-319-13987-6
Springer Cham Heidelberg New York Dordrecht London

Library of Congress Control Number: 2014956367

LNCS Sublibrary: SL 7 – Artificial Intelligence

Typesetting: Camera-ready by author, data conversion by Scientific Publishing Services, Chennai, India

Printed on acid-free paper

Springer is part of Springer Science+Business Media (www.springer.com)

Preface

The Conference on Technologies and Applications of Artificial Intelligence (TAAI) entered its 19th year, 5 years after its internationalization in 2010. TAAI 2014, held during November 21–23, known as the biggest AI academic event in Taiwan, was organized by the National Taiwan University of Science and Technology.

TAAI 2014 gathered participants from universities, research institutes, and industry together to present, discuss, and address the cutting edge of technologies and applications in AI. The conference provides an international platform for the sharing of original research results and practical development experiences among researchers and application developers from the many AI-related areas including machine learning, data mining, statistics, computer version, Web intelligence, information retrieval, and computer games.

This year the conference was fortunate to have six keynote speeches, a panel discussion, an international track with two invited sessions organized by the Institute of Statistical Science, Academia Sinica, one international workshop, a domestic track, demonstrations of intelligent multimedia systems with human interactions, computer game tournaments, a poster session, and a special exhibition of research results from the Intelligence Computing Area of the Ministry from Science and Technology.

We thank Prof. Sarit Kraus (Israel), Prof. Lichen Fu (Taiwan), Prof. Chunnan Hsu (USA), Dr. Wei-Ying Ma (China), Prof. Mark Schmidt (Canada), and Prof. Masahiko Inami (Japan) for their keynote speeches at TAAI 2014. The conference also featured insightful panel discussions on the latest research areas and topics in AI. Prof. Shou-de Lin chaired the panel discussion on industrial opportunities for AI people with the following panelists: Dr. Wei-Ying Ma from MSRA, Dr. Edward Chang from HTC Inc., Dr. Peter Wu from ASUS Cloud Corporation, Dr. Chih-Han Yu from Appier, and Prof. Chih-Jen Lin from NTU. We thank them.

This year the international Program Committees were formed by 82 researchers. We received 93 submissions to the international track, domestic track, and international workshops. Submissions to the international track received more than three reviews on average, and 35 papers are published in the conference proceedings, including 23 regular and, four short presentations at the conference as well as eight workshop papers. We are grateful to Springer for publishing these selected papers in the prestigious *Lecture Notes in Artificial Intelligence* series. The publication chair, Prof. Shin-Ming Cheng, completely devoted himself to ensure that all camera-ready versions were submitted in a timely and error-free manner. It is one of the important requirements for having high-quality conference proceedings. We must thank all the authors who submitted their excellent research work to TAAI 2014. We owe a great debt to all

Program Committee members for undertaking the reviewing in a timely manner. Their contribution helped TAAI 2014 be a high-quality international conference.

The local arrangements chair, Prof. Kai-Lung Hua, the Taiwanese Association for Artificial Intelligence assistant Miss Siao-Nong Chen, and Miss Ya-Lin Shao provided all the support needed for a successful conference. Needless to say, there are still many colleagues and friends who helped us in immeasurable ways. We are also grateful to them all.

Last but not the least, we would like to thank the following leading-edge organizations, and government agencies, whose generous support contributed to the success of TAAI 2014: National Taiwan University of Technologies, Taiwanese Association for Artificial Intelligence, ACM Taipei, Ministry of Science and Technology, Research Center for Information Technology Innovation Academic Sinica, National Taiwan University, Intel-NTU CCC Center and Ministry of Education. The industrial sponsors were Bridgewell Inc. and Vpon Inc. Their involvement in TAAI 2014 and their support of the conference is especially appreciated and demonstrates their commitment to the future of AI.

November 2014

Jane Yung-Jen Hsu
Yuh-Jye Lee
Hsing-Kuo Pao
Hsuan-Tien Lin
Hui-Huang Hsu
Tzong-Han Tsai
Chuan-Kang Ting

Organization

Program Committee

Bao Rong Chang	National University of Kaohsiung, Taiwan
Chia-Hui Chang	National Central University, Taiwan
Ching-Lueh Chang	Yuan Ze University, Taoyuan, Taiwan
Chuan-Hsiung Chang	Institute of Biomedical Informatics, National Yang Ming University, Taiwan
Ee-Chien Chang	Naional University of Singapore
Kuang-Yu Chang	
Xiaojun Chang	Northwest University
Berlin Chen	National Taiwan Normal University, Taiwan
Bo-Nian Chen	Institute for Information Industry
Chi-Yuan Chen	NIU
Chun-Hao Chen	Tamkang University, Taiwan
Ho-Lin Chen	
Hwann-Tzong Chen	National Tsing Hua University, Taiwan
Jr-Chang Chen	Chung Yuan Christian University, Taiwan
Jrchang Chen	Chung Yuan Christian University, Taiwan
Kuan-Ta Chen	Academia Sinica, Taiwan
Ling-Jyh Chen	Academia Sinica, Taiwan
Rung Ching Chen	Chaoyang University of Technology, Taiwan
Shang-Tse Chen	Georgia Institute of Technology, Taiwan
Sheng-Wei Chen	Academia Sinica, Taiwan
Shih-Hsin Chen	
Yi-Shin Chen	National Tsing Hua University, Taiwan
Ying-Ping Chen	National Chiao Tung University, Taiwan
Hsu-Yung Cheng	National Central University, Taiwan
Shin-Ming Cheng	National Taiwan University of Science and Technology
Wen-Huang Cheng	Academia Sinica, Taiwan
Chao-Kai Chiang	University of Leoben
Chuan-Wen Chiang	National Kaohsiung First University of Science and Technology, Taiwan
I-Jen Chiang	Graduate Institute of Biomedical Informatics, Taipei Medical University, Taiwan
Tsung-Che Chiang	National Taiwan Normal University
Been-Chian Chien	National University of Tainan, Taiwan

Chun-Wei Lin	Harbin Institute of Technology Shenzhen Graduate School, China
Grace Lin	Institute for Information Industry
Hsuan-Tien Lin	National Taiwan University, Taiwan
Hwei Jen Lin	Tamkang University, Taiwan
Jerry Chun-Wei Lin	Harbin Institute of Technology Shenzhen Graduate School, China
Koong Lin	National University of Tainan, Taiwan
Shou-De Lin	National Taiwan University, Taiwan
Shun-Shii Lin	National Taiwan Normal University, Taiwan
Wen-Yang Lin	National University of Kaohsiung, Taiwan
Yen-Yu Lin	Academia Sinica, Taiwan
Chao-Lin Liu	National Chengchi University, Taiwan
Rey-Long Liu	Tzu Chi University, Taiwan
Ching-Hu Lu	Yuan Ze University, Taiwan
Zhiyong Lu	National Center for Biotechnology Information, National Institutes of Health, USA
Mitsunori Matsushita	Kansai University, Japan
Jia-Yu Pan	Google, Inc.
Hsing-Kuo Kenneth Pao	National Taiwan University of Science and Technology, Taiwan
Pradeep Kumar Ray	School of Information Systems, Technology and Management, University of New South Wales, Australia
Man-Kwan Shan	National Chengchi University, Taiwan
Yasuyuki Shirai	JST-ERATO MINATO Discrete Structure Manipulation System Project
Chih-Hua Hana Tai	National Taipei University, Taiwan
Asufumi Takama	Tokyo Metropolitan University, Japan
Chuan-Kang Ting	CCU
Chun-Wei Tsai	NIU
Ming-Feng Tsai	National Chengchi University, Taiwan
Richard Tzong-Han Tsai	National Central University
Yu Tsao	Research Center for Information Technology Innovation (CITI) at Academia Sinica, Taiwan
Hao-Chuan Wang	National Tsing Hua University, Taiwan
Jenq-Haur Wang	National Taipei University of Technology, Taiwan
Ju-Chiang Wang	National Taiwan University, Taiwan
Leon Wang	National University of Kaohsiung, Taiwan
Yu-Chiang Frank Wang	Academia Sinica, Taiwan

Chih-Hsuan Wei	National Center for Biotechnology Information, National Institutes of Health, USA
Paul Weng	LIP6
Sai-Keung Wong	National Chiao Tung University, Taiwan
Wing-Kwong Wong	National Yunlin University of Science & Technology, Taiwan
Brandon Shan-Hung Wu	National Tsing Hua University, China
Chih-Hung Wu	National University of Kaohsiung, Taiwan
Ic Wu	National Chiao Tung University, Taiwan
Jiann-Ming Wu	
Shih-Hung Wu	Chaoyang University of Technology, Taiwan
Yi-Leh Wu	National Taiwan University of Science and Technology, Taiwan
Cheng-Zen Yang	Yuan Ze University, Taiwan
De-Nian Yang	Academia Sinica, Taiwan
Mi-Yen Yeh	Institute of Information Science, Academia Sinica, Taiwan
Yi-Ren Yeh	Chinese Culture University
Shi-Jim Yen	National Dong Hwa University, Taiwan
Show-Jane Yen	Ming Chuan University, Taiwan
Chih-Wei Yi	National Chiao Tung University, Taiwan
Daisaku Yokoyama	The University of Tokyo, Japan
Hsiang-Fu Yu	
Zhi-Hui Zhan	Sun Yat-sen University, China
Jun Zhang	
Min-Ling Zhang	Southeast University
	Ming Chuan University, Taiwan

Additional Reviewers

Chang, Yung-Chun	Lien, I-Chan
Gobbel, Glenn	Liu, Shaowu
Groza, Tudor	Shih, Meng Jung
Ho, Yao-Hua	Stubbs, Amber
Hur, Junguk	Tsai, Ming-Lun
Jonnagaddala, Jitendra	Tsai, Yi-Lin
Lai, Po-Ting	Wang, Yu-Chun
Li, Qian	Wu, Chia-Chi
Liao, Xin-Lan	Zhang, Chuan-Bin

Table of Contents

Age and Gender Estimation Using Shifting and Re-scaling of Local Regions

Nawwar Ali, Chi-Fu Lin, Yuh-Shen Hsiung, Yun-Che Tsai, and Chiou-Shann Fuh

Department of Computer Science and Information Engineering,
National Taiwan University, Taipei 10617, Taiwan (R.O.C)
{nawwar.ali.j,daky1983,bear8039,jpm9ie8c}@gmail.com,
fuh@csie.ntu.edu.tw

Abstract. A method for estimating age and gender using multiple local patches is proposed in this thesis. We use the histogram of rotation-invariant local binary pattern as our features to train the SVM model. We further introduce the shifting and scaling of the local patches to enhance the accuracy of the estimation. Our proposed method not only provides accurate results but also can be incorporated with other methods to further improve their accuracy.

Keywords: Age and Gender Estimation, Local Invariant Local binary patterns, Support Vector Regression, Haar Cascades, integral image, Supervised Descent Method.

1   Introduction

Age and gender estimation is an important research topic in computer vision today; it could be hard for humans to estimate the age and gender correctly, and automating the process could offer many advantages. Age and gender estimation is to label a face image automatically with the correct gender and the exact age or the age group of the individual face.

Age estimation in humans is an ability that is developed early in life and it can be fairly accurate. However it is usually more accurate in the estimator's own kind, i.e. if you try to estimate somebody's age who is in your own age group and race and shares with you the same gender you achieve better accuracy than other people. Humans could use some other factors other than the face to estimate the age, such as the overall posture, hair color, and facial hair.

Some of the applications for such system would be to limit access for services to users of a certain age; such as the sale of alcohol or tobacco or access to certain website, or it could be used to retrieve photos of yourself when you were a certain age. It could be used to allow different Graphical User Interface (GUI) to different users, if the user appears to be of an older age the interface would use bigger size text.

Some of the challenges for accurate age detection are that aging is uncontrollable non-linear process and that different people seems to age at different speeds. Another problem is that the available databases for labeled facial images leave much be

S.-M. Cheng and M.-Y. Day (Eds.): TAAI 2014, LNAI 8916, pp. 1–13, 2014.
© Springer International Publishing Switzerland 2014

desired. Ideally we would have the face of each person throughout his whole life; at least one picture per year, but most databases have pictures of people at a certain age only. Moreover, the images at higher ages are especially rare.

The goal of this paper is to implement an age and gender estimation algorithm using frontal facing facial images where the input would be an image and the output would be estimation for the age and the gender, respectively.

2   Related Works

There are many aging face models. The models recognized in [6] are:

- Anthropometric Model.
- Active Appearance Model.
- Aging Pattern Subspace.
- Age Manifold.
- Appearance Model.

Once we get our aging feature representation, the next step would be to estimate the age. The choice of your aging feature representation should affect our choice for age estimation algorithm, for example if we had strong facial features our age estimation algorithm should be simple and if we choose simple facial features our age estimation algorithm should be complex.

While gender classification is clearly a classification problem (Only two classes to choose from; male and female). The question that begs itself is whether age estimation is a classification problem or a regression problem. Age estimation can be looked at as a pattern recognition task where each age label can be viewed as a class; therefor, age estimation can be looked at as a classification problem. Another way to look at the problem is that age numbers are a set of sequential numbers; therefore, age estimation can be considered as a regression problem.

Thus age estimation can be viewed as a classification or a regression problem. To find out which is more suitable, we need to try both of them on the same databases to see the performance difference. Guo et al. [10, 11] did that and they chose Support Vector Machine (SVM) as the classifier and Support Vector Regression (SVR) as the regressor. They used the same image database for both experiments to evaluate their performance. The result depended on which database they used, on the YGA database the SVM outperformed the SVR. While with the FG-NET [5] database, it was the other way around. This leads to suggest that it might be wise to combine classification and regression for higher robustness and to get benefit from both methods.

3   Background

3.1   Face Detection Using Haar Cascades

To estimate the age and gender, we need to find the location of the face first. One of the methods to detect faces is using Haar Feature-based cascade classifiers [24]. It is a machine learning based approach where a cascade function is trained with negative and positive samples and then could be used to detect objects in other images.

3.2 Landmark Extraction Using Supervised Descent Method

We will describe our method to detect the landmark points on the face, which is Supervised Descent Method (SDM) and its Applications to Face Alignment [23]. The main difference between SDM and other gradient descent methods is that during training, the SDM learns a sequence of descent directions that minimize the mean of Non-linear Least Squares (NLS) functions sampled at different points. Then in testing, the SDM minimizes the NLS objective using the learned descent directions.

The training begins with finding the face in the training images, and then the initial shape estimate is given by centering the mean face at the square. Then the translational and scaling differences between the initial and manually labeled landmarks are computed. Then Scale Invariant Feature Transform (SIFT) [21] descriptors are computed on 32 x 32 pixel local patches. The SIFT features offer robust representation against illumination changes. The goal is to learn a sequence of descent directions and re-scaling factors such that it produces a sequence of updates starting from the initial estimate that converges to the ground truth location.

3.3 Rotation Invariant Local Binary Pattern

Local Binary Pattern (LBP) is a texture operator that was first introduced by Ojala et al. [19] based on the assumption that texture has locally two complementary aspects: a pattern and strength. One of the most attractive features of LBP is its robustness to gray-scale changes caused by differences in illumination.

3.4 Support Vector Machines

Support Vector Machines (SVMs)[1][4] are a useful technique for data classification and regression. Given a set of training samples each labeled with a class label and a set of features. The goal is to find a model to predict the label for the test data given only the features for the test data.

4 Methodology

4.1 Overview

Our age and gender estimation system uses frontal face images for training and testing. The first step is to detect whether or not a face exists and find its location using the Haar cascades. After that, we find the cranio-facial landmarks on the face using the supervised gradient descent method, so we can separate the face into different regions. After separating the face into different regions of interest (left eyebrow, right eyebrow, left eye, right eye, nose, and mouth), we begin to extract features, the features we choose are the histogram of the rotation-invariant local binary pattern.

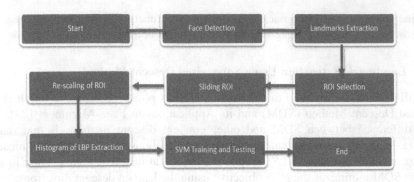

Fig. 1. The flow of our proposed algorithm

For added robustness, we add a sliding window for each region of interest where we slide each window by a certain amount. This way we get 9 windows or patches from each region of interest, and we take the average of their histograms as the feature describing the region of interest.

To capture the largest amount of details possible, we rescale each region of interest multiple times and apply the LBP operator once on each scale. For example, we rescale each window to 0.8 of its original size and apply LBP on it, then we rescale the window to 1.2 of its original size and apply LBP. This allows us to capture different levels of details from the image.

Once we have features ready and paired up with the proper label (representing either gender or age), we use SVM for training and testing.

4.2 Regions of Interest(ROI) Selection

There is a huge variation between faces. To solve the challenges that come with that, such as the alignment of facial features, we choose to focus on local regions around main facial features. To select these regions accurately we use the landmark points acquired by the supervised descent method.

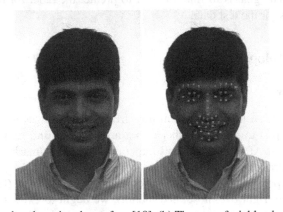

Fig. 2. (a) Facial landmarks pointed on a face [18]. (b) The same facial landmarks numbered.

We try to use landmark points that do not change positions with the change of facial expression. For example, the width of the eye always stays the same, but the height changes depending on whether the eyelids are closed or not. Thus we try not to use the landmark points that change positions easily.

Table 1. Facial landmarks-dependent ROI boundaries. The notation $p_{n,\{x,y\}}$ represents the x and y coordinates from the n-th facial landmark.

	Left Bound	Upper Bound	Width	Height
Left Eyebrow	$p_{1,x} - 0.25$ $* (p_{5,x} - p_{1,x})$	$\min(p_{2,y}, p_{3,y}, p_{4,y})$	$1.5 * (p_x^5 - p_x^1)$	$0.5 * (p_{5,x} - p_{1,x})$
Right Eyebrow	$p_{6,x} - 0.25$ $* (p_{10,x} - p_{6,x})$	$\min(p_{7,y}, p_{8,y}, p_{9,y})$	$1.5 * (p_{10,x} - p_{6,x})$	$0.5 * (p_{10,x} - p_{6,x})$
Left Eye	$p_{20,x} - 0.5$ $* (p_{23,x} - p_{20,x})$	$((p_{21,y} + p_{22,y} + p_{24,y} + p_{25,y})$ $/4))$ $-0.6(p_{23,x} - p_{20,x})$	$1.9 * (p_{23,x} - p_{20,x})$	$1.4 * (p_{23,x} - p_{20,x})$
Right Eye	$p_{26,x} - 0.5$ $* (p_{29,x} - p_{26,x})$	$((p_{27,y} + p_{28,y} + p_{30,y} + p_{31,y})/4)$ $-0.6(p_{29,x} - p_{26,x})$	$1.9 * (p_{29,x} - p_{26,x})$	$1.4 * (p_{29,x} - p_{26,x})$
Nose	$p_{15,x} - 0.35$ $* (p_{19,x} - p_{15,x})$	$p_{12,y} - 0.1 * (p_{17,y} - p_{12,y})$	$1.7 * (p_{19,x} - p_{15,x})$	$1.2 * (p_{17,y} - p_{12,y})$
Mouth	$p_{32,x} - 0.25$ $* (p_{38,x} - p_{32,x})$	$p_{12,y} + 1.1 * (p_{17,y} - p_{12,y})$	$1.5 * (p_{38,x} - p_{32,x})$	$p_{41,y} + p_{35,y} - 2 * (p_{12,y}$ $+ 1.1 * (p_{17,y} - p_{12,y})))$
Face	$p_{11,x} - 3$ $* (p_{23,x} - p_{20,x})$	$p_{11,y} - 1.5 * (p_{17,y} - p_{12,y})$	$6 * (p_{23,x} - p_{20,x})$	$4 * (p_{17,y} - p_{12,y})$

The bounding boxes used to crop out the ROI are shown in Table 4-1. They are based on several ratios in the face that remain steady throughout the change of facial expressions, such as the width of the eye or the height of the nose.

4.3   Feature Extraction

We use the histogram of the rotation-invariant LBP to describe each ROI. Since every face is different, and to work around alignment issues, we use local regions. However, within each region there is variation in position and shape. To solve the problem of alignment in local scale, we introduce a sliding window in Fig. 5.

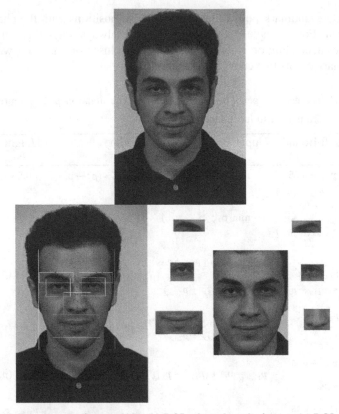

Fig. 3. (a) Face image of a man [18]. (b) ROI selected on the image. (c) ROI cropped.

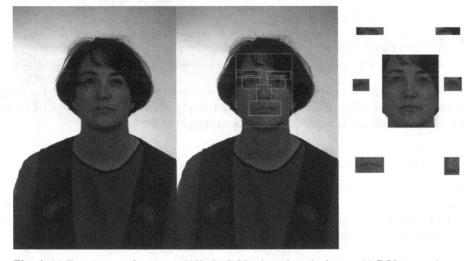

Fig. 4. (a) Face image of a women [18]. (b) ROI selected on the image. (c) ROI cropped.

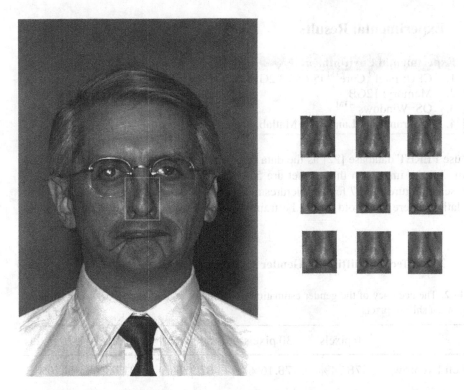

Fig. 5. (a) Face image of a man with the nose region highlighted [18]. (b) The 9 cropped areas taken by sliding the original ROI by *s* pixels (9 pixels in this example).

We start with the original position of the patch and move it to the left by *s* pixels and upwards by *s* pixels. Then we increment the *x* and *y* position by *s* pixels independently three times. This way, we have 9 patches around the original one. This should solve any alignment issues in the local scale.

Before we apply the LBP operator, we rescale each patch multiple times (in our experiments, we take 3 sizes). We use bilinear interpolation to resize each patch. Once we have the resized patches ready we can apply the invariant LBP operator.

4.4 SVM Training and Region Voting

Once we have each shifted and scaled patch ready, we apply the rotation-invariant LBP. We take the histogram of the rotation-invariant LBP and average it out across each region and normalize it to its size. This will be our feature vector describing each region.

The next step is to train using the SVM for gender and SVR for age. We use LIBSVM [2] for the implementation of the SVM and SVR. Each region would have its own classifier and its own decision. The final decision (estimation) would be decided by a majority vote where each region would cast its vote (male or female in case of gender classification). Each region has an equally weighted vote, and since we are using 7 regions, there would be no ties.

5   Experimental Results

Experimental Environment
1. CPU: Intel® Core™ i5-650 3.2GHz processor
2. Memory: 12GB
3. OS: Windows 7™
4. Programming Language: Matlab, C++, Python.

We use FERET database [22] as the data set for our age and gender estimation algorithm. All the images in the test set are 512x768 pixels. The data set contains 2722 grey-scale pictures: 1007 female pictures and 1715 male pictures. We use 5-fold cross validation where each fold would be trained on 2178 images and tested on 544 images.

5.1   The Effect of Shifting on Gender Estimation

Table 2. The accuracy of the gender estimation on different regions separately using different amounts of shift in pixels

	0 pixels	30 pixels	60 pixels	90 pixels	120 pixels
Left Eyebrow	78.54%	78.46%	82.93%	81.53%	74.70%
Right Eyebrow	78.20%	80.62%	82.65%	84.09%	76.53%
Left Eye	71.94%	76.90%	82.46%	87.75%	82.76%
Right Eye	72.42%	74.43%	83.55%	86.47%	85.79%
Nose	71.91%	73.83%	79.91%	85.59%	86.61%
Mouth	78.12%	81.40%	86.87%	87.53%	84.87%
Face	86.60%	87.29%	88.42%	80.91%	66.73%
Voting	89.12%	88.95%	90.91%	91.05%	85.58%

We expected the best results would be in the region of 10 to 20 pixels shift, this way all the patches would overlap with the original patch (Fig. 5). However, as we keep increasing the shifting amount, the results keep getting better and would only drop off when the patches would start shifting to the outside of the face regions. The cause of this is that all areas of the face carry information about gender and age. Moreover, when there is less overlapping between regions, we can extract more information that can lead to better estimations.

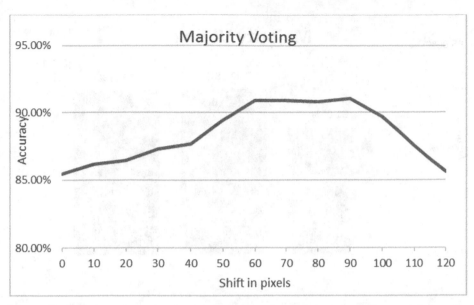

Fig. 6. The accuracy of gender classification from the voting of the different regions using different shift amounts. The best result is at 90 pixels shift, 91.05%.

5.2   The Effect of Scaling on Gender Estimation

In this section, we will show the added benefit of using multiple scales. In the following table (5-2), the first column shows the results without any scaling done. Meanwhile the second column shows the results when each patch is scaled to 0.8 of its original size and 1.2 of its original size along with no scaling. The third bar shows the result with scaling to 0.5 of the original patch size and 1.5 of the original patch size along with no scaling.

Table 3. The accuracy of the gender classification on different regions separately using different scales and a shift of 90 pixels

	[1.0]	[0.8, 1.0, 1.2]	[0.5 ,1.0, 1.5]
Left Eyebrow	81.53%	83.44%	84.67%
Right Eyebrow	84.09%	85.09%	85.68%
Left Eye	87.75%	89.03	88.73%
Right Eye	86.47%	88.59%	88.61%
Nose	85.59%	86.54%	85.94%
Mouth	87.53%	88.93%	89.51%
Face (60 pixel shift)	88.42%	89.49%	88.72%
Voting	91.05%	92.88%	92.78%

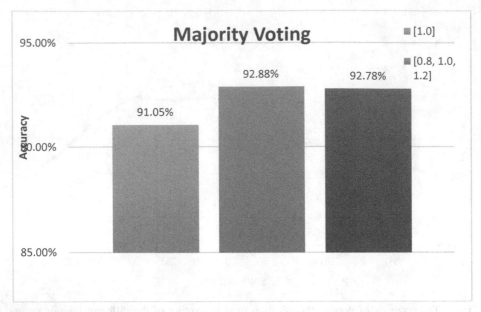

Fig. 7. The accuracy of gender classification from the voting of the different regions using multiple scales

5.3   Age Estimation Results

For age estimation, we use the same algorithm as the gender classification algorithm with using SVR instead of SVM. We measure the age estimation accuracy in mean absolute error in years (lower is better).

Table 4. The accuracy of the age estimation on different regions separately using different scales and a shift of 90 pixels

	[1.0]	[0.8, 1.0, 1.2]
Left Eyebrow	8.654	8.760
Right Eyebrow	8.931	8.873
Left Eye	7.804	7.493
Right Eye	7.745	7.613
Nose	7.766	7.491
Mouth	8.315	8.298
Face	7.955	7.785
Average	8.167	8.044

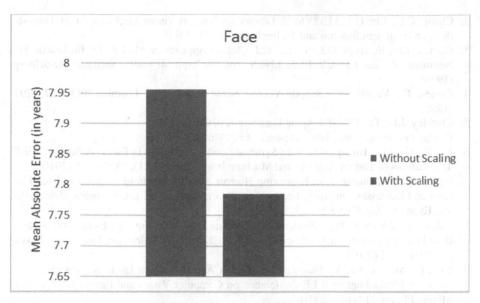

Fig. 8. The accuracy of age classification from the face region (single patch) with shifting of 60 pixels

6   Conclusion and Future Work

Age and gender estimation is a challenging problem due to the non-linearity of the aging and the subtle difference between individuals. In this thesis we propose an age and gender estimation algorithm based on the fusion of multiple local patches. We further demonstrated the effectiveness of shifting and scaling the local patches to further increase the accuracy of the performance.

During our experiments, we find out that increasing the size of the shifting beyond overlapping helped increases the accuracy. This helps to demonstrate that all patches of the face (instead of just the main facial features) hold information that can help with the estimation of age and gender. Using this information the algorithm could be further modified to include other patches to increase the accuracy.

Acknowledgement. This research was supported by the Ministry of Science and Technology of Taiwan, R.O.C., under Grants NSC 102-2221-E-002 -177 and MOST 103-2221-E-002-188, and by   Winstar Technology, Test Research, Qisda, Lumens Digital Optics, PolarLink, and Lite-on.

References

1. Boser, B.E., Guyon, I., Vapnik, V.: A Training Algorithm for Optimal Margin Classifiers. In: Proceedings of the Annual Workshop on Computational Learning Theory, Pittsburgh, PA, pp. 144–152 (1992)

2. Chang, C.C., Lin, C.J.: LIBSVM: A Library for Support Vector Machines. ACM Transactions on Intelligent Systems and Technology 2, 1–27 (2011)
3. Cootes, T.F., Edwards, G.J., Taylor, C.J.: Active Appearance Models. In: Burkhardt, H., Neumann, B. (eds.) ECCV 1998. LNCS, vol. 1407, pp. 484–498. Springer, Heidelberg (1998)
4. Cortes, C., Vapnik, V.: Support-Vector Network. Machine Learning 20(3), 273–297 (1995)
5. Crowley, J.L.: The FG-NET Aging Database (2010), http://www-prima.inrialpes.fr/FGnet/
6. Fu, Y., Guo, G., Huang, T.S.: Age Synthesis and Estimation via Faces: A Survey. IEEE Transactions on Pattern Analysis and Machine Intelligence 32(11), 1955–1976 (2010)
7. Fu, Y., Xu, Y., Huang, T.S.: Estimating Human Ages by Manifold Analysis of Face Pictures and Regression on Aging Features. In: Proceedings of IEEE Conference Multimedia and Expo, Beijing, China, pp. 1383–1386 (2007)
8. Fukai, H., Takimoto, H., Mitsukura, Y., Fukumi, M.: Apparent Age Estimation System Based on Age Perception. In: Proceedings of SICE Annual Conference, Takamatsu, Japan, pp. 2808–2812 (2007)
9. Guo, G., Mu, G., Fu, Y., Huang, T.S.: Human Age Estimation Using Bio Inspired Features. In: Proceedings of IEEE Conference on Computer Vision and Pattern Recognition, Miami, FL, pp. 112–119 (2009)
10. Guo, G., Fu, Y., Dyer, C., Huang, T.S.: Image-Based Human Age Estimation by Manifold Learning and Locally Adjusted Robust Regression. IEEE Transactions on Image Processing 17(7), 1178–1188 (2008)
11. Guo, G., Fu, Y., Huang, T.S., Dyer, C.: Locally Adjusted Robust Regression for Human Age Estimation. In: Proceedings of IEEE Workshop on Applications of Computer Vision, Copper Mountain, CO, pp. 1–6 (2008)
12. Geng, X., Zhou, Z.-H., Zhang, Y., Li, G., Dai, H.: Learning from Facial Aging Patterns for Automatic Age Estimation. In: Proceedings of ACM Conference on Multimedia, Santa Barbara, CA, pp. 307–316 (2006)
13. Gonzalez-Ulloa, M., Flores, E.S.: Senility of the Face – Basic Study to Understand the Causes and Effects. Plastic and Reconstructive Surgery 36, 239–246 (1965)
14. Hayashi, J., Yasumoto, M., Ito, H., Koshimizu, H.: A Method for Estimating and Modeling Age and Gender Using Facial Image Processing. In: Proceedings of Seventh International Conference on Virtual Systems and Multimedia, Berkeley, CA, pp. 439–448 (2001)
15. Kwon, Y., Lobo, N.: Age Classification from Facial Images. In: Proceedings of IEEE Conference on Computer Vision and Pattern Recognition, Seattle, WA, pp. 762–767 (1994)
16. Lanitis, A., Taylor, C., Cootes, T.: Toward Automatic Simulation of Aging Effects on Face Images. IEEE Transactions on Pattern Analysis and Machine Intelligence 24(4), 442–455 (2002)
17. Lowe, D.G.: Distinctive Image Features from Scale-Invariant Keypoints. International Journal of Computer Vision 60(2), 91–110 (2004)
18. NIST.: The FERET Database (2001), http://www.itl.nist.gov/iad/humanid/feret/
19. Ojala, T., Pietikäinen, M., Harwood, D.: A Comparative Study of Texture Measures with Classification Based on Feature Distributions. Pattern Recognition 29, 51–59 (1996)
20. Ojala, T., Pietikäinen, M., Mäenpää, T.: Multiresolution Gray-Scale and Rotation Invariant Texture Classification with Local Binary Patterns. IEEE Transactions on Pattern Analysis and Machine Intelligence 4(7), 971–987 (2002)

21. Ramanathan, N., Chellappa, R.: Modeling Age Progression in Young Faces. In: Proceedings of IEEE Computer Vision and Pattern Recognition, New York, vol. 1, pp. 387–394 (2006)
22. Suo, J., Wu, T., Zhu, S., Shan, S., Chen, X., Gao, W.: Design Sparse Features for Age Estimation Using Hierarchical Face Model. In: Proceedings of IEEE Conference on Automatic Face and Gesture Recognition, Amsterdam, Netherland, pp. 1–6 (2008)
23. Xiong, X., De la Torre Frade, F.: Supervised Descent Method and Its Applications to Face Alignment. In: Proceedings of IEEE International Conference on Computer Vision and Pattern Recognition, Portland, OR, pp. 532–539 (2013)
24. Viola, P., Jones, M.: Rapid Object Detection Using a Boosted Cascade of Simple Features. In: Proceedings of IEEE Conference on Computer Vision and Pattern Recognition, Kauai, HI, vol. 1, pp. 511–518 (2001)

Manipulating Information Providers Access to Information in Auctions

Shani Alkoby[1], David Sarne[1], and Esther David[2]

[1] Department of Computer Science
Bar-Ilan University, Ramat-Gan, Israel
[2] Department of Computer Science
Ashkelon Academic College, Ashkelon, Israel
shani.alkoby@gmail.com
sarned@cs.biu.ac.il
astrdod@acad.ash-college.ac.il

Abstract. Information purchasing is a crucial issue that auctioneers have to consider when running auctions, in particular in auction settings where the auctioned item's value is affected by a common value element. In such settings it is reasonable to assume the existence of a self-interested information provider. The main contribution of the information provider may be the elimination of some uncertainty associated with the common value of the auctioned item. The existence of an information provider does not necessarily impose the use of its services. Moreover, in cases in which the auctioneer decides to purchase information, it is not always beneficial for him to disclose it. In this work, we focus on environment settings where the information that may purchased still involves some uncertainty. The equilibrium analysis is provided with illustrations that highlight some non-intuitive behaviors. In particular, we show that in some cases it is beneficial for the auctioneer to initially limit the level of detail and precision of the information he may purchase. This can be achieved, for example, by limiting the information provider's access to some of the data required to determine the exact common value. This result is non-intuitive especially in light of the fact that the auctioneer is the one who decides whether or not to use the services of the information provider; hence having the option to purchase better information may seem advantageous.

Keywords: auction, common value, self interested auctioneer, information provider.

1 Introduction

One of the main crucial issues that an auction mechanism designer should take into account is information disclosure. Namely, what part of the information should be revealed in order to maximize the auctioneer's target utility which can either be related to the auctioned good's expected revenue in case of a self-interested designer or social welfare in cases in which the auction designer acts as

S.-M. Cheng and M.-Y. Day (Eds.): TAAI 2014, LNAI 8916, pp. 14–25, 2014.

the social planner. Many researchers have explored this issue in both theoretical and empirical manners [9,12]. In particular, this issue becomes more relevant in auction settings where the auctioned item involves an uncertain common value element [11,29,14,13,20,21,4]. For example, the board of a firm for sale can choose which part of the firm's client list or its sales forecast will be disclosed to the potential buyers. The decision regarding the information disclosure directly affects bidders' valuation of the auctioned item and consequently also the winner's determination and the auctioneer's expected revenue.

More often, information regarding the common value element is not available to the auctioneer before the auction. However, the auctioneer may use some relevant expert services termed external information provider. This situation is common in scenarios where information discovery involves special expertise or equipment the auctioneer does not own. Specifically, in the scenario of a firm for sale, the information may pertain to the financial stability of key clients of the firm, hence typically offered for sale in the form of business analysts' reports. In such situations the auctioneer's responsibility is to decide both whether to purchase the information and whether to disclose it fully or partially to bidders when purchased. Such scenarios become much more complex when the information provider acts strategically, controlling the accuracy of the information provided and its price.

Prior work in such settings assumed strategic behavior on the auctioneer and the information provider sides. However, the auctioneer's strategy was limited to the choice of the information to be disclosed to the buyers [4,11] while the information provider's strategy was limited to setting the price of the information provided (i.e., assume the information provided is fully certain and captures the exact common value [34]).

In this paper we extend the model to the more realistic case, where the information provider cannot guarantee the identification of the true common value, but rather can offer a more precise estimate of this variable. In particular we focus on the case in which the information provider can only eliminate some of the possible values and cannot fully distinguish between others. For example in the example of the firm, it is possible that the information provider will be able to classify customers as "good" and "bad" where each category spans a wide range of possible values. Similarly, it is possible that the information provider will be able to distinguish between strong and weak sales forecasts, but will not be able to differentiate between a wide range slightly above or below the average sales figures.

To this end, the paper's contribution is twofold:

- We augment the three-ply equilibrium analysis (considering the strategic behavior of the information provider, the auctioneer and the bidders) to cases where the information provider can reduce the uncertainty associated with the common value rather than provide its true value.
- We illustrate a beneficial, yet somewhat non-intuitive, strategic behavior of the auctioneer. In particular, this behavior is the auctioneer's choice to intentionally limit the information provider's (e.g., the analyst) ability to

distinguish between values. This becomes possible when the information provider's ability to provide accurate information depends on inputs received from the auctioneer. For example, in the sale of the firm example, the board can decide to provide the analyst with accurate, yet aggregative, information, such that the information provider can estimate future sales as weak or strong rather than a certain figure from a wider range of values. The non-intuitiveness of doing this is attributed to the fact that at the end of the day the information provider's information is offered for sale to the auctioneer herself, thus by restricting the information provider's ability to distinguish between values the auctioneer restricts himself by not having the choice of purchasing more accurate information.

The paper is structured as follows. In the following section we provide a formal presentation of the model. Then, we present an equilibrium analysis and illustrate the potential profit for the auctioneer from influencing the accuracy of the information that can be provided by the information provider. Finally we conclude with a review of related work and a discussion on the main findings.

2   The Model

Our model considers an auctioneer offering a single item for sale to n bidders using a second-price sealed-bid auction (with random winner selection in case of a tie). The auctioned item is assumed to be characterized by some value X (the "common value"), which is a priori unknown to both the auctioneer and the bidders [16,17]. The only information publicly available with regard to X is the set of possible values it can obtain, denoted $X^* = \{x_1, ..., x_k\}$, and the probability associated with each value, $Pr(X = x)$ ($\sum_{x \in X^*} Pr(X = x) = 1$). Bidders are assumed to be heterogeneous in the sense that each is associated with a type T that defines her valuation of the auctioned item (i.e., her "private value") for any possible value that X may obtain. We use the function $V_t(x)$ to denote the private value of a bidder of type $T = t$ if the true value of the item is $X = x$. It is assumed that the probability distribution of types, denoted $Pr(T = t)$, is publicly known, however a bidder's specific type is known only to herself.

The model assumes the auctioneer can obtain information related to the value of X from an outside source, denoted "information provider", by paying a fee C that is set by the information provider. Similar to prior models (e.g., [34]), and for the same justifications given there, it is assumed that the option of purchasing the information is available only to the auctioneer, though the bidders are aware of the auctioneer's option to purchase such information. In its most general form, the information provided by the information provider is a subset $X' \subset X^*$, ensuring that one of the values in X' is the true common value. This is usually the case when the information provider cannot distinguish between some of the possible outcomes however can eliminate others. Therefore, the information provider will provide a subset $X' \in D = \{X_1, ..., X_l\}$ where D is the set of possible subsets of X^*, each containing values between which the information provider cannot distinguish, such that $\cup_{X_i \in D} X_i = X^*$ and $X_i \cap X_j = \emptyset$, $\forall i, j$.

If the information is purchased, the auctioneer, based on the subset obtained, can decide either to disclose the information to the bidders or keep it to herself (hence disclosing $\emptyset$). If she discloses the information, then presumably the information received from the information provider is disclosed as is (i.e., truthfully and symmetrically to all bidders), e.g., if the auctioneer is regulated or has to consider her reputation. Finally, it is assumed that all players (auctioneer, bidders and the information provider) are self-interested, risk-neutral and fully rational agents, and are acquainted with the general setting parameters: the number of bidders in the auction, n, the cost of purchasing the information, C, the possible subsets that may be obtained by the information provider, D, the discrete random variables X and T, their possible values and their discrete probability distributions.

The above model generalizes the one found in [11,29] in the sense that it requires that the auctioneer decide whether or not to purchase the external information rather than assume that she initially possesses it. Similarly, it generalizes the work in [34] in the sense that it allows the information provider to provide a subset of values rather than the specific true value.

3 Analysis

Our analysis uses the concept of mixed Bayesian Nash Equilibrium. Since the auctioneer needs to decide both whether to purchase the information and if so whether to disclose the information received, we can characterize her strategy using $R^{auc} = (p^a, p_1^a, ..., p_l^a)$ where p^a is the probability she will purchase the information from the information provider and p_i^a ($1 \leq i \leq l$) is the probability she will disclose to the bidders the subset received if that subset is X_i. The dominating bid of a bidder of type t, when subset X' is received (including the case where $X' = \emptyset$, i.e., no information is disclosed), denoted $B(t, X')$, is the expected private value calculated by weighing each private value $V_t(x)$ according to the post-priori probability of x being the true common value given the information X', denoted $Pr(X = x | X')$ [11], i.e.: $B(t, X') = \sum_{x \in X^*} V_t(x) \cdot Pr(X = x | X')$. If the auctioneer discloses a subset $X' \subset X^* \neq \emptyset$ then $Pr(X = x | X') = \frac{Pr(X=x)}{\sum_{y \in X'} Pr(X=y)}$ for any $x \in X'$ and $Pr(X = x | X') = 0$ otherwise. If no information is disclosed ($X' = \emptyset$) then $Pr(X = x | X' = \emptyset)$ needs to be calculated based on the bidders' belief of whether information was indeed purchased and if so, whether that value is intentionally not disclosed by the auctioneer. Assume the bidders believe that the auctioneer has purchased the information from the information provider[1] with a probability of p and that if indeed purchased then if the information received was the subset X_i then it will be disclosed to the

---

[1] Being rational, all bidders hold the same belief in equilibrium.

bidders with a probability of p_i. In this case the probability of any value $x \in X_i$ being the true common value is given by:

$$Pr(X{=}x|X'{=}\emptyset) = \frac{Pr(X=x)(p(1-p_i)+(1-p))}{(1-p)+p\sum_{X_j}(1-p_j)\sum_{y\in X_j}Pr(X=y)} \tag{1}$$

The term in the numerator is the probability that x is indeed the true value however the subset it is in is not disclosed. If indeed x is the true value (i.e., with a probability of $Pr(X = x)$) then it is not disclosed either when the information is not purchased (i.e., with a probability of $(1-p)$) or when purchased but not disclosed (i.e., with a probability of $p(1-p_i)$). The term in the denominator is the probability information will not be disclosed. This happens when the information is not purchased (i.e., with a probability $(1-p)$) or when the information is purchased however the auctioneer does not disclose the subset received (i.e., with a probability of $p\sum(1-p_j)\sum_{y\in X_j}Pr(X=y)$). Further on in the paper we refer to the strategy where information is not disclosed as an empty set. The bidders' strategy, denoted R^{bidder}, can thus be compactly represented as $R^{bidder} = (p^b, p_1^b, ..., p_k^b)$, where p^b is the probability they assign to information purchased and p_i^b is the probability they assign to the event that the information is indeed disclosed if purchased and becomes X_i.

In order to formalize the expected second-best bid if the auctioneer discloses the subset X' we apply the calculation method given in [34] but replace the exact value x with a subset X'. We first define two probability functions. The first is the probability that given that the subset disclosed by the auctioneer is X', the bid placed by a random bidder equals w, denoted $g(w, X')$, given by: $g(w, X') = \sum_{B(t,X')=w} Pr(T = t)$. The second is the probability that the bid placed by a random bidder equals w or below, denoted $G(w, X')$, given by: $G(w, X') = \sum_{B(t,X')\leq w} Pr(T = t)$.

The auctioneer's expected profit when disclosing the subset X', denoted $ER_{auc}(X')$, equals the expected second-best bid:

$$ER_{auc}(X') = \sum_{w\in\{B(t,X')|t\in T\}} w(\sum_{k=1}^{n-1} n \binom{n-1}{k})$$

$$(1{-}G(w,X'))(g(w,X'))^k(G(w,X') - g(w,X'))^{n-k-1} \tag{2}$$

$$+ \sum_{k=2}^{n} \binom{n}{k}(g(w,X'))^k(G(w,X') - g(w,X'))^{n-k})$$

The calculation iterates over all of the possible second-best bid values, assigning to each its probability of being the second-best bid. As we consider discrete probability functions, it is possible to have two bidders place the same highest bid (in which case it is also the second-best bid). For any given bid value, w, we therefore consider the probability of either: (i) one bidder bidding more than w, $k \in 1, ..., (n-1)$ bidders bidding exactly w and all of the other bidders bidding less than w; or (ii) $k \in 2, ..., n$ bidders bidding exactly w and all of the others bidding less than w.

Consequently, the auctioneer's expected revenue from the auction itself (i.e., excluding the payment C to the information provider), when the auctioneer uses $R^{auc} = (p^a, p_1^a, ..., p_k^a)$ and the bidders use R^{bidder}, denoted $ER(R^{auc}, R^{bidder})$, is given by:

$$ER(R^{auc}, R^{bidder}) = p^a \sum_{i=1}^{l} \sum_{x \in X_i} Pr(X = x) p_i^a \cdot ER_{auc}(X_i)$$

$$+ ((1-p^a) + p^a \sum_{i=1}^{l} \sum_{x \in X_i} Pr(X = x)(1 - p_i^a)) \cdot ER_{auc}(\emptyset)$$

(3)

where $ER_{auc}(X_i)$ is calculated according to (2) (also in the case where $X_i = \emptyset$). Consequently the auctioneer's expected benefit, denoted $EB(R^{auc}, R^{bidder})$, is given by $EB(R^{auc}, R^{bidder}) = ER(R^{auc}, R^{bidder}) - p^a * C$.

A stable solution in terms of the mixed Bayesian Nash Equilibrium in this case is necessarily of the form $R^{auc} = R^{bidder} = R = (p, p_1, ..., p_l)$ (because otherwise, if $R^{auc} = R' \neq R^{bidder}$ then bidders necessarily have an incentive to deviate to $R^{bidder} = R'$), such that: (a) for any $0 < p_i < 1$ (or $0 < p < 1$): $ER_{auc}(\emptyset, R) = ER_{auc}(X_i)$ (or $ER_{auc}(\emptyset, R^{bidder}) = ER_{auc}((1, p_1, ..., p_l), R^{bidder}))$; (b) for any $p_i = 0$ (or $p = 0$): $ER_{auc}(\emptyset, R^{bidder}) \geq ER_{auc}(X_i)$ (or $ER_{auc}(\emptyset, R^{bidder}) \geq ER_{auc}((1, p_1, ..., p_l), R^{bidder})$); and (c) for any $p_i = 1$ (or $p = 1$): $ER_{auc}(\emptyset, R^{bidder}) \leq ER_{auc}(X_i)$ (or $ER_{auc}(\emptyset, R^{bidder}) \leq ER_{auc}((1, p_1, ..., p_l), R^{bidder})$. The proof for this derivation is similar to the proof given in [34] (see page 39), with the exception that instead of referring to individual values of X we refer to subsets of values X_i. Therefore we need to evaluate all the possible solutions of the form $(p, p_1, ..., p_l)$ that may hold (where each probability is either assigned 1, 0 or a value in-between). Each mixed solution of these $2 \cdot 3^k$ combinations (because there is only one solution where $p = 0$ is applicable) should be first solved for the appropriate probabilities according to the above stability conditions. Since the auctioneer is the first mover in this model (deciding on whether or not to purchase information), the equilibrium used is the stable solution for which the auctioneer's expected profit is maximized.

We note that if the information is provided for free ($C = 0$) then information is necessarily obtained and the resulting equilibrium is equivalent to the one given in [11] for the pure Bayesian Nash Equilibrium case and in [29] for the mixed Bayesian Nash Equilibrium case. Similarly, if $|X_i| = 1 \; \forall i$ is enforced (i.e., the information provider provides the exact value of X) then the resulting equilibrium is the same as the one given in [34].

4   Influencing the Information Provider's Capabilities to Distinguish between Values

As discussed in the introduction, in various settings the auctioneer can influence the information provider's ability to distinguish between different values the common value obtains. In this section we consider the case where the auctioneer has full control over the structure of D, i.e., the division of X^* into disjoint subsets, each composed of values which the information provider cannot distinguish between.

Limiting the information provider's ability to distinguish between values may seem non-intuitive in the sense that it limits the auctioneer's strategy space when it comes to disclosing this information to bidders, if it is purchased. Nevertheless, in many settings the strategy of constraining the information provider's input can actually play into the hands of the auctioneer and improve her expected profit. This phenomenon is illustrated in Figure 1, which depicts the auctioneer's expected profit (vertical axis) as a function of the information purchasing cost (horizontal axis), for several possible divisions of X^* into subsets of non-distinguishable values. The setting used for this example is given in the table below the graph. It is based on three bidders, where each can be of four different types. The first column of the table depicts the different bidder types and the second column gives their probability. Similarly, the second and third rows depict the different possible values of X (denoted x_1, x_2, x_3 and x_4) and their probabilities. The remaining values are the valuations that bidders of different types assign different possible values of the parameter X. For example, if a bidder is of type 3, then her valuation of x_2 is 59.

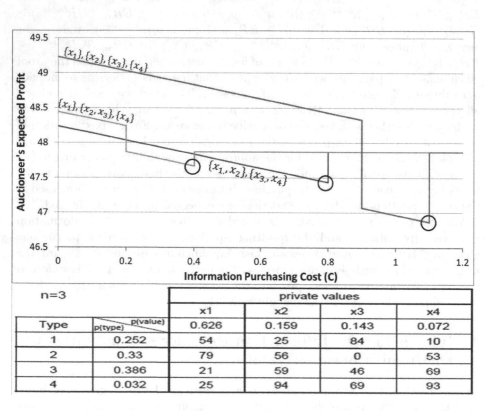

n=3		private values			
		x1	x2	x3	x4
Type	p(type) p(value)	0.626	0.159	0.143	0.072
1	0.252	54	25	84	10
2	0.33	79	56	0	53
3	0.386	21	59	46	69
4	0.032	25	94	69	93

Fig. 1. The auctioneer's expected profit as a function of the information purchasing cost for different divisions of X^* into subsets of non-distinguishable values

Each of the three graphs given in the figure relates to different possible divisions, d of X^* (marked next to it), depicting the expected profit of the auctioneer in the equilibrium resulting in the specific cost of information on the horizontal axis. In this example the resulting equilibrium is always based on pure strategies (i.e., $p, p_i \in \{0, 1\}$) and the points of discontinuity in the curve represent the transition from one equilibrium to another. In particular, for C values in which the curve decreases, the equilibrium is based on always purchasing the information (though not necessarily disclosing all subsets). This happens when the cost of purchasing the information justifies its purchase, i.e., for relatively small C values. The non-decreasing part of the curve is associated with an equilibrium in which the information is essentially not purchased.

As can be seen from the figure, for any cost of purchasing the information $0.9 < C < 1.1$, the auctioneer is better off not allowing the information provider to distinguish between all values: the division $d = \{\{x_1\}, \{x_2\}, \{x_3\}, \{x_4\}\}$ is dominated by $d' = \{\{x_1\}, \{x_2, x_3\}, \{x_4\}\}$ and $d'' = \{\{x_1, x_2\}, \{x_3, x_4\}\}$. The explanation for this interesting phenomenon lies in the different costs of the transition between equilibria due to stability considerations. With fully distinguishable values, it is possible that a desired solution which yields the auctioneer a substantial expected profit is not stable (e.g., in our case when $0.9 < C < 1.1$ the solution is that the information is not purchased at all), whereas with inaccurate information the solution is stable and holds as the equilibrium.

In particular, in our example, when the information provider acts fully strategically, i.e., sets the price of information to the maximum possible price for which the information will still be purchased (the C value in which the equilibrium changes from purchase to not purchase the information, marked with circles in the graphs) the auctioneer will gain (and the information provider will essentially lose) from restricting the information provider's ability to distinguish between values. For example, with $\{\{x_1\}, \{x_2, x_3\}, \{x_4\}\}$ the information will be priced at $C = 0.4$ yielding the auctioneer an expected profit of 47.6 (compared to $C = 1.1$ and a profit of 46.8 in the "fully distinguishable" case).

5   Related Work

Auctions are an effective means of trading and allocating goods whenever the seller is unsure about buyers' (bidders') exact valuations of the sold item [24,25]. The advantage of many auction mechanism variants in this context is in the ability to effectively extract the bidders' valuations [23,32], resulting in the most efficient allocation. Due to its many advantages, this mechanism is commonly used and researched and over the years has evolved to support various settings and applications such as on-line auctions [22,27,19,37,36], matching agents in dynamic two-sided markets [5], resource allocation [31,30,7] and even for task allocation and joint exploration [15,26]. In this context great emphasis has been placed on studying bidding strategies [40,38,3], the use of software agents to represent humans in auctions [6], combinatorial auctions [39] and the development of auction protocols that are truthful [5,8,7,2] and robust (e.g., against false-name bids in combinatorial auctions [41]).

The case where there is some uncertainty associated with the value of the sold (auctioned) item is quite common in the literature on auctions. Most commonly it is assumed that the value of the auctioned item is unknown to the bidders at the time of the auction and bidders may only have an estimate or some privately known signal, such as an expert's estimate, that is correlated with the true value [17,24]. Many of the works using uncertain common value models assumed asymmetry in the knowledge available to the bidders and the auctioneer regarding the auctioned item, typically having sellers more informative than bidders [1,11]. As such, much emphasis was placed on the role of information revelation [28,33,9,12,14,13,20,21]. In particular, several authors have considered the computational aspects of such models where the auctioneer needs to decide on the subsets of non-distinguishable values to be disclosed to the bidders [11,29,10]. Nonetheless, all these works assume the auctioneer necessarily obtains the information and that the division into non-distinguishable groups, whenever applicable, is always a priori given to the bidders. Furthermore, not disclosing any information (signal) is not allowed in these works. Our problem, on the other hand, does not require that the auctioneer possess (or purchase) the information in the first place, and allows the auctioneer the decision of whether or not to disclose any value even if the information is purchased. In particular, when no information is disclosed bidders cannot distinguish between the information not being purchased in the first place and the information is purchased but the value is not disclosed. More importantly, none of the prior work considers the option of influencing the ability of the information provider to distinguish between different values.

Prior work that considers a three-ply equilibrium in settings where information can be potentially purchased from an external information provider assumes the information provider can always supply the true common value [34]. Moreover, this work does not allow any influence whatsoever on the auctioneer's strategy over the ability to distinguish between different values. Work in other domains that did consider selective information disclosure, e.g., for comparison shopping agents [18] or for sharing data for user modeling [35] is very far in terms of the principles used, and cannot be applied in our case. On the whole, despite the many prior models that consider a subset of our model's characteristics, to the best of our knowledge, an analysis that addresses all of the different aspects included in our model does not exist in the literature.

6   Conclusions and Future Work

In this paper we advance the state of the art by providing a three player equilibrium analysis that allows the ability of influencing the auctioneer's expected profit through controlling the granularity and accuracy of the information offered for sale. The presence of information providers in multi agent systems has become substantial and consequently, enforces the reconsideration of the equilibrium where this time such options are taken into account. The information providers may be individuals with specific expertise who offer their services for a fee (e.g. an analyst) or large information service providers such as carfax.com or credit report companies. It is commonly assumed that these information providers indeed can control the level of accuracy they offer their customers. Moreover, the accuracy of the information provided depends on the customer's cooperation and the level of the inputs she provides. Against this background, the importance of this equilibrium construction and analysis for auctioneers or the information providers is clear, especially, in terms of the ability to control the granularity in which information is provided.

Here, we show an interesting phenomenon where the auctioneer may benefit in cases where the information provider cannot fully identify the exact state of nature, even though the information is eventually offered exclusively to the auctioneer. This phenomenon is explained by the stability requirement – beneficial solutions that could not hold with the complete ("perfect") information scheme, because of stability considerations, are found to be stable once the information being offered for sale is constrained.

Acknowledgment. This work was supported in part by the Israeli Science Foundation grant no. 1083/13.

References

1. Akerlof, G.: The market for "lemons": Quality uncertainty and the market mechanism. The Quarterly Journal of Economics 84(3), 488–500 (1970), http://www.jstor.org/stable/1879431
2. Azoulay, R., David, E.: Truthful and efficient mechanisms for site oriented advertizing auctions, multiagent and grid systems. An International Journal Press 10(2), 67–94 (2014)
3. Bagnall, A., Toft, I.: Autonomous adaptive agents for single seller sealed bid auctions. Autonomous Agents and Multi-Agent Systems 12(3), 259–292 (2006)
4. Board, S.: Revealing information in auctions: the allocation effect. Economic Theory 38(1), 125–135 (2009)
5. Bredin, J., Parkes, D., Duong, Q.: Chain: A dynamic double auction framework for matching patient agents. Journal of Artificial Intelligence Research (JAIR) 30, 133–179 (2007)
6. David, E., Azoulay-Schwartz, R., Kraus, S.: Bidding in sealed-bid and english multi-attribute auctions. Decision Support Systems 42(2), 527–556 (2006)
7. David, E., Manisterski, E.: Strategy proof mechanism for complex task allocations in prior consent for subtasks completion environment. In: IAT, pp. 209–215 (2013)
8. Dobzinski, S., Nisan, N.: Mechanisms for multi-unit auctions. Journal of Artificial Intelligence Research (JAIR) 37, 85–98 (2010)
9. Dufwenberg, M., Gneezy, U.: Information disclosure in auctions: an experiment. Journal of Economic Behavior & Organization 48(4), 431–444 (2002)
10. Dughmi, S., Immorlica, N., Roth, A.: Constrained signaling for welfare and revenue maximization. ACM SIGecom Exchanges 12(1), 53–56 (2013)
11. Emek, Y., Feldman, M., Gamzu, I., Leme, R., Tennenholtz, M.: Signaling schemes for revenue maximization. In: Proceedings of the 12th ACM Conference on Electronic Commerce (EC 2012), pp. 514–531 (2012)

12. Eső, P., Szentes, B.: Optimal information disclosure in auctions and the handicap auction. The Review of Economic Studies 74(3), 705–731 (2007)
13. Ganuza, J.-J., Penalva, J.S.: Signal orderings based on dispersion and the supply of private information in auctions. Econometrica 78(3), 1007–1030 (2010)
14. Ganuza Fernández, J.J.: Ignorance promotes competition: An auction model with endogenous private valuations (2005)
15. Gerkey, B., Mataric, M.: Sold!: auction methods for multirobot coordination. IEEE Transactions on Robotics 18(5), 758–768 (2002)
16. Goeree, J., Offerman, T.: Efficiency in auctions with private and common values: An experimental study. American Economic Review 92(3), 625–643 (2002)
17. Goeree, J., Offerman, T.: Competitive bidding in auctions with private and common values. The Economic Journal 113, 598–613 (2003)
18. Hajaj, C., Hazon, N., Sarne, D., Elmalech, A.: Search more, disclose less. In: Proceedings of the Twenty-Seventh AAAI Conference on Artificial Intelligence (2013)
19. Hajiaghayi, M., Kleinberg, R., Mahdian, M., Parkes, D.: Online auctions with re-usable goods. In: Proceedings of the Sixth ACM Conference on Electronic Commerce (EC 2005), pp. 165–174 (2005)
20. Jewitt, I., Li, D.: Cheap-talk information disclosure in auctions. Tech. rep., Working paper (2012)
21. Johnson, J.P., Myatt, D.P.: On the simple economics of advertising, marketing, and product design. The American Economic Review, 756–784 (2006)
22. Juda, A., Parkes, D.: An options-based solution to the sequential auction problem. Artificial Intelligence 173(7-8), 876–899 (2009)
23. Klemperer, P.: Auction theory: A guide to the literature. Journal of Economic Surveys 13(3), 227–286 (1999)
24. Klemperer, P.: Auctions: Theory and Practice. Princeton University Press (2004)
25. Krishna, V.: Auction Theory. Academic Press (2002)
26. Lagoudakis, M., Markakis, E., Kempe, D., Keskinocak, P., Kleywegt, A., Koenig, S., Tovey, C., Meyerson, A., Jain, S.: Auction-based multi-robot routing. In: Proceedings of Robotics: Science and Systems, pp. 343–350 (2005)
27. Lavi, R., Nisan, N.: Competitive analysis of incentive compatible on-line auctions. In: Proceedings of the Second ACM Conference on Electronic Commerce (EC 2000), pp. 233–241 (2000)
28. Milgrom, P., Weber, R.: A theory of auctions and competitive bidding. Econometrica 50(5), 1089–1122 (1982)
29. Miltersen, P., Sheffet, O.: Send mixed signals: earn more, work less. In: Proceedings of the 13th ACM Conference on Electronic Commerce(EC 2012), pp. 234–247 (2012)
30. Ng, C., Parkes, D., Seltzer, M.: Virtual worlds: fast and strategyproof auctions for dynamic resource allocation. In: Proceedings Fourth ACM Conference on Electronic Commerce (EC 2003), pp. 238–239 (2003)
31. Nisan, N.: Algorithms for selfish agents. In: Meinel, C., Tison, S. (eds.) STACS 1999. LNCS, vol. 1563, pp. 1–15. Springer, Heidelberg (1999)
32. Parkes, D., Shneidman, J.: Distributed implementations of vickrey-clarke-groves mechanisms. In: Proceedings of the Third International Conference on Autonomous Agents and Multiagent Systems (AAMAS 2004), vol. 1, pp. 261–268 (2004)
33. Perry, M., Reny, P.: On the failure of the linkage principle in multi-unit auctions. Econometrica 67(4), 895–900 (1999)
34. Sarne, D., Alkoby, S., David, E.: On the choice of obtaining and disclosing the common value in auctions. Artificial Intelligence 215, 24–54 (2014)

35. Sarne, D., Grosz, B.J.: Sharing experiences to learn user characteristics in dynamic environments with sparse data. In: Proceedings of the Sixth International Joint Conference on Autonomous Agents and Multiagent Systems (AAMAS 2007), pp. 202–209 (2007)
36. Sarne, D., Hadad, M., Kraus, S.: Auction equilibrium strategies for task allocation in uncertain environments. In: Klusch, M., Ossowski, S., Kashyap, V., Unland, R. (eds.) CIA 2004. LNCS (LNAI), vol. 3191, pp. 271–285. Springer, Heidelberg (2004)
37. Sarne, D., Kraus, S.: Solving the auction-based task allocation problem in an open environment. In: Proceedings of the Twentieth National Conference on Artificial Intelligence and the Seventeenth Innovative Applications of Artificial Intelligence Conference (AAAI 2005), pp. 164–169 (2005)
38. Stone, P., Schapire, R., Littman, M., Csirik, J., McAllester, D.: Decision-theoretic bidding based on learned density models in simultaneous, interacting auctions. Journal of Artificial Intelligence Research 19(1), 209–242 (2003)
39. Tennenholtz, M.: Tractable combinatorial auctions and b-matching. Artificial Intelligence 140(1/2), 231–243 (2002)
40. Vetsikas, I., Jennings, N.: Bidding strategies for realistic multi-unit sealed-bid auctions. Autonomous Agents and Multi-Agent Systems 21(2), 265–291 (2010)
41. Yokoo, M., Sakurai, Y., Matsubara, S.: Robust combinatorial auction protocol against false-name bids. Artificial Intelligence 130(2), 167–181 (2001)

High-Efficiency Remote Cloud Data Center Backup with Intelligent Parameter Adaptation

Bao Rong Chang[1,*], Hsiu-Fen Tsai[2], Cin-Long Guo[1], Chia-Yen Chen[1], and Chien-Feng Huang[1]

[1] Department of Computer Science and Information Engineering, National University of Kaohsiung 81148, Taiwan
{brchang,m1015504,ayen,cfhuang15}@nuk.edu.tw
[2] Department of Marketing Management, Shu Te University, Kaohsiung 82445, Taiwan
soenfen@stu.edu.tw

Abstract. This paper aims to realize high efficient remote cloud data center backup using HBase and Cassandra, and in order to verify the high efficiency backup they have applied Thrift Java for cloud data center to take a stress test by performing strictly data read/write and remote backup in the large amounts of data. In order to optimize traffic flow of data center backup, adaptive network-based fuzzy inference system (ANFIS) along with particle swarm optimization (PSO) has been employed to off-line tune seamless handoff and network traffic flow. Finally, in terms of the effectiveness-cost evaluation to assess the remote database backup, a cost-performance ratio has been evaluated for several benchmark databases and the proposed ones. As a result, the proposed HBase approach outperforms the other databases.

Keywords: NoSQL Database, HBase, Cassandra, Remote Data Center, Backup, ANFIS-PSO, Thrift Java.

1 Introduction

In recent years, cloud services [1][2] are applicable in our daily lives. Many traditional services such as telemarketing, television and advertisement are evolving into digitized formats. As smart devices are gaining popularity and usage, the exchange of information is no longer limited to just desktop computers, but instead, information is transferred through portable smart devices [3][4], so that humans can receive prompt and up-to-date information anytime. This leads to the emergence of non-relational databases, of which many notable NoSQL databases that are currently being used by enterprises are HBase [5], Cassandra [6], and Mongo [7].

This paper will implement data center remote backup using two remarkable NoSQL databases HBase and Cassandra, and perform stress tests with a large scale of data, for instances, read, write, and remote data center backup. Furthermore, in order to maintain data center backup over internet smoothly, we proposed an intelligent

---

* Corresponding author.

S.-M. Cheng and M.-Y. Day (Eds.): TAAI 2014, LNAI 8916, pp. 26–35, 2014.
© Springer International Publishing Switzerland 2014

adaptation scheme, an adaptive network-based fuzzy inference system (ANFIS) [8] together with particle swarm optimization (PSO) approach [9], which has employed for tuning seamless handoff and control traffic flow between different data centers.The experimental results of remote data center backup using HBase and Cassandra will show the assessment of their effectiveness and efficiency based on cost-performance ratio [10].

2   Large-Scale Database in Data Center

This paper will realize remote data center backup for the two distributed databases HBase and Cassandra. Both designs achieved two of the three characteristics that are consistency (C), availability (A), and partition tolerance (P) in C.A.P theory [11]. HBase, a distributed database, works under the master-slave [12] framework, where the master node assigns information to the slave node to realize the distributed data storage, meanwhile emphasizing on consistency and partition tolerance characteristics. Regarding remote data center backup, a certain data center with HBase has the following advantages: (1) retain data consistency, (2) activate instant reading or writing of massive information, (3) access to large-scale unstructured data, (4) expand new slave nodes, (5) provide computing resources, and (6) prevent a single-node failure problems in the cluster.

Cassandra, a distributed database, works under the peer-to-peer (P2P) [13] framework, where each node contains totally identical backup information to realize the distributed data storage with uninterrupted services, at the same time emphasizing on availability and partition tolerance characteristics. As for remote data center backup, a certain data center with Cassandra has the following advantages: (1) each node shares equal information, (2) cluster setup is quick and simple, (3) dynamically expand new nodes, (4) each node has the equal priority of its precedence, and (5) cluster does not have a single-node failure problem.

3   Remote Data Center Backup

3.1   Remote HBase and Cassandra Data Centers Backup

In remote HBase data center backup architecture [14], the master cluster and slave cluster must possess its own independent Zookeeper in a cluster [15]. The master cluster will establish a copy code for the data center, and designate the location of the replication, so to achieve offsite or remote data center backup between different sites.

In remote Cassandra data center backup architecture [16], Cassandra is of peer-to-peer (P2P) framework connects all nodes together. When information is written into data center A, a copy of the data is immediately backed up into a designated data center B, as well, each node can designate a permanent storage location in a rack [17].

This paper expands the application of a single-cluster replication mechanism to the replication of data center level. Through adjusting the replication mechanism between data center and nodes, the corresponding nodes from two independent data centers are connected and linked through SSH protocol, and then information is distributed and written into these nodes by master node or seed node to achieve remote data center backup.

3.2   Cross-Platform Data Transfer Using Apache Thrift

Apache Thrift [18] was developed by the Facebook team [19], and it was donated to the Apache Foundation in 2007 to become one of the open source projects. Thrift was designed to solve Facebook's problem of large number of data transfers between various platforms and distinct programming languages, and thus cross-platform RPC protocols. Thrift supports a number of programming languages [20], such as C++, C#, Cocoa, Erlang, Haskell, Java, Ocami, Perl, PHP, Python, Ruby, and Smalltalk. With binary high performance communication properties, Thrift supports multiple forms of RPC protocol acted as a cross-platform API. Thrift is also a transfer tool suitable for large amounts of data exchange and storage [21]; when comparing with JSON and XML, its performance and capability of large-scale data transfer is clearly superior to both of them. The Input Code is the programming language performed by the Client. The Service Client is the Client side and Server side code framework defined by Thrift documents, and read()/write() are codes outlined in Thrift documents to realize actual data read and write operations. The rest are Thrift's transfer framework, protocols, and underlying I/O protocols. Using Thrift, we can conveniently define a multi-language service system, and select different transfer protocol. The Server side includes the transfer protocol and the basic transfer framework, providing both single and multi-thread operation modes on the Server, where the Server and browser are capable of interoperability concurrently.

4   Research Method

4.1   Implementation of HBase and Cassandra Data Centers

The following procedures will explain how to setup HBase and Cassandra data centers using CentOS 6.4 system, and achieve remote backup. Next, this paper will test the performance of data centers against reading, writing and remote backup of large amounts of information.

(1) CentOS's firewall is strictly controlled, to use the transfer ports, one must pre-set the settings that is a snapshot from the webpage of CentOS's firewall in Chinese version.

(2) IT manager setup HBase and Cassandra data centers and examine the status of all nodes.

(3) Forms with identical names must be created in both data centers in HBase system. The primary data center will execute command (add_peer) [14], and backup the information onto the secondary data center.

(4) IT Manager edits Cassandra's file content (cassandra-topology.properties), then sets the names of the data center and the storage location of the nodes (rack number).

(5) IT manager edits Cassandra's file content (cassandra.yaml), and then changes the content of endpoint_snitch [16] to PropertyFileSnitch (data center management mode).

(6) IT manager executes command (create keyspace test with strategy_options ={DC1:2,DC2:1} and placement_strategy='NetworkTopologyStrategy') in Cassandra's primary data center, and then creates a form and initialize remote backup.

(7) IT manager eventually has to test the performance of writing, reading, and offsite data backup against large amounts of information using Thrift Java.

4.2   Intelligent Parameter Adaptation

In order to maintain the smooth remote backup over internet, we focus on the quality of services (QoS) about the data transmission and receipt. In other words, we have to deal with the crucial problems about jitter, loss, latency, and throughput. This paper introduces an intelligent adaptation for tuning data transmission and receipt parameters appropriately in both datacenters. As shown in Fig. 1 the diagram illustrates an intelligent adaptation using an adaptive network-based fuzzy inference system (ANFIS) [8] along with particle swarm optimization (PSO) [9] approach, where C, D, W, R, and M denote the normalized CPU clock rate, the size of SDRAM, network bandwidth, the ratio of read to write operation, and the number of message, respectively, to adjust remote backup parameters in HBase, i.e., the time interval between RegionServer and master as well as the ratio of read to write operation in system. It is noted that PSO approach is utilized to search the optimal weight parameters of ANFIS. Besides, the same scheme of ANFIS is applied for tuning remote backup parameters in Cassendra, namely the maximum size of commitlog space in memory, the maximum throughput in read/write operation, and the percentage of cache release for saving the out of bound of Java heap as shown in Fig. 2 where N represents the number of read plus write operation instead of R in Fig. 1. We have collected a lot of data by the manner of trial-and-error during the experiments. Once the data collection has completed, those of data have been put into the ANFIS for training and validating so that we can get a trained ANFIS system for infer the key parameters such as

(1) hbase.regionserver.msginterval,
(2) hbase.ipc.server.callqueue.read.ratio,
(3) commitlog_total_space_in_mb,
(4) compaction_throughput_mb_per_sec, and
(5) reduce_cache_capacity_to.

After that, the remote data center backup has been tested in the cloud computing system based on web interface and as a result it performs very well on HBase and Cassendra data center backup remotely.

4.3   Performance Index, Total Cost of Ownership, and Cost-Performance Ratio

Eq. (1) calculates the average access time (AAT) for each data size. In Eq. (1), AAT_{ijk} represents average access time with the same data size, and N_{ik} represents the current data size. The following three formulae will evaluate the performance index (PI) [1][2]. Eq. (2) calculates the data center's average access times overall $\overline{AAT_{s_{jk}}}$ for each test (i.e. write, read, remote backup), in which $AAT_{s_{ijk}}$ represents the average access time of each data size, please refer back to Eq. (1). Eq. (3) calculates the data center's normalized performance index. Eq. (4) calculates the data center's performance index overall, SF_1 is constant value and the aim is to quantify the value for observation.

$$AAT_{s_{ijk}} = \frac{AAT_{ijk}}{N_{ik}}, \text{ where } i = 1,2,...,l, \; j = 1,2,...,m, \; k = 1,2,...,n \tag{1}$$

$$\overline{AAT_{s_{jk}}} = \sum_{i=1}^{l} \omega_i \cdot AAT_{s_{ijk}}, \text{ where } j = 1,2,...,m, \; k = 1,2,...,n, \; \sum_{i=1}^{l} \omega_i = 1 \tag{2}$$

$$\overline{PI_{jk}} = \frac{\dfrac{1}{\overline{AAT_{s_{jk}}}}}{\underset{h=1,2,...,m}{MAX}\left(\dfrac{1}{\overline{AAT_{s_{hk}}}}\right)}, \text{ where } j = 1,2,...,m, \; k = 1,2,...,n \tag{3}$$

$$PI_j = \left(\sum_{k=1}^{n} W_k \cdot \overline{PI_{jk}}\right) \cdot SF_1, \text{ where } j = 1,2,...,m, \; k = 1,2,...,n, \; SF_1 = 10^2, \; \sum_{k=1}^{n} W_k = 1 \tag{4}$$

The total cost of ownership (TCO) [1][2] is divided into four parts: hardware costs, software costs, downtime costs, and operating expenses. The costs of a five-year period $Cost_{jg}$ are calculated using Eq. (5) where the subscript j represents various data center and g stands for a certain period of time. Among it, we assume there is an annual unexpected downtime, $Cost_{downtime\,for\,server_a}$, the monthly expenses $Cost_{monthly_b} \cdot period$, including machine room fees, installation and setup fee, provisional changing fees, and bandwidth costs.

$$Cost_{jg} = \sum_{a} Cost_{downtime\,for\,server_a} + \sum_{b} Cost_{monthly_b} \cdot period + \sum_{c} Cost_{hardware_c} + \sum_{d} Cost_{software_d}, \tag{5}$$

$$\text{where } j = 1,2,...,m, \; g = 1,2,...,o$$

This section defines the cost-performance ratio (C-P ratio) [10], CP_{jg}, of each data center based on total cost of ownership, CP_{jg}, and performance index, PI_j, as shown in Eq. (6). Eq. (6) is the formula for C-P ratio where SF_2 is the constant value of scale factor, and the aim is to quantify the C-P ratio within the interval of (0,100] to observe the differences of each data center.

$$CP_{jg} = \frac{PI_j}{Cost_{jg}} \cdot SF_2, \tag{6}$$

$$\text{where } j = 1,2,...,m, \; g = 1,2,...,o, \; SF_2 = 10^4$$

5 Experimental Results and Discussion

This section will go for the remote data center backup, the stress test, as well as the evaluation of total cost of ownership and performance index among various data centers. Finally, the assessment about the effectiveness and efficiency among various data centers have done well based on cost-performance ratio. All of tests have performed on IBM X3650 Server and IBM BladeCenter. The copyrights of several databases applied in this paper have Apache HBase and Apache Cassandra are of NoSQL database proposed this paper, but otherwise Cloudera HBase, DataStax Cassandra, and Oracle MySQL are alternative databases.

5.1 Intelligent Parameter Adaptation

In order to improve the quality of services (QoS) on remote data center backup, we have to deal with the crucial problems about jitter, loss, latency, and throughput in this experiment. According to the diagram as shown in Figs. 1 and 2, an intelligent adaptation using an adaptive network-based fuzzy inference system (ANFIS) with particle swarm optimization (PSO) approach is employed, which have utilized the CPU clock rate, the size of SDRAM, NIC bandwidth, message, the ratio of read to write operation per second or the number of read plus write operation per second, and the number of messages per second, respectively, as listed in Tables 1 and 2, to adjust two parameters (1) hbase.regionserver.msginterval and (2) hbase.ipc.server.callqueue.read.ratio in HBase and three parameters (1) commitlog_total_space_in_mb, (2) compaction_throughput_mb_per_sec, and (3) reduce_cache_capacity_to in Cassandra, as shown below in Figs 3 and 4.

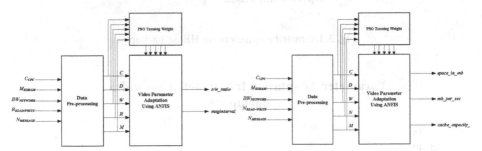

Fig. 1. Intelligent parameter adaptation for remote HBase backup

Fig. 2. Intelligent parameter adaptation for remote Cassandra backup

Table 1. Five operational mode for HBase backup

Operational Mode	CPU Clock Rate (MHZ)	Size of DRAM (GByte)	Band Width (Mbps)	Read/Write Ratio (per sec)	Message (per sec)
1	2400	32	77.79	0.9	15
2	2300	32	77.79	0.5	5
3	2200	32	77.79	0.7	9
4	2100	32	77.79	0.8	12
5	2000	32	77.79	0.6	7

Table 2. Five operational mode for Cassandra backup

Operational Mode	CPU Clock Rate (MHZ)	Size of DRAM (GByte)	Band Width (Mbps)	Read+Write (per sec)	Message (per sec)
1	2400	32	77.79	3150	15
2	2300	32	77.79	2900	5
3	2200	32	77.79	3000	9
4	2100	32	77.79	2850	12
5	2000	32	77.79	2950	7

Parameter Adaptation for Remte HBase Backup

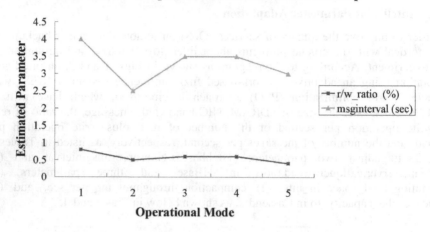

Fig. 3. Estimated parameters for HBase backup

Parameter Adaptation for Remote Cassandra Backup

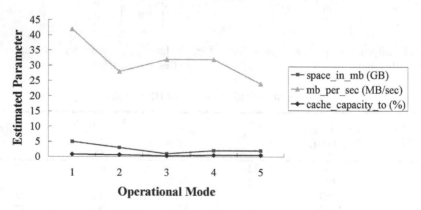

Fig. 4. Estimated parameters for Cassandra backup

5.2   Stress Test of Data Read/Write and Data Center Backup

Writing and reading tests of large amounts of information are originating from various database data centers. A total of four varying data sizes were tested, and the average time of a single datum access was calculated for each.

(1) Data centers A and B perform large amounts of information writing test through Thrift Java. Five consecutive writing times among various data centers were recorded for each data size. We substitute the results into Eq. (1) to calculate the average time of a single datum write for each type of data center.
(2) Data centers A and B perform large amounts of information reading test through Thrift. Five consecutive reading times among various data centers were recorded for each data size. We substitute the results into Eq. (1) to calculate the average time of a single datum read for each type of data center.

The remote backup testing tool, Thrift Java, is mainly used to find out how long will it take to backup each other's data remotely between data centers A and B. As a matter of fact, tests show that the average time of a single datum access for the remote backup of Apache HBase and Apache Cassandra only takes a fraction of mini-second. Further investigations found that although the two data centers are located in different network domains, they still belonged to the same campus network. The information might have only passed through the campus network internally, but never reach the internet outside, leading to speedy the remote backup. Nonetheless, we do not need to setup new data centers elsewhere to conduct more detailed tests because we believe that information exchange through internet will get the almost same results just like performing the remote backup tests via intranet in campus. Five consecutive backup times among various data centers were recorded for each data size. We substitute the results into Eq. (1) to calculate the average time of a single datum backup for each type of data center.

5.3   Cost-Performance Ratio Assessment

The following subsection will evaluate the performance index. We first substitute in the average execution times into Eq. (2) to find the normalized performance index of data centers for each test. Next we substitute the numbers into Eq. (3) to find average normalized performance index. Finally, we substitute the numbers into Eq. (4) to find the performance index of data centers as listed in Table 3. The total cost of ownership (TCO) includes hardware costs, software costs, downtime costs, and operating expenses. TCO over a five-year period is calculated using Eq. (5), and has listed in Table 4. We estimate an annual unexpected downtime costing around USD$1000; the monthly expenses includes around USD$200 machine room fees, installation and setup fee of around USD$200/time, provisional changing fees of around USD$10/time, and bandwidth costs. In Eq. (6) the formula assesses the cost-performance ratio, CP_{jg} , of each data center according to total cost of ownership, $Cost_{jg}$, and performance index, PI_j . Therefore we substitute the numbers from Tables 3 and 4 into Eq. (6) to find the cost-performance ratio of each data center as listed in Table 5.

Table 3. Performance index

DataBase	Performance Index
Apache HBase	93
Apache Cassandra	80
Cloudera HBase	54
DataStax Cassandra	51
Oracle MySQL	18

Table 4. Total cost of ownership over a 5-year period (unit: USD)

DataBase	1st Year	2nd Year	3rd Year	4th Year	5th Year
Apache HBase	12686	10020	10020	10097	10171
Apache Cassandra	12686	10020	10020	10097	10171
Cloudera HBase	14240	12373	12373	12050	12109
DataStax Cassandra	14190	12727	12727	12209	12313
Oracle MySQL	15030	13373	13373	13450	13524

Table 5. C-P ratio over a 5-year period

DataBase	1st Year	2nd Year	3rd Year	4th Year	5th Year
Apache HBase	74	93	93	93	92
Apache Cassandra	63	80	80	79	78
Cloudera HBase	38	44	44	45	45
DataStax Cassandra	36	40	40	42	42
Oracle MySQL	12	14	14	13	13

6   Conclusion

This paper realizes the remote data backup for HBase and Cassandra data centers, and has employed adaptive network-based fuzzy inference system (ANFIS) along with particle swarm optimization (PSO) to off-line tune seamless handoff and control network traffic flow. As a result both HBase and Cassandra yield the best C-P ratio when comparing with the others, provided that this paper indeed gives us an insight into the topic of remote data center backup.

Acknowledgments. This work is fully supported by the National Science Council, Taiwan, Republic of China, under grant number MOST 103-2221-E-390-011.

References

1. Chang, B.R., Tsai, H.-F., Chen, C.-M.: Empirical Analysis of Server Consolidation and Desktop Virtualization in Cloud Computing. Mathematical Problems in Engineeringarticle ID 947234, 11 pages (2013)

2. Chang, B.R., Tsai, H.-F., Chen, C.-M.: High-Performed Virtualization Services for In-Cloud Enterprise Resource Planning System. Journal of Information Hiding and Multimedia Signal Processing 5(4), 614–624 (2014)
3. Chang, B.R., Tsai, H.-F., Chen, C.-M., Huang, C.-F.: Intelligent Adaptation for UEC Video/Voice over IP with Access Control. International Journal of Intelligent Information and Database Systems 8(1), 64–80 (2014)
4. Chen, C.-Y., Chang, B.R., Huang, P.-S.: Multimedia Augmented Reality Information System for Museum Guidance. Personal and Ubiquitous Computing 18(2), 315–322 (2014)
5. Carstoiu, D., Lepadatu, E., Gaspar, M.: Hbase-non SQL Database, Performances Evaluation. International Journal of Advanced Computer Technology 2(5), 42–52 (2010)
6. Lakshman, A., Malik, P.: Cassandra: A Decentralized Structured Storage System. ACM SIGOPS Operating Systems Review 44(2), 35–40 (2010)
7. O'Higgins, N.: MongoDB and Python: Patterns and Processes for the Popular Document-Oriented Database. O'Reilly Media Inc., Sebastopol (2011)
8. Jang, J.-S.R.: ANFIS: Adaptive Network-Based Fuzzy Inference System. IEEE Transactions on System, Man and Cybernetics 23(3), 665–685 (1993)
9. Pousinho, H.M.I., Mendes, V.M.F., Catalão, J.P.S.: A hybrid PSO–ANFIS approach for short-term wind power prediction in Portugal. Energy Conversion and Management 52(1), 397–402 (2011)
10. Chang, B.R., Tsai, H.-F., Chen, C.-M.: Assessment of In-Cloud Enterprise Resource Planning System Performed in a Virtual Cluster. Mathematical Problems in Engineering, article ID 947234, 11 pages (2014)
11. Pokorny, J.: NoSQL Databases: A Step to Database Scalability in Web Environment. International Journal of Web Information Systems 9(1), 69–82 (2013)
12. Giersch, A., Robert, Y., Vivien, F.: Scheduling Tasks Sharing Files on Heterogeneous Master–Slave Platforms. Journal of Systems Architecture 52(2), 88–104 (2006)
13. Chakravarti, A.J., Baumgartner, G., Lauria, M.: The Organic Grid: Self-Organizing Computation on A Peer-to-Peer Network. IEEE Transactions on Systems, Man and Cybernetics, Part A: Systems and Humans 35(3), 373–384 (2005)
14. George, L.: HBase: the definitive guide. O'Reilly Media Inc., Sebastopol (2011)
15. Okorafor, E., Patrick, M.K.: Availability of Jobtracker Machine in Hadoop/Mapreduce Zookeeper Coordinated Clusters. Advanced Computing: An International Journal 3(3), 19–30 (2012)
16. Parthasarathy, V.: Learning Cassandra for Administrators. Packt Publishing Ltd., Birmingham (2013)
17. Gu, Y., Grossman, R.L.: Sector: A High Performance Wide area Community Data Storage and Sharing System. Future Generation Computer Systems 26(5), 720–728 (2010)
18. Slee, M., Agarwal, A., Kwiatkowski, M.: Thrift: Scalable Cross-Language Services Implementation. Facebook White Paper 5, 8 pages (2007)
19. Maver, J.J., Cappy, P.: Essential Facebook Development: Build Successful Applications for the Facebook Platform. Addison-Wesley Professional, Boston (2009)
20. Murthy, R., Goel, R.: Low-Latency Queries on Hive Warehouse Data. XRDS: Crossroads. The ACM Magazine for Students 19(1), 40–43 (2012)
21. Ramo, A.C., Diaz, R.G., Tsaregorodtsev, A.: DIRAC RESTful API. Journal of Physics: Conference Series 396(5), ID: 052019 (2012)

An Interaction Pattern Kernel Approach for Protein-Protein Interaction Extraction from Biomedical Literature

Yung-Chun Chang[1,2], Yu-Chen Su[2], Nai-Wen Chang[1,3], and Wen-Lian Hsu[1]

[1] Institute of Information Science, Academia Simica
No. 128, Sec. 2, Academia Rd., Taipei City 11529, Taiwan (R.O.C)
[2] Department of Information Management, National Taiwan University
No. 1, Sec. 4, Roosevelt Rd., Taipei City 10617, Taiwan (R.O.C)
[3] Graduate Institute of Biomedical Electronics and Bioinformatics
No. 1, Sec. 4, Roosevelt Rd., Taipei City 10617, Taiwan (R.O.C)
{changyc,hsu}@iis.sinica.edu.tw,
{b99705029,d00945020}@ntu.edu.tw

Abstract. Discovering the interactions between proteins mentioned in biomedical literature is one of the core topics of text mining in the life sciences. In this paper, we propose an interaction pattern generation approach to capture frequent PPI patterns in text. We also present an interaction pattern tree kernel method that integrates the PPI pattern with convolution tree kernel to extract protein-protein interactions. Empirical evaluations on LLL, IEPA, and HPRD50 corpora demonstrate that our method is effective and outperforms several well-known PPI extraction methods.

Keywords: Text Mining, Protein-Protein Interaction, Interaction Pattern Generation, Interaction Pattern Tree Kernel.

1 Introduction

With a rapidly growing number of research papers, researchers have difficulty finding the papers that they are looking for. Relationships between entities, mentioned in these papers, can help biomedical researchers find the specific papers they need. Among biomedical relation types, protein–protein interaction (PPI) extraction is becoming critical in the field of molecular biology due to demands for automatic discovery of molecular pathways and interactions in the literature. The goal of PPI extraction is to recognize various interactions, such as transcription, translation, post translational modification, complex and dissociation between proteins, drugs, or other molecules from biomedical literature.

Most PPI extraction methods can be regarded as supervised learning approaches. Given a training corpus containing a set of manually-tagged examples, a supervised classification algorithm is employed to train a PPI classifier to recognize whether an interaction exists in the text segment (e.g., a sentence). Feature-based approaches and

S.-M. Cheng and M.-Y. Day (Eds.): TAAI 2014, LNAI 8916, pp. 36–46, 2014.

kernel-based approaches are frequently used for PPI extraction. Feature-based methods exploit instances of both positive and negative relations in a training corpus to identify effective text features for protein-protein interaction extraction. For instance, Van et al. [16] propose a rich-feature-based kernel which applies feature vectors in combination with automated feature selection for protein-protein interaction extraction. In addition, a co-occurrence-based method is introduced by Airola et al. [1], which explores co-occurrence features of dependency graphs for representing the sentence structure.

However, feature-based methods often have difficulty finding effective features to extract entity relations. In order to address this problem, the kernel-based methods have been proposed to implicitly explore various features in a high dimensional space by employing a kernel to directly calculate the similarity between two objects. In particular, kernel-based methods can be effective in reducing the burden of feature engineering for structured objects in Natural Language Processing (NLP) research, such as the tree structure in PPI extraction. For instance, Erkan et al. [6] define two kernel functions based on the cosine similarity and the edit distance among the shortest paths between protein names in a dependency parse tree. Moreover, Satre et al. [19] develop a system called AkanePPI, which extracts features using the combination of a deep syntactic parser to capture the semantic meaning of the sentences with a shallow dependency parser for the tree kernels, in order to automatically create rules to identify pairs of interacting proteins from a training corpus.

Current research attempt to use tree kernel-based methods mainly due to its capability to effectively utilize the structured information derived from sentences, especially for the constituent dependencies knowledge. Vishwanathan et al. [17] propose a subtree (ST) kernel which considers all common subtrees in the tree representation of two compared sentences. Here a subtree comprises a node with all its descendants in the tree, and two subtrees are identical if labels of the node and order of their children are identical for all nodes. Likewise, Collins et al. [3] introduce a subset tree (SST) kernel that relaxes the constraint that requires all leaves to be included in the substructures at all times. In the meanwhile it preserves the grammatical rules. For a given tree node, either none or all of its children have to be included in the resulting subset tree. In addtion, Moschitti et al. [13] adopt a partial tree kernel (PT) which is more flexible by virtually allowing any tree sub-structures; the only constraint is the order of child nodes must be identical. Both SST and PT kernels are convolution tree kernels. Kuboyama et al. [9] propose a spectrum tree kernel (SpT) which put emphasis on the simplest syntax-tree substructures among these four tree kernels. It compares all directed vertex-walks, that is, sequences of edge connected syntax tree nodes, of length q as the unit of representation. When comparing two protein pairs, the number of shared sub-patterns called tree q-grams are measured as similarity score.

To extract PPI from biomedical literature effectively, we modeled interaction extraction as a classification problem. We proposed an interaction pattern generation approach to capture frequent PPI patterns. Furthermore, to identify interactions between proteins, we developed an interaction pattern tree kernel that integrates the shortest path-enclosed tree (SPT) structure with generated PPI patterns to support vector machines (SVM). The results of experiments demonstrate that the iterative pattern tree kernel method is effective in extracting PPI. In addition, the proposed interaction pattern generation approach successfully exploits the interaction semantics of text by capturing frequent PPI patterns. Consequently, the method outperforms the tree kernel-based PPI method [3, 9, 13, 17]; the feature-based PPI method [1, 16]; and the shortest path-enclosed tree (SPT) detection method which is widely used to identify relations between named entities.

2   Our System Architecture

Figure 1 shows the proposed interaction extraction method, which is comprised of two key components: *interaction pattern generation* and *interaction pattern tree construction*. We regard interaction extraction as a classification problem. The interaction pattern generation component aims to automatically generate representative patterns of mention interactions between proteins. Then, the interaction pattern tree construction integrates the syntactic and content information with generated interaction patterns for representation of text. Finally, the convolution tree kernel measures similarity between interaction pattern tree structures for SVM to classify interactive expressions. We discuss each component in detail in the following sections.

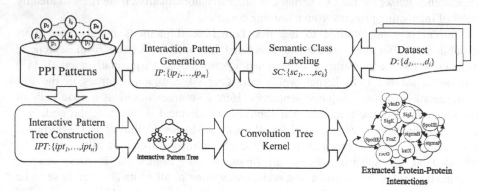

Fig. 1. The interaction extraction method

3   Interaction Pattern Generation

The human perception of a protein-protein interaction is obtained through the recognition of important events or semantic contents to rapidly narrow down the scope of possible candidates. For example, when an expression contains strongly correlated words like "*beta-catenin*", "*alpha-catenin 57-264*" and "*binding*" simultaneously, it is natural to conclude that this is a protein-protein interactive expression, with a less likelihood of a non-interactive one. This phenomenon can explain how humans can skim through an article to quickly capture the interactive expression. In light of this rationale, we proposed an interaction pattern generation approach that aims to automatically generate representative patterns from sequences of expression of protein-protein interactions.

We formulate interaction pattern generation as a frequent pattern mining problem. First of all, the instances undergo the semantic class labeling process. To illustrate the process of semantic class labeling, consider the instance I_n = "*Abolition of the gp130 binding site in hLIF created antagonists of LIF action*", as shown in Fig. 2. First, "*gp130*" and "*hLIF*" are two given protein names, as tagged *PROTEIN1* and *PROTEIN2* respectively. Then, we stem remaining tokens by using porter stemming algorithm [15]. Finally, trigger words "bind" and "antagonist" are labeled with their corresponding types by using our compiled trigger word list which extracts from a BioNLP corpus [8]. Evidently the SCL can group the synonyms together by the same label. This enables us to find distinctive and prominent semantic classes for PPI expression in the following stage.

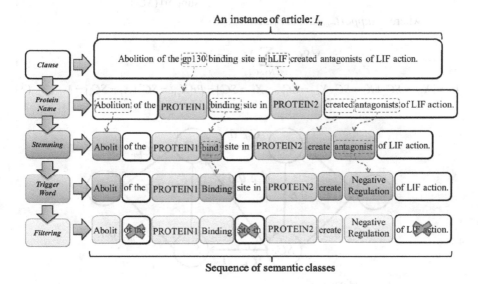

Fig. 2. Semantic class labeling process

After labeling semantic classes, we based on the co-occurrence of semantic classes to construct a graph to describe the strength of relations between them. Since semantic classes are of an ordered nature, the graph is directed and can be made with association rules. In order to avoid the generation of frames with insufficient length, we empirically set the minimum support of a semantic class as 20 and minimum confidence as 0.5 in our association rules. Thus, an association rule can be represented as (1). Fig. 3 is an illustration of a semantic graph. In this graph, vertices (SC_x) represent semantic classes, and edges represent the co-occurrence of two classes, SC_i and SC_j, where SC_i precedes SC_j. The number on the edge denotes the confidence of two connecting vertices. After constructing all of the semantic graphs, we then generate semantic frames by applying the random walk theory [13] in search of high frequency and representative classes for each topic. Let a semantic graph G be defined as $G=(V,E)$ ($|V|=p$, $|E|=k$), a random walk process consisting of a series of random selections on the graph. Every edge (SC_n, SC_m) has its own weight M_{nm}, which denotes the probability of a semantic class SC_n, followed by another class SC_m. For each class, the sum of weight to all neighboring classes $N(SC_n)$ is defined as (2), and the whole graph's probability matrix is defined as (3). As a result, a series of a random walk process becomes a Markov Chain. According to [4], the cover time of a random walk process on a normal graph is $\forall SC_n, C_{SC_n} \leq 4k^2$. We select frequent semantic classes and their neighborhoods as start nodes of a random walk process. We can conclude that using random walk to find frequent patterns on the interactive graph would help us capture even the low probability combinations and shorten the processing time.

$$\text{confidence}(SC_i \Rightarrow SC_j) = P(SC_j|SC_i) = \frac{\text{support}(SC_i \cup SC_j)}{\text{support}(SC_i)}, \tag{1}$$

where $support_{min}=20$, $confidence_{min}=0.5$

$$\forall SC_n \sum_{m \in N(SC_n)} M_{nm} = 1 \tag{2}$$

$$Pr = [X_{t+1} = SC_m \mid X_t = SC_n, X_{t-1} = SC_k, ..., X_0 = SC_i] = Pr[X_{t+1} = SC_m \mid X_t = SC_n] = M \tag{3}$$

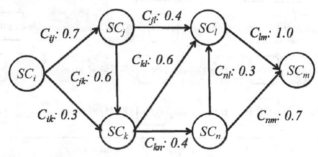

Notation:
SC: Semantic Class C_{pq}: Confidence ($SC_p \Rightarrow SC_q$)

Fig. 3. An interactive graph for pattern generation

Although the random walk process can help us generate frames from frequent patterns in semantic graphs, it can also create some redundancy. Hence, a merging procedure is required to eliminate the redundant results by retaining the patterns, with long length and high coverage, and dispose of bigram patterns that are completely covered by another pattern. For example, the pattern [PROTEIN1]->[Binding] is completely covered by the pattern [PROTEIN1]->[Binding]->[Regulation]->[Transcription]->[PROTEIN2]. Thus, the former pattern is incorporated. Otherwise, if a bigram pattern partially overlaps with another, the overlapping part is concatenated to form a longer pattern. For instance, the pattern [Positive_regulation]->[Regulation] partially overlaps with [Regulation]->[Gene_expression]->[PROTEIN1], thus the two patterns are merged into another single pattern

[*Positive_regulation*]->[*Regulation*]-> [*Gene_expression*]->[*PROTEIN1*]. Moreover, the reduction of the semantic classes space provided by pattern selection is critical. It allows the execution of more sophisticated text classification algorithms, which lead to improved results. Those algorithms cannot be executed on the original semantic classes space because their execution time would be excessively high, making them impractical [1]. Therefore, to select patterns closely associated with an interaction would improve the performance of PPI extraction. We use the pointwise mutual information (PMI) [1], a popular statistical approach used in feature selection, to discriminate semantic classes for PPI instances. Given a training dataset comprised of positive instances, the PMI calculates the likelihood of the occurrence of a semantic class in the expressions of PPI. A semantic class with a large PMI value is thought to be closely associated with the interaction. Lastly, we rank the interaction patterns in the training dataset based on a sum of semantic classes PMI values and retain the top 20 for representing protein-protein interactions.

4   Interaction Pattern Tree Construction

A PPI instance is represented by the interaction pattern tree (IPT) structure, which is the shortest path-enclosed tree (SPT) of the instance enhanced by following steps. To facilitate comprehension of the construction process, the positive instance shown in Fig. 4(a), which mentions the interaction between "AVP" and "PKC", serves as an example.

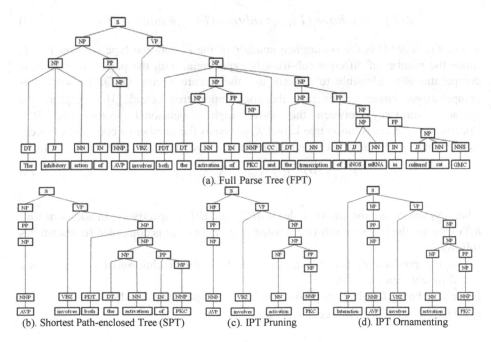

Fig. 4. The interaction pattern tree construction procedure for a PPI instance "The inhibitory action of AVP involves both the activation of PKC and the transcription of iNOS mRNA in cultured rat GMC"

In [15], the authors show that the SPT is effective in identifying the relation between two entities mentioned in a segment of text. Given an instance, therefore we first construct the smallest common sub-tree including the two proteins. In other words, the sub-tree is enclosed by the shortest path linking the two proteins p_i and p_j in the parse tree, which as shown in Fig. 4(b). Next, in order to make the IPT concise and clear, we remove indiscriminative IPT elements. Frequent words are not useful for expressing interactions between proteins. For instance, the word "*both*" in Fig. 4(c) is a common word and cannot discriminate interactive expressions. To remove stop words and the corresponding syntactic elements from the IPT, we sort words according to their frequency in the text corpus. Then, the most frequent words are used to compile a stop word list. Moreover, to refine the list, protein names and verbs are excluded from it because they are key constructs of protein-protein interactions. Finally, the generated interaction patterns can help us capture the most prominent and representative patterns for expressing PPI. Highlighting interaction patterns closely associated with PPIs in an IPT would improve the interaction extraction performance. For each IPT that matched an interaction pattern, we add an IP tag as a child of the tree root to incorporate the interactive semantics into the IPT structure (as shown in Fig. 4(d)).

A convolution kernel aims to capture structured information in terms of substructures. Generally, we can represent a parse tree T by a vector of integer counts of each sub-tree type (regardless of its ancestors):

$$\phi(T) = (\#subtree_1(T),...,\#subtree_i(T),...,\#subtree_n(T)), \qquad (4)$$

where $\#subtree_i(T)$ is the occurrence number of the ith sub-tree type ($subtree_i$) in T. Since the number of different sub-trees is exponential with the parse tree size, it is computationally infeasible to directly use the feature vector $\phi(T)$. To solve this computational issue, we leverage the convolution tree kernel [3] to capture the syntactic similarity between the above high dimensional vectors implicitly. Specifically, the convolution tree kernel K_{CTK} counts the number of common sub-trees as the syntactic similarity between two rich interactive trees IPT_1 and IPT_2 as follows:

$$K_{CTK}(IPT_1, IPT_2) = \sum_{n_1 \in N_1, n_2 \in N_2} \Delta(n_1, n_2), \qquad (5)$$

where N_1 and N_2 are the sets of nodes in IPT_1 and IPT_2 respectively. In addition $\Delta(n_1, n_2)$ evaluates the common sub-trees rooted at n_1 and n_2 and is computed recursively as follows:

(1) if the productions (i.e. the nodes with their direct children)at n_1 and n_2 are different, $\Delta(n_1, n_2) = 0$;

(2) else if both $n1$ and $n2$ are pre-terminals (POS tags), $\Delta(n_1, n_2)=1 \times \lambda$;

(3) else calculate $\Delta(n_1, n_2)$ recursively as:

$$\Delta(n_1, n_2) = \lambda \prod_{k=1}^{\#ch(n_1)} (1 + \Delta(ch(n_1,k), ch(n_2,k))), \qquad (6)$$

where #$ch(n_1)$ is the number of children of node n_1; $ch(n, k)$ is the kth child of node n; and $\lambda(0<\lambda<1)$ is the decay factor used to make the kernel value less variable with respect to different sized sub-trees. The parse tree kernel counts the number of common sub-trees as the syntactic similarity measure between two relation instances. The time complexity for computing this kernel is $O(|N_1| \cdot |N_2|)$.

5   Experiments

5.1   Experimental Setting

We evaluated our method with three publicly available corpora that contain PPI annotations: LLL [13], IEPA [4] and HPRD50 [6] (the distribution of corpora are shown as the Fig.5). All the corpora are parsed using Stanford parser (http://nlp.stanford.edu/software/lex-parser.shtml) to generate the output of parse tree and part-of-speech tagging. In our implementation, we use Moschitti's tree kernel toolkit [1] to develop the convolution kernel of an IPT. To derive credible evaluation results, we utilize the 10-fold cross validation method [1] on all of the corpora. This guarantees the maximal use of the available data and allows comparison to the earlier relevant work. The evaluation metrics are the precision rate, recall rate, and F1-measure [1]. The F1 value is used to determine relative effectiveness of the compared methods. We exploit the macro-averaged score to indicate the overall performance across three different corpora for each evaluation metric.

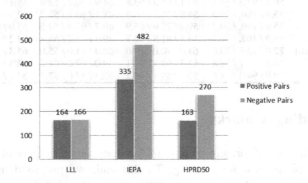

Fig. 5. Distribution of 3 corpora used for performance evaluation of PPI extraction

5.2   Results and Discussion

The proposed interaction pattern tree kernel uses the PPI patterns to enhance the SPT. In the following, we compare it with several feature-based and kernel-based PPI extraction methods reported by [17] to demonstrate the effectiveness. As shown in Table 1, the proposed method significantly outperforms SPT and AkanePPI. Furthermore, the syntax tree-based kernel methods (ST, SST, PT, and SpT) only examine the syntactic structures of text and cannot sense the semantics of protein interactions. By contrast, our method analyzes the semantics and content (i.e., PPI patterns) of text to identify protein-protein interactions. Hence, our performance is superior to that of them. It is noteworthy that syntax tree-based kernel methods oftentimes are just on par with the co-occurrence approach in terms of F1-measure. On the very small LLL, their results practically coincide with co-occurrence. The rich-feature-based and Cosine also outperform SPT, AkanePPI and syntax tree-based kernel methods as it incorporates dependency features to distinguish protein-protein interactions. Although Cosine can accomplish higher performance by further considering term weighting, it is difficult to represent word relations. By contrast, our method can extract word semantics, and generate PPI patterns that can capture long distance relations among them. Consequently, we can achieve a better outcome than other methods.

To summarize, the proposed interaction pattern tree kernel approach successfully integrates the syntactic and semantic information in text to identify protein-protein interactions. Hence, it achieves the best performance among the compared methods, as shown in Table 1.

Table 1. The interaction extraction performance of the compared methods

System	LLL	IEPA	HPRD50	Macro-average
	Precision, Recall, F1-measure (%)			
SPT	56.4 / 96.1 / 69.6	55.5 / 28.8 / 37.1	46.2 / 13.4 / 20.8	52.7 / 46.1 / 42.5
AkanePPI [19]	**76.7** / 40.2 / 52.8	**66.2** / 51.3 / 57.8	52.0 / 55.8 / 53.8	**65.0** / 49.1 / 54.8
co-occ. [1]	55.9 / **100.** / 70.3	40.8 / **100.** / 57.6	38.9 / **100.** / 55.4	45.2 / **100.** / 61.1
PT [13]	56.2 / 97.3 / 69.3	63.1 / 66.3 / 63.8	54.9 / 56.7 / 52.4	58.1 / 73.4 / 61.8
SST [3]	55.9 / **100.** / 70.3	54.8 / 76.9 / 63.4	48.1 / 63.8 / 52.2	52.9 / 80.2 / 62.0
ST [17]	55.9 / **100.** / 70.3	59.4 / 75.6 / 65.9	49.7 / 67.8 / 54.5	55.0 / 81.1 / 63.6
SpT [9]	55.9 / **100.** / 70.3	54.5 / 81.8 / 64.7	49.3 / 71.7 / 56.4	53.2 / 84.5 / 63.8
rich-feature-based [16]	72.0 / 73.0 / 73.0	64.0 / 70.0 / 67.0	**60.0** / 51.0 / 55.0	65.3 / 64.7 / 65.0
Cosine [6]	70.2 / 81.7 / **73.8**	61.3 / 68.4 / 64.1	59.0 / 67.2 / 61.2	63.5 / 72.4 / 66.4
Our method	59.9 / 94.4 / 71.6	52.2 / 88.1 / **65.2**	59.3 / 83.0 / **67.3**	57.1 / 88.5 / **68.0**

6   Concluding Remarks

Automated extraction of protein-protein interactions is an important and widely studied task in biomedical text mining. To this end, we proposed an interaction pattern generation approach for acquiring PPI patterns. We also developed a method that combines the shortest path-enclosed tree structure with the generated PPI patterns to analyze the syntactic, semantic, and content information in text. It then exploits the derived information to identify protein-protein interactions in biomedical literatures. Our experiment results demonstrate that the proposed method is effective and also outperforms well-known PPI extraction methods.

In the future, we will investigate the syntactic dependency tree in text to incorporate further syntactic and semantic information into the interactive pattern tree structures. We will also utilize information extraction algorithms to extract interaction tuples from positive instances and construct an interaction network of proteins.

Acknowledgements. This research was supported by the National Science Council of Taiwan under grant NSC102-3113-P-001-006, MOST103-2319-B-010-002 and MOST103-3111-Y-001-027.

References

1. Airola, A., Pyysalo, S., Björne, J., Pahikkala, T., Ginter, F.: All-paths graph kernel for protein-protein interaction extraction with evaluation of cross-corpus learning. BMC Bioinformatics 9, S2 (2008)
2. Baeza-Yates, R., Ribeiro-Neto, B.: Modern Information Retrieval: The Concepts and Technology Behind Search. Addison Wesley (2011)
3. Collins, M., Duffy, N.: Convolution kernels for natural language. In: Proceedings of Annual Conference on Neural Information Processing Systems, pp. 625–632 (2001)
4. Cooper, C., Frieze, A.M.: The cover time of random regular graphs. SIAM Journal on Discrete Mathematics 18, 728–740 (2005)
5. Ding, J., Berleant, D., Nettleton, D., Wurtele, E.: MEDLINE: abstracts, sentences, or phrases? In: Proceedings of Pacific Symposium on Biocomputing, pp. 326–337 (2002)
6. Erkan, G., Özgür, A., Radev, D.R.: Semi-supervised classification for extracting protein interaction sentences using dependency parsing. In: Proceedings of the 2007 Joint Conf. on Empirical Methods in Natural Language Processing and Computational Natural Language Learning, pp. 228–237 (2007)
7. Fundel, K., Küffner, R., Zimmer, R.: RelEx – Relation extraction using dependency parse trees. Bioinformatics 23(3), 365–371 (2007)
8. Kim, J.D., Ohta, T., Pyysalo, S., Kano, Y., Tsujii, J.: Overview of BioNLP'09 shared task on event extraction. In: Proceeding of the Workshop on Current Trends in Biomedical Natural Language Processing: Shared Task, pp. 1–9 (2009)
9. Kuboyama, T., Hirata, K., Kashima, H., Aoki-Kinoshita, K.F., Yasuda, H.: A spectrum tree kernel. Information and Media Technologies 2, 292–299 (2007)
10. Lovász, L.: Random walks on graphs: a survey, vol. 2, pp. 1–46. Janos Bolyai Mathematical Society, Budapest (1993)
11. Manning, C.D., Schütze, H.: Foundations of statistical natural language processing, 1st edn. MIT Press, Cambridge (1999)
12. Moschitti, A.: A study on convolution kernels for shallow semantic parsing. In: Proceedings of the 42nd Annual Meeting of the Association for Computational Linguistics, pp. 21–26 (2004)
13. Moschitti, A.: Efficient convolution kernels for dependency and constituent syntactic trees. In: Fürnkranz, J., Scheffer, T., Spiliopoulou, M. (eds.) ECML 2006. LNCS (LNAI), vol. 4212, pp. 318–329. Springer, Heidelberg (2006)
14. Nédellec, C.: Learning language in logic-genic interaction extraction challenge. In: Proceedings of the 4th Learning Language in Logic Workshop, pp. 31–37 (2005)
15. Porter, M.F.: An algorithm for suffix stripping. In: Jones, K.S., Willet, P. (eds.) Readings in Information Retrieval. Morgan Kaufmann, San Francisco (1997)
16. Van Landeghem, S., Saeys, Y., De Baets, B., Van de Peer, Y.: Extracting protein-protein interactions from text using rich feature vectors and feature selection. In: Proceedings of 3rd International Symposium on Semantic Mining in Biomedicine, pp. 77–84 (2008)
17. Tikk, D., Thomas, P., Palaga, P., Hakenberg, J., Leser, U.: A Comprehensive Benchmark of Kernel Methods to Extract Protein–Protein Interactions from Literature. PLoS Computational Biology 6(7), 1–19 (2010)

18. Vishwanathan, S.V.N., Smola, A.J.: Fast kernels for string and tree matching. In: Proceedings of Neural Information Processing Systems (NIPS 2002), pp. 569–576 (2002)
19. Satre, R., Sagae, K., Tsujii, J.: Syntactic features for protein-protein interaction extraction. In: Proceedings of the 2nd International Symposium on Languages in Biology and Medicine, pp. 6.1-6.14 (2007)

Section Heading Recognition in Electronic Health Records Using Conditional Random Fields

Chih-Wei Chen[1], Nai-Wen Chang[2,3], Yung-Chun Chang[4], and Hong-Jie Dai[1,*]

[1] Graduate Institute of Biomedical Informatics, College of Medical Science and Technology,
Taipei Medical University, Taiwan
[2] Institution of Information Science, Academia Sinica, Taiwan
[3] Graduate Institute of Biomedical Electronics and Bioinformatics,
National Taiwan University, Taiwan
[4] Institute of Information Science, Academia Simica, Taiwan
{cwchen123,naiwun}@gmail.com, changyc@iis.sinica.edu.tw,
hjdai@tmu.edu.tw

Abstract. Electronic health records (EHRs) contain a wealth of information, such as discharge diagnoses, laboratory results, and pharmacy orders, which can be used to support clinical decision support systems and enable clinical and translational research. Unfortunately, the information is represented in a highly heterogeneous semi-structured or unstructured format with author- and domain-specific idiosyncrasies, acronyms and abbreviations. To take full advantage of health data, text-mining techniques have been applied by researchers to recognize named entities (NEs) mentioned in EHRs. However, the judgment of clinical data cannot be known solely from the NE level. For instance, a disease mention in the section of past medical history has different clinical significance when mentioned in the family medical history section. To obtain high-quality information and improve the understanding of clinical records, this work developed a machine learning-based section heading recognition system and evaluated its performance on a manually annotated corpus. The experiment results showed that the machine learning-based system achieved a satisfactory F-score of 0.939, which outperformed a dictionary-based system by 0.321.

Keywords: Information Extraction, Natural Language Processing, Electronic Health Record, Section Recognition.

1 Introduction

Electronic health records (EHRs) promote the access, retrieval and sharing of clinical information. Nevertheless, the records of EHRs are stored in free-text form, which becomes difficult to acquire meaningful data and information from EHRs. Applying natural language processing (NLP) techniques to EHRs can facilitate the gathering of significant facts, assist clinical decision support and foster analysis and research from

---

* Corresponding author.

S.-M. Cheng and M.-Y. Day (Eds.): TAAI 2014, LNAI 8916, pp. 47–55, 2014.

EHRs. Apparently, recognition of clinical entities such as drugs and diseases in clinical narratives is one of the fundamental tasks for clinical NLP systems. Several clinical NLP systems, such as MedLEE (Friedman, Shagina et al. 2004), MetaMap (Aronson 2001), and cTAKES (Savova, Masanz et al. 2010) have been developed to support the clinical entity recognition task. However, the judgment of clinical data cannot be known solely from named entity level. For instance, "coronary heart disease" has different clinical significance in the section of past medical history or family medical history. The frequent use of author- and domain-specific idiosyncrasies, acronyms and abbreviations that exist in different parts of an EHR also increases difficulty for NLP systems to understand the semantics. For example, the acronym "BS" means "blood sugar" in the laboratory section, but indicates "bowel sounds" in the section of abdominal exams (Denny, Miller et al. 2008).

The task of recognizing section heading can improve the understanding of clinical records and aid the disambiguation of the meaning of information (Denny, Miller et al. 2008). Unfortunately, recognition of section headings appears to be a challenging task. First of all, the names of section headings do not follow a universal system. For the section of a chief problem, "chief complaint", "presenting complaint", "presenting problems", "reason for encounter", or even the use of abbreviation "CC" may be a possible name. Furthermore, the hierarchies of sections vary from record to record. For instance, "Laboratory section" and "radiology section" may be two separated parts, or both may be put together under the "data section". "Impression and assessment" may be separated individually or merged together into one section. Occasionally, the same section name can infer different definitions. "CC" can refer to "chief complaint" in a discharge summary, or "carbon copy" in a clinical narrative written in email. "Impression" might mean the overall diagnosis of a patient, or the subsection of image studies. Therefore, section recognition entirely based on dictionaries or patterns may not always work. In light of this issue, this work compiled a section recognition corpus on top of the dataset released by the i2b2 2014 shared task (Stubbs, Kotfila et al. 2014) and presented a machine learning approach based on the linear chain conditional random fields (CRF) model (Lafferty, McCallum et al. 2001)to deal with the section heading recognition task for EHRs. A set of features were proposed and their effectiveness were studied in this work.

2   Methodology

2.1   Section Heading Corpus Generation

To the best of the authors' knowledge, currently there is no openly available corpus annotated with medical section heading information. Therefore, this work used a section heading corpus from the dataset of Track 2 of the i2b2 2014 shared-task (Stubbs, Kotfila et al. 2014). The section heading strings in the clinical note section header terminology (SecTag) (Denny, Miller et al. 2008) were used to tag all plausible candidate headings mentioned in EHRs. Afterwards, the machine-generated annotations were manually corrected by the first author of this paper, who is a doctor of medicine.

For our manual annotation of EHRs, only the topmost section headings are annotated; if there are section headings whose contents also belong to a superior section or can be viewed as subsections themselves, these headings are removed from the annotations regardless of their section level in other EHRs. For example, in an EHR, if both "laboratory" and "radiology" appeared and can be considered as subsections of "data", then only the superior section "data" is annotated. But if "laboratory" and "radiology" are two separate sections without a superior section that covers them, both sections are annotated. In another case, "impression" is annotated if it is the topmost section; however, if the content of the "impression" section clearly contains the data of certain reports, such as X-ray or echography, and its description was followed by section headings like "cardiac echography" or "chest X-ray", then the annotation of the "impression" section is removed. In addition, if the name of a topmost section consists of two merged concepts, it is still annotated as one section. For instance, some EHRs join "impression" and "plan" as one section "impression/plan", while others may separate "plan" from "impression".

2.2   Section Heading Recognition

For a given EHR, the raw text was extracted and the original line breaks were retained. The text distinguished by the line breaks was processed by the MedPost tagger (Smith, Rindflesch et al. 2004) to further split it into lines of texts that consist of tokens. Each line was then aligned with experts' annotations to generate the training instances for CRF. This work employed the IOB tag scheme to represent the annotations for section heading; the B tag indicates the beginning of a section heading boundary, the I tag indicates contents inside the boundary of a section heading, and the O tag means contents outside of a section heading. Figure 1 illustrates an example, in which the assigned tag is highlighted in bold.

Record/**B** date/**I**:/**I** 2149-03-19/**O**

Reason/**B** for/**I** visit/**I** 67/**O**yo/**O** man/**O** with/**O** DM/**O** , /**O**...
Patient/**O** was/**O** in/**O** his/**O** ...

...

Selected/**B** recent/**I** labs/**I**chem/**O** 7/**O** : /**O** 140/**O** //**O** 4.0/**O** //**O**...

Fig. 1. A sample EHR annotated with section heading information

For each token, a set of features were extracted and the CRF model was used to build the section heading recognizer. The following subsections elaborate the features developed for this work.

Word Features
Apparently, the word of a target token and words preceding or following the target token can be useful for determining the target token's assigned tag. This work used

the content window size of five to extract word features, including the two preceding words, the current word, and the two following words.

The advantages of normalizing words when encoding them as features haven been shown in many sequential labeling tasks (Tsai, Sung et al. 2006). Therefore, this work normalized all words within a context window by transforming all words into lower cases and encoded all numeric values as the value 1.

Dictionary Features

The strings of the "str" column in the SecTag section header terminology were collected to compile a dictionary for our dictionary features. For all collected section heading strings, this work calculated their existing position information within the dictionary, and encoded the position information using 3 bits. Table 1 shows the encoded results. Based on the dictionary and position information, this work developed two dictionary features. One is the dictionary matching feature, whose value is 1 if the current word is a substring of the terms in our dictionary. The other is the dictionary position feature, whose value is the encoded position information if the current word is matched with our dictionary.

Table 1. Position Information

Encoded Position Information	Description
001	The term only appeared in the first token among all section headings.
010	The term only appeared in the middle token among all section headings.
100	The term only appeared in the last token among all section headings.
011	The term appeared in the first/middle token among all section headings.
110	The term appeared in the middle/last token among all section headings.
101	The term appeared in the first/last token among all section headings.
111	The term appeared in the first/middle/last token among all section headings.

In addition, in the SecTag terminology, section headings were defined within a hierarchy, and associated with a level information to indicate their location within a tree. Each heading string was also normalized to a unique string, which enables us to find the same section heading represented in different names. The normalized section strings and the associated level information were encoded as features.

Affix Features

An affix refers to a morpheme that is attached to a base morpheme to form a word. This work employed two types of affixes: prefixes and suffixes. Some prefixes and suffixes can provide good clues for classifying section headings. For example, words which end in "Hx" are related to medical historical information, such as PSurHx refers to the "past surgical history" section. This work used the length of 2 characters for prefixes and suffixes.

Orthographic Features
The surface strings of the section headings in an EHR may vary, but still follow certain rules established by usage. The orthographic features were developed to capture the subtle writing style. Each orthographic feature is implemented by using regular expressions to capture writing rules of section headings in terms of spelling, hyphenation, and capitalization. If the current word matches the defined orthographic feature, its feature value is 1; otherwise, the value is 0.

Layout Features
Given the variety of the layouts of EHRs, the original line breaks of the raw text can guide the machine learning model to determine the section headings that lead section blocks. This work developed layout features to capture the line break information. In our implementation, for a given split sentence, if its previous line in the original raw text was an empty line, the value of the layout feature is 1, otherwise it is 0. Take the third line of Figure 1 as an example. The value of the layout feature with block size 1 would be 1, but the value of the fourth line is 0. The block size for the layout features was set to six, meaning that for a given sentence, the preceding and the following three lines were considered.

3 Experiment

3.1 Dataset

The Track 2 dataset released by the i2b2 2014 shared-task was used in this work. The dataset was preliminarily divided into three subsets: set1 (521 records), set2 (269 records) and testing set (514 records). After the manual annotation of section headings was completed, the dataset contains a total of 1304 medical records annotated with 13,962 section headings.

This work analyzed the compiled corpus and generated the following statistics of existing section headings. Among all annotated sections, 803 (5.7%) are the "chief complaints" section, which was found to be presented in several alternative spellings such as CC, chief, and reason. 843 (6.0%) are the "present illness" section. 2,701 (19%) are "personal histories", which may include subsections like social history, medication, allergy, substance, marital status, activity and general health status. 486 (3.4%) are "family histories",1,104 (7.9%) are "physical examinations", 401 (2.8%) are "laboratory examinations", and 87 (< 1.0%) are "radiology reports". 103 (< 1.0%) are "data" sections, which include laboratory and radiology results. 884 (6.3%) are "diagnosis" or "impressions", 468 (3.3%) are "plans" or "recommendations", and the remaining 6,081 (43.6%) are other section names, including patient name, physician name, hospital name, identity number, carbon copy, merged sections such as "assessment and plan", and so on.

In our experiment, the set1 data was used as the training set for the CRF model; the set2 data set was used to develop features. Finally, the testing set was used to test the performance of the developed model trained on set1.

3.2   Evaluation Schemes

The standard recall, precision and F-measure metrics (RPF) were used to evaluate the performance of the developed CRF model and its comparison with a dictionary-based method.

$$\text{Precision} = \frac{\text{the number of correctly recognized Section Heading chunks}}{\text{the number of recognized Section Heading chunks}}$$

$$\text{Recall} = \frac{\text{the number of correctly recognized Section Heading chunks}}{\text{the number of true Section Heading chunks}}$$

This work defines a correctly recognized section-heading chunk (a true positive case) as a case in which the text span of the recognized section heading is completely matched with the span of the manually annotated heading. Therefore, a false positive (FP) case includes any unmatched section headings generated by the computer.

3.3   Experiment Configurations and Results

This work developed a dictionary-based method based on the maximum matching algorithm as a baseline system to compare its performance with that of the CRF-based method. Three dictionaries were used by the dictionary-based methods: the SecTag section header terminology (the "SecTag" configuration), the section heading names collected from the training[1] set (the "Training" configuration), and the union of the two dictionaries (the "SecTag+Training" configuration). In addition, to study the effect of the proposed layout features, this work trained two CRF models; one is the model with all proposed feature sets (CRF-based+Layout Features), and the other excluded the layout features (CRF-based).

The experimental results of the five configurations are shown in Table 2. The best recall on both datasets was achieved by the dictionary-based method without using the section names from SecTag. However, the CRF-based method noticeably outperforms the dictionary-based methods in terms of P and F-scores.

On the test dataset, the best CRF-configuration achieved a P-score of 0.955, which outperforms the best configuration of the dictionary-based method by 0.496. With the layout feature, both precision and recall of the CRF-based method can be improved by 0.112 and 0.174, respectively. CRF-based methods with layout features achieved the best performance in terms of PRF. Similar observations can also be examined on the development set.

---

[1] When testing on the test set, the section names from set 2 were also added into the dictionary.

Table 2. Performance comparison among different methods

DataSet	Config.	P (%)	R (%)	F (%)
Set2 (Develop. Set)	Dictionary-based (SecTag)	38.09	67.44	48.69
	Dictionary-based(Training)	**47.24**	**98.88**	**63.93**
	Dictionary-based(SecTag+Training)	46.05	93.65	61.74
	CRF-based	94.47	91.87	93.15
	CRF-based + Layout Features	**94.67**	**94.15**	**94.41**
Test	Dictionary-based (SecTag)	38.43	69.1	49.39
	Dictionary-based(Training)	**45.9**	**95**	**61.89**
	Dictionary-based(SecTag+Training)	44.56	89.28	59.45
	CRF-based	94.33	90.74	92.5
	CRF-based + Layout Features	**95.45**	**92.48**	**93.94**

4   Discussion

As shown in the previous section, CRF-based methods evidently outperformed the dictionary-based approach. The diversity of section heading names of EHRs is a key issue that resulted in the huge performance gap between CRF- and dictionary-based methods. A physician can combine any section heading names in an EHR to form a new section, or insert any supplemental information in a section heading. For example, the bold texts in the two sections "Meds (**confirmed with patient**)" and "DATA (**08/25/61**):". These cases cannot be dealt by the dictionary-based method, since there are no dictionaries that can cover all of these variations. By contrast, the CRF model is capable of identifying these names, because the sequential labelling formulation can model the dependency between tokens. In addition, the results showed that the inclusion of the terminology from SecTag resulted in a decreased precision. This is caused by the various section headings of different granular levels within the SecTag content. For example, it includes terms like "toenail exam" and "muscle tone exam", which usually does not belong to the topmost section headings.

On the other hand, the results of CRF-based section recognition are not completely flawless. A comparison of the "CRF-based" configuration with the "CRF-based+Layout feature" indicates that adding the layout feature enables the CRF model to recognize section headings that did not appear in the training set. For example, section headings such as "HCP/FAMILY CONTACT", "INDICATIONS FOR TPN", "Allergies or adverse reactions" "Course on floor" and "Oncology CONSULTATION NOTE" were not present in the training set, but with their clear layout, the model with our layout features is able to recognize them.

Finally, this work conducted error analysis on the predicted results of our best configuration "CRF-based+Layout features", and categorized the errors into two categories: false negative (FN) and FP cases. The following subsections discuss them respectively.

4.1   False Negative Error Cases

The test set contains some topmost section headings that are rarely used in EHRs. These headings, such as "microbiology" and "habits", only appeared a few times in the training set. Due to the sparseness of these section names, it is difficult for the machine learning-based section tagger to recognize these instances. We also observed that some records adopted non-standard or idiosyncratic topmost section headings along with abbreviations, which made it difficult to recognize them. Some non-standard section headings or abbreviations found in the test set include: "All" for "allergy" and "ROS" for "Review of Systems".

4.2   False Positive Error Cases

Occasionally, the trained CRF-based section tagger recognizes non-section parts or probable subsection headings of an EHR, which become the main source of FP cases. For example, in the following snippet of a record: "The patient is a 75-year-old white female with past medical history significant for throat cancer," the tagger erroneously recognized the non-section description "medical history" as a section heading. In addition, some section headings, such as "laboratory", can be topmost section headings in one EHR, but are not topmost sections in the other EHRs. This may also contribute to the occurrence of FP/FN cases.

5   Conclusion

This work presented a CRF-based method with a set of features developed for recognizing section headings in EHRs. The experiment results showed that the proposed CRF-based method evidently outperforms the dictionary-based approach in terms of precision and F-scores. The proposed layout features, which captured the line break information, can model the original layout given by medical doctors with the intention of increasing readability. Implementing the layout features into our method resulted in an improvement of the performance of section heading recognition, which can be observed from the experiment results. Nevertheless, issues including the varieties of section heading hierarchies among different EHRs and the arbitrary naming in section headings, such as non-standard section heading abbreviations, still remain to be challenging problems for section heading recognition.

References

1. Aronson, A.: Effective Mapping of Biomedical Text to the UMLS Metathesaurus: The MetaMap Program. Journal of Biomedical Informatic 35, 17–21 (2001)
2. Denny, J.C., Miller, R.A., Johnson, K.B., Spickard III, A.: Development and evaluation of a clinical note section header terminology. In: AMIA Annu. Symp. Proc., pp. 156–160 (2008)
3. Friedman, C., Shagina, L., Lussier, Y., Hripcsak, G.: Automated encoding of clinical documents based on natural language processing. J. Am. Med. Inform. Assoc. 11(5), 392–402 (2004)

4. Lafferty, J., McCallum, A., Pereira, F.: Conditional random fields: Probabilistic models for segmenting and labeling sequence data. In: Proceedings of the 18th International Conference on Machine Learning (ICML), pp. 282–289 (2001)
5. Savova, G.K., Masanz, J.J., Ogren, P.V., Zheng, J., Sohn, S., Kipper-Schuler, K.C., Chute, C.G.: Mayo clinical Text Analysis and Knowledge Extraction System (cTAKES): architecture, component evaluation and applications. Journal of the American Medical Informatics Association 17(5), 507–513 (2010)
6. Smith, L., Rindflesch, T., Wilbur, W.J.: MedPost: a part-of-speech tagger for bioMedical text. Bioinformatics 20(14), 2320–2321 (2004)
7. Stubbs, A., Kotfila, C., Xu, H., Uzuner, O.: Practical applications for NLP in Clinical Research: the 2014 i2b2/UTHealth shared tasks. In: Proceedings of the i2b2 2014 Shared Task and Workshop Challenges in Natural Language Processing for Clinical Data (2014)
8. Tsai, R.T.-H., Sung, C.-L., Dai, H.-J., Hung, H.-C., Sung, T.-Y., Hsu, W.-L.: NERBio: using selected word conjunctions, term normalization, and global patterns to improve biomedical named entity recognition. BMC Bioinformatics7(suppl. 5), S11 (2006)

Detecting Spam on Twitter via Message-Passing Based on Retweet-Relation

Pei-Chi Chen[1], Hahn-Ming Lee[1,2], Hsiao-Rong Tyan[3], Jain-Shing Wu[1,4], and Te-En Wei[1]

[1] Dept. Computer Science and Information Engineering
National Taiwan University of Science and Technology, Taiwan
{m10115081,hmlee,d9807501}@mail.ntust.edu.tw
[2] Institute of Information Science
Academia Sinica, Taiwan
[3] Dept. of Information and Computer Engineering
Chung Yuan Christian University, Taiwan
tyan@ice.cycu.edu.tw
[4] CyberTrust Technology Institute
Institute for Information Industry, Taiwan
jsw@iii.org.tw

Abstract. Due to the popularity of Twitter, it attracts malicious users' interests. Most of previous approaches relied on account-based features such as message similarity between tweets, following-followers ratio, and so on. Account-based features can be easily manipulated by spam accounts. Spam collusion is a new way to escape the detection mechanisms. Therefore, we need an advanced mechanism to identify the spam collusion relations.

We exploit spam campaign which spreads spam tweets. We focus on the tweet with the high retweet count. We create the message-passing graph via the retweet relations, following relations, and retweet time, then we extract the time evolution feature in the aspect of graph structure. The latent behavior indexing technique is used to extract critical concepts for spam collusion recognition. We collect 5 million tweets from May 14, 2014 to July 15, 2014 and the ground-truth has been labeled by domain experts. Our approach can achieve 86% accuracy.

Keywords: spam detection, information propagation, social network.

1 Introduction

In recent years, Twitter has become one of the most popular social networking sites. It allows users to read and send messages which are less than 140 characters, known as "tweets". With tremendous growing availability of Twitter, it also attracts malicious users' attentions. A previous research [3] showed that nearly 50% of users on social networking sites click on the links which posted by their friend accounts, even if they do not meet that friend in real life. This has revealed

S.-M. Cheng and M.-Y. Day (Eds.): TAAI 2014, LNAI 8916, pp. 56–65, 2014.

a phenomenon that spammers can inveigle victims easily through social media platforms.

In 2009, the first revolutionary malware called KOOBFACE successfully and continuously propagated through social networks [1]. This malware using fraudulent messages with harmful link that taking victims to a site which uploads malware to victims' computers. In the past few years, many researchers focused on detecting spam accounts individually by using effective account features. Stringhini et al. [16] proposed some features based on the result of data analysis, including the following and follower ratio, URL ratio, and content similarity between tweets. These features can be evaded. For example, the following and follower ratio can be easily manipulated by follower Yang et al. [24] proposed Criminal account Inference Algorithm (CIA) based on the closeness of social relationships. However, friend relations can be easily forged through the follower markets.

A spam post on social media can potentially reach thousands or millions of users. According to the "2013 State of Social Media Spam" research report from Nexgate, they got the following key findings [12]:

- Only 15% of all social spams have a link that can be detected as spam, so it is harder to detect social spam.
- During the first half of 2013, there has been a 355% growth of social spam.

Therefore finding spam tweets with the spam collusion mask becomes an important issue.

2 Background and Related Work

2.1 Types of Social Spam

Social media contain many kinds of social spams. The most common ones are link spam and text spam.

Link spam: This type of spam may be just a link with no surrounding text. Curious and unsuspecting users click on this link, then the users will be redirected to a malicious website. This website may contain advertisements or malicious software which spammers can profit from it.

Text spam: Spam content is usually very charming. Some text spam request the recipient to respond to the spammer via a private message in order to obtain detailed information [12].

2.2 Spammers on Twitter

In social network sites, following and follower counts may influence the ranking of tweets by search engines [7]. Thus, spammer began to acquire more following and follower counts. Yang et al. [24] conducted in-depth analysis of spam accounts community on Twitter. They found out that spam accounts community was made up of spam accounts and spam collusion accounts community. Spam collusion accounts are those users who have close relationship with spammers.

2.3   Individual Detection Mechanisms

Stringhini et al. [16] proposed some features which are following and follower ratio, the frequency of user that posted tweets including URL, message similarity between tweets, friend choice (whether the user used a list of names to pick its friends or not), the number of messages sent and friend number. Shekar et al. [14] used specific keywords to filter the pharmaceutical spam on Twitter. Thomas et al. [18] detected link spam on Twitter messages via a real-time system. Lee and Kim [10] developed a WarningBird system to discover correlated URL redirect chains. Once the malicious links be detected, it will be reported and added to the blacklist. So spammer could not use this link to acquire victims.

Most of these works detected Twitter spam accounts individually, instead of focusing on observing collusive spammers. They needed to renew effective features at regular intervals so that can quickly adjust features to spam accounts' new behaviors. Therefore, detecting spammers individually is not the best mechanism.

2.4   Collusive Spammers Detection Mechanisms

To find out more robust features, there are some researchers began to look at the issue from another side. Yardi et al. [25] designed ten new detection features including graph-based features (local clustering coefficient, betweenness centrality, and bi-directional links ratio), neighbor-based features (average neighbors' followers, average neighbors' tweets, and followings to median neighbors' followers), automation-based features (the usage frequency related to Twitter API) and timing-based feature (the speed an account follows others). Song et al. [15] devoted to the relations between spam senders and receivers such as the shortest paths, minimum cut and random walk. The reason why they choose those features was spammers usually can not establish robust relationships with their neighbors.

Most of the methods relied on accounts' following and follower relations. If Twitter changes their detecting strategies, spammers may change their actions. Hence, we try to find out the feature of spam accounts' campaigns that can not be simply transformed.

3   Message-Passing Graph Analyzer

3.1   Concept of Proposed Methodology

Many researches [9,4,6] focused on analyzing retweeting behavior of users on Twitter. The concept of spam collusion was proposed by Ghosh et al. [7] and Yang et al. [24] in recent year. But both of Ghosh et al. and Yang et al. did not consider the spammers' automatically retweet behavior. Therefore, we use retweet relations and the time evolution features.

Since the spam flooding, Twitter defined rules to stop spammers growth rate. The first policy is to limit users to aggressively follow others. That means an account has followed 2,000 users, the number of additional accounts it can follow is limited to its follower number [21]. In order to break the limit of 2000 following, spammer began to become others' followers and spam collusions formed. We observed that the retweet behaviour of spam collusion accounts can be classified into the following two types:

a) Only retweet massive spam tweets from a specific group of spammers.
b) Not only retweet a large number of spam tweets but also post spam tweets.

The other important rule to avoid spammers is to limit the maximum number of tweets per day. Because of this, spammers can not continue to send junk tweets. To let more victims see spam tweets, spammers use spam collusion accounts. We can use this behavior characteristic to recognize Twitter spam.

Kwak et al. [9] discovered that half of retweets occur within an hour, and 75% within a day. Their observation indicated that a "window of survival", from one hour to one day, where a certain tweet gets a higher chance to be retweeted [13]. Therefore, to capture the time evolution features, we decide to analyze the information diffusion in an hour. Then we propose our system called Message-passing Graph Analyzer (Figure 1) to recognize the Twitter spam without the spam collusion mask.

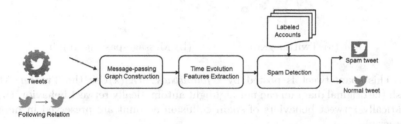

Fig. 1. The system architecture of our proposed system.

The first component is Message-passing Graph Construction. Through the Twitter API [20] we can obtain tweet information. We exploit the unique ID of the source tweet to aggregate tweets into a group. Then we extract the retweeters' Twitter ID and the time the retweeter retweeted the source tweet. We also add following relations to build the message-passing graph. The second component is Time Evolution Features Extraction. We extract three graph structure based features from the graph, which are degree variance, clustering coefficient and the number of triangles in the graph. Then we combine the features of the same tweets between different time interval into a time evolution feature. The last part of the system is Spam Detection that using labeled spammers' and normal accounts' information to train the model.

3.2   Message-Passing Graph Construction

We use the time sequence of retweeters' ID to create a message-passing graph representation of the Twitter social network in form of $G(V, E)$, where

- Node V : The set of nodes V represents unique users' Twitter ID.
- Edge E : An *edge* $(i,\ j) \in E$ between two nodes v_i, v_j could represent a retweet relation. The retweet relations are the combination of following relations and retweet time.

As shown in Figure 2(a) and 2(b), the message-passing graph of a spam looks different to its Twitter graph. For a normal tweet, the two graph looks alike. This is helpful for spam detection.

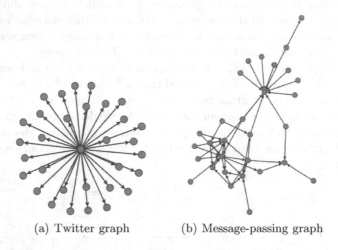

(a) Twitter graph   (b) Message-passing graph

Fig. 2. This spam tweet is posted by @*followback_707*. (a)Use the Twitter API to establish the original diagram can not highlight automatically retweet behavior. (b) The automatically retweet behaviors of spam collusion account are preserved in message-passing graph.

3.3   Time Evolution Features Extraction

Graph-Based Features. As we consider treat the whole Twitter social network as a directed graph $G(V,\ E)$, there are several graph-based features we can use:

Average clustering coefficient : The clustering coefficient C_u of a node u is defined as shown in Equation 1:

$$C_u = \frac{2\,T_u}{deg(u)(deg(u) - 1)} \tag{1}$$

where $u \in$ V, $deg(u)$ is the number of neighbours of u and T_u is the number of connected pairs between all neighbours of u [22,2]. Spammers or spam collusion accounts usually blindly retweet the tweets which were posted by small communities. Therefore, their retweet relations are with with very high overlapping probability. We use average clustering coefficient of a graph which is written in Equation 2 to replace the clustering coefficient:

$$AC = \frac{1}{n} \sum_{u \in G} C_u \tag{2}$$

where u is a node in the message-passing graph and $u \in V$, n is the total number of nodes.

Transitivity : As shown in Equation 3, the denominator represents the number of triangles in the graph, and the numerator is the number of triads in the graph which means two edges with a shared vertex [11]:

$$Trans = 3 \times \frac{number\_of\_triangles}{number\_of\_triads} \tag{3}$$

Comparing with the legitimate tweets, the message-passing graphs of spam tweets has higher transitivity.

Degree variance : The variance is the degree of dispersion in a set of data. We want to use variance to measure the vertex, which is defined as shown in Equation 4:

$$DV = \frac{1}{n} \sum_{i=1}^{n} \left(deg(i) - \overline{deg} \right)^2 \tag{4}$$

where $deg(i)$ is the degree value of i-th node and $\overline{deg}$ is the average degree value of all the nodes in the message-passing graph. This metric is to measure whether the message-passing graph has small community or not. The degree variance of legal tweets is higher than the degree variance of spam tweets.

Extractor Based on Time Evolution Feature. In our system, we set the unit time interval as five minutes which means we divide an hour into twelve blocks. For each block we construct the message-passing graph and extract the graph-based features which are average clustering coefficient, transitivity and degree variance from it. The equation is as shown in Equation 5:

$$G_j^i = < ac_j^i, trans_j^i, dv_j^i > \tag{5}$$

$\forall\ ac_j^i \in$ AC, $\forall\ trans_j^i \in$ Trans, $\forall\ dv_j^i \in$ DV, G represents the message-passing graph, where i is i-th time interval block and j represents the index value of tweet ID. When considering the time range, we can combine those features into the time evolution feature ω_j. Let $\omega_j = <G_j^1, G_j^2, G_j^3,...,G_j^m>$ denotes the time evolution feature of a tweet which index value is j, where m is the total number of time interval block, and here the value of m is twelve. Then we can get matrix M as shown in Equation 6:

$$M = [\omega_1, \omega_2, \dots, \omega_p]^T \tag{6}$$

where p is the total number of tweets.

3.4   Spam Detection

After establishing the message-passing graph, extracting graph-based features, combining into the time evolution feature and get matrix M, the final step of our system is to identify spam. We use labeled accounts information and employ *Singular Value Decomposition (SVD)* method to train the latent semantic indexing as shown in Equation 7:

$$M = U \times \Sigma \times V^T \tag{7}$$

where U and V are orthogonal matrices, Σ is the diagonal matrix which consists of singular vectors. For a tweet to be added, we extract the time evolution feature ω_{add}, then we use Equation 8 to convert coordinates.

$$\omega_{convert} = \omega_{add} \times (V^T)^{-1} \times (\Sigma)^{-1} \tag{8}$$

4   Experiments

4.1   Experiment Design

We use WEKA [23] to run clustering and classification algorithms. In the Message-passing Graph Analyzer, we set the unit interval as five minutes. Therefore, we made the experiments through changing different parameters to show the sensitivity of our system. By searching for specific keywords in the Twitter stream [17], we could collect the retweets. There were about 2.3 million spam tweets and 2.7 million normal tweets collected between May 14, 2014 and July 15, 2014. The data which were collected before June 22th were for training, the remaining data were for testing. The rules about how we identified spam were as follows:

a) A few weeks later, we re-examined whether the account had been suspended or not. If it had been suspended by Twitter, we labeled it as spam.
b) The profile of the account contained some keywords or hashtag such as "follow".
c) The screen name of the account contained some keywords like "follow" or "followback".
d) Some spammers used confusion word to set their screen name. For example, they replaced the character o with zero, e.g., F0llowerz.
e) The screen name of the account like @follow_♯, where ♯ was a digit number represented the accounts could generate by script [8].

In addition, we also need to identify some normal Twitter tweets. The rules about how we identified normal tweets were as follows:

a) We checked the Twitter profile of accounts contained the blue verified badge [19] or not, if they contained the blue verified badge then we labeled them as a normal account.
b) Manually checking the contents of the tweets were legal or spam.

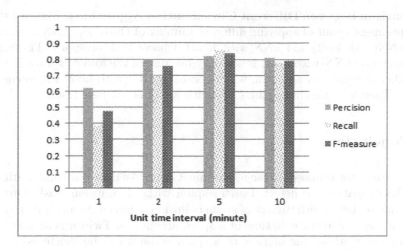

Fig. 3. Effectiveness of unit time interval selection

4.2 Effectiveness Analysis

Effectiveness of Unit Time Interval Selection. Figure 3 shows the experiment results of applying different unit time interval values to Message-passing Graph Analyzer. If the unit time interval is too small, the automatically retweet behavior of spam collusion accounts were not obvious. At the beginning, the message-passing graphs of some spam tweets were similar to normal tweets. When the unit time interval is set as five minutes, we get the best precision and recall rate from our experiment results. If the unit time interval is too large, the message-passing graphs contained more noisy nodes and effected the graph-based features. Thus, the precision and recall rate declined slightly.

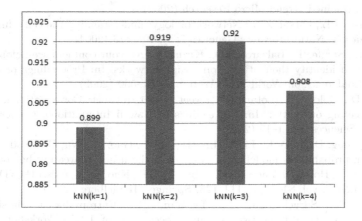

Fig. 4. The accuracy in different methods

Comparison between Different Classification Algorithms. Figure 4 shows the experiment result of applying different number of clusters of kNN algorithm. Both kNN(with k=2) and kNN(with k=3) achieve high accuracy. The reason why we choose kNN(with k=3) is not only because of the lower FP rate but also the higher accuracy. In addition, when choosing kNN(with k=2) will encounter a draw. Therefore, we choose the kNN(with k=3) as our best result.

5 Conclusions

In this work, we propose Message-passing Graph Analyzer, a combination of graph-based features to detect Twitter spam without collusion mask. Our system is able to distinguish variant of spam collusion behavior. Stringhini et al. [16] observed that the average lifetime of a spam account on Twitter is 31 days. But by using our method, the lifetime of a spam account can be shortened in 1 to 2 hours. Due to the limitations of Twitter we can only construct the proximate message-passing graph. But there are many researches focused on analyzing retweet behavior and inferred the possible information diffusion direction, such as Du et al. [5] utilized the user activity time to infer the retweet behavior. Therefore, we may further improve the message-passing graphs to that the graphs more complete.

Acknowledgments. This research is supported in part by the Ministry of Science and Technology of Taiwan under grants number MOST 102-2218-E-011-011 MY3.

References

1. Baltazar, J., Costoya, J., Flores, R.: The real face of koobface: The largest web 2.0 botnet explained. Trend Micro Research (2009)
2. Barabasi, A.L., Oltvai, Z.N.: Network biology: understanding the cell's functional organization. Nature Reviews Genetics 5(2), 101–113 (2004)
3. Bilge, L., Strufe, T., Balzarotti, D., Kirda, E.: All your contacts are belong to us: automated identity theft attacks on social networks. In: Proceedings of International Conference on World Wide Web, pp. 551–560 (2009)
4. Boyd, D., Golder, S., Lotan, G.: Tweet, tweet, retweet: Conversational aspects of retweeting on twitter. In: Proceedings of Hawaii International Conference on System Sciences, pp. 1–10 (2010)
5. Du, J., Song, D., Liao, L., Li, X., Liu, L., Li, G., Gao, G., Wu, G.: ReadBehavior: Reading probabilities modeling of tweets via the users' retweeting behaviors. In: Tseng, V.S., Ho, T.B., Zhou, Z.-H., Chen, A.L.P., Kao, H.-Y. (eds.) PAKDD 2014, Part I. LNCS, vol. 8443, pp. 114–125. Springer, Heidelberg (2014)
6. Ghosh, R., Surachawala, T., Lerman, K.: Entropy-based classification of 'retweeting' activity on twitter. In: Proceedings of KDD Workshop on Social Network Analysis (2011)

7. Ghosh, S., Viswanath, B., Kooti, F., Sharma, N.K., Korlam, G., Benevenuto, F., Ganguly, N., Gummadi, K.P.: Understanding and combating link farming in the twitter social network. In: Proceedings of International Conference on World Wide Web, pp. 61–70 (2012)
8. Jiang, M., Cui, P., Beutel, A., Faloutsos, C., Yang, S.: Detecting suspicious following behavior in multimillion-node social networks. In: Proceedings of the Companion Publication of the International Conference on World Wide Web Companion, pp. 305–306 (2014)
9. Kwak, H., Lee, C., Park, H., Moon, S.: What is twitter, a social network or a news media? In: Proceedings of International Conference on World Wide Web, pp. 591–600 (2010)
10. Lee, S., Kim, J.: Warningbird: A near real-time detection system for suspicious urls in twitter stream. IEEE Transactions on Dependable and Secure Computing 10(3), 183–195 (2013)
11. Netowrkx: Netowrkx, https://networkx.github.io/
12. Nexgate: 2013 state of social media spam, http://nexgate.com/wp-content/uploads/2013/09/Nexgate-2013-State-of-Social-Media-Spam-Research-Report.pdf
13. Peng, H.K., Zhu, J., Piao, D., Yan, R., Zhang, Y.: Retweet modeling using conditional random fields. In: Proceedings of IEEE International Conference on Data Mining Workshops, pp. 336–343 (2011)
14. Shekar, C., Wakade, S., Liszka, K.J., Chan, C.C.: Mining pharmaceutical spam from twitter. In: Proceedings of International Conference on Intelligent Systems Design and Applications, pp. 813–817 (2010)
15. Song, J., Lee, S., Kim, J.: Spam filtering in twitter using sender-receiver relationship. In: Sommer, R., Balzarotti, D., Maier, G. (eds.) RAID 2011. LNCS, vol. 6961, pp. 301–317. Springer, Heidelberg (2011)
16. Stringhini, G., Kruegel, C., Vigna, G.: Detecting spammers on social networks. In: Proceedings of Annual Computer Security Applications Conference, pp. 1–9 (2010)
17. Stringhini, G., Wang, G., Egele, M., Kruegel, C., Vigna, G., Zheng, H., Zhao, B.Y.: Follow the green: growth and dynamics in twitter follower markets. In: Proceedings of ACM SIGCOMM Conference on Internet Measurement, pp. 163–176 (2013)
18. Thomas, K., Grier, C., Ma, J., Paxson, V., Song, D.: Design and evaluation of a real-time url spam filtering service. In: Proceedings of IEEE Symposium on Security and Privacy, pp. 447–462 (2011)
19. Twitter: About verified accounts, https://support.twitter.com/articles/119135
20. Twitter: Rest api v1.1 resources, https://dev.twitter.com/docs/api/1.1
21. Twitter: Twitter limits (api, updates, and following), https://support.twitter.com/articles/15364
22. Watts, D.J., Strogatz, S.H.: Collective dynamics of 'small-world' networks. Nature 393(6684), 440–442 (1998)
23. Witten, I.H., Frank, E., Hall, M.A.: Data Mining: Practical machine learning tools and techniques, 3rd edn. Morgan Kaufmann (2011)
24. Yang, C., Harkreader, R., Zhang, J., Shin, S., Gu, G.: Analyzing spammers' social networks for fun and profit: a case study of cyber criminal ecosystem on twitter. In: Proceedings of International Conference on World Wide Web, pp. 71–80 (2012)
25. Yang, C., Harkreader, R.C., Gu, G.: Die free or live hard? Empirical evaluation and new design for fighting evolving twitter spammers. In: Sommer, R., Balzarotti, D., Maier, G. (eds.) RAID 2011. LNCS, vol. 6961, pp. 318–337. Springer, Heidelberg (2011)

An Improved Multi-Objective Genetic Model for Stock Selection with Domain Knowledge

Shin-Shou Chen[1], Chien-Feng Huang[2], and Tzung-Pei Hong[1, 2]

[1] Department of Computer Science and Engineering,
National Sun Yat-Sen University, Kaohsiung, 804, Taiwan
[2] Department of Computer Science and Information Engineering,
National University of Kaohsiung, Kaohsiung, 811, Taiwan
cronus4619@hotmail.com, {cfhuang15,tphong}@nuk.edu.tw

Abstract. In the past, we employed a multi-objective genetic algorithm (MOGA) for optimization of model parameters and feature selection, and then devised a stock scoring mechanism to rank and select stocks for forming a portfolio. With each chromosome representing a feasible portfolio, that adopted multi-objective genetic algorithm (MOGA) model thus decided good portfolios by considering their return and risk. In this paper, we further improve upon the MOGA model using financial knowledge to help selection of beneficial portfolios. Especially, we refine the evaluation criteria with the assistance of relevant domain knowledge from investment. Based on the promising results, we expect this improved MOGA methodology to advance the current state of research in soft computing for real-world stock selection applications.

Keywords: stock selection, genetic algorithms, feature selection, multi-objective optimization.

1 Introduction

Stock selection has been an important and challenging task in the area of investment. Researchers from the field of artificial intelligence have made several attempts to tackle this task. One of the most known methods is genetic algorithm [6], which simulates the process of biological evolution to solve optimization problems. In the early works, the study of portfolio optimization typically centered around one single objective, i.e., the return of portfolios. In this context, the goal of stock selection may aims at maximizing the expected return of individual stocks in order to obtain the maximal actual return of portfolio. To improve the performance of the single-objective GA-based models, multi-objective methods that consider two competitive goals of return and risks simultaneously have been developed.

In this study, we extend our previous multi-objective GA-based method [2] for increasing investment return and reducing the risk. In the previous approach, we used the non-dominated sorting to find non-dominated solutions. In that treatment, the portfolios with low risk but negative return might be generated, this might lead to bankruptcy over the course of investment. In order to mitigate this problem, in this

S.-M. Cheng and M.-Y. Day (Eds.): TAAI 2014, LNAI 8916, pp. 66–73, 2014.
© Springer International Publishing Switzerland 2014

paper, we reset the scores of these portfolios to zero to prevent these solutions from being selected. In addition, although the traditional crowding distance method chooses significant solutions on the same front, these solutions typically lack meaningful advantage in the sense of investment. In this study we thus propose to assign higher weights to the portfolios of higher return per unit of risk and come up with the MOGA method to construct more profitable portfolios.

With the domain knowledge, we thus improve the score calculation of stocks. Our experimental results show that our method provides significant improvement over the previous one in terms of the return and risk on investment. The goal of this study is to shed more light on the complex characteristics of stock selection in order to advance the current state of computational finance using AI-based methodologies.

2   Related Works

The class of genetic algorithms was first proposed by Holland [6] according to the principle of natural selection and has been a widely used approach for optimization that can be used to improve investment decisions. Pereira [15] presented a discussion of the advantages of using the GA in the complex optimization problems that arise in financial markets, and showed that the performance can be improved when using binary encoding in the algorithm. Chiang [3] applied some fundamental analysis indicators and the GA to evaluate the quality of stocks and showed his proposed model is effective in financial markets. Kim and Han [10] proposed a different GA-based approach for dimension reduction and the determination of connection weights for ANNs, in order to predict the price movements of stock index. Orito and Yamazaki [14] calculated the contribution rate from the portfolio, and combined this with the weight of appropriate risk to set the fitness value. Lai et al. [11] used a double-stage GA to select stocks from the Shanghai stock exchange from 2001 to 2004, and found that this approach was more suitable for financial applications than fuzzy or artificial neural networks. More recently, Huang et al. [7, 8, 9] proposed two hybrid versions of the SVM and fuzzy-based GA models for stock selection. Using certain statistical tests, Huang et al. provided evidence that their models considerably outperformed the relevant benchmark.

As to the multi-objective genetic approaches, NSGA-II, a fast and elitist multi-objective genetic algorithm proposed by Deb et al. [4], is one of the most well-known. This method combines non-dominated sorting and crowding distance. For portfolio optimization, Hoklie and Zuhal [5] used Markowitz's method [13] and the two objectives of return and risk to solve the problem of multi-objective portfolio construction. Bermudez et al. [1] presented a fuzzy ranking procedure for the portfolio selection problem. They used the trapezoidal fuzzy numbers to evaluate return and risk, and then used non-dominated sorting as well as the risk aversion to compose the optimal portfolios. Li and Xu [12] proposed a multi-objective portfolio selection model with fuzzy random returns and quantified the return, risk, and liquidity of a portfolio to select the best solution.

In this study, we propose an improved MOGA method with some financial knowledge in criteria evaluation to make it more suitable for stock selection than our previous work [2]. We also employ stock datasets of twenty years of time in order to conduct a more convincing statistical validation of the effectiveness of our approach.

3   Our Proposed Algorithm

This section describes our proposed algorithm for the construction of our stock scoring model, optimized by the GA and the corresponding extension of our previous model [2] in the context of multi-objective optimization. The algorithm is presented as follows:

1. Devise a chromosome that consists of three portions — the feature selection F, the stock sorting indicators I and the feature weights W. A chromosome is represented by a binary coding scheme.

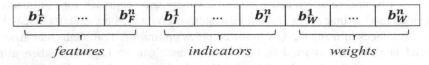

Fig. 1. Chromosome encoding

In Figure 1, n is the number of fundamental variables (features). b_F^1 through b_F^n are defined for candidate features 1 through n, where 1 or 0 corresponds to the feature being selected or not. b_I^1 through b_I^n are defined as the sorting indicators, where 0 represents the higher the value of the variable, the better; and 1 represents the opposite case. b_W^1 through b_W^n are defined as the encoding of the set of weights W. Figure 2 shows the detailed binary encoding for the weight of each individual variable, where the value of b_W^n (the weight for variable n) in Fig. 1 is encoded by loci $b_{W_n}^1$ through $b_{W_n}^l$.

$$\boxed{b_{W_1}^1 \quad \cdots \quad b_{W_1}^l \quad b_{W_2}^1 \quad \cdots \quad b_{W_2}^l \quad b_{W_n}^1 \quad \cdots \quad b_{W_n}^l}$$

Fig. 2. Detailed encoding of the weighting terms

The portion in the chromosome representing the genotype of weight W is transformed into the phenotype as follows:

$$y = min_y + \frac{d}{2^l - 1} \times (max_y - min_y), \tag{1}$$

where y is the corresponding phenotype for the particular weight; min_y and max_y are the minimum and maximum of the parameters; d is the corresponding decimal value, and l is the length of the block used to encode the weight in the chromosome.

2. Let W_j denote the weight of the j-th variable. The total score of stock i at time t, $y_{i,t}(W)$, can be defined as:

$$y_{i,t}(W) = \sum_j W_j X_{i,j,t},\qquad(2)$$

where W is the vector of the weights of the input features. Given the scores for all stocks, the ranking of a stock can be defined as:

$$\alpha_{i,t}(W) = \rho\left(y_{i,t}(W)\right),\qquad(3)$$

where $\rho(\cdot)$ is a ranking function so that $\alpha_{i,t} \in N$ is the ranking of stock i at time t, and $\alpha_{i,t} \geq \alpha_{j,t}$ if $y_{i,t} \geq y_{j,t}$.

3. Use rankings from step 2 to select the top-ranked m stocks as components of a portfolio. The performance of a portfolio can be evaluated by averaging the actual returns of the stocks in the portfolio, which is defined as:

$$\overline{R_t} = \frac{1}{m}\sum_{i=1}^{m} R_t(s_{i,t}),\qquad(4)$$

where $s_{i,t}$ is the i-th ranked stock at time t; $R_t(\cdot)$ is the actual return for a stock at time t and $\overline{R_t}$ is the average return over all the m stocks in the portfolio at time t.

4. Use the following two objectives to evaluate the performance of a stock selection model.

- The cumulative total (compounded) return:

$$R_c = \prod_{t=1}^{n} \overline{R_t},\qquad(5)$$

where R_c is defined as the product of the average yearly return, $\overline{R_t}$, of the stocks in a portfolio over n consecutive years.

- The standard deviation of $\overline{R_t}$ as the measure of risk:

$$\bar{x} = \frac{1}{n}\sum_{t=1}^{n} \overline{R_t},\qquad(6)$$

$$\sigma = \sqrt{\frac{1}{n}\sum_{t=1}^{n}(\overline{R_t} - \bar{x})^2},\qquad(7)$$

where $\bar{x}$ is defined as the mean of $\overline{R_t}$; $\overline{R_t}$ is the average return of all the m stocks in the portfolio at time t.

5. With return and risk, use the non-dominated sorting and crowding distance [4] to calculate the scores for all portfolios, in which the ranking of a portfolio can be defined as:

$$i_{score} < j_{score}$$

$$\text{if } (i_{rank} < j_{rank}) \text{ or } \left((i_{rank} = j_{rank}) \text{ and } (i_{distance} > j_{distance})\right),$$

where i_{score} and j_{score} are defined as the scores of portfolios i and j; i_{rank} and j_{rank} are defined as the non-dominated (front) rankings of portfolios i and j; and $i_{distance}$ and $j_{distance}$ are defined as the crowding distances of portfolios i and j. We also use the following two rules inspired from financial knowledge to improve the scoring model:

(1) Removing the portfolio with negative returns, i.e.,

$$\text{if } R_c \leq 0, \text{ then } i_{score} = 0.$$

(2) Adjusting the return by risk (similar to the idea of the Sharpe ratio), i.e.,

$$f = \frac{\sqrt[n]{R_c}}{\sigma}; \tag{8}$$

$$i_{score'} < j_{score'} \text{ if } i's f < j's f,$$

where R_c is the cumulative total return by Eq. (5); i_{score} is defined as the score of portfolio i; $i_{score'}$ is defined as the modified score; σ is the standard deviation of all the average yearly returns; and n is the number of years.

6. According to step 5, define the fitness of a chromosome as the function of the annualized return and the risk of a portfolio, as follows:

$$\text{fitness}_i = i_{score} + i_{score'}, \tag{9}$$

where i_{score} is the final score of portfolio i defined by step 5; $i_{score'}$ is the modified score of portfolio i defined by step 5, as well.

7. Repeat the following until a sufficient number of offspring are generated.

— Select one pair of chromosomes as parents;
— Apply crossover;
— Apply mutation.

In this study, we use the tournament selection scheme, and one-point crossover scheme with rate of 0.7, and the mutation rate of 0.005 are used.

8. Replace the parents with the offspring to generate a new generation of chromosomes.
9. Return to step 2 until the termination conditions are met (we use 50 generations as the termination condition for this study).

4   Experimental Results

To further obtain the performance discrepancy of our method and the others, we use the 14 fundamental variables and the half-yearly returns of stocks from textile sector in Taiwan's stock market for years ranging from 1992 to 2012.

In order to provide a statistical validation for the effectiveness of our proposed model, the datasets are divided into two parts for training and testing: the first n periods of the data is used to train the model and the remaining data is used to for validation. For instance, the data of 1992 through 1996 can be used for training, and the data for the remaining years (1997-2012) can be used to test the models learned in the training stage.

Table 1 show an illustration of the CV's used for this study. For example, for the yearly data, CV=5 means the data of the first 5 years (years 199206 through 199406) is used for training and the other years are used for testing.

Table 1. Periods of CV

CV	199206	199212	199306	199312	199406	......	201206	201212
4	training				testing			
5	training					testing		
...	training						testing	
41	training							testing

We compare the performance discrepancy of the benchmark, our previous method [2], and our current MOGA method. Here the benchmark means the annualized return from selecting all the stocks in the sector. Figures 3 and 4 provide the comparison of annualized returns for the textile industry for the training and the testing phases, respectively. As can be seen, the proposed model acquired in the training phase signifi cantly outperforms both the benchmark and our previous method in all of the CV's. Furthermore, these trained models by our method are also able to outperform the other two methods in all of the CV's in the testing phase.

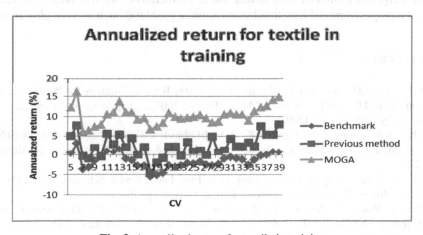

Fig. 3. Annualized return for textile in training

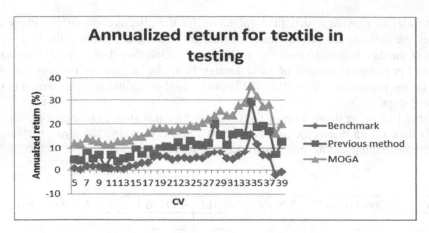

Fig. 4. Annualized return for textile in testing

5   Conclusions

In our proposed MOGA here, we mainly use NSGA-II to study the effect of the two competitive objectives of return and risk, and then refine the method with the assistance of relevant domain knowledge from investment. Especially, we reset the scores of the portfolios with low risk but negative return to zero to prevent them from being selected and assign higher weights to the portfolios of higher return per unit of risk to construct more profitable portfolios. The experimental results showed that the MOGA method significantly outperformed the benchmark. In the future, we intend to employ other sophisticated versions of the MOGA, such as the MOEA/D to substitute the simple weight-sum MOGA used in this study. Furthermore, we will attempt to generalize the proposed model here to other investment problems such as asset allocation.

References

1. Bermudez, J.D., Segura, J.V., Vercher, E.: A Fuzzy Ranking Strategy for Portfolio Selection Applied to the Spanish Stock Market. In: The 2007 IEEE International Conference on Fuzzy Systems, pp. 1–4 (2007)
2. Chen, S.S., Huang, C.F., Hong, T.P.: A Multi-objective Genetic Model for Stock Selection. In: The 27th Annual Conference of the Japanese Society for Artificial Intelligence (2013)
3. Chiang, C.H.: Using Genetic Algorithms to Find Fundamental Selection and Technical Timing Rules. Master Thesis, National Central University (2002)
4. Deb, K., Pratap, A., Agarwal, S., Meyarivan, T.: A Fast and Elitist Multiobjective Genetic Algorithm: NSGA-II. The 2002 IEEE Transactions on Evolutionary Computation 6(2), 182–197 (2002)
5. Hoklie, Z.L.R.: Resolving Multi Objective Stock Portfolio Optimization Problem Using Genetic Algorithm. In: The Second International Conference on Computer and Automation Engineering, vol. 2, pp. 40–44 (2010)

6. Holland, J.H.: Adaptation in Natural and Artificial Systems. University of Michigan Press (1975)
7. Huang, C.F.: A Hybrid Stock Selection Model Using Genetic Algorithms and Support Vector Regression. Applied Soft Computing 12(2), 807–818 (2012)
8. Huang, C.F., Chang, B.R., Cheng, D.W., Chang, C.H.: Feature Selection and Parameter Optimization of a Fuzzy-based Stock Selection Model using Genetic Algorithms. International Journal of Fuzzy Systems 14(1), 65–75 (2012)
9. Huang, C.F., Chang, C.H., Chang, B.R., Cheng, D.W.: A Study of a Hybrid Evolutionary Fuzzy Model for Stock Selection. In: The 2011 IEEE International Conference on Fuzzy Systems, pp. 210–217 (2011)
10. Kim, K.J., Han, I.: Genetic Algorithms Approach to Feature Discretization in Artificial Neural Networks for the Prediction of Stock Price Index. Expert Systems with Applications 19(2), 125–132 (2000)
11. Lai, K.K., Yu, L., Wang, S., Zhou, C.: A Double-Stage Genetic Optimization Algorithm for Portfolio Selection. In: King, I., Wang, J., Chan, L.-W., Wang, D. (eds.) ICONIP 2006. LNCS, vol. 4234, pp. 928–937. Springer, Heidelberg (2006)
12. Li, J., Xu, J.: Multi-Objective Portfolio Selection Model with Fuzzy Random Returns and a Compromise Approach-Based Genetic Algorithm. Information Sciences 220, 507–521 (2013)
13. Markowitz, H.M.: Portfolio Selection: Efficient Diversification of Investment. Wiley, New York (1959)
14. Orito, Y., Yamazaki, G.: Index Fund Portfolio Selection by Using GA. In: The 2001 IEEE International Conference on Computational Intelligence, pp. 118–122 (2001)
15. Pereira, R.: Genetic Algorithm Optimisation for Finance and Investments. Discussion Paper, La Trobe University (2000)

Bayesian Variable Selection for Multi-response Linear Regression

Wan-Ping Chen[1], Ying Nian Wu[1], and Ray-Bin Chen[2]

[1] Department of Statistics,
University of California, Los Angeles, CA, USA
[2] Department of Statistics,
National Cheng Kung University, Tainan, Taiwan, ROC

Abstract. This paper studies the variable selection problem in high dimensional linear regression, where there are multiple response vectors, and they share the same or similar subsets of predictor variables to be selected from a large set of candidate variables. In the literature, this problem is called multi-task learning, support union recovery or simultaneous sparse coding in different contexts. In this paper, we propose a Bayesian method for solving this problem by introducing two nested sets of binary indicator variables. In the first set of indicator variables, each indicator is associated with a predictor variable or a regressor, indicating whether this variable is active for any of the response vectors. In the second set of indicator variables, each indicator is associated with both a predicator variable and a response vector, indicating whether this variable is active for the particular response vector. The problem of variable selection can then be solved by sampling from the posterior distributions of the two sets of indicator variables. We develop the Gibbs sampling algorithm for posterior sampling and demonstrate the performances of the proposed method for both simulated and real data sets.

Keywords: Multi-task learning, Support union recovery, Simultaneous sparse coding.

1 Introduction

Variable selection is a fundamental problem in linear regression, especially in modern applications where the number of predictor variables or regressors can exceed the number of observations. Under the sparsity assumption that the number of active variables is small, it is possible to select these active variables even if the number of candidate variables is very large.

During the past decade, the problem of variable selection in high dimensional linear regression has been intensely studied in statistics, machine learning and signal processing. Many variable selection methods have been developed, such as the Lasso by Tibshirani (1996) [14], SCAD by Fan and Li (2001) [5], elastic net by Zou and Hastie (2005) [19], and MCP by Zhang (2010) [18]. In addition to these penalized least squares methods, Bayesian approaches have also been proposed, for example, stochastic search variable selection (SSVS) by George and McCulloch (1993) [7], Gibbs variable selection (GVS) by Dellaportas et al. (2000) [4], and RVM by Tipping (2005) [15].

S.-M. Cheng and M.-Y. Day (Eds.): TAAI 2014, LNAI 8916, pp. 74–88, 2014.

Variable selection methods have also been proposed for group sparsity. For example, Yuan and Lin (2006) [17] proposed the group Lasso method under the group sparsity assumption. Simon et al. (2013) [13] generalized group Lasso to sparse group lasso. In the Bayesian framework, Farcomeni (2010) [6] proposed a Bayesian constrained variable selection approach that can also be used for group selection. Raman et al. (2009) [12] proposed a Bayesian group Lasso method by extending the standard Bayesian Lasso. Chen et al. (2014) [3] introduced a Bayesian approach for the sparse group selection problem.

The linear regression problems treated by the above methods usually involve a single response vector. In some applications, there can be multiple response vectors, and these response vectors may be explained by the same or similar subsets of variables to be selected from a large set of candidate variables. Such shared sparsity pattern enables different response vectors to collaborate with or to borrow strength from each other to select the active variables. Such a problem has been studied by Tropp et al. (2006) [16] under the name of simultaneous sparse coding, where each response vector is a signal, each predictor vector is a base signal or an atom, and the collection of all the base signals form a dictionary. The goal is to select a small number of base signals from the dictionary to represent the observed signals. The problem has also been studied by Lounici et al. (2009) [9] under the name of multi-task learning, where the regression of each response vector on the predictor variables is considered a single task. Obozinski et al. (2011) [10] studied this problem under the name of support union recovery, where the word "support" means the subset of variables selected for a response vector, and "support union" means the union of subsets of variables selected for all the response vectors. If the supports of different response vectors are similar, then the union of the supports will only be slightly bigger than the supports of individual response vectors.

In this paper, we propose a Bayesian method for solving the above support union recovery problem, by assuming two nested sets of binary indicator variables. In the first set of indicators, each indicator is associated with a variable, indicating whether this variable is active for any of the response vectors. The set of variables whose indicators are 1's then become the union of the supports. In the second set of indicators, each indicator is associated with both a variable and a response vector, indicating whether this variable is active for explaining the particular response vector. So the second set of indicators gives us the supports of individual response vectors. Variable selection can then be accomplished by sampling from the posterior distributions of the two sets of indicators. We develop the Gibbs sampling algorithm for posterior sampling and demonstrate the performances of the proposed method for both simulated and real data sets.

2   Problem Setup and the Model

Consider the following multiple response model:

$$Y = XB + W, \tag{1}$$

where $Y = [Y_1, \cdots, Y_M]$ is an $n \times M$ response matrix of observations, $X = [X_1, \cdots, X_p] \in \mathbb{R}^{n \times p}$ is the fixed $n \times p$ design matrix, $B = [\beta_1, \cdots, \beta_M]$ is a $p \times M$

matrix of the unknown regression coefficients, and $W = [\omega_1, \cdots, \omega_M] \in \mathbb{R}^{n \times M}$ is the corresponding noise matrix. Here the error term ω_m is an $n \times 1$ noise vector that follows a multivariate normal distribution with zero mean vector and covariance matrix $\sigma^2 I_n$, where I_n is the n-dimensional identify matrix. Thus a group of M response vectors are to be regressed on the same design matrix X. The model can also be written as

$$Y_m = X\beta_m + \omega_m \sim N_n(X\beta_m, \sigma^2 I_n), \, m = 1, \cdots, M, \tag{2}$$

where $\beta_m = (\beta_{1,m}, \cdots, \beta_{p,m})'$ is the coefficient vector for the m-th response vector Y_m. Then the estimation of each column of B, β_m, is a single linear regression problem with response vector Y_m and design matrix X, and can be solved individually. However, in this paper, we solve the M individual regression problems together by exploiting the similarities among β_m, or by imposing constraints on the matrix B.

In particular, we are interested in the variable selection problem for th multi-response model (2). Suppose S_m is the support set for the m-th response vector, i.e.

$$S_m = \{j \in \{1, \cdots, p\} | \beta_{j,m} \neq 0\}. \tag{3}$$

In some applications, S_m should be the same or similar for different m. Thus it is more benefit to identify the set of variables which are related to any of the multiple response vectors simultaneously than to identify S_m separately. Thus similar to Obozinski et al. (2011) [10], we target the "support union recovery" problem, i.e., we want to recover the union of the support sets, i.e.

$$S = \bigcup_m S_m = \{(j,m) | \beta_{j,m} \neq 0, j \in \{1, \cdots, p\}, m \in \{1, \cdots, M\}\}.$$

In this paper, a Bayesian approach is adopted and the corresponding Bayesian algorithms are proposed to recover the unknown support set S.

3   Bayesian Methods for Support Recovery

3.1   Group-Wise Gibbs Sampler

In support union recover problem, Obozinski et al. (2011) [10] set the group structure for each variable across multiple response vectors, and the group Lasso approach was adopted. Consider the corresponding Bayesian approach. It is straightforward to apply Bayesian group selection algorithm to replace the group Lasso approach. Thus one set of the indicators is defined to denote whether X_j is active or not. Similar to group Lasso, we want to select the "best" subset of variables from $X_1, \cdots, X_p$ to explain the multiple responses $Y_1, \ldots, Y_M$ simultaneously.

First, following SSVS in George and McCulloch (1993) [7], a $p \times 1$ vector of indicator variables, $\delta = (\delta_1, \ldots, \delta_p)'$, is introduced to indicate which variables are selected. It is defined as:

$$\delta_j = \begin{cases} 1, & \text{if } X_j \text{ is selected or active} \\ 0, & \text{if } X_j \text{ is not selected or inactive} \end{cases} \quad j = 1, \cdots p. \tag{4}$$

Consider the prior assumption for (δ_j, β_j). The prior distribution of δ_j is assumed to follow the Bernoulli distribution with $P(\delta_j = 0) = \theta_j$, and $P(\delta_j = 1) = 1 - \theta_j$. Then the prior distribution of the coefficient $\beta_{j,m}$ given the indicator δ_j is set as

$$\beta_{j,m}|\delta_j \sim (1 - \delta_j)\gamma_0 + \delta_j N(0, \tau_{j,m}^2), m = 1, \cdots, M, \tag{5}$$

where γ_0 is a point mass at 0. That is if X_j is inactive, i.e. $\delta_j = 0$, then $\beta_{j,m} = 0$ for all $m = 1, \ldots, M$. Otherwise $N(0, \tau_{j,m}^2)$ is the prior distribution of $\beta_{j,m}$. We also assume that the prior distribution of $(\delta_j, \beta_{j,m})$ are independent for $m = 1, \cdots, M, j = 1, \ldots, p$, and they are independent of the prior distribution of the residual variance σ^2, which is assumed to follow an inverse Gamma distribution, $\sigma^2 \sim IG(a/2, b/2)$.

Based on the prior assumptions, the sampling scheme of component-wise Gibbs sampler in Chen et al. (2011) [2] is modified. We sample $(\delta_j, \beta_{j,1}, \ldots, \beta_{j,M})$ one at a time by fixing the other components $(\delta_{-j}, \beta_{-j,m})$, where δ_{-j} denotes all the indicators except δ_j, and $\beta_{-j,m}$ denotes all the coefficients for Y_m except $\beta_{j,m}$. Therefore in the Gibbs sampler, we need to compute the posterior probability $P(\delta_j = 1|, \boldsymbol{Y}, \delta_{-j}, \{\beta_{-j,m}, m = 1, \cdots, M\}, \sigma)$, where the calculation of the likelihood ratio

$$\tilde{Z}_j = \frac{P(\boldsymbol{Y}|\delta_j = 1, \delta_{-j}, \{\beta_{-j,m}, m = 1, \cdots, M\}, \sigma)}{P(\boldsymbol{Y}|\delta_j = 0, \delta_{-j}, \{\beta_{-j,m}, m = 1, \cdots, M\}, \sigma)}$$

is the key step. Due to the independent assumption of $Y_1, \cdots, Y_M$, it is easy to show that

$$\begin{aligned}\tilde{Z}_j &= \prod_{m=1}^{M} \frac{P(Y_m|\delta_j = 1, \delta_{-j}, \beta_{-j,m}, \sigma)}{P(Y_m|\delta_j = 0, \delta_{-j}, \beta_{-j,m}, \sigma)} \\ &= \prod_{m=1}^{M} \frac{\int P(Y_m|\delta_j = 1, \delta_{-j}, \beta_{j,m}, \beta_{-j,m}, \sigma)P(\beta_{j,m}|\delta_j = 1)d\beta_{j,m}}{\int P(Y_m|\delta_j = 0, \delta_{-j}, \beta_{j,m}, \beta_{-j,m}, \sigma)P(\beta_{j,m}|\delta_j = 0)d\beta_{j,m}} \\ &= \prod_{m=1}^{M} \frac{\sigma}{\sqrt{X_j'X_j\tau_{j,m}^2 + \sigma^2}} \cdot \exp\left\{\frac{(R_{j,m}'X_j)^2\tau_{j,m}^2}{2\sigma^2(\sigma^2 + X_j'X_j\tau_{j,m}^2)}\right\}\end{aligned}$$

where $R_{j,m} = Y_m - \sum_{i \neq j} X_i\beta_{i,m}$. Define $r_{j,m} = \frac{R_{j,m}'X_j\tau_{j,m}^2}{\sigma^2 + X_j'X_j\tau_{j,m}^2}$, and $\sigma_{j,m}^{\star 2} = \frac{\sigma^2\tau_{j,m}^2}{X_j'X_j\tau_{j,m}^2 + \sigma^2}$. We then can rewrite $\tilde{Z}_j$ as

$$\tilde{Z}_j = \prod_{m=1}^{M} \sqrt{\sigma_{j,m}^{\star 2}/\tau_{j,m}^2} \exp\left\{\frac{r_{j,m}^2}{2\sigma_{j,m}^{\star 2}}\right\}. \tag{6}$$

The group-wise Gibbs sampler is described in Algorithm 1. In practice, we start from the null model and then iterate the steps in Algorithm 1 to generate the posterior samples of δ_j, β_j for the posterior inference.

Algorithm 1: Group-Wise Gibbs Sampler for Support Recovery

1. Randomly select a variable X_j. Compute $R_{j,m} = Y_m - \sum_{i \neq j} X_i \beta_{i,m}$, for $m = 1, \cdots, M$.
2. Compute the likelihood ratio $\tilde{Z}_j$ according to Eq. (6), and then evaluate the posterior probability of δ_j

$$P(\delta_j = 1 | \boldsymbol{Y}, \delta_{-j}, \{\beta_{-j,m}, m = 1, \cdots, M\}, \sigma) = \frac{(1 - \theta_j)\tilde{Z}_j}{(1 - \theta_j)\tilde{Z}_j + \theta_j}. \quad (7)$$

3. Sample δ_j based on the posterior probability in (7). If $\delta_j = 0$, then set $\beta_{j,m} = 0$, $m = 1, \cdots, M$, otherwise, sample $\beta_{j,m} \sim N(r_{j,m}, \sigma_{j,m}^{*2})$.
4. After repeat above steps for all variables, compute the current residual matrix, $Res = \boldsymbol{Y} - \boldsymbol{XB}$. Then sample $\sigma^2 \sim IG(\frac{a+n}{2}, \frac{\sum(diag(Res'Res))/M+b}{2})$. Go to Step 1.

3.2 Two-Layer Structure and Two-Layer Gibbs Sampler

In the group selection methods, once a variable, X_j, is selection, then X_j is active for all the responses, $Y_1, \ldots, Y_M$. However, we can further assume that the selected variable might not be active for all response vectors simultaneously. In other words, we are interested in finding the best union of support sets, S, and we also assume that the variable in S might be inactive for some response vectors. Therefore, unlike the single indicator set-up in the group-wise Gibbs sampler, two nested sets of binary indicator variables are used. The first set of indicators, $\delta = (\delta_1, \cdots, \delta_p)'$ is associated with variables, $X_1, \ldots, X_p$, respectively, and δ_j is defined to indicate if the variable, X_j, is active for any of the response vectors. Specifically if $\delta_j = 1$, then the variable X_j is selected, and $\delta_j = 0$ otherwise. In the second indicator set, each indicator is associated with a variable and a response vector, indicating whether this variable is active for explaining the particular response vector. Thus for each variable X_j, we define the indicator vector $\eta^{(j)} = (\eta_{j,1}, \cdots, \eta_{j,M})$, and if $\eta_{j,m} = 1$, the variable X_j is active for the m-th response, Y_m, and $\eta_{j,m} = 0$ otherwise.

Similar to the group-wise Gibbs sampler, the prior distribution of δ_j is also assumed to follow the Bernoulli distribution with $P(\delta_j = 0) = \theta_j$ and $P(\delta_j = 1) = 1 - \theta_j$, i.e. $Ber(1 - \theta_j)$. Consider the prior assumption for the second set of indicators. Following Chen et al. (2014) [3], the prior distribution of the indicator in the second set, $\eta_{j,m}$, is chosen as a mixture distribution depended on the indicator in the first set: δ_j, and is represented as

$$\eta_{j,m} | \delta_j \sim (1 - \delta_j)\gamma_0 + \delta_j Ber(1 - \rho_{j,m}), \quad (8)$$

where $P(\eta_{j,m} = 0) = \rho_{j,m}$. Based on Eq. (8), if the j-th variable, X_j, is not selected in S, i.e. $\delta_j = 0$, then $\eta_{j,m} = 0$ for all $m = 1, \ldots, M$, however, when $\delta_j = 1$, $\eta_{j,m}$ still could be 0 or 1 due to the Bernoulli prior distribution. Then for the coefficient, $\beta_{j,m}$, given the indicators δ_j and $\eta_{j,m}$, the prior distribution of $\beta_{j,m}$ can be defined as

$$\beta_{j,m} | \delta_j, \eta_{j,m} \sim (1 - \delta_j \eta_{j,m})\gamma_0 + \delta_j \eta_{j,m} N(0, \tau_{j,m}^2). \quad (9)$$

That is the prior of $\beta_{j,m}$ is $N(0, \tau_{j,m}^2)$ only when $\delta_j = 1$ and $\eta_{j,m} = 1$, i.e. X_j is in S and is active for the m-th response, Y_m. Otherwise $\beta_{j,m}$ is set to be zero. In fact, this coefficient prior has also been used in Chen et al. (2014) [3]. For the prior assumption on the noise variance σ^2, as usual, we choose the inverse gamma conjugate prior $\sigma^2 \sim \text{IG}(a/2, b/2)$. Finally in the prior distribution, $(\delta_j, \eta_{j,m}, \beta_{j,m}), j = 1, \ldots, p$ are assumed to be independent and given $\delta_j = 1$, $(\eta_{j,m}, \beta_{j,m})$, $m = 1, \ldots, M$ are assumed to be independent of each others, too.

Based on the prior set-up, we can use Gibbs sampler to draw posterior samples of the indicators and the coefficients. Similar to group-wise Gibbs sampler in Algorithm 1, the key step is to compute the likelihood ratios of the indicators in the first and second sets respectively, and then the posterior probabilities for $\delta_j = 1$ and $\eta_{j,m} = 1$ can be computed accordingly. Thus we can sample these indicators from the corresponding posterior Bernoulli distributions. First, consider the multi-response model in Eq. (1). Based on the assumption of independence between $Y_1, \cdots, Y_M$, the likelihood ratio Z_j of the variable X_j is represented as

$$Z_j = \frac{P(\mathbf{Y}|\delta_j = 1, \delta_{-j}, \{\beta_{-j,m}, m = 1, \cdots, M\}, \sigma)}{P(\mathbf{Y}|\delta_j = 0, \delta_{-j}, \{\beta_{-j,m}, m = 1, \cdots, M\}, \sigma)} = \prod_{m=1}^{M} \frac{P(Y_m|\delta_j = 1, \delta_{-j}, \beta_{-j,m}, \sigma)}{P(Y_m|\delta_j = 0, \delta_{-j}, \beta_{-j,m}, \sigma)}.$$

Let $k = \{(k_1, \cdots, k_M) : k_m = 0 \text{ or } 1, m = 1, \cdots, M\}$ denote the set of all possible combinations of $(\eta_{j,1}, \cdots, \eta_{j,M})$. It is easy to show that

$$Z_j = \sum_{k=(k_1, \cdots, k_M)} (\prod_{m=1}^{M} b_{j,k_m}),$$

where

$$b_{j,k_m} = \frac{\int P(Y_m|\beta_{j,m}, \eta_{j,m} = k_m, \delta_j = 1, \delta_{-j}, \beta_{-j,m}, \sigma) P(\beta_{j,m}, \eta_{j,m} = k_m|\delta_j = 1) d\beta_{j,m}}{P(Y_m|\delta_j = 0, \delta_{-j}, \beta_{-j,m}, \sigma)}.$$

If $k_m = 0$, then we can simply obtain $b_{j,k_m=0} = \rho_{j,m}$. When $k_m = 1$, then

$$
\begin{aligned}
b_{j,k_m=1} &= \frac{\frac{(1-\rho_{j,m})}{\sqrt{2\pi\tau_{j,m}^2}} \int \exp\left\{-\frac{1}{2\sigma^2}(R_{j,m} - \beta_{j,m}X_j)'(R_{j,m} - \beta_{j,m}X_j) - \frac{\beta_{j,m}^2}{2\tau_{j,m}^2}\right\} d\beta_{j,m}}{\exp\left(-\frac{1}{2\sigma^2}R_{j,m}'R_{j,m}\right)} \\
&= \frac{(1 - \rho_{j,m})\sigma}{\sqrt{X_j'X_j\tau_{j,m}^2 + \sigma^2}} \cdot \exp\left\{\frac{(R_{j,m}'X_j)^2\tau_{j,m}^2}{2\sigma^2(\sigma^2 + X_j'X_j\tau_{j,m}^2)}\right\} \\
&= (1 - \rho_{j,m}) \times \sqrt{\sigma_{j,m}^{*2}/\tau_{j,m}^2} \exp\left\{\frac{r_{j,m}^2}{2\sigma_{j,m}^{*2}}\right\}.
\end{aligned}
$$

Thus the likelihood ratio Z_j of the indicator δ_j can be represented as

$$Z_j = \sum_{k=(k_1, \cdots, k_M)} \left\{\prod_{m=1}^{M}\left[\left((1 - \rho_{j,m}) \times \sqrt{\sigma_{j,m}^{*2}/\tau_{j,m}^2}\exp\left\{\frac{r_{j,m}^2}{2\sigma_{j,m}^{*2}}\right\}\right)^{k_m} \cdot \rho_{j,m}^{(1-k_m)}\right]\right\}.$$

$$(10)$$

Once X_j is not selected, then we can simply set $\eta_{j,m} = 0$ and $\beta_{j,m} = 0$ for all $m = 1, \ldots, M$. Otherwise, if the variable X_j is included in S, i.e. $\delta_j = 1$, then we need to check if X_j is active or not for each individual response Y_m separately. Following the component-wise Gibbs sampler in Chen et al. (2011) [2], the likelihood ratio $Q_{j,m}$ of the variable X_j with respect to the m-th model, Y_m, is computed and can be shown as

$$
\begin{aligned}
Q_{j,m} &= \frac{P(Y_m|\eta_{j,m} = 1, \eta_{-j,m}, \beta_{-j,m}, \sigma, \delta_j = 1)}{P(Y_m|\eta_{j,m} = 0, \eta_{-j,m}, \beta_{-j,m}, \sigma, \delta_j = 1)} \\
&= \frac{\sigma}{\sqrt{X_j'X_j\tau_{j,m}^2 + \sigma^2}} \cdot \exp\left\{ \frac{(R_{j,m}'X_j)^2\tau_{j,m}^2}{2\sigma^2(\sigma^2 + X_j'X_j\tau_{j,m}^2)} \right\} \\
&= \sqrt{\sigma_{j,m}^{*2}/\tau_{j,m}^2}\, \exp\left\{ \frac{r_{j,m}^2}{2\sigma_{j,m}^{*2}} \right\}.
\end{aligned}
\tag{11}
$$

Based on both likelihood ratio functions, Eq. (10) and Eq. (11), the corresponding posterior probabilities of $\delta_j = 1$ and $\eta_{j,m} = 1$ can be derived. The proposed Gibbs sampling algorithm is summarized in Algorithm 2. Note that we would start from the null model by setting $\delta_j = 0$; $\eta_{j,m} = 0$ and $\beta_{j,m} = 0$ for all j and m. Based on our experiences, this initial model works well.

Algorithm 2: The Two-Layer Gibbs Sampler for Support Recovery

1. Randomly select a variable X_j. Compute $R_{j,m} = Y_m - \sum_{i\neq j} X_i\beta_{i,m}$ for $m = 1, \cdots, M$.
2. Compute the likelihood ratio Z_j according to Eq. (10), and then evaluate the posterior probability of δ_j

$$
P(\delta_j = 1|Y, \delta_{-j}, \{\beta_{-j,m}, m = 1, \cdots, M\}, \sigma) = \frac{(1 - \theta_j)Z_j}{(1 - \theta_j)Z_j + \theta_j}.
\tag{12}
$$

3. Sample δ_j based on the posterior probability in Eq. (12). If $\delta_j = 0$, then set $\eta_{j,m} = 0$ and $\beta_{j,m} = 0$, for all $m = 1, \cdots, M$. Otherwise, for each $m = 1, \cdots, M$, compute the likelihood ratio $Q_{j,m}$ according to Eq. (11), and sample $\eta_{j,m}$ based on the posterior probability

$$
P(\eta_{j,m} = 1|Y_m, \eta_{-j,m}, \beta_{-j,m}, \sigma) = \frac{(1 - \rho_{j,m})Q_{j,m}}{(1 - \rho_{j,m})Q_{j,m} + \rho_{j,m}}.
\tag{13}
$$

If $\eta_{j,m} = 0$, set $\beta_{j,m} = 0$; otherwise, sample $\beta_{j,m} \sim N(r_{j,m}, \sigma_{j,m}^{*2})$.
4. After repeat above steps for all variables, compute the current residual matrix, $Res = Y - XB$. Then sample $\sigma^2 \sim IG(\frac{a+n}{2}, \frac{\sum(diag(Res'Res))/M+b}{2})$. Go to Step 1.

3.3   Sample Version of Two-Layer Gibbs Sampler

In Algorithm 2, the computation of Z_j in Eq. (10) involves 2^M cases and can be computational expensive, especially when the number of the responses, M, is large. To save computational cost, instead of deciding whether the j-th variable, X_j, is selected or not based on the posterior probability in Eq. (12) directly, we adopt another method as below. If the current variable is not selected in the union of the support sets, i.e., $\delta_j = 0$, we propose to active this variable first by setting $\delta_j = 1$, and sample the individual indicators $\eta_{j,m}$ and coefficients $\beta_{j,m}$ from the corresponding conditional distributions via the component-wise Gibbs sampling approach in Chen et al. (2011) [2], i.e. the Step 3 in Algorithm 2. We then decide whether to keep the sampled indicators and coefficients via the Metropolis-Hastings acceptance-rejection rule. Conversely, if the variable is selected in S, i.e. $\delta_j = 1$, we then propose to turn down this indicator by switching δ_j to 0, and setting all the corresponding indicators $\eta_{j,m}$ and coefficients $\beta_{j,m}$ to be zero. Therefore, we determine whether to accept this proposal or not via the Metropolis-Hastings acceptance-rejection rule, too. Thus this proposed method can be treated as the sample version of the two-layer Gibbs sampler. The details of these stages are shown in the following.

Let $\Theta_j = (\delta_j, \eta^{(j)}, \beta^{(j)})$ be the parameter set for the jth variable, X_j, where $\eta^{(j)} = (\eta_{j,1}, \cdots, \eta_{j,M})$, and $\beta^{(j)} = (\beta_{j,m}, \cdots, \beta_{j,M})$ are the corresponding second-layer indicators and coefficients. The proposed transition of Θ_j can be defined as

$$T(\Theta_j^0 \to \Theta_j^1) = P(\hat{\beta}^{(j)}, \hat{\eta}^{(j)} | R^{(j)}, \delta_j = 1, \sigma) \tag{14}$$

$$T(\Theta_j^1 \to \Theta_j^0) = 1, \tag{15}$$

where $\Theta_j^0 = (\delta_j = 0, \eta^{(j)} = \mathbf{0}, \beta^{(j)} = \mathbf{0})$, $\Theta_j^1 = (\delta_j = 1, \hat{\eta}^{(j)}, \hat{\beta}^{(j)})$, $R^{(j)} = (R_{j,1}, \cdots, R_{j,M})$, and $\{\hat{\beta}^{(j)}, \hat{\eta}^{(j)}\}$ are sampled from the joint posterior distribution. Here $T(\Theta_j^0 \to \Theta_j^1)$ is the proposal distribution for changing δ_j from 0 to 1, and $T(\Theta_j^1 \to \Theta_j^0)$ is the proposal distribution to switch δ_j to 0. Suppose the variable X_j is not included in S currently, i.e. $\delta_j = 0$. Then after sampling $\hat{\eta}_{j,m}$ and $\hat{\beta}_{j,m}$ by setting $\delta_j = 1$, we calculate the acceptance probability $\hat{A}_j$ as:

$$
\begin{aligned}
&\hat{A}_j(\Theta_j^0 \to \Theta_j^1) \\
&= \frac{P(\Theta_j^1)}{P(\Theta_j^0)} \cdot \frac{T(\Theta_j^1 \to \Theta_j^0)}{T(\Theta_j^0 \to \Theta_j^1)} \\
&= \frac{P(\delta_j=1, \hat{\eta}^{(j)}, \hat{\beta}^{(j)} | \mathbf{Y}, \delta_{-j}, \eta^{(-j)}, \beta^{(-j)}, \sigma)}{P(\delta_j=0, \eta^{(j)}=\mathbf{0}, \beta^{(j)}=\mathbf{0} | \mathbf{Y}, \delta_{-j}, \eta^{(-j)}, \beta^{(-j)}, \sigma)} \cdot \frac{1}{P(\hat{\beta}^{(j)}, \hat{\eta}^{(j)} | R^{(j)}, \delta_j=1, \sigma)} \\
&= \left(\prod_{m=1}^{M} \frac{P(Y_m | \hat{\beta}_{j,m}, \hat{\eta}_{j,m}, \delta_j=1, \delta_{-j}, \beta_{-j,m}, \sigma) P(\hat{\beta}_{j,m}, \hat{\eta}_{j,m} | \delta_j=1)}{P(Y_m | \delta_j=0, \delta_{-j}, \beta_{-j,m}, \sigma)} \right) \times \frac{1 - \theta_j}{\theta_j} \\
&\quad \times \frac{1}{\prod_{m=1}^{M} P(\hat{\beta}_{j,m} | \hat{\eta}_{j,m}, R_{j,m}, \delta_j = 1, \sigma) P(\hat{\eta}_{j,m} | R_{j,m}, \delta_j = 1, \sigma)} \\
&= \prod_{m=1}^{M} \left[\left(\frac{1 - \rho_{j,m}}{p_{j,m}} \cdot \frac{\sigma_{j,m}^*}{\tau_{j,m}} \cdot \exp\left(-\frac{\sigma^2 + \tau_{j,m}^2 X_j' X_j}{2\tau_{j,m}^2 \sigma^2} \hat{\beta}_{j,m}^2 + \frac{R_{j,m}' X_j}{\sigma^2} \hat{\beta}_{j,m} \right. \right. \right. \\
&\quad \left. \left. \left. + \frac{(\hat{\beta}_{j,m} - r_{j,m})^2}{2\sigma_{j,m}^{*2}} \right) \right)^{\hat{\eta}_{j,m}} \right] \times \prod_{m=1}^{M} \left[\left(\frac{\rho_{j,m}}{1 - p_{j,m}} \right)^{(1 - \hat{\eta}_{j,m})} \right] \cdot \frac{1 - \theta_j}{\theta_j} \tag{16}
\end{aligned}
$$

where $p_{j,m} = P(\eta_{j,m} = 1|R_{j,m}, \delta_j = 1, \sigma) = \frac{(1-\rho_{j,m})Q_{j,m}}{(1-\rho_{j,m})Q_{j,m}+\rho_{j,m}}$, $\eta^{(-j)}$ denotes all the second-layer indicator vectors except $\eta^{(j)}$, and $\beta^{(-j)}$ denote all the coefficient vectors except $\beta^{(j)}$. So based on Metropolis-Hastings acceptance-rejection rule, we accept the proposed samples, $\delta_j = 1$ and $(\beta^{(j)}, \eta^{(j)}) = (\hat{\beta}^{(j)}, \hat{\eta}^{(j)})$, with probability $P_{add} = \min\{1, \hat{A}_j\}$. Otherwise if the variable X_j is active already, that is $\delta_j = 1$, then based on the current $\beta^\star_{j,m}$ and $\eta^\star_{j,m}$, $m = 1, \cdots, M$, we have

$$
\begin{aligned}
&\hat{D}_j(\Theta^1_j \to \Theta^0_j) \\
&= \frac{P(\Theta^0_j)}{P(\Theta^1_j)} \cdot \frac{T(\Theta^0_j \to \Theta^1_j)}{T(\Theta^1_j \to \Theta^0_j)} \\
&= \prod_{m=1}^{M} \left[\left(\frac{p_{j,m}}{1-\rho_{j,m}} \cdot \frac{\tau_{j,m}}{\sigma^\star_{j,m}} \cdot \exp\left(\frac{\sigma^2 + \tau^2_{j,m}X'_jX_j}{2\tau^2_{j,m}\sigma^2}\beta^{2\star}_{j,m} - \frac{R'_{j,m}X_j}{\sigma^2}\beta^\star_{j,m} \right. \right. \right. \\
&\qquad\qquad \left. \left. \left. - \frac{(\beta^\star_{j,m} - r_{j,m})^2}{2\sigma^{\star 2}_{j,m}} \right) \right)^{\eta^\star_{j,m}} \right] \times \prod_{m=1}^{M} \left[\left(\frac{1-p_{j,m}}{\rho_{j,m}} \right)^{(1-\eta^\star_{j,m})} \right] \cdot \frac{\theta_j}{1-\theta_j}. \quad (17)
\end{aligned}
$$

Thus the probability of accepting the proposal to remove the variable X_j from S is $P_{del} = \min\{1, \hat{D}_j\}$.

The modified algorithm is shown in Algorithm 3. As mentioned before, in this algorithm, component-wise Gibbs sampler is used to generate the proposal samples of $\eta_{j,m}$ and $\beta_{j,m}$ for the corresponding response Y_m individually.

Algorithm 3: Sample Version of Two-Layer Gibbs Sampler for Union Support Recovery

1. Randomly select a variable X_j. Compute $R_{j,m} = Y_m - \sum_{i \neq j} X_i\beta_{i,m}$ for $m = 1, \cdots, M$.

2. If $\delta_j = 0$, sample $\{(\hat{\eta}_{j,m}, \hat{\beta}_{j,m}), m = 1, \cdots, M\}$ based on the component-wise Gibbs sample (Step 3 in Algorithm 2) through $R_{j,m}$. Compute $\hat{A}_j$ in Eq. (16). Switch δ_j from 0 to 1 with probability $P_{add} = \min\{1, \hat{A}_j\}$. If $\delta_j = 1$, set $\eta_{j,m} = \hat{\eta}_{j,m}$, $\beta_{j,m} = \hat{\beta}_{j,m}$, $m = 1, \cdots, M$.

3. If $\delta_j = 1$, suppose the current coefficients and indicators in the second layer are $\beta_{j,m} = \beta^\star_{j,m}$ and $\eta_{j,m} = \eta^\star_{j,m}$, $m = 1, \cdots, M$. Compute $\hat{D}_j$ in Eq. (17). Change δ_j from 1 to 0 with the probability $P_{del} = \min\{1, \hat{D}_j\}$. If the proposal is rejected, it means the variable X_j is kept in the union model. Then we can re-sample $\eta_{j,m}$ and $\beta_{j,m}$, $m = 1, \cdots, M$ for each individual regression model according to the component-wise Gibbs sampler by $R_{j,m}$.

4. After repeat above steps for all variables, compute the current residual matrix, $Res = Y - XB$. Then sample $\sigma^2 \sim IG(\frac{a+n}{2}, \frac{\sum(diag(Res'Res))/M+b}{2})$. Go to Step 1.

4 Simulated Example

In this section, we illustrate the performance of the proposed two-layer Gibbs sampler via a simulated example. In this example, we set $M = 15$ and there are $p = 200$ predictor variables of length $n = 80$. The variables are defined by

$$X_j = G_j + kG,$$

where $k = 2$ is a pre-specified constant, and G_j's and G are independently generated from multivariate normal distribution with zero mean vector and identical covariance matrix I_{80}. In the setting, the correlation between any two variables is 0.8. The true active variable set was $\{X_7, X_8, X_9, X_{11}, X_{12}, X_{13}\}$, i.e. $S = \{7, 8, 9, 11, 12, 13\}$, and the corresponding coefficients of 15 single regression models are shown in Table 1. The other coefficients are all set to be zero. Then each response is generated according to the linear model $Y_m = X\beta_m + \omega_m$, where $\omega_m \sim N_{80}(0, I_{80})$.

The sample version of two-layer Gibbs sampler, Algorithm 3, is used in this example. The prior parameters are set as $\theta_j = 0.5$, $\rho_{j,m} = 0.5$, $\tau_{j,m}^2 = 20$ for all $j \in \{1, \cdots, 200\}, m \in \{1, \cdots, 15\}$, and $a = b = 0.001$ as the non-informative parameter for inverse gamma prior of σ^2. The initial model is set as the null model, i.e. $\delta_j = 0$; $\eta_{j,m} = 0$ and $\beta_{j,m} = 0$ for all j and m. Totally we run 3000 sweeps. After discarding the first 2000 sweeps, samples collected from the last 1000 sweeps are used for the inference about support union recovery. First the posterior probabilities $P(\delta_j = 1|\mathbf{Y})$ and $P(\eta_{j,m} = 1|\delta_j = 1, \mathbf{Y})$ are estimated based on the posterior samples, and then for the posterior inference, the median probability criterion is used according to Barbieri and Berger (2004) [1]. Thus the threshold probabilities for including predictor in the shared and individual model are both set to 0.5, i.e. $\hat{P}(\delta_j = 1|\mathbf{Y}) \geq 0.5$ and $\hat{P}(\eta_{j,m} = 1|\delta_j = 1, \mathbf{Y}) \geq 0.5$.

The posterior probabilities of $\hat{P}(\delta_j = 1|\mathbf{Y})$ are shown in Figure 1. In fact, the posterior probabilities of $X_7, X_8, X_9, X_{11}, X_{12}$ and X_{13} are all higher than 0.5. Therefore, the selection result of the support union recovery agrees the true model.

Then $\hat{P}(\eta_{j,m} = 1|\delta_j = 1, \mathbf{Y})$ for $j \in S$ are shown in Figure 2. For those nonzero coefficients in Table 1, all corresponding indicators in the second set have posterior probability larger than 0.5. Therefore, based on the median probability criterion, these are treated as active. In particular, $\beta_{8,6} = 0.4$, $\beta_{9,5} = 0.4$, $\beta_{9,6} = 0.4$, $\beta_{9,9} = 0.5$, and $\beta_{9,14} = 0.5$ are relatively smaller values. However, the corresponding posterior

Table 1. The true coefficients of the union of the support sets S in the simulated example

X_j	$\beta_{j,1}$	$\beta_{j,2}$	$\beta_{j,3}$	$\beta_{j,4}$	$\beta_{j,5}$	$\beta_{j,6}$	$\beta_{j,7}$	$\beta_{j,8}$	$\beta_{j,9}$	$\beta_{j,10}$	$\beta_{j,11}$	$\beta_{j,12}$	$\beta_{j,13}$	$\beta_{j,14}$	$\beta_{j,15}$
X_7	0.9	1.7	0	1.2	0.5	0	2.1	0.7	0	0.8	0.8	2.5	0	0	0.9
X_8	0.9	1.7	2.2	1.2	0	0.4	2.1	0.7	0	0.8	0.8	2.5	1.3	0	0
X_9	0.9	1.7	0	0	0.5	0.4	2.1	0	0.5	0.8	0.8	2.5	0	0.5	0
X_{11}	0	0	0	0	1.3	0	0	0	0	0	0	0	0	0	0
X_{12}	0	0	0	0	0	0	0	0	0.7	0	0	0	0	0	0
X_{13}	0	0.6	0	0	0	0.5	0	0	0	0	0	0	0	0	0

probabilities of $\eta_{8,6}$, $\eta_{9,5}$, $\eta_{9,6}$, and $\eta_{9,9}$ are still larger than 0.5. Thus the proposed two-layer Gibbs sampler can successfully recover supports correctly. The posterior means of the coefficients for the selected variables are also shown in Table 2.

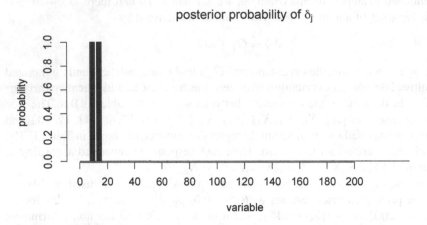

Fig. 1. The posterior probabilities of δ_j: $\hat{P}(\delta_j = 1|\boldsymbol{Y})$ estimated by the two-layer Gibbs sampler in the simulated example

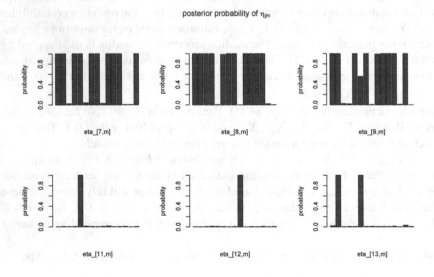

Fig. 2. The posterior probabilities of $\eta_{j,m}$: $\hat{P}(\eta_{j,m} = 1|\delta_j = 1, \boldsymbol{Y})$ obtained by the two-layer Gibbs sampler in the simulated example

To compare with the other approaches, first the group-wise Gibbs sampler, Algorithm 1, is used for the same simulation data. In the group-wise Gibbs sampler, indicator variables, $\delta_j, j = 1, \cdots, p$, are only adopted in the model. To implement this algorithm, the prior parameters set-up are chosen the same as these in the two-layer Gibbs sampler, and the median probability criterion is also adopt for the posterior

Table 2. The estimated coefficients by the sample version of the two-layer Gibbs sampler, Algorithm 3, in the simulated example

X_j	$\hat\beta_{j,1}$	$\hat\beta_{j,2}$	$\hat\beta_{j,3}$	$\hat\beta_{j,4}$	$\hat\beta_{j,5}$	$\hat\beta_{j,6}$	$\hat\beta_{j,7}$	$\hat\beta_{j,8}$	$\hat\beta_{j,9}$	$\hat\beta_{j,10}$	$\hat\beta_{j,11}$	$\hat\beta_{j,12}$	$\hat\beta_{j,13}$	$\hat\beta_{j,14}$	$\hat\beta_{j,15}$
X_7	0.85	1.78	0	1.20	0.47	0	2.18	0.63	0	0.71	0.92	2.31	0	0	0.78
X_8	0.94	1.68	2.20	1.23	0	0.44	2.06	0.75	0	0.76	0.83	2.59	1.30	0	0
X_9	0.91	1.61	0	0	0.52	0.20	2.03	0	0.46	0.96	0.64	2.73	0	0.55	0
X_{11}	0	0	0	0	1.30	0	0	0	0	0	0	0	0	0	0
X_{12}	0	0	0	0	0	0	0	0	0.73	0	0	0	0	0	0
X_{13}	0	0.57	0	0	0	0.52	0	0	0	0	0	0	0	0	0

Table 3. The estimated coefficients by the group-wise Gibbs sampler, Algorithm 1, in the simulated example

X_j	$\hat\beta_{j,1}$	$\hat\beta_{j,2}$	$\hat\beta_{j,3}$	$\hat\beta_{j,4}$	$\hat\beta_{j,5}$	$\hat\beta_{j,6}$	$\hat\beta_{j,7}$	$\hat\beta_{j,8}$	$\hat\beta_{j,9}$	$\hat\beta_{j,10}$	$\hat\beta_{j,11}$	$\hat\beta_{j,12}$	$\hat\beta_{j,13}$	$\hat\beta_{j,14}$	$\hat\beta_{j,15}$
X_7	0.85	1.88	-0.19	1.13	0.79	0.22	2.19	0.61	0.40	0.71	0.92	2.30	-0.05	0.06	0.77
X_8	0.95	1.89	2.17	1.16	0.40	0.53	2.06	0.73	0.17	0.73	0.83	2.59	1.41	0.11	0.05
X_9	0.91	1.77	0.22	0.16	0.92	0.39	2.02	0.05	0.57	0.97	0.64	2.74	-0.10	0.41	-0.04

inference. The simulation result is summarized as follows. Only three variables, X_7, X_8, X_9, are identified as active variables and the posterior means of the nonzero coefficients are show in Table 3. Thus this group-wise Gibbs sampler has the under-selection problem for active variables. The reason is due to the weak group signal for the variables X_{11}, X_{12}, X_{13} because X_{11} and X_{12} are active for Y_5 and Y_9 respectively and X_{13} is only important for Y_2 and Y_6.

In addition to Bayesian approaches, we also compare the simulation results with the Lasso type method. Here the sparse group Lasso function, *mc_sgLeastRin.m*, in SLEP MATLAB toolbox [8] is used for this simulation study. The active variables are determined if at least one of the Lasso coefficient estimations is nonzero. Consider active variable selection results. In addition to the true 6 active variables, there are 14 other variables treated as active. So it has the over-selection problem for the union of the support sets. Focus on the true active variable set, S. The coefficient estimations, $\hat\beta_{j,m}$ for $j \in S$ and $m = 1, \ldots, 15$, are shown in Table 4, and we also find out the over-selection problem for the each response vector individually.

5   Application in Image Analysis

In this section, a real image example is used to illustrate the performance of the proposed Bayesian algorithm. There are five cup images, i.e. $M = 5$, as shown in Figure 3. Based on the sparse coding theory of Olshausen and Field (1996) [11], an image **I** can be represent as a linear composition of Gabor wavelet elements

$$\mathbf{I} = \sum_{j=1}^{p} c_j G_j + U, \tag{18}$$

Table 4. The estimated coefficients by sparse group Lasso in the simulated example

X_j	$\hat\beta_{j,1}$	$\hat\beta_{j,2}$	$\hat\beta_{j,3}$	$\hat\beta_{j,4}$	$\hat\beta_{j,5}$	$\hat\beta_{j,6}$	$\hat\beta_{j,7}$	$\hat\beta_{j,8}$	$\hat\beta_{j,9}$	$\hat\beta_{j,10}$	$\hat\beta_{j,11}$	$\hat\beta_{j,12}$	$\hat\beta_{j,13}$	$\hat\beta_{j,14}$	$\hat\beta_{j,15}$
X_7	0.74	1.63	0	1.18	0.42	0	1.76	0.55	0.13	0.66	0.70	2.26	0	0	0.59
X_8	0.70	1.45	1.83	0.74	0	0.17	1.83	0.43	0	0.62	0.54	2.27	1.95	0	0
X_9	0.71	1.62	0	0	0.29	0.41	1.86	0	0.34	0.51	0.42	2.07	0.04	0.25	0
X_{11}	0	0	0	0	0.86	0	0	0	0	0	0.04	0	0	0	0
X_{12}	0	0.01	0	0	0	0	0	0	0.06	0.01	0	0	0	0	0
X_{13}	0	0.24	0	0	0	0.16	0.01	0	0.03	0	0	0.04	0	0	0

where $\{G_j, j = 1, \ldots, p\}$ is a dictionary of Gabor basis functions defined on the same domain as $\mathbf{I}$, $\{c_j, j = 1, \ldots p\}$ are the coefficients, and U is the unexplained residual image. In this case, the basis functions are treated as representational features and assumed over-complete.

Each cup image is represented as $(50 \times 50) \times 1$ image vector, and the Gabor basis dictionary are defined as

$$g(u, v) = \exp\left[-\frac{1}{2}(\sigma_u u^2 + \sigma_v v^2)\right] \cos\left[\frac{2\pi u}{\lambda}\right],$$

$$u = u_0 + x_1 \cos\theta - x_2 \sin\theta,$$

$$v = v_0 + x_1 \sin\theta - x_2 \cos\theta,$$

where (u_0, v_0) has same domain as image, $\sigma_u = 1$, $\sigma_v = \sqrt{2}$, $\lambda = \sqrt{2\pi}$, and $\theta = \{k/5 \times \pi, k = 0, 1, \cdots, 4\}$. Thus, totally 12500 Gabor basis functions are chosen in this real example.

In the sample version of two-layer Gibbs sampler, we choose the same prior parameters as those in simulation study, and keep last 2000 draws from the total 5000 sweeps as the posterior samples. Figure 4 show the recovered cup images. Using Two-layer structure, the recovered figure not only reveal the shape of cup, but also the different logo on each cup.

Fig. 3. The original cup images

Fig. 4. The recovered cup images

6   Conclusion

In this paper, a Bayesian variable selection method is studied for recovering the union of support sets. Here the two nested sets of indicators are augmented into the multi-response linear regression model, and thus we do not only recover the union of the support sets, S, but also determine if the variables are active or not for the particular response. Two Gibbs sampling methods are introduced for the posterior sampling. The results of the simulation study and the image example demonstrate the performances of the proposed Bayesian approach.

The following are some directions for future work. Firstly the set-up of the prior parameters is still an issue, especially for $\tau_{j,m}$, because based on our experience, the selection results can be sensitive to the values of $\tau_{j,m}$. Secondly in this paper, we consider the homoscedastic model, i.e. the covariance matrix of the error vector in each single task share the same identity matrix. How to extend the proposed method to the heteroscedastic multi-response model can be an interesting project. Finally the asymptotical property of the proposed Bayesian method needs to be investigated.

References

1. Barbieri, M., Berger, J.O.: Optimal predictive model selection. Annals of Statistics 32, 870–897 (2004)
2. Chen, R.-B., Chu, C.H., Lai, T.Y., Wu, Y.N.: Stochastic Matching Pursuit for Bayesian Variable Selection. Statistics and Computing 21, 247–289 (2011)
3. Chen, R.B., Chu, C.H., Yuan, S., Wu, Y.N.: Bayesian sparse group selection (preprint 2014)
4. Dellaportas, P., Forster, J.J., Ntzoufras, I.: Bayesian variable selection using the gibbs sampler. In: Dey, D.K., Ghosh, S., Mallick, B. (eds.) Generalized Linear Models: A Bayesian Perspective, pp. 271–286. Marcel Dekker, New York (2000)
5. Fan, J., Li, R.: Variable selection via nonconcave penalized likelihood and its oracle properties. Journal of the American Statistical Association 96, 1348–1360 (2001)
6. Farcomeni, A.: Bayesian constrained variable selection. Statistica Sinica 20(3), 1043–1062 (2010)
7. George, E.I., McCulloch, R.E.: Variable Selection via Gibbs Sampling. Journal of the American Statistical Association 88, 881–889 (1993)
8. Liu, J., Ji, S., Ye, J.: SLEP: Sparse Learning with Efficient Projections. Arizona State University (2009)
9. Lounici, K., Pontil, M., Tsybakov, A.B., van de Geer, S.: Taking advantage of sparsity in multi-task learning. In: Proceedings of the 22nd Conference on Information Theory, pp. 73–82 (2009)
10. Obozinski, G., Wainwright, M.J., Jordan, M.I.: Support union recovery in high-dimensional multivariate regression. The Annals of Statistics 39(1), 1–47 (2011)
11. Olshausen, B., Field, D.: Emergence of simple-cell receptive field properties by learning a sparse code for natural images. Nature 381, 607–609 (1996)
12. Raman, S., Fuchs, T.J., Wild, P.J., Dahl, E., Roth, V.: The Bayesian group-lasso for analyzing contingency tables. In: Proceedings of the 26th Annual International Conference on Machine Learning, ICML 2009, pp. 881–888. ACM, New York (2009)
13. Simon, N., Friedman, J., Hastie, T., Tibshirani, R.: A sparse group lasso. Journal of Computational and Graphical Statistics 22(2), 231–245 (2013)

14. Tibshirani, R.: Regression shrinkage and selection via the Lasso. Journal of the Royal Statistical Society. Series B (Methodological), 267–288 (1996)
15. Tipping, M.E.: Sparse Bayesian Learning and the Relevance Vector Machine. Journal of Machine Learning Research 1, 211–244 (2001)
16. Tropp, J.A.: Just relax: convex programming methods for identifying sparse signals in noise. IEEE Transactions on Information Theory 52(3), 1030–1051 (2006)
17. Yuan, M., Lin, Y.: Model selection and estimation in regression with grouped variables. J. R. Stat. Soc. Ser. B Stat. Methodol. 68(1), 49–67 (2006)
18. Zhang, C.-H.: Nearly unbiased variable selection under minimax concave penalty. The Annals of Statistics 38(2), 894–942 (2010)
19. Zou, H., Hastie, T.: Regularization and variable selection via the elastic net. Journal of the Royal Statistical Society: Series B (Statistical Methodology) 67(2), 301–320 (2003)

Mining Frequent Patterns with Multiple Item Support Thresholds in Tourism Information Databases

Yi-Chun Chen, Grace Lin, Ya-Hui Chan, and Meng-Jung Shih*

Advanced Research Institute, Institute for Information Industry, Taipei, 105 Taiwan, R.O.C.
{divienchen,gracelin,yhchan,mengjungshih}@iii.org.tw

Abstract. Frequent pattern mining is an important model in data mining. Certain frequent patterns with low minimum support can provide useful information in many real datasets. However, the predefined minimum support value as a threshold needs to be set properly, or it may cause rare item problem. A too high threshold causes missing of rare items, whereas a too low threshold causes combinatorial explosion. In this paper, we proposed an improved FP-growth based approach to solve the rare item problem with multiple item supports, where each item has its own minimum support. Considering the difficulty of setting appropriate thresholds for all items, an automatic tuning multiple item support (MIS) approach is proposed, which is based on Central Limit Theorem. A series of experimental results on various tourism information datasets shows that the proposed approach can enhance frequent pattern mining with better efficiency and efficacy.

Keywords: frequent pattern mining, multiple item support, automatic turning minimum support.

1 Introduction

Frequent patterns are an important class of regularities that exist in databases. Since it was first introduced in [1], the problem of mining frequent patterns has received a great deal of attention [3]. Most of the frequent pattern mining algorithms (e.g., Apriori [2] and FP-growth [4]) use the single minimum support framework to discover complete set of frequent patterns, where the setting of minimum support (min_sup) plays the key role to this model's success. The frequent patterns discovered with this framework satisfy *downward closure property*. That is, "all non-empty subsets of a frequent pattern must also be frequent." This property holds the key for minimizing the search space in all of the single min_sup based frequent pattern mining algorithms [2, 3]. However, this algorithm has a strong assumption that all items in the data are of the same nature and/or have similar frequencies in the database. This is generally way from features of data in real applications. In many applications, some items appear very frequently in the data, while others rarely appear. A valuable part is on these rare items, which appear with low frequency and may be missed easily. Frequent patterns containing rare items usually can

---

* Corresponding author.

S.-M. Cheng and M.-Y. Day (Eds.): TAAI 2014, LNAI 8916, pp. 89–98, 2014.

reveal information with high profitable potential for further decision support. This kind of phenomenon is often seen in consumer market. The necessities, consumables and low-price products such as bread or jam are bought frequently, but luxury goods, electric appliance and high-price such as bed or fridge are generally bought once for a long period. In such a situation, if the min_sup is set too high, all of the frequent patterns containing rare items will be missed. On the other hand, if the min_sup is set too low, many meaningless frequent patterns will be included and misleading focus. The problem to find mining frequent patterns containing both frequent and rare items with "single min_sup framework" is so called as the *rare item problem*.

For addressing rare item problem, B. Liu et al.[7] proposed mining frequent patterns with "multiple min_sup framework", with which each pattern can satisfy a different min_sup depending upon the items within it. The frequent patterns discovered through "multiple min_sup framework" do not satisfy downward closure property and therefore deemed not applicable for minimizing the search space in multiple min_sup based frequent pattern mining algorithms. An Apriori-based algorithm known as Multiple Support Apriori (MSApriori) was proposed in this literature to find frequent patterns with "multiple min_sup framework"[7]. Also, two FP-growth based algorithms, Conditional Frequent Pattern-growth (CFP-growth) [5] and CFP-growth++ [6], have been proposed to mine frequent patterns. Since downward closure property no longer holds in "multiple min_sup framework," the CFP-growth algorithm [5] has to carry out exhaustive search in the constructed tree structure. In [6], it proposed an improved CFP-growth approach, CFP-growth++, by introducing four pruning techniques to reduce the search space. Multiple min_sup framework is reasonable but brings another question: users generally have trouble specifying "good" support value for each item--they need constantly tune the support value. Updating items' min_sup is a costly work—it takes time and efforts to scan database and then to execute the mining algorithm once again—and thus not appropriate to rerun so frequently. Therefore, it is necessary to design a maintenance approach for specifying min_sup automatically.

This study proposes an automatic tuning multiple item support (MIS) approach, with an illustrative example on tourism information database. We firstly categorized the data from the tourism information database to five classes, who, what, when, where and why, according to predefined ontology structure which constructed by domain experts. Fig. 1 illustrates the ontology schema applied in this case. As a general database in real world, tourism information database contains abundant data of popular sites on holidays, with significantly less records on items not so popular—frequencies of items vary widely and it is a rare item problem. Moreover, the cost of tuning multiple minimum supports is far higher than those of tuning single minimum support, because it is to tune all min_sup thresholds for all different items, which is large in number. Therefore, we developed an improved CFP-growth++ approach to solve the rare item problem with multiple item supports. An automatic tuning MIS approach is designed based on the Central Limit Theorem [8]. A series of experimental results on various tourism information datasets shows that the proposed approach can enhance frequent pattern mining with better efficiency and efficacy.

The remaining of the paper is organized as follows. In section 2, we explain the necessary background. In section 3, we proposed improved CFP-growth++ approach to mine both frequent and rare patterns. Experimental results are discussed in section 4. Finally, the conclusion and future work is drawn in section 5.

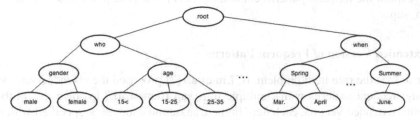

Fig. 1. An ontology schema for tourism information database

2   Problem Definition

In this section, we discuss rare item problem and extended version of frequent patterns on multiple min_sups.

Table 1. Encoded transaction database

TID	Items	Items (ordered by MIS value)
1	{111, 121, 211, 21*}	{21*, 111, 211, 121}
2	{111, 121, 221, 22*}	{111, 22*, 221, 123}
3	{111, 123, 212, 21*}	{21*, 111, 212, 123}
4	{112, 122, 222, 22*}	{112, 22*, 222, 122}
5	{112, 122, 211, 21*}	{112, 21*, 211, 122}
6	{112, 122, 222, 22*}	{112, 22*, 222, 122}
7	{111, 123, 211, 21*}	{21*, 111, 211, 123}
8	{112, 123, 211, 21*}	{112, 21*, 211, 123}
9	{112, 123, 222, 22*}	{112, 22*, 222, 123}
10	{112, 123, 212, 21*}	{112, 21*, 212, 123}

2.1   Rare Item Problem

There are mostly non-uniform in nature containing both frequent and rare items in real world datasets. If the frequencies of items in a database vary widely, the following issues will be encountered while mining frequent patterns under single min_sup framework:

1. If min_sup is set too high, the frequent patterns containing rare items will not be exploited.
2. If min_sup is set too low, it can find frequent patterns that involve both frequent and rare items. However, it can also cause combinatorial explosion, generating too many meaningless frequent patterns.

Example 1. Consider the database shown in Table 1. At high min_sup, say min_sup = 4, we will miss the frequent patterns involving the rare items {221} and {222}. In order to exploit the frequent patterns containing {221} and {222}, we have to specify low min_sup.

2.2 Extended Version of Frequent Patterns

In order to face the rare item problem, B. Liu et al. [7] proposed the extended version of mining frequent patterns with "multiple min_sup framework" to solve this problem. In this extended version, each item in the transaction database is specified with a support constraint known as *minimum item support* (MIS, in short). Moreover, the min_sup of a itemset is represented with minimal MIS value among all its items.

$$MIN(X) = \min(MIS(i_1), MIS(i_2), \ldots, MIS(i_k)) \tag{1}$$

where $X = \{i_1, \ldots, i_k\}$, $1 \leq k \leq n$, is a pattern and $MIS(i_j)$, $1 \leq j \leq k$, means the MIS of an item $i_j \in X$.

This extended model enables users to generate rare item rules without causing frequent items to generate too many meaningless patterns. However, in real-world applications, users cannot specify applicable min_sup at once and always tune MIS of each item constantly. It is very time-consuming and costly because it must rescan database many times. Therefore, in this paper, an automatic tuning MIS approach is proposed. The concept of the Central Limit Theorem is utilized to specify MIS values automatically. We clarify the Central Limit Theorem in Theorem 1.

Theorem 1. (Central Limit Theorem)
Given certain conditions, the arithmetic mean of a sufficiently large number of iterates of independent random variables, each with a well-defined expected value and variance, will be approximately normally distributed. [8]

That is, suppose that a sample is obtained containing a large number of observations, the central limit theorem says that the computed values of the average will be distributed according to the normal distribution. Moreover, in our ontology, it can divide into different taxonomies and each of them is independent of each other. According to the 68-95-99.7 rule which means nearly all values lie within three standard deviations of the mean in a normal distribution, we can know that if MIS value = mean-standard deviation, approximately 84% item combinations will be found. Therefore, it can avoid that occur combinatorial explosion, producing too many meaningless frequent patterns. We define the MIS value of each item as follows:

$$\mu(i_j) = \frac{1}{N}\sum_{j=1}^{N} Sup(i_j) \tag{2}$$

$$MIS(i_j) = \mu(i_j) - \sqrt{\frac{1}{N}\sum_{j=1}^{N}\left(Sup(i_j) - \mu(i_j)\right)^2} \tag{3}$$

$\mu(i_j)$ means the average frequency of the items $i_1, \ldots, i_N$, where items $i_1, \ldots, i_N$ belong to the same level nodes of each category in the ontology.

3   Algorithm

The proposed approach is an improvement over CFP-growth++ algorithm proposed in [6]. The basic concepts of the algorithm can be decomposed into three stages: (1) construction of MIS-tree (2) generating compact MIS-tree and (3) mining frequent patterns from the compact MIS-tree.

A detailed description of the algorithm is given in Algorithm 1 and Algorithm 2. First, we construct MIS-tree. The MIS-tree consists of two components: prefix-tree structure and MIS header table. The prefix-tree structure is similar to FP-tree structure [4]. The difference is that items in the MIS-tree are ordered in descending order according to their MIS values. Each entry in the MIS header table consists of three fields: item, the MIS value of each item, and head of node link which point to the first node in the MIS-tree with that item. The following example is used to illustrate the MIS-tree construction process.

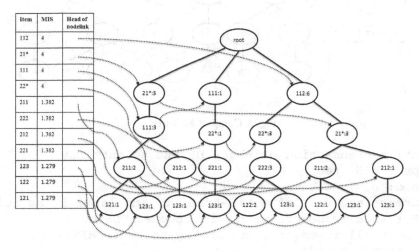

Item	MIS	Head of nodelink
112	4	
21*	4	
111	4	
22*	4	
211	1.382	
222	1.382	
212	1.382	
221	1.382	
123	1.279	
122	1.279	
121	1.279	

Fig. 2. Initial MIS-tree

Example 2. Following the example above, let us consider the database shown in Table 1. The MIS value of each item is shown in the MIS header table in Fig. 2, which is computed by using equation 3. According to Algorithm 1, the items in each transaction (see the third column in Table 1) and the order of item list in MIS header table are arranged in decreasing order according to their MIS value.

Next, a MIS-tree is created as follows. First, the root node is created. Then, the scan of the first transaction leads to the construction of the first branch of the tree with four nodes <21*:1>, <111:1>, <211:1> and <121:1>. The second transaction containing the items '111', '22*', '221' '123' will result in a branch where '111' is linked to root node, '22*' is linked to '111', '221' is linked to '22*' and '123' is linked to '221'. The remaining transactions in TDB can be done in the same way. To facilitate tree traversal, a MIS header table is built in which each item points to its occurrences in the MIS-tree via the head of node link. Moreover, nodes with the same item are linked in sequence via such node links. After scanning all the transactions in Table 1, we will get the initial MIS-tree shown in Fig. 2.

To decrease the search space, the compact MIS-tree is generated by pruning items with supports less than MIN value and merging nodes with the same item name. For example, we remove the nodes with items, 121 and 221, and the complete and compact MIS-tree is shown in Fig. 3.

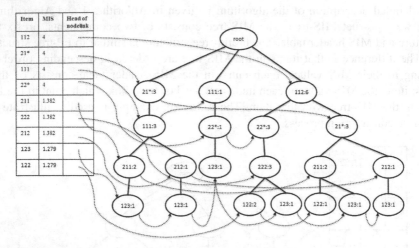

Fig. 3. Compact MIS-tree

```
Input: a transaction database DB and an ontology
Output: MIS-tree
Method:
1. Create the root of a MiS-tree, T, and label it as null
2. For each Transaction, tₙ, in encoded TDB do
3.  Sort all items in tₙ according to their MIS(i)in
    deccending order
4.  Count the support values of any item i, denoted as
    Sup(i) in tₙ.
5.  Insertion(tₙ[p|P], T), where p is the first element
    and P is the remaining list.
6. End for
7. For each item ₤ in unfrequent itemset F do where F is
   the set of items with support smaller than MIN(F)
8.  Delete the entry in the header table with item_name =
    ₤
9.  Pruning(T, ₤)
10.End for
11.Get MIN frequent item header table
12.Merge(T)
Procedure Insertion(tₙ[p|P], T)
1. While P is not empty
```

```
2.    If T has a child N = p
3.      N.count++
4.    Else
5.      Creat a new node N, N.count =1
6.      Let its parent link be linked to T
7.      Let its node-link be linked to the nodes with the
        same item-name via the node-link structure
8.  End while
Procedure Pruning(T, i_j)
1. For each node n in the node-link i_j in T do
2.    If n is a leaf
3.      Remove n
4.    Else
5.      Remove n && its parent link will be linked to its
        child
6. End for
Procdeure Merge(T)
1. For each i_j in MIN frequent item header table do
2.    If there are childnodes with the same item name
3.      Merge these childnodes
4.      Set the count as the summation of these nodes' count
5. End for
```

Table 2. All conditional pattern bases and conditional frequent patterns

Item	MIS	Cond. Pattern bases	Cond. Frequent patterns
122	1.279	<112, 22*, 223: 2>, <112, 21*, 211: 1>	{222, 122:2}, {22*, 122:2}, {112, 122:2}, {22*, 222, 122:2}, {112, 222, 122:2}, {112, 22*, 122:2}, {112, 22*, 222, 122:2}
123	1.279	<21*, 111, 211:1>, <21*, 111, 212:1>, <111, 22*:1>, <112, 22*, 222: 1>, <112, 21*, 211:1>, <112, 21*, 212:1>	{112, 123:3}, {21*, 123:4}, {111, 123:3}, {22*, 123:2}, {211, 123:2}, {212, 123:2}, {112, 21*, 123:2}, {21*, 111, 123:2}, {21*, 211, 123:2}, {21*, 212, 123:2}
212	1.382	<21*, 111>, <112, 21*>	{21*, 212:2}
222	1.382	<112, 22*>	{112, 222:3}, {22*, 222:3}, {112, 22*, 222:3}
211	1.382	<21*, 111>, <112, 21*>	{21*,211:4}, {111, 211:2}, {112, 211:4}, {21*, 111, 211:2}, {112, 21*, 211:2}
22*	4	<111>, <112>	Φ
111	4	<21*>	Φ
21*	4	<112>	Φ
112	4	Φ	Φ

The procedure for mining the complete set of frequent patterns from compact MIS-tree is shown in Algorithm 2. The process of mining frequent patterns is described as follows. Consider the item '122' that has lowest MIS among all items in the compact MIS tree. It occurs in two branches of compact MIS-tree, <112, 22*, 223, 122: 2>, <112, 21*, 211, 122: 1>. Consider the item '122' as a suffix item , its conditional prefix paths are <112, 22*, 223: 2> and <112, 21*, 211: 1>, which form the conditional pattern base. As the compact MIS-tree is constructed, '122' will have MIN value among all items in its conditional pattern base. Therefore, using MIS value of '122' as the conditional min_sup, conditional MIS-tree is generated with <112, 22*, 223: 2> and <112, 21*, 211: 1>. The rightmost column of Table 2 lists all the frequent patterns. Similar process is repeated for other remaining items in the compact MIS-tree to discover the complete set of frequent patterns. The complete set of frequent patterns is shown in Table 2.

```
Algorithm 2 CFP-growth++
Input : MIS-tree, a set of MIN frequent items F, MIS(iⱼ)
of each item iⱼ in F
Output : the complete set of all iⱼ's conditional frequent
itemsets
Method :
1.  For each item iⱼ in the header of Tree do
2.    Set conditional min_sup, Cmin_sup = MIS(iⱼ)
3.    If iⱼ is a frequent item
4.      Generate pattern β= iⱼ∪α with support = iⱼ.support.
5.      Construct β's conditional pattern base and β's
      conditional MIS-tree T_β
6.      If T_β≠Φ
7.        CFPGrowth++( T_β, β, Cmin_sup)
8.  End for
Procedure CFPGrowth++(Tree, α, Cmin_sup)
1.  For each item iⱼ in the header of Tree do
2.    Generate pattern β= iⱼ∪α with support = iⱼ.support.
3.    Construct β's conditional pattern base and β's
    conditional MIS-tree T_β
4.    If T_β≠Φ
5.      If T_β contains a single path P
6.        For each combination γ of the nodes in the path P
      do
7.          Generate pattern γ∪β with support = minimum
    support count of nodes in γ.
8.        End for
9.      Else
10.       CFPGrowth++( T_β, β, Cminsup).
11.   End for
```

4   Experimental Results

This section describes a set of experiments performed to assess the benefit of our approach. We compare the method proposed in [7] to assign MIS values to items with our approach. The method [7] is as follows:

$$\text{MIS}(i_j) = \begin{cases} \sigma \times f(i_j) & \sigma \times f(i_j) > MIN \\ MIN & otherwise \end{cases} \tag{4}$$

The $f(i_j)$ is the actual frequency of item i_j in the TDB. *MIN* denotes the user-specified least minimum item support value of all items. $\sigma(0 \leq \sigma \leq 1)$ is a parameter that controls how the MIS values for items should be related to their frequencies. If $\sigma = 0$, we have only one min_sup, MIN, which is the same as the traditional frequent pattern mining. If $\sigma = 1$ and $f(i_j) > MIN$, $f(i_j)$ is the MIS value for item i_j. The approaches are implemented in Java and all the experiments are performed in an Intel Core i7 2.90GHz with 7.7 GB of memory, and running on Windows 7.

For our experiments, we generated a number of data sets from the tourism information database to test our approach. For each point of interest (poi, in short), we used other four categories from ontology, who, when, why and what, which are utilized to describe poi to construct a dataset. Here, we use the results from one data set to illustrate. The others are similar and thus omitted. The number of transaction is 97. We set up MIN values =1. Fig. 4 shows the number of frequent patterns found. We let $\sigma = 1/\alpha$ and vary α from 1 to 5. We see from Fig. 4 that the number of frequent patterns is significantly reduced by the method proposed in [7] when α is not too large. The number of frequent patterns found by our approach is close to the average of number of frequent patterns found by the method proposed in [7]. This result indicates that it can prevent to generate meaningless frequent patterns by using our maintenance method for automatic min_sup specifying.

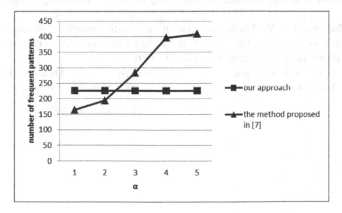

Fig. 4. POI dataset

5   Conclusions

This paper has proposed how to mine frequent pattern containing both frequent and rare items with multiple min_sups and presented a maintenance method for automatic min_siup specifying without rescanning database. We have implemented the improved CFP-growth++ method. By conducting experiments on tourism information dataset, the effectiveness of the maintenance method for automatic min_sup specifying is shown experimentally and practically.

There remain some problems that are worth studying in the future. First, the MIS-tree maintenance problem will be considered. Since the database is updated continuously, how to maintain the MIS-tree structure is an interesting problem. Second, we are planning to use the concept of frequent closed pattern to make the mining process efficiently.

References

1. Agrawal, R., Imieliński, T., Swami, A.: Mining association rules between sets of items in large databases. SIGMOD Rec. 22, 207–216 (1993)
2. Agrawal, R., Srikant, R.: Fast algorithms for mining association rules in large databases. In: Proc. Of the 20th International Conference on Very Large DataBases, pp. 487–499 (1994)
3. Han, J., Cheng, H., Xin, D., Yan, X.: Frequent pattern mining: current status and future directions. Data Min. Knowl. Discov. 15(1), 55–86 (2007)
4. Han, J., Pei, J., Yin, Y., Mao, R.: Mining frequent patterns without candidate generation: A frequent-pattern tree approach. Data Min. Knowl. Discov. 8(1), 53–87 (2004)
5. Hu, Y.-H., Chen, Y.-L.: Mining association rules with multiple minimum supports: a new mining algorithm and a support tuning mechanism. Decis. Support Syst. 42(1), 1–24 (2006)
6. Kiran, B.U., Reddy, P.K.: Novel techniques to reduce search space in multiple minimum supports-based frequent pattern mining algorithms. In: EDBT/ICDT 2011 Proceedings of the 14th International Conference on Extending Database Technology, Pages, pp. 11–20 (2011)
7. Liu, B., Hsu, W., Ma, Y.: Mining association rules with multiple minimum supports. In: KDD 1999: Proceedings of the fifth ACM SIGKDD International Conference on Knowledge Discovery and Data Mining, pp. 337-341 (1999)
8. Rice, J.: Mathematical statistics and data analysis, vol. 2. Duxbury Press (1995) ISBN 0-534-20934-3

Bio-inspired Evolutionary Computing
with Context-Awareness and Collective-Effect

Yi-Ting Chen[1], Jeng-Shyang Pan[1], Shu-Chuan Chu[2], and Mong-Fong Horng[1,*]

[1] Department of Electronics Engineering,
National Kaohsiung University of Applied Sciences, Kaohsiung, Taiwan
[2] Department of Computer Sciences
Flinders University, Australia
ytchen@bit.kuas.edu.tw

Abstract. In this study, an innovative conception is conceived to break the development bottleneck of the traditional ECs at present. This innovative conception is bio-inspired evolutionary computing with context-awareness and collective-effect called as Next-Generation ECs (EC 2.0). For the property of context-awareness in EC 2.0, the individuals are able to observe environmental information by physic property. And, the individual can regularly and closely move to objective. In addition, the individual behaviors in collective-effect include competition, cooperation and conflict. The conflict behaviors of individuals such as difference, contradiction or inconsistence are considered to design the search strategy. The proposed guidable bat algorithm (GBA) is the paradigm of EC 2.0. The bats governed by GBA are able to rapidly and precisely discover the global optimal solution. The simulation results show that the solving efficiency and solution quality of GBA are better than BA's, even well-known HBA's.

Keywords: Next-Generation Evolutionary Computing (EC 2.0), Bio-Inspired Evolutionary Computing, Context-Awareness, Collective-Effect, Guidable Bat Algorithm (GBA).

1   Introduction

Optimization problem in real-world is more complex and has attracted a lot of researchers to search for efficient problem-solving methods. Evolutionary computing is the better solution to solve the optimization problems and widely applied in various applications such as big data analysis [1, 2]. Swarm-based evolutionary computation consists of individuals to become an adaptive system [3-5]. The data structure of solution represents an individual for the optimization problem in CE. Then, the fitness function is used to evaluate the quality of individuals. Each individual searches the best solution by an evolution procedure. In the traditional ECs, the individuals are advanced by the cooperation and competition such as communication with each other

---

* Corresponding author.

S.-M. Cheng and M.-Y. Day (Eds.): TAAI 2014, LNAI 8916, pp. 99–113, 2014.
© Springer International Publishing Switzerland 2014

and tracking the best individual. And, the fitness value is the unique condition to individual evolution. All individuals compete and cooperate to improve their own quality decided by fitness value. However, the individual evolution only counts on competition and cooperation to cause that the similarity among individual is quite high. The individuals tend to falling into local optimal solution in the higher similarity.

However, for the aspect of sociology, the conflict between individuals in an organization is the main motivation of advancement in Conflict Theory. The cooperation, competition and conflict are required to progress the evolution of organization simultaneously. A harmonious organization lacks of innovation and motivation to impede the development. And the individual in a harmonious organization does not contribution to innovation, problem-solving, and creativity. The conflict is able to motive individuals to think innovation and renovate organization. The conflict is produced by character difference, behavior inconsistency, strategic discrepancy and all that. The organization will be substantially advanced by conflict to increase competitiveness and enhance quality. The conflict behavior can benefit the organization development through the evolution of organization culture, nice communication, organization recombination and encouragement competition if the conflict strategies are properly utilized. Therefore, the healthful conflict benefits the organization development.

According to above description about the organization advancement in sociology, the conflict behavior is studied to create a novel conception of collective-effect in this study. The conflict is caused by (1) the individuals seek different objectives, (2) the behaviors between individuals are inconsistent or exclusionary, (3) the adopted strategies are contradictive among individuals in an organization. In EC, a population is regarded as an organization. The individuals cooperate and compete for each other so that the individuals are very similar. The higher similarity causes the lower diversity of population to deteriorate the performance efficiency. Hence, the conflict behavior is considered to increase the difference of individual in a population. The individuals in a population cooperate, compete and conflict each other to advance the population diversity in the proposed Next-Generation ECs (EC 2.0).

Bat Algorithm (BA) is a new evolutionary computing technology and proposed by Xin-She Yang in 2010 [6]. In this study, the search strategies of evolution in BA are improved by the properties of context-awareness and collective-effect to design Guidable Bat Algorithm (GBA). Therefore, GBA is a typical paradigm of EC 2.0. The bats governed in guidable search with context-awareness are able to regularly move based on Doppler Effect. Moreover, in divers search, the conflict conception is considered in the property of collective-effect. The bats select new location according to the difference between their own location and another location. The conflict conception enable to increases the population diversity to enhance the performance efficiency of GBA. This study is the first to employ conflict behaviors of individuals as a kind of collective-effect in swarms. The conceived EC 2.0 is close to real world.

In the rest of this paper, related work about BA and its development are reviewed in Section 2. A paradigm of EC 2.0, GBA, applied to solve the optimization problems is presented in Section 3. The evolutionary steps of GBA are also elaborated in detail in this section. In Section 4, there is a series of simulation to verify the performance of GBA. The performance evaluation is expressed in this section. And, these simu-lated results are compared with BA and HBA. Finally, the conclusions of this study are summarized in Section 5.

2   Related Work

Bat Algorithm (BA) is a bio-inspired algorithm proposed by Xin-She Yang to solve optimization problems of single objective and multi-objectives [6, 7]. And, BA is investigated in depth and is applied [8]. All bats have an ability of echolocation. Bats randomly fly in the velocity (v_i) with frequency (f_{min}), varying wavelength (λ), adjust-able pulse emission rate (r_i) and changeable loudness (A_0) at position (x_i) to search the prey. The frequency f_i in bat i is assumed to range from f_{min} to f_{max}. The loudness is assumed between 1 and 2 as well as decreases from a large positive A_0 to a minimum constant value A_{min}. The pulse emission rate is set between 0 and 1.

The frequency only depends on a randomly vector from a uniform distribution. The movement of bats is unable to adjust its velocity according to the distance between bats and objective appropriately. The echo time is adopted to aid the more accurate measurement of distance between bats and objective. This bat algorithm with echo-aided is called as EABA [9]. In EABA, the velocity of each bat not only considers the frequency of ultrasound but takes the echo time into account to properly adjust movement of bats. The bats emit an ultrasound to the objective to calculate the echo time between its position and the objective's position as Eq. (1). The longer echo time is, the farther the distance is. At this moment, the bats should increase its velocity to quickly approach to the objective. On the contrary, the bats should decrease its veloci-ty to discover the better position near the objective when the echo time is shorter. The velocity is adjusted by the measured echo time as shown in Eq. (2).

$$T_i = \frac{2(x_i^{t-1} - x_*)}{V}, V = 340(m/s) \tag{1}$$

$$v'^t_i = v_i^t + (v_i^t \times T_i) \tag{2}$$

where T_i is the echo time between the ith bat and current global best solution, V is the propagation of sound in temperature is 25°C. The velocity (v_i^t) is from frequency. Then, the velocity (v'^t_i) is obtained by velocity (v_i^t) and echo time (T_i). The echo time is used to measure the distance from bat to objective. The bats can accurately move by the echo-aided to reduce the error caused by random frequency. This pro-posed EABA improves the performance of the original bat algorithm.

Echolocation is an important feature of bat behavior. That means, bats emit an ul-trasound and listen to the echo bouncing back from obstacles while flying. This algo-rithm obtained good results in dealing with lower-dimensional optimization problems, but may become problematic for higher-dimensional problems because it tends to converge very fast initially. In order to improve bat algorithm behavior for higher-dimensional problems, the original bat algorithm was hybridized with the strategies of differential evolutions (DE), called hybrid bat algorithm (HBA) [10]. HBA has been proved on a standard set of benchmark functions taken from literatures. And, the experimental results show that the proposed HBA can significantly improve the performance of the original bat algorithm, which can be very useful for the future.

The original bat algorithm was hybridized by the differential evolutions (DE). DE is a typical evolutionary algorithm with differential mutation, crossover and selection that was successfully applied to continuous function optimization, proposed by Storn and Price [11-13]. HBA differs from the original BA in local search step. A random solution is selected and modified by "DE/rand/1/bin" strategy of DE. The differential mutation randomly selects two solutions and adds a scaled difference between them to produce the third solution. This mutation can be expressed as follows:

$$u_i^{(t)} = w_{r_0}^{(t)} + F(w_{r_1}^{(t)} - w_{r_2}^{(t)}), \quad for\ i=1,...,\ PS \tag{3}$$

where $u_i^{(t)}$ is the candidate solution presented by the ith bat at iteration t, generated by mutation and PS is the population size. $F \in [0.1, 1.0]$ is the mutation rate as a scaling factor to scale the adjustment. The variables, r_0, r_1 and r_2, are random integers from 1 to PS. w is the bat in a population. This intention of HBA is to produce a position of bat different from the position of all bats in a population.

Uniform crossover is employed as a differential crossover by the DE. The trial vector is built out of parameter values that have been copied from two different solutions. This crossover can be expressed as follows:

$$z_{i,j}^{(t)} = \begin{cases} u_{i,j}^{(t)} & if\ rand_i(0,1) \le CR\ or\ j = j_{rand} \\ w_{i,j}^{(t)} & otherwise \end{cases} \tag{4}$$

where j is the jth dimension in bat i. z is a new solution generated by crossover of the original position and the solution generated by mutation. $CR \in [0.0, 1.0]$ is the crossover rate and controls the fraction of parameters that are copied to the trial solution. Note, the relation $j = j_{rand}$ assures that the trial vector is different from the original solution $Y^{(t)}$. In [10], the strategy "DE/rand/1/bin" is applied to produce the variety of trial position and denotes that the base vector is randomly selected, 1 vector difference is added to it, and the number of modified parameters in mutation vector follows binomial distribution. This operation in HBA benefits the information gathering for population to produce a better position of bats. Then, differential selection can be expressed as follows:

$$w_i^{(t)} = \begin{cases} z_i^{(t)} & if\ f(Z^{(t)}) \le f(Y^{(t)}) \\ w_i^{(t)} & otherwise \end{cases} \tag{5}$$

where f is the fitness function used to evaluate the quality of position for each bat in HBA. If the quality of new position generated by crossover is better than the quality of the original position, the bat will move to the new position. Otherwise, the bats stay in the current position. In HBA, an operator of DE is applied in local search to gather the information. The various positions of bats are produced by information gathering to improve the solving efficiency in BA.

3   Guidable Bat Algorithm is Applied in Solving Optimization Problems

In BA, the frequency of bat is generated by a random vector with uniform distribution. This randomly generated frequency effortlessly makes aimless search of bats to deteriorate the evolution quality of algorithm. And, there are no exclusive rules to steer the bats toward the correct direction during movement procedure. These situations deteriorate the evolution quality to search the global optimal solution for algorithm. In order to overcome these disadvantages to enhance the solving efficiency, a guidable bat algorithm with frequency shift based on Doppler Effect is proposed in this study.

The principles of Doppler Effect and conflict behavior are applied in BA to invent an innovative bio-inspired EC approach called as Guidable Bat Algorithm (GBA) as shown in Fig. 1. This conception mainly provides a regular rule based on Doppler Effect to guide the bats toward the correct direction in guidable search. The bats governed in GBA are able to fast and accurately discover the global optimal solution. A regular rule is able to move the step of bats according to the distance between the bats and the current best bat appropriately.

In the traditional EC such as particle swarm optimization (PSO) [14, 15], the particles learn and communicate experience with each other. The particles only use the fitness value to evaluate the quality of position. As well as, the fly direction of all particles depend on the best particle. Hence, the particles are very similar so that the particles easily fall into local optimal solutions. In order to overcome this disadvantage. In divers search of GBA, the conflict behavior is considered to design the search strategy to strengthen the ability of global search for bats. The bats search new location by considering the similarity between their own location and another location. Therefore, the population is comprised by diversity bats to search wider region.

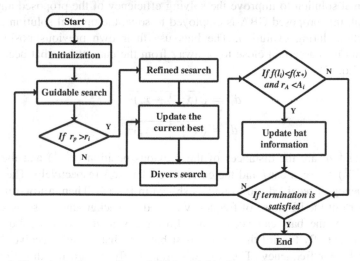

Fig. 1. Flowchart of a paradigm of GBA with bio-inspired evolutionary computing

Step 1. Initialization

The parameters are specified including iteration, population size and dimension of search space for algorithm. Then, for the properties of bat such as the frequency, velocity, previous position, current position, location, loudness and emission pulse rate are initialized. In GBA, the position of bats represents a potential solution in a solution space. Then, the fitness function is designed for the target problem and used to evaluate the quality of position. Each bat has its fitness evaluated by the defined fitness function. In this study, the proposed algorithm is used to discover the minimum solution of continuous functions. Hence, the smaller the fitness value is, the better the position is.

Step 2. Guidable Search

Doppler Effect is employed to establish a regular rule of bat movement in GBA. The bats governed by GBA are able to adjust their velocity by frequency shift with Doppler Effect. This frequency shift depends on Doppler Effect caused by velocity between the bats and the current best bat. When the bats are close to the current best bat, the bats should receive the ultrasound with higher frequency. The bats use this higher frequency of the ultrasound to accelerate the velocity. The acceleration is able to assist the bats quickly flying toward the direction of the current best bat. The bats attempt to find a better position than the current best bat according to this direction. On the contrary, when the bats run away from the current best bat, the bats will receive an ultrasound with lower frequency. The bats should use this frequency to derive the velocity. The bats slowly move to explore a better position than their own position along the path of the current best bat. In guidable search, the velocity of bats is adjusted by frequency shift of the received ultrasound wave to approach to a better position. This novel movement benefits the bats to quickly and accurately explore the global optimal solution to improve the solving efficiency of the proposed algorithm. In additional, this proposed GBA is employed to solve the optimal solution of continuous function during evolution. The bats use their own previous positions and current position to ascertain close to or away from the current best bat according to Eq. (6) and Eq. (7).

$$d_i'^t = \sqrt{(\tilde{x}_i^{t-1} - x_*)^2} \tag{6}$$

$$d_i^t = \sqrt{(x_i^{t-1} - x_*)^2} \tag{7}$$

where $d_i'^t$ and d_i^t are the distances of the previous position $(\tilde{x}_i^{t-1})$ and the current position (x_i^{t-1}) between bat i and the current best bat (x_*) respectively. The bats obtain a frequency of received ultrasound as shown in Eq. (8). Then, a low filter is utilized to filter out the LF noise of frequency caused by background noise as shown in Eq. (9). Hence, the bats can accurately adjust the velocity given by Eq. (10). If $d_i^t \leq d_i'^t$, the bats fly toward the current best bat. The bats should receive the ultrasound with higher frequency. The bats will quickly fly toward the direction of the current best bat to find a better position than the current best bat according to this direction. On the contrary, if $d_i^t > d_i'^t$, the bats fly away from the current best bat. The bats receive the ultrasound with lower frequency. The bats should decelerate to explore a better position than their own position along the path of the current best bat.

$$\hat{f}_i^t = \begin{cases} (V + v_i^{t-1})/(V - v_*)]\hat{f}_i, & if\ d_i^t \leq d_i'^t \\ [(V - v_i^{t-1})/(V + v_*)]\hat{f}_i, & if\ d_i^t > d_i'^t \end{cases} \tag{8}$$

$$f_i^t = (f_i^{t-1} + \hat{f}_i^t)/2 \tag{9}$$

$$v_i^t = v_i^{t-1} + (x_i^{t-1} - x_*)f_i^t \tag{10}$$

where $\hat{f}_i^t$ is the frequency caused by Doppler Effect for bat i at iteration t. V is the propagation speed of sound in 25°C. In this study, V is set 340 m/s. v_i^{t-1} is the velocity of bat i at iteration t-1. $\hat{f}_i$ is the frequency of emitted ultrasound for the bats and be assumed from f_{min} to f_{max} with uniform distribution in [0, 1]. v_* is the velocity of the current best bat. f_i^t is the new frequency obtained by the past frequency (f_i^{t-1}) and the frequency ($\hat{f}_i^t$) caused by Doppler Effect of bat i at iteration t. The velocity (v_i^t) is modified by the distance between bat i and the current best bat, as will at the new frequency (f_i^t).

Besides, there is no exclusive rule to steer the bats move forward the correct direction in BA. The bats managed in GBA utility the velocity and their own current position to explore the location (l_i^t). If the quality of explored location is better than their current positions, the bats will update their own current position with the new found locations and the original current positions will be the previous positions as Eq. (11). Otherwise, the bats stay at their own position as shown in Eq. (12) and Eq. (13). As a result, this searching policy provides the proper frequency and suitable velocity to guide the bats toward correct direction to follow the current best bat.

$$l_i^t = x_i^{t-1} + v_i^t \tag{11}$$

$$x_i^t = \begin{cases} l_i^t, & if\ f(l_i^t) < f(x_i^{t-1}) \\ x_i^{t-1}, & otherwise \end{cases} \tag{12}$$

$$\tilde{x}_i^t = \begin{cases} x_i^{t-1}, & if\ f(l_i^t) < f(x_i^{t-1}) \\ \tilde{x}_i^{t-1}, & otherwise \end{cases} \tag{13}$$

The bats use the modified velocity (v_i^t) to explore new location (l_i^t) based on the position (x_i^{t-1}). If the new location is better than their own position (x_i^{t-1}), the bat will update their own position (x_i^t) with the new found location (l_i^t). Then, the original position (x_i^{t-1}) will be the previous position ($\tilde{x}_i^t$) according to Eq. (13).

Step 3. Refined Search

In BA, there is a condition, $r_p > r_i$, to decide whether the bats execute the local search or not. Thus, this condition is referred in the proposed algorithm to provide obvious performance comparison with original BA. If a random value (r_p) is greater than the emission pulse rate (r_i) of the bats, the bats will carry out the refined search designed. In other words, the execution probability of refined search is $1-r_i^t$ for each bat. In this step, the bats attempt to find a better location by slightly explore near the current best bat. In BA, the bats slightly move based on the average loudness (A') of all the bats at iteration t to search a better location near the current best bat. However, the average loudness is decreasing with the iterations increasing. The smaller the average loudness is, the narrower the search region is. The search region of bats is centralized near the current best bat. This centralized search easily makes bats falling into the local optimal solution. In GBA, the bats search a better location near the current best bat according to their frequency by Eq. (14). The movement do not be seriously affected by iteration in proposed approach. The search region is elastic to enhance the possibility with position updating.

$$l_i^t = x_* + \varepsilon f_i^t, \quad \varepsilon = [-1,1] \tag{14}$$

where x_* is the current best bat. ε is the random number with uniform distribution. f_i^t is the frequency of bat i at iteration t. l_i^t is the found new location by slight movement.

Step 4. Update the Current Best Bat

The current best bat may be replaced due to the position updating of some bats. Once the current best bat is changed, the flight direction of bats toward the current best bat will be different next iteration. The current best bat with the finest quality is selected after comparing with all position of bats as shown in Eq. (15). This current best bat will lead other bats toward the search direction of global optimal solution.

$$x_* = x_i^t, \quad if \; fit(x_i^t) < fit(x_*) \tag{15}$$

Step 5. Divers Search

Divers search is an early-stage resolution to conflict between bats, proposed in this paper. When the bats are trapped in conflict solution, a divers search is involved in GBA to strengthen the global search. The velocity of bats will be randomly modified to search new location by Eq. (16). There are three exploration strategies including excavate near position, excavate near location and disorder, to be adopted according to a random value (R) for each dimension as shown in Eq. (17), if R=1, the bat explore new location based on its current position. If R=2, the bat explores new locations near its current location. The bats attempt to carefully discover the better position near their own position and location in these two exploration strategies. Otherwise, when R=3, the bat randomly selects a location in solution space to exploit new search region.

$$v_{i,j}^t = \sigma v_{i,j}^t, \quad \sigma \in [-2,2] \tag{16}$$

$$\tilde{l}_{i,j}^t = f(x) = \begin{cases} x_{i,j}^{t-1} + v_{i,j}^t, & if \ R = 1 \\ l_{i,j}^{t-1} + v_{i,j}^t, & if \ R = 2 \\ random(), & if \ R = 3 \end{cases} \tag{17}$$

where $v_{i,j}^t$ is the j-th dimensional velocity of bat i at iteration t and is modified by a random value, σ, from a uniform distribution. $\tilde{l}_i^t$ is the new location of bat by three designed strategies. As a result, a new found location consist of different elements from position, location and random for the bat to deviate the search direction of bats. The divers search benefits the bats to exploit new search region to avoid falling into a local optimal solution. Then, the cosine similarity is utilized to analyze the similarity of the new location and original location of a bat as Eq. (18).

$$Cos\_sim\left(l_i^t, \tilde{l}_i^t\right) = \frac{\sum_{j=1}^d l_j^t \times \tilde{l}_j^t}{\sqrt{\sum_{j=1}^d l_j^{t^2}} \times \sqrt{\sum_{j=1}^d \tilde{l}_j^{t^2}}} \tag{18}$$

Cos_sim is the similarity of a new location and a current location. If the similarity of bat is greater than the similarity threshold (T_{sim}), the bat is still search the location around their own location after the search direction of bat suffers violent disturb by designed strategies. This bat will discover a new location through tracking for the current best bat to fast approach to the current best bat as shown in Eq. (19). T_{sim} is the similarity threshold.

$$l_i^t = \begin{cases} \tilde{l}_i^t, & If \ c_{sim} \leq T_{sim} \\ x_* c_{sim} + x_i^t (1 - c_{sim}), & If \ c_{sim} > T_{sim} \end{cases} \tag{19}$$

Step 6. Update Bat Information

This bat will update its properties to afresh adjust status, including loudness (A_i) and emission pulse rate (r_i) according to Eq. (20). This new current best bat with better status will lead all bats toward new search direction to explore new area. The loudness and emission pulse rate of bats will be updated when (1) the current best bat is updated in divers search and (2) the random number (r_A) between 0 and 1 is smaller than the loudness (A_i) of bat i.

$$A_i^t = \alpha A_i^{t-1}, \quad r_i^t = r_i^0 [1 - exp(-\gamma t)] \tag{20}$$

Step 7. Termination

All bats carry out Step 2-6 to indicate that iterations have been finished. All bats will be back to Step 2 to start next iteration repeatedly until the condition of termination is satisfied. When the termination is satisfied, the final current best bat is regarded as the global best bat and its position is the derived global optimal solution of the optimization problem in this evolution.

4   Simulation Results

Two benchmark functions are used to validate the performance of the proposed algorithm [16]. These selected benchmark functions are described in details as follows.

- Griewangk Function

This function is similar to the Rastrigin function. There are many widespread local minima distributed regularly as shown in Fig. 2. It is defined as follows,

$$f_1(x) = \frac{1}{4000} \sum_{i=1}^{n} x_i^2 - \prod_{i=1}^{n} \cos\left(\frac{x_i}{\sqrt{i}}\right) + 1$$

$$for -600 \le x_i \le 600, for \; i = 1, \dots, n. \tag{21}$$

The global minimum $f_1(x) = 0$ is obtainable when $x_i = 0$, $i=1,\dots,n$. There are 191 local minimal as $d=1$ in this function. The number of local minima exponentially increases with d. When the number of local minima fast increases, the global optimal solution becomes extremely difficult to detect as d increment. The number of local minima is more than the Rastrigin function. And the local minimal are distributive in whole solution space. The ability of escapement from local optimal solution for the proposed algorithm will be demonstrated by this function.

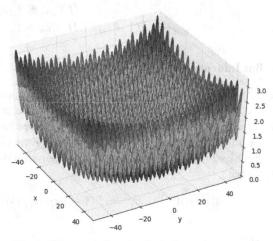

Fig. 2. Griewangk function in 2-dimension

- Ackley Function

Ackley function is based on the gradient and widely used as test function of multi-modal as shown in Fig. 3. This function is with a cosine wave of moderate amplitude modulated with an exponential function. Ackley function is composed of a plane-like outer region and a control hole or peak where modulations by the cosine wave become more and more influential. A typical Ackley function is as follows,

$$f_2(x) = -a \cdot exp\left(-b \cdot \sqrt{\frac{1}{n}\sum_{i=1}^{n} x_i^2}\right) - exp\left(\frac{1}{n}\sum_{i=1}^{n} cos(cx_i)\right) + a + exp(1)$$

$$for \ -32.768 \le x_i \le 32.768, \ i = 1, ..., n. \tag{22}$$

The parameters of this function are recommended to set a=20, b=0.2, c=2π. The global minimum $f_2(x) = 0$ is located on $x_i = 0$ for $i=1,...,n$. This function produces moderate complications in the search of optimal solutions. Due to multiple local optima, the algorithm only based on the gradient will be trapped in local optimal solution. However, the ability of search and analysis in wider area is helpful to algorithms that will be able to cross the valley among the optima and to achieve better results.

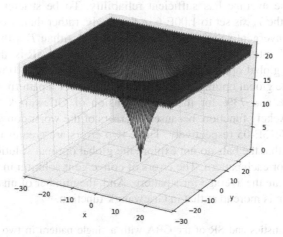

Fig. 3. Ackley function in 2-dimension

The initial parameters are the same as the original bat algorithm in [6] including population size, frequency range, emission pulse rate and loudness. Then, the previous position, current position, location, velocity, emission pulse rate and loudness of each bat are randomly generated in initialization. There are two kinds of dimensions (d=64, 128) to produce the different complexity for two benchmark functions. The dimension increment leads to the expanded solution space which requires more time to discover the global optimal solution in these functions. In this simulation, the highest dimension is set according to the previous work [6].

The initial positions of bats are randomly generated and regarded as a pattern. A pattern is executed by 1000 iteration as a round to obtain a convergent solution. And, this pattern is repeated examined by 100 rounds to derive the statistics include average error (*Avg.*), standard deviation (*Std.*) maximum (*Max.*) and minimum (*Min.*). These statistics appraise the solving efficiency of GBA. The *Avg.* presents the quality of convergent solution found by GBA. The *Std.*, *Max.* and *Min.* are applied to support the reliability of average error. The *Std.* is variance of convergent solutions found in

100 rounds. The smaller the *Std.* is, the higher the reliability is. The *Max.* and *Min.* are the best and the worst convergent solutions in 100 rounds respectively. A tolerable threshold (T_{tor}) is utilized to determine the acceptance of a solution. If the average error of solution is less than T_{tor}, the global optimal solution is found in an iteration limitation. The evolution is successful in this round. And, *SR.* is defined as following:

$$SR = \frac{no.of\ success}{no.of\ round} \tag{23}$$

The statistics of convergent solution with the single pattern for two benchmark function with different dimensions are shown in Table 1. *Avg.* mainly appraises the quality of convergent solution. The smaller *Avg.* implies the smaller the average errors of converged solution is and the better the performance of algorithm. The convergent solution is 5.41E-6 occurred in Ackley function with d=128. The errors of these cases slightly rise in the case of 128-dimension functions. In addition, the *Std.* is very small. The average has sufficient reliability. To be stricter than the previous works [6, 10], the T_{tor} is set to 1.00E-6 in this study, rather than 1.00E-05. If the average error of convergent solution in an evolution is less than T_{tor}, the bats successfully finds the global optimal solution in a round. The higher the SR is, the better the ability of discovering global optimal solution for bats are. The SR is 100% to indicate that the bats find the global optimal solution in all rounds for a pattern. On the other hand, the SR is 91% and 73% for the 128-dimension of Griewangk function and 128-dimension of Ackely function, because the errors of the worst convergent solution are 3.36E-05 and 6.13E-05 respectively. These two errors are greater than tolerable threshold to imply that the bats do not explore the global optimal solution in a small number of rounds for each pattern. The errors of convergent solution in these unsuccessful rounds deteriorate the average for a pattern. And, the number of unsuccessful round in Ackley function is more than that in Griewangk function.

Table 1. The statistics and SR of the GBA with a single pattern in two benchmark function with two kinds of dimensions

benchmark	Griewangk		Ackley	
Dimension	**64**	**128**	**64**	**128**
Avg.	2.90E-16	1.31E-06	3.46E-10	5.41E-06
Std.	0.00E+00	4.37E-06	1.05E-09	8.52E-06
Max.	1.50E-14	3.36E-05	6.34E-09	6.13E-05
Min.	0.00E+00	3.23E-18	2.37E-15	1.19E-08
SR.	100%	91%	100%	73%

In order to confirm the solving efficiency of proposed bat algorithm in this study, the GBA is compared with HBA and BA in 10, 20 and 30 dimensions with an iteration limitation. The simulation results of HBA and BA are provided by [10]. In [10], the iteration limitations are separately set to 1000, 2000 and 3000 for 10, 20 and 30 dimensions to verify the quality of global optimal solution. And each function is executed 25 rounds to derive the statistics in these three kinds of dimensions. The parameters of Griewangk function and Ackley function in this study are the same as [10]. Therefore, these two functions are adopted to the comparison of solving efficiency for GBA, HBA and BA in these three kinds of dimensions. The simulation results of compared three algorithms are shown in Table 2.

The purpose is to compare the quality of global optimal solution between GBA, HBA and BA in an iteration limitation. For BA, there are severe average errors of global optimal solution in these three kinds of dimensions for these two examined functions. Therefore, these iteration limitations are insufficient to discover the eligible global optimal solution. Furthermore, the HBA is proposed to improve the quality of global optimal solution in an iteration limitation. The strategies of differential evolution are applied to reform the local search in BA to design HBA. The average error of global optimal solution is decreased so that it is noticeably improved in HBA, particularly for Griewangk function shown in Table 2. These simulation results prove that HBA based on DE applied in local search benefits the improvement of quality with global optimal solution.

Table 2. The statistics comparison of BA, HBA, and GBA in benchmark functions with various dimensions

Algorithm	Function	Statistics	d=10	d=20	d=30
BA	Griewangk	Min.	3.29E+01	8.77E+01	1.58E+02
		Max.	1.73E+02	1.43E+02	4.18E+02
		Avg.	8.30E+01	1.46E+00	1.51E+02
		Std.	6.94E+01	1.64E+01	1.52E+01
	Ackley	Min.	1.37E+01	2.15E+02	3.39E+02
		Max.	2.00E+01	5.87E+02	7.82E+02
		Avg.	1.75E+01	3.38E+02	4.67E+02
		Std.	1.73E+01	1.80E+01	1.76E+01
HBA	Griewangk	Min.	2.25E-09	1.01E-07	6.38E-06
		Max.	3.97E-05	2.96E+01	3.57E+01
		Avg.	3.18E-06	8.56E-07	6.42E-05
		Std.	1.14E-07	2.17E+00	3.12E+00
	Ackley	Min.	6.31E-04	3.70E-05	5.43E-04
		Max.	2.00E+01	5.48E+01	9.85E+01
		Avg.	1.16E+01	3.82E-05	2.53E-03
		Std.	1.78E+01	1.95E+01	1.94E+01
GBA	Griewangk	Min.	0.00E+00	0.00E+00	0.00E+00
		Max.	0.00E+00	0.00E+00	0.00E+00
		Avg.	0.00E+00	0.00E+00	0.00E+00
		Std.	0.00E+00	0.00E+00	0.00E+00
	Ackley	Min.	1.45E-16	1.45E-16	1.45E-16
		Max.	1.12E-14	1.86E-14	2.97E-14
		Avg.	1.24E-15	3.36E-15	6.04E-15
		Std.	0.00E+00	0.00E+00	0.00E+00

According to the simulation results, HBA provides a good solving efficiency and is a ponderable challenge target. Although HBA displayed a good solving efficiency, the quality of global optimal solution in GBA is outstandingly meliorated than it is in HBA. And the iteration limitation is only set to 1000 in these three kinds of dimension for GBA. Therefore, GBA not only represents a better quality of global optimal solution but also requires a less iteration. In addition, the quality of global optimal solution in HBA is steadier than it is in BA because the statistics including *Max.*, *Min.* and *Std.* are smaller. This smaller statistics benefits to enhance the reliability for quality of the global optimal solution. As a whole, in [6], the simulation results show that BA is better than GA and PSO. And in [10], the HBA improves the solving efficiency of BA. Then, an innovative guidable bat algorithm is proposed in this study. This proposed algorithm is a perfect swarm-based evolutionary computation and better than the above algorithms by the demonstration of simulation results.

5   Conclusions

In this study, GBA based on Doppler Effect is proposed to improve the solving efficiency of BA. The bats in GBA have the ability of guidance by frequency shift based on Doppler Effect toward the correct direction in guidable search. Moreover, both refined search and divers search are employed to reinforce the ability of local search and global search. The bats are able to discover the eligible position to upgrade the position of the current best bat in a short time. Therefore, the bats are able to rapidly and precisely to discover the global optimal solution to augment the solving efficiency of the proposed GBA. GBA is a perfect evolutionary computation and better than the other algorithms such as GA, PSO, BA and HBA by the demonstration of simulation results. Hence, the features of context-awareness and collective-effect in EC 2.0 benefit the performance efficiency of the global optimal solution. In addition, the cooperation, competition and conflict are not only to balance the operation but also to speed up the advancement in organization. Additionally, how to adjust the individual behavior with cooperation, competition and conflict to maintain the population advancement will be valuable and difficult topic for the technology of ECs in future.

Acknowledgement. The authors would like to express their sincere thanks to Ministry of Science and Technology, Taiwan (ROC), for financial support under the grants NSC 102-2218-E-151 -005 and MOST 103-2221-E-151 -041 -.

References

1. Mukhopadhyay, A., Maulik, U., Bandyopadhyay, S., Coello Coello, C.A.: A Survey of Multiobjective Evolutionary Algorithms for Data Mining: Part I. IEEE Transactions on Evolutionary Computation 18(1), 4–19 (2014)
2. Mukhopadhyay, A., Maulik, U., Bandyopadhyay, S., Coello Coello, C.A.: A Survey of Multiobjective Evolutionary Algorithms for Data Mining: Part II. IEEE Transactions on Evolutionary Computation 18(1), 20–35 (2014)

3. Yan, P., Hideyuki, T.: A survey on accelerating evolutionary computation approaches. In: Proceeding of International Conference of Soft Computing and Pattern Recognition (SoCPaR), pp. 201–206 (2011)
4. Asadul Islam, M., Mashrur-E-Elahi, G.M., Hashem, M.M.A.: A new distributed evolutionary computation technique for Multi-Objective Optimization. In: Proceeding of IEEE International Conference on Computer and Communication Engineering (ICCCE), pp. 1–6 (2010)
5. Komar, M., Grbic, D., Cupic, M.: Solving exam timetabling using distributed evolutionary computation. In: Proceeding of the 33rd International Conference on Information Technology Interfaces (ITI), pp. 301–306 (2011)
6. Yang, X.-S.: A New Metaheuristic Bat-Inspired Algorithm. In: González, J.R., Pelta, D.A., Cruz, C., Terrazas, G., Krasnogor, N. (eds.) NICSO 2010. SCI, vol. 284, pp. 65–74. Springer, Heidelberg (2010)
7. Yang, X.S.: Bat Algorithm for multi-objective optimization. International Journal of Bio-Inspired Computation 3(5), 267–274 (2011)
8. Wang, G., Guo, L.H., Duan, H., Liu, L., Wang, H.: A Bat Algirthm with Mutation for UCAV Path Planning. The Scientific World Journal 2012, 1–15 (2012)
9. Chen, Y.T., Lee, T.F., Horng, M.F., Pan, J.S.: An Echo-Aided Bat Algorithm to Support Measurable Movement for Optimization Efficiency. In: Proceeding of IEEE International Conference on Systems, Man, and Cybernetics (SMC2013), pp. 806–811 (2013)
10. Wang, G., Guo, L.H.: A Novel Hybrid Bat Algorithm with Harmony Search for Global Numberical Optimization. Journal of Applied Mathematics 2013, 1–21 (2013)
11. Das, S., Suganthan, P.N.: Differential evolution: A survey of the state-of-the-art. IEEE Transactions on Evolutionary Computation 15(1), 4–31 (2011)
12. Storn, R., Price, K.: Differential evolution simiple and efficient heuristic for global optimization over continuous spaces. Journal of Global Optimization 11(4), 341–359 (1997)
13. Qu, B.Y., Suganthan, P.N., Liang, J.J.: Differential Evolution With Neighborhood Mutation for Multimodal Optimization. IEEE Transactions on Evolutionary Computation 16(5), 601–614 (2012)
14. Kennedy, J., Eberhart, R.C.: Particle swarm optimization. In: Proceeding of IEEE International Conference on Neural Network, vol. 4, pp. 1942–1948 (1995)
15. Horng, M.F., Chen, Y.T., Chu, S.C., Pan, J.S., Liao, B.Y.: An Extensible Particles Swarm Optimization for Energy-Effective Cluster Management of Underwater Sensor Networks. In: Proceeding of Second International Conference on Computational Collective intelligence (ICCCI), pp. 109–116 (2010)
16. Molga, M.: Smutnicki. C.: Test functions for optimization needs (2005), http://www.zsd.ict.pwr.wroc.pl/files/docs/functions.pdf

Expert-Based Fusion Algorithm of an Ensemble of Anomaly Detection Algorithms

Esther David[1], Guy Leshem[1], Michal Chalamish[1], Alvin Chiang[2],
and Dana Shapira[3]

astrdod@acad.ash-college.ac.il, leshemg@cs.bgu.ac.il,
{michal.chalamish,alvin.chiang.180,shapird}@gmail.com

[1] Department of Computer Science, Ashkelon Academic College, Ashkelon, Israel
[2] Department of Computer Science and Information Engineering, National Taiwan University of Science and Technology, Taiwan
[3] Department of Computer Science, Ariel University, Israel

Abstract. Data fusion systems are widely used in various areas such as sensor networks, robotics, video and image processing, and intelligent system design. Data fusion is a technology that enables the process of combining information from several sources in order to form a unified picture or a decision. Today, anomaly detection algorithms (ADAs) are in use in a wide variety of applications (e.g. cyber security systems, etc.). In particular, in this research we focus on the process of integrating the output of multiple ADAs that perform within a particular domain. More specifically, we propose a two stage fusion process, which is based on the expertise of the individual ADA that is derived in the first step. The main idea of the proposed method is to identify multiple types of outliers and to find a set of expert outlier detection algorithms for each type. We propose to use semi-supervised methods. Preliminary experiments for the single-type outlier case are provided where we show that our method outperforms other benchmark methods that exist in the literature.

Keywords: Anomaly Detection Algorithms, Cluster, Ensemble, Outlier, Scores.

1 Introduction

According to the current state of the art, a wide range of anomaly detection algorithms (ADA) are proposed in various disciplines such as statistics, data mining, machine learning, information theory and spectral decomposition [1], which are also known as outlier detection algorithms [2]. Given the decisions of multiple ADAs, which all operate in the same environment, in this research we aim to confront the challenge of integrating the individual decisions into a final unified representative decision. Specifically, we are interested in non-stationary (i.e., unstable and unexpected) environments where the algorithms improve the decision making process using partial feedback given to them sporadically (that is, at unknown times) and the correctness of the feedback is also unknown [18].

S.-M. Cheng and M.-Y. Day (Eds.): TAAI 2014, LNAI 8916, pp. 114–123, 2014.

The need for such a fusing system stems from the fact that there are many ADAs that suffer from a certain percentage of error. By fusing and aggregating the outputs of multiple ADAs we aim to minimize the error percentage as much as possible. In other words we intend to maximize the recall rate of the process. An illustrative example is the case where a computer system administrator aims to identify and block any offensive attack on his computer system or any malicious program [19–22]. Another noncriminal example of an anomaly detection scenario is the case where countries with high typhoon vulnerability aim to identify approaching storms and to act in such a way that will minimize potential damage [23].

An ideal ADA satisfies the conditions of (i) having a True Positive Rate (TPR) equal to 1 (the TPR indicates the portion of accurate positive instances of all positive instances that were classified as positive; this measurement is also known as the recall rate or alternatively the sensitivity rate) and (ii) having a False Positive Rate (FPR) equal to 0 (the FPR is the portion of positive instances that were misclassified as positive of all positive classified instances (the FPR is also known as the false alarm rate).

Assuming that a set of ADAs do not overlap and are independent we may use a simple OR operation among them in order to fuse them. Namely, it is sufficient that a single ADA decides a certain input instance is an outlier in order to have the final decision of an outlier. Unfortunately, this assumption is far from applicable. Therefore, in this paper we propose a fusing method that will achieve a false alarm rate smaller than each of individual ADA.

Against this background, in this paper we propose a two phase mechanism. In the first step an offline process will take place to classify all the given ADAs into clusters based on their expertise. In the second phase an online and continuous process will take place in which we aim to fuse the decision of all the ADAs in a way that promotes the expert ADAs that were identified in the previous phase for each given type of outlier.

Next we provide a preliminary experiment that deals with the case of a single type of outlier. Here we focus on a more basic debate that exists in the literature about the process of unifying the scores given by different ADAs taken from different scales and ranges termed the normalization phase. We show a way to overcome the problem of normalization by using ranking in its place, which was found to perform better than the normalization.

The paper is structured as follows. In section 2 we describe the current state of the art. In section 3 we provide details about the general fusing structure. Then, in section 4 we describe our proposed expertise based fusing mechanism. In section 5 we describe our simulation and provide initial results. Finally we conclude in section 6 and discuss future work.

2   Related Work

Information or data fusion has been widely researched in the last decade [3, 4]. According to Ahmed and Pottie [4], data fusion is the process by which a data from a multitude of sensors is used to yield an optimal estimate of a specified state vector pertaining to the observed system, whereas sensor administration is the design of communication and control mechanisms for the efficient use of distributed sensors with regard to power, performance, reliability, etc. In this paper we deal with a special case of information fusion which is decision fusion [5]. In information fusion the goal is to fuse complex noisy information provided by multi-sources or multi sensors, of distributed networks, to produce a single unified information model (e.g., vision systems, sonar, robotic platform, weather prediction [4]). However, in our case of decision fusion, we aim to integrate the multiple decisions we receive from the ADAs into a single decision that will be more accurate than the decision of each ADA itself. Each of the ADAs provides a decision in a binary form or in a score form. The special characteristics of our decision fusion problem make most of the available information fusion methods irrelevant.

Next we provide some background on the way an ensemble of methods of the same type can be used to improve the efficiency and correctness of the decision making as we suggest by the term fusion. The first use of such an ensemble was in the classification domain. Building an ensemble of single classifiers to gain an improved effectiveness has a rich tradition and sound theoretical background [6–8]. The idea of using an ensemble can also be found in the clustering domain. [6, 9]. Next, in the domain of anomaly detection or also known as outlier detection algorithms, most of the efforts have been invested in the development of new methods for outlier detection. Only very few preliminary studies have attempted to use the notion of ensemble in order to compose a group of outlier detection algorithms in order to create a meta outlier that will perform better [10–13]. Going back to ensemble in classification, the main insight from using ensemble in the classification domain is that for an ensemble to outperform each of the individual classifier requires that they are (i) accurate (i.e., at least better than random); (ii) diverse (i.e., making different errors with new instances). These conditions are necessary and sufficient. When these conditions are satisfied the majority voting rule of the ensemble also may be correct [6]. In conclusion, the rule of thumb in constructing a meaningful ensemble is to choose members that make uncorrelated errors. We have followed this principle in composing our ensemble of outlier detection algorithms/ADAs.

Some information fusion methods are based on weighting techniques of varying degrees of complexity [4]. For example, Berger [14] discusses a majority voting technique based on a probabilistic representation of information. In our work we also consider a weighting method that is basically based on expertise associated with the multiple ADAs.

3   Fusion Structure

In this paper we assume that there is a set of N ADAs whereby each monitors the same system, aiming to detect an outlier event or data. Each individual ADA performs based on different methods. According to Chandola [15] three types of anomaly detection algorithms exist, which were defined by him as follows:

1. **Point Anomalies:** If an individual data instance can be considered as anomalous with respect to the rest of data, then the instance is termed a point anomaly. This is the simplest type of anomaly and is the focus of the majority of research on anomaly detection (e.g. a fraudulent credit card transaction).
2. **Contextual Anomalies:** The anomalous behavior is determined using the values for the behavioral attributes within a specific context. For example, suppose an individual usually has a weekly shopping bill of 100 except during the Christmas week, when it reaches 1000. A new purchase of 1000 in a week in July will be considered a contextual anomaly, since it does not conform to the normal behavior of the individual in the context of time even though the same amount spent during the Christmas week would be considered normal.
3. **Collective Anomalies:** If a collection of related data instances is anomalous with respect to the entire data set, it is termed a collective anomaly .e.g. a low value for an abnormally long period of time where the low value is not, in itself, anomalous or a typical Web-based attack by a remote machine followed by copying of data from the host computer to a remote destination via ftp.

In our research we will focus on ADAs of the first type i.e., point anomaly detection.

This group of ADAs is also termed an ensemble of ADAs. From this ensemble we aim to fuse scores/decisions to reach the final score/decision. We assume the input data to be behavioral which is characterized by being temporal and sequential. We define an outlier to be an input instance that substantially differs from previous time series data for which no a priori knowledge exists. An example of an outlier in the Web-based environment is a data package in the flow between two remote computers that contains a malicious attack. Another example in the weather monitoring domain system may be out of range attribute values that may indicate an approaching storm.

The output of each ADA may use a different scoring/ranking range. Therefore, in order to enable a meaningful integration or fusion of these values we first must use a normalization phase that will keep a proportion across the ADAs' scores. The simplest way of bringing outliers scores onto a normalized scale is to apply a linear transformation such that the minimum (maximum) occurring score is mapped to 0 (1). [11]. In the experiment section we show that ranking may replace the normalization and even outperform it.

4   Expertise Based Fusion Algorithm

In this section we present our method for fusing the score/decision of an ensemble of ADAs. Our leading/base assumption is that there might be multiple types of outliers and that there may be some ADAs that will be experts in the detection of a certain type or multiple types of outliers, but with a very low prediction ability regarding other types of outliers.

The motivation for the assumption of having multiple types of outliers in a certain monitored data, stems from the domain of web-based attacks from remote computers that can be for example of multiple types of Trojans (we have a huge dataset that includes for example temporal data flow consisting of around 13 types of Trojans). To this end, we propose a two stage expertise based fusion protocol:

1. **Offline Stage:** Identify groups/clusters of outliers within an initial data set and associate expert ADAs with each of the outlier clusters, based on their classification/decision on the instances of the initial data set. Namely, if an ADA exists, such that in most cases it has correctly classified a certain outlier type than it will be considered an expert for that type of outlier. Moreover a certain ADA may be found to be expert for multiple outlier types. At the end of this phase we should have a set of outlier types and for each such outlier type we should have a list (which might be empty) of ADAs that are associated with it and are assumed to be expert in detecting it.

2. **Online Phase:** For any new given instance, identify its nearest outlier cluster/type, then using an **expertise based weighting function** combine the decisions, in order to reach the final decision/score. The expertise based weighting function aims to promote the decision of the ADAs that were found to be experts for the given instance's type. Thus, we aim to achieve a more accurate decision.

The offline stage may be performed using either supervised or unsupervised methods. The motivation for using an unsupervised offline stage is the common assumption that in some environments (e.g., big data) in which anomaly detection algorithms perform, the anomalies are not expected and are unknown; therefore it is impossible to assume we have tagged or classified data that can be used.

For the supervised case we propose to reveal the list of anomaly types (if available). Next, for each anomaly type and for each instance of it in the available data, compare the score/decision of each member of the ensemble (i.e., an ADA member) to the accurate decision. Each ADA algorithm that was found to have a relatively high performance with regard to a certain outlier type will be referred to as an expert for that particular anomaly type.

For the unsupervised case, on the other hand, the process of identifying experts is much more complicated. In particular, in order to overcome the fact that the initial data set is not classified/tagged we will follow a procedure that was proposed by Schubert et al. [6]. According to the initialization procedure of Schubert in order to identify the anomaly instances we will take the k top scored instances according to each ADA. Next, we collect the instances identified by each ADA (using the union set) to create the group of outliers. Once this initialization classification is derived, we continue with identifying the expertise of each ADA similar to the supervised case.

In the online phase, for each new given instance, E we propose to calculate the nearest anomaly cluster and this similarity measurement s and the specific most similar cluster SC will define the expertise based weighting function's parameters. Given these notations, the fused score for a certain instance E will be calculated as follows:

FusedScore(E)=s*[average score of expertsADAs(SC)]+(1-s)*[average score of unexpertsADAs(SC)]

5   Preliminary Experiment

In this section we limit ourselves to the case of a single outlier type. For this case we describe the Union Voting Fusion method that basically aims to overcome the normalization issue.

5.1   The Union Voting Fusion Algorithm

The scores from each ADA are converted to rankings. Then these rankings are combined into a (inverse) suspicious score by taking the k-th highest rank from the group of the ADAs. This is interpreted as at least k ADAs having a consensus that the final rankings of the data are not too suspicious. For example, if an instance's final suspicious score is 10, then k of the classifiers agree that this instance deserves to be on a top-10 outlier list.

It is preferable to combine rankings rather than the raw scores due to the fact that the scores cannot be interpreted in the same way. The rankings obtained in this manner are more robust than the individual rankings of the outlier detectors because they are smoothed out.

Table 1. Scores table

Instance	Score 1	Score 2	Score 3
A	0.5 (1st)	0.75 (3rd)	0.9 (1st)
B	0.4 (2nd)	0.9 (2nd)	0.8 (3rd)
C	0.3 (3rd)	0.95 (1st)	0.85 (2nd)
D	0.2 (4th)	0.3 (4th)	0.2 (5th)
E	0.1 (5th)	0.1 (5th)	0.25 (4th)

Example. If we do a "one-vote union", we take the smallest ranking as the ranking of the 3-detector ensemble. i.e.
A : min(1,3,1) = 1
B : min(2,2,3) = 2
C : min(3,1,2) = 1
... and so on

Instances with the score n appeared in the top-n outlier list of at least 1 detector. In other words the "one-union" means that it is sufficient to be considered by at least one ADA classifier.

Similarly, for an "x-vote union" we take the x-th smallest ranking as the score of the ensemble. e.g. Union-2

A : min2(1,3,1) = 1

B : min2(2,2,3) = 2

C : min2(3,1,2) = 2 Points with the score n appeared in the top-n outlier list of at least x detectors.

The ALOI Outlier Data-Set was used for the experiment. Some details are given below:

1. The ALOI [17] dataset is a set of 110250 color images taken from 1000 small objects under varying conditions (i.e., approximately 100 pictures per object).
2. In order to be appropriate for use as an outlier dataset, the ALOI dataset was converted into an RGB histogram form, with 3 bins for each color channel, and the number of images was reduced to 50000, with 1508 outliers.
3. To create these outliers, 1-5 images taken from the photo galleries of 562 objects such that there were a total of 1508 images to be used as the outliers. While the other image galleries were left intact to serve as non-outliers. The result was a dataset of 50000 with a dimensionality of 27.

For our candidate algorithms we used KNN, Aggregated KNN, LOF [24], LDOF[25] and LoOP[11], which all have a single parameter k. k was adjusted from 3 to 30 for a total of 5*28 = 140 candidates.

In the comparison made we compared our proposed "one union vote"(at least one ADA has marked it as an outlier), the "140-union vote" (all the ADAs agree that a certain instance is an outlier, where we use 140 versions of various ADAs), the greedy fusion proposed by [6], and the simple average of all ADAs termed the "Mean Ensemble". We also include the result of initializing the greedy ensemble method using the labels themselves. This is obviously not possible in practice and is done to get the upper bound on performance for benchmarking. The performance of the various methods are measured by the ROC curve. The Receiver-Operator Curve (ROC) graphically displays a classifier's TPR vs. it's FPR as the discrimination threshold is varied. It is often used to compare the goodness of the rankings, scores, or probabilities produced by different classifiers. The curve always starts at the bottom left (0,0) and ends at (1,1) representing the extremes of a threshold so high that no instances will be considered positive, and a threshold so low such that all instances become positive.

The ROC of an ideal classifier reaches TPR=1 when FPR=0 (is tight with the y-axis and the top left corner), implying that there exists a decision threshold where the classes are split perfectly. In terms of rankings, this means all instances of the positive class are ordered before the negative class. The area-under-curve of this ideal ROC curve is the area of the entire plot and is taken to be 1, normalized. A classifier that randomly labels instances as positive or negative will have a ROC curve approaching the diagonal and an AUC of 0.5.

Since there may not be a pre-specified acceptable rate of false positives or a decision threshold, oftentimes the area-under-curve(AUC) is used as a crude way

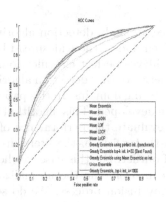 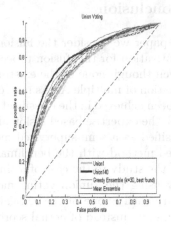

Fig. 1. ROC Curves and Union Voting

Table 2. AUC results for different ensemble

Ensemble System	AUC
KNN Ensemble	0.6388
Agg KNN Ensemble	0.6703
LOF Ensemble	0.7802
LDOF Ensemble	0.7479
LoOP Ensemble	0.7966
Greedy Ensemble, Original Method (using best k found)	0.7971
Greedy Ensemble w/ Perfect Initialization (Labels as Target Vector)	0.8048
Greedy Ensemble using Mean Ensemble as Target Vector	0.7861
Union Voting1	0.7438
Union Voting140	0.8009

of comparing the performance of two classifiers on the whole. Given a positive
and negative example, the AUC can be interpreted as the probability of the
positive example receiving a higher score than the negative example. From the
AUCs values listed in Table. 2 we can see that by requiring a high degree of
consensus between the anomaly detector models (Union Voting 140), we prevent
any one detector from mislabeling the data as outlier and so reduce the false
positive rate. This effect is more convincingly demonstrated in the right side of
Fig. 1 where we show the "rise" in the curve when we switch from a simple union
(Union Voting 1, green curve) to Union Voting 140 (blue curve). (The dotted
blue green curves show Union Voting with thresholds in-between 1 and 140.)

6 Conclusion

In this paper we consider the Fusion of multiple anomaly detection algorithm. The motivation for this fusion process has evolved due to the widespread belief that even though none of the existing ADAs achieves perfect classification, the combination of multiple ADAs may create a superior outlier detection algorithm as has been achieved in the classification and clustering domains. In this paper we describe the expertise based fusion algorithm we developed. This algorithm may be classified as a semi-supervised method. To evaluate the performance of the proposed method with the benchmark method that exists in the literature, we limited the study to the case of a single type of outlier. For this case we showed that by using the /union voting method, we can overcome the normalization problem which is one of the critical parts in any fusion process. We do so by using ranking instead of actual scores. Thus we demonstrated that our method outperforms the benchmark method from the literature.

References

1. Chandola, V., Banerjee, A., Kumar, V.: Outlier detection: A survey. ACM Computing Surveys (2007) (to appear)
2. Petrovskiy, M.I.: Outlier detection algorithms in data mining systems. Programming and Computer Software 29(4), 228–237 (2003)
3. Zhang, L., Leung, H., Chan, K.C.C.: Information fusion based smart home control system and its application. IEEE Transactions on Consumer Electronics 54(3), 1157–1165 (2008)
4. Ahmed, M., Pottie, G.: Fusion in the context of information theory. Distributed Sensor Networks, 419–436 (2005)
5. Jeon, B., Landgrebe, D.A.: Decision fusion approach for multitemporal classification. IEEE Transactions on Geoscience and Remote Sensing 37(3), 1227–1233 (1999)
6. Schubert, E., et al.: On Evaluation of Outlier Rankings and Outlier Scores. In: SDM (2012)
7. Dietterich, T.G.: Ensemble methods in machine learning. Multiple classifier systems, pp. 1–15. Springer, Heidelberg (2000)
8. Tan, A.C., Gilbert, D.: Ensemble machine learning on gene expression data for cancer classification (2003)
9. Balke, W.-T., Kießing, W.: Optimizing multi-feature queries for image databases. In: Proc. of the Intern. Conf. on Very Large Databases (2000)
10. Asuncion, A., Newman, D.: UCI machine learning repository (2007)
11. Kriegel, H.-P., Kröger, P., Schubert, E., Zimek, A.: Interpreting and unifying outlier scores. In: Proc. SDM, pp. 13–24 (2011)
12. Lazarevic, A., Kumar, V.: Feature bagging for outlier detection. In: Proc. KDD, pp. 157–166 (2005)
13. Nguyen, H.V., Ang, H.H., Gopalkrishnan, V.: Mining outliers with ensemble of heterogeneous detectors on random subspaces. In: Kitagawa, H., Ishikawa, Y., Li, Q., Watanabe, C. (eds.) DASFAA 2010. LNCS, vol. 5981, pp. 368–383. Springer, Heidelberg (2010)

14. Berger, T.M., Durrant-Whyte, H.F.: Model distribution in decentralized multi-sensor data fusion. In: American Control Conference. IEEE (1991)
15. Chandola, V.: Anomaly detection for symbolic sequences and time series data. Diss. University of Minnesota (2009)
16. Kriegel, H.-P., et al.: Interpreting and Unifying Outlier Scores. In: SDM (2011)
17. Geusebroek, J.M., Burghouts, G.J., Smeulders, A.: The Amsterdam Library of Object Images. Int. J. Computer Vision 61(1), 103–112 (2005)
18. Grnitz, N., Kloft, M.M., Rieck, K., Brefeld, U.: Toward supervised anomaly detection. arXiv preprint arXiv:1401.6424 (2014)
19. Rajab, M.A., et al.: CAMP: Content-Agnostic Malware Protection. In: NDSS (2013)
20. Rieck, K., et al.: Automatic analysis of malware behavior using machine learning. Journal of Computer Security 19(4), 639–668 (2011)
21. Jang, J., Brumley, D., Venkataraman, S.: Bitshred: feature hashing malware for scalable triage and semantic analysis. In: Proceedings of the 18th ACM Conference on Computer and Communications Security. ACM (2011)
22. Egele, M., et al.: A survey on automated dynamic malware-analysis techniques and tools. ACM Computing Surveys (CSUR) 44(2), 6 (2012)
23. Thom, D., et al.: Spatiotemporal anomaly detection through visual analysis of geolocated twitter messages. In: 2012 IEEE Pacific Visualization Symposium (PacificVis). IEEE (2012)
24. Breunig, M.M., Kriegel, H.-P., Ng, R.T., Sander, J.: LOF: identifying density-based local outliers. SIGMOD Rec. 29(2) (May 2000)
25. Zhang, K., Hutter, M., Jin, H.: A New Local Distance-Based Outlier Detection Approach for Scattered Real-World Data. In: Proceedings of the 13th Pacific-Asia Conference on Advances in Knowledge Discovery and Data Mining, PAKDD 2009 (2009)

Painting Using Genetic Algorithm
with Aesthetic Evaluation of Visual Quality

Sheng-Yu Feng and Chuan-Kang Ting

Department of Computer Science and Information Engineering
National Chung Cheng University, Taiwan
{fsy102m,ckting}@cs.ccu.edu.tw

Abstract. Creating art using artificial intelligence technologies is an emerging research topic. In particular, evolutionary computation has achieved several promising results in generating visual art and music. Evaluation of the items generated by evolutionary algorithms is a key issue at computational creativity. Interactive evolutionary algorithms are widely used to address this issue by incorporating human feedback in the fitness evaluation. However, this manner suffers from fatigue and decreasing sensitivity after long-term evaluation, which is commonly required in evolutionary algorithms. This paper proposes using an aesthetic evaluation of visual quality in the fitness evaluation for genetic algorithm (GA) to create paintings. Specifically, the fitness function considers two features for aesthetics. The generative ecosystemic art system, EvoEco, is applied as a test bench for the proposed method. Experimental results show that the proposed GA can generate satisfactory paintings by using aesthetic evaluation.

1 Introduction

Computational creativity has received increasing attention owing to the advance of artificial intelligence technologies. Creativity involves with the generation of appropriate novelty and represents some ideas based on previous works [2]. Several artificial intelligence technologies have been applied to achieve creativity by computers. In particular, using evolutionary computation to generate artworks, create visual art, and compose music has gained considerable promising results [4,10,13]. Evolutionary algorithms (EAs) are nature-inspired global search approaches and have succeeded in solving a variety of complex optimization problems. EAs manipulate a set of chromosomes representing candidate solutions and change them by mimicking the evolutionary operators in nature, such as selection, crossover, and mutation. The candidate solutions are evaluated by the fitness function. Following Darwin's theory "Survival of the Fittest," the chromosomes with relatively high fitness values are selected to survive into the next generation.

Fitness evaluation plays an important role in EAs because it guides the search direction. In computational creativity using EAs, it ordinarily lacks a specific fitness function for evaluating chromosomes. Human feedback is commonly used as

S.-M. Cheng and M.-Y. Day (Eds.): TAAI 2014, LNAI 8916, pp. 124–135, 2014.
© Springer International Publishing Switzerland 2014

an interactive fitness evaluation to address this issue. That is, human users act like the fitness function to assign fitness values or to select parents and survivors for EAs. This manner is useful since it combines the search capability of EAs and aesthetic taste of human. However, EAs usually require thousands or even million times of fitness evaluation, which makes interactive EAs impractical due to the fatigue and decreasing sensitivity of human beings after long-term evaluation. The interactive EAs for creativity, therefore, have to compromise with small population and short run. Some studies attempt to avoid user's fatigue. For example, Machwe and Parmee [12] used meta-feature clustering to learn and predict user's judgment. Llor et al. [11] applied support vector machine to synthesize the subjective fitness function. Kowaliw et al. [7] developed the EvoEco system to automatically detect and emphasize creative designs. A potential issue at these methods is that users may need to spend more time in fitness evaluation once the prediction results are wrong and needed to be corrected. Some research works on design of fitness functions that can emulate human aesthetic preference by using machine learning technologies such as neural networks [1] and coevolutionary algorithm [5]. Recently, Liu and Ting [9,10] proposed using objective evaluation metrics instead of human feedback to address this issue. They designed the fitness function based on music theory to evaluate the compositions and achieved satisfactory results.

This study aims to generate paintings by EA with aesthetic evaluation. Specifically, we develop a genetic algorithm (GA) and propose using aesthetic visual quality of paintings for fitness evaluation. In performance assessment, we implement the EvoEco system, an EA-based image generator, and replace its interactive EA with the proposed method. The resultant paintings show the effectiveness of the proposed GA with aesthetic evaluation. The remainder of this paper is organized as follows. Section 2 introduces the EvoEco system that uses an interactive EA to generate images. Section 3 presents our proposed GA and describes the structure of chromosomes and the fitness function based on aesthetic visual quality. Section 4 presents and compares the generated paintings. Finally, Section 5 draws the conclusions of this study.

2   Creativity and the EvoEco System

Regarding creativity, Dorin and Korb claimed that "Creativity is the introduction and use of a framework that has a relatively high probability of producing representations of patterns that can arise only with a smaller probability in previously existing frameworks" [3]. According to this definition, they built the EvoEco system to generate images. EvoEco is a multi-agent ecosystemic platform based on interactive EA to evolve into generative art. The system consists of two parts: the ecosystemic (generative) stage transforms a genome into a phenotype (image), and the evolutionary stage selects and evolves chromosomes.

Following the EA framework, an image is represented as a chromosome in EvoEco. A chromosome is composed of k agents and each agent is in charge of painting during its lifetime. The evolutionary process of EvoEco to generate images is as follows:

1. Randomly determine the background color of each chromosome.
2. Chromosomes serve as agents to paint during their life time.
3. Mutation and crossover are performed on the chromosomes.

Note that in EvoEco the fitness of images is evaluated by users. When the generated image is good, users can terminate the system. Figure 1 shows the EvoEco system and some evolving images.

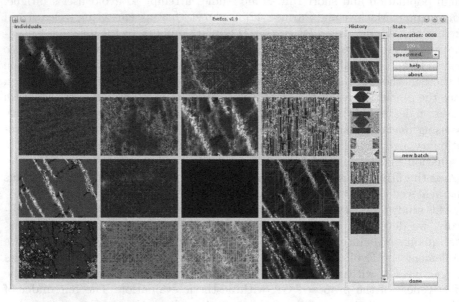

Fig. 1. Screenshot of the EvoEco system. The left frame shows the population of 16 chromosomes. The middle frame shows the history of previous eight choices. The right frame shows the control panel.

3   The Proposed Method

Genetic algorithm (GA) is a well-known EA and has shown its effectiveness on a variety of optimization problems. The general principle of GA is to simulate the mechanisms of natural evolution, such as selection, crossover, and mutation [6]. Based on Darwin's theory "Survival of the Fittest," GA is believed to be capable of evolving candidate solutions into better ones. To solve an optimization problem, GA represents candidate solutions as chromosomes, for which the encoding scheme is essentially related to the problem to be solved. Compared to conventional search methods, GA manipulates a set (population) of chromosomes in the search process. The fitness function is used to evaluate the quality (fitness) of candidate solutions (chromosomes). For a maximization problem, higher fitness implies better solution quality.

The evolutionary process of GA begins with initialization of the population. Then GA embarks on reproduction to generate new candidate solutions: First, the selection operator picks two chromosomes from the population to serve as parents. The two parents carry out the crossover operator to produce their off-spring, where the crossover rate defines the probability to perform crossover. Afterward, mutation is performed with a probability, i.e., mutation rate, on the offspring to slightly change some genes. The above reproduction process repeats until the set of offspring is filled. Following "Survival of the Fittest," the survivor operator picks the fittest chromosomes out of the offspring population with (or without) the primitive population to survive and constitute the population for the next generation.

Design of GA for a given problem concerns representation, fitness function, selection, crossover, and mutation operators. The following describes our design of GA for generation of paintings.

3.1 Representation

A chromosome in the GA represents multiple agents to generate images. Formally, a chromosome I is represented by

$$I = (k, (ind_H, ind_S, ind_B), a^1, \ldots, a^k),$$

where $k \in \{2, \ldots, 6\}$ is the number of agents, (ind_H, ind_S, ind_B) indicates the background color, and $a^1, \ldots, a^k$ are painters.

The agents paint by assigning colors at some pixels. An agent can be defined by

$$a = (sD, delay, (a_H, a_S, a_B), a_{dir}, life),$$

where $sD \in \{0, \ldots, 8\}$ denotes the starting direction, $delay \in [0, 0.5]$ determines whether the agent paints this pixel or not, and $life$ is the agent's moving time. The terms (a_H, a_S, a_B) and a_{dir} is generated by a GP-tree, which indicates the color to paint at the current pixel and the direction for the subsequent move.

In the beginning, each agent randomly generates a GP-tree. Then, agents conduct the following actions at every time step:

1. Collect data from its local neighborhood as input.

   An agent will collect data from its Moore neighborhood (see Fig 2). These data, including eight directions and eight colors, are used to calculate the following input variables:
   - (H_c, S_c, B_c): The hue (H), saturation (S), and brightness (B) values of the pixel at the agent's current location
   - (H_p, S_p, B_p): The hue, saturation, and brightness values of the pixel at the agent's previous location
   - $(H_{mean}, S_{mean}, B_{mean})$: The mean hue, saturation, and brightness values of the agent's neighborhood
   - (ind_H, ind_S, ind_B): The chromosome's initial background color
   - d_p: The agent's previous direction

- B_{max}, B_{min}: Maximum and minimum brightness values among the agent's neighborhood
- *rand*: a uniformly random number in the range $[0, 1]$

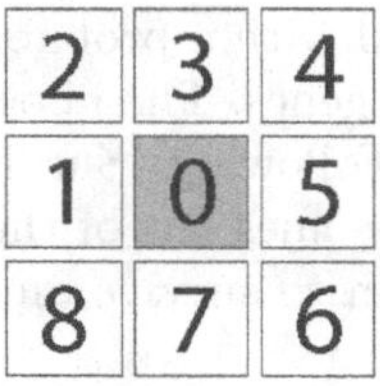

Fig. 2. Moore neighborhood and directions

2. Calculate output values from the inputs.

   The output values are computed by the agent's GP-tree and the 16 inputs. In this study, we introduce uncertainty in determining the direction to diversify the generated patterns. The output values include new hue a_H, saturation a_S, brightness a_B, and direction a_{dir}, which are used to determine the agent's next pixel to move to. Note that the hue, saturation, and brightness values might be out of bounds $[0, 1]$ and are thus truncated by discarding the integer part and negative sign. The direction is also regularized to $\{0, \ldots, 8\}$ by the remainder of dividing $(100 \cdot a_{dir})$ by nine. Table 1 lists the functions used for the GP-trees. An example GP-tree is given in Fig. 3.

Table 1. Function set used in the GP

Function	Action (on two inputs x and y)
add	$x + y$
sub	$x - y$
mult	xy
const	returns the associated constant value
max	$\max(x, y)$
min	$\min(x, y)$
sin	$\sin(x)$
id	x
div	$\begin{cases} 1 & y < 0.0001 \\ x/y & \text{otherwise} \end{cases}$
incdec	$\begin{cases} x + 1/8 & y > 0.5 \\ x - 1/8 & \text{otherwise} \end{cases}$
mean	$\frac{x+y}{2}$

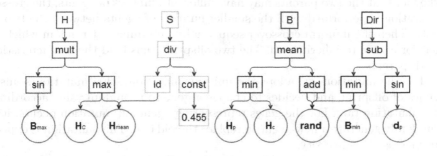

$$a_H = \sin(B_{\max}) * \max(H_c, H_{\mathrm{mean}})$$

$$a_S = H_{\mathrm{mean}}/0.455$$

$$a_B = \frac{1}{2}(\min(H_p, H_c) + rand + B_{\min})$$

$$a_{dir} = \min(rand, B_{\min}) - \sin(d_p)$$

Fig. 3. An example GP-tree for the four outputs a_H, a_S, a_B, and a_{dir}

3. Color the current pixel according to the output variables.

   For a pixel, each agent will probabilistically decide whether to paint it or not. The color to paint for the current pixel is determined by (a_H, a_S, a_B) from step 2.

4. Move to the next pixel in the direction given by output.

   Each agent will move to the next pixel according to direction a_{dir}, no matter the current pixel is colored or not. This study develops two strategies for the moving direction, i.e., deterministic and uncertain direction. The first strategy moves the agent to the pixel in the direction of a_{dir} deterministically. In the second strategy, the nine directions can be selected for the agent to move, where the a_{dir} direction has a high probability 1/2 while each of the remaining eight directions has a low probability 1/16 to be selected as the moving direction. This uncertainty in the moving direction is expected to diversify the generated patterns.

3.2 Genetic Operators

The genetic operators of GA include parent selection, crossover, mutation, and survival selection. In this study, we employ the k-tournament selection in view of its recognized performance. The proposed GA uses a 5-tournament selection, which selects the best of 5 randomly picked chromosomes as a parent. Performing this selection twice gains a pair of parents for subsequent crossover and mutation.

This study adopts the well-known uniform crossover for the GA. Considering the fact that the two parents may have different numbers of agents, the crossover operation is performed with the smaller number of agents between the two parents. Then the uniform crossover sequentially determines at random which parent for a gene to inherit from. The two offspring thus hold the characteristics of both parents.

For the mutation, we adopt the uniform mutation. This mutation scans the genes of offspring and decides to change a gene to a random value according to the mutation rate. For the genes representing agents, if mutation occurs, it will randomly generate a new agent to replace the old one. This mutation is expected to increase the diversity.

As for survival selection, this study utilizes the $(\mu + \lambda)$ strategy to keep elitists among the population.

3.3   Fitness Function

In this study, we propose using two measures of visual quality, i.e., edge distribution and line intersection, in place of human feedback to evaluate the quality of painting.

Edge Distribution

In evaluating the fitness of a painting, we first consider that the important regions should have more focus points. Li et al. [8] have validated the utility of this feature. Given that our painting comprises the results from several agents coloring the canvas pixel by pixel and thus has interactions, we remove the Gaussian smoothing filtering used in the original method and keep the edge noises to increase edge points in the generated paintings.

Specifically, we convert the image from HSB scheme to gray channels and then apply a 3×3 Laplacian filter on it (cf. Fig. 4). Afterward, we calculate the area of the smallest bounding box and its ratio to the whole area. The bounding box is defined as the rectangle that contains 81% edge points [8]. Figure 5 shows the original image and the image after applied with Laplacian filter and its bounding box. According to the test in [8], high-quality paintings have a low ratio, whereas low-quality paintings have a high ratio. Therefore, we define the complement of

-1	-1	-1
-1	8	-1
-1	-1	-1

Fig. 4. Discrete approximation to the Laplacian filter

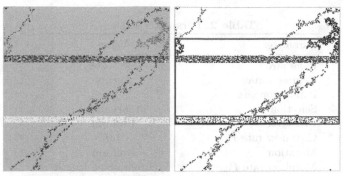

(a) The better image that has a smaller bounding box

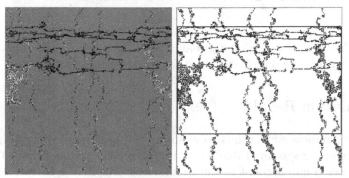

(b) The worse image that has a larger bounding box

Fig. 5. Laplacian filter example

this ratio as the first part of fitness evaluation and compute it by

$$f_{\text{edge}} = 1 - \frac{W_b H_b}{W H},$$

where W_b and H_b denote the width and height of the bounding box, and W and H are the width and height of the image, respectively.

Line Intersection

In the light of the proposed painting method, it is desired to have more interaction between agents. The interaction level of agents is reflected on the number of line intersections in the image. Accordingly, we define the second part of fitness evaluation by

$$f_{\text{intersect}} = \frac{\#\text{intersections}}{W H}.$$

The fitness value of a painting is defined by

$$F = f_{\text{edge}} + f_{\text{intersect}}.$$

Table 2. Parameter setting

Parameter	Value
Paint size	256×256
Representation	Agents
Population size	10
Selection	5-tournament
Crossover	Uniform
Crossover rate P_c	1.0
Mutation	Uniform
Mutation rate P_m	5/chromosome_length
Survivor	$\mu + \lambda$
Termination	10 generations

The objective of GA is to find the paintings that maximize the above fitness value considering edge distribution and line intersection.

4   Simulation Results

This study conducts simulations to examine the performance of the proposed GA-based painting system. Table 2 lists the parameter setting for the GA. Two factors are taken into account in the simulations: The first is the use of smooth rule; the second is the presence of uncertainty in the moving direction. The study investigates the results from the four combinations of these two factors.

1) No Smoothing + Deterministic Direction

We first experimented with drawing a pixel in a deterministic direction without performing the smoothing rule at each step. The color of a pixel is calculated according to its neighbors' information. The simulation results in Fig. 6a shows that the generated patterns lack diversity. This is caused by the use of deterministic direction for drawing pixels, which results in many straight lines in the patterns. To address the monotony issue, we adopt the smoothing rule and enable uncertainty in the direction to move.

2) Smoothing + Deterministic Direction

Figure 6b presents the results of drawing a pixel in a deterministic direction with smoothing at each step. The generated patterns are similar with Fig. 6a because the moving directions are deterministic. However, the gaps between pixels are moderated by smoothing among neighbors. It helps to generate smoother and more harmonious patterns in Fig. 6b than the patterns in Fig. 6a.

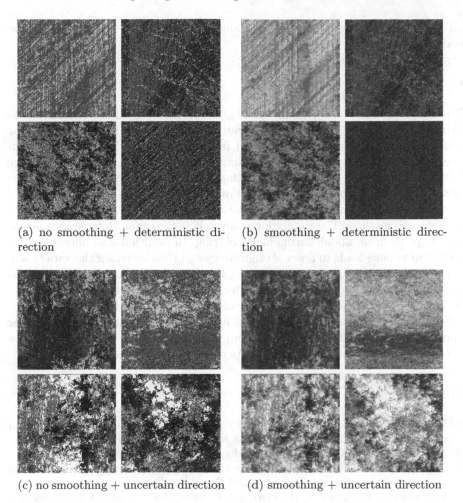

(a) no smoothing + deterministic direction

(b) smoothing + deterministic direction

(c) no smoothing + uncertain direction

(d) smoothing + uncertain direction

Fig. 6. Simulation results

3) No Smoothing + Uncertain Direction

The results in Fig. 6c are generated by drawing pixels in uncertain directions without smoothing. The effect of applying uncertainty in moving direction is obvious: Comparing the patterns in Figs. 6a–6c, uncertain directions lead to high variety and fewer straight lines in the generated patterns. This outcome is preferable for visual experience.

4) Smoothing + Uncertain Direction

Finally, Fig. 6d shows the patterns generated by drawing a pixel in an uncertain direction with smoothing at each step. The results reflect the effects of smoothing and uncertainty: The generated patterns have fewer straight lines due to uncertainty in moving; furthermore, smoothing contributes to harmonious and moderate coloring.

5 Conclusions

This study proposes using visual quality as the fitness evaluation criterion to address the issues of fatigue and decreasing sensitivity at interactive EAs for computational creativity. The proposed fitness function is based on two measures of visual quality, i.e., edge distribution and line intersection. The edge distribution considers the ratio of bounding box area to the whole area. The line intersection reflects the interaction level of agents.

Simulations are conducted on the EvoEco system to investigate the effects of the proposed method. The simulation results show that smoothing among neighbors helps to bring about harmonious coloring. In addition, the uncertainty in moving directions leads to fewer straight lines and thus increases the variety and diversity of generated patterns. In general, these two factors and the proposed fitness function based on visual quality achieve satisfactory patterns, which validate the effectiveness of EAs and aesthetic evaluation on computational creativity.

Future work includes some directions. First, the fitness function can consider more aesthetic evaluation metrics. Second, design of genetic operators based on aesthetic evaluation is promising for EAs to generate satisfactory artworks.

References

1. Baluja, S., Pomerleau, D., Jochem, T.: Towards automated artificial evolution for computer-generated images. Connection Science 6(2), 325–354 (1994)
2. Boden, M.A.: The Creative Mind: Myths and Mechanisms. Basic Books (1991)
3. Dorin, A., Korb, K.B.: Improbable creativity. In: Proceedings of the Dagstuhl International Seminar on Computational Creativity (2009)
4. Fernandes, C.M., Mora, A.M., Merelo, J.J., Rosa, A.C.: Kants: A stigmergic ant algorithm for cluster analysis and swarm art. IEEE Transactions on Evolutionary Computation 44(6), 843–856 (2013)
5. Greenfield, G.: Co-evolutionary methods in evolutionary art. In: The Art of Artificial Evolution, pp. 357–380 (2008)
6. Holland, J.: Adaptation in Natural and Artificial Systems. University of Michigan Press (1975)
7. Kowaliw, T., Dorin, A., McCormack, J.: Promoting creative design in interactive evolutionary computation. IEEE Transactions on Evolutionary Computation 16(4), 523–536 (2012)
8. Li, C., Chen, T.: Aesthetic visual quality assessment of paintings. IEEE Journal of Selected Topics in Singal Processing 3(2), 236–252 (2009)
9. Liu, C.-H., Ting, C.-K.: Polyphonic accompaniment using genetic algorithm with music theory. In: Proceedings of the 2012 IEEE Congress on Evolutionary Computation (2012)
10. Liu, C.-H., Ting, C.-K.: Evolutionary composition using music theory and charts. In: Proceedings of the 2013 Computational Intelligence for Creativity and Affective Computing (2013)

11. Llorà, X., Sastry, K., Goldberg, D.E., Gupta, A., Lakshmi, L.: Combating user fatigue in igas: Partial ordering, support vector machines, and synthetic fitness. In: Proceedings of the 2005 Conference on Genetic and Evolutionary Computation, vol. 2, pp. 1363–1370 (2005)
12. Machwe, A.T., Parmee, I.C.: Reducing user fatigue within an interactive evolutionary design system using clustering and case-based reasoning. Engineering Optimization 41(9), 871–887 (2009)
13. Valdez, M.G., Guervós, J.J.M., Trujillo, L., de Vega, F.F., Romero, J.C., Mancilla, A.: Evospace-i: a framework for interactive evolutionary algorithms. In: Proceedings of the 2013 Genetic and Evolutionary Computation Conference, pp. 1301–1308 (2013)

Solving PERT Problems Involving Type-2 Fuzzy Uncertainty: An Approach

Juan Carlos Figueroa-García, Iván Darío Jiménez-Medina,
and Rausses Danilo Rojas-Olaya

Universidad Distrital Francisco José de Caldas, Bogotá - Colombia
jcfigueroag@udistrital.edu.co
ivan.d-7@hotmail.com
rausses.rojas@aiesec.net

Abstract. This paper proposes a method for solving the PERT (Program Evaluation and Review Technique) problem that involves uncertainty coming from the perception of multiple experts about the activities. The experts opinions over the duration of an activity is represented by interval Type-2 Fuzzy Sets (IT2FSs). Four linear programming models based on the α-cuts done over the duration of the activities of the project are proposed and solved, keeping fuzzy information coming from the experts into the solution.

Keywords: PERT, Interval Type-2 Fuzzy Sets, Linear Programming.

1 Introduction

The CPM (Critical Path Method) allows us to plan a project when the activity times are considered as deterministic, it helps to make a fairly accurate estimate of the duration of the project (see [1], and Kelley [2]). Duration of activities are not well known in all projects, so the PERT technique has been independently but contemporaneously developed with the CPM method (see [3]), as a tool to handle probabilistic uncertainty over the activities times through the beta distribution, thereby driving a degree of uncertainty.

There are some criticisms about the statistical assumptions of the PERT method, and some authors have questioned the applicability of the beta distribution to estimate the duration of activities (see MacCrimmon & Ryavec [4], and Shipley, De korvin & Omer [5]). As an alternative to estimate the duration of activities, triangular and trapezoidal distributions has been used for, but inference for activity times requires a measurement process, or a posterior frequency distribution as pointed out by Chen [6], so in practice some projects does lack of historical data and it is not possible to infer distributions, this is the case where subjectivity of the experts comes as the only available information.

Fuzzy set theory has been proposed by Lotfi A. Zadeh in 1965 [7], thus the concept of fuzzy PERT has been proposed by Fargier, Galvagnon & Dubois [8], Hsiau & Li [9], Wang & Hao [10] in which activity times are represented by *fuzzy sets*, these fuzzy sets come from the opinion of only one expert, or the agreement of several experts. McCahon [11] developed a fuzzy project network analysis by fuzzifying the activity times in project-network analysis.

S.-M. Cheng and M.-Y. Day (Eds.): TAAI 2014, LNAI 8916, pp. 136–144, 2014.

Several problems have been identified in the application of fuzzy PERT. Chen & Wang [12] proposed an algorithm for finding multiple possible critical paths using fuzzy sets. Fargier, Galvagnon & Dubois [8] found that while it is easy to compute fuzzy earliest starting dates of tasks in the critical path method, the problem of determining latest starting dates and slack times is much more tricky, and he treated this problem with serial-parallel graphs framed on the theory of possibility. Chanas & Zielinski [13] proposed the application of the Zadeh's extension principle to the concept of criticality of a route, and a method for calculating the degree of criticality through linear programming. Chen [6] proposed an approach based on the fuzzy extension principle and a pair of linear programs parameterized by possibility levels α to analyze a critical path.

This paper proposes an extension to the PERT problem involving the opinion of multiple experts who estimate activity times. The ambiguity of the experts and the uncertainty associated with the discrepancy among them is represented by IT2FSs. Based on the results of Chen [6], an optimization model was designed to address the PERT problem with multiple experts, using a simulated scenario where multiple experts give their opinions through optimist and pessimist activity times of a project.

This paper is structured as follows: in Section 2, we provide some basic concepts about Type-2 fuzzy sets. In Section 3, we introduce the Fuzzy PERT problem and its mathematical model. In Section 4, we propose a method and a model to solve fuzzy PERT problem involving Type-2 fuzzy activity times alongside a numerical example. Finally, concluding remarks are presented in Section 5.

2   Basic Concepts

A fuzzy set, namely A, is a generalization of a *Crisp* or Boolean set. It is defined over a universe of discourse X by a *Membership Function* namely $\mu_A(x)$ that takes values in the interval [0,1]. A fuzzy set A may be represented as a set of ordered pairs of a generic element x and its degree of membership, $\mu_A(x)$, i.e.,

$$A = \{(x, \mu_A(x)) \mid x \in X\} \tag{1}$$

2.1 α-Cuts

One of the most important concepts of fuzzy sets is the concept of α-cut and the *strong* α-cut. Given a fuzzy set A defined over X and $\alpha \in [0, 1]$ the α-cut, $^{\alpha}A$, and the *strong* α-cut, $^{\alpha+}A$, is defined as follows

$$^{\alpha}A = \{x \mid A(x) \geq \alpha\} \tag{2}$$

That is, the α-cut of a fuzzy set A is the crisp set $^{\alpha}A$ that contains all the elements of the power set X whose memberships in A are greater or equal than α (see Klir [15]).

2.2 Representation of Fuzzy Sets

The principal role of α-cuts and strong α-cuts in fuzzy set theory is their capability to represent fuzzy sets. To represent fuzzy sets by its α-cuts it is needed to convert each of the α-cuts to a special fuzzy set $_\alpha A$, defined as follow

$$_\alpha A(x) = \alpha \cdot {}^\alpha A(x) \tag{3}$$

This representation is usually referred to as decomposition of A. In the following, three decomposition theorems of fuzzy sets are shown [15].

Theorem 21 *(First Decomposition Theorem). For every $A \in F(X)$,*

$$A = \bigcup_{\alpha A \in [0,1]} {}_\alpha A,$$

where $_\alpha A$ is defined by equation 3 and $\cup$ denotes the standard fuzzy union.

2.3 Extension Principle for Fuzzy Sets

It is said that a crisp function

$$f : X \rightarrow Y \tag{4}$$

is fuzzified when it is extended to act on fuzzy sets defined on X and Y. That is, the fuzzified function, for which the same symbol f is usually used, has the form:

$$f : F(X) \rightarrow F(Y) \tag{5}$$

Then, the *Extension Principle* allows us to compute fuzzy functions from crisp ones:

$$[f(A)](y) = \sup_{x|\,y=f(x)} A(x) \tag{6}$$

2.4 Interval Type-2 Fuzzy Sets

A Type-2 fuzzy set is a collection of infinite Type-1 fuzzy sets into a single fuzzy set. It is defined by two membership functions (upper and lower MFs) which shape the footprint of uncertainty (FOU). Mendel [16] define the FOU as the union of all primary membership degrees, the upper membership function (UMF) as a subset that has the maximum membership degree of the footprint of uncertainty and the lower membership function (LMF) as a subset that has the minimum membership degree of the footprint of uncertainty. An IT2FS is described as:

$$\tilde{A} = \int_{x \in X} \int_{u \in J_x} 1/(x,u) = \int_{x \in X} \left[\int_{u \in J_x} 1/u \right] /x, \tag{7}$$

where x is the *primary variable*, J_x an interval in $[0,1]$, is the *primary membership* of x, u is the *secondary variable*, and $\int_{u \in J_x} 1/(x,u)$ is the *secondary membership function* (MF) at x. Equation (7) means that $\tilde{A} : X \longrightarrow \{[a,b] : 0 \le a \le b \le 1\}$. Uncertainty about $\tilde{A}$ is conveyed by the union of all of the primary membership function called *Footprint Of Uncertainty* of $\tilde{A}$ (see Mendel [16]).

$$FOU(\tilde{A}) = \bigcup_{x \in X} J_x \qquad (8)$$

The $FOU(\tilde{A})$ can be seen in Figure 1. It is bounded by an upper MF (UMF) $\overline{\mu}_{\tilde{A}}(x)$ and a lower MF (LMF) $\underline{\mu}_{\tilde{A}}(x)$, both of which are T1FSs; consequently, the membership degree of each element of an IT2FS is an interval $[\underline{\mu}_{\tilde{A}}(x), \overline{\mu}_{\tilde{A}}(x)]$ (see Wu & Mendel [17]).

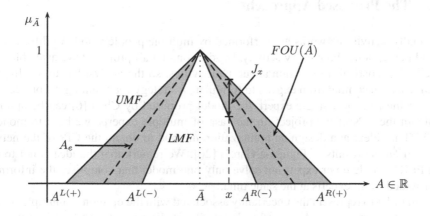

Fig. 1. Interval Type-2 Fuzzy set $\tilde{A}$

3   Fuzzy PERT Problem

The PERT method requires a probabilistic distribution (usually Beta) of time duration for each activity, seen as a random variable. The Beta distribution is described by three parameters; optimistic, expected and pessimistic values, but sometimes it is hard to obtain data to compute it. In recent years, some PERT methods based on the theory of fuzzy sets (see Wang & Hao [10], McCahon [11], Chen & Wang [12], Glisovic, Bojovic & Milenkovic [14], which include numerical imprecision that comes from non probabilistic uncertainty (associated with the perception of an expert about the project).

Chen [6] proposed an interesting version of the CPM, considering fuzzy parameters in the objective function as follows:

$$\tilde{D} = \sup_{d \in R^+, (ij) \in S} \min \left\{ \tilde{T}_{ij} \mid d = y_n - y_1 \right\}$$

$$s.t \qquad (9)$$

$$y_j \geq y_i + \tilde{T}_{i,j} \, \forall \, (i,j) \in S$$

$$y_i, y_j \in \mathbb{R} \, \forall \, (i,j) \in S$$

where y_j is the occurrence time of the node j, node i precedes node j, y_n is the starting time of the last activity, and y_1 is the starting time of the first activity, S is the set of all active nodes of the project. The activity times are defined by a fuzzy set $\tilde{T} : A \rightarrow \mathcal{F}(R^+)$, $\mathcal{F}(R^+)$ is the set of non-negative fuzzy numbers, thus $\tilde{T}_{ij}$ is the fuzzy duration time of activity $(i, j) \in S$, and its membership function is $\mu_{\tilde{T}_{ij}}(t_{ij})$.

This way, we propose a model and an algorithm based on the representation theorem and the decomposition of fuzzy set to solve a PERT problem where activities times are defined by the knowledge of multiple experts. Next sections show the obtained results.

4   The Proposed Approach

Usually, activity networks are performed by multiple people who have different ideas and perceptions about every activity. In addition, not all projects have available and/or reliable statistical information about its activities, so the analyst has to use linguistic information coming from experts to formulate a strategy for planning the project.

In the case of a single expert, the model proposed by Chen [6] can be applied to obtain the CPs of the project. In the case of multiple experts, we have to model the PERT problem and design an optimization method to obtain the CPs of the network, based on the results of Figueroa-García [20]. We remark that the idea is not to solve a PERT problem per expert but solve only one model that comprises the information provided by all experts at the same time.

In order to represent the uncertainty associated with the opinion of multiples experts, we assume an expected time of each activity of the project, and based on this value we select a discrete group of experts to ask them about two sentences: optimist and pessimist time of each activity. Once we get their opinion, we can build a Triangular Type-1 Fuzzy Set (T1FS) for each expert. Now, having m-fuzzy sets for each activity we can use the representation theorem to describe the set $\tilde{T}$ (see Liu & Mendel [18]):

$$\tilde{T} = \bigcup_{e=1}^{m} T^e \tag{10}$$

where m is the total amount of T1FSs and T^e is a T1FS provided by the expert e (a.k.a. embedded fuzzy set). Now, we represent every set $\tilde{T}_{ij}$ using five parameters as follows:

$$\tilde{T}_{ij} = (t_{ij}^{L+}, t_{ij}^{L-}, \bar{t}_{ij}, t_{ij}^{R-}, t_{ij}^{R+}) \tag{11}$$

where t_{ij}^{L+} is the minimum optimistic time, t_{ij}^{L-} is the maximum optimistic time, $\bar{t}_{ij}$ is the expected time, t_{ij}^{R-} is the minimum pessimistic time and t_{ij}^{R+} is the maximum pessimistic time provided by the experts.

Figure 1 shows an example of a triangular IT2FS bounded by a UMF $\overline{\mu}_{\tilde{T}}(t_{ij})$ and LMF $\underline{\mu}_{\tilde{T}}(t_{ij})$. To build the membership function of the total duration time of the project $\mu_{\tilde{D}}(d)$, it is necessary to derive its α-cuts. The α-cut of $\tilde{T}_{ij}$ is defined as follows:

$$^\alpha\tilde{T}_{ij} = \left[\left[(T_{ij})_\alpha^{L+}, (T_{ij})_\alpha^{L-} \right], \left[(T_{ij})_\alpha^{R-}, (T_{ij})_\alpha^{R-} \right] \right] \tag{12}$$

These intervals indicate where the values of t_{ij} lie at possibility α. Based on the Zadeh's extension principle, the fuzzy set $\mu_{\tilde{D}}(d)$ can be defined as:

$$\mu_{\tilde{D}}(d) = \sup_{d \in R^+, (ij) \in S} \min_{(ij) \in S} \left\{ \mu_{\tilde{T}_{ij}} \mid d = y_n - y_1 \right\} \tag{13}$$

To find the membership function $\mu_{\tilde{D}}(d)$, we need to compute the left external bound D_α^{L+}, the left internal bound D_α^{L-}, the right internal bound D_α^{R-} and the right external bound D_α^{R+} of the α-cut of $\mu_{\tilde{D}}(d)$, using the following models:

$$D_\alpha^{L+} = \min\{y_n - y_1 \mid y_j \geq y_i + (T_{i,j})_\alpha^{L+}; \, y_i, y_j \in R \,\forall\, (i,j) \in S\} \tag{14}$$

$$D_\alpha^{L-} = \min\{y_n - y_1 \mid y_j \geq y_i + (T_{i,j})_\alpha^{L-}; \, y_i, y_j \in R \,\forall\, (i,j) \in S\} \tag{15}$$

$$D_\alpha^{R-} = \min\{y_n - y_1 \mid y_j \geq y_i + (T_{i,j})_\alpha^{R-}; \, y_i, y_j \in R \,\forall\, (i,j) \in S\} \tag{16}$$

$$D_\alpha^{R+} = \min\{y_n - y_1 \mid y_j \geq y_i + (T_{i,j})_\alpha^{R+}; \, y_i, y_j \in R \,\forall\, (i,j) \in S\} \tag{17}$$

where y_j represents the occurrence time of the node j, the node i precedes the node j, and the value of $y_n - y_1$ represents the duration of the project, since y_n is the starting time of the last activity, and y_1 is the starting time of the first activity. The objective of the dual problem is to find the required minimal duration time such that all precedence relationships among the different activities are satisfied, and each constraint specifies the precedence relationships among activities.

4.1 An Example

Consider a project whose network is shown in Figure 2 (proposed by Chen [6]). The activity times are IT2FSs coming from the opinion of eight experts who provided their optimistic and pessimistic perceptions which composes the FOU of each $\tilde{T}_{ij}$, and the fuzzy activity times, shapes and parameters are presented in Table 1.

Here, $L_{ij}(x)$ is the left shape, and $R_{ij}(x)$ is the right shape of the set $\tilde{T}_{ij}$. After solving the models proposed in (14), (15), (16), and (17), we have obtained the results shown in Table 2.

Now, we can derive $\mu_{\tilde{D}}(d)$ through the extension principle, $D_\alpha^{L-}, D_\alpha^{R-}, D_\alpha^{L+}$, and D_α^{R+}. The obtained results are shown in Figure 3.

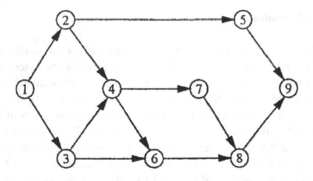

Fig. 2. The network structure of the example (taken from Chen [6])

Table 1. Parameters and shapes of the example

$\tilde{T}_{ij}$	UMF	LMF	$L_{ij}(x)$	$R_{ij}(x)$
$\tilde{T}_{12} =$	$(1, 1.5, 1, 1)$	$(1, 1.5, 0.8, 0.8)$	$L_{12}(x) = \max(1 - x^2, 0)$	$R_{12}(x) = \max(0, 1 - x)$
$\tilde{T}_{13} =$	$(2, 3, 0.3, 2.4)$	$(2, 3, 0, 2)$	$L_{13}(x) = \exp^{-x}$	$R_{13}(x) = \max(0, 1 - x)$
$\tilde{T}_{24} =$	$(0, 0, 0, 0)$	$(0, 0, 0, 0)$	$L_{24}(x) = \max(0, 1 - x)$	$R_{24}(x) = \max(0, 1 - x)$
$\tilde{T}_{25} =$	$(2, 3, 1.4, 2.3)$	$(2, 3, 1, 2)$	$L_{25}(x) = \max(0, 1 - x^4)$	$R_{25}(x) = \exp^{-x}$
$\tilde{T}_{34} =$	$(0, 0, 0, 0)$	$(0, 0, 0, 0)$	$L_{34}(x) = \max(0, 1 - x)$	$R_{34}(x) = \max(1 - x^2, 0)$
$\tilde{T}_{36} =$	$(6, 7, 0.5, 2.5)$	$(6, 7, 0, 2)$	$L_{36}(x) = \exp^{-x^2}$	$R_{36}(x) = \max(1 - x^2, 0)$
$\tilde{T}_{46} =$	$(5, 5, 1.1, 1.2)$	$(5, 5, 1, 1)$	$L_{46}(x) = \max(0, 1 - x)$	$R_{46}(x) = \max(0, 1 - x^4)$
$\tilde{T}_{47} =$	$(9, 9, 1.4, 1.6)$	$(9, 9, 1, 1)$	$L_{47}(x) = \max(0, 1 - x^4)$	$R_{47}(x) = \exp^{-x}$
$\tilde{T}_{59} =$	$(8, 9, 2.3, 4.7)$	$(8, 9, 2, 4)$	$L_{59}(x) = \max(0, 1 - x^4)$	$R_{59}(x) = \max(1 - x^2, 0)$
$\tilde{T}_{68} =$	$(4, 4, 2.6, 2.8)$	$(4, 4, 2, 2)$	$L_{68}(x) = \max(1 - x^2, 0)$	$R_{68}(x) = \max(0, 1 - x^4)$
$\tilde{T}_{78} =$	$(3, 4, 2.5, 0.3)$	$(3, 4, 2, 0)$	$L_{78}(x) = \max(0, 1 - x)$	$R_{78}(x) = \max(0, 1 - x^4)$
$\tilde{T}_{89} =$	$(6, 9, 2.2, 3.7)$	$(6, 9, 2, 3)$	$L_{89}(x) = \max(1 - x^2, 0)$	$R_{89}(x) = \exp^{-x^2}$

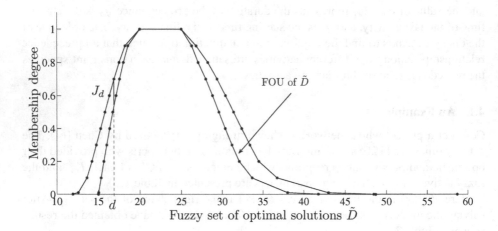

Fig. 3. Fuzzy set $\tilde{D}$ composed from optimal project times

4.2 Analysis of Results

The shape of the left function for the optimal solution shows the same critical path (1-3-4-7-8-9) for several α-cuts, the minimal optimistic time for the external left function and the internal left function is approximately 12 and 15 respectively. Table 2 shows that the project has three possible CPs (1-2-4-7-8-9), (1-3-4-7-8-9), (1-3-6-8-9) which can occur anytime in the project, so the analyst should pay attention to CPs and their activities when performing the project to identify when a CP will switch to another one.

The internal right bound presents a different CP (1-3-6-8-9) from 0.1 to 0.8 α-cut and its maximal pessimistic time is approximately 49, the external right bound presents a similar behavior changing the CP from 0.2 to 0.9 α-cut and its maximal pessimistic time is approximately 59.

Table 2. Results of the optimization process

α	D_α^{L-}	CP	D_α^{R-}	CP	D_α^{L+}	CP	D_α^{R+}	CP
1	20	1-3-4-7-8-9	25	1-3-4-7-8-9	20	1-3-4-7-8-9	25	1-3-4-7-8-9
0.9	18.6052	1-3-4-7-8-9	26.27914	1-3-4-7-8-9	18.2354	1-3-4-7-8-9	26.8061	1-3-6-8-9
0.8	18.0368	1-3-4-7-8-9	27.04905	1-3-6-8-9	17.513	1-3-4-7-8-9	28.2183	1-3-6-8-9
0.7	17.5645	1-3-4-7-8-9	27.96728	1-3-6-8-9	16.9019	1-3-4-7-8-9	29.3713	1-3-6-8-9
0.6	17.1398	1-3-4-7-8-9	28.79961	1-3-6-8-9	16.342	1-3-4-7-8-9	30.4124	1-3-6-8-9
0.5	16.7449	1-3-4-7-8-9	29.59367	1-3-6-8-9	15.8092	1-3-4-7-8-9	31.4027	1-3-6-8-9
0.4	16.3707	1-3-4-7-8-9	30.38111	1-3-6-8-9	15.2888	1-3-4-7-8-9	32.3826	1-3-6-8-9
0.3	16.012	1-3-4-7-8-9	31.19447	1-3-6-8-9	14.7676	1-3-4-7-8-9	33.3926	1-3-6-8-9
0.2	15.6654	1-3-4-7-8-9	32.08625	1-3-6-8-9	14.2254	1-3-4-7-8-9	34.4981	1-3-6-8-9
0.1	15.3286	1-3-4-7-8-9	33.65486	1-3-6-8-9	13.6085	1-3-4-7-8-9	36.7508	1-3-4-7-8-9
0.01	15.0325	1-3-4-7-8-9	38.02307	1-3-4-7-8-9	12.558	1-3-4-7-8-9	42.9836	1-3-4-7-8-9
0.001	15.0033	1-2-4-7-8-9	41.79054	1-3-4-7-8-9	11.9045	1-3-4-7-8-9	48.4745	1-3-4-7-8-9
0.00001	15	1-2-4-7-8-9	48.6921	1-3-4-7-8-9	11.9	1-3-4-7-8-9	58.675	1-3-4-7-8-9

The uncertainty associated to multiple experts allows to know other critical path (1-3-6-8-9) which is important in order to ensure a suitable development of the project. The activity 3-6 has the biggest influence in the project when the perception of experts is pessimistic with a membership degree from 0.1 to 0.9.

Note that every point (optimal solution) allowable into the support of $\tilde{D}$ has a set of memberships $u \subset J_d$ (see Figure 3). This means that every solution is satisfactory to all experts in different degrees.

5 Concluding Remarks

IT2FSs are useful to represent the uncertainty associated to the opinion of multiple experts, or the ambiguity of a single expert regarding their activities times. A PERT problem can be solved when linguistic uncertainty appears through linear optimization tools that lead to a set of possible choices which conforms the solution of the problem.

We have solved a PERT problem with no statistical information, using linguistic information coming from people considered as experts of the system. This kind of information has been handled through IT2FSs and optimization tools to find a set of possible choices of CPs. This means that the analyst can see the project in different scenarios and predict the behavior of the system through its CPs.

The proposal obtains an FOU that characterizes the optimal solution, which means that the decision maker can manage the project in a more suitable way based on information coming from experts.

Different fuzzy measures can be used to solve the uncertain PERT problem. Other representations can be performed using the fuzzy measures of an IT2FS (see Wu & Mendel [17]), and centroid based optimization can be performed using the results of Figueroa-García [19,20]. Different LP models can be formulated for this problem, so our proposal is just one approach to the problem.

References

1. Project Management Institute.: Project Management Body Of Knowledge (PMBOK) Guide. Fifth Edition, EE.UU (2004)
2. Kelley, J., Walker, M.: Critical-path planning and scheduling. In: Eastern Joint IRE-AIEE-CM Computer Conference, pp. 160–173 (1959)
3. USA Navy Defense Technical Information Center: PERT Summary Report, Phase 1. EE.UU (1959)
4. MacCrimmon, K., Ryavec, C.: An Analytical Study of PERT Assumptions. United States Air Force Project RAND (1962)
5. Shipley, M., De Korvin, A., Omer, K.: BIFPET methodology versus PERT in project management: fuzzy probability instead of the beta distribution. Engineering and Technology Management 14 (1997)
6. Chen, S.-P.: Analysis of Critical Paths in a Project Network with Fuzzy Activity Times. European Journal of Operational Research 183, 442–459 (2007)
7. Zadeh, L.A.: Fuzzy Sets. Information and Control 8, 338–353 (1965)
8. Fargier, H., Galvagnon, V., Dubois, D.: Fuzzy PERT in series-parallel graphs. In: Ninth IEEE International Conference on Fuzzy Systems, vol. 2, pp. 717–722 (2000)
9. Hsiau, H., Lin, R.C.: A Fuzzy PERT Approach to Evaluate Plant Construction Project Scheduling Risk Under Uncertain Resources Capacity. Journal of Industrial Engineering and Management. 2, 31–47 (2013)
10. Wang, J.-H., Hao, J.: Fuzzy Linguistic PERT. IEEE Transactions on Fuzzy Systems 15, 133–144 (2007)
11. McCahon, C.S.: Using PERT as an Approximation of Fuzzy Project-Network Analysis. IEEE Transactions on Engineering Management 40, 146–153 (1993)
12. Chen, S.-M., Wang, C.-Y.: Finding Multiple Possible Critical Paths Using Fuzzy PERT. IEEE Transactions on Systems, Man, and Cybernetics 31, 930–937 (2001)
13. Chanas, S., Zielinski, P.: Critical path analysis in the network with fuzzy activity times. Fuzzy Sets and Systems 122, 195–204 (2001)
14. Glisovic, N., Bojovic, N., Milenkovic, M.: Decision Support System for a Project Activity Time Forecasting Based on Fuzzy Pert Method. In: 32nd Int. Conf. on information Technology Interfaces, pp. 231–236 (2010)
15. Klir, G., Yuan, B.: Fuzzy Sets and Fuzzy Logic. Prentice Hall PTR (1995)
16. Liang, Q., Mendel, J.M.: Interval Type-2 Fuzzy Logic Systems: Theory and Design. IEEE Transactions on Fuzzy Systems 8, 535–550 (2000)
17. Wu, D., Mendel, J.M.: Uncertainty measures for interval type-2 fuzzy sets. Information Sciences 177, 5378–5393 (2007)
18. Liu, F., Mendel, J.M.: Encoding Words Into Interval Type-2 Fuzy Sets Using an Interval Approach. IEEE Transactions On Fuzzy Systems 16, 1503–1521 (2008)
19. Figueroa-García, J.C.: A general model for Linear Programming with Interval Type-2 fuzzy technological coefficients. In: 2012 Annual Meeting of the North American Fuzzy Information Processing Society (NAFIPS) (2012)
20. Figueroa-García, J.C.: An approximation method for Type Reduction of an Interval Type-2 fuzzy set based on α-cuts. In: Proceedings of FEDCSIS 2012 (2012)

Time Series Classification with Temporal Bag-of-Words Model

Zi-Wen Gui[1] and Yi-Ren Yeh[2]

[1] Department of Computer Science and Information Engineering
National Taiwan University of Science and Technology, Taipei, Taiwan
[2] Department of Applied Mathematics
Chinese Culture University, Taipei, Taiwan

Abstract. Time series classification has attracted increasing attention in machine learning and data mining. In the analysis of time series data, how to represent data is a critical step for the performance. Generally, we can regard each time stamp as a feature dimension for time series data instance. However, this näive representation might be not suitable for data analysis due to the over-fitting of data. To address this problem, we proposed a temporal bag-of-words representation for time series classification. A codebook is generated by the representative subsequences from the time series data. Consequently, we encode a time series data instance by the codebook, which describes different local patterns of time series data. In our experiments, we demonstrate that our proposed method can achieve better results by comparing with competitive methods.

Keywords: time series data, representation, classification, bag-of-words.

1 Introduction

Time series classification has been an important task in many machine learning tasks, such as speech recognition or sensor data analysis. By comparing with other types of data, time series data suffer from highly intra-class variability where patterns might be sifted in time. As a result, näive representation (i.e., using a timestamp as a feature dimension) of time series might not be suitable for data analysis [5]. Dynamic Time Warping (DTW) is proposed to address the intra-class variations of time-series patterns [2,9]. DTW measures the similarity between time series data with an automatic time alignment by a dynamic programming approach. However, previous studies showed that using a high level representation to measure similarity will be more appropriate for time series data [7,8,6,4]. Similar to [7,6], our work is based on the Bag-of-Words (BoW) model which aims to represent an object by feature vectors of subobjects. It is also worth noting that BoW representations are widely used in computer vision due to the promising performance [1,3]. In our BoW model, subsequences of all time seres data instances are extracted for feature learning (i.e., generating a codebook). Once we obtain the codebook, the time series data instance can be represented by the distribution of learned codewords (i.e., the histogram of codewords). The framework is illustrated in Fig. 1. We first generate the codebook

S.-M. Cheng and M.-Y. Day (Eds.): TAAI 2014, LNAI 8916, pp. 145–153, 2014.

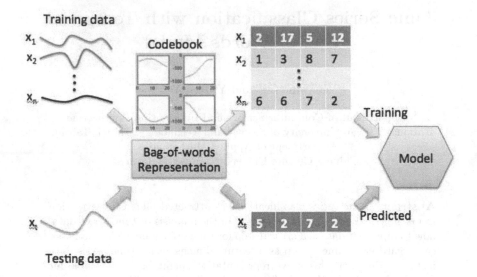

Fig. 1. Illustration of our framework

by representative subsequences. All the time series data instances are converted to an $\mathbb{R}^k$ by the learned codebook with k codewords. That is, we summarize how many codewords are used for a time series data instance and conclude the representation with the histogram of the codewords. Then we apply classification methods, such as support vector machine, to the time series data with BoW representation.

2   Bag-of-Words Model for Time Series Classification

Suppose a time series instance is originally represented by $\mathbf{x^i} = (x_1^i, x_2^i, ..., x_p^i)$ where we have p timestamps for each instance. Each time series instance $\mathbf{x}^i$ is associated with a class label y^i for $i = 1, 2, ..., n$ and $y^i \in \{1, 2, ..., C\}$ where n is the number of instances and C is the number of class labels. As we mentioned, directly representing a time series in this p-dimensional space might be too specific to describe a time series appropriately. In this section, we will address how to apply BoW for representation of time series data, and present the details for the codebook learning and representation encoding.

2.1   Codebook Learning

Due to the intra-class variability, using global properties for times series data might not be suitable for the classification. The local patterns could be applied for improving the recognition performance. Therefore, we represent each time series data instance by feature vectors derived from subsequences. It is worth

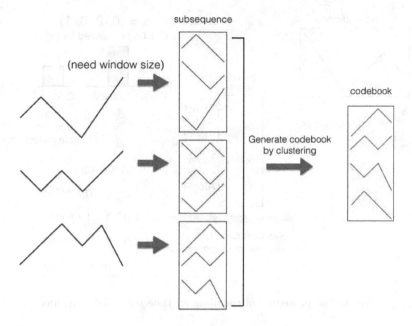

Fig. 2. Codebook Generation

noting that a subsequence is a subinterval of a time series data instance. For example a subsequence is represented as $\mathbf{x}^i = (x_2, x_3, x_4)$ with a window size 3.

To extract representative local patterns, we first extract subsequences from all the time series data instances by a sliding window for each time series data instance. More specifically, we will extract $p - w + 1$ subsequences from each time series data instance and we will have $n(p - w + 1)$ subsequences from the training data. Note that w is the window size. The clustering algorithms can be applied to find the local patterns. In our experiments, we use k-means to cluster these subsequences with d centroids. All these centroids are regarded as codewords of the codebook $\mathbf{D} \in \mathbb{R}^{w \times d}$. The process is shown in Fig 2. In the following, we will address how to use these features to describe a time series instance.

2.2 Feature Encoding with Codebook

We assume that a codebook $\mathbf{D} \in \mathbb{R}^{w \times d}$ is learned. As we mentioned above, the codewords of a codebook can be viewed as features of time series data instances. Each feature (codeword) is represented as a local pattern which could improve the ability to define the class. Thus, how to utilize these local patterns is critical step for new representation.

For BoW model in text classification, we investigate the histogram of the words in a document. That is, we utilize the distribution of the words in the dictionary to classify the unlabeled document. Similar to text classification, we also aim to check the distribution of local patterns (i.e., the codewords) for a

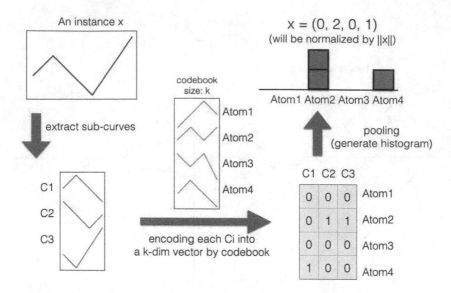

Fig. 3. The procedure of encoding an time series data instance

time series data instance (see Fig 3). First, we also extract $p - w + 1$ subsequences (i.e., $c_1, c_2, ..., c_{p-w+1}$) from each time series data instance by the same sliding window. To aggregate the information of these collected subsequences, we encode each subsequence into a d-dimensional vector $\mathbf{h} = (h_1, h_2, ..., h_d)$. More specifically, we map each subsequence to the closest centroid and encode the corresponding dimension with one. That is, by given a subsequences $\mathbf{c}$, the formal definition of the encoding vector $\mathbf{h}$ is expressed as follows:

$$h_i = \begin{cases} 1 & \text{if } \mathbf{c} \text{ is closest to } i\text{th centroid,} \\ 0 & \text{others.} \end{cases} \quad (1)$$

For example, if a subsequence is closest to the 3th centroid with 5 centroids which concluded by the clustering algorithm, we will encode the subsequence as $(0, 0, 1, 0, 0)$.

Once we have encoded all the subsequences within a time series data instance with $p - w + 1$ vectors, we summarize the information by computing the histogram of the d features (codewords). As shown in Fig 3, the original time series data instance $\mathbf{x}$ can be extracted with three subsequences. By encoding each subsequence into a 4-dimensional vectors, we can compute the histogram for the codewords. By aggregating the encoding vectors with sum, the original time series data instance is represented as $(0, 2, 0, 1)$. While encoding all the time series data instances, the standard learning models can be applied for further analysis, such as classification. It is also worth noting that the normalization will be applied for a more robust representation.

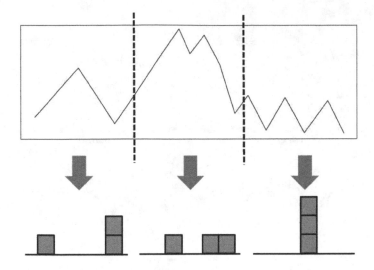

Fig. 4. The procedure of temporal bag of words

3   Bag-of-Words Model with Temporal Information

As presented in the previous section, Bow models utilize the distribution of local patterns (or histogram of codewords) to provide a more robust data representation for time series data. However, describing time series data by the histogram might lose the temporal information within a time series data instance. A local pattern appears in the early or late stage within a time series data instance might have different information for classifying an instance. For example, considering a opening/closing trajectory (as shown in Fig. 5), a spike appear in late stage might provide more discriminative information for the classification. In BoW models, the local patterns are aggregated without considering this temporal information. That is, some informative local patterns, which appear in a particular period, will not be emphasized in BoW representation models.

To consider the temporal information with BoW models, we split a time series data instance into n intervals (segments). Suppose we have a time series data instance $\mathbf{x}^i = (x_1^i, x_2^i, ..., x_p^i)$. The instance $\mathbf{x}^i$ will be split into $\mathbf{s}^1, \mathbf{s}^2, ...,$ and $\mathbf{s}^n$ where each interval have $\frac{p}{n}$ timestamps (i.e., $\mathbf{x}^i = (\mathbf{s}_1^i, \mathbf{s}_2^i, ..., \mathbf{s}_{p/n}^i)$). After splitting time series data, we apply BoW models to each interval. More specifically, for the jth interval, we collect subsequences from the jth interval of all training data, and generate a codebook for this interval. We can have local histogram $\mathbf{h}_j^i$ to represent $\mathbf{s}_j^i$ for the jth interval (see Fig. 4). Our temporal BoW model consider the histogram of local patterns with different stages (i.e., different intervals) within time series data. By comparing with applying BoW models to full sequence, our proposed method could capture the behaviors of the data at different stages, and provide a more discriminative ability for the classification. In our experiments, we also demonstrate that taking the temporal information

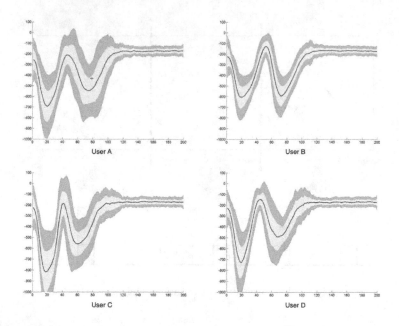

Fig. 5. Examples in our door opening/closing trajectory dataset

into account will improve the performance by comparing with the standard BoW model.

In our temporal BoW model, n histograms are generated for a time series data instance. How to combine these histograms will also be an interesting issue. Many feature fusion methods have also been proposed to address this problem [10]. In our experiments. we simply concatenate all the histograms. More specifically, a instance $\mathbf{x}^i \in \mathbb{R}^p$ is represented by $[\mathbf{h}_1^i, \mathbf{h}_2^i, \dots, \mathbf{h}_n^i] \in \mathbb{R}^{n \times d}$.

4   Experiments

4.1   Data Description

In our experiments, we apply our proposed method to user identification by door opening/closing trajectory. To collect the time series data, we adopt 3-axis accelerometer to collect 4 users opening/closing trajectories. The sampling rate of accelerometer is 50 Hz (i.e., 20 timestamps within a second). In order to collect full sequence of operation for door opening/closing, the sensor records each trajectory by 10 seconds while the door is opened. Thus, we have 200 timetamps in each time series data instance. We collect 100 records of opening/closing trajectory for each user. It is worth noting that the quantity of acceleration is affected by the relative position of the door since the sensor is attached on the door. As a result, the Z-axis is might not help for the recognition since we will only sensing small values from this axis . Furthermore, the X-axis and Y-axis will present

Table 1. The comparison results with averaged recognition rate and standard deviation. Raw data represents using the original representation without preprocessing. PCA + SVM represents applying PCA as preprocessing where the number is the projected dimensionality. BoW+SVM represents apply BoW model with SVM where d is codebook size and w is the window size. tBoW+SVM is our proposed method.

Method	Raw Data	PCA(100)+SVM	BoW+SVM (w:20,d:32)	BoW+SVM (w:40,d:64)	tBoW+SVM (w:20,d:32,4 segments)
Recognition rate	0.7410 (0.0152)	0.7308 (0.0146)	0.8277 (0.0148)	0.8538 (0.0104)	0.8819 (0.0107)

symmetric opening/closing trajectory. For the sake of the simplicity, we only use the data from the Y-axis in our experiments. The Fig 5 shows some examples in our door opening/closing trajectory dataset.

4.2 Experimental Results

In our experiments, we use linear support vector machine (SVM) as our classification model. To determine the appropriate parameter C in SVM, we perform a grid search from $C = \{2^0, 2^1, 2^2, ..., 2^9\}$ with the cross-validation. For the evaluation, we compare our proposed method with different representations. One is using the original representation without preprocessing. The other is applying Principal Component Analysis (PCA) as the preprocessing. Note that we project our data noto the 50 and 100 principal components in our experiments. For our methods, we use k-means clustering algorithm to extract the codebook. For the sizes of sliding window and codebook, we use two pairs in our experiments: (w, d) = (20, 32) and (40, 64). For experiments, we randomly split 80% of the data for training and the remaining 20% for testing. We repeat this process five times and report the average error rates.

Table 1 shows the experimental results for the five different settings, including ours. As observed, our method achieved improved error rates by comparing with other methods. By comparing PCA with using raw data, we could see that PCA perform worse than using raw data. The worse performance shows that it might lose some local information while project the data note the principal space. Comparing BoW with using raw data, the improved performance is significant. These results confirmed that represent by the distribution of local patterns could provide a more discriminative ability for time series data. While the standard BoW improved the performance, our temporal BoW (tBoW) model achieved the best performance. Comparing the results shown in Tabel 1, taking the temporal information was able to improve the recognition performance. It is also worth noting that the performance of using larger codebook and window sizes is better while applying BoW to full sequence. This shows that 2 seconds (40 timestamps) might be more suitable for a larger trajectory where one second(20 timestamps) might be too short to present the local patterns. However, apply BoW model to an interval, which contains only $\frac{p}{n}$ timestamps, one second(20 timestamps) will be more appropriate for the shortertrajectory.

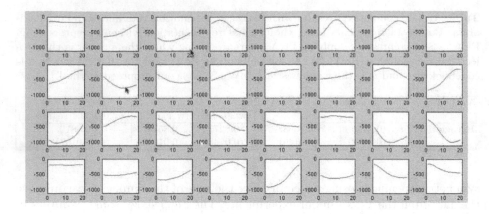

Fig. 6. An example for the codebook

In Fig 6, we also present a particular learned codebook with $d = 32$ and $w = 20$ in our experiment. By comparing with global properties of using original representation, we can observe that these codewords could capture the local patterns within the time series data instances. Utilizing these local patterns with the encoding concept could provide a more high level descriptor for the data in which one can avoid the over-fitting issue from the original representation.

5   Conclusion

We utilized the bag-of-words model to represent the time series data. With the learned codebook, we summarize each original time series data instance by a histogram. This provides a high level description by these local patterns (codewords) which can capture more discriminative information for classification tasks. Experiments on door opening/closing trajectory confirmed that our proposed method achieved improved recognition accuracy than using the original representation. This also shows an appropriate representation of time series data is important for time series data analysis.

References

1. Babenko, B., Yang, M.-H., Belongie, S.: Robust object tracking with online multiple instance learning. IEEE Transactions on Pattern Analysis and Machine Intelligence 33(8), 1619–1632 (2011)
2. Ding, H., Trajcevski, G., Scheuermann, P., Wang, X., Keogh, E.: Querying and mining of time series data: experimental comparison of representations and distance measures. Proceedings of the VLDB Endowment 1(2), 1542–1552 (2008)
3. Fergus, R., Perona, P., Zisserman, A.: Object class recognition by unsupervised scale-invariant learning. In: Computer Vision and Pattern Recognition (2003)

4. Geurts, P.: Pattern extraction for time series classification. In: Siebes, A., De Raedt, L. (eds.) PKDD 2001. LNCS (LNAI), vol. 2168, p. 115. Springer, Heidelberg (2001)
5. Gudmundsson, S., Runarsson, T.P., Sigurdsson, S.: Support vector machines and dynamic time warping for time series. In: International Joint Conference on Neural Networks (2008)
6. Nanopoulos, A., Grabocka, J.: Lars schmidt-thieme: Invariant time-series classification. In: ECML/PKDD (2012)
7. Lin, J., Li, Y.: Finding structural similarity in time series data using bag-of-patterns representation. In: Winslett, M. (ed.) SSDBM 2009. LNCS, vol. 5566, pp. 461–477. Springer, Heidelberg (2009)
8. Lin, J., Li, Y.: Finding structural similarity in time series data using bag-of-patterns representation. In: Winslett, M. (ed.) SSDBM 2009. LNCS, vol. 5566, pp. 461–477. Springer, Heidelberg (2009)
9. Rakthanmanon, T., Campana, B., Mueen, A., Batista, G., Westover, B., Zhu, Q., Zakaria, J., Keogh, E.: Searching and mining trillions of time series subsequences under dynamic time warping. In: ACM SIGKDD International Conference on Knowledge Discovery and Data Mining (2012)
10. Yeh, Y.-R., Lin, T.-C., Chung, Y.-Y., Wang, Y.-C.F.: A novel multiple kernel learning framework for heterogeneous feature fusion and variable selection. IEEE Transactions on Multimedia 14(3), 563–574 (2012)

A Frame-Based Approach for Reference Metadata Extraction

Yu-Lun Hsieh[1], Shih-Hung Liu[1], Ting-Hao Yang[1], Yu-Hsuan Chen[1],
Yung-Chun Chang[1], Gladys Hsieh[1], Cheng-Wei Shih[1], Chun-Hung Lu[2],
and Wen-Lian Hsu[1]

[1] Institute of Information Science, Academia Sinica, Taipei, Taiwan
{morphe,journey,tinghaoyang,smallright,changyc,gladys,
dapi,hsu}@iis.sinica.edu.tw
[2] Innovative Digitech-Enabled Applications & Services Institute, III, Taiwan
enricoghlu@iii.org.tw

Abstract. In this paper, we propose a novel frame-based approach
(FBA) and use reference metadata extraction as a case study to demonstrate its advantages. The main contributions of this research are
three-fold. First, the new frame matching algorithm, based on sequence
alignment, can compensate for the shortcomings of traditional rule-based
approach, in which rule matching lacks flexibility and generality. Second,
an approximate matching is adopted for capturing reasonable abbreviations or errors in the input reference string to further increase the coverage of the frames. Third, experiments conducted on extensive datasets
show that the same knowledge framework performed equally well on various untrained domains. Comparing to a widely-used machine learning
method, Conditional Random Fields (CRFs), the FBA can drastically
reduce the average field error rate across all four independent test sets
by 70% (2.24% vs. 7.54%).

Keywords: Reference Metadata Extraction, Knowledge representation,
Frame-based approach.

1 Introduction

In natural language processing (NLP), an important task is to recognize various linguistic expressions. Many such expressions can be represented as rules or
templates. These templates are matched by computer to identify those linguistic objects in text. However, in the real world, there always seem to be many
exceptions or variations not covered by rules or templates. A typical approach
to cope with this situation is either to produce more templates or to relax the
constraints of the templates (e.g., by inserting optionals or wild cards). But the
former produces many case-by-case templates that could create more conflicts;
and the latter could lead to lots of false positives, namely, matched but undesirable linguistic expressions. Thus, the inflexibility of rule-based systems has
troubled the NLP as well as the artificial intelligence (AI) communities for years

S.-M. Cheng and M.-Y. Day (Eds.): TAAI 2014, LNAI 8916, pp. 154–163, 2014.

so as to make people think that, rule-based approach is not suitable for NLP or AI in general. On the other hand, fine-grained linguistic knowledge cannot be easily captured by current machine learning models, which often resulted in less desirable recognition accuracy. Therefore, how to make the best out of rule-based and statistical approaches has always been a challenging task. In light of this, we propose a novel frame-based approach (FBA) and use reference metadata extraction (RME) as a case study to demonstrate its advantages.

The task of RME is to automatically extract the metadata of input reference or citation strings[1], where metadata is defined as a set of structured data, such as the author, title, etc. However, automatic RME often struggles with the variations between field separators. For example, the author and title fields can be separated by spaces or periods, while the volume and issue fields can be separated by braces or parentheses [1]. Moreover, RME is a punctuation-sensitive task, since the missing punctuations between and/or within fields often cause ambiguity. Even within each field, there can be punctuation and spacing differences. To further complicate this problem, there are many drastically different citation styles (i.e., different field orders).

The main contributions of this research are three-fold. First, the new frame matching algorithm, based on sequence alignment, can compensate for the shortcomings of traditional rule-based approach, in which rule matching lacks flexibility and generality. Second, an approximate matching is adopted for capturing reasonable abbreviations or errors in the input reference string to further increase the coverage of the frames. Third, experiments conducted on extensive datasets show that the same knowledge framework performed equally well on various untrained domains.

2   Related Work

Previous work can roughly be divided into three categories: machine learning based, template-based, and knowledge-based (or rule-based) methods. The machine learning based approach, which casts RME as a sequential labeling or classification problem in token level, take advantage of the probabilistic estimation based on training sets of tagged bibliographical data. [11] use the Hidden Markov Model to extract important fields from the headers of computer science research papers. [8] apply classifier such as the support vector machine (SVM) for this task. [10] employ CRFs to extract various common fields from the headers and citations of research papers. The template-based approach contains the BibPro system [2] and those developed by [3] and [6]. They use a template mining approach for citation extraction. The BibPro system transforms citation strings into protein-like sequence and uses Basic Local Alignment Search Tool (BLAST) to find the highest similarity score for predicting fields of a citation string. [6] use three templates for extracting information from citations. The advantage of such models is its efficiency. Thirdly, the knowledge-based methods include

---

[1] The two terms "reference" and "citation" will be used interchangeably in this paper.

CiteSeer [7], InfoMap [12,5] and Flux-CiM [4]. CiteSeer can identify titles, authors and page numbers by exploiting heuristic rules. InfoMap is an ontological knowledge representation and inference framework that provides an integrated environment (accompanied by Compass [12], a knowledge base editing tool), for extracting citation information. The Flux-CiM is an unsupervised knowledge-based approach by automatically collect pairs as knowledge base and a series of matching strategies are designed for capturing reference metadata [4].

These methods have their own merits and drawbacks. Machine learning based approaches can achieve substantial performance without much human involvement. However, they suffer from the data sparseness problem and the lack of the ability to make generalizations [9]. Once the domain of the task is changed, the models need to be re-trained to obtain satisfactory results. On the contrary, the main shortcoming of the template-based or knowledge-based methods is the need of human effort, which motivated us to develop the FBA to ease this annoyance.

3   Frame-Based Approach (FBA)

The FBA for RME consists of two main steps. The first one is to represent the information in the reference by frames and related bigram statistics. The next step is a hierarchical frame matching for extracting the desired metadata from reference strings.

3.1   Frame Representation for RME

The FBA is a hierarchical frame-slot combination scheme, in which a frame can serve as a description as well as organization of a certain piece of knowledge, and the slots indicate essential components in a frame. The conceptualization of a "reference" is a frame consisting of slots such as Author, Title, Volume, and so on. Within each slot, e.g., Volume, there can be another frame with its corresponding slots, viz. prefix keywords and the following digits. We can recursively defined knowledge until reasonable basic units of a frame are completed. Since regular reference strings are sequences of literal and number chunks, we naturally separate the concept of a reference string into these two parts. Specifically, the literal part contains author, title, and journal slots, and the number part contains volume, issue, page, and year slots. An overview of hierarchical frame representation of the reference domain is shown in Figure 1. "SLOT" and "PATTERN" represent slots and patterns, respectively, for the corresponding frame. The possible orders of slots are represented using patterns. For instance, in an author frame, if the associated slots are first, middle, and last name, then one possible order of slots to constitute this author frame is the left-to-right order of first, middle, and last name slots. In sum, a frame is a formulation containing the main constituents and their possible orders of appearance.

3.2   Slot Identification of the Literal Part in RME

The extraction of the literal part can be viewed as a boundary identification problem, and we explore some useful empirical cues to serve this purpose. Some

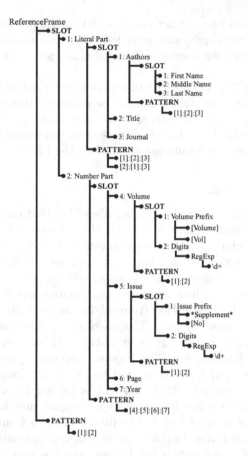

Fig. 1. An illustration of the frame-slot representation of the RME domain knowledge

pre-collected dictionaries are used to tag author, title and journal as A, T, and J, respectively. A reference string is first tokenized by whitespace, and then the dictionaries are used to assign single or multiple tags for each token. Subsequently, frequent trigram tags are examined to generate frames such as "AAT", "TTA" and "TTJ". In addition, 40% of the titles in the training data are enclosed by quotation marks, so they are used to designate the boundary of T and J. Furthermore, over 60% of the year field exists between A and T, according to previous analysis [5]. Thus, it is also included as an indicator of boundary.

Authors are usually either "F M L" or "L, F M", in which "F", "M", and "L" indicate first, middle, and last name, respectively. Most author names in references would be written following a consistent style and abbreviation convention. Hence, abbreviation patterns can be used to determine the end of the author field.

For the title, the length of the title in a normal reference string is often more than three words, and few punctuations, such as commas or periods, would occur within the title. In contrast, punctuations, especially commas, are commonly used to separate author names. Therefore, we calculate the distance between any two punctuations and extract possible title segments with a length longer than four, i.e. this segment contains at least four consecutive words. For each possible title segment, we compute the confidence score by checking the title dictionary.

To enhance the FBA, we also create a plug-in mechanism to allow the use of other resources to perform slot tagging. For example, through the use of pre-collected dictionaries such as journal name lists from the web, we can easily broaden our knowledge base. In this way, we can incorporate other techniques, such as statistical models, to further strengthen the FBA.

3.3   Frame Matching

We propose an alignment-based matching algorithm that enables a single frame to match multiple similar expressions with high accuracy. Each frame contains a collection of slot relations and related bigram statistics. A slot can be a word, phrase, semantic category, or another frame concept. Unlike normal template-based approaches, we utilize slot relations as scoring criteria during matching. During the matching procedure, we score possible candidate frames depending on matched slots, slot relations and insertions/deletions/substitutions. Each exactly matched slot gets a score of four. The score of an insertion is calculated by gathering its left (resp. right) bigram statistics with its neighboring left (resp. right) slots in the training set. The bigram frequency gives a way to assign the insertion scores, which are truncated to fall in the ranges from -10 to 2. Deletions are less common in RME and will be assigned a score from -10 to 0. A substitution is either a partial match or a category match of the slot, which is usually assigned a score of 1 or 2. The final score of a frame is the sum of all the scores within this frame. In this way, we can capture most of the variations of a certain concept using only a few frames, and the score can determine the most likely match. A frame concept described above is more general than rules, in that, different expressions of the same concept can likely be captured by one frame. Such generality might slightly sacrifice precision, but tends to get a much higher recall. Note that the number of frames adopted tends to be proportional to the number of reference styles rather than the size of the training set.

3.4   Examples of Insertion, Deletion and Substitution for a Frame

Consider a frame involving three components V, I, and P, (i.e. Volume, Issue, and Page, respectively), which are arranged in this order from left to right. Suppose we have a reference string "38, ,115–126", in which V and P are identified, but I is missing (a deletion). There may be various punctuations between V and P (insertions). An insertion can be given a positive score if it tends to collocate with its left or right matched components, such as punctuations in this case, (otherwise, negative). A deletion can be harmful if slot I contains a key component for the frame. Note that many such key components can be pre-specified in the frame. Furthermore, in another example like "38, suppl 2, 115–126", a match for slot I can be found by partial matching for the word "supplement" rather than exact matching (substitution). A probable substitution is considered helpful in matching and given a positive score that is lower than that of an exact match. After all these scores are determined, the score of the matched frame is obtained.

To recap, consider the cases shown in Table 1, in which authors contain different styles and even some errors like two consecutive commas. A rule-based approach like [5] must enumerate all possible combinations of insertions or deletions, making it hard to handle unseen cases or unexpected errors. However, FBA can tackle such variations, in that, it can capture multiple forms of the same reference concept in one compact frame (e.g. $F{:}M{:}L$). Since multiple rules can be facilitated by the same frame, the number of frames could be exceedingly small, which is indeed the case shown in Table 1. Though the precision of FBA might be slightly sacrificed, the recall is much higher. Consequently, human labor is drastically reduced in FBA approach.

Table 1. Comparison of rule- and frame-based method for various number part and one author in literal part of reference string (including errors)

Rule-based: One rule for each case (to list just a few)	Frame-based: One frame to cover all cases	Rule-based: One rule for each case (to list just a few)	Frame-based: Two frames to cover all cases
Vol. 38, no. 2, pp. 115–126		K.C. Wang	
Volume 38, suppl 2, p. 11–126		Yue-Kuen Kwok	
38, 2, 115–126		H.-J. Li	
38(2):115–126		Yen, Jerome	
38(2:115–126	$V : I : P$	Burghard von Karger	$F : M : L$
38.2, 115-126		Tung X. Bui	$L : F : M$
38 115–126		Bui, Tung X.	
38,, 2,,, 115–126		Li,, H.-J.	
38:2:115–126		Chen.. S. L.	

4 Experiments

4.1 Experiment Setup

First of all, 30,000 reference records were retrieved from publicly available digital libraries on the web, and 5,076 bibliographic (journal) styles are collected from EndNote[2]. The reference strings were generated from each of those 5,076 journal styles. We then randomly selected 10,000 and 20,000 strings for training (denoted as the TrainingSet) and test (denoted as the EndNoteSet), respectively. In addition, we used the BibPro set [2] consisting of 10,000 reference strings with six journal styles, and the FluxHS [4] set containing 2,000 journal reference strings in health science domain. Finally, we randomly collected 1,500 journal reference strings from multiple researchers websites to be the "free style set". Hence, there are one training set and four test sets for FBA and CRFs.

---

[2] http://endnote.com/downloads/styles

The resources (dictionaries) used in FBA were collected from WordNet[3], DBLP[4], and the Internet. We parsed individual words in authors' name, title and journal names from DBLP to form part of the author, title, and journal dictionaries. A family name list containing 71,475 entries was collected from the Internet[5]. We then aggregated these resources into corresponding dictionaries for author, title, and journal field, which contain 308,157, 73,683, and 32,305 words, respectively.

The baseline system was built by conditional random fields (CRFs)[6], which is widely-used and well-practiced for sequential labeling problem in various natural language applications. The same resources were used to train both FBA and CRFs. For the training of CRFs, we adopted the features in [10], except for their external resources that we could not obtain.

In contrast to previous RME evaluations, which used word and/or field accuracy, we evaluate the performance using field error rate (FER), as in (1),. The reason is that most accuracies are close to 100%, so the reduction in the error rate can more faithfully reflect the improvement.

$$FER = 1 - \left(\frac{Number\ of\ correctly\ extracted\ fields}{Total\ number\ of\ fields} \right) \times 100\% \qquad (1)$$

4.2 Experiment Results

At the outset, we evaluated training set performance (regarded as the inside test) for FBA and CRFs. As shown in Table 2, the overall field error rates of FBA and CRFs are 2.05% and 7.15%, respectively. CRFs performs well in the literal part and some of the number part. However, FBA is slightly better than CRFs in the number part, yet this condition is reversed in the literal part.

For the EndNote test set performance as depicted in Table 3, FBA is better than CRFs for all fields with the overall field error rate being 2.29%, which is a 5.22% improvement over CRFs. Since this test set has the same journal styles as in the training set, both FBA and CRFs could achieve stable results. From the observation of performances achieved by CRFs in training and EndNote set, the performance of the number part is lower. A reasonable explanation is that some number part of reference is whitespace-free, but CRFs is tokenized by whitespace, which could lead to the prediction error of CRFs. This would require some post-processing to get partial result in the number part. If one could design a more sophisticated tokenization strategy unaffected by punctuations, then the performance of CRFs could be further enhanced.

Next, we compared the performance of the baseline CRFs and those reported by [2] in the BibPro set, which only contains six journal styles from the 5,076 generated journal styles. Table 4 indicates that FBA has a stable performance

---

[3] http://wordnet.princeton.edu

[4] http://dblp.uni-trier.de/xml

[5] http://www.last-names.net,http://genforum.genealogy.com/surnames

[6] http://crfpp.googlecode.com

Table 2. Average field error rates achieved by FBA and CRFs in the training set. (5076 styles)

TrainingSet, 10,000	Author	Title	Journal	Volume	Issue	Page	Year	Average
FBA	0.60	0.84	0.78	3.06	4.09	3.56	1.43	**2.05**
CRFs	0.20	0.30	2.60	17.30	8.40	15.20	6.10	7.15

Table 3. Average field error rates achieved by FBA and CRFs in EndNote style set. (5076 styles)

EndNoteSet, 20,000	Author	Title	Journal	Volume	Issue	Page	Year	Average
FBA	0.82	1.13	0.94	3.34	3.96	4.51	1.35	**2.29**
CRFs	1.20	1.80	3.20	16.70	9.10	14.00	6.60	7.51

Table 4. Average field error rates achieved by FBA, CRFs, and Chen et al. in BibPro set. (6 styles)

BibProSet, 10,000	Author	Title	Journal	Volume	Issue	Page	Year	Average
FBA	0.52	1.52	1.78	2.73	2.92	1.95	1.89	**1.90**
CRFs	2.50	4.00	2.30	4.70	5.00	1.80	18.50	5.54
Chen et al. 2012	1.77	5.07	7.80	2.41	6.62	1.90	0.90	3.78

Table 5. Average field error rates achieved by FBA, CRFs, and Cortez et al. in FluxHS set

FluxHS, 2,000	Author	Title	Journal	Volume	Issue	Page	Year	Average
FBA	7.47	10.33	5.66	2.06	-	1.05	0.15	3.81
CRFs	10.30	14.20	3.20	11.20	-	10.70	10.50	8.58
Flux (Cortez et al. 2007)	1.00	5.60	7.00	2.30	-	0.50	0.40	**2.40**

Table 6. Average field error rates achieved by FBA and CRFs in free style set

FreeStyleSet, 1,500	Author	Title	Journal	Volume	Issue	Page	Year	Average
FBA	0.91	0.82	2.69	2.09	1.79	3.28	1.09	**1.81**
CRFs	9.90	28.90	14.60	19.70	29.40	22.10	14.10	19.80

similar to those of the training and the EndNote set, and achieves better results over CRFs and the BibPro system of [2]. The overall field error rates of FBA, CRFs, and BibPro system are 1.90%, 5.54%, 3.78%, respectively.

In Table 5, we compared the unsupervised knowledge-based approach proposed by [4] (denoted as Flux) as well as the baseline CRFs in the FluxHS dataset. Note that this dataset does not contain issues of a reference. The overall field error rates achieved by FBA, CRFs and Flux are 3.81%, 8.58% and 2.40%, respectively. The performance of FBA remains better than that of CRFs, but a little worse than that of the Flux system. One possible explanation is that this dataset is in the health science domain, and there are many special terms used in this dataset not available for either FBA or CRFs whose title dictionary is collected from general-purpose words in the WordNet. Thus, domain dictionaries are required for FBA and CRFs to achieve better performance.

Finally, to validate the effectiveness of FBA in general, we created a "free style set" by randomly selecting 1,500 journal reference strings from researchers websites. Many of these researchers use their own favorite styles. As we can see in Table 6, the performance of FBA remains stable and is better than that of CRFs. These results indicate that the performance of machine learning models could easily be affected by unseen journal styles. In contrast, FBA appears to be more tolerable. Since this free style set is quite different from the training set, and can be treated as individualized journal styles, the performance on this dataset could indicate how a system would perform in case it is adopted as a web service.

We also list some errors predicted by CRFs to analyze its deficiency. As observed in Table 7, CRFs fails to recognize the author due to that only the field label ("A","T" and so on) be provided in the training set. We believe that if we spend lots of effort to label the fine-grained features such as "First", "Last", "Generation", etc, the performance of CRFs could be improved. In contrast, FBA can easily incorporate such fine-grained feature without much effort.

All in all, experiment results showed that FBA performed equally well on trained and various untrained test domains. It can reduce the weighted average field error rate across all four test sets by around 70% (2.24% vs. 7.54%) when compared to CRFs.

Table 7. The examples for the prediction error of CRFs

Reference string	Predicted author by CRFs
Dupavcova, Jitka and Wets, Roger: Asymptotic behavior of statistical...	Dupavcova, Jitka and Wets
E.D. Falkenberg and Pols, R. van der and Weide, Th.P. van der, Under-standing process structure...	E.D. Falkenberg and Pols, R. van der and Weide
Michael S. Kogan and Freeman L. Rawson, III: The design of Operating System...	Michael S. Kogan and Freeman L. Rawson

5 Conclusions

We proposed a frame-based approach (FBA) by taking reference metadata extraction as a case study to show its merits. FBA is designed to compensate for the shortcomings while retaining the strengths of traditional rule-based approach in that, the fuzzy nature of frame matching can capture reasonable variations in the input text to further increase the coverage of the frames. Our experiment results indicate that the FBA is superior to other widely-used machine learning (e.g., CRFs) and template-based (e.g., BibPro) methods.

There are three directions for future research. First, we plan to extend this framework to other reference styles such as conference proceeding, book chapter and technical report. Second, we are applying this flexible FBA to other fundamental NLP tasks, such as named entity recognition. Lastly, since current FBA still needs some personel involvement for frame pattern generation, we are in an attempt to develop an unsupervised frame pattern generation mechanism through data mining and/or clustering techniques in order to construct a fully automatic FBA approach.

Acknowledgments. This study is conducted under the "NSC 102-3114-Y-307-026 A Research on Social Influence and Decision Support Analytics" of the Institute for Information Industry which is subsidized by the National Science Council.

References

1. Agichtein, E., Ganti, V.: Mining reference tables for automatic text segmentation. In: Proceedings of the ACM SIGKDD International Conference on Knowledge Discovery and Data Mining, pp. 20–29 (2004)
2. Chen, C.C., Yang, K.H., Chen, C.L., Ho, J.M.: BibPro: A citation parser based on sequence alignment. IEEE Transactions on Knowledge and Data Engineering 24(2), 236–250 (2012)
3. Chowdhury, G.: Template mining for information extraction from digital documents. Library Trends 48, 182–208 (1999)
4. Cortez, E., da Silva, A.S., Goncalves, M.A., Mesquita, F., de Moura, E.S.: FLUX-CiM: Flexible unsupervised extraction of citation metadata. In: Proceedings of the Seventh ACM/IEEE CS Joint Conf. Digital Libraries, pp. 215–224 (2007)
5. Day, M.Y., Tsai, T.H., Sung, C.L., Hsieh, C.C., Lee, C.W., Wu, S.H., Wu, K.P., Ong, C.S., Hsu, W.L.: Reference metadata extraction using a hierarchical knowledge representation framework. Decision Support Systems 43, 152–167 (2007)
6. Ding, Y., Chowdhury, G., Foo, S.: Template mining for the extraction of citation from digital documents. In: Proceedings of the Second Asian Digital Library Conference, pp. 47–62 (1999)
7. Giles, C.L., Bollacker, K.D., Lawrence, S.: CiteSeer: An automatic citation indexing system. In: Proceedings of the Third ACM Conference on Digital Libraries, pp. 89–98 (1998)
8. Han, H.C., Giles, L., Manavoglu, E., Zha, H., Zhang, Z., Fox, E.A.: Automatic document metadata extraction using support vector machines. In: Proceedings of the Third ACM/IEEE-CS Joint Conference on Digital libraries, pp. 37–48 (2003)
9. Mitchell, T.M.: Machine Learning. McGraw-Hill, Inc. (1997)
10. Peng, F., McCallum, A.: Accurate information extraction from research papers using conditional random fields. In: Proceedings of the Human Language Technology Conference and North American Chapter of the Association for Computational Linguistics (HLT-NAACL), pp. 320–336 (2004)
11. Seymore, K., McCallum, A., Rosenfeld, R.: Learning hidden markov model structure for information extraction. In: Proceedings of the AAAI-99 Workshop on Machine Learning for Information Extraction, pp. 37–42 (1999)
12. Wu, S.H., Tsai, T.H., Hsu, W.L.: Domain event extraction and representation with domain ontology. In: Proceedings of the IJCAI 2003 Workshop on Information Integration on the Web, Acapulco, Mexico (2003)

Wonders of Seabed: Difficulty Evaluation of Management Games Using Neural Network

Cheng-Yi Huang, Yi-Chen Lee, Chia-An Yu,
Yi-Zheng Lee, and Sai-Keung Wong*

National Chiao Tung University, Taiwan (R.O.C.)
cswingo@cs.nctu.edu.tw

Abstract. In management games, players enjoy developing the virtual objects, such as avatars, farms, villages, cities, resources, etc. Usually, the management games do not have a time limit to play. Players know little about how much time that they need to devote in order to quickly build up the virtual objects. This paper studies about the difficulty level of the management games. That is, under a limit amount of time, how far a player can develop the objects. We propose to adopt a neural network to evaluate the difficulty of such kind of games. There is a diverse set of features supported by management games. Thus, we have developed a manageable management game called Wonders of Seabed. Our game is a 3D game and the game story happens at the seabed. Players need to develop a city by managing different resources. Our method can adjust the game difficulty for the players.

Keywords: management games, game balance, game evaluation, neural network, game difficulty.

1 Introduction

Games are useful for people to learn knowledge and they are widely used for educational and training purposes [2][6]. Serious games are also considered for healthcare training [7]. Management games enable players to acquire knowledge and they have educational purposes. Management games have become popular since SimCity. Management games enable players to develop the virtual farms, cities and other virtual items. Players can create any items supported in the games and gradually upgrade the items. The players have fun by organizing and beautifying the virtual items in the game. However, management games could be time consuming and tedious to play. It would take a long time to collect the required items.

We take SimCity as an example. In SimCity, the tax policy is employed to control the development of the cities. A player acts as a government agent. He or she establishes different policy rules to improve the income. Almost all the money is collected from taxes of citizens. If the tax rates are too high in the

---

* Corresponding author.

S.-M. Cheng and M.-Y. Day (Eds.): TAAI 2014, LNAI 8916, pp. 164–177, 2014.

early development stages of the game, the city population would not increase fast enough. Sooner or later, the city would bankrupt since the population is too low for the city to develop. The player must balance the tax rates and expenses to make the citizens happy. While the city is developed, the tax rates should not be too low in the later stages. If the tax rates are too low, there would be insufficient budget to maintain the development of the city even though the citizens are happy. In addition, there are many custom laws that are used for collecting maintenance fees. Players may come up with some sophisticated strategies so as to get as much budget as possible in a short time. In management games, as there are different combinations of strategies to develop virtual items, players enjoy very much in playing this kind of games. Furthermore, if the simulated environment of the games is based on examples in real life, the players also acquire new knowledge while they play the games. However, the major problem of this kind of games is that there is no clue about how long it would take to develop the virtual items to a certain level.

In this paper, we propose to use a neural network to evaluate the difficulty of management games. Based on the evaluation score, we can adjust the difficulty level of the game to suit for the players expectation. There are a vast amount of different management games that have a diverse set of features. We have developed our in-house management game called Wonders of Seabed. We have built a manageable set of features so that we can easily evaluate the progress of the game. While players develop the cities, we evaluate the players financial strategy and adjust the difficulty level of the game. If the players cannot earn enough money at early stages, the game difficulty level would be lowered. On the other hand, if the players could find out a good strategy to play the game, our system would adjust the settings to increase the difficulty level. Thus, our game would achieve a better gaming experience for players.

The organization of the remaining sections of this paper is as follows. Section 2 reviews the previous work. Section 3 covers our game system architecture, implementation and the game rules. Section 4 presents the method for evaluating the game difficulty. Section 5 presents our results and finally Section 6 concludes this paper.

2   Related Work

There are techniques which have been developed for balancing game difficulty. For example, the artificial intelligence technique was adopted to switch the difficulty of the game based on a finite state machine [10]. The range of game difficulty could also be dynamically adjusted according to the fitness values of players [15]. An extending reinforcement learning technique can provide dynamic game balancing [5]. The basic idea is to employ reinforcement learning policy to monitor the game difficulty level that fits the players. In [3], a reinforcement learning technique evaluates the players satisfaction level to achieve challenge-sensitive game balancing. The dynamic game balancing scheme is designed for fighting games. A quantitative modeling technique was proposed to satisfy or entertain players [1]. A challenge-sensitive technique was present to balance the game difficulty level in battle games [4]. In [17], adaptive algorithms were developed to adapt to the playing performance of players to achieve difficulty control. The proposed algorithms were tested on a real-time driving game.

Some techniques are developed based on particle swarm optimization (PSO) to achieve game balance. For example in [8], the powers of two teams are evaluated based on PSO in a role-playing game. In [14], the neural network approach and particle swarm optimization approach were compared. A case study of n-queens problem using PSO was conducted in chess games [9]. Neural networks are also employed in game evaluation. For example, neural network was employed in video games [16], chess games [18] and rules based approach for the self-learning evaluation [13].

3   System Architecture

In this section, we describe the system architecture of a management game, the game rules and the implementation of the system.

We have developed a manageable management game called *Wonders of Seabed* for studying the game difficulty level. We build the game scene under the water. There are four major parameters to control the development of the city: tax, maintenance fee, celebration fee, and human resource fee. Players are required to control these four parameters to achieve certain goals within a given amount of time duration. We integrate our game with a neural network to evaluate the game difficulty level for a player. Our system is able to adjust the game difficulty level to meet the player's expectation. Our game features automatic generated scenes so that a player can enjoy the flourish of his/her own city with only some adjustment of income/outcome. Furthermore, our game would adjust the difficulty to higher level if advanced players want to have a challenging game. In other words, heavy gamers may face a harsh environment while new gamers can have a prosper city with little effort.

3.1   Wonders of Seabed: How to Play

In Wonders of Seabed, the city is divided into four major areas: a residential area, a commercial area, agricultural area, and an administrative center. In each area, there are parameters that the players need to control to improve the income of each area. We hope players could learn how to manage a city by controlling the parameters and gradually understand how to develop a city successfully in a long run.

To develop the city, players need to balance four key values every game month: tax, maintenance fee, celebration fee and human resource fee. A game month is 30 seconds (i.e., half minute) in real world. We describe each of the key values.

Tax. The tax income is the total income of the government unit from the commercial area, agriculture area and residential area. Tax is the main income in this game. If players set the tax to be too high, 'economic recession' may happen. It means that the income from tax will be decreased because citizens do not have enough money to pay tax. Subsequently, the population of the city would decrease as citizens choose to leave the city.

Maintenance Fee. The maintenance fee is the expense that is regularly incurred to maintain the city. For example, if there is sufficient amount of maintenance fee, the city area would be clean. The maintenance fee is used to hire cleaners. If players allocate the maintenance fee below a certain threshold, the number of cleaners would become fewer and fewer. Consequently, the city areas would become dirty, resulting in a 'messy' city. This messy event would lead to the deterioration of the environment. The total income is decreased due to this messy event. The government unit would need to raise money to restore the city environment.

Celebration Free. A celebration event is an event held by the government unit. The purpose of this event is to give a chance for citizens to relax and also encourage them to work hard. If the government unit spends sufficient amount of money to hold parties, citizens would be happy, thereby leading to double the income.

Human Resource Free. The factor of human resource is about public affairs that are managed by the government unit. If there is less human resource, an event called 'wrong policy' would happen. Players should make sure that human resource is kept above a reasonable standard. When a 'wrong policy' occurs, a quarter of the income would be lost.

3.2 Game Implementation

This section presents the implementation of the game. We build the game as a 3D game. There are agents, fish, 3D models of different buildings. Our game runs at real time rate. Players can interact with the game via mouse and keyboard controls. We apply different techniques to control crowd simulation, fish school simulation, and game balance. Figures 1 shows the objects used in the four areas.

In the part of crowd simulation, we apply the A* algorithm to compute the movement of crowd. At the beginning of the game, we record all the possible paths which are computed by using the A* algorithm. Thus, the agents (or citizens) can be animated on the paths based on their current positions and destinations, e.g., walking to farms and returning houses. To avoid collision between agents, our system dynamically adjusts their movement direction if they would collide with each other. After the collision events are resolved, the agents continue to move based on the pre-computed paths.

To simulate a school of fish, we compute the distance between fish. We also compute the distance between each fish and a group of fish. The fish reaction is performed according to the distance between fish and the group [11]. Figure 2 shows the fish reaction behaviors. Basically, we apply repulsive force to push away the approaching fish for avoiding collision. We ignore the details about the mathematical models about controlling the orientation and movement of agents and fish in this paper.

Fig. 1. Virtual objects in Wonders of Seabed. Top, from left to right: resident area and commercial area. Bottom: agricultural area and administrative area. In the residential area, there are sphere-like objects which are agents. We have implemented the caustics effect [12] (i.e., brighter regions) to enhance the attractiveness of the scene.

4   Evaluation Method Using Neural Network

We integrate a neural network with our game system. We apply the neural network to evaluate the game difficulty level based on the players' current performance. Then, our system would adjust the game difficulty level to suit for the players' expectation (see Fig. 3). We hope by doing so that the players would enjoy in playing this kind of management games. While a player develops the virtual city, he/she only knows the outcomes of the city. There are five outcomes of the city in each month. They are stated as follows:

1. money earned in this month? (an integer)
2. is 'economic recession' event happening? (a boolean)
3. is 'messy' event happening (a boolean)
4. is 'happy citizen' event happening (a boolean)
5. is 'wrong policy' event happening (a boolean)

Thus, we use these five outcomes and pass them as inputs to the neural network. We use the neural network to evaluate the expected achievement of the player which reflects the game difficulty level with respect to the player. There are four output of the neural network which are: 1) tax, 2) maintenance fee, 3) celebration fee, and 4) human resource fee.

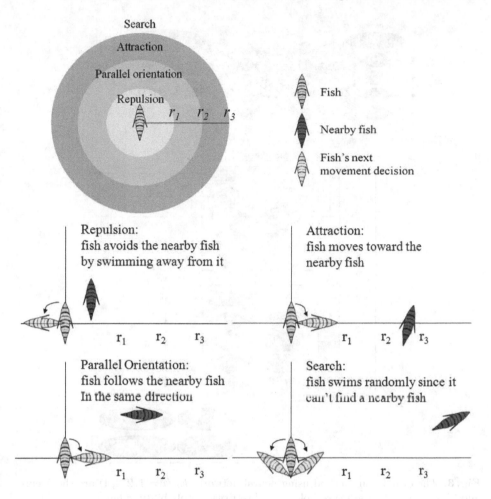

Fig. 2. Modeling fish behaviours based on a distance map

The evaluation process of the game difficulty level is divided into three steps: 1) input generation, 2) neural network forwarding, and 3) neural network back propagation.

In the first step, we compute the four initial values which are tax rate, maintenance fee, celebration fee, and human resource fee. Then, we generate the inputs with the following rules:

1. If the tax is larger than T_{tax}, it has a chance to occur the economic recession event. The player should pay an amount of money P_{eco} as penalty if the economic recession event occurs.
2. There is a chance that a messy event would occur if the assigned maintenance fee is less than $T_{maintain}$. The player should pay P_{messy} as penalty if the messy event occurs.

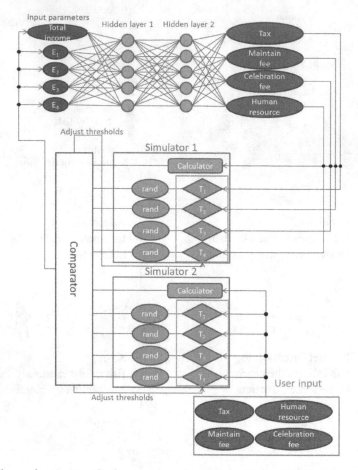

Fig. 3. The evaluation method using neural network. E_i ($i = 1, 2, 3, 4$) are the events and T_j ($j = 1, 2, 3, 4$) are thresholds. *rand* returns a probability value.

3. If celebration fee is bigger than T_{cele}, it has chance to occur a *happy citizen event*. A happy citizen event leads to that the income for the government is doubled for this month.
4. If the human resource fee is less than T_{human}, it has a chance to occur a *wrong policy event*. A wrong policy event would make a loss of a quarter of the income.

The percentage of the chance is decided by the value of the parameters (see Figure 4). One may employ a sophisticated probability model or based on a real statistics to compute the probability for an event to occur. This is beyond the scope of this paper.

In the second step, we multiply each input with the weight and add bias. Then, the result is fed as input to the neural network. After that, we use a discriminant function to get the outcomes of the current developed city.

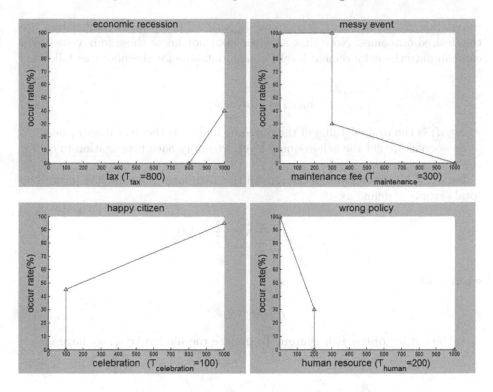

Fig. 4. Probability models for the economic recession event, the messy event, the happy citizen event and the wrong policy event

An output of a neuron is computed as follows:

$$o_j^{(r)} = f(s_j^{(r)}) \tag{1}$$

$$s_j^{(r)} = \alpha \sum_i^{K^{(r-1)}} w_{j,i}^{(r)} o_i^{(r)} + b_j^{(r)} \tag{2}$$

$$f(x) = \frac{1}{1 + e^{-x}} \tag{3}$$

where $K^{(r-1)}$ is the number of neurons of the $(r-1)$-th layer, $o_i^{(r-1)}$ is the i-th output of the $(r-1)$-th layer, $w_{j,i}^{(r)}$ is the weight from the i-th neuron at the $(r-1)$-th layer to the j-th neuron at the (r)-th layer, α is a scalar and $b_j^{(r)}$ is the j-th bias of the r-th layer. Note that:

$$f'(x) = f(x) * (1 - f(x)). \tag{4}$$

In the third step, we calculate the expectation achievement level of the player based on the player's current achievement. This is done by computing the difference between the outputs of the neural network and the four default threshold values (i.e., T_{tax}, $T_{maintain}$, T_{cele}, and T_{human}). These four default values are the desired outcomes. Note that a player does not know these four values. We can compute the achievement level for each outcome for the player as follows:

$$a_{level} = -(d_j - o_j), \tag{5}$$

where d_j is the desired value of the outcome and o_j is the actual outcome.

As soon as we get the achievement level, we apply back propagation to evolve the neural network.

Let $K^{(L)}$ be the number of neurons in the L-th layer, i.e., the last layer. The total error J is define as:

$$J = \frac{1}{2} \sum_{j=1}^{K^{(L)}} e_j^2, \tag{6}$$

where e is:

$$e_j = d_j - o_j. \tag{7}$$

o_j is the output of the j-th neuron. To update the hidden layer, we have

$$\frac{\partial J}{\partial o_j^{(r)}} = \sum_{k=1}^{K^{(r+1)}} \frac{\partial J}{\partial o_k^{(r+1)}} * f'(s_k^{(r+1)}) * w_{kj}^{(r+1)}, \tag{8}$$

$$\Delta w_{ji}^{(r)} = \left[\sum_{k=1}^{K^{(r+1)}} \frac{\partial J}{\partial o_k^{(r+1)}} * f'(s_k^{(r+1)}) * w_{kj}^{(r+1)} \right] * f'(s_j^{(r)}) * o_i^{(r-1)} \tag{9}$$

where $w_{ji}^{(r)}$ is the change of the weight from i-th neuron to the j-th neuron of the r-th layer. $o_k^{(r+1)}$ is the output of the k-th neuron in the $(r+1)$-th layer.

For the last layer, i.e., L-th layer, we have

$$\frac{\partial J}{\partial o_k^{(L)}} = -(d_k - o_k). \tag{10}$$

The weight changes are computed as follows:

$$\Delta w_{kj}^{(L)} = \frac{\partial J}{\partial o_k^{(L)}} * f'(s_k^{(L)}) * o_j^{(L-1)}. \tag{11}$$

We can use the following formula to update all the weights:

$$\mathbf{w}(t+1) = w(t) - \eta * \Delta \mathbf{w},$$

where t is the current step, η is the learning rate (0.3 in our system), and $\Delta \mathbf{w}$ is the change of the weight vector.

After finishing all the three steps, our system learns the settings about the tax, maintenance fee, and so on. And then the process is repeated until the termination condition is satisfied. During the iterations, we record the total amount of money that would be earned. This total amount of money indicates whether or not the game rules are too difficult or not for the player. Our system can then adjust thresholds when necessary to suit for the player's expectation achievement level.

5   Result and Discussion

We performed experiments to evaluate the game difficulty levels in several examples. The number of the evaluation iterations of the neural network was set to 100. Different game time limits were employed. A game time limit is the time duration for playing a game. We recorded the average total incomes, as shown in Table 1. One month game time is set as 30 seconds in real life. Our observations are stated as follows:

1. In Table 1(A), for the first 20 months, the total income is always negative. From 15 months to 20 months, the total income is increasing because the neural network learned better than before. So we could say that players start to know how to balance the parameters to get more income starting from the 20-th month. If we set the stage goal to be 20,000 dollar, a player needs 40 months to clear the stage. In other words, in real life time, the player takes 20 minutes to clear the stage. Based on our experimental results, we can use the neural network to control how long a player needs to clear a stage.

Table 1. Experiment Results

A. $(T_{tax}, T_{maintain}, T_{cele}, T_{human}) = (750,250,100,50)$									
Time to play (month)	10	15	20	30	40				
Average total income	-4804	-5125	-3241	5392	20670				

B. $(T_{tax}, T_{maintain}, T_{cele}, T_{human}) = (750,250,500,500)$									
Time to play (month)	10	15	20	30	40				
Average total income	-5927	-6340	-3515	1592	16213				

C. $(T_{tax}, T_{maintain}, T_{cele}, T_{human}) = (850,100,500,500)$									
Time to play (month)	10	15	20	30	40				
Average total income	-694	1224	6359	20350	40583				

D. $(T_{tax}, T_{maintain}, T_{cele}, T_{human}) = (850,100,100,50)$									
Time to play (month)	10	15	20	30	40				
Average total income	-159	3301	8507	22027	44412				

E. $(T_{tax}, T_{maintain}, T_{cele}, T_{human}) = (600,400,400,400)$									
Time to play (month)	10	15	20	30	40	50	60	70	80	90	100
Average total income	-10428	-13219	-16452	-18420	-16153	-13271	-7164	1654	5427	7278	21462

2. From Table 1(A) and Table 1(B), we can see that the effect of T_{cele} and T_{human} is not so obvious for improving the total income. However, it can increase slightly the time that the player needs to clear the stage.
3. Consider the results in Table 1(B) and Table 1(C) as examples. The larger the range between T_{tax} and $T_{maintain}$ is, the earlier the average total income becomes positive. So, the difference between T_{tax} and $T_{maintain}$ affects greatly the amount of money earned.

6   Conclusions

We have developed a management game and proposed to use a neural network to evaluate the difficulty level for players. Our management game is a real time 3D game. Players can control a government unit to develop a city. Our game has four major areas: a residential area, a commercial area, agricultural area, and an administrative center. The players need to maximize the income within a game time limit. We have applied the neural network to learn how to play the game. Our system computes an expected income within a game time duration. We can estimate the amount of time that a player needs to take to clear a stage. Thus, we can evaluate the game difficulty level with respect to a player while the game is running.

Our approach has limitations. The complexity of the game rules is simple in our game. There are only four parameters to control. If the complexity of the game grows higher, our approach may not be adequate to evolve the neural network to successfully play the game. This is due to that the output may be highly non-linear with respect to the input data. The probability functions are not smooth in our game and they affect the learning speed of the neural network. Furthermore, the major parameters would be changed over time while the player develops the city. The weights of the neural network are not useful anymore after the major parameters are changed. The neural network must be trained again. In the future, we would like to tackle these limitations.

Acknowledgements. We would like to thank the anonymous reviewers for their constructive comments. This work was partially supported by the National Science Council of ROC (Taiwan) under the grant no. NSC 102-2221-E-009-103-MY2 and the Ministry of Science and Technology of ROC (Taiwan) under the grant no. MOST 103-2221-E-009-122-MY3 and 103-2815-C-009-031-E.

References

1. Real-time game adaptation for optimizing player satisfaction. IEEE Transactions on Computational Intelligence and AI in Games 1(2), 121–133 (2009)
2. Game object model version ii: a theoretical framework for educational game development. Educational Technology Research and Development 55(1) (2007)
3. Andrade, G., Ramalho, G., Gomes, S., Corruble, V.: Dynamic game balancing: An evaluation of user satisfaction. In: AAAI Conference on Artificial Intelligence and Interactive Digital Entertainment, pp. 3–8 (2006)

4. Andrade, G., Ramalho, G., Santana, H., Corruble, V.: Challenge-sensitive action selection: an application to game balancing. In: IEEE/WIC/ACM International Conference on Intelligent Agent Technology, pp. 194–200 (2005)
5. Andrade, G., Ramalho, G., Santana, H., Corruble, V.: Extending reinforcement learning to provide dynamic game balancing. In: Proceedings of the Workshop on Reasoning, Representation, and Learning in Computer Games, 19th International Joint Conference on Artificial Intelligence (IJCAI), pp. 7–12 (2005)
6. Bellotti, F., Kapralos, B., Lee, K., Moreno-Ger, P., Berta, R.: Assessment in and of serious games: An overview. Adv. in Hum.-Comp. Int. 2013, 1:1–1:11 (2013)
7. de Ribaupierre, S., Kapralos, B., Haji, F., Stroulia, E., Dubrowski, A., Eagleson, R.: Healthcare training enhancement through virtual reality and serious games 68, 9–27 (2014)
8. Fang, S.-W., Wong, S.-K.: Game team balancing by using particle swarm optimization. Knowledge-Based Systems 34, 91–96 (2012)
9. Hu, X., Eberhart, R.C., Shi, Y.: Swarm intelligence for permutation optimization: a case study of n-queens problem. In: Proceedings of the 2003 IEEE Swarm Intelligence Symposium, pp. 243–246 (2003)
10. Hunicke, R., Chapman, V.: Ai for dynamic difficulty adjustment in games. In: Challenges in Game Artificial Intelligence AAAI Workshop, pp. 91–97 (2004)
11. Huth, A., Wissel, C.: The simulation of the movement of fish schools. Journal of Theoretical Biology 156(3), 365–385 (1992)
12. Iwasaki, K., Dobashi, Y., Nishita, T.: Efficient rendering of optical effects within water using graphics hardware. In: Proceedings of Ninth Pacific Conference on Computer Graphics and Applications, pp. 374–383 (2001)
13. Lee, C.-C.: A self-learning rule-based controller employing approximate reasoning and neural net concepts. International Journal of Intelligent Systems 6(1), 71–93 (2007)
14. Messerschmidt, L., Engelbrecht, A.: Learning to play games using a pso-based competitive learning approach. IEEE Transactions on Evolutionary Computation 8(3), 280–288 (2004)
15. Spronck, P., Sprinkhuizen-Kuyper, I., Postma, E.: Difficulty scaling of game ai. In: Proc. Fifth Int'l Conf. Intelligent Games and Simulation, pp. 33–37 (2004)
16. Stanley, K.O.: Evolving neural network agents in the nero video game. In: Proceedings of the IEEE 2005 Symposium on Computational Intelligence and Games, pp. 182–189 (2005)
17. Tan, C.-H., Tan, K.-C., Tay, A.: Dynamic game difficulty scaling using adaptive behavior-based ai. IEEE Transactions on Computational Intelligence and AI in Games 3(4), 289–301 (2011)
18. Thrun, S.: Learning to play the game of chess. Advances in Neural Information Processing Systems 7, 1069–1076 (1995)

Appendix

We show some of 3D and rendering results of our game in this section. Figure 5 is a far view of our game. A billboard is placed at the back of the scene. The texture of the billboard is seamlessly matched at the boundary of the ground texture. Figure 6 shows the agents moving on the road. The paths of the agents are pre-computed. Figure 7 shows the fish and agent models. We hope that while the players play the game, they can also enjoy seeing the sea life.

Fig. 5. The screenshot of our game system. Our management game is a real time 3D game. There are bubbles, buildings, fish and farms in the scene.

Fig. 6. The agents move on the road

Fig. 7. Fish and agents. (a) Fish in the search state. (b) agents avoid collision. (c) Fish following. (d) the fish model.

Semi-supervised Dimension Reduction with Kernel Sliced Inverse Regression

Chiao-Ching Huang[1] and Kuan-Ying Su[2]

[1] Department of Computer Science and Information Engineering,
National Taiwan University,
[2] National Taiwan University of Science and Technology, Taipei, Taiwan

Abstract. This study is an attempt to draw on research of semi-supervised dimension reduction. Many real world problems can be formulated as semi-supervised problems since the data labeling is much more challenging to obtain than the unlabeled data. Dimension reduction benefits the computation performance and is usually applied in the problem with high dimensional data. This paper proposes a semi-supervised dimension reduction achieved with the kernel sliced inverse regression (KSIR). The prior information is applied to estimate the statistical parameters in the KSIR formula. The semi-supervised KSIR performs comparably to other established methods but much more efficient.

1 Introduction

Dimension reduction is one of the most important research topic in the machine learning and data mining domains for improving computation performance and achieving data visualization. In machine learning, tasks can be classified according to the availability of labeled data, so called the supervised information. Semi-supervised learning (SSL) investigate the problems which only part of the original input data is labeled. Although the supervised learning, so called as classification, is learned from the totally labeled data then predicting unlabeled data, SSL focus on the problem consisted of most unlabeled data and few labeled ones. Real world physical problems usually belong to SSL since the data is readily available but the labeled data is fairly expensive to obtain.

Existing dimension reduction methods can also be categorized into supervised, semi-supervised, and unsupervised according to the existence of labeled data. Fisher Linear Discriminant (FLD) [3] is one of the supervised dimension reduction methods which tries to extract the optimal discriminant vectors with the supervised information. An example of unsupervised dimension reduction method is the well-known Principle Component Analysis (PCA) [5]. It repeatedly finds the principle components, the orthogonal projections, with preserving the covariance structure of data without any labeled information.

Although the PCA [5] is an unsupervised dimension reduction method, which tries to retain the covariance arrangement of original data without the class information, the Sliced Inverse Regression (SIR)[8] exploits the prior knowledge for the dimension reduction. As an supervised dimension reduction method,

S.-M. Cheng and M.-Y. Day (Eds.): TAAI 2014, LNAI 8916, pp. 178–187, 2014.
© Springer International Publishing Switzerland 2014

SIR extracts the effective dimension reduction (*e.d.r*) subspace via using the known class information as the responses in the regression formula. A noted semi-supervised dimension reduction method was proposed in [13] which exploited the pairwise constraint as the semi-supervised information and formulated as an object function for optimization. Using pairwise constraint for dimension reduction could be found in[10].

In this paper, the notation of data is defined as: $A = [\mathbf{x_1}^\top; \cdots ; \mathbf{x}_n^\top] \in \mathbb{R}^{n \times p}$ be the data matrix of input attributes and $y = [y_1; ...; y_n] \in \mathbb{R}^n$ be the corresponding response, the labels. In semi-supervised problems, large portion of Y is unknown but fixed.

2   Supervised Kernel SIR for Dimension Reduction

Sliced inverse regression (SIR) [8] shows that the *e.d.r*. subspace can be estimated from the leading directions, the most informative directions in the input pattern space, in the central inverse regression function with the largest variation. SIR finds the dimension reduction directions by solving the following generalized eigenvalue problem:

$$\Sigma_{E(A|Y_J)}\beta = \lambda \Sigma_A \beta, \tag{1}$$

where Σ_A is the covariance matrix of A, Y_J denotes the membership in J slices, and $\Sigma_{E(A|Y_J)}$ denotes the between-slice covariance matrix based on sliced means given by

$$\Sigma_{E(A|Y_J)} = \frac{1}{n} \sum_{j=1}^{J} n_j(\bar{x}^j - \bar{x})(\bar{x}^j - \bar{x})^\top. \tag{2}$$

Here $\bar{x} = \frac{1}{n}\sum_{i=1}^n x^i$ is the grand mean, $\bar{x}^j = \frac{1}{n_j}\sum_{i \in S_j} x^i$ is the mean value of the jth slice, S_j is the index set for jth slice, n_j is the size of jth slice. Note that the slices are sliced from A according to responses Y.

In supervised problems, $\bar{x}^j$ is simply the class mean of input attributes for the jth class in which the slices are replaced by the classes. An equivalent way to modeling SIR by the following optimization problem:

$$\max_{\beta \in \mathbb{R}^p} \beta^\top \Sigma_{E(A|Y_J)}\beta \text{ subject to } \beta^\top \Sigma_A \beta = 1 \tag{3}$$

The solution, denoted by β_1, givens the first *e.d.r*. direction such that slice means projected along β_1 are most spreading out, where β_1 is normalized with respect to the sample covariance matrix Σ_A. Repeatedly solving this optimization problem with the orthogonality constraints $\beta_k \Sigma_A \beta_l = \delta_{k,l}$, where $\delta_{k,l}$ is the Kronecker delta, and the sequence of solution $\beta_1, ...\beta_d$ forms the *e.d.r*. basis. Some insightful discussion on the SIR methodology and applications can be found in [12, 8].

Since the classical SIR is designed to find a linear transformation from input space to a low dimensional subspace which retains as much information as possible for the output variable y, it may perform poorly in the non-linear tasks. To solve the linearity problem, the kernel sliced inverse regression (KSIR)[11] is proposed to describe key features by few nonlinear components [12]. Let ϕ be a nonlinear mapping and the kernel function $K(\mathbf{x}^\top, \mathbf{z}) = \phi(\mathbf{x})^\top \phi(\mathbf{z})$. KSIR finds the dimension reduction directions by solving the following generalized eigenvalue problem with the kernel method:

$$\Sigma_{E(K|\mathbf{y})}\beta = \lambda \Sigma_K \beta \tag{4}$$

where $K = K(A, A^\top) \in \mathbb{R}^{n \times n}$, Σ_K is the sample covariance matrix of K, and $\Sigma_{E(K|Y_J)}$ denotes the between-slice sample covariance matrix based on the kernelized slice means given by

$$\Sigma_{E(K|Y_J)} = \frac{1}{n} \sum_{j=1}^{J} n_j (\bar{K}^j - \bar{K})(\bar{K}^j - \bar{K})^\top, \tag{5}$$

where $\bar{K} = \frac{1}{n}\sum_{i=1}^{n} K(\mathbf{A}, \mathbf{x}_i)$ and $\bar{K}^j = \frac{1}{n_j}\sum_{i=1}^{n_j} K(\mathbf{A}, \mathbf{x}_i^j)$ is the kernelized slice mean of the jth slice.

Although full kernel matrix computation is time- and memory-consuming and the effective rank of the covariance matrix of kernel data is quite low in the real world applications, these leads to numerical instability and poor estimates of the *e.d.r.* directions. An appropriate solution is to find a reduced-column approximation to K, denoted by $\tilde{K}$ which provides a good approximation, as demonstrated by the reduced support vector machine (RSVM) [7]. The main characteristic is the reduction of the full and dense kernel matrix K from $n \times n$ to $n \times \tilde{n}$, where $\tilde{n}$ is the size of randomly selected subset of kernel matrix. This reduced matrix is much smaller thus the optimization problem can be solved faster. The reduced kernel technique can also be applied to KSIR application. Let $\tilde{A} \in \mathbb{R}^{\tilde{n} \times d}$ be the reduced set, and the reduced KSIR can be formulated as follows:

$$\Sigma_{E(\tilde{K}|Y_J)}\tilde{\beta} = \lambda \Sigma_{\tilde{K}}\tilde{\beta}, \tag{6}$$

where $\tilde{\beta} \in \mathbb{R}^n$ and $\tilde{K} = K(A, \tilde{A}^\top)$, $\tilde{n} \ll n$.

Since the rank of the between-slice covariance of kernel data, $E(K|y)$ in Equation (5), is $(J-1)$, we do not need to solve the whole eigenvalue decomposition problem for this $n \times \tilde{n}$ matrix. Instead, the reduced singular value decomposition (SVD) technique is used to solve for the leading $(J-1)$ components to save computing time.

3   Semi-supervised KSIR for Dimension Reduction

In the supervised dimension reduction via KSIR, the *e.d.r.* subspace is generated by solving a generalized eigenvalue problem. Based on this property of KSIR, we can apply the KSIR from supervised dimension reduction to semi-supervised (SS) dimension reduction approach [9]. In a SS problem, given a small portion of labeled data instances and abundant unlabeled data instances, we try to find a decision function for predicting the labels of new data instances. We assume that the small portion of labeled instances can reflect the statistical structure of the entire data; the global physical meaning can be preserved through sampling without losing much information.

We first use a toy example to experiment the variation using different amount of labeled instance to generate the KSIR $e.d.r.$ subspace. In the experiment, we use the different portions ($t\%$, $t=10, 20, ... 100$) of labeled instances to build the kernelized covariance matrix and find the KSIR projection direction $u_{t\%}$, then using this direction $u_{t\%}$ to project one of cluster mean onto 2D space. Figure 1 visualizes the data distribution of projecting the different portion of data into 2D space. The color dots means different amount of labeled join to generate KSIR directions computing and the big black dot means the entire labeled data to build the KSIR direction which is ground truth here. The distribution of using small portion of labeled data of KSIR direction varies big because of random sampling. Table 1 shows that the numerical result representing the distribution of the project using different portion of labeled data to calculate the KSIR direction. The cluster mean in this toy example somehow means that the original data. No matter from the graphical or from the numerical result, the observation shows that the mean by different amount of labeled data changes slightly.

Table 1. The Average and Standard Deviation of distance to the actual means after projection with different amount of labeled data

Label %	Average	Standard Deviation	Label %	Average	Standard Deviation
10%	1.0558	0.5190	20%	0.6110	0.4009
30%	0.4133	0.3532	40%	0.3317	0.3421
50%	0.2429	0.2957	60%	0.1474	0.1781
70%	0.1133	0.1522	80%	0.0972	0.1334
90%	0.0495	0.0267	100%	0.0000	0.0000

Therefore, it is assumed that the small amount of labeled instances can strongly react the distribution of entire labeled data according to above observations. In this SS problem setting, our methods are based on the constraint that the more uniformly the labelled data distributed, the better estimation of the slice mean would be achieved. The kernalized covariance matrix and the between-class covariance matrix for generating the $e.d.r.$ subspace in KSIR are estimated by the small portion of labeled data in the semi-supervised dimension reduction.

Table 2. The summary of the data sets used in experiments

Data set	instance	dimension	classes	Data set	instance	dimension	classes
USPS	11,000	256	10	PIE CMU	1,700	1,024	5
COIL20	1,440	1,024	20	Adult	4,521	14	2
Text	1,946	7,511	2	COLT 98	1,051	4,840	2

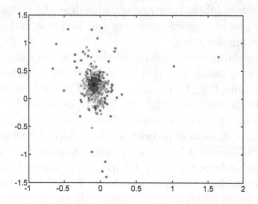

Fig. 1. Data distribution of projecting the different portion of data into 2D space

Here we reformulate semi-supervised dimension reduction which inhert the supervised KSIR. K denotes the kernelized entire dataset and K_ℓ denotes kernelized labelled dataset. The goal becomes to solve the following generality eigenvalue problem:

$$\Sigma_{E(K|Y_J)}\beta = \lambda\Sigma_K\beta. \tag{7}$$

And the between-class covariance will be

$$\Sigma_{E(K|Y_J)} = \frac{1}{n}\sum_{j=1}^{J} n_j(\bar{K_\ell}^j - \bar{K})(\bar{K_\ell}^j - \bar{K})^\top \tag{8}$$

where $\bar{K}$ is the grand mean computed through the kernelized entire dataset, including labelled and unlabelled data, $\bar{K_\ell}^j$ is the sample mean for the jth slice, estimated by the kernelized labeled data of jth slice.

In the observation of solving eigenvalue decomposition problem, the effective rank of the covariance matrix of kernel data is quite low, so we take only top $J-1$ components for KSIR computing, where the J is the number of classes. This restricts its use in binary classification problems since only one-direction can be obtained, which will drop much information in the *e.d.r.* subspace. Basic clustering approach is applied to force training data separate to more classes for finding the KSIR directions. With believe of high dimension data can describe the data more accurate, for the training data with labeled information in binary classification, we use K-means to partition positive instances into two different clusters for each class.Then, using those four classes as their new label for KSIR to compute the $J-1$ direction(we got 3 direction in this example). After getting the direction, the data is put back to the original one and use the original label information for SVM to classify. Thus, we can give more descriptive variables for the classification purpose.

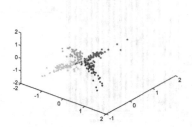

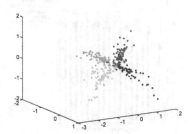

(a) 30% of labeled data to computing
KSIR direction on PIE CMU dataset

(b) Entire labeled data to computing
KSIR direction PIE CMU dataset

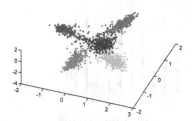

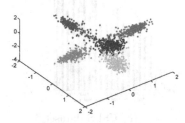

(c) 30% of labeled data to computing
KSIR direction on USPS dataset

(d) Entire labeled data to computing
KSIR direction on USPS dataset

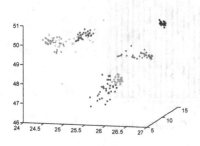

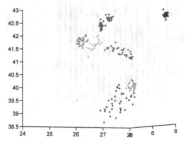

(e) 40% of labeled data to computing
KSIR direction on COIL20 dataset

(f) Entire labeled data to computing
KSIR direction on COIL20 dataset

Fig. 2. Distribution of dimensionalit reduction result by using small amount of labeled
data and entire labeled set to generate the KSIR direction in 3D space

4   Experiment Results

In our experiments, we use the linear smooth support vector machine (SSVM)
in [6] as our classifier. To compare the performance of KSIR algorithm with
other SSL algorithms, we test it on 6 public available real world datasets shown

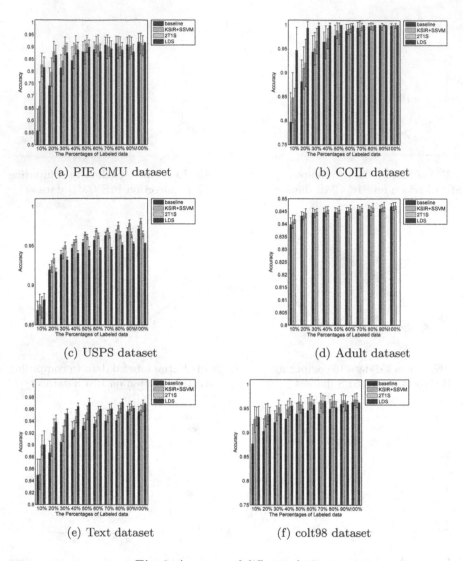

(a) PIE CMU dataset

(b) COIL dataset

(c) USPS dataset

(d) Adult dataset

(e) Text dataset

(f) colt98 dataset

Fig. 3. Accuracy of different datasets

in Table 2. The dimension reduction result project data into 3D by computing KSIR with small amount and entire labeled instances are shown in Figures 2. It illustrates that small amount labeled data is enough to estimated a $e.d.r.$ subspace.

In order to evaluate the overall performance of our semi-supervised KSIR method, we compare it with several state-of-the-art semi-supervised algorithms including the RSVM based two-teachersone-student semi-supervised learning algorithm (2T1S) in[1] and low density separation (LDS) in [2] and a pure supervised benchmark given by running a nonlinear SSVM [6] classifier trained on

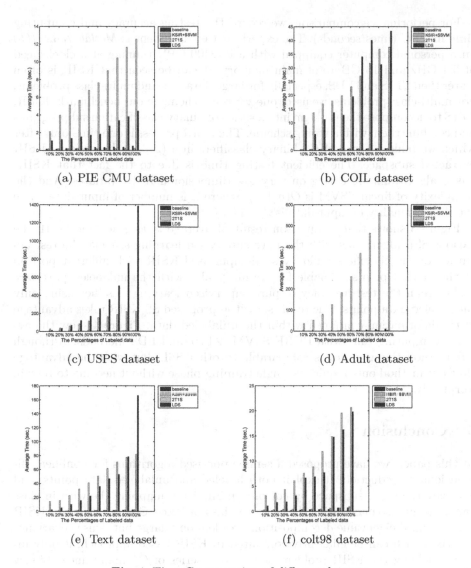

(a) PIE CMU dataset

(b) COIL dataset

(c) USPS dataset

(d) Adult dataset

(e) Text dataset

(f) colt98 dataset

Fig. 4. Time Consumption of different datasets

a fully labeled dataset. We adopt Gaussian kernel functions, and the uniform design(UD) model selection method[4] on 5-fold cross validation to select the penalty parameter(c) and Gaussian kernel width parameter(γ). Each experiment executes 50 times by randomly selecting the training labeled set to build the model. We use one-tenth of the data as our testing set and the other ninetenths of the data as our training set. Note that as the percentage of labeled instances in the training set changes, the entire training and testing data sets remain the same for the entirety of that experiment.

For performance comparison, we record the testing accuracy and computing time in CPU times(seconds). The experiment environment is *Matlab 7(R2010b)* on a personal computer equipped with a i5-2400 CPU running at a clockspeed of 3.1 GHz and 16 GByte of main memory. It can be seen that KSIR is often faster then 2T1S and LDS, especially for large data sets and multi-class problems. For multi-class problems, we used 'one-vs.-one' scheme in our benchmark, KISR, 2T1S to decompose the problem into a series of binary classification subprograms and combine them with a voting scheme. The KSIR process is one-time-only after which we build a series of C_2^J binary classifiers in a $(J-1)$-dimensional KSIR extracted subspace. The efficient testing time is due to the fact that KSIR-based algorithms are acting on very low-dimensional KSIR variates. And the complexity of linear SSVM is $O(n+1)$, where n is number of input data (here the dimensionality of input data is $J-1$).

Figure 3 shows that comparison result of average testing accuracy with the various SSL algorithms with the pure supervised learning scheme.The test accuracy of the classifiers build by semi-supervised KSIR with different portion of the labeled points available for training (also with the unlabeled part) are higher than the test accuracy of pure supervised learning classifier using only the labeled data points. The result show the proposed SS KSIR takes advantage of the information contained within the unlabeled data. Figure 4 show the average computing time with PURE SSVM, 2T1S, and LDS methods. Although our method the accuracy is comparable to other SSL, but with the advantage that our method only requires a single training phase without needing to retrain iteratively.

5   Conclusion

In this paper, we have proposed a semi-supervised algorithms for nonlinear dimensionality reduction. It exploit both labeled and unlabeled data points, and generate the *e.d.r.* subspace by not only minimizing mapping the with-in class variance but also maximizing the between-class variance. Computationally, KSIR is a standard eigenvalue decomposition problem on a large but dense covariance matrix, which can be efficiently computed.In KSIR-based approach, it only involves solving the KSIR problem once and a series of C_2^J many linear binary SVMs in a $(J-1)$-dimensional space. Our method can preserve the intrinsic structure of the data set as shown in the result. Experimental results on single training time for the semi-supervised classificaiton problem retrieval demonstrate the effectiveness of our algorithm. Although the accuracy of our method cannot be as high as another methods, but it save more than 10 times of computing time. This is because our approach only needs a single training pass to compute the directions unlike traditional SSL/transductive learning approaches which usually require many iterations

References

[1] Chang, C.-C., Pao, H.-K., Lee, Y.-J.: An rsvm based two-teachers–one-student semi-supervised learning algorithm. Neural Networks 25, 57–69 (2012)

[2] Chapelle, O., Zien, A.: Semi-supervised classification by low density separation (2004)

[3] Fisher, R.A.: The use of multiple measurements in taxonomic problems. Annals of Eugenics 7, 179–188 (1936)

[4] Huang, C.-M., Lee, Y.-J., Lin, D., Huang, S.-Y.: Model selection for support vector machines via uniform design. Computational Statistics & Data Analysis 52(1), 335–346 (2007)

[5] Jolliffe, I.: Principal component analysis. Wiley Online Library (2005)

[6] Lee, Y.-J., Mangasarian, O.: SSVM: A smooth support vector machine for classification. Computational Optimization and Applications 20(1), 5–22 (2001)

[7] Lee, Y.-J., Mangasarian, O.L.: Rsvm: Reduced support vector machines. In: Proceedings of the first SIAM International Conference on Data Mining, pp. 5–7. SIAM (2001)

[8] Li, K.-C.: Sliced inverse regression for dimension reduction. Journal of the American Statistical Association 86(414), 316–327 (1991)

[9] Su, K.-Y.: Kernel sliced inverse regression (ksir) for semi-supervised learning. Master thesis, NTUST (2014)

[10] Tang, W., Zhong, S.: Pairwise constraints-guided dimensionality reduction. In: SDM Workshop on Feature Selection for Data Mining (2006)

[11] Wu, H.-M.: Kernel sliced inverse regression with applications to classification. Journal of Computational and Graphical Statistics 17(3) (2008)

[12] Yeh, Y.-R., Huang, S.-Y., Lee, Y.-J.: Nonlinear dimension reduction with kernel sliced inverse regression. IEEE Transactions on Knowledge and Data Engineering 21(11), 1590–1603 (2009)

[13] Zhang, D., Zhou, Z.-H., Chen, S.: Semi-supervised dimensionality reduction. In: SDM, pp. 629–634. SIAM (2007)

Identifying Transformative Research in Biomedical Sciences

Yi-Hung Huang[1,2], Ming-Tat Ko[2], and Chun-Nan Hsu[3]

[1]Department of Computer Science, National Taiwan University, Taipei 106, Taiwan
[2]Institute of Information Science, Academia Sinica, Taipei 115, Taiwan
[3]Division of Biomedical Informatics, Department of Medicine, UC San Diego, La Jolla, CA 92093
d98922025@csie.ntu.edu
http://www.csie.ntu.edu.tw/

Abstract. Transformative research refers to research that shifts or disrupts established scientific paradigms. Identifying potential transformative research early and accurately is important for funding agencies and policy makers to maximize the impact of their investment. It also helps scientists identify and focus their attention on promising emerging works and thus improve their productivity. This paper will describe a systematic approach to address this need. We will focus on biomedical sciences for its highest impact. Our key idea is that transformative research creates an observable disruption in the structure of information cascades, the chains of citations that can be traced back to the papers establishing some scientific paradigm, which measure the attention the scientific community pays to this paradigm. Therefore, a disruption occurs when the challenger shifts the attention of the community away from the established paradigm. Our experimental results show that such a disruption is visible soon after the challenger's introduction.

Keywords: Citation Analysis, Network Data Analysis, Transformative Research.

1 Introduction

Transformative research refers to research driven by ideas that lead to emerging concepts, approaches, and/or new subfields of research that shifts or disrupts an established scientific paradigm. According to Thomas Kuhn's influential book titled *The Structure of Scientific Revolutions* [1], the progress of science is a non-incremental process propelled by paradigm shifts. Recently, government funding in research is under increasing scrutiny. The challenge is how to maximize return of investment of research budgets. Funding transformative research is generally agreed as an effective strategy and has been officially placed at the top priority of funding decision by National Institute of Health (NIH) and National Science Foundation (NSF) [2]. Systematically identifying transformative research accurately and early is therefore more critical than ever. This also applies to scientists, who need to constantly monitor the most recent transformative research in related fields to stay competitive in the forefront of their respective fields.

S.-M. Cheng and M.-Y. Day (Eds.): TAAI 2014, LNAI 8916, pp. 188–197, 2014.

This project aims at a data-driven approach to the problem of transformative research identification. Specifically, we will focus on the biomedical sciences. One of the most active and heavily funded areas, the biomedical sciences impact both public health and economy. Recognizing this need and opportunity, NIH has established a new office called Office of Portfolio Analysis (OPA) in 2011 responsible for applying data-driven approaches to funding prioritization and resulting impact evaluation. In a pilot study [3], we have developed a preliminary approach to quantifying transformative research with a *disruption score* and showed that the method can successfully identify transformative scientific papers that disrupt established paradigms in Physics and Computer Science. In this paper, we will show that the disruption score is an accurate early indicator of a successful transformative research in biomedical sciences as well, regardless of whether the challenger paradigm is an instant hit or a classic whose contribution is formally recognized with a Nobel Prize decades later. In addition, this paper will present a model-based approximation algorithm to accelerate the computation of disruption scores for the first time.

Our approach is novel because it measures disruption in terms of a competition between information cascades using a recently developed framework to quantitatively characterize growing information cascades [4]. Using this framework we are able to target transformative challengers of dominant paradigms, rather than investigate them in isolation, as was done by prior studies. This allows us to separate influential research that reinforces dominant paradigms from those that transform them. The field of Bibliometrics in Information and Library Science focuses on measuring scientific impact of research but rarely targets transformative research explicitly. Scientific impact is usually measured by citation counts, and citations-based measures, such as the h-index [5], are widely used to evaluate the productivity of scientists. Disruptions of citation cascade growth of well-established, field-defining papers usually represent an event of "paradigm shift," "breakthrough," emergence of a "disruptive idea," and a successful "transformative research." The closest studies to the proposed work include [6] and [7]. Mazloumian *et al.* [6] characterize how citations are boosted when a work is recognized by a Nobel prize. Their goal is to characterize changes in citation patterns after a transformative research work is recognized, rather than detecting them in advance. Chen [7] describes the use of a time progressive co-citation network to reveal "intellectual turning point" papers, which include hubs, landmarks and pivot nodes in the network. Those are characteristic of highly influential works or works that bridge two important fields. However, they do not explicitly identify how one dominant paradigm is challenged by transformative research like the research here.

2   Approach

2.1   Overview

Figure 1 illustrates the idea behind our method. In (a), we show a citation network, where node 1 and 2 are papers advocating some dominant scientific

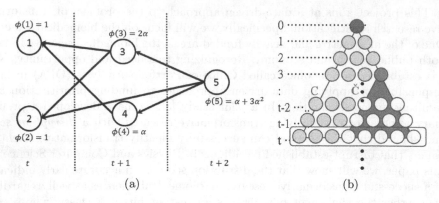

(a)   (b)

Fig. 1. (a) An example of **cascade** and ϕ values in an information network. (b)**Information disruption** by a challenger in an information cascade. The seed of an established paradigm, marked in red, creates a cascade as it is cited by other papers, while a challenger, marked in blue, disrupts the cascade of the seed.

paradigm, and a link from node 3 to 1, means paper 3 cites paper 1. This representation can be generalized to other communication networks, $e.g.$, where nodes are social media users sharing information with followers. The cascade function $\phi(j)$ of a paper j is defined as the sum of $\alpha\phi(i)$ for all papers i that j cites and α is a constant damping factor. For example, $\phi(5) = \alpha\phi(2)+\alpha\phi(3)+\alpha\phi(4) = \alpha + 2\alpha^2 + \alpha^2 = \alpha + 3\alpha^2$. We set $\alpha = 0.5$ in all of our experiments.

Consider Figure 1(b). The cascade C of the seed paper (red node) is the network connecting all papers to the seed via citations. A challenger (blue node) is a paper that advocates a new paradigm. It attracts citations from papers in the cascade, shown as white nodes with blue background, leaving the complement cascade consisting of green nodes. When the challenger represents a noncompeting idea, though there will be papers that cite both seed and challenger, they will not interfere with the growth of the cascade of the seed.

In contrast, a transformative challenger will disrupt the growth of the established paradigm. Without considering the challenger, it may appear that the established paradigm continues to prosper, as its cascade continues to grow, but subtracting part of the cascade taken over by the challenger will reveal that the growth of the remaining cascade (green nodes) slows. In this case, the community's attention shifts to papers that support the challenger paradigm. This can be measured by comparing the growth of the average ϕ over time for all papers in the cascade and the papers in the complement cascade (green nodes).

Formally, a citation network is a directed graph $G = (V, E)$ where V is the set of papers and E is the set of edges indicating citations made by papers. A link $(i \leftarrow j) \in E$ denotes that paper j cites paper i, $cite(j)$ denotes the set of all papers that j cites and $cited(i)$ the set of all papers that cite i. V_t is the set of papers published at time t. We assume that if $(i \leftarrow j) \in E$ and $i \in V_t$ and $j \in V_{t'}$ then $t < t'$. That is, no new paper should be cited by an older paper.

Given one or more papers $S \in V$, a cascade C is a subgraph that contains all citation chains that end at S. The set S is called the *seed* or *root* of the cascade. The seed indirectly exerts influence on all papers in the cascade, but influence decays with the distance to the seed. For a node j in the cascade, the cascade generating function [4] $\phi(j)$ summarizes the structure of the cascade, i.e., all citation chains, up to that point. The cascade generating function quantifies the influence of S on node j, and is defined recursively by

$$\phi(j) := \begin{cases} 1 & \text{if } j \in S \\ \sum_{i \in cite(j)} \alpha \phi(i) & \text{otherwise,} \end{cases} \tag{1}$$

where α is a constant damping factor. Figure 1(a) shows an example cascade and the ϕ values for its nodes. For a paper j published after T time steps (*e.g.*, years) from the publication of the seed, $\phi(j)$ can be written as $\phi(j) = \sum_{p=0}^{T} a_p \cdot \alpha^p$, where the coefficient a_p is the number of distinct paths of length p from one of the seeds to j. The impact of α is that the smaller the value of α, the higher the penalty against long paths. Though it is also possible to assign a unique α_{ij} for each link, assigning a constant 0.5 for all links to control its impact works well in our experiments.

2.2 Cascade Disruption

Consider Figure 1(b). C is the entire cascade rooted by the seed paper. Let $C^{(c)}$ denote the cascade originating from the challenger. We define the *residue cascade*, denoted by $\widetilde{C}$, as the complement subgraph of C obtained by subtracting $C^{(c)}$ from C, *i.e.*,

$$\widetilde{C} := C - (C \cap C^{(c)}) = C \setminus C^{(c)}.$$

By definition, references of papers in $\widetilde{C}$ can only be traced back to the seed papers but not the challenger. We note that it is not necessary for the challenger to be in C. The blue nodes in Figure 1(b) are the root node(s) of the intersection of C and $C^{(c)}$.

Let C_t be the set of papers in cascade C published at time t, *i.e.*, nodes in the bottom red box in Figure 1(b). The average of the cascade function ϕ of papers in C_t is defined by

$$\Phi_t(C) := \frac{1}{|C_t|} \sum_{j \in C_t} \phi(j) = \sum_{p=0}^{t} \overline{a_p} \cdot \alpha^p, \tag{2}$$

where $\overline{a_p}$ is the average of the coefficient a_p in Eq. (2) for j in C_t, and $\overline{a_p}$ indicates on average number of distinct citation chains of length p from papers published at time t to the seeds. The variable Φ_t can be interpreted as an indicator of the seed papers' influence at time t. Let t_0 be the publication time of the challenger paper, the *disruption score* is defined as

$$\delta(\tau) := \sum_{t=t_0}^{t_0+\tau} \log \frac{\Phi_t(C)}{\Phi_t(\widetilde{C})} = \sum_{t=t_0}^{t_0+\tau} \left(\log \Phi_t(C) - \log \Phi_t(\widetilde{C}) \right). \tag{3}$$

To obtain the disruption score, we need to compute ϕ of the nodes in the cascade. A citation network is a directed acyclic graph if cycles are considered as errors. From Eq. (1), traversing the citation network in a topological order [8] and updating ϕ values along the way will guarantee that no backtracking is necessary to compute all ϕ values for all nodes. Therefore, we can apply topological sorting to compute ϕ and obtain the disruption scores. The time complexity of topological sorting is $O(|V_C| + |E_C|)$, which is linear to the sum of the number of nodes and edges in cascade C.

2.3   Model-Based Approximation

Computation of the scores must be efficient given ever-growing number of biomedical sciences papers and citations. One challenge of the proposed approach is that the computation of the cascade structure and pairwise comparison can be intractable. We have several strategies to accelerate the computation. One strategy is to avoid exhaustive pairwise comparison by reusing intermediate results. Suppose we would like to rank 100 candidate challengers by their disruption scores. A brute-force approach is to compute the residue cascades for each of the candidates. By sorting these candidates in their topological order in the citation network, the ϕ values computed for the upstream candidates can be reused for the downstream candidates and significantly reduce the computational costs.

Another strategy is by approximation, where we can take advantage of the fact that citations decay exponentially over time to estimate the size of cascades. Computing average cascade Φ can be intractable. A brute-force algorithm to compute Φ is to traverse the citation network and update ϕ for each node visited by a topological sorting algorithm. Such an exhaustive search algorithm slows down as the size of the citation network increases exponentially in recent years. Arbesman [9] shows that, for any paper, the longer away from the citing paper, the less likely that the paper will be cited, and the decay is approximately exponential. Also, modern papers cite more often and the average citations increase each year. The result suggests that it is possible to model the citation counts accurately and we will take advantage of that to derive an approximation algorithm to accelerate the computation of cascade overtaking. We now present accurate approximation algorithms scalable to very large scale citation networks by taking advantage of properties of Φ.

It has been suggested that citation counts of papers decay exponentially over time [9] and the rate of decay can be estimated accurately. We plotted the curves of the annual average citation count of the papers in the APS citation network dataset as shown in Figure 2, which shows that the longer away from the citing paper, the less likely that the paper will be cited, and the decay is approximately exponential. Also, modern papers cite more often and the average citations increase each year. The plot suggests that it is possible to model the citation counts accurately and we will take advantage of that to derive an approximation algorithm to accelerate the computation of cascade overtaking.

Given a cascade C, We model the number of citations by a function $\Gamma_C(t, \tau)$, the average citations from papers published in time t to papers published τ time

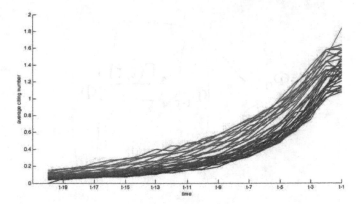

Fig. 2. Average citations of papers in the APS citation network dataset. Each curve is for the papers published in one year from 1970 (darkest) to 2009 (brightest). The curve plots the change of the average citations to the past years. The horizontal-axis indicates how many year from the publication time t.

steps (*i.e.*, year, in this case) early. $\Gamma_C(t, \tau)$ can be estimated and presented as a data point on a curve in the plot.

Consider the problem of computing Φ. If we consider paper $j \in C_t$ as a random variable, then $\Phi_t(C)$ is by definition the expectation of $\phi(j)$. The number of citations from j to papers published in time $t - \tau$ will also be a random variable and its expectation will be $\Gamma_C(t, \tau)$. Then the expected contribution of these citations to $\phi(j)$ will be $\Gamma_C(t, \tau) \cdot \alpha \cdot \Phi_{t-\tau}(C)$ approximately. Figure 3 illustrates this idea. Therefore, we can derive an approximation of Φ as follows:

$$\Phi_t(C) = \mathbb{E}_{j \sim C_t}[\phi(j)]$$

$$= \mathbb{E}_{j \sim C_t}\left[\sum_{\tau=1}^{t} \alpha \sum_{i \in C_{t-\tau}} I[i \in cite(j)]\phi(i)\right]$$

$$= \sum_{\tau=1}^{t} \alpha (\mathbb{E}_{i \sim C_{t-\tau}}[\sum I[i \in cite(j)]]\mathbb{E}_{i \sim C_{t-\tau}}[\phi(i)] + \mathrm{cov}_{i \sim C_{t-\tau}}[\sum I[i \in cite(j)], \phi(i)]) \quad (4)$$

$$\approx \sum_{\tau=1}^{t} \alpha \Gamma_C(t, \tau)\Phi_{t-\tau}(C). \quad (5)$$

We note that $I[s]$ is the identity function that returns 1 if the parameter s is true and 0 otherwise. The difference between the approximation (5) and (4) is the sum of the covariance terms in (4). These terms are zero under the assumption that the cascade function value ϕ of a paper, which depends on how many papers it cites, and how often it is cited in the future, are uncorrelated. The assumption is reasonable and can be confirmed empirically. Therefore, we expect that the approximation error will be negligible.

Compared to an exhaustive search algorithm, computing $\Phi_t(C)$ using Eq. (5) reduced the complexity from exponential to quadratic. Since the equation is defined recursively, there are plenty of room to optimize its implementation.

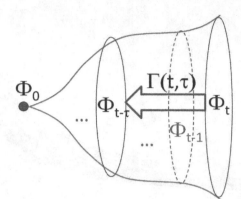

Fig. 3. Estimating average cascade function values Φ by modeling citation counts Γ

The preprocessing step that estimates Γ requires to visit each node once and therefore its time complexity is linear to the size of the citation network.

3 Experimental Results

Here we report our results of testing if the approach works in the biomedical sciences, too. Our citation data is from PubMed (`www.ncbi.nlm.nih.gov/pubmed`), which provides E-utilities, an application programming interface service that allows users to query for its contents, including a "cited_in" list for each article, via a computer program remotely.

We plot the growth of $\Phi_t(C)$ (red curve) and $\Phi_t(\tilde{C})$ (green curve), as illustrated in Figures 4, where we also show the growth of the challenger cascade $\Phi_t(C^{(c)})$ (blue curve) for reference. The value of Φ_t for both the seed (red) and challenger (blue) papers may both grow rapidly, but the growth of the residue cascade will start to flatten out and drop if the challenger successfully shifts the attention of the community. Otherwise, the green curve will continue to grow. The disruption score can be visualized as the area between the red and green curves in Figures 4 from t_0 to $t_0 + \tau$. The disruption score allows us to identify and measure the impact of the challenger paper.

Our first case is the confirmation of *Helicobacter Pylori* as the major cause of peptic ulcer by Marshall and Warran in 1984 [10]. Prior to their work, the established paradigm believed that excess acid in the stomach was the cause and the standard treatment is antacid. Marshall and Warren's early manuscripts were rejected because previous studies had established that discoveries of bacteria in patients of peptic ulcer were due to contamination [11–13]. Unlike the case of high-temperature superconductivity, which was widely recognized as a breakthrough and immediately become an instant hit, Marshall and Warran's work is a contrast case and perfect to test if our approach can detect their work as transformative even though their contribution was not recognized for a Nobel Prize until 2005.

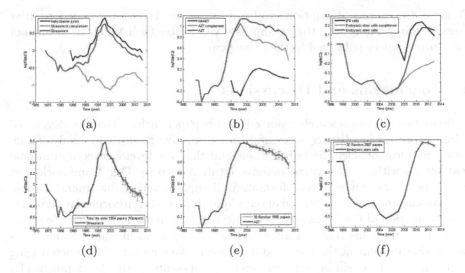

Fig. 4. Transformative research in the biomedical sciences. (a) and (d) shows the case of H. Pylori vs. traditional stress/acid paradigm; (b) and (e) shows the case of HAART vs. AZT for AIDS therapy; (c) and (f) shows iPS vs. embryonic stem cells.Notice the split between the red curves and green curves, indicating cascade disruption.

Figure 4(a) and (d) shows that Marshall and Warran's 1984 papers created a cascade disruption much wider than 30 related papers published in the same year. The gap (dropping of the green curve) can be observable as early as 1985, right after its publication.

To test the specificity of cascade interruption, we randomly selected 30 highly cited papers published in the same year as each of the transformative research papers that we selected. These randomly selected papers served as negative controls. We plot the growth of their cascades and computed the means and standard deviations of the average cascades of these 30 challengers and the green curve shows those for their residue cascades, as shown in Figure 4(d). The curves show that though the growth of their cascades varies widely (blue curve), the complements of the dominating cascade are hardly disrupted (green curve).

We tested two other renown cases of transformative research in the biomedical sciences: HAART vs. AZT for the treatment of AIDS and induced pluripotent stem cells (iPS) vs. embryonic stem cells. Zidovudine or azidothymidine (AZT) [14, 15] is the first approved drug in the U.S. for AIDS therapy. However, the best AZT can do is to slow down virus replication but never completely cure the disease until a "cocktail" therapy known as highly active antiretroviral therapy (HAART) was proposed by David D. Ho *et al.* [16]. Research on the stem cells used to require a technique that derives the stem cells from early-stage embryo [17] and raised ethical concerns.iPS [18, 19] is a breakthrough that allows for derivation of stem cells without the controversial use of embryos. As shown in

Figure 4, the cascade disruption can be observed for the cases of transformative research immediately (our time stamp is a year) after their publication but not for control papers published in the same year.

4 Conclusions and Discussions

Contributions of the research reported in this paper include that we developed a framework for identifying successful transformative research by analyzing citation patterns of scientific publications and that we developed computational scalable algorithms to analyze massive citation records. Our framework that considers a paradigm shift as information disruption will enable quantification, comparison, and characterization of paradigm shifts and transformative research. The foundation of the framework is a function that characterizes cascade structures. Exploring this function allows us to develop efficient and scalable algorithms that implement the proposed framework. We have presented encouraging results here and we will build on the success and complete the development of a theory of transformative research as our future work.

Acknowledgments. The project is supported in part by grant 100-2221-E-014-MY3 from the National Science Council, Taiwan, to YHH and MTK and the Big Data to Knowledge (BD2K) Data Discovery Index Coordination Consortium (BioCaddie) from the National Institute of Health, USA, to CNH. The authors would like to thank Professor Y.-T. Liu at the Moores Cancer Center, UC San Diego, for his comments and help with the early draft of this manuscript.

References

1. Kuhn, T.S.: The Structure of Scientific Revolutions, 3rd edn. University of Chicago Press (December 1996)
2. National Science Board (U.S.). Enhancing support of transformative research at the National Science Foundation [electronic resource]. National Science Foundation, Arlington, VA (2007)
3. Huang, Y.H., Hsu, C.-N., Lerman, K.: Identifying Transformative Scientific Research. In: Proc. of IEEE International Conference on Data Mining (ICDM) (2013)
4. Ghosh, R., Lerman, K.: A framework for quantitative analysis of cascades on networks. In: Proceedings of Web Search and Data Mining Conference (WSDM) (February 2011)
5. Hirsch, J.E.: An index to quantify an individual's scientific research output. Proceedings of the National Academy of Sciences 102(46), 16569–16572 (2005)
6. A. Mazloumian, Y.-H. Eom, D. Helbing, S. Lozano, S. Fortunato: How Citation Boosts Promote Scientific Paradigm Shifts and Nobel Prizes. PLoS ONE 6(5), e18975+ (2011)
7. Chen, C.: Searching for intellectual turning points: Progressive knowledge domain visualization. Proceedings of the National Academy of Sciences of the United States of America, 101(suppl. 1), 5303–5310 (2004)

8. Kahn, A.B.: Topological sorting of large networks. Communications of the ACM 5(11), 558–562 (1962)

9. Arbesman, S.: The Half-life of Facts: Why Everything We Know Has an Expiration Date, 1st edn. Current Hardcover (September 2012)

10. Marshall, B.J., Warren, J.R.: Unidentified curved bacilli in the stomach of patients with gastritis and peptic ulceration. Lancet, 1(5), 1311-5 (1984)

11. Palmer, E.D.: Investigation of the gastric mucosa spirochetes of the human. Gastroenterology 27(2), 218–220 (1954)

12. Patrick, W.J., Denham, D., Forrest, A.P.: Mucous change in the human duodenum: a light and electron microscopic study and correlation with disease and gastric acid secretion. Gut 15(10), 767–776 (1974)

13. Steer, H.W., Colin-Jones, D.G.: Mucosal changes in gastric ulceration and their response to carbenoxolone sodium. Gut 16(8), 590–597 (1975)

14. Mitsuya, H., Weinhold, K.J., Furman, P.A., St Clair, M.H., Lehrman, S.N., Gallo, R.C., Bolognesi, D., Barry, D.W., Broder, S.: 3'-azido-3'-deoxythymidine (bw a509u): an antiviral agent that inhibits the infectivity and cytopathic effect of human t-lymphotropic virus type iii/lymphadenopathy-associated virus in vitro. Proceedings of the National Academy of Sciences, 82(20):7096–7100 (1985)

15. Furman, P.A., Fyfe, J.A., St Clair, M.H., Weinhold, K., Rideout, J.L., Freeman, G.A., Lehrman, S.N., Bolognesi, D.P., Broder, S., Mitsuya, H.: Phosphorylation of 3'-azido-3'-deoxythymidine and selective interaction of the 5'-triphosphate with human immunodeficiency virus reverse transcriptase. Proceedings of the National Academy of Sciences 83(21), 8333–8337 (1986)

16. Perelson, A.S., Neumann, A.U., Markowitz, M., Markowitz, M., Leonardy, J.M., Ho, D.D.: Hiv-1 dynamics in vivo: Virion clearance rate, infected cell lifespan, and viral generation time. Science 271, 1582–1586 (1996)

17. Thomson, J.A., Itskovitz-Eldor, J., Shapiro, S.S., Waknitz, M.A., Swiergiel, J.J., Marshall, V.S., Jones, J.M.: Embryonic stem cell lines derived from human blastocysts. Science 282(5391), 1145–1147 (1998)

18. Takahashi, K., Tanabe, K., Ohnuki, M., Narita, M., Ichisaka, T., Tomoda, K., Yamanaka, S.: Induction of pluripotent stem cells from adult human fibroblasts by defined factors. Cell 131(5), 861–872 (2007)

19. Takahashi, K., Yamanaka, S.: Induction of pluripotent stem cells from mouse embryonic and adult fibroblast cultures by defined factors. Cell 126(5), 663–676 (2006)

A Weight-Sharing Gaussian Process Model Using Web-Based Information for Audience Rating Prediction

Yu-Yang Huang[1], Yu-An Yen[1], Ting-Wei Ku[1], Shou-De Lin[1],
Wen-Tai Hsieh[2], and Tsun Ku[2]

[1] Dept. of Computer Science and Information Engineering,
National Taiwan University, Taipei, Taiwan
[2] Institute for Information Industry, Taipei, Taiwan
{myutwo150,lovelove6402,martin79831}@gmail.com,
sdlin@csie.ntu.edu.tw,
{wentai,cujing}@iii.org.tw

Abstract. In this paper, we describe a novel Gaussian process model for TV audience rating prediction. A weight-sharing covariance function well-suited for this problem is introduced. We extract several types of features from Google Trends and Facebook, and demonstrate that they can be useful in predicting the TV audience ratings. Experiments on a dataset consisting of daily dramas show that the proposed model outperforms the other conventional models given the same feature set.

Keywords: Time Series, Gaussian Process, Audience Rating Prediction.

1 Introduction

Time series analysis is an active research area with many real-world applications including price forecasting [12] and sales prediction [9]. A typical method relies on historical data sequences to predict upcoming data points. In this paper, we focus on television audience rating prediction. The goal is to accurately predict the rating of an upcoming TV episode, and to analyze the most crucial factors that cause the audience ratings to fluctuate.

Gaussian Process Regression (GPR) [16] is used to predict the audience ratings. We analyze variants of GPR models, and propose a weight-sharing kernel to deal with the overfitting issue caused by the increasing number of hyperparameters. The experiments show that, with the weight-sharing technique applied, our GPR model outperforms the other competitors in predicting the audience ratings.

Furthermore, we propose three novel types of features to boost the prediction performance. Different from previous works, our model relies not only on classic time series features such as historical ratings, but also on features extracted from social networks and search engines. For example, trend information from Google Trends, opinion polarity and popularity information from Facebook are used in the prediction. We show how such information can be adapted in the proposed GPR model.

S.-M. Cheng and M.-Y. Day (Eds.): TAAI 2014, LNAI 8916, pp. 198–208, 2014.

The main contributions of this work are summarized as follows:

- We modify a standard kernel of GPR model to avoid overfitting, and make it more suitable for the TV audience rating prediction problem.
- We propose three novel types of web-based features: trend features, social network features, and opinion features for better performance.
- We conduct experiments to verify the validity of the model and features.

2   Related Work

Audience rating prediction is treated as a time series forecasting problem in the field of statistics and data analysis. Well-known models such as autoregressive model, moving average model, or the hybrid (ARIMA), or the more advanced ones such as generalized autoregressive conditional heteroskedasticity (GARCH) [2] and the nonlinear extension of it (NGARCH) [12] are all plausible models that can be applied. However, those models may not be the best choice for audience rating prediction because they do not consider specific characteristic of the ratings. Researchers have shown that using time-based and program-based covariates provides a more effective way to forecast the audience ratings [5, 6] than general time series models, as these models consider correlations between rating, genre, show duration, live status, etc.

Another serious drawback of general time series models is that they cannot consider external features such as information from social media and search engine. Such external and social information has been shown effective in forecasting. In [1], a work using chatters from Twitter to predict future revenue of movies is proposed. The works in [4, 8] propose to perform audience rating prediction utilizing the count of posts and comments from social media. Our work further extends the idea to exploit opinion mining and search engine such as Google Trends to enhance the prediction performance.

3   Framework and Features

In this paper, the TV audience rating prediction problem is modeled as a supervised learning task. To forecast near-future ratings, historical data together with the following listed features are used as the training input for the models.

1. Basic Time Series Features

Similar to other basic time series forecasting models, the ratings of the previous episodes, the rating of the first episode, and binary indicator variables corresponding to weekdays are used as features.

2. Social Network Features

Nowadays, TV companies often host "Fan Pages" on social networking sites such as Facebook. On these pages, companies run promotional campaigns, face-to-face events, polls, and provide previews of the next episodes. Also, it provides a platform for the fans to interact with each other and show their support or oppose to the show.

To model such effects, the daily cumulative numbers of "posts", "shares", "likes", "comments" on the official Facebook Fan Pages of the dramas are included as features.

3. Opinion Polarity Features

Users may express their thoughts toward a show via a Facebook Fan Page, and such opinions will have influence on others' opinions. For example, if most of the fans are looking forward to the upcoming episode, it will be reasonable to assign a higher audience rating for the new episode. Thus we propose to analyze the polarity (i.e. positive or negative) of users' posts and replies on Facebook fans page. We use the daily cumulative number of positive and negative words in both posts and comments as the opinion polarity features.

4. Trend Features

Google Trends is a useful tool provided by Google Inc. to investigate the popularity of a keyword in a region. Given certain time period, it gives the number of searches for a keyword relative to the total number of searches across this period. The displayed number is normalized such that the highest number is equal to 100 and the lowest number is equal to zero. For each drama, we collect time series data from Google Trends for three different sets of keywords. We use drama name as well as actor/actress's name as queries in Google Trends to obtain the corresponding features.

4   Methodology

4.1   Gaussian Process Regression (GPR)

A typical regression problem can be formulated as

$$y = f(\mathbf{x}) + \varepsilon \tag{1}$$

where $\mathbf{x}$ is the input vector, y is the observed target value, and f is a function that models the underlying process of generating the data points $\{(\mathbf{x}_i, y_i): i = 1, \dots, N\}$. An additive independent and identically distributed Gaussian noise $\varepsilon \sim \mathcal{N}(0, \sigma_n^2)$ is assumed.

There are two equivalent ways to derive the predictive distribution for Gaussian process regression, namely the weight-space view and the function-space view [13]. In the following paragraphs, we will give a brief introduction to the main concepts of GPR in the function-space.

A random process $f = \{f(\mathbf{x}): \mathbf{x} \in \mathcal{X}\}$ is defined as a collection of random variables $f(\mathbf{x})$ indexed by an ordered set $\mathcal{X}$. In the audience rating prediction problem, we consider the input space $\mathcal{X} \subseteq \mathfrak{R}^d$, where d is the dimension of input vectors. The random variable $f(\mathbf{x})$ therefore represent the value of the random function f evaluated at the data point $\mathbf{x}$. If normality is assumed, the random process is called a *Gaussian process* (GP). An important property of GP is that any finite collection of the random variables $f(\mathbf{x})$ will be jointly normally distributed.

A Gaussian process is completely defined by its second-order statistics. The mean function and the covariance function of a Gaussian process can be defined as follows:

$$m(\mathbf{x}) = E[f(\mathbf{x})] \tag{2}$$

$$k(\mathbf{x}, \mathbf{x}') = E[(f(\mathbf{x}) - m(\mathbf{x}))(f(\mathbf{x}') - m(\mathbf{x}'))] \tag{3}$$

and $f \sim \mathcal{GP}(m(\mathbf{x}), k(\mathbf{x}, \mathbf{x}'))$. Without loss of generality, it is common to consider GPs with mean function $m(\mathbf{x}) \equiv 0$ to simplify the derivation. In this case, a GP is fully specified given its covariance function.

Since it is infeasible to consider all possible random functions, certain assumptions must be made when making inference. By restricting the underlying function f to be distributed as a GP, the number of choices is reduced. Furthermore, a Gaussian predictive distribution can be derived in closed-form under such assumption. If we consider only zero-mean Gaussian processes, then for a test input $\mathbf{x}^*$, the mean and variance of the predictive distribution can be computed as follows [16]:

$$\mu(\mathbf{x}^*) = \mathbf{k}^T K^{-1} \mathbf{y} \tag{4}$$

$$\sigma^2(\mathbf{x}^*) = k(\mathbf{x}^*, \mathbf{x}^*) - \mathbf{k}^T K^{-1} \mathbf{k} \tag{5}$$

where $\mathbf{k} = \left(k(\mathbf{x}^*, \mathbf{x}_1), ..., k(\mathbf{x}^*, \mathbf{x}_N)\right)^T$, $K = \left[K_{ij}\right]$ is the covariance matrix of training input vectors with $K_{ij} = k(\mathbf{x}_i, \mathbf{x}_j)$, and $\mathbf{y} = (y_1, y_2, ..., y_N)^T$ is a vector of training target values. The point prediction is commonly taken to be the mean of the predictive distribution, i.e. $y^* = \mu(\mathbf{x}^*)$.

4.2   Weight-Sharing Kernel

The covariance function is also called the *kernel* of a GP. As previously mentioned, the behavior of a zero-mean GP can be fully specified provided its covariance function. For regression problems, we want to assign similar prediction values to two input vectors that are close in space. In other words, if two similar time series are observed, the model should be able to give similar predictions. A widely used kernel possessing this property is the radial basis function (RBF) kernel, which is called a squared exponential (SE) kernel in GP literature. It has the form

$$k(\mathbf{x}, \mathbf{x}') = \exp\left(-\frac{1}{2}\sum_{i=1}^{d} \frac{(x_i - x'_i)^2}{l_i^2}\right) \tag{6}$$

where x_i is the i-th dimension of vector $\mathbf{x}$ and d is the dimension of input vectors.

There are d hyperparameters $\boldsymbol{\theta} = (l_1, l_2, ... l_d)^T$ for this kernel. The hyperparameters are called the *characteristic length-scales*. It serves as a distance measure along the i-th dimension. The effect of these hyperparameters can be shown more clearly if we rewrite Eq. 6 as

$$k(\mathbf{x}, \mathbf{x}') = \prod_{i=1}^{d} \exp\left(-\frac{(x_i - x'_i)^2}{2l_i^2}\right). \tag{7}$$

If the characteristic length-scale for the i-th dimension is large, the i-th exponential term will be close to zero, and the covariance will be independent of that input dimension. This is a form of *automatic relevance determination* (ARD) [11] or "soft" feature selection. When we are estimating the hyperparameters, the irrelevant input dimensions will be ignored by fitting the length-scales to a relatively large value. However, this type of kernel introduces one parameter per input dimension. The common problem of overfitting is severe if we are dealing with high-dimensional inputs [3]. This is especially the case for time series prediction. If we have M types of co-varying features, and for each of them we consider only T time steps before current prediction, the total number of features is $d = M \times T$, which will increase rapidly as we consider longer historical sequences. This will limit the power of the time series model in that it must either include less features or use shorter historical sequences. Furthermore, the time needed to train an ARD kernel is significantly longer than its isotropic counterpart (i.e. setting $l_1 = l_2 = \cdots = l_n = l$). The isotropic SE kernel, although usually performs well, suffers from its inability to distinguish the importance of different input dimensions. Therefore, we propose a *weight-sharing kernel* that strikes a balance between the two.

In the field of time series prediction, the input features usually come from co-varying time sequences and therefore are naturally grouped. For example, the features extracted from Google Trends can be viewed as a feature group. The main idea is to reduce the number of hyperparameters by sharing the same length-scale among features belonging to the same group, while at the same time possessing the ability to determine the importance of different groups of features.

The kernel consists of a weighted sum of SE kernels:

$$\begin{aligned}
k(\mathbf{x}, \mathbf{x}') = \sum_{g \in G_T} v_g \exp\left(-\frac{1}{2l_g^2} \sum_{i=1}^{d_g} (x_i - x'_i)^2\right) \\
+ \sum_{g \in G_{T'}} v_g \exp\left(-\frac{1}{2} \sum_{i=1}^{d_g} \frac{(x_i - x'_i)^2}{l_{i,g}^2}\right).
\end{aligned} \tag{8}$$

The first term is a weighted sum of isotropic SE kernels which are designed for time co-varying features. We denote the set of time co-varying feature groups (i.e. "*Opinion*", "*Google Trends*", "*Facebook*") as G_T. For each feature group g, the number of features in the group is denoted as d_g, and the overall importance of the group is v_g. The same length scale l_g is shared among all features belonging to the group. This can significantly reduce the number of hyperparameters.

The second term of the kernel is a weighted sum of ARD SE kernels. We use $G_{T'}$ to denote the set of time-invariant feature groups, or features that require a separate length-scale for each dimension to function properly (e.g. *"First Episode rating"*, *"Past 3 Episodes ratings"* and *"Weekdays"*). Usually, the number of time-invariant features is much less than the time co-varying features, so this term would not add too many hyperparameters to the model.

As a brief example, assume that we consider M co-varying time sequences, each of them is of length T. In our case $T = 4$ and there are $M = 11$ time co-varying features (4 from *"Opinion"*, 3 from *"Google Trends"*, and 4 from *"Facebook"*). An ARD kernel will have 44 hyperparameters to be learnt, making the inference slow and the prediction inaccurate. On the other hand, the weight-sharing kernel introduces 2 hyperparameters (i.e. l_g and v_g) for each feature group, merely 6 in total. With the weight-sharing kernel applied, the inference is much faster and, as will be shown in the Experiment section, a better performance is achieved.

4.3   Training

In general, the hyperparameters of a Gaussian process model can be learnt by maximizing the marginal likelihood or by using Markov chain Monte Carlo methods such as slice sampling [10]. We adopt in this work the maximum marginal likelihood framework, also known as Type-II maximum likelihood (ML-II) or empirical Bayes.

In the ML-II framework, the hyperparameters are chosen by maximizing the probability of observing target values $\mathbf{y}$ given the input $X = \{\mathbf{x}_i : i = 1, \dots, N\}$. Let $\mathbf{f} = (f(\mathbf{x}_1), f(\mathbf{x}_2), \dots, f(\mathbf{x}_N))^T$ be a vector of function values evaluated at the N training input data points. Since the function $f \sim \mathcal{GP}(m(\mathbf{x}), k(\mathbf{x}, \mathbf{x}'))$ is a random function sampled from a GP, the vector $\mathbf{f}$ is an N-dimensional normally distributed random vector, i.e. $\mathbf{f}|X \sim \mathcal{N}(0, K)$. The exact form of the marginal likelihood is given by marginalizing over the random vector $\mathbf{f}$:

$$p(\mathbf{y}|X, \boldsymbol{\theta}) = \int p(\mathbf{y}|\mathbf{f}, X) p(\mathbf{f}|X, \boldsymbol{\theta}) \, d\mathbf{f} \qquad (9)$$

where $\boldsymbol{\theta}$ is a vector of hyperparameters of the kernel. From Eq. 1 it is clear that $\mathbf{y} \sim \mathcal{N}(0, K_y)$, where $K_y = K + \sigma_n^2 I$. It follows that the log marginal likelihood is

$$\log p(\mathbf{y}|X, \boldsymbol{\theta}) = -\frac{1}{2}\mathbf{y}^T K_y^{-1}\mathbf{y} - \frac{1}{2}\log|K_y| - \frac{n}{2}\log 2\pi . \qquad (10)$$

To find the best hyperparameters with ML-II, we must take the derivatives of the log marginal likelihood with respect to the hyperparameters, as shown below:

$$\frac{\partial}{\partial \theta_j}\log p(\mathbf{y}|X, \boldsymbol{\theta}) = \frac{1}{2}\mathbf{y}^T K_y^{-1}\frac{\partial K_y}{\partial \theta_j}K_y^{-1}\mathbf{y} - \frac{1}{2}\mathrm{tr}\left(K_y^{-1}\frac{\partial K_y}{\partial \theta_j}\right). \qquad (11)$$

The above computations involve matrix inversion, which takes $O(N^3)$ time complexity. It often limits the use of GP models to small data sets, or approximation methods must be sought [14]. However, in our problem, the length of each drama usually does not exceed a few tens of episodes. Since time complexity is not a big issue for this application, we use exact inference in all the following experiments.

To avoid being trapped to local minima, we randomly initialize the hyperparameters and run the optimization multiple times. The set of hyperparameters yielding the highest marginal likelihood is selected as the final model to perform prediction.

5   Experiments

In this section we first introduce our dataset and the evaluation metric. Then we compare our model with other competitors. Finally we conduct a quantitative analysis on the usefulness of selected features.

5.1   Dataset and Evaluation Metrics

Four *daily dramas*, which are broadcast only on weekdays, are chosen as the experiment dataset. We collect Facebook Fan Page statistics, opinion polarities, and Google Trends information to create the features. All features are standardized. A brief summary for the dataset is listed in Table 1.

Table 1. Basic information about the dramas

Drama	#Episode	Broadcast period	Average Rating	Std.
D1	80	2012/04/10 ~ 2012/07/30	1.819	0.263
D2	82	2012/07/31 ~ 2012/11/26	1.941	0.201
D3	90	2012/06/27 ~ 2012/10/30	1.485	0.226
D4	84	2011/12/13 ~ 2012/04/09	2.540	0.754

We perform sequential prediction for all experiments. That is, to predict the rating of episode k of drama D1, we first train our model using data from the first k-1 episodes of D1 and data from the other dramas. For Facebook Fan Page statistics, opinion polarities, and Google Trends features, we use the values from the broadcasting day and three days prior to it. To evaluate the usefulness of different feature combinations, we also train models on all possible combinations of features.

The mean absolute percentage error (MAPE) is used as the evaluation metric since it is the most commonly used metric for the audience rating prediction problems.

$$MAPE = \frac{100\%}{N} \sum_{i=1}^{N} \left| \frac{y_i - p_i}{y_i} \right| \tag{12}$$

5.2 Comparison of the Models

We compare the proposed model with three other models as described below.

1. Support Vector Regression (SVR) [15]. This model solves the following regression problem:

$$min_{w} \frac{1}{2} w^T w + C \sum_{i=1}^{N} \frac{1}{y_i} \xi_\epsilon (w; x_i, y_i) \tag{13}$$

Note that Eq. 13 is different from the original form as there is an additional $1/y_i$ term added to optimize the MAPE. We tried both linear and polynomial transformation, and use LIBLINEAR [7] for the experiment. After several trials, we choose the regularization parameter C=1.

2. GP_ard. GPR with ARD SE kernel. (Eq. 6)
3. GP_iso. GPR with isotropic SE kernel. (Eq. 6, with $l_1 = l_2 = \cdots = l_n = l$)

There are six types of features, namely social network features (from Facebook), opinion features, trend features, ratings from previous three episodes, rating of the first episode, and weekday indicator variables. Therefore, there are total $2^6 - 1 = 63$ different combinations of features. Table 2 shows the average MAPE of all feature combinations for each drama. We also rank the MAPE obtained from different models, and then compute the average value. The result is shown in Table 3. Our model outperforms baseline models in terms of both MAPE and ranking.

Table 2. Average MAPE of all possible feature combinations

Model \ Drama	D1	D2	D3	D4	Avg.
SVR	0.1132	0.1027	0.1300	0.1396	0.1214
GP_ard	0.1124	0.0928	0.1297	0.1162	0.1128
GP_iso	0.1165	0.0959	0.1357	0.1158	0.1160
Our Model	0.1163	0.0918	0.1276	0.1117	**0.1118**

Table 3. Average ranking of all feature combinations

Model \ Drama	D1	D2	D3	D4	Avg.
SVR	2.1904	3.3492	2.1587	3.0952	2.6984
GP_ard	2.4365	2.2619	2.9444	2.6349	2.5694
GP_iso	2.7540	2.4683	2.5635	2.4365	2.5556
Our Model	2.6190	1.9206	2.3333	1.8333	**2.1766**

Then, we compare our modified GP model with the two standard GP-based competitors, GP_ard and GP_iso. Since the best feature combination is fairly different for each drama, a general scenario is considered, where all available features are used in the prediction. With the capability to estimate the relative importance of different groups of features and to avoid overfitting, the proposed weight-sharing method outperforms the other standard GP-based models. Results are shown in Table 4.

Table 4. Average MAPE using all features

Model / Drama	D1	D2	D3	D4	Avg.
GP_ard	0.1015	0.0887	0.1001	0.1184	0.1022
GP_iso	0.1018	0.0833	0.0929	0.0973	0.0938
Our Model	0.0991	0.0794	0.0911	0.0869	**0.0891**

5.3   Feature Analysis

In this section, we study the usefulness of the features based on our proposed model. As previously mentioned, the features are categorized into six types, as shown in the first column of Table 5. Holding the rest of the features identical, we compare the performance with and without a certain type of features. If the resulting error is lower when a certain type of features is used, we define it as a "win". Conversely, if the error is higher, then we define it as a "lose". For instance, with all other conditions the same, if removing Facebook features results in a higher MAPE for D1, then a "lose" is assigned.   Since there are total 63 different combinations of features, 31 comparisons are made for each drama. The winning percentages $\left(= \frac{W}{W+L} \times 100\%\right)$ for each type of the features are shown in Table 5. The higher the winning percentage, the more useful it is. We can observe that the previous ratings and weekday information are overall the most important features, while most of the features except opinion feature generally improves the performance.

Table 5. Winning percentage with or without a certain type of features

Winning Percentage (%)	D1	D2	D3	D4	TOTAL
Opinion	26	58	42	55	45
Google Trends	58	35	74	77	61
Facebook	29	71	87	55	60
Ratings of previous three episodes	100	100	100	100	100
Rating of the first episode	71	61	97	42	68
Weekday	81	100	100	84	91

6   Conclusion

In this paper, we present a weight-sharing Gaussian process model for the TV audience rating prediction problem. Also, we extract three types of web-based features for this task, namely Facebook Fan Page statistics, opinion polarities, and Google Trends. A series of experiments on a dataset consisting of four popular Chinese dramas are made to investigate the usefulness of these features. With the weight-sharing kernel applied, the proposed model yields lower error rates than the other baseline models in predicting the audience ratings.

Acknowledgement. This study is conducted under the "Social Intelligence Analysis Service Platform" of the Institute for Information Industry which is subsidized by the Ministry of Economy Affairs of the Republic of China.

References

1. Asur, S., Huberman, B.A.: Predicting the future with social media. In: Proceedings of the 2010 IEEE/WIC/ACM International Conference on Web Intelligence and Intelligent Agent Technology, WI-IAT 2010, vol. 01, pp. 492–499. IEEE Computer Society, Washington, DC (2010), http://dx.doi.org/10.1109/WI-IAT.2010.63
2. Bollerslev, T.: Generalized autoregressive conditional heteroskedasticity. Journal of Econometrics 31(3), 307–327 (1986)
3. Cawley, G.C., Talbot, N.L.: On over-fitting in model selection and subsequent selection bias in performance evaluation. The Journal of Machine Learning Research 11, 2079–2107 (2010), http://dl.acm.org/citation.cfm?id=1756006.1859921
4. Cheng, Y.H., Wu, C.M., Ku, T., Chen, G.D.: A predicting model of tv audience rating based on the facebook. In: International Conference on Social Computing (SocialCom), pp. 1034–1037. IEEE (2013)
5. Danaher, P., Dagger, T.: Using a nested logit model to forecast television ratings. International Journal of Forecasting 28(3), 607–622 (2012)
6. Danaher, P.J., Dagger, T.S., Smith, M.S.: Forecasting television ratings. International Journal of Forecasting 27(4), 1215–1240 (2011)
7. Fan, R.E., Chang, K.W., Hsieh, C.J., Wang, X.R., Lin, C.J.: Liblinear: A library for large linear classification. The Journal of Machine Learning Research 9, 1871–1874 (2008), http://dl.acm.org/citation.cfm?id=1390681.1442794
8. Hsieh, W.T., Chou, S.C.T., Cheng, Y.H., Wu, C.M.: Predicting tv audience rating with social media. In: Proceedings of the IJCNLP 2013 Workshop on Natural Language Processing for Social Media (SocialNLP), pp. 1–5. Asian Federation of Natural Language Processing, Nagoya (2013), http://www.aclweb.org/anthology/W13-4201
9. Luxhøj, J.T., Riis, J.O., Stensballe, B.: A hybrid econometric-neural network modeling approach for sales forecasting. International Journal of Production Economics 43(2), 175–192 (1996)
10. Murray, I., Adams, R.P.: Slice sampling covariance hyperparameters of latent gaussian models. In: Advances in Neural Information Processing Systems, pp. 1723–1731 (2010)
11. Neal, R.M.: Bayesian Learning for Neural Networks. Springer-Verlag New York, Inc., Secaucus (1996)

12. Posedel, P.: Analysis of the exchange rate and pricing foreign currency options on the croatian market: the ngarch model as an alternative to the black-scholes model. Financial Theory and Practice 30(4), 347–368 (2006)
13. Rasmussen, C., Williams, C.: Gaussian Processes for Machine Learning. The MIT Press, Cambridge (2006)
14. Schwaighofer, A., Tresp, V.: Transductive and inductive methods for approximate gaussian process regression. In: Advances in Neural Information Processing Systems (2003)
15. Vapnik, V.: The Nature of Statistical Learning Theory. Springer (2000)
16. Williams, C.K.I., Rasmussen, C.E.: Gaussian processes for regression. In: Advances in Neural Information Processing Systems, pp. 514–520. MIT Press (1996)

Adaptive Affinity Propagation Clustering in MapReduce Environment

Wei-Chih Hung[1], Yuan-Cheng Liu[1], Yi-Leh Wu[1],
Cheng-Yuan Tang[2], and Maw-Kae Hor[3]

[1]Department of Computer Science and Information Engineering,
National Taiwan University of Science and Technology, Taipei, Taiwan
[2]Department of Information Management, Huafan University, New Taipei City, Taiwan
[3]Kainan University, Taoyuan, Taiwan
ywu@csie.ntust.edu.tw

Abstract. The Affinity Propagation (AP) is a clustering algorithm based on the concept of "message passing" between data points. Unlike most clustering algorithms such as k-means, the AP does not require the number of clusters to be determined or estimated before running the algorithm. There are implementation of AP on Hadoop, a distribute cloud environment, called the Map/Reduce Affinity Propagation (MRAP). But the MRAP has a limitation: it is hard to know what value of parameter "preference" can yield an optimal clustering solution. The Adaptive Affinity Propagation Clustering (AAP) algorithm was proposed to overcome this limitation to decide the preference value in AP. In this study, we propose to combine these two methods as the Adaptive Map/Reduce Affinity Propagation (AMRAP), which divides the clustering task to multiple mappers and one reducer in Hadoop, and decides suitable preference values individually for each mapper. In the experiments, we compare the clustering results of the proposed AMRAP with the original MRAP method. The experiment results support that the proposed AMRAP method outperforms the original MRAP method in terms of accuracy.

Keywords: Affinity propagation, Map/Reduce, Hadoop, clustering algorithm.

1   Introduction

The Affinity Propagation (AP) [1] is a clustering algorithm that requires no pre-set number of clusters K. The AP is a fast clustering algorithm especially in the case of large number of clusters. Speed, general applicability and good performance are its advantages. The AP works based on similarities between pairs of data points, and simultaneously considers all the data points as the potential cluster centers, called exemplars. There are two kinds of message exchanged between data points, and each takes into account a different kind of competition. Messages can be combined at any stage to decide which points are exemplars; and for the non-exemplar points, which exemplar it belongs to. The "responsibility" $r(i, k)$, sent from data point i to candidate exemplar point k, reflects the accumulated evidence for how well-suited point k

S.-M. Cheng and M.-Y. Day (Eds.): TAAI 2014, LNAI 8916, pp. 209–218, 2014.

is to serve as the exemplar for point i, taking into account other potential exemplars for point i. The "availability" $a(i,k)$, sent from candidate exemplar point k to point i, reflects the accumulated evidence for how appropriate it would be for point i to choose point k as its exemplar, taking into account the support from other points that point k should be an exemplar. The AP searches for clusters through an iterative process until a high-quality set of exemplars and corresponding clusters emerges. In the iterative process, identified exemplars start from the maximum n exemplars to fewer exemplars until m exemplars appear and remain unchanged any more. The m clusters found based on m exemplars are the clustering solution of the AP.

Based on the original AP, there are many improvements to make AP more efficient. He et al. [2] presented a method which is called "Adaptive Affinity Propagation" to search the range of "preference" that AP needs then find a suitable value which can optimize the result of AP. The "preference" value is important in AP to decide the result is good or not. A more suitable preference value makes the clusters assignment more reasonable.

To implement the AP on Map/Reduced architecture [3], we employ the Apache Hadoop [4]. The Apache Hadoop is an open-source software framework for storage and large-scale processing of data sets on clusters of commodity hardware. The Hadoop is an Apache top-level project being built and used by a global community of contributors and users. The Map/Reduce is a programming model and an associated implementation for processing and generating large data sets with a parallel, distributed algorithm [5-7] on a cluster.

To combine the AP and Hadoop, there is a method called the Map/Reduce Affinity Propagation (MRAP) [9]. We propose to combine the Adaptive Affinity Propagation [8] (AAP) the MRAP on Hadoop called the Adaptive Map/Reduce Affinity Propagation (AMRAP). The proposed AMRAP is implemented on Hadoop and can determine the range of preference for the optimal value. The experimental results show that the proposed AMRAP method outperforms the standard affinity propagation with Map/Reduce clustering method.

The main contributions of this works are as follows:

1. The proposed AMRAP method produces clusters with higher recall and precision because of better preference values selection.
2. The proposed AMRAP method is faster, in terms of overall execution time, than other traditional AP methods.

The rest of the paper is organized as follows. In section 2, we present the concept and theory on the proposed method, and give the algorithm details. We conduct experimental study of the proposed Adaptive Map/Reduce Affinity Propagation and compare with the MRAP on real-world data sets in section 3 and conclude the paper in section 4.

2   Algorithm of Affinity Propagation

In this section, we first introduce how the AP works and discuss how to find a better preference value that the AP required. Second, we discuss how to improve the AP in the Map/Reduce environment and what we try to change in the architecture.

2.1   Affinity Propagation

The AP takes as input a collection of real-valued similarities between data points, where the similarity $s(i, k)$ indicates how well the data point with index k is suited to be the exemplar for data point i. When the goal is to minimize squared error, each similarity is set to a negative squared error (Euclidean distance).For points x_i and x_k:

$$s(i, k) = -||x_i . x_k||^2 \tag{1}$$

Rather than requiring that the number of clusters be pre-specified, affinity propagation takes as input a real number $s(k, k)$ for each data point k so that data points with larger values of $s(k, k)$ are more likely to be chosen as exemplars. These values are referred to as "preferences." The number of identified exemplars (number of clusters) is influenced by the values of the input preferences, but also emerges from the message-passing procedure. If a priori, all data points are equally suitable as exemplars, the preferences should be set to a common value, and this value can be varied to produce different numbers of clusters. The shared value could be the median of the input similarities (resulting in a moderate number of clusters) or their minimum (resulting in a small number of clusters).

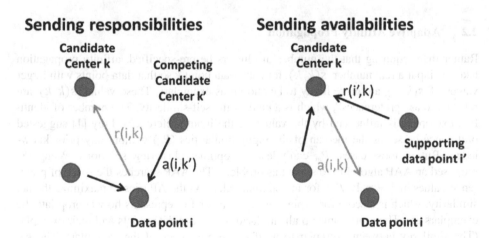

Fig. 1. The messages ("responsibility" $r(i, k)$ and "availability" a(i, k)) passing between any two points

There are two kinds of message exchanged between data points, and each takes into account a different kind of competition. Messages can be combined at any stage to decide which points are exemplars and, for every other point, which exemplar it belongs to. The "responsibility" $r(i, k)$, sent from data point i to candidate exemplar point k, reflects the accumulated evidence for how well-suited point k is to serve as the exemplar for point i, taking into account other potential exemplars for point i. The "availability" $a(i, k)$, sent from candidate exemplar point k to point i, reflects the accumulated evidence for how appropriate it would be for point i to choose point k as its exemplar, taking into account the support from other points that point k should be an exemplar. $r(i, k)$ and $a(i, k)$ can be viewed as log-probability ratios. To begin with, the availabilities are initialized to zero: $a(i, k) = 0$. Then, the responsibilities are computed using the rule:

$$r(i, k) \leftarrow s(i, k) - \max_{k' \neq k} \{a(i, k') + s(i, k')\} \qquad (2)$$

In the first iteration, because the availabilities are zero, $r(i, k)$ is set to the input similarity between point i and point k as its exemplar, minus the largest of the similarities between point i and other candidate exemplars. This competitive update is data-driven and does not take into account how many other points favor each candidate exemplar. In later iterations, when some points are effectively assigned to other exemplars, their availabilities will drop below zero as prescribed by the update rule below. These negative availabilities will decrease the effective values of some of the input similarities $s(i, k')$ in the above rule, removing the corresponding candidate exemplars from competition. For $k = i$, the responsibility $r(k, k)$ is set to the input preference that point k be chosen as an exemplar, $s(k, k)$, minus the largest of the similarities between point i and all other candidate exemplars. This "self-responsibility" reflects the accumulated evidence that point k is an exemplar, based on its input preference tempered by how ill-suited it is to be assigned to another exemplar.

2.2   Adaptive Affinity Propagation

Rather than requiring that the number of clusters be pre-specified, affinity propagation takes as input a real number $s(k, k)$ for each data point k so that data points with larger values of $s(k, k)$ are more likely to be chosen as exemplars. These values $s(k, k)$ are referred to as "preferences", which is a kind of the self-similarity. The number of identified exemplars is influenced by the values of the input preferences. Frey [1] suggested preference be set as the median of the input similarities (P_m) without any prior knowledge. But in most cases, P_m can't lead to optimal clustering solutions. Wang [8] proposed an AAP algorithm to solve this problem. The AAP searches the space of preference values in $[-\infty, P_m/2]$ for the optimal value. As the AP tries to maximize the net similarity, which is a score for explaining the data, and it represents how appropriate the exemplars are. The score sums up all similarities between data points and their exemplar (The similarity between exemplar to itself is the preference of the exemplar). The AP aims at maximizing the net similarity and tests each data point whether it is an exemplar. Therefore, the method which is using for computing the range of preferences can be developed.

The maximum preference (P_{max}) in the range is the value which clusters the N data points into N clusters, and this is equal to the maximum similarity, since a preference lower than that would make the object better to have the data point associated with that maximum similarity assigned to be a cluster member rather than an exemplar. The derivation for P_{min} is similar to P_{max}. Compute dpsim1 = $\max_j \{\sum_j s(i,j)\}$, dpsim2 = $\max_{i \neq j} \{\sum_j \max\{s(i,k)\}, s(j,k)\}$, Compute the minimal value of preference $P_{min} = dpsim1 - dpsim2$.

After computing the range of preferences, we can scan through preferences space to find the optimal clustering result. Different preferences would lead to different cluster results. Cluster validation techniques are used to evaluate which clustering result is optimal for the datasets. The preference step is very important to scan the space adaptively, where $P_s = (P_{max} - P_{min})/N$. To sample the whole space, we set the base of scanning step as $P_s = (P_{max} - P_{min})/N$.

We employ the global silhouette index as the validity indices. The silhouette index is introduced by Rousseeuw [12] as a general graphical aid for interpretation and validation of cluster analysis, which provides a measure of how well a data point is classified when it is assigned to a cluster in according to both the tightness of the clusters and the separation among clusters.

The global silhouette index is defined as follows:

$$GS = \frac{1}{n_c}\sum_{j=1}^{n_c} S_j \tag{3}$$

Local silhouette index is defined as:

$$S_j = \frac{1}{r_j}\sum_{i=1}^{r_j} \frac{b(i)-a(i)}{\max\{b(i),a(i)\}} \tag{4}$$

Where r_j is the count of the objects in class j, $a(i)$ is the average distance between object i and the objects in the same class j, $b(i)$ is the minimum average distance between object i and objects in class closet to class j. The largest global silhouette index indicates the best clustering quality and the optimal number of clusters [12-13]. A series of global silhouette index Sil values corresponding to clustering result with different number of cluster are calculated. The optimal clustering result is found when Sil is largest.

The AAP clustering method steps are as follow:

Step1: Apply Preferences Range algorithm to computing the range of preferences:

$$[P_{min}, P_{max}] \tag{5}$$

Step2: Initialize the preferences:

$$preference = P_{min} - P_s \tag{6}$$

Step3: Update the preferences:

$$preference = preference + P_s \tag{7}$$

Step4: Apply the AP algorithm to generating K clusters.
Step5: Terminate until Sil is largest.

2.3   Adaptive Map/Reduce Affinity Propagation

We employ the Adaptive Affinity Propagation to extend previous work [9]. There are multiple mappers and two reducers in the proposed environment settings. We can increase the number of mappers at will, which means the proposed method is scalable.

At the beginning, the input data will be processed for initial similarity and preference values. Each mapper can process the input data at the same time. We divide the input data into small size randomly, source input data and divided input data are both in the HDFS. The suitable preference values can be decided by employing the AAP method individually on each mapper.

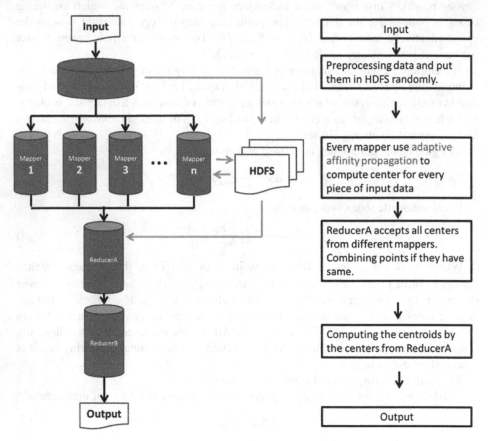

Fig. 2. The framework of Adaptive Map/Reduce Affinity Propagation

The AAP steps of the proposed AMRAP clustering method are as follow:
Step1: Initialize $s(k,k)$ to zero:

$$s(k,k) = 0 \qquad (8)$$

Step2: Compute the maximal preference:

$$P_{max} = max\{s(i,k)\} \qquad (9)$$

Step3: Compute the minimal preference:

$$dpsim1 = \max_j\{\textstyle\sum_j s(i,j)\} \tag{10}$$

$$dpsim2 = \max_{i \neq j}\{\textstyle\sum_k \max\{s(i,k), s(j,k)\}\} \tag{11}$$

Step4: Compute the minimal preference:

$$P_{min} = dpsim1 - dpsim2 \tag{12}$$

Step5: Compute the step:

$$P_{step} = (P_{max} - P_{min})/N \tag{13}$$

Step6: Initialize the preferences:

$$preference = P_{min} - P_{step} \tag{14}$$

Step7: Update the preferences:

$$preference = preference + P_{step} \tag{15}$$

The range of preference value will between P_{min} and P_{max}.

In the mapping stage, every mapper will get different divided data from the HDFS and processing the AP using the assigned input data set. And then each mapper decides its own similarity matrix and preference values. After AP, the mappers will get their own results just like single node processing. So that each mapper has its own information like centers and key values. Mappers send this information to the next reducing stage., where <key, i, k> means point i's center is point k.

All parameters transmit among multiple mappers and the reducer. The Map/Reduce unit will collect the values with the same key value and process the values at the same time.

The mappers need to process their own data isolatedly. There are two restrictions using AP on Map/Reduce. First, there are many iterations in AP. If the mappers transmit information to each other, unpredictable cost may occur. Second, in this Map/Reduce architecture, every mapper is processing independently. It cannot transmit data to other mappers.

There are two parts in the reducing stage. First, the ReducerA collects the information from each mapper, and using this information to calculate the center points then sends the result to ReducerB. Second, the ReducerB collects all centers of clusters, that each mapper maybe calculates different centers. To decide the suitable centroid of centers from ReducerA, we use

$$\text{Centroid} = \frac{c_1 + c_2 + \cdots + c_k}{k} \tag{16}$$

After merge clusters, the points of the merged clusters will have the same unique key value if the points are in the same cluster. Clustered points and their centers combine the output result.

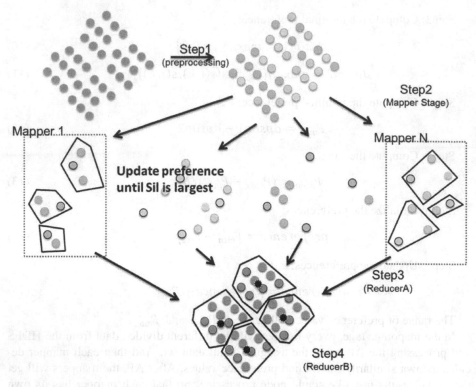

Fig. 3. Processing steps of the proposed Adaptive Map/Reduce Affinity Propagation

3   Evaluation and Experiments

There are total nine machines employed in our experimental environment. One machine serves as the master and the other eight machines are slaves. All of these machines are with CPU: Intel® Core™2 Quad Processor Q6600 (8M Cache, 2.40 GHz, 1066 MHz FSB), RAM: DDR2-800 2G * 2. We chose five datasets from the UC Irvine Machine Learning Repository [10] and the Yale Face Database [11].

3.1   Accuracy Result

The dimension of the Iris dataset is 4. As shown in Table 1, the AMRAP, MRAP and the Canopy initialed Map/Reduce K-means method produce similar accuracy when the dimensionality is low.

The dimension of the Wine quality dataset is 11. As shown in Table 2, the result is that the precision rate and the recall rate decrease significantly. The proposed AMRAP method produces more stable clustering output than the MRAP and Canopy initialed Map/Reduce K-means when the data dimensionality increases.

Table 1. Accuracy of Iris dataset

	MRAP		K-means (Canopy initial)		AMRAP	
	Precision	Recall	Precision	Recall	Precision	Recall
Cluster1	0.690	0.980	0.723	0.940	0.980	1
Cluster2	1	1	1	1	0.742	0.980
Cluster3	0.97	0.56	0.914	0.64	1	0.667
Average	0.887	0.847	0.877	0.860	0.907	0.882

Table 2. Accuracy of SatImage dataset

	MRAP		K-means (Canopy initial)		AMRAP	
	Precision	Recall	Precision	Recall	Precision	Recall
Cluster1	0.75	0.1472	0.0615	1	0.441	0.533
Cluster2	0.4665	0.1584	0.0745	0.1123	0.371	0.485
Cluster3	0.4474	0.2253	0	0	0.588	0.521
Cluster4	0.1823	0.3643	0	0	0.352	0.56
Cluster5	0.0543	0.4629	0	0	0.493	0.68
Average	0.466	0.267	0.026	0.22	0.449	0.556

4   Conclusions and Future Work

We propose the Adaptive Map/Reduce Affinity Propagation (AMRAP) method implemented on Hadoop. The main differences between the proposed AMRAP with Map/Reduce Affinity Propagation (MRAP) is that the proposed AMRAP can decide suitable preference values automatically. The proposed AMRAP also inherits the multi-processing advantage that is scalable with added machines. And on this architecture, the proposed AMRAP method can process large dataset with good performance unlike the one node system.

But some problems persist in our experiments. If the reducer task takes longer than 600 seconds the job will be killed because of time-out. Currently we try to increase the max time-out into 1800 seconds, but the problem still persists. We will next employ the SIFT dataset which is composed from images. Each image has different number of SIFT features with 128 dimensions. And the SIFT dataset is expected to have million to billion number of SIFT features. We will employ the proposed AMRAP to analyze the large SIFT dataset and solve the time-out problem in the future.

Acknowledgement. This work was partially supported by the Ministry of Science and Technology, Taiwan, under the Grants No. NSC102-2221-E-011-134, NSC102-2221-E-211-012, and NSC102-2119-M-424-001.

References

1. Frey, B.J., Dueck, D.: Clustering by Passing Messages Between Data Points. Science 315, 972–976 (2007)
2. He, Y.C., Chen, Q.C., Wang, X.L., Xu, R.F., Bai, X.H., Meng, X.J.: An adaptive affinity propagation document clustering. Informatics and Systems (INFOS), pp. 1-7 (March 2010)
3. Dean, J., Ghemawat, S.: MapReduce: simplified data processing on large clusters. Communications of the ACM 51(1), 107–113 (2008)
4. Hadoop, http://hadoop.apache.org (referenced on March 1, 2013)
5. Bhandarkar, M.: MapReduce programming with apache Hadoop. In: Parallel & Distributed Processing (IPDPS), pp. 19–23 (April 2010)
6. Maurya, M., Mahajan, S.: Performance analysis of MapReduce programs on Hadoop cluster. In: Information and Communication Technologies (WICT), pp. 505–510 (2012)
7. Lynch, N.A.: Distributed Algorithms. Morgan Kaufmann (1996)
8. Wang, K., Zhang, J., Li, D., Zhang, X., Guo, T.: Adaptive Affinity Propagation Clustering. Acta Automatica Sinica 33(12), 1242–1246 (2007)
9. Hung, W.C., Chu, C.Y., Wu, Y.L., Tang, C.Y.: Map/Reduce Affinity Propagation Clustering Algorithm. In: International Conference on Control, Robotics and Cybernetics (ICCRC 2014)(August 2014)
10. UCI Machine Learning Repository, http://archive.ics.uci.edu/ml/ (referenced on March 1, 2013)
11. The Yale Face Database, http://cvc.yale.edu/projects/yalefaces/yalefaces.html (referenced on March 1, 2013)
12. Rousseeuw, P.J.: Silhouettes: a graphical aid to the interpretation and validation of cluster analysis. Computational and Applied Mathematics 20, 53–65 (1987)
13. Dudoit, S., Fridlyand, J.: A prediction-based resampling method for estimating the number of clusters in a dataset. Genome Biology 3(7) (2002)

HTNSystem: Hypertension Information Extraction System for Unstructured Clinical Notes

Jitendra Jonnagaddala[1,2,3], Siaw-Teng Liaw[2,*], Pradeep Ray[3], Manish Kumar[1], and Hong-Jie Dai[4,*]

[1] Translational Cancer Research Network
UNSW Australia
[2] School of Public Health and Community Medicine
UNSW Australia
[3] Asia-Pacific Ubiquitous Healthcare Research Centre
UNSW Australia
{z3339253,siaw,p.ray,manish.kumar}@unsw.edu.au
[4] Graduate Institute of Biomedical Informatics, College of Medical Science and Technology
Taipei Medical University, Taipei, Taiwan, R.O.C.
hjdai@tmu.edu.tw

Abstract. Hypertension (HTN) relevant information has great application potential in cohort discovery and building predictive models for prevention and surveillance. Unfortunately most of this valuable patient information is buried in the form of unstructured clinical notes. In this study we present HTN information extraction system called HTNSystem which is capable of extracting mentions of HTN and inferring HTN from BP lab values. HTNSystem is a rule based system which implements MetaMap as a core component together with custom built BP value extractor and post processing components. It is evaluated on a corpus of 514 clinical notes (82.92% F-measure). HTNSystem is distributed as an open source command line tool available at https://github.com/TCRNBioinformatics/HTNSystem.

Keywords: Hypertension, Blood pressure, Information extraction, Rule based, Apache UIMA, Apache Ruta, Text mining.

1 Introduction

Hypertension (HTN) or high blood pressure (HBP) is one of the major public health burdens in developing and developed countries. It is estimated that there will be 60% increase in adults with hypertension by year 2025[1, 2]. HTN is also a leading risk factor for many cardio vascular diseases (CVD) and kidney diseases [1]. Any patient information relevant to HTN has great application potential in cohort discovery and building predictive models for prevention and surveillance. In general, most of this valuable patient information is buried in the form of unstructured clinical notes scattered across various electronic health records (EHR) or electronic medical records

---

* Corresponding authors.

S.-M. Cheng and M.-Y. Day (Eds.): TAAI 2014, LNAI 8916, pp. 219–227, 2014.

(EMR) systems [3]. Researchers often spend lot of time and resources in extracting patient information from unstructured clinical notes. Specifically, it is more challenging and tedious to extract HTN information manually as the HTN information is usually mentioned in multiple records for a single patient. At the same time, coding this HTN information to standard ontologies like SNOMED-CT adds another burden to the manual extraction.

Simple clinical text mining techniques can be employed to extract HTN information very easily from unstructured clinical notes. There are various tools to extract HTN information from unstructured clinical notes or biomedical text. However, these tools have limited capabilities in extracting HTN information. For example, MetaMap [4] is a popular biomedical text information extraction system which is capable of identifying HTN mentions but can't infer HTN information based on medications or lab values. On the other hand, there are rule based tools that can recognize blood pressure (BP) values or medications but not capable of inferring whether the values or medications are relevant to HTN [5-7]. In other words, these systems can not differentiate between high BP and low BP. In addition, differences in what range of BP values are considered as HTN vary from country to country. In this study, we present a simple HTN information extraction system called HTNSystem which is capable of extracting mentions of hypertension and inferring HTN information from BP lab values from unstructured clinical notes. HTNSystem is a rule-based information system which implements MetaMap as a core component together with a custom built BP value extractor and rule-based post processing components. The BP value extractor component was originally built as part of TMUNSW system developed for 2014 i2b2/UTHealth Shared-Task 2 and 4 [8, 9]. As part of HTNSystem the old BP value extractor is significantly improved to increase performance (more details in results section). Overall, HTNSystem is generic and highly configurable allowing end users and developers to customize HTNSystem according to their preferences or suggested clinical guidelines.

2   Materials and Methods

2.1   2014 i2b2/UTHealth Shared-Task 2 Corpus

The 2014 i2b2/UTHealth Shared-Task 2[1] corpus is a clinical data set distributed by organizers [10]. The corpus represents longitudinal data of diabetic patients collected for the purpose of identifying CVD risk factors. It was distributed as a part of shared Task in three sets. Table 1 presents a summary level statistics of the corpus. Two training sets consist of 521 and 269 unstructured clinical notes (from here on referred as records) respectively and a test set with 514 records. The records in the training data set were distributed in XML (Extensible Markup Language) format and included annotations on CVD risk factors. Each record in the corpus was manually annotated by three different annotators. The risk factors identified in the corpus were Hypertension, Diabetes, Obesity, Medication, Coronary artery disease and Smoking history. Three

---

[1] https://www.i2b2.org/NLP/HeartDisease/

annotators separately annotated hypertension information for patient in the corpus by identifying mentions and also considering BP values from which HTN can be inferred. Few examples of BP values from which HTN can be inferred found in corpus are – "BP: 158/72","blood pressure 149/96","Blood pressure is elevated at 188/92" and "BP unchanged at 145/70".

Table 1. Summary of 2014 i2b2/UTHealth Share-Task 2 corpus

Data set	Number of records	Number of HTN Annotations
Training Data 1	521	580
Training Data 2	269	291
Test Data	514	537

2.2   MetaMap

MetaMap is a highly configurable dictionary-based tool which maps biomedical text to UMLS Metathesaurus [4]. MetaMap parses input text into noun phrases and forms variants from these terms like alternate spelling, abbreviations, synonym, inflection and derivation. These variants are used to form a candidate set of Metathesaurus terms and scores are computed on the strength of mapping from the variants to each candidate term. Even though MetaMap was built to process biomedical text, it is also widely used in processing clinical notes [11]. MetaMap is freely distributed, but an UMLS license is required to run it locally or use the available web interface[2]. The current MetaMap version available is MetaMap 14 released on 10th of August 2014. MetaMap can also be used as an UIMA analysis engine using MetaMap UIMA wrapper[3]. The MetaMap UIMA annotator is based on Apache UIMA framework[4] and encodes named entities that can be used as part of UIMA component. The MetaMap UIMA annotator requires existing local MetaMap, UIMA framework and SDK, MetaMap Java API, and Java Runtime environment installed. The current version of this annotator is the 2014 MetaMap UIMA annotator. For developing HTNSystem, we used MetaMap 14 on Windows Server 2012 with JDK 1.8 and UIMA Java Framework V2.6.0 and MetaMap 14 Java API.

2.3   Apache Ruta

Apache UIMA Ruta[5] is a rule-based scripting language designed to rapidly develop rule-based text mining applications within the UIMA system. UIMA Ruta rules defines a pattern of annotation and if this pattern applies then the action of the rule are

---

[2] http://ii.nlm.nih.gov/Interactive/UTS_Required/metamap.shtml
[3] http://metamap.nlm.nih.gov/UIMA.shtml
[4] https://uima.apache.org/
[5] https://uima.apache.org/ruta.html

performed on matched annotations which may be subjected to additional rules. A rule is composed of a sequence of rule elements, and each rule element basically has a matching condition, an optional quantifier of a list of conditions and list of actions. The actions of rules are applied only when all rule elements of the rule have successfully matched .We used RUTA Version 2.2.0 for developing our HTNSystem. We developed RUTA rules using RUTA-eclipsed-based tooling workbench and later this was packaged as UIMA component in to HTNSystem. Using RUTA not only allowed us to rapidly develop rules but it also allowed us to maintain interoperability with other UIMA-framework-based systems.

2.4   HTNSystem Design

HTNSystem is a generic Hypertension Information extraction system, which can be used to extract hypertension information contained within records. HTNSystem is distributed as free and open source command line tool[6] with various configuration options, which enable users to configure and control output from each component in the system. HTNSystem is designed with MetaMap and Apache RUTA as backbone mainly to take advantage of their UIMA nature. This design allows authors to address the shortcomings of MetaMap in identifying HTN information by using Apache RUTA. Figure 1 below illustrates the workflow and components within the system. HTNSystem consist of two major modules, the concept recognition module and the post processing module.

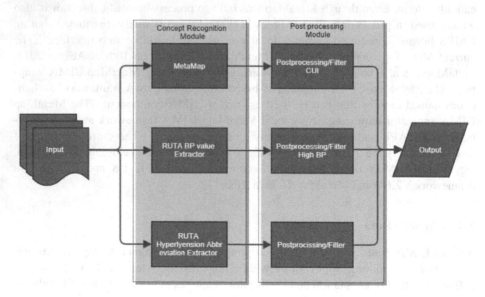

Fig. 1. HTNSystem workflow and components design overview

---

[6] https://github.com/TCRNBioinformatics/HTNSystem

Concept Recognition Module. This module extracts hypertension concept mentions from inputted records using MetaMap and apache RUTA-based components. The MetaMap component of this system needs to be installed separately as it requires separate licensing. The configuration file has an option for MetaMap mmserver host IP address and port which users need to configure based on their MetaMap installation configuration. Optionally, users need to configure word sense disambiguation (WSD) server information if required. By default the HTNSystem is restricted to find concepts relevant to SNOMEDCT_US only, however users can configure to use other available vocabularies from UMLS. The configuration file also contains lists of common unique identifiers (CUIs)[7] for identifying Hypertension concepts, the CUIs presented in Table 2 are based on our analysis of the corpus and it covers almost all relevant hypertension concepts. However, if required, users can also add additional CUIs to this list based on individual requirements.

The Ruta BP value extractor component extracts BP mentions and its associated values based on Ruta scripts. HTNSystem infers a BP value as HTN, if the systolic BP is greater than 140 or diastolic BP is greater than 90. HTNSystem also allows users to configure these value ranges in configuration files. This component is a completely rule-based component and from our analysis of the corpus, Ruta BP value extractor component is able to extract most of the BP values. The Ruta script shown in figure 2 is capable of identifying mentions of BP values like "BP: 158/72","blood pressure 149/96","Blood pressure is elevated at 188/92" and "BP unchanged at 145/70". The Ruta-based Hypertension abbreviation extractor extracts Hypertension-related abbreviations like "ht" for hypertension and "hbp" for high blood pressure.

Table 2. Default list of HTN relevant UMLS CUIs in HTNSystem

Term	UMLS CUI
Hypertensive disease	C0020538
Benign hypertension	C0264637
Essential hypertension	C0085580
Endocrine hypertension	C0264641
Malignant hypertension	C0020540
Systolic hypertension	C0221155
Diastolic hypertension	C0235222
Secondary hypertension	C0155616
Secondary benign hypertension	C0155620
Malignant secondary hypertension	C0155617
Secondary diastolic hypertension	C0264647

Post-processing Module. Post-processing module in the HTNSystem is a combination of custom built Java based components. These components act like a filtering system which filters out concept and mentions relevant to HTN. The CUI filter within

---

[7] http://www.nlm.nih.gov/research/umls/new_users/glossary.html#c

this module identifies only CUIs relevant to HTN concepts. The BP value filter identifies the BP mentions which are higher than user specified BP values. The components also identify HTN relevant abbreviations based on context. For example, we identified that "ht" is used as abbreviation for both height and hypertension. This filter analyzes the context of "ht" based on preceding and succeeding word tokens in sentences and then filters out cases that were not HTN. For example, in the two sentences, like "His ht was 165cms" and "He was diagnosed with ht" where "ht" can be identified as height and hypertension respectively using our context-based filters. The output from the HTNSystem is written to a CSV file which contains filename, annotated text, and text boundaries for each of the identified and inferred HTN mentions.

```
DECLARE systolic,diastolic,valueSeparator,separator,Bpvalue;
BOOLEAN flag = true;
WORDLIST htAbbrList = 'HypertensionAbbr.txt';
Document{-> MARKFAST(hypertension, htAbbrList,true)};
DECLARE bp , blood, pressure;
W{REGEXP("BP",flag) -> MARK(bp)};
W{REGEXP("blood",flag) -> MARK(blood)};
W{REGEXP("pressure",flag) -> MARK(pressure)};
blood + pressure {-> MARK(bp, 1,2)};
//value separator
SPECIAL{REGEXP("=") -> MARK(separator)};
COLON{-> MARK(separator)};
//BP Value
NUM{REGEXP(".{2,3}") -> MARK(systolic)} ;
NUM{REGEXP(".{2,3}") -> MARK(diastolic,1,2)} ;
//valueSeparator
SPECIAL{REGEXP("/") -> MARK(valueSeparator)};
systolic+ valueSeparator+ diastolic {-> MARK(Bpvalue, 1, 2, 3)};
bp+ separator + Bpvalue {-> MARK(BpAnnotation, 1, 2, 3,4,5)};
bp+ W*Bpvalue {-> MARK(BpAnnotation,1,5)} ;
```

Fig. 2. Sample Ruta Script used to identify BP values

3   Results

The performance metrics of our previous system in extracting HTN information on test set is presented in Table 3. These evaluation results are calculated based on the gold standard annotations provided by the 2014 i2b2/UTHealth Shared-Tasks organizers. As shown in Table 3, our previous system had acceptable recall but low precision. This is mainly due to the fact that the system identified a large number of HTN mentions and BP values, which are ignored by the annotators of i2b2. For example, a record might include HTN information mentioned under family history, which may not be a representation of the patient's HTN information.

We performed an extensive manual error analysis on the previous system and identified improvement gaps. The gaps for improvement included leveraging on contextual information, resolving disambiguation in abbreviations and additional dictionary look up entries for HTN mentions and BP values. These gaps are addressed in the new HTNSystem by adding additional components and modules. For example, the system failed to identify and infer HTN information in "Initial blood pressure systolic 218 was reduced to 190 range". Adding additional Ruta rules based on error analysis, the HTNSystem was able to identify these annotations. The previous system identified "blood pressure and improved with carotid sinus massage during exam on 01/96" as blood pressure value of 01/96 which is actually a date value. These false positives were filtered out using more robust context-based rules and filtering built into HTNSystem components. As a result of this, the performance of the current HTNSystem is significantly improved as it evident from F-measure score. It correctly identified 471 HTN mentions out of 537 achieving a recall of 0.8770 and a precision of 0.7863 with false positive and false negative counts at 128 and 66 respectively. The overall performance metrics on test set are illustrated in Table 3 based on the provided gold standard annotations. This significant improvement in the system can be attributed because of improved BP value extractor component and addition of new context based BP value abbreviation and post processing components developed in this work.

Table 3. TMUNSW & HTNSystem performance metrics for HTN mentions

System	TP	FP	FN	Precision	Recall	F-measure
TMUNSW	421	336	116	0.556	0.783	0.650
HTNSystem	471	128	66	0.7863	0.877	0.829

4   Discussion

In this study, we presented HTNSystem, a highly configurable and generic information extraction system capable of extracting HTN information from records. HTNSystem is a package of custom built components and MetaMap. The HTNSystem had a good overall performance on the corpus, but the results may vary depending on the corpus. The performance of the HTNSystem is very similar to the performance of other systems. However, these systems extracted either HTN mentions or BP values [5, 6, 12, 13]. The BP of a patient can be elevated due to various reasons and the HTNSystem didn't consider HTN medications or treatment information to infer HTN. We selected a few of such records and tried to identify rules or context patterns but unfortunately didn't find enough information to classify those mentions as HTN. The performance of the system can be further improved by testing the system on other corpuses [12, 13]. The system demonstrates the feasibility of its application in identifying HTN as a risk factor for other diseases and identifying cohorts based on HTN information.

The HTN annotations made by HTNSystem were manually reviewed and was discovered that the system missed few HTN mentions in sentences like "blood pressure, and found it to be 220/140", in this case the system failed to identify BP value because the text contained special characters. This situation can be handled by implementing a few pre-processing steps to identify special character tokens and remove them. This should allow HTNSystem to identify HTN mentions in text containing special characters. Furthermore, we also found that the system was not able to identify systolic or diastolic blood pressure as alone. For example, the system failed to identify HTN information in sentences with mentions like "SBP 140s". The other case where our system failed to identify blood pressure value is when these value are given as a range like "150-160/78-82". Also, the system was not able to resolve hypertension mention when there were presence of two BP values, for example "170/85 in her left arm and 165/70 in her right". We also identified that there were few occasions where HTNSystem falsely identified hypertension. For example, "blood pressure and heart rate with a goal blood pressure less than 120/80" this text string should not be annotated as just BP value and infer it is not HTN. We believe that the above mentioned situations can be handled by employing more sophisticated contextual rules using section information of the records.

HTNSystem used MetaMap as one of the component in concept recognition module mainly to take advantage of MetaMap UMLS CUI normalization capabilities. However, authors have experienced various performance issues using MetaMap API. The performance issues of MetaMap are also observed in other studies [14, 15]. In future, we would like to investigate various options to address current limitations of HTNSystem and at the same time improve its performance. Specifically, to explore the option of replacing MetMap mmserver component with NCBO Annotator [16, 17], and integrate HTN medication and treatment information to infer HTN at record summary level and build a sectionizer like SecTag [18] component to identify complex contextual rules.

5   Conclusion

In conclusion, HTNSystem, a HTN information extraction system for unstructured clinical notes, was developed in this study. The system is highly configurable and easy to integrate into other information extraction systems. The HTNSystem was evaluated on 2014 i2b2/UTHealth shared task 2 corpus and it successfully extracted and inferred HTN information with over 80% F-measure. It is useful for cohort discovery and predictive modeling in HTN or in other diseases where HTN is a risk factor. It is evident that the performance of the system can be further improved and we plan to extend the system with more frame-based pattern matching contextual rules.

Acknowledgments. This project was supported by a Cancer Institute NSW's translational cancer research center program grant. The authors would also like to thank the organizers of 2014 i2b2/UTHealth Shared-Tasks.

References

1. Kearney, P.M., et al.: Global burden of hypertension: analysis of worldwide data. The Lancet 365(9455), 217–223 (2005)
2. Organization, W.H., I.S.O.H.W Group: World Health Organization (WHO)/International Society of Hypertension (ISH) statement on management of hypertension. Journal of hypertension 21(11), 1983–1992 (2003)
3. Murdoch, T.B., Detsky, A.S.: The inevitable application of big data to health care. JAMA 309(13), 1351–1352 (2013)
4. Aronson, A.R., Lang, F.-M.: An overview of MetaMap: historical perspective and recent advances. Journal of the American Medical Informatics Association 17(3), 229–236 (2010)
5. Turchin, A., et al.: Using regular expressions to abstract blood pressure and treatment intensification information from the text of physician notes. Journal of the American Medical Informatics Association 13(6), 691–695 (2006)
6. Turchin, A., Pendergrass, M.L., Kohane, I.S.: DITTO–a Tool for Identification of Patient Cohorts from the Text of Physician Notes in the Electronic Medical Record. In: AMIA Annual Symposium Proceedings. American Medical Informatics Association (2005)
7. Xu, H., et al.: MedEx: a medication information extraction system for clinical narratives. Journal of the American Medical Informatics Association 17(1), 19–24 (2010)
8. Chang, N.-W., et al.: TMUNSW System for Risk Factor Recognition and Progression Tracking. In: Proceedings of the 2014 i2b2/UTHealth Shared-Tasks and Workshop on Challenges in Natural Language Processing for Clinical Data (2014)
9. Jonnagaddala, J., et al.: Coronary heart disease risk assessment from unstructured clinical notes using Framingham risk score. In: Proceedings of the 2014 i2b2/UTHealth Shared-Tasks and Workshop on Challenges in Natural Language Processing for Clinical Data (2014)
10. Stubbs, A., et al.: Practical applications for NLP in Clinical Research: the 2014 i2b2/UTHealth shared tasks (2014)
11. Jonnagaddala, J., et al.: TMUNSW: Disorder Concept Recognition and Normalization in Clinical Notes for SemEval-2014 Task 7. In: 8th International Workshop on Semantic Evaluation (SemEval 2014), Dublin, Ireland, August 23-24. ACL Anthology (2014)
12. Greenberg, J.O., et al.: Meaningful measurement: developing a measurement system to improve blood pressure control in patients with chronic kidney disease. Journal of the American Medical Informatics Association, p. amiajnl-2012-001308 (2013)
13. Voorham, J., Denig, P.: Computerized Extraction of Information on the Quality of Diabetes Care from Free Text in Electronic Patient Records of General Practitioners. Journal of the American Medical Informatics Association 14(3), 349–354 (2007)
14. Gooch, P., Roudsari, A.: A tool for enhancing MetaMap performance when annotating clinical guideline documents with UMLS concepts (2011)
15. Osborne, R.M., Aronson, A.R., Cohen, K.B.: A repository of semantic types in the MIMIC II database clinical notes. In: ACL 2014, p. 93 (2014)
16. Jonquet, C., Shah, N.H., Musen, M.A.: The open biomedical annotator. Summit on Translational Bioinformatics, 56 (2009)
17. Roeder, C., et al.: A UIMA wrapper for the NCBO annotator. Bioinformatics 26(14), 1800–1801 (2010)
18. Denny, J.C., et al.: Evaluation of a method to identify and categorize section headers in clinical documents. Journal of the American Medical Informatics Association 16(6), 806–815 (2009)

Monte-Carlo Tree Reductions
for Stochastic Games

Nicolas Jouandeau[1] and Tristan Cazenave[2]

[1] LIASD, Université de Paris 8, France
n@ai.univ-paris8.fr
[2] LAMSADE, Université Paris-Dauphine, France
cazenave@lamsade.dauphine.fr

Abstract. Monte-Carlo Tree Search (MCTS) is a powerful paradigm for perfect information games. When considering stochastic games, the tree model that represents the game has to take chance and a huge branching factor into account. As effectiveness of MCTS may decrease in such a setting, tree reductions may be useful. Chance-nodes are a way to deal with random events. Move-groups are another way to deal efficiently with a large branching factor by regrouping nodes. Group-nodes are regrouping only reveal moves and enable a choice between reveal moves and classical moves. We present various policies to use such reductions for the stochastic game CHINESE DARK CHESS. Move-groups, chance-nodes and group-nodes are compared.

1 Introduction

CHINESE DARK CHESS (CDC) is a popular stochastic two player game in Asia that is most commonly played on a 4x8 rectangular board where players do not know payoff of reveal moves. The 2 players (called black and red) start with the same set of pieces. Before the first move, players do not know their colors. The first player move defines the first player color. Then pieces can capture other pieces according to their values and their positions. Even if reveal moves imply a huge number of possible boards, classical moves can lead to similar positions during the game and capturing rules are different for each piece [7]. As Monte Carlo Tree Search (MCTS) techniques deal with nodes statistics, blindness goes along with branching factor. MCTS programs seem to be promising in CDC. In TCGA 2012, one participant was a MCTS program. In TCGA 2013, five participants, including the winner called *DarkKnight*, were MCTS programs. In TCGA 2014, the alpha-beta program *Yahari* won the competition ahead of *DarkKnight*. As CDC has a huge branching due to the revealing moves, we try to reduce the revealing moves dependency by applying different ways of regrouping nodes. In the context of stochastic games, we believe that a better understanding of MCTS behavior is needed. We show in this paper 3 different MCTS implementations, called move-groups, chance-nodes and group-nodes, that are using longer playouts, the same playout policy and no heuristic playouts.

S.-M. Cheng and M.-Y. Day (Eds.): TAAI 2014, LNAI 8916, pp. 228–238, 2014.
© Springer International Publishing Switzerland 2014

Section 2 describes related works. Section 3 presents move-groups, chance-nodes and group-nodes principles applied to MCTS algorithms and different regrouping policies. Section 4 shows experimental results. At the end, section 5 concludes.

2 Related Works

In this section we expose related works on creating nodes and regrouping them in CDC and in stochastic games.

Most previous works related to CDC consider openings building [2], endgames building [3–5], sub-problems resolution [6]. Due to a long expertise in *alpha-beta*, most programs use the minimax extension to games of chance called *expecti-max* [7] with its common pruning extensions *Star1* and *Star2* [8]. It remains that MCTS programs are highly sensitive to their parameters [1].

Move-groups have been proposed in [10] to address the problem of MCTS in games with a high branching factor. When there are too many moves, it can be a good heuristic to regroup the statistics of moves that share some properties. For example in the game of Amazons where the branching factor can be of the order of a thousand of moves, a natural way to reduce the branching factor is to separate the queen move from the stone placement. In the imperfect information game Dou Di Zhu, Information Set [11] has been combined with move-groups: the player first chooses the base move and then the kicker, as two separate consecutive decision nodes in the tree. Move-groups have also been analyzed on an abstract game [12].

Chen *et al.* [7] used *alpha-beta* algorithm with different revealing policies combined with the *initial-depth flipping* method to reduce the branching factor.

Yen *et al.* [1] presented a non-deterministic MCTS with chance-nodes [13]. They create shorter simulation by moderating the three policies named *Capture First*, *Capture Stronger Piece First* and *Capture and Escape Stronger Piece First*.

Jouandeau and Cazenave [9] presented MCTS influence of various playout size, of basic or advanced policies and with heuristic playouts. They studied group constitution related to position's pieces. They showed that relevant playout sizes, policies and heuristic playouts are not equivalent for chance-nodes and group-nodes.

More generally, MCTS has been successfully applied in the past to other multi-player perfect information stochastic games with different regrouping optimizations.

In BACKGAMMON, Monte Carlo playouts have been parallelized to evaluate a position. As playing a position depends on dices, random dices sequences have been also evaluate in parallel. As the number of possible moves increases when dices are doubles, states evaluation can be divided in 2 sub-problems [14] : the first without double dices and the second with double dices. In other words, they distinguished states in 2 groups : light states that have small branching factor and heavy states that have huge branching factor.

In SCRABBLE, simulations are restricted inside a directed acyclic graph to produce existing words [15].

In POKER, betting strategies depends on the gamestate [16] (that can be Pre-Flop, Flop, River). During these gamestates, players' hands are consistent with their actions. Thus simulations are limited to special tracks that are defined by players' hands.

These contributions in other stochastic games show that biased sampling according to particular things of gamestates and regrouping possibilities has been used to settle efficient MCTS playouts.

3   Regrouping Nodes

In this section, we present the use of chance-nodes, move-groups and group-nodes principles applied to MCTS.

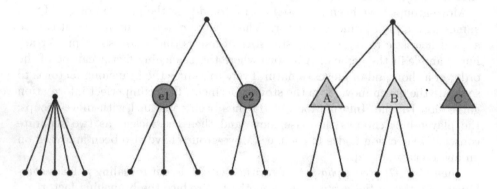

Fig. 1. Common, chance-nodes and move-groups representations

Figure 1 show the differences between representations of a common tree, a tree with chance-nodes and a tree with move-groups. With chance-nodes and move-groups, branching factor reductions can arise. With chance-nodes (related to a game where possible moves are partly defined by rolling a dice), events $e1$ and $e2$ are selecting possible next nodes. With move-groups, children are divided between categories (here 3 categories A, B and C) to perform a smart descent towards the best leaf. When these categories are defined by the moves coordinates in the board, move-groups are called group-nodes.

The main loop of MCTS applied to perfect information games is presented in Alg. 1. It is a statistical search based on 3 steps called *selection*, *expansion* and *backpropagation*, also guided by random games (*i.e.* playouts). The tree expansion is performed to evaluate the current most promising node. The main loop presented is limited to *nbPlayouts* iterations but it can be an anytime process. It can start from an empty tree with its root node only or from a tree filled by previous MCTS loops. The use of such procedure is consistent if and only if the root node is not a *endgame* position (*i.e.* root is not a solved problem). This process can lead to the insertion of 1 to *nbPlayouts* nodes. The select function takes the current tree $\mathcal{T}$ as input and performs descent toward the best node q and returns the move m to produce a new node. Then the **expand** function applies m to q and produces q_{new}. Starting from this new node q_{new}, a playout helps to collect statistical information of q_{new}. Then **backpropagation** function insert q_{new} in the tree $\mathcal{T}$ as statistically informed node and backpropagates q_{new} results of its parents. If during the descent, this q_{new} node is a winning leaf, this leaf is updated and future tree expansions are expected to perform different descents and select different nodes. According to this exclusion of endgames inside $\mathcal{T}$, the **select** function detailed in Alg. 2 always selects node q with at most 1 move. It selects the best node q_{best} from all possible moves m from q or it breaks at the first node $(q + m)$ not in $\mathcal{T}$.

---

input : $\mathcal{T}$ the current tree
output: $\mathcal{T}$ expanded with 1 to $nbPlayouts$ nodes

for $nbPlayouts$ **do**
  (q , m) $\leftarrow$ **select** ($\mathcal{T}$) ;
  q_{new} $\leftarrow$ **expand** (q , m) ;
  res $\leftarrow$ **playout** (q_{new}) ;
  backpropagate (q_{new} , res) ;

Algorithm 1. Classical MCTS applied to perfect information games

---

input : $\mathcal{T}$ the current tree
output: (q , m) where $q \in \mathcal{T}$ and q to expand by applying a move m

$q \leftarrow root$;
while *true* **do**
  $q_{best} \leftarrow \{\emptyset\}$;
  foreach *move m from q* **do**
    if $(q + m) \notin \mathcal{T}$ **then return** (q, m) ;
    $q_{best} \leftarrow$ **best** (q_{best} , $(q+m)$) ;
  $q \leftarrow q_{best}$;

Algorithm 2. Select function of classical MCTS

Considering stochastic games and modifications of tree's representation that are arising with chance-nodes and move-groups usage :

- the **select** function may distinguish types of nodes.
- the endgame shortcut assertion is no more true. Thus endgames can be selected inside **select** function. It implies modifications in main loop and in **select** function.

```
input  : T the current tree
output: T expanded with nbPlayouts iterations
for nbPlayouts do
    ( q , m ) ← select ( T ) ;
    if m ≠ {∅} then
        q_new ← expand ( q , m ) ;
        res ← playout ( q_new ) ;
        backpropagate ( q_new , res ) ;
    else
        res ← result ( q ) ;
        backpropagate ( q , res ) ;
```

Algorithm 3. MCTS applied to stochastic games

The modified main loop is presented in Alg. 3. Even if a descent can lead to an endgame, stochastic games can lead to different events during the descent, that should lead to unevaluated parts of T. The *selection* process is guided by nodes scores and by stochastic events. Thus the statistical scoring process can be applied systematically during *nbPlayouts* iterations, to insert 0 to *nbPlayouts* nodes in T. In such games, *expansion*, *playout* and *backpropagation* are applied only if the selected move m differs from $\{\emptyset\}$.

The modified `select` function with chance-nodes is presented in Alg. 4. At each iteration, the state of the node is checked : if it is a chance-node, then the `dice` function adds an external event to q. If no move is available from q, then $\{\emptyset\}$ is returned as move m to apply. If q is not in T, then q is inserted and the move returned to apply to q is its first move. Thus each time this node is selected, it will try to add another move from q before looking for the best children of q to descend one more time in T.

The modified `select` function with move-groups is presented in Alg. 5. The process is divided between 3 cases :

- there is *no move from q*, that is equivalent to no group available. The process breaks and the tuple (q , $\{\emptyset\}$) is returned.
- 1 *move-group g exists from q*, which means that this group contains at least 1 move. In this case, the process tries to evaluate all possible moves of the move-group g.
- if 2 or more move-groups exists from q, then the process tries to select the first group without a move. If all groups have 1 or more moves, then the best group $\mathcal{M}_{best}$ is selected and 1 move from this group is considered. If this move is not in T, then it returns the tuple (q , m). This process implies to check the intersection between a move-group and T. The `one-move` function defines the policy to generate and add new moves in T.

The modified `select` function with group-nodes is presented in Alg. 6. Revealing moves are regrouped by position. Each position to reveal leads to different

---

input : $\mathcal{T}$ the current tree
output: (q, m) where $q \in \mathcal{T}$ and q to expand by applying a move m

$q \leftarrow root$;
while *true* **do**
  if *q is a chance-node* **then** $q \leftarrow q + $ dice ( ) ;
  else
    if *no move from q* **then break** ;
    if $q \notin \mathcal{T}$ **then**
      | *insert q in* $\mathcal{T}$;
      | **return** (q , *first move from q*) ;
    else
      | $q_{best} \leftarrow \{\emptyset\}$;
      | **foreach** *move m from q* **do**
        | **if** $(q + m) \notin \mathcal{T}$ **then return** (q, m) ;
        | $q_{best} \leftarrow$ best (q_{best} , $(q + m)$) ;
      | $q \leftarrow q_{best}$;
return (q , $\{\emptyset\}$) ;

Algorithm 4. Select function with chance-nodes

---

input : $\mathcal{T}$ the current tree
output: (q, m) where $q \in \mathcal{T}$ and q to expand by applying a move m

$q \leftarrow root$;
while *true* **do**
  if *no move from q* **then break** ;
  if *only 1 move-group g exists from q* **then**
    $q_{best} \leftarrow \{\emptyset\}$;
    foreach *move m of g from q* **do**
      | **if** $(q + m) \notin \mathcal{T}$ **then return** (q, m) ;
      | $q_{best} \leftarrow$ best (q_{best} , $(q + m)$) ;
    $q \leftarrow q_{best}$;
  else
    $\mathcal{M}_{best} \leftarrow \{\emptyset\}$;
    foreach *move-group* $\mathcal{M}$ *from q* **do**
      | **if** $\mathcal{M} \cap \mathcal{T} = \emptyset$ **then**
        | *add* **one-move** *of* $\mathcal{M}$ *in* $\mathcal{T}$;
        | **return** (q , m) ;
      | $\mathcal{M}_{best} \leftarrow$ best ($\mathcal{M}$, $\mathcal{M}_{best}$) ;
    $m \leftarrow$ **one-move** *of* $\mathcal{M}_{best}$;
    if $(q + m) \notin \mathcal{T}$ **then return** (q, m) ;
    $q \leftarrow q + m$;
return (q , $\{\emptyset\}$) ;

Algorithm 5. Select function with move-groups

input : $\mathcal{T}$ the current tree
output: (q, m) where $q \in \mathcal{T}$ and q to expand by applying a move m

$q \leftarrow root$;
while *true* **do**
    if *no move from q* **then break** ;
    $q_{best} \leftarrow \{\emptyset\}$;
    foreach *possible move m from q* **do**
        if *m is a classical move* **then**
            if $(q + m) \notin \mathcal{T}$ **then return** (q, m) ;
            $q_{best} \leftarrow$ best (q_{best} , $(q + m)$) ;
        else if *m is a reveal move* **then**
            $q_{new} \leftarrow$ revealRandomlyAt (q, m);
            if $q_{new} \notin \mathcal{T}$ **then return** (q, m) ;
            $q_{best} \leftarrow$ best (q_{best} , q_{new}) ;
    $q \leftarrow q_{best}$;
return (q , $\{\emptyset\}$) ;

Algorithm 6. Select function with group-nodes

boards. Thus a board with 3 known pieces with 4 possible moves each and with 10 unrevealed pieces will have 12 children for its known pieces and 10 children for its unrevealed pieces. As revealing positions can leads to different boards, possible moves are always recomputed with group-nodes. The select function returns the first unevaluated classical move or the first unevaluated reveal move from the current best node in the tree. The function revealRandomlyAt applies a random reveal at the position m. As revealed pieces will be different, sub-groups will be also different. Thus the group-nodes regrouping policy produced an approximate evaluation of groups.

In this paper, we investigate the way that groups constitution influence MCTS performances in CDC stochastic game. To achieve this, we consider different regrouping policies and different generating policies inside groups:

- revealed group or unrevealed group : these 2 groups are simply defined on the board by revealed and unrevealed pieces. Using these 2 groups, we tried to generate randomly new moves (abrev. *move-group-random*) and to cycle over the considered move-group's elements (abrev. *move-group-cycle*).
- revealed pieces or unrevealed group : this is equivalent to group-nodes. Unrevealed pieces are considered randomly inside the unrevealed group and revealed pieces are considered individually (abrev. *group-nodes*).

4 Experiments

In the first experiment, we compare the 5 regrouping policies *move-groups-random*, *move-groups-cycle-R*, *move-groups-cycle-M*, *group-nodes* and *chance-nodes* to a random player and to a reference player *rand-mm*. The policies *move-groups-cycle-R* and *move-groups-cycle-M* are respectively starting by reveal moves and by real moves. Thus *move-groups-cycle-R* is more dependant on the number of revealing possibilities than *move-groups-cycle-M*. The reference player *rand-mm* simply plays randomly when pieces are unrevealed and otherwise applies minimax to find the best move. In our experiments, UCT (abrev. Upper Confidence bounds applied to Trees) values are computed with

$$(v/(v+d)) + \sqrt{K * log(n)/(v+d)}$$

with n simulations, v wins, d losses and K equals to 0.3. As capture has been proven to contribute in better MCTS evaluations [1, 9], captures are preferred to random moves inside playouts.

As playouts can finish with a draw endgame and are evaluated without heuristic function, we extended the draw rule inside playouts to 640 turns to produce more informed playouts. Results presented in all tables involve 500 games in which half are achieved with one player as first and half are achieved with the other player as first. Games are played with 0.01[sec] per move and with 1[sec] per move.

Table 1. Games against random-player and random-minimax player

Policy	Against *rand*			Against *rand-mm*		
	win	lost	draw	win	lost	draw
with 0.01[sec] per move						
move-groups-random	194	0	306	90	95	315
move-groups-cycle-R	81	0	419	100	400	0
move-groups-cycle-M	202	0	298	100	150	250
group-nodes	314	0	186	1	238	261
chance-nodes	360	0	140	191	13	296
with 1[sec] per move						
move-groups-random	291	0	209	140	42	318
move-groups-cycle-R	64	0	436	0	437	63
move-groups-cycle-M	282	0	218	205	14	281
group-nodes	353	0	147	49	15	436
chance-nodes	393	0	107	249	3	248

Results of table 1 confirm that the *move-groups-cycle-R* policy of cycling on moves and starting by reveal moves is not a good policy. As similar results are obtained with *move-groups-random* and *move-groups-cycle-M*, the knowledge introduced with cycling and starting by known pieces is inefficient to do better than a random selection. Results show that *chance-nodes* are more effective than others with simple playouts (*i.e.* no heuristic evaluation function inside playouts).

In the second experiment, we enhanced these 5 policies by using minimax as the reference player *rand-mm* do. When all pieces are revealed, enhanced

Table 2. Using minimax at the end

Policy	Against *rand-mm*		
	win	lost	draw
with 0.01[sec] per move			
move-group-random-mm	169	1	330
move-group-cycle-R-mm	186	2	312
move-group-cycle-M-mm	166	0	334
group-nodes-mm	24	5	471
chance-nodes-mm	240	0	260
with 1[sec] per move			
move-group-random-mm	265	0	235
move-group-cycle-R-mm	290	0	210
move-group-cycle-M-mm	293	0	207
group-nodes-mm	121	0	379
chance-nodes-mm	310	0	190

players apply minimax to find the best move. Policies are used when pieces are unrevealed and otherwise a minimax search is done. These modified players *move-groups-random-mm*, *move-groups-cycle-R-mm*, *move-groups-cycle-M-mm*, *group-nodes-mm* and *chance-nodes-mm* are compared to *rand-mm* player.

Results of table 2 show that adding minimax search in the perfect information part of games improves all the players. This enhancement makes *chance-nodes-mm* the best player with 0.01[sec] and 1[sec] per move. In case of 1[sec] per move, *move-groups-cycle-R-mm* and *move-groups-cycle-M-mm* are closed to *chance-nodes-mm*. In all these experiments, *rand-mm* obtains quasi null scores.

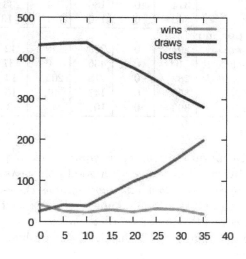

Fig. 2. *chance-nodes-mm* with X random plies against *chance-nodes-mm*

In the third experiment, we evaluate the contribution of chance-nodes by gradually introducing random moves. The figure 2 shows the performance of *chance-nodes-mm* against himself. The second player is weakened with a random move during X first turns. Players are evaluated in 500 games, with 1[sec] per move, from 0 to 35 random moves. It shows that performances are equal when *chance-nodes-mm* plays randomly during its 10 first moves. After 10 first random moves, losts increase and draws decrease. It shows chance-nodes contribution while some unrevealed pieces remain. After 20 turns, the game has more chance to be fully revealed. It shows that similar gain is achieved in the perfect information part of the game. As there are 32 unrevealed positions at the beginning of the game, *chance-nodes* contributes effectively at least in managing 12 unrevealed pieces.

5 Conclusion

Monte-Carlo Tree Search (MCTS) is a powerful paradigm for perfect information games. When considering stochastic games, the tree model that represents the game has to take chance and a huge branching factor into account. We have presented 3 ways to regroup nodes and their consequences to MCTS algorithm and the descent function. We have compared different regrouping policies and different generating policies in CHINESE DARK CHESS games. Experiments show that without heuristic function evaluation, *chance-nodes* regrouping policy is the best for the stochastic part of the game and that adding minimax search in the perfect information part of the game improves all players.

References

1. Yen, S.-J., Chou, C.-W., Chen, J.-C., Wu, I.-C., Kao, K.-Y.: The Art of the Chinese Dark Chess Program DIABLE. In: Chang, R.-S., Jain, L.C., Peng, S.-L. (eds.) Advances in Intelligent Systems & Applications. SIST, vol. 20, pp. 231–242. Springer, Heidelberg (2013)
2. Chen, B.-N., Hsu, T.-S.: Automatic Generation of Chinese Dark Chess Opening Books. In: 8th Int. Conf. on Computers and Games (CG 2013) (2013)
3. Chen, J.-C., Lin, T.-Y., Hsu, S.-C., Hsu, T.-S.: Design and Implementation of Computer Chinese Dark Chess Endgame Database. In: TCGA Computer Game Workshop (TCGA 2012) (2012)
4. Saffidine, A., Jouandeau, N., Buron, C., Cazenave, T.: Material Symmetry to Partition Endgame Tables. In: 8th Int. Conf. on Computers and Games (CG 2013) (2013)
5. Chen, J.-C., Lin, T.-Y., Chen, B.-N., Hsu, T.-S.: Equivalence Classes in Chinese Dark Chess Endgames. IEEE Trans. on Computational Intelligence and AI in Games (TCIAIG-2014) (2014)
6. Chang, H.-J., Hsu, T.-S.: A quantitative study of 2 × 4 chinese dark chess. In: van den Herik, H.J., Iida, H., Plaat, A. (eds.) CG 2013. LNCS, vol. 8427, pp. 151–162. Springer, Heidelberg (2014)
7. Chen, B.-N., Shen, B.-J., Hsu, T.-S.: Chinese Dark Chess. ICGA Journal 33(2), 93 (2010)

8. Ballard, B.W.: The *-minimax search procedure for trees containing chance nodes. Artifical Intelligence 21, 327–350 (1983)
9. Jouandeau, N., Cazenave, T.: Small and large MCTS playouts applied to Chinese Dark Chess stochastic game. In: ECAI 3th Int. Computer Games Workshop 2014 (CGW 2014) (2014)
10. Childs, B.E., Brodeur, J.H., Kocsis, L.: Transpositions and move groups in Monte Carlo tree search. In: IEEE Symp. On Computational Intelligence and Games (CIG 2008), pp. 389–395 (2008)
11. Cowling, P.I., Powley, E.J., Whitehouse, D.: Information Set Monte Carlo Tree Search. IEEE Trans. on Computational Intelligence and AI in Games 4(2), 120–143 (2012)
12. Van Eyck, G., Müller, M.: Revisiting move groups in monte-carlo tree search. In: van den Herik, H.J., Plaat, A. (eds.) ACG 2011. LNCS, vol. 7168, pp. 13–23. Springer, Heidelberg (2012)
13. Lanctot, M., Saffidine, A., Veness, J., Archibald, C., Winands, M.: Monte Carlo *-Minimax Search. In: 23rd Int. Joint Conf. on Artificial Intelligence (IJCAI 2013) (2013)
14. Van Lishout, F., Chaslot, G., Uiterwijk, J.W.H.M.: Monte-Carlo Tree Search in Backgammon. In: Int. Computer Games Workshop (CGW 2007), pp. 175–184 (2007)
15. Sheppard, B.: World-championship-caliber Scrabble. Artificial Intelligence 134, 241–275 (2002)
16. Billings, D., Davidson, A., Schaeffer, J., Szafron, D.: The Challenge of Poker. Artificial Intelligence 134, 201–240 (2002)

LAW: Link-AWare Source Selection
for Virtually Integrating Linked Data

Xuejin Li[1], Zhendong Niu[1], Chunxia Zhang[2], and Xiaoyang Wang[1]

[1] School of Computer Science, Beijing Institute of Technology
xuejinli7@gmail.com
zniu@bit.edu.cn
qduwxy@126.com
[2] School of Software, Beijing Institute of Technology
cxzhang@bit.edu.cn

Abstract. With the wide adoption of linked data principles, a large amount of structural data have emerged on World Wide Web. These data are interlinked and form a Web of Data. Yet, so far, only little attention has been paid to the effect of links on federated querying. This work presents LAW, a novel link-aware approach for federated SPARQL queries over the Web of Data. The source selection module (called LAWS) of LAW can be directly combined with existing federated query engines in order to achieve the same query recall values while querying fewer datasets. We extend three well-known federated query engines with LAWS and compare our extensions with the original approaches. The comparison shows that LAWS can greatly reduce the number of queries sent to the endpoints, while keeping high query recall values. Therefore, it can significantly improve the performance of federated query processing engines. We also have implemented LAW as an independent system. A wide experimental study shows that LAW has higher performance than state-of-the-art federated query systems.

Keywords: federated query processing, SPARQL, Web of Data.

1 Introduction

With the wide adoption of linked data principles, the World Wide Web has evolved from a global information space of linked documents to one where both documents and data are linked [2]. A large amount of structural data on the Web enable new types of applications which can aggregate data from different data sources and integrate fragmentary information from multiple sources to achieve a more complete view. Answering queries across multiple distributed Linked Data sources is a key challenge for developing this kind of applications.

Federated querying over the distributed data sources is called *virtual data integration*. User queries are decomposed into several sub-queries that are distributed to autonomous data sources which execute these sub-queries and return the results which are integrated locally. There are a high number of links in the

S.-M. Cheng and M.-Y. Day (Eds.): TAAI 2014, LNAI 8916, pp. 239–248, 2014.

Web of Linked Data. Yet, so far, only little attention has been paid to the effect of links between datasets on federated querying.

In this paper, we presents LAW, a link-aware approach to source selection for federated querying over the Web of Data. We redefine the RDF graph as the RDF *triple link graph* to reveal links between triples in one single dataset or multiple datasets. We also define basic graph patterns in SPARQL as *triple pattern link graph* to reveal links between triple patterns. To bridge the gap of triple link graphs and triple pattern link graphs, we design a special statistical model called *property link graph* to approximate links between real linked data. Moreover, LAW also provides a distributed join execution mechanism that minimises network traffic during executing selection plans.

Our main contribution presented in this paper is threefold. (1) We formalize the RDF triple link graph and triple pattern graph. (2) We propose an efficient approach of source selection. (3) We perform a comprehensive simulation study based on the real dataset to evaluate our approaches.

The remainder of this paper is structured as follows. In Section 2 we review related works. In Section 3 we present the background knowledge. Section 4 describes the statistical model. Source selection and the execution of selection plans are presented in Section 5. An evaluation of our approach is given in Section 6. Finally, we conclude and discuss future directions in Section 7.

2   Related Works

DARQ [8] extends the popular query processor Jena ARQ to an engine for federated SPARQL queries. It requires users to explicitly supply a configuration file which enables the query engine to decompose a query into sub-queries and optimize joins based on predicate selectivity. SemWIQ [6] requires all subjects must be variables and for each subject variable its type must be explicitly or implicitly defined. Additional information (another triple pattern or DL constraints) is needed to tell the type for the subject of a triple pattern. It uses these additional information and extensive RDF statistics to decompose the original user query. DARQ [8] and SemWIQ [6] potentially assume that RDF triples are independent from each other: if the property or subject class of one triple pattern is defined by one dataset, then they are relevant. FedX[10] also potentially adopts triple independency assumption. It asks all known data sources by SPARQL ASK query form whether they contain matched data for each triple pattern presented in a user query. FedSearch[7] is based on FedX and extends it with sophisticated static optimization strategies. If the amount of known data sources is very large(it is common in an open setting), the query performance may leave much to be desired. SPLENDID [5] relies on the VOID descriptions existing in remote data sources. However, a VOID description is not an integral part of Linked Data principles[1].

In other cases, users are required to provide additional information to determine the relevant data sources. For instance, [13] theoretically describes a solution called Distributed SPARQL for distributed SPARQL query on the top of the Sesame RDF repository. Users are required to determine which SPARQL endpoint the sub-queries should be sent to by the GRAPH graph pattern. The association between graph names and respective SPARQL endpoints at which they reside is explicitly described in a configuration file. The W3C SPARQL working group has defined a federation extension for SPARQL 1.1 [4]. However, remote SPARQL queries require the explicit notion of endpoint URIs. The requirement of additional information imposes further burden on the user. On the other hand, the proposed approach hardly imposes any restrictions on user queries.

The link-aware source selection approach is firstly proposed by Stuckenschmidt [12]. They use predicate path index hierarchies of datasets for source selection. This approach requires predicates of triple patterns must be bounded, and then limits the variety of user queries.

3 Preliminary

The Resource Description Framework (RDF) is a language for representing information about resources in the World Wide Web [?]. By using IRIs to identify things, it provides a simple way to make statements about Web resources. An RDF statement has three parts: subject, predicate(also called property) and object. Formally, RDF triples are defined as:

Definition 1. *Assume that I(IRIs), B(Blank nodes) and L(RDF literals) are pairwise disjoint infinite sets. An RDF statement can be represented as a tuple: $(s, p, o) \in (I \cup B) \times I \times (I \cup B \cup L)$. In this tuple, s is the subject, p is the predicate and o is the object. The tuple representing an RDF statement is called a RDF triple, simply called triple.*

A set of triples can be represented as a RDF graph, where the nodes are its subjects and objects and predicates are represented as directed arcs(edges) which point from subjects to objects. A RDF graph shows the entity-property-values and relations between entities. However, it does not explicitly reveals relations between triples. From the view of link relations, we define a set of triples as a RDF *triple link graph*, where nodes are triples; A triple link graph is a directed graph in which if two triples share at least one resource, then a typed edge linking them is built. For example, two triples (exm:person1 foaf:name "lixj") and (exm:person1 foaf:age 34) are linked by an edge labeled by SS, i.e. they share the same subject.

In SPARQL, the basic graph pattern(BGP) is the fundamental block to build other complex graph patterns, and consists of a set of triple patterns. In distributed SPARQL queries, a triple pattern tp is relevant to a set S of datasets, written as tp^S. We define a BGP associated with relevant datasets to be a *triple pattern link graph*, as following:

Definition 2. *A triple pattern link graph G is an ordered pair (V, E), where V is a set of distinct triple patterns(associated with relevant datasets) and E is a set* *of distinct triple pattern pairs. For each ordered pair* $(v_i, v_j) \in E$, $v_i \in V, v_j \in V$, v_i *and* v_j *share at least one variable.*

Familiar with triple link graphs, edges in triple pattern link graphs have types.

Definition 3. *A selection plan* p_G *for* G *is a triple pattern link graph, where a triple pattern is relevant to one single dataset. The result set of* p_G *are the integration of matched data of triple patterns over their respective relevant datasets.*

Definition 4. *The set* P_G *is the selection plan space of* G. *A selection plan* $p_G \in P_G$ *is an element of this space. The size of* P_G *is the total number of selection plans for* G.

Given a BGP $B = \{tp_1^{S_1}, tp_2^{S_2}, ..., tp_n^{S_n}\}$, the size of P_G is $|S_1| \times |S_2| \times ... \times |S_n|$, where $|S_i|$ is the cardinality of S_i. The optimization problem for B is to prune P_G and exclude any $p_G \in P_G$ whose result set potentially being empty.

4   Statistical Model

To bridge the gap between triple link graphs and triple pattern link graphs, we develop *property link graphs*. Firstly, the property set P of a dataset is collected. Then, for each property $p \in P$, we compute its domain D and range R; a property tuple (D, p, R) is constructed. We define a set $\mathcal{U}$ of property tuples to be a graph U as a set of connected property link graphs. The elements $u \in \mathcal{U}$ are the components of U. For each pair (u_i, u_j) are disconnected. The property link graph of one dataset may link to ones of other datasets. Consequently, links between property link graphs reveal the links between real linked data.

Generally, linked data sources do not explicitly declare domains and ranges of properties. The domain of a property p in one dataset S can be fetched in S by the SPARQL query: SELECT ?d WHERE { ?s p ?o. ?s rdf:type ?d.}. The object of a triple may be a URI or a Literal. Hence, the class the object o of a triple in one dataset S is computed as : (1) if o is a URI, the class of o is fetched in S or from other dataset by dereferencing the URI; if the class of o is not explicitly defined by rdf:type, then o is assigned a common class rdfs:Resource. (2) if o is a typed literal, the class of o is the type of the literal; if o is a plane literal, o is assigned a common class rdfs:Literal.

5   Source Selection and Execution of Selection Plans

To find relevant datasets according to property link graphs, triple patterns are translated to property tuple patterns. For example, a triple pattern (?person foaf:age "34"^^xsd:integer) is translated to the tuple pattern (?person foaf:age {xsd:integer}). If the property tuple pattern of a triple pattern has matched property tuples on the property link graph of a dataset, then we can state that the triple pattern is relevant to this dataset.

By matching property tuple patterns on property link graphs, the relevant datasets and the sets of property tuples for each triple pattern are decided. Then, for each selection plan $p_G \in P_G$, if two triple patterns are joined and their matched property tuples are not joined, then the edge linking them is deleted from p_G. Finally, if p_G become a unconnected graph, then it is excluded from P_G.

For a selection plan, triple patterns relevant to the same dataset are sent together(as a conjunctive query) to the relevant dataset, thus executing them in a single subquery at the respective endpoint. The result set of a selection plan is produced by joining all subqueries.

We implement distributed join operations using an optimizing version of nest-loop join. Subqueries are ordered according to a heuristics-based cost estimation. We use the variable counting technique proposed in [11]. Our algorithm uses a variation of the technique proposed in [10] and is depicted in Algorithm 1. Firstly, It selects the subquery with minimum cardinality(line 3) and append it to the result list(line 4). Then, it selects the subquery from the remaining subqueries which has minimum join cardinality with the last subquery in the result list (line 7-8) and append it to the end of the result list(line 9).

Algorithm 1. Executing A Selection Plan

1: order($sqs : list\ of\ n\ joint\ subqueries$)
2: $result \leftarrow \varnothing$
3: $mincard \leftarrow min(card(sqs[1 - n]))$
4: $result \leftarrow result + \{sqs[j]\}$//j is the index of subquery with minimum cardinality
5: $sqs \leftarrow sqs \backslash sqs[j]$
6: **while** $sq \neq \varnothing$ **do**
7:     $q \leftarrow result[result.len - 1]$
8:     $mincost \leftarrow card(q \bowtie sqs[i])$//i is the index of subquery which has the minimum join cardinality with q
9:     $result \leftarrow result + \{sqs[i]\}$
10:    $sqs \leftarrow sqs \backslash sqs[i]$
11: **end while**
12: **return** $result$

---

6   Experimental Study

In this section we present an experimental evaluation of the LAW approach.

6.1   As an Extension of Other Query Engines

The presented source selection approach(called LAWS) can combine with other query engines. We implemented our source selection approach on top of three different federated query engines: DARQ [8], SPLENDID [5], and FedX [10] and compare our extensions with the original approaches.

Benchmark Setup. As a basis for our evaluation we use FedBench [9], a comprehensive benchmark suite which focuses on analyzing the efficiency and effectiveness of federated query processing strategies over semantic data. FedBench covers a broad range of scenarios and provides a benchmark driver to perform the benchmark in an integrative manner. The overview of the data sets is shown in Table 1(a) in terms of number of triples(#Triples). Queries are shown in Table 1(b) in terms of number of patterns in the WHERE clause and size of results.

Table 1. FedBench datasets and queries

(a) Datasets

Dataset	#Triples
DBpedia	43.6M
NYTimes	335k
LinkedMDB	6.15M
Jamendo	1.05M
Geo Names	108M
SW DogFood	104k
KEGG	1.09M
Drugbank	767k
ChEBI	7.33M

(b) Queries

Query	#Patterns	#Results
CD1	3	90
CD2	3	1
CD3	5	2
CD4	5	1
CD5	4	2
CD6	4	11
CD7	4	1
LS1	2	1159
LS2	3	333
LS3	5	9054
LS4	7	3
LS5	7	393
LS6	5	28
LS7	5	144

Due to the unpredictable availability and latency of the original SPARQL endpoints of the benchmark dataset we used local copies of them which were hosted on five 64bit Intel(R) Xeon(TM) CPU 3.60GHz server instances running Sesame 2.4.2 with each instance providing the SPARQL endpoint for one life science and for one cross domain dataset. The evaluation was performed on a separate server instance with 64bit Intel(R) Xeon(TM) CPU 3.60GHz and a 100Mbit network connection.

Experimental Results. We define $R = \frac{N_e}{N_E}$ and $P = \frac{N_e}{N}$ to measure the quality of source selection, where N_e is the number of effective selection plans generated by query systems and N_E is the number of all effective selection plans that a query should have, N is the number of all selection plans generated by query systems. An effective selection plan means that its result set is not empty.

These three engines and LAW have 100% recall of source selection for all queries. So, we only discuss the result of precision. Table 2 shows the precision of the three federated query engines and LAW. DARQ does not support CD1 and LS2 due to unbound predicates. We can see that LAWS can effectively improve the precision of source selection, thus enable fewer subqueries federation. With

Table 2. Precision of Source Selection(%)(– means not supported)

Query	DARQ	SPLENDID	FedX	LAWS
CD1	–	10	30	33.3
CD2	12.5	100	100	100
CD3	11.4	100	12.5	100
CD4	0.7	100	1.56	100
CD5	12.5	100	12.5	100
CD6	2.8	5.56	5.56	25
CD7	3.1	25	3.13	100
LS1	50	100	100	100
LS2	–	10	10	50
LS3	1.4	100	12.5	100
LS4	11.1	100	100	100
LS5	1.4	12.5	12.5	100
LS6	1.4	12.5	12.5	100
LS7	25	50	25	100
avg.	11.11	58.97	31.27	86.31

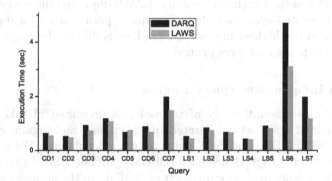

Fig. 1. Query execution time of DARQ and its LAWS extension

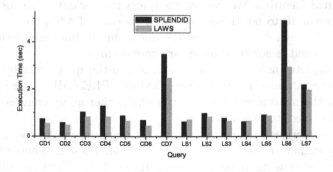

Fig. 2. Query execution time of SPLENDID and its LAWS extension

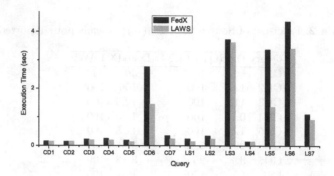

Fig. 3. Query execution time of FedX and its LAWS extension

the LAWS extension, the precision of source selection increases by a percentage of 75.2, 55.04 and 27.34 respective for DARQ, FedX and SPLENDID.

We also measured the average query execution time in each of the federated query approaches and also in their LAWS extension. Figures 1, 2 and 3 show the results. We can see that LAWS improves the query performance for most of the cases. For twelve of the benchmark queries, LAWS improved the query execution times of all federated systems tested. The query performance for queries CD7 and LS6 showed the highest improvements. This is due to the large number of source selection plans that were pruned.

6.2   As an Independent Query Engine

For a widely experimental study of technologies presented in this paper, we have implemented LAW as a federated query engine, and, again, compare it with DARQ, SPLENDID and FedX using another Benchmark. For our tests we adopt the Berlin SPARQL Benchmark (BSBM) [3]. The BSBM executes a mix of 12 SPARQL queries over generated sets of RDF data; the datasets are scalable to different sizes based on a scaling factor. The hardware environments used by BSBM is the same as the one where FedBench is deployed.

Experimental Results. We execute the query mix for datasets generated with scaling factors of 10 to 60; these datasets have sizes of 4,971 to 26,108 triples, respectively. For each dataset we run the query mix 6 times where the first run is for warm up and is not considered for the measures.

Figure 4 depicts the average times to execute the query mix by LAW and the other three federated query engines: DARQ, SPLENDID and FedX. As can be seen from the measures, LAW is better than other query engines for all mix queries with respect to execution times.

Table 3 summarizes the average number of requests sent to the data sources during query evaluation in the SPARQL federation. These numbers immediately explain the improvements in query performance of LAW. With our optimization techniques, LAW is able to minimize the number of selection plans necessary to process the queries.

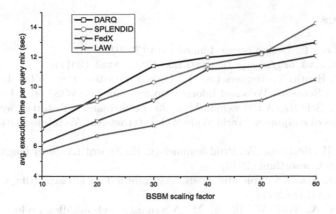

Fig. 4. Average times to execute the BSBM query mix

Table 3. Average Number of Requests

	DARQ	SPLENDID	FedX	LAW
Q1	2	2	5	1
Q2	35	12	22	6
Q3	92,358	689	172	8
Q4	22,331	1,810	696	4
Q5	1	1	2	1
Q6	28,673	1,574	233	6
Q7	1,879	3,231	1,674	4
Q8	35,832	2,785	1,346	4
Q9	1	1	1	1
Q10	4,582	2,056	2,897	4
Q11	X	18,542	2343	4
Q12	1,478	983	486	6

7 Conclusions

In this paper we presented LAW, an approach for link-aware federated querying over the Web of Data. LAW is based on property link graphs approximating triple link graphs. We evaluated our approach against DARQ, SPLENDID and FedX. The evaluation shows that by using the LAWS extension the query execution times were improved in most of the cases. Wide experiments based on BSBM show that LAW as an independent query engine has higher performance than the other three federated query systems.

Acknowledgment. This work was supported by the National Natural Science Foundation of China (no. 61370137, 61272361) and the 111 Project of Beijing Institute of Technology.

References

1. Berners-Lee, T.: Design issues: Linked data (2006), http://www.w3.org/DesignIssues/LinkedData.html (2011)
2. Bizer, C., Heath, T., Berners-Lee, T.: Linked data-the story so far. International Journal on Semantic Web and Information Systems (IJSWIS) 5(3), 1–22 (2009)
3. Bizer, C., Schultz, A.: Benchmarking the performance of storage systems that expose sparql endpoints. World Wide Web Internet And Web Information Systems (2008)
4. Garlik, S.H., Seaborne, A., Prud hommeaux, E.: Sparql 1.1 query language. World Wide Web Consortium (2013)
5. Görlitz, O., Staab, S.: Splendid: Sparql endpoint federation exploiting void descriptions. In: COLD (2011)
6. Langegger, A., Wöß, W., Blöchl, M.: A semantic web middleware for virtual data integration on the web. In: Bechhofer, S., Hauswirth, M., Hoffmann, J., Koubarakis, M. (eds.) ESWC 2008. LNCS, vol. 5021, pp. 493–507. Springer, Heidelberg (2008)
7. Nikolov, A., Schwarte, A., Hütter, C.: FedSearch: Efficiently combining structured queries and full-text search in a SPARQL federation. In: Alani, H., Kagal, L., Fokoue, A., Groth, P., Biemann, C., Parreira, J.X., Aroyo, L., Noy, N., Welty, C., Janowicz, K. (eds.) ISWC 2013, Part I. LNCS, vol. 8218, pp. 427–443. Springer, Heidelberg (2013)
8. Quilitz, B., Leser, U.: Querying distributed rdf data sources with sparql. In: Bechhofer, S., Hauswirth, M., Hoffmann, J., Koubarakis, M. (eds.) ESWC 2008. LNCS, vol. 5021, pp. 524–538. Springer, Heidelberg (2008)
9. Schmidt, M., Görlitz, O., Haase, P., Ladwig, G., Schwarte, A., Tran, T.: FedBench: A benchmark suite for federated semantic data query processing. In: Aroyo, L., Welty, C., Alani, H., Taylor, J., Bernstein, A., Kagal, L., Noy, N., Blomqvist, E. (eds.) ISWC 2011, Part I. LNCS, vol. 7031, pp. 585–600. Springer, Heidelberg (2011)
10. Schwarte, A., Haase, P., Hose, K., Schenkel, R., Schmidt, M.: FedX: Optimization techniques for federated query processing on linked data. In: Aroyo, L., Welty, C., Alani, H., Taylor, J., Bernstein, A., Kagal, L., Noy, N., Blomqvist, E. (eds.) ISWC 2011, Part I. LNCS, vol. 7031, pp. 601–616. Springer, Heidelberg (2011)
11. Stocker, M., Seaborne, A., Bernstein, A., Kiefer, C., Reynolds, D.: Sparql basic graph pattern optimization using selectivity estimation. In: Proceedings of the 17th International Conference on World Wide Web, pp. 595–604. ACM (2008)
12. Stuckenschmidt, H., Vdovjak, R., Houben, G.J., Broekstra, J.: Index structures and algorithms for querying distributed rdf repositories. In: Proceedings of the 13th International Conference on World Wide Web, pp. 631–639. ACM (2004)
13. Zemánek, J., Schenk, S., Svatek, V.: Optimizing sparql queries over disparate rdf data sources through distributed semi-joins. In: International Semantic Web Conference (Posters & Demos) (2008)

Hybridizing Infeasibility Driven and Constrained-Domination Principle with MOEA/D for Constrained Multiobjective Evolutionary Optimization

Huibiao Lin[1,4], Zhun Fan[1,4,*], Xinye Cai[2], Wenji Li[1,4],
Sheng Wang[1,4], Jian Li[3,4], and Chengdian Zhang[1,4]

[1] School of Engineering, Shantou University, Guangdong, 515063 P.R. China
{zfan,13hblin,12cwang2,chengdianzhang}@stu.edu.cn,
wenji_li@126.com
[2] College of Computer Science and Technology, Nanjing University of Aeronautics
and Astronautics,Nanjing, Jiangsu, 210016 P.R. China
xinye@nuaa.edu.cn
[3] College of Science, Shantou University, Guangdong, 515063 P.R. China
lijian@stu.edu.cn
[4] Guangdong Provincial Key Laboratory of Digital Signal and Image Processing Techniques,
Shantou University, Guangdong, 515063 P.R. China

Abstract. This paper presents a novel multiobjective constraint handling approach, named as MOEA/D-CDP-ID, to tackle constrained optimization problems. In the proposed method, two mechanisms, namely infeasibility driven (ID) and constrained-domination principle (CDP) are embedded into a prominent multiobjective evolutionary algorithm called MOEA/D. Constrained-domination principle defined a domination relation of two solutions in constraint handling problem. Infeasibility driven preserves a proportion of marginally infeasible solutions to join the searching process to evolve offspring. Such a strategy allows the algorithm to approach the constraint boundary from both the feasible and infeasible side of the search space, thus resulting in gaining a Pareto solution set with better distribution and convergence. The efficiency and effectiveness of the proposed approach are tested on several well-known benchmark test functions. In addition, the proposed MOEA/D-CDP-ID is applied to a real world application, namely design optimization of the two-stage planetary gear transmission system. Experimental results suggest that MOEA/D-CDP-ID can outperform other state-of-the-art algorithms for constrained multiobjective evolutionary optimization.

Keywords: Multiobjective evolutionary algorithm, Infeasibility driven, Constrained -domination principle, Constrained multiobjective optimization, Penalty functions.

---

* Corresponding author.

S.-M. Cheng and M.-Y. Day (Eds.): TAAI 2014, LNAI 8916, pp. 249–261, 2014.

1   Introduction

Most Real world optimization problems require simultaneous treatment of multiple objectives [1], and involve a number of inequality and/or equality constraints which the optimal solutions must satisfy. A generic constrained multiobjective optimization problem can be formulated as follows:

$$
\begin{aligned}
Min. \quad & f_i(\vec{x}), && i = 1,2,\cdots m, \\
S.t. \quad & g_j(\vec{x}) \leq 0, && j = 1,2,\cdots,p \\
& h_j(\vec{x}) = 0, && j = p+1,\cdots,m
\end{aligned}
\tag{1}
$$

where $\vec{x}$ is the vector of the solutions $(\vec{x} = (x_1, x_2, ..., x_n))$ and $x \in \Omega \subseteq \Re^n, \Omega$ is the set of feasible solutions that satisfy p inequality constraints and $(m-p)$ equality constraints and $\Re^n$ is a n-dimension rectangular space confined by the low boundary and upper boundary of $\vec{x}$ as follows.

$$
l_k \leq x_k \leq u_k, \qquad l \leq k \leq n
\tag{2}
$$

where l_k and u_k are the lower boundary and upper boundary for a decision variable x_k respectively. Usually, equality constraints are transformed into inequality form as follows.

$$
\mid h_j \mid - \varepsilon \leq 0, \qquad j = p+1, ..., m
\tag{3}
$$

where ε is an allowed positive tolerance value.

Over the recent years, constraint handling has become an active area of research for which numerous approaches have been proposed. Some of the commonly used constraint-handling techniques are listed below.

a. Penalty functions methods: Penalty functions methods are one of the most commonly adopted forms of constraint handling[2] [15]. This method uses the constraint violation to punish infeasible solutions. In this approach, the fitness of infeasible solutions is degraded using a sum of constraint violations. The penalty functions methods may work quite well for some constraint handling problem; however, some additional parameters are required in implementations of most penalty functions schemes. The result of the optimization process is known to be highly sensitive to these parameters. As a result, the choice of these parameters is very critical to the success of penalty functions methods for constrained optimization problems.

b. Ranking approaches: In order to eliminate the need for a penalty parameter, Runarsson and Yao [2] introduced a stochastic ranking method based on the objective function and constraint violation values, where a probability parameter is used to determine if the comparison is to be based on objective or constraint violation values. Besides, methods based on the preference of feasible solutions over infeasible solutions have been proposed. For example, Deb [3] [18] proposed a constrained-domination principle that is a feasibility-driven rule to compare individuals.

c. Maintaining infeasible solutions: A few researchers have proposed maintaining a proportion of infeasible solutions in the population during the course of evolution. For single-objective optimization, Coello Coello [4] proposed splitting the population into various subpopulations, each of which uses either the objective or one of the constraints as the fitness function to increase the diversity. Mezura and Coello [5] introduced an archive of infeasible solutions in which the "best" infeasible solution determined by its objective function value is allowed to be copied into the next generation. Cai and Wang [6] suggested a modification of Mezura and Coello [5] approach by using a non-dominated ranking for all the solutions. To focus the search on constraint boundaries with an aim of achieving good quality feasible as well as marginally infeasible solutions, Infeasibility Driven Evolutionary Algorithm (IDEA) was proposed in [7]. IDEA uses a constraint violation measure which firstly ranked the solutions according to each constraint violation, then the sum value of the relative ranking number is defined as a extensional objective function to evolve;thus delivering good quality feasible solutions as well as marginally infeasible solutions for trade-off considerations. This method adds an objective function, also increase the objective space search difficulty.

d. Hybrid methods: A dynamic hybrid framework is proposed by Wang and Cai [15] [16]. The proposed framework consists two major component: global search model and local search model. The search engine used differential evolution [17] , and the selection mechanism of individuals is carried out under pareto-domination concept. This framework has the advantage of implementing global and local search dynamically based on the feasibility proprotion in the current population.

In this paper, Infeasibility driven and constrained-domination principles are embedded into MOEA/D. This constraint handling approach intrinsically treats constraint violation and aggregation function values separately and keeps a balance between exploration and exploitation in the evolution process, wherein a number of infeasible solutions are merged with feasible solutions to evolve and update offspring. Experimental results on several benchmark problems show that the approach performs more effectively and efficiently than the other methods for constrained multi-objective optimization in comparison. The performance of the algorithm is also illustrated using a real-world constraint optimization problem i.e. the two-stage planetary gear transmission system optimization [8] [12].

The remainder of the paper is organized as follows. The details of the proposed algorithm are presented in Section 2 while the experimental results and performance of the algorithm are presented in Section 3. Our proposed MOEA/D_CDP_ID is applied to the two-stage planetary gear transmission system optimization in Section 4. Finally, the paper concludes with some final remarks.

2   The Proposed Approach

The proposed approach extends the ability of MOEA/D [1] [17] to deal with constrained multiobjective optimization problems. Infeasibility driven [7] and constrained-domination principle [3] are embedded to MOEA/D. The details of the proposed schemes are discussed below:

2.1   Constraint Violation

Constraint violation (CV) [2] is a scalar value derived through the summation of total violations of the inequality and equality constraints. If CV equals to zero, the solution is feasible. The degree of constraint violation of an individual on the jth constraint is defined as:

$$G_j(\vec{x}) = \begin{cases} \max\{0, g_j(\vec{x})\}, & 1 \le j \le l \\ \max\{0, |h_j(\vec{x})| - \delta\}, & l+1 \le j \le m \end{cases} \quad (4)$$

In the proposed approach, the degree of constraint violation of an individual is defined as:

$$G(\vec{x}) = \sum_{j=1}^{m} G_j(\vec{x}) / \max(G_j(\vec{x})) \quad (5)$$

2.2   Constrained-Domination Principle

Constrained-domination principle (CDP) [3] defines a domination relation of two solutions in constraint handling problem. A solution A is said to constrained-dominate a solution B, if any of the following conditions is true.

1) Solutions A and B are both feasible and solution A dominates solution B.
2) Solutions A and B are not both feasible, but solution A has a smaller overall constraint violation.

In the proposed approach, CDP is used as a basic comparison mechanism to conduct population update in the MOEA/D. the pseudo code of CDP is shown in algorithm 1.

Algorithm 1. CDP in population update in MOEA/D

1: if $G(x_j) = G(x_{j+1}) = 0$ then
2:      if $f(x_j) > f(j+1)$ then
3:          swap (x_j, x_{j+1}) ;
4:      end if
5: else
6:      if $G(x_j) > G(x_{j+1})$ then
7:          swap (x_j, x_{j+1}) ;
8:      end if
9: end if

2.3   Infeasibility Driven

Infeasibility driven (ID) is a mechanism for constrained handling problem first proposed in Infeasibility Driven Evolutionary Algorithm (IDEA) [7]. ID first evolves a child population and merges the parent population with the child population into a new extended set. Then, the combined population is divided into a feasible set and an infeasible set by constraint violations. When creating the second generation, a certain percentage of feasible solutions (×) and marginally (say, 20%) infeasible solutions (*) are adopted into the new population to evolve. As the presence of infeasible solutions in each population might drives the child populations (C) onto the constraint boundaries where the optimal solutions may exist, as indicated in Figure 1. In infeasibility driven mechanism, infeasible and feasible solutions need to be ranked using original objectives and constraint violation. One ranking scheme is called infeasibility driven ranking. As is shown in Figure 2, in CDP the feasible and infeasible sets are separately ranked using nondominated crowding sorting. We need to define a parameter α that is used to identify the proportion of the infeasible solutions to be retained in the population. If the population size is N, the number of feasible and infeasible solutions in the population are respectively denoted as $(1 - \alpha) \times N$ and $\alpha \times N$.

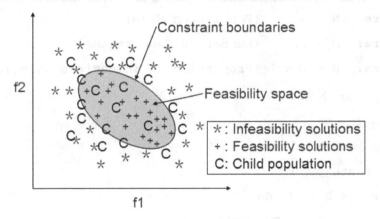

Fig. 1. Illustration of Infeasibility Driven (ID) Mechanism

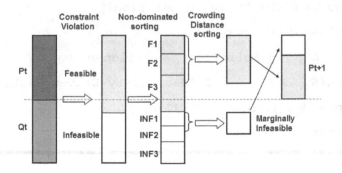

Fig. 2. Infeasibility Driven Ranking

Meanwhile, the infeasible solutions selected first receive a higher rank than the feasible solutions. It is notable that there are some special cases in ranking. For example, if the number of infeasible set is less than $\alpha \times N$, then all the infeasible set are selected. The rest of the solutions are selected from the feasible set by nondominated crowding sorting. If the number of feasible set has fewer than $(1 - \alpha) \times N$, then all the infeasible solutions are ranked by nondominated crowding sorting, and $\alpha \times N$ infeasible solutions are selected. In that case, all the feasible solutions are selected and the rest are filled with the selected infeasible solutions.

Hybridizing infeasibility driven (ID) and constrained-domination principle (CDP) with MOEA/D leads to a new algorithm MOEA/D-CDP-ID for constrained multi-objective evolutionary optimization. The child population Qt is first evolved from parents by MOEA/D-CDP, wherein the CDP mechanism is used to make pair-wise comparisons between individuals for population update in MOEA/D. Then the ID mechanism is applied to the combined population to obtain the offspring population Pt+1. The pseudo code of MOEA/D-CDP-ID is shown in Algorithm 2.

Algorithm 2. MOEA/D-CDP-ID

Require: N   {Population Size}

Require: $N_G > 1$ {Number of Generations}

Require: $0 < \alpha < 1$ {Proportion of infeasible solutions}

1: $N_{inf} = \alpha \times N$

2: $N_f = N - N_{inf}$

3: $pop_1 = $ Initialize()

4: Evaluate(pop_1)

5: **for** $i = 2$ to N_G **do**

6:     $childpop_{i-1} = $ Evolve(pop_{i-1})

        {MOEA/D-CDP Evolve population}

7:     Evaluate($childpop_{i-1}$)

8:     $(S_f, S_{inf}) = $ Split($pop_{i-1} + childpop_{i-1}$)

9:     Rank(S_{inf}, S_f)   { Infeasibility Driven Ranking }

11:    $pop_i = S_{inf} (1:N_{inf}) + S_f (1:N_f)$

12: **end for**

---

3   Experimental Study

In order to evaluate the performance of the proposed algorithm, we tested its performance on several widely used benchmark problems. The parameters' settings are given in Table 1. Features of the selected test problems are listed in Table 2. The aim of the experiment is to test if the ID mechanism added to MOEA/D-CDP or NSGAII-CDP is effective and can help improve the performance of the algorithms. We therefore compared the performance of MOEA/D-CDP-ID with MOEA/D-CDP, and NSGAII-CDP-ID with NSGAII-CDP.

Table 1. Parameter Settings

1	Population size (N)	100
2	Maximal number of generations	500
3	Neighborhood size(T)	20
4	Crossover rate(CR)	0.5
5	Mutation rate(F)	0.5
6	Probability of selecting mating parents from neighborhood	0.9
7	Number of runs:	30
8	Proportion of infeasible solutions(α):	0.2
9	FEmax:	50000

In this study, hypervolume metric [9] is used to compute the performance of the proposed algorithm MOEA/D-CDP-ID, as well as the abovementioned algorithms MOEA/D-CDP, NSGAII-CDP-ID, and NSGAII-CDP. The larger the hypervolume mean value, the better quality of the obtained non-dominated set. The experimental results in table 3 show that the hypervolume mean value is larger when the ID mechanism is added to MOEA/D-CDP and NSGAII-CDP for the test functions OSY, wherein the biggest hypervolume mean value is achieved in MOEA/D-CDP-ID. In the test function CONSTR, the hypervolume mean value in MOEA/D-CDP-ID is larger than MOEA/D-CDP. In addition, the hypervolume mean values are almost equal in NSGAII-CDP-ID and NSGAII-CDP. In this test function, the biggest hypervolume mean value is also achieved in MOEA/D-CDP-ID. In the test function SRN, when the ID mechanism is added to MOEA/D-CDP and NSGAII-CDP, the hypervolume mean values also become larger, even though in this case the biggest hypervolume mean value is achieved in NSGAII-CDP-ID. Based on the above results, it can be safely concluded that the ID mechanism is effective to help the constrained multiobjective optimization algorithms to achieve better performance. In addition, embedding the ID and CDP mechanisms in MOEA/D can lead to effective new algorithm for handling constrained multiobjective optimization problems.

Table 2. Summary of Test Problem

problem	obj/D	Search Range	Constraints	
			Ineq.	Eq.
CONSTR	2/2	[0.1,1],[0,5]	2	0
SRN	2/2	$[-20,20]^D$	2	0
OSY	2/6	[0,10],[0,10],[1,5] [0,6],[1,5],[0,10]	6	0

Table 3. Mean and standard deviation of hypervolume metric values obtained by four Algorithm for benchmark problems

Instance Hypervolume (Runs=30)	CONSTR (ref [1,10])		SRN (ref [300,150])		OSY (ref [0,200])	
	mean	std	mean	std	mean	std
MOEA/D-CDP-ID	**1.054e+1**	3.95e-1	**6.66e+5**	1.07e+5	**1.58e+5**	1.15e+5
MOEA/D-CDP	1.049e+1	5.49e-3	3.48e+5	3.01e+4	7.42e+4	2.21e+4
NSGAII-CDP-ID	1.050e+1	5.34e-3	**9.00e+5**	9.46e+4	**1.35e+5**	6.29e+4
NSGAII-CDP	1.051e+1	2.881e-3	6.98e+5	7.09e+4	7.82e+4	7.42e+3

4   Engineering Optimization Problem

4.1   Two-Stage Planetary Gear Transmission System Optimization Problems

The design problem of two-stage planetary gear transmission system is a ten-variable and bi-objective constrained multiobjective optimization problem [8] [12]. The goal of the design is to minimize volume and the maximize efficiency of the two-stage planetary gear transmission system.

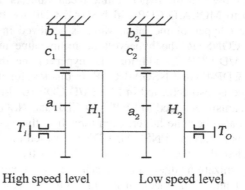

High speed level   Low speed level

Fig. 3. Two-stage planetary gear transmission system

The two-stage planetary gear transmission system is shown in Fig.3 [8]. The design variables of the problem are: the gear width of the two-stage gear($0 \leq B_1 \leq 100$ and $0 \leq B_2 \leq 180$), the module of two stage gear($2 \leq m_1 \leq 10$ and $2 \leq m_2 \leq 10$), the tooth number of two-stage sun gear($14 \leq Z_{a1} \leq 30$ and $14 \leq Z_{a2} \leq 30$), the tooth number of two-stage annular gear($0 \leq Z_{b1} \leq 160$ and $0 \leq Z_{b2} \leq 160$), and the tooth number of two-stage planetary gear($14 \leq Z_{c1} \leq 50$ and $14 \leq Z_{c2} \leq 60$). The vector of the design variables can be defined as follows:

$$X = [x_1 \; x_2 \; x_3 \; x_4 \; x_5 \; x_6 \; x_7 \; x_8 \; x_9 \; x_{10}]^T = [B_1 \; B_2 \; m_1 \; m_2 \; Z_{a1} \; Z_{b1} \; Z_{c1} \; Z_{a2} \; Z_{b2} \; Z_{c2}]^T$$

The two objective functions are defined as follows:
Minimize the volume of the two-stage planetary gear transmission system:

$$V_s = V_{a1} + V_{a2} + V_{b1} + V_{b2} + V_{c1} + V_{c2}$$

$$\approx \sum_{i=1}^{2} \frac{\pi}{4} B_i m_i^2 (Z_{ai}^2 + n_i Z_{ci}^2 + 9 Z_{bi} - 30.2)$$

(6)

Maximize the efficiency of the two-stage planetary gear transmission system:

$$\eta_{a1H2} = \eta_{a1H1}^{b1} \eta_{a2H2}^{b2} = \left[1 - \frac{p_1}{1 + p_1} \varphi^{H1}\right]\left[1 - \frac{p_2}{1 + p_2} \varphi^{H2}\right]$$

(7)

where :

$$p_1 = \frac{Z_{b1}}{Z_{a1}}, p_1 = \frac{Z_{b2}}{Z_{a2}}$$

$$\varphi^H = \varphi_{za}^H + \varphi_{zb}^H + \varphi_n^H, \varphi_{za}^H = \frac{\pi}{2} \varepsilon f_k \left[\frac{1}{Z_a} + \frac{1}{Z_c}\right], \varphi_{zb}^H = \frac{\pi}{2} \varepsilon f_k \left[\frac{1}{Z_c} - \frac{1}{Z_b}\right]$$

φ_n^H is the bearing loss coefficient. n_i is the number of i-stage planetary gear, i.e. $n_1 = n_2 = 3$.

The two-stage planetary gear transmission system is subject to many constraints on gear ratio and adjoining condition of the gears, strength and dimension of the gears, and concentric condition for installation, etc. The lower value of volume means lower mass of the system that leads to lower production cost. Maximizing efficiency is important because maximum efficiency leads to least power consumption for transmission and corresponding savings in the operating costs. The constraint conditions are listed as follows:

$$g_1 = \left| 0.0357 \frac{(x_5 + x_6)(x_8 + x_9)}{x_5 x_8} - 1 \right| - 0.04 \qquad g_2 = 2 + x_7 - (x_5 + x_7)\sin\frac{\pi}{n_1}$$

$$g_3 = 2 + x_{10} - (x_8 + x_{10})\sin\frac{\pi}{n_2} \qquad g_4 = 659130\sqrt{\frac{x_6 - x_5}{x_6 x_3^2 x_5^2 x_1 n_1}} - 1100$$

$$g_5 = 659130\sqrt{\frac{(x_9 - x_8)(x_6 + x_5)}{x_9 x_4^2 x_8^2 x_2 x_5 n_2}} - 1100 \qquad g_6 = \frac{7455600}{x_3^2 x_5 x_1 n_1} - 525$$

$$g_7 = \frac{7455600(x_6 + x_5)}{x_4^2 x_5 x_8 x_2 n_2} - 525 \qquad g_8 = 0.8 - \frac{x_3 x_6}{x_4 x_9}$$

$$g_9 = \frac{x_3 x_6}{x_4 x_9} - 1.2$$

$$h_{10} = x_5 + 2x_7 - x_6 \qquad\qquad h_{11} = x_8 + 2x_{10} - x_9$$

The optimization problem is stated using the state variables X and the constraint conditions based on functions (6) (7) as follows:

$$\text{Min.} \qquad f_1(X) = 0.8754(x_1 x_3^2(x_5^2 + n_1 x_7^2 + 9x_6 - 30.2) + x_2 x_4^2(x_8^2 + n_2 x_{10}^2 + 9x_9 - 30.2))$$

$$\text{Min.} \qquad f_2(X) = -(1 - 0.1178 x_6 \frac{\frac{1}{x_5} + \frac{2}{x_7} - \frac{1}{x_6}}{x_5 + x_6}) \times (1 - 0.1178 x_9 \frac{\frac{1}{x_8} + \frac{2}{x_{10}} - \frac{1}{x_9}}{x_8 + x_9})$$

$$\text{S.t.} \qquad g_i(X), \quad for \quad i = 1,2,...,9$$

$$h_j(X), \quad for \quad j = 10,11$$

$$X = [x_1 \quad x_2 \quad x_3 \quad x_4 \quad x_5 \quad x_6 \quad x_7 \quad x_8 \quad x_9 \quad x_{10}]^T$$

(8)

It is noted that for the second objective function a minus sign is added to convert the original maximization objective to the minimization objective.

4.2 Multiobjective Optimization Results

A population of 100 solutions was allowed to evolve over 500 generations. The same parameters were used for both MOEA/D-CDP and MOEA/D-CDP-ID. In this case study, The experimental results of using MOEA/D-CDP-ID for optimizing the two-stage planetary gear transmission system are also provided. Figure 4 shows the final Pareto front obtained in a typical run, which indicates that MOEA/D-CDP-ID outperforms the MOEA/D-CDP.

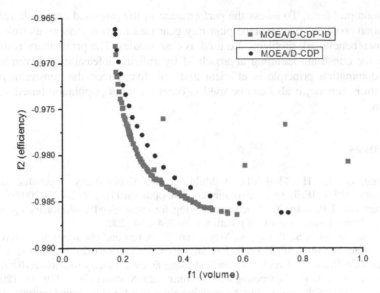

Fig. 4. Final non-dominated fronts for the two-stage planetary gear transmission system optimization using MOEA/D-CDP-ID compared to MOEA/D-CDP

We conducted experiments for 30 runs to verify the results. In the study, a reference point of [5, 5] is used, which is taken by estimating the maximum value of each objective across the runs. As shown in Table 4, MOEA/D-CDP-ID achieves higher values of hypervolume [9] and smaller values of Inverted Generational Distance(IGD) [13] and Averaged Hausdorff Distance(ΔP) [14] as compared to MOEA/D-CDP. Because the smaller value of IGD and Hausdorff Distance the better the performance of the algorithm, we can conclude that MOEA/D-CDP-ID outperforms MOEA/D-CDP.

Table 4. Mean and standard devation of metric values obtained by MOEA/D-CDP-ID compared to MOEA/D-CDP on the two-stage planetary gear transmission system optimization

Instance (Runs=30)	Hypervolume (ref[5,5])		IGD		ΔP(P=2)	
	mean	std	mean	std	mean	std
MOEA/D-CDP-ID	**5.63e+1**	2.09e+1	**2.87e-2**	3.59e-2	**1.07e-2**	1.67e-2
MOEA/D-CDP	4.43e+1	1.66e+1	3.90e-2	8.83e-2	2.78e-2	6.94e-2

5   Conclusions

In this paper, two mechanisms, namely infeasibility driven and constrained-domination principle are embedded within the framework of multi-objective evolutionary algorithm based on decomposition (MOEA/D) [1] to deal with constrained multiobjective optimization problems. To assess the performance of the proposed approach, real-world optimization problems of two-stage planetary gear transmission system, as well as three well-known benchmark problems are used as case studies. The preliminary results indicate that the constraint handling approach of hybridizing infeasibility driven and constrained-domination principle is efficient and effective. Since the constraint handling mechanism is generic, it also can be used in other forms of population based stochastic algorithms.

References

[1] Zhang, Q., Li, H.: MOEA/D: A Multiobjective Evolutionary Algorithm Based on Decomposition. IEEE Trans. Evolutionary Computation 11(6), 712–731 (2007)

[2] Runarsson, T.P., Yao, X.: Stochastic ranking for constrained evolutionary optimization. IEEE Trans. Evolutionary Computation 4(3), 284–294 (2000)

[3] Deb, K., Agrawal, S., Pratap, A., Meyarivan, T.: A fast and elitist multiobjective genetic algorithm: NSGA-II. IEEE Trans. Evolutionary Computation 6(2), 182–197 (2002)

[4] Coello Coello, C.A.: Constraint-handling using an evolutionary multiobjective optimization technique. Civil Engineering and Environmental Systems 17(4), 319–346 (2000)

[5] Hamida, S.B., Schoenauer, M.: An adaptive algorithm for constrained optimization problems. In: Deb, K., Rudolph, G., Lutton, E., Merelo, J.J., Schoenauer, M., Schwefel, H.-P., Yao, X. (eds.) PPSN 2000. LNCS, vol. 1917, pp. 529–538. Springer, Heidelberg (2000)

[6] Cai, Z., Wang, Y.: A Multiobjective Optimization-Based Evolutionary Algorithm for Constrained Optimization. IEEE Transactions on Evolutionary Computation 10(6), 658–675 (2006)

[7] Ray, T., Singh, H.K., Isaacs, A., Smith, W.: Infeasibility driven evolutionary algorithm for constrained optimization. In: Mezura-Montes, E. (ed.) Constraint-Handling in Evolutionary Optimization. SCI, vol. 198, pp. 145–165. Springer, Heidelberg (2009)

[8] Hu, Q., Min, R.: Mult-i objective optimal design study of the two-stage planetary gear transmission system s based on the MATLAB. Modern Manufacturing Engineering (3), 98–101 (2008)

[9] Zitzler, E., Thiele, L., Laumanns, M., Fonseca, C.M., Grunert da Fonseca, V.: Performance Assessment of Multiobjective Optimizers: An Analisis and Review. Computer Engineering and Networks Laboratory, ETH Zurich, Tech. Rep. 139 (June 2002)

[10] Liu, C.-A.: New Multi-Objective Constrained Optimization Evolutionary Algorithm. In: Proc. 3rd Int. Conf. Innovative Computing Information and Control ICICIC 2008 (2008)

[11] Liu, M., Zou, X., Chen, Y., Wu, Z.: Performance assessment of DMOEA-DD with CEC 2009 MOEA competition test instances. In: Proc. IEEE Congress Evolutionary Computation CEC 2009, pp. 2913–2918 (2009)

[12] del Castillo, J.M.: The Analytical Expression of the Efficiency of Planetary Gear Trains. Mechanism and Machine Theory (37), 197–214 (2002)

[13] Coello Coello, C.A., Cruz Cort´es, N.: Solving Multiobjective Optimization Problems using an Artificial Immune System. Genetic Programming and Evolvable Machines 6(2), 163–190 (2005)

[14] Schütze, O., Esquivel, X., Lara, A., Coello, C.A.C.: Using the averaged hausdorff distance as a performance measure in evolutionary multiobjective optimization. IEEE Trans. Evolutionary Computation 16(4), 504–522 (2012)

[15] Wang, Y., Cai, Z.: Combining multiobjective optimization withdifferential evolution to solve constrained optimization problems. IEEE Trans. Evolutionary Computation 16(1), 117–134 (2012a)

[16] Wang, Y., Cai, Z.: A dynamic hybrid framework for constrained evolutionary optimization. IEEE Trans. Syst. Man Cybern. Part B Cybern. 42(1), 203–217 (2012b)
[17] Li, H., Zhang, Q.: Multiobjective optimization problems with complicated Pareto sets, MOEA/D and NSGA-II. IEEE Trans. Evolutionary Computation 13(2), 284–302 (2009)
[18] Deb, K.: An efficient constraint handling method for genetic algorithms. Comput. Meth. Appl. Mech. Eng. 186, 311–338 (2000)

A Transfer-Learning Approach to Exploit Noisy Information for Classification and Its Application on Sentiment Detection

Wei-Shih Lin[1], Tsung-Ting Kuo[1], Yu-Yang Huang[1], Wan-Chen Lu[2], Shou-De Lin[1]

[1] Department of Computer Science & Information Engineering, National Taiwan University
{r00922013,d97944007,r02922050,sdlin}@csie.ntu.edu.tw
[2] Telecommunication Laboratories, Chunghwa Telecom Co., Ltd
janelu@cht.com.tw

Abstract. This research proposes a novel transfer learning algorithm, Noise-Label Transfer Learning (NLTL), aiming at exploiting noisy (in terms of labels and features) training data to improve the learning quality. We exploit the information from both accurate and noisy data by transferring the features into common domain and adjust the weights of instances for learning. We experiment on three University of California Irvine (UCI) datasets and one real-world dataset (Plurk) to evaluate the effectiveness of the model.

Keywords: Transfer Learning, Sentiment Diffusion Prediction, Novel Topics.

1 Introduction

This paper tries to handle the situation where there is no sufficient expert-labelled, high quality data for training by exploiting low-quality data with imprecise features and noisy labels. We generalize the task as a classification with noisy data problem, which assumes both features and labels of some training data are noisy, similar to [1]. More specifically, we have two different domains of labeled training data. The first we call it the high-quality data domain, which contains data of high quality labels and fine-grained features. We assume it is costly to obtain such data, therefore only a small amount of it can be obtained. The other is called the low-quality data domain, which contains noisy data and coarse-grained features. Unlike high quality data, the volume of this data can be large.

The example we use throughout this paper to describe our idea is the compulsive buyer prediction problem given transaction data from different online stores (e.g. Amazon, eBay, etc.). Let us assume the users' transaction records from different online websites are obtained as our training data to train a model for compulsive buyer classification. As shown in Fig. 1, there are some common features for users across these stores, such as gender and month or birth. However, there are also features that are common across different stores but have different granularity due to different registration processes. For instance, age can be exact (e.g. 25 years old) or in a range (e.g. 20~30), and same situation applies to locale and job categories.

S.-M. Cheng and M.-Y. Day (Eds.): TAAI 2014, LNAI 8916, pp. 262–273, 2014.
© Springer International Publishing Switzerland 2014

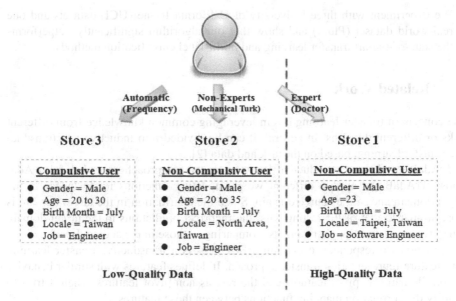

Fig. 1. An Example of Compulsive User Prediction

Assume we ask experts to annotate whether a person is a compulsive buyer based on the transaction and content information of a more fine-grained dataset from a particular store. This dataset is considered the high-quality data. For the data with coarse-grained features, we can hire non-experts (e.g., through Mechanical Turk) or exploit some indicators such as shopping frequency and quantity to label data. Such data (we call it low-quality data) might not be as accurate and precise as the high-quality data, but can potentially boost the learning performance under the assumption that there is only few high-quality data available. Training a classifier using such data is non-trivial because (1) the features/labels in the low-quality domain might not be precise/correct, and (2) the data distribution in the low-quality training domain and the testing domain might not be identical.

In this paper, we propose a novel transfer learning algorithm, Noisy-Label Transfer Learning (NLTL). First, we identify the mapping function between features from different domains. Next, we learn the importance of instance based on the labels from the different domain of data. Finally, we exploit the learnt importance of instances to improve the prediction accuracy. To summarize, the main contributions of this paper are as follows:

- We introduce a novel and practical classification task given noisy data. In this problem, only small amount of correctly labeled data along with large amount of roughly labeled data are available for training.
- We propose a transfer learning approach to solve the above-mentioned problem, and provide a practical application scenario on sentiment diffusion prediction.

- We experiment with three University of California Irvine (UCI) datasets and one real-world dataset (Plurk) and show that our algorithm significantly outperforms the state-of-the-art transfer learning and multi-label classification methods.

2   Related Work

The concept of transfer learning lies in leveraging common knowledge from different tasks or different domains. In general, it can be divided into inductive and transductive transfer learning, based on the task and data [2].

TrAdaBoost [3] is an inductive instance transfer approach extended from Ada-Boost. TrAdaBoost applies different weight-updating functions for instances in the target domain and in the source domain. Since the distribution in the target domain is more similar to that of the testing data, the incorrect predictions in the target domain generally are assigned higher weights, comparing to those in the source domain.

Structural Correspondence Learning (SCL) [4] is a transductive transfer learning with feature-representation transfer approach. It defines features with similar behavior in both domains as pivot features and the rest as non-pivot features. Then it tries to identify the correlation mapping functions between these features.

Our proposed algorithm belongs to transductive transfer learning, which applies both instance and feature-representation transfer. However, the most important difference is that we deal with items that have diverse labels in different domains. Those items are used to serve as a bridge to connect different domains.

3   Methodology

3.1   Problem Definition

We start by formulating the problem. Suppose a high-quality domain dataset D_H and N different low-quality domain dataset D_{L_j}, where $1 \leq j \leq N$, are given. We define high-quality domain data as $D_H = \{(x_{H_1}, y_{H_1}), ..., (x_{H_{n_H}}, y_{H_{n_H}})\}$, where n_H is the number of instance in D_H, $x_{H_i} \in X_H$ represent the features of an instance, and $y_{H_i} \in Y_H$ is the corresponding label. Here we assume low-quality domain data can come from multiple sources, defined as $D_L = \{D_{L_1}, ..., D_{L_N}\}$ and $|D_L| = n_L$. The low-quality domain data from each source can be presented as $D_{L_j} = \{(x_{L_{j_1}}, y_{L_{j_1}}), ..., (x_{L_{j_{n_{L_j}}}}, y_{L_{n_{L_j}}})\}$, where n_{L_j} is the number of instance in D_{L_j}, $x_{L_{ji}} \in X_{L_j}$, and $y_{L_{ji}} \in Y_{L_j}$. Moreover, we assume that instances in D_H contain high quality labels and fine-grained features and those in D_L have coarse-grained features and noisy labels. Note that in general we assume $n_H \ll n_L$, as obtaining high quality data is more expensive and time-consuming.

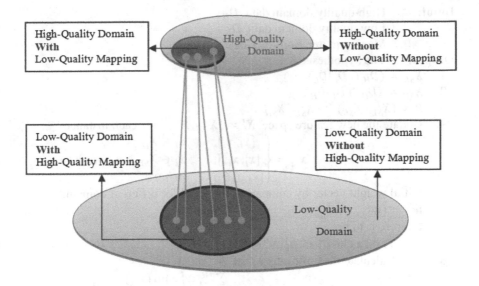

Fig. 2. Sketch Illustration for Instances

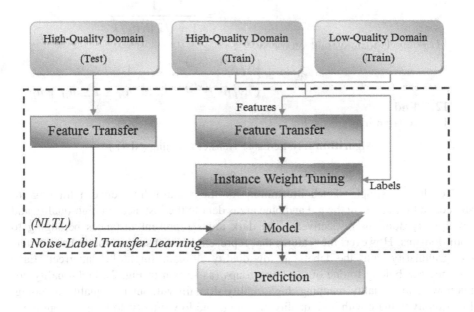

Fig. 3. Algorithm Architecture

Input: High-quality domain data D_H.
              Low-quality domain data D_L.
              Maximum iterations of AdaBoost k.

Output: The hypothesis h.

1. $X_{SL} = (D_H \cap D_L | D_L)$
2. $X_{SH} = (D_H \cap D_L | D_H)$
3. $\theta = (X_{SL}^T \cdot X_{SL})^{-1} \cdot X_{SL}^T \cdot X_{SH}$
4. Update the new feature space $X' = \{X'_H, X'_L\}$ for each instance:

$$x'_i = \begin{cases} [x_i, x_i], & x_i \in X_H \\ [x_i, x_{i*}], & x_i \in X_{SL} \wedge x_i \text{ maps to } x_{i*} \\ [x_i, x_i \theta], & others \end{cases}$$

5. Initial weight vector by comparing the label for different domain:
   $w^1 = (w_1^1, \dots, w_{n_H + n_L}^1)$.
6. **For** $t = 1$ to k:
7.   Train a classifier $h_t : X' \rightarrow [0, 1]$.
8.   Calculate the error rate ϵ_t of h_t on X'_H:

$$\epsilon_t = \frac{\sum_{i=1}^{n_H} w_i^t \cdot |h_t(x'_i) - y_i|}{\sum_{i=1}^{n_H} w_i^t}$$

9.
$$\beta_t = \frac{\epsilon_t}{1 - \epsilon_t}$$

10.
$$\beta = \frac{1}{1 + \sqrt{2 \ln n_L / k}}$$

11.   Update weight vector w^{t+1}:

$$w_i^{t+1} = \begin{cases} w_i^t \beta_t^{-|h_t(x'_i) - y_i|}, & 1 \le i \le n_H \\ w_i^t \beta^{|h_t(x'_i) - y_i|}, & n_H \le i \le n_H + n_L \end{cases}$$

12. **End**
13. **Return** hypothesis h_k.

Algorithm 1. Noise-Label Transfer Learning (NLTL)

We show a simple sketch illustration for the relationship between training instances in Fig. 2, where the red and blue areas denote the instances in high-quality and low-quality domains respectively. The dark areas represent instances belonging to both domains. However, the features that represent these instances might have different granularity, and the labels in low-quality domain might be incorrect. Each instance can belong to one of the four groups (as shown in Fig. 2), high-quality domain with low-quality mapping, high-quality domain without low-quality mapping, low-quality domain with high-quality mapping, and low-quality domain without high-quality mapping. Finally, the task to be solved is defined as given $D_{H_{train}}$ and $D_{L_{train}}$, learn an accurate classifier to predict $D_{H_{test}}$.

3.2 Noise-Label Transfer Learning (NLTL)

We propose NLTL, which is a transfer learning model to solve the above-mentioned problem. The overall architecture is shown in Fig. 3. The idea is to transfer information from low-quality domain data to improve the prediction in high-quality domain which has insufficient training instances. Note that for each object, we may integrate corresponding instances from multiple low-quality data sources. NLTL first uses instances existing in both high-quality and low-quality domains as a bridge to identify the correlation between coarse-grained and fine-grained features. Then it learns the weight of instances from each domain to train a binary classifier to predict testing data in the high-quality domain. It should be noted that we perform feature transfer on both training and testing data, however, only training data are used to learn the weight of instances since testing data are not labeled. We define NLTL in Algorithm 1. Feature transfer is performed using Structural Corresponding Learning (SCL) [4] (Step 1 to Step 4, see 3.3), and TrAdaBoost [3] is used to tune the weight of instances (Step 5 to Step 12, see 3.4).

3.3 Feature Transferring

We want to handle the problem that the quality of features in low-quality domain is not as good as that in high-quality domain in terms of granularity. The goal is to identify a mapping function to project the features in the low quality domain to the high quality domain, by changing their distributions.

We propose a method based on Structural Corresponding Learning (SCL) [4]. The intuition is to identify the correspondences among the features from different domains by modeling their correlation with features that have similar distribution in both domains. To transfer the low-quality data into high-quality domain, for each feature in the low-quality domain, it is necessary to find its mapping to the more fine-grained high-quality domain. Here we propose to create a prediction model to perform the mapping. That is, for each feature in the high-quality domain, we create a classification or regression model, for categorical and numerical features respectively, to predict its value given each corresponding instance in the low-quality domain. Assume an user u appears in both high-quality domain (its feature vector, denoted as u_{s1}, is {"Male", "22", "May", "Taipei", "Software Engineer"}) and low-quality domain (feature vector denoted as u_{s2} , which is {"Male", "20 to 30", "May", "Taiwan", "Engineer"}). u_{s1} will of course be used as the training example to learn a compulsive user model, but we want to use u_{s2} as well to enlarge the training set. Therefore, for each feature in the high-quality domain, we create a classifier that maps u_{s2} to a corresponding value. In our example, we will build 4 classifiers and 1 regressor (for 'age' feature), each of which takes an instance in u_{s2} as input and output the possible assignment for the fine-grained feature.

We denote these models as mapping function θ, and it models the correlation between the features from different domain. In the experiment we use linear regression to learn θ.

$$\theta = (X_{SL}^T \cdot X_{SL})^{-1} \cdot X_{SL}^T \cdot X_{SH}$$

where X_{SL} denotes features with instances in the low-quality domain that have high-quality mapping, and X_{SH} denotes features with instances in the high-quality domain that have low-quality mapping.

Finally, we create a new feature space, which is twice in length comparing to the original feature space, for the processed instances. The instances are processed in three different ways. 1) For instances appear in both low-quality and high-quality domains, we concatenate the corresponding low-quality features with the original high-quality features. 2) For instances that only appear in high-quality domains, we simply copy the features and concatenate them to the end. 3) For instances that only appear in low-quality domain, we first generate the corresponding mapping to the high-quality domain, and then treat it like case 2.

3.4   Instance Weight Tuning

We are now ready to exploit the instances from both domains to train a classifier. However, it is apparent that the instances from high-quality and low-quality domains should not be treated equally during training. Here we propose a method to adjust the initial weights on each instance according to the following heuristics.

- Instances in the high-quality domain should have higher weights. Furthermore, if the corresponding low-quality instances also contain identical label, the weight is even higher.
- For instances in the low-quality domain that can be mapped to high-quality domain with the same labels, their weights should be greater than the weights of the instances that cannot be mapped to high-quality domain.

We order the instances based on the above heuristics, and assign initial weight as $W_i = W_{i-1} \times \alpha$ where $\alpha < 1$, W_i and W_{i-1} stands for instances of order i and i-1. W_i represents the set of weights to the instances. After setting initial instance weights, we apply TrAdaBoost [3] to tune the weights iteratively. The intuition of TrAdaBoost is to use different weight-updating function for different domain data. More specifically, we increase the weight more if the instance is predicted incorrectly in high quality domain. The assumption of this setting is that the data in low-quality domain does not have as high confidence score as those in high-quality domain. The formulas of TrAdaBoost to update the instance weights are as follows:

$$w_i^{t+1} = \begin{cases} w_i^t \beta_t^{-|h_t(x_i)-y_i|}, \text{ in high-quality domain} \\ w_i^t \beta^{|h_t(x_i)-y_i|}, \text{ in low-quality domain} \end{cases}.$$

where β and β_t are multiplier calculated by error rates and traditional AdaBoost.

Table 1. Experiment Results in AUC

	CTG	Magic	Wine
High-Quality	88.35%	75.49%	69.95%
Low-Quality_1	85.58%	76.91%	73.89%
Low-Quality_2	85.14%	58.81%	66.28%
All Instance	89.20%	78.22%	75.37%
TrAdaBoost	89.56%	81.28%	76.52%
SCL	86.58%	76.04%	69.42%
Label-Powerset	85.77%	78.82%	71.29%
NLTL	**91.83%**	**81.71%**	**76.63%**

4   Experiments

4.1   Dataset and Settings

We test our model on three datasets (CTG, Magic, and Wine) collected from UCI Machine Learning Repository [5]. We preprocess the labels to binary classes in our experiment. The three datasets contain 2126, 19020, and 6497 instances and 21, 10, and 11 features, respectively. For each dataset, we use original features and labels as high-quality domain data. To generate noisy low-quality domain data, we randomly pick c% of instances, flip their labels, and modify their features to be coarser. For example, for a numerical feature, we quantize its values into K groups, and assign the medium value for each group as the new feature value. In our experiment, we generate two low-quality domain datasets with $(c, K) = (20, 5)$ and $(c, K) = (50, 10)$. To reflect the fact that correctly labeled data are rare, we randomly choose 10% of high-quality domain data for training and keep the remaining for testing. We use 4-fold cross validation for evaluation.

We choose area under ROC curve (AUC) as the evaluation metric because of data imbalance. We rank the testing instances base on the predicted positive probability, and then compare it to the ground truths to produce AUC. For weight tuning, we manually assign the largest weight to 10 and α to 0.7. That is, the second largest weight is 7, third is 4.9, and so on. We compare our model with three types of algorithms, traditional non-transfer learning (High-Quality, Low-Quality_1, Low-Quality_2 and All Instance), transfer learning (TrAdaBoost and SCL), and multi-label (Label-Powerset) algorithms.

4.2   Results

We show the results comparing other baselines to NLTL in Table 1. The best results are marked in bold.

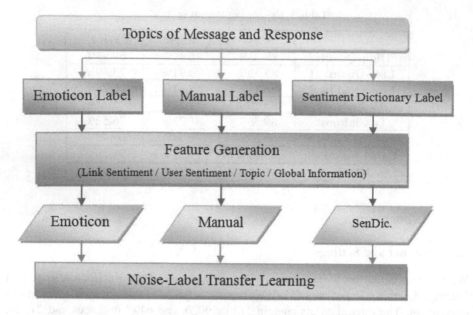

Fig. 4. Framework of Sentiment Diffusion Prediction with NLTL

The results show that NLTL outperforms the competitors for all dataset, especially for CTG. It also shows that by exploiting low-quality domain data, NLTL is useful and can improve the result using only high-quality domain data (denoted as High-Quality in Table 1) up to 6.7% in terms of AUC. On the other hand, NLTL combines the advantages of TrAdaBoost and SCL. It considers not only features but also labels to the same items together. The improvement of NLTL over baseline algorithms shows that both features and labels information from low-quality domain data are important and useful.

5   Sentiment Diffusion Prediction on Novel Topics

In this section, we use NLTL to handle a novel real-world sentiment diffusion prediction problem. Sentiment prediction aims at predicting whether an opinion is positive or negative [6]. However, in this application, we are interested in predicting the diffusion of sentiment through social networks. In other words, we emphasize on sentiment "diffused" rather than sentiment "expressed" by a user. Analyzing sentiment diffusion allows us to understand how people react to other people's comments on micro-blog platforms.

Traditional sentiment prediction uses a variety of textual or linguist information as features [6]. Such solution has a serious drawback as it is unable to handle new topics that appear rarely. On the other hand, Kuo et al. [7] propose a method to predict the diffusion on novel topics utilizing latent and social features. Rather than predicting the existence of diffusion, we extend [7] to predict the diffusion of sentiments.

Our framework applies NLTL as shown in Fig. 4. We first provide high-quality and low-quality labels using three methods, and then the features are generated as described before. Finally, we learn a classifier using both high-quality and low-quality domain data, and show that low-quality domain data is useful in improving the performance.

5.1 Labeling

We provide high-quality labels (manual labeling) as well as low-quality labels (using emoticon and sentiment dictionary). The low-quality labeling methods are automatic and low-cost but the result may contain noises.

- **Emoticon Labeling.** We first manually classify the emoticons which are clearly positive or negative. Then, we use the emoticons to decide the label (positive or negative) of the diffusions.
- **Manual Labeling.** Human annotators are asked to label whether the content is positive, negative, or unknown.
- **Sentiment Dictionary Labeling.** We construct a sentiment dictionary and label the diffusions based on the voting of the words in the sentiment dictionary.

5.2 Dataset

We first identify 100 top discussion topics from Plurk micro-blog site [8]. We collect the messages and responses from users who discuss about those topics in the period from 01/2011 to 05/2011. A diffusion of sentiment is denoted as (x, y, t, s), which means user x posts a message of topic t, and user y responses x with sentiment s (positive or negative, labeled by different methods introduced in 5.1). This dataset contains 699,985 objects, thus is not practical to label them all manually. We choose 17% of the objects to be labeled manually, while other objects are labeled using emoticon and sentiment dictionary. Finally, we obtain 82,277 diffusions from manual labeling, 117,876 diffusions from emoticon labeling, and 396,370 diffusions from sentiment dictionary labeling.

5.3 Feature Generation

To perform sentiment prediction, we design the following features. We divide the proposed features into four types as follows.

- **Link Sentiment Information.** The link sentiment information describes the tendency of each link in the network to be positive or negative for a given topic. For a link, link sentiment score (LS) is calculated by comparing the number of times that a positive or negative content is diffused. That is, we increase LS by one for each positive diffusion and decrease LS by one for each negative diffusion.

Table 2. Sentiment Diffusion Prediction results

	All Features	**Best Features**
High-Quality	62.90%	65.04%
Low-Quality_1	61.73%	65.36%
Low-Quality_2	63.47%	66.26%
All Instance	62.13%	64.25%
SCL	61.65%	62.33%
TrAdaBoost	61.84%	65.27%
Label-Powerset	59.58%	62.59%
NLTL	**64.21%**	**68.30%**

- **User Sentiment Information.** Similar to link sentiment information, user senti-ment information models the tendency of each user to reply to positive/negative posts. For a user, we generate the user sentiment score according to sender aspect (USS), receiver aspect (USR), and sender-receiver aspect ($USSR$). More specifical-ly, for USS we only consider the number of positive and negative posts sent by us-er, and ignore those received by this user. On the other hand, USR only considers the number of positive and negative posts received by user. $USSR$ considers both aspects.
- **Topic Information.** We follow the same approach described in [7] to extract latent topic signature (TG) features. Besides TG, we also extract topic similarity (TS) features weighted by link sentiment information and user sentiment information. There are four features generated based on topic similarity, topic similarity for link sentiment ($TSLS$), topic similarity for user sentiment with sender aspect ($TSUSS$), topic similarity for user sentiment with receiver aspect ($TSUSR$), and topic similar-ity for user sentiment with sender-receiver aspects ($TSUSSR$).
- **Global Information.** We extract global social features such as in-degree (ID), out-degree (OD), and total-degree (TD) from social network. Note that these three fea-tures remain the same for different labeling methods; thus, we utilize them as pivot features in SCL and NLTL algorithms.

5.4   Results

The experiment setting of sentiment diffusion prediction task is the same as that de-scribed in Section 4. We compare NLTL that utilizes three sources to the competi-tors as described in 4.1. We run the experiment on two set of feature combinations: using all features and the best feature combination chosen using wrapper-based for-ward selection method [9]. The result shows that NLTL is able to integrate the infor-mation of features and labels to outperform the competitors by a large margin.

6   Conclusion

In this paper, we propose a novel prediction problem together with a transfer learning algorithm to solve it. We serve the objects which have multiple labels as a bridge and transfer knowledge from different data domains. We update instance weights and transfer features by comparing labels and features in high-quality domain and low-quality domain simultaneously. The experiment result shows NLTL consistently outperforms the competitors. Furthermore, we propose a real-world task of sentiment diffusion prediction that can benefit from our framework. Our experiments demonstrate how such problem can be formulated into a noisy-label prediction task that can be solved using NLTL.

Acknowledgement. This work is primarily supported by a grant from Telecommunication Laboratories, Chunghwa Telecom Co., Ltd under the contract No. TL-103-8201.

References

1. Sáez, J.A., Galar, M., Luengo, J., Herrera, F.: Tackling the Problem of Classification with Noisy Data Using Multiple Classifier Systems: Analysis of the Performance and Robustness. In: Information Science (2013)
2. Pan, S.J., Yang, Q.: A Survey on Transfer Learning. IEEE Transactions on Knowledge and Data Engineering 22, 1345–1359 (2010)
3. Dai, W., Yang, Q., Xue, G., Yu, Y.: Boosting for Transfer Learning. In: Proceedings of the 24th International Conference on Machine Learning, pp. 193–200 (2007)
4. Blitzer, J., McDonald, R., Pereira, F.: Domain Adaptation with Structural Correspondence Learning. In: Proceedings of the 2006 Conference on Empirical Methods in Natural Language Processing, pp. 120–128 (2006)
5. Bache, K., Lichman, M.: UCI Machine Learning Repository. University of California, School of Information and Computer Science, Irvine (2013)
6. Meng, X., Wei, F., Liu, X., Zhou, M., Li, S., Wang, H.: Entity-Centric Topic-Oriented Opinion Summarization in Twitter. In: Proceedings of the 18th ACM SIGKDD International Conference on Knowledge Discovery and Data Mining, pp. 379–387 (2012)
7. Kuo, T.-T., Hung, S.-C., Lin, W.-S., Peng, N., Lin, S.-D., Lin, W.-F.: Exploiting Latent Information to Predict Diffusions of Novel Topics on Social Network. In: Proceedings of the 50th Annual Meeting of the Association for Computational Linguistics, pp. 344–348 (2012)
8. Kuo, T.-T., Hung, S.-C., Lin, W.-S., Lin, S.-D., Peng, T.-C., Shih, C.-C.: Assessing the Quality of Diffusion Models Using Real-World Social Network Data. Technologies and Applications of Artificial Intelligence (TAAI) 2011, 200–205 (2011)
9. Kohavi, R., John, G.H.: Wrappers for feature subset selection. Artificial Intelligence 97(1), 273–324 (1997)

A Framework for Personalized Diet and Exercise Guideline Recommendation

Yu-Feng Lin[1], Cheng-Hao Chu[1], Bo-Hau Lin[1], Yi-Ching Yang[2], Vincent S. Tseng[1,*],
Miin-Luen Day[3], Shyh-Chyi Wang[3], and Kuen-Rong Lo[3]

[1] Department of Computer Science and Information Engineering,
National Cheng Kung University, Tainan, Taiwan
[2] Department of Family Medicine, National Cheng Kung University Hospital,
Tainan, Taiwan
[3] Telecommunication Laboratories, Chunghwa Telecom Co., Ltd.
tsengsm@mail.ncku.edu.tw

Abstract. Due to the popularity of information sources on medical educational sites, people are becoming to pay more attention on individual health care and disease prevention. According to the report of regular comprehensive physical examination or daily self-measurement using medical devices, now people can clearly understand the vital signs and physiological changes in order to detect the disease and treatment. Although a number of health management systems provided from medical institutions have been developed for recording the daily health measurements, users still have to take the record to medical institutions and ask for self-care guidelines from health care providers. This paper thus proposes a novel framework of virtual assistant system for personal health management, which can analyze the report of regular comprehensive physical examination to calculate the health risk and provide personalized health care services for users in terms of diet and exercise guideline recommendation.

Keywords: Personalized healthcare services, diet and exercise guideline recommendation, comprehensive physical examination, virtual assistant system.

1 Introduction

Due to the busy and high pressure modern life, many people cannot keep the healthy living style and tend to be in lack of exercise with eating disorders. Consequently, the populations of chronic illness (e.g., hypertension, diabetes and metabolic syndrome) are getting more and young [1]. If people can maintain a healthy lifestyle (e.g., through diet and exercise), as well as control their glucose, blood lipids, blood pressure and waist circumference, chronic illness can be effectively prevented. Hence, self-health management is very important in preventing chronic illness [1, 2, 3, 9]. With vigorous development of the Internet, public knowledge of self-health management and individual health care have been put on the websites, and people can clearly understand that how to manage self-health. However, even though a number of health

---

* Corresponding author.

S.-M. Cheng and M.-Y. Day (Eds.): TAAI 2014, LNAI 8916, pp. 274–283, 2014.

management systems provided from medical institutions have been developed for recording the daily self-measurement by users, users still have to take the record to medical institutions and ask for self-care guidelines from health care providers [2, 9, 10, 11].

In this paper, we propose a novel framework of virtual assistant system for personal health management, which can analyze the report of regular comprehensive physical examination to calculate the health risk and provide personalized health care services for users in terms of diet and exercise guideline recommendation. In addition, this paper also designs a module for supervising and reminding users to meet the recommended plans of personalized diet and exercise guidelines. However, achieving these aims was not an easy task, due to following reasons: First, the design of system involves the integration of clinic experience and knowledge, computer and information technology, as well as human-machine interface. Second, the vital signs and physiological changes of interest vary among users, and so the recommending diet and exercise guideline module of the system need to be personalized for different users.

To address these issues, a novel framework is proposed for constructing a *Virtual Assistant System for Personal health management*, called *VASP*. The major contributions of this work are as follows:

I.   This study is the first to target the topic of automatic recommendation of personalized diet and exercise guidelines according to the analysis of the individual report of regular comprehensive physical examination.

II. The idea of an active database which automatically executes specified actions when specified conditions arise is employed to set the individual plans from users to supervise and remind them for meeting the recommended diet and exercise guidelines.

The remainders of this paper are organized as follows. We describe related works in Section 2. Then, the proposed framework is introduced in details in Section 3. Conclusions and future works are given in Section 4.

2   Related Works

Recently, many medical institutions can provide various services and resources for personal health management on the Internet [1, 2, 5, 6, 9, 10, 11]. In this aging society, the remote monitor system is needed for the elderly home care, and the system can help medical experts efficiently maintain their patients or avoid the elderlies on the danger. A part of existing remote monitor systems already supports various wearable devices to collect the vital signs from the users. The vital signs can be uploaded to the database of the remote monitor system provided by medical institutions. The experts then analyze the vital signs to determine the health state of their patients on real time.

Although the remote monitor system can automatically send alarms when the vital signs are abnormal, those systems do not assess the health risk and give users some guidelines for the risk [6, 7, 8, 12, 13]. The personal health management system is a platform for the users to request the assessment of health risk from the data of users' physical examination. The personal health management system provided by the medical institutions or companies on the website is the personal health analysis and management system for the patients or employees. The personal health management systems can assess the health risk from the report of regular comprehensive physical examination upload by the users or vital signs collected by wearable devices [7, 8]. According to the result of health risk assessment, a part of the health management systems can recommend an improvement plan for users. The improvement plan aims to provide the guidelines which can be used to reduce the health risk.

The representative application of the existing personal health management system is the employee health management system [9]. The employee health management system provides the companies to analyze health risk of their employees. The results of analyzing health risk can be used to understand employee health not only for themselves but also their employers. Some employee health management systems target the metabolic syndrome as the early stage of chronic diseases for monitoring health state of the employees. The employees upload their reports of regular comprehensive physical examination to this system for analyzing the health risk. The users get their analysis report created by the employee health management system. The analysis report includes the health risk and recommended guidelines. But the employee health management systems are only applied in the companies.

iHealth365 [10] is one of personal health management systems, and it is a platform for medical institutions or companies to management health of customers or employees. iHealth365 system allows users to upload their report of regular comprehensive physical examination and analyze the vital signs of the report, and it also provides not only the assessment of health risk but also the health data visualization and remind system to supervise the users. Furthermore, the smart phone app of the iHealth365 for the users can get an improvement plan to maintain their health. The experts also can use this system to help their patients on real time when the patients give the feedbacks. The iHealth365 also provides a function for collecting data from the wearable devices. But iHealth365 system does not automatically provide personal diet and exercise guidelines, and it still needs medical experts to analyze the report to suggest the personal guidelines.

In general, those personal health management systems provide monitoring the health state of users and create the assessment of health risk. And then the users search guidelines from the database of the systems or get an improvement plan which includes the recommended guidelines. The users can comply with the improvement plan commended by the systems. Therefore, the users maintain their health state by themselves. Furthermore, the scalability of the systems should be considered, because some of those systems only target the specific diseases, like metabolic syndrome, Fatty Liver, or Cancers. The existing systems are recommending the guidelines in fixed or for specific diseases. The systems should allow the users to search the database of the systems. There are no systems only using physical examination data and automatically create the personal improvement plan for the users. In the real applications, the real-time remind is needed for supervising the users but the existing systems do not include in their framework.

3   Framework Design

This section first describes the design of *VASP*, based on the framework shown in Figure 1. It then presents an overview of using *VASP*, and introduces the functions of the system when implemented on a website. Finally, we explain the personalized diet and exercise guideline recommendation (abbreviated as *DEG*) used for analyzing the individual report of regular comprehensive physical examination and offering related guidelines to users.

3.1   Overview of System Workflow

Traditionally, users have a report of comprehensive physical examination from medical institutions, and then find out the meanings of the report on the internet or websites provided from medical institutions in Taiwan. If users want to understand how to have diet and exercise guidelines for health according to the report, they have to go to medical institutions and ask for self-care guidelines from health care providers. Furthermore, health care providers usually rely on experience to tell whether user's physical examination items are normal or not and recommend the guidelines for users, without the use of any references. This is inconvenient, and can lead to a lower quality of providing health care.

To solve these problems, *VASP* designs diet and exercise guideline recommendation (abbreviated as *DEG*) to automatically analyze the report of comprehensive physical examination and recommend the guidelines for users, so that users do not need to go to medical institutions to get this information. In addition, *DEG* provides a simple way to let health care providers can easily transfer their knowledge of health care into *VASP*.

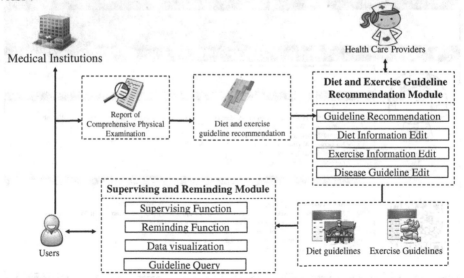

Fig. 1. The framework of *VASP*

Also, we consider that in the future the supervising and reminding module can be combined to mobile devices for supervising and reminding users to meet the recommended guidelines everytime and everywhere. We thus provide an automated logging guidelines service with QR codes. The use of a QR code automates the procedure of downloading users' recommended guidelines, and users thus have an easy way to get them and do not access via network. We expect that users only use mobile devices to scan the QR code, and the recommended guidelines can be loaded to app on the devices.

3.2   Diet and Exercise Guideline Recommendation Module

The diet and exercise guideline recommendation module has following major functions: guideline recommendation, diet information edit, exercise information edit, and disease guideline edit. These functions are explained in the following:

Guideline Recommendation. Guideline recommendation is the core of the design module, and it can recommend personal guidelines for users according to the report of comprehensive physical examination, as shown in Figure 2. In the designs, in addition to the full guidelines that can be automatically recommended, medical experts or health care providers can adjust the priority of guidelines in order to more adapt to users.

Diet Information Edit. The diet information edit function aims to let medical experts or health care providers update the diet information, and the information can be connected to diet guidelines via this function. In addition, the input type of batch file is also designed for information sequence creator.

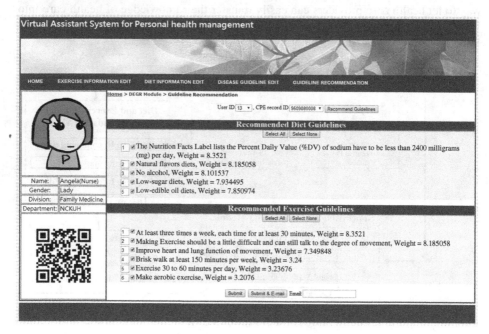

Fig. 2. Screenshots of guideline recommendation function

Exercise Information Edit. The function design of exercise information edit is same as diet information edit. It is worth mentioning that exercise information considers the MET values for calculating calorie and applying to lose weight.

Disease Guideline Edit. This function provides medical experts or health care providers to update disease data online. The disease data is a connection that how the disease is related to physical examination items. In the website, they can choose the physical examination item to edit.

3.3   Supervising and Reminding Module

This module is designed for supervising and reminding users, and the module has following major functions: supervising function, reminding function, data visualization, and guideline query. In order to automatically supervising and reminding users to meet their personal recommended diet and exercise guidelines, an active database is utilized for achieving the purpose. An active database considers an event-driven architecture which can respond to conditions both inside and outside the database.

Supervising Function. This function aims to supervise users to fill out the daily diet and exercise suggestions on time, and the function designs different basic supervising time by general users' life style. In addition, users can adjust and set the supervising time according to their special life style. The function supervises users until the reminding time, and the reminding function is triggered.

Reminding Function. Once users forget to fill out the daily diet and exercise suggestions for a while time, the reminding function is triggered to automatically remind users to fill out the daily diet and exercise suggestions. In addition, the system also sends the weekly-report to user.

Data Visualization. Data visualization employs line graphs to visualize the data in order to make the data more readable, user then can intuitively interpret the line graphs. Users record the daily diet and exercise suggestions, and the daily records then are saved to the database and are shown through data visualization function. The function provides line graphs and record lists so that users can easily check their records of diet and exercise guidelines been done. With regard to the line graphs, it can present records of diet and exercise guideline of users by dates. With the record lists, users can choose the date to show what they have done in that day.

Guidelines Query. Guideline Query provides users to search their guideline history. The function of guidelines query provides users with an offline database of guidelines, so that they can find this information accessibly. In order to meet the users' requirements, the query results show not only the corresponded guidelines but the suggested food and sports related to guidelines.

3.4   Guideline Generator

This subsection introduces diet and exercise guideline recommendation (*DEG*), with a related flowchart shown in Figure 3. In the knowledge collection phase, the impact of diet and exercise guidelines to different physical examination items can be collected and built by medical experts or health care providers into a database. After this, the guidelines for users can be recommended in the guideline recommendation phase. Then, we shall describe in detail the different processes involved in *DEG*.

Let $\{DG_1, DG_2, ..., DG_{|DG|}\}$ and $\{EG_1, EG_2, ..., EG_{|EG|}\}$ be two finite sets of guidelines, where DG_i and EG_j are diet and exercise guidelines for all $1 \leq i \leq |DG|$ and $1 \leq j \leq |EG|$, and $|DG|$ and $|EG|$ are numbers of diet and exercise guidelines respectively. Let $PEI_{n,k}$ be the n-level of the k-th physical examination item in a report, where $|SI|$ is number of physical examination items in a report and $|NL|$ is a user-specified value of levels of a physical examination item for discretizing the vital sign of physical examination item for all n $(1 \leq n \leq |NL|)$ and k $(1 \leq k \leq |SI|)$. For example, Table 1 lists examples of discretization of physical examination items.

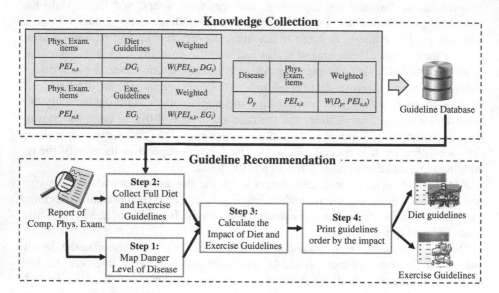

Fig. 3. Flowchart of diet and exercise guideline recommendation (*DEG*)

Table 1. Examples of discretization of blood pressure, oxygen, and heart rate standards

ID	Physical Examination Item	Type	Standard	Notation
1	Systolic of Blood Pressure	Prehypertension	120 - 139 (mmHg)	$PEI_{1,1}$
		Stage 1 hypertension	140 - 159 (mmHg)	$PEI_{2,1}$
		Stage 2 hypertension	≥ 160 (mmHg)	$PEI_{3,1}$
2	Oxygen	Mild hypoxemia	< 94%	$PEI_{1,2}$
		Moderate hypoxemia	< 89%	$PEI_{2,2}$
		Severe hypoxemia	< 75%	$PEI_{3,2}$
3	Heart Rate	Tachycardia	> 100 (bpm)	$PEI_{1,3}$
		Bradycardia	< 60 (bpm)	$PEI_{2,3}$
		......		

The design of guideline recommendation takes into account two impacts: (1) diet or exercise guidelines (*DG* or *EG*) with regard to physical examination items (*PEI*); and (2) physical examination items with regard to the diseases (*D*). The processes of guideline recommendation are explained in more detail below.

Step 1. Map Danger Level of Disease. According to the physical examination items users have, *DEG* first maps the danger level $PEI_{n,k}$ bases on the vital sign of each physical examination item, and collects the corresponding weighted DPW_t of $PEI_{n,k}$ related a disease D_p defined by medical experts or health care providers.

Step 2. Collect Full Diet and Exercise Guidelines. According to the danger level $PEI_{n,k}$, *DEG* then collects DG_i and EG_j, as well as the corresponding weighted DW_t and EW_t related to the examination items.

Step 3. Calculate the Impact of Diet and Exercise Guidelines. Given a diet or exercise guideline *G* and the corresponding weighted $W(PEI_k, G)$ with regard to a set of physical examination items $\{ PEI_1, PEI_2,..., PEI_y\}$ for all k $(1 \leq k \leq y)$. The impact of *G* with regard to the disease *D* is denoted as $I(G, D)$ and is defined as:

$$I(G, D) = \sum_{k=1}^{y} W(PEI_k, G) * W(D, PEI_k).$$

Step 4. Print Guidelines Order by the Impact. Last, the guidelines are arranged in descending impact calculated by step 3, and users can request to only print top-k guidelines or satisfying guidelines on a given impact threshold.

Example 1. Table 2 and Table 3 show examples of diet guidelines and diseases corresponding to physical examination items, respectively. The impact of guidelines "No alcohol (DG_1)" with regard to the disease "Cardiovascular Disease (D_1)" is $I(DG_1, D_1)=0.2*2.5 + 0.8*5.2 + 0.5*3.7=6.51$. In addition, the impact of DG_2 w.r.t. the (D_1) is 3.34.

Table 2. Example of exercise guidelines corresponding to physical examination items

Phys. Exam. Items (notation)	Diet Guidelines (notation)	Weighted
Moderate hypoxemia ($PEI_{2,2}$)	No alcohol (DG_1)	2.5
	Low-edible oil diets (DG_2)	1
Tachycardia ($PEI_{1,3}$)	No alcohol (DG_1)	3.7
	Low-edible oil diets (DG_2)	1
Stage 2 hypertension ($PEI_{3,1}$)	No alcohol (DG_1)	5.2
	Low-edible oil diets (DG_2)	3.3
	Natural flavors diets (DG_3)	1.7

Table 3. Example of diseases corresponding to physical examination items

Deseases	Phys. Exam. Items (notation)	Weighted
Cardiovascular Disease (D_1)	Stage 2 hypertension ($PEI_{3,1}$)	0.8
	Moderate hypoxemia ($PEI_{2,2}$)	0.2
	Tachycardia ($PEI_{1,3}$)	0.5

4   Conclusion and Future Work

This work presented a novel framework called *VASP (Virtual Assistant System for Personal health management)* in order to provide effective personalized health care with analyzing the report of regular comprehensive physical examination. In addition, this work also designed a diet and exercise guideline recommendation module to effectively collect the impact of diet and exercise guidelines on different physical examination items by medical experts, as well as discussed with medical experts to provide an impact calculation of guidelines for recommending personal guidelines for users. We expect that the proposed framework can significantly reduce the loads of healthcare providers and can help them improve the efficiency and quality of patient care.

With regard to future developments, the implemented system will be subjected to a practical evaluation by medical experts, health care providers and users/patients to get useful feedback and suggestions on the system. In addition, we would apply institutional review board for our framework to prove that *VASP* is feasible for use in a clinical environment.

Acknowledgments. This research was partially supported by Chunghwa Telecom Co., Ltd., Taiwan, Republic of China.

References

1. Health Promotion Administration, Ministry of Health and Welfare, http://health99.hpa.gov.tw/TXT/HealthyHeadLineZone/HealthyHe adlineDetai.aspx?TopIcNo=5170 (accessed onAugust 8, 2014)
2. Department of Health, Taipei City Government, http://telecare.taipei.gov.tw/hlc/PW2/PW2_MENU.do?forward=PW 2_B01_01_Q00 (accessed onAugust 8, 2014)
3. Wu, C.-H., Fang, K.-T., Chen, T.-C.: Applying data mining for prostate cancer. In: The International Conference on New Trends in Information and Service Science, Beijing, pp. 1063–1065 (2009)
4. Tsai, C.-H., Lin, G.-D.: Prevalence of the Metabolic Syndrome in Individuals Seeking for Health Examination. Ching Medical Journal, 10–16 (2006)
5. Lin, F.-Y., Hwu, Y.-J., Chen, Y.-O.: Data Mining Technology Applied to Adult Check-Up Data. Journal of Nursing and Healthcare Research 6(2), 117–124 (2010)
6. Lin, Y.-S.: Apply the Health Examination Data to Construct Colorectal Cancer Prediction Models. Master Thesis, Industrial Engineering and Management, Chaoyang University of Technology (2011)
7. Lan, G.-C., Lee, C.-H., Wu, J.-S., Li, H.-C., Ho, S.-H., Tseng, V.S.: A Framework for Personalized Health Trend Analysis. In: The 10th International Symposium on Pervasive Systems, Algorithms, and Networks, pp. 405–410 (2009)
8. Lin, Y.-F., Shie, H.-H., Yang, Y.-C., Tseng, V.S.: Design of a Real-Time and Continua-based Framework for Care Guideline Recommendation. International Journal of Environmental Research and Public Health (IJERPH) 11(4), 4262–4279 (2014)
9. HealthVault, https://www.healthvault.com/tw/en (accessed on August 8, 2014)

10. iHealth365, http://www.ihealth365.com.tw/ (accessed on August 8, 2014).
11. Platform of cloud Health, Qisda Corp., http://fet.qissense.com/ (accessed on September 22, 2013)
12. Lin, L-Y.: Metabolic Syndrome, http://www.ym.edu.tw/hc/hc3/hc32/960502%20metabolic%20syndrome.pdf (accessed on August 8, 2014)
13. Yang, Y.-C.: Definition, Physiological Mechanisms and Epidemiology of metabolic syndrome. Taiwan Medical Journal 51(11) (2008)

A Robust Learning-Based Detection
and Tracking Algorithm

Dini Nuzulia Rahmah, Wen-Huang Cheng, Yung-Yao Chen, and Kai-Lung Hua

National Taiwan University of Science and Technology, Taipei, Taiwan
hua@mail.ntust.edu.tw

Abstract. Object tracking in video is a challenging problem in several applications such as video surveillance, video compression, video retrieval, and video editing. Tracking an object in a video is not easy due to loss of information caused by illumination changing in a scene, occlusions with other objects, similar target appearances, and inaccurate tracker responses. In this paper, we present a novel object detection and tracking algorithm via structured output prediction classifier. Given an initial bounding box with its position, we first divide it into sub-blocks with a predefined size. Next, we extract the features from each sub-blocks with Haar-like features method. And then we learn those features with a structured output prediction classifier. We treat the sub-blocks obtained from the initial bounding box as positive samples and then randomly choose negative samples from search windows defined by the specific area around the bounding box. After that, we obtain prediction scores for each sub-blocks both from positive and negative samples. We construct a region-graph with sub-blocks as nodes and classifier's score as weight to detect the target object in each frame. Our experimental results show that the proposed method outperforms state-of-the-art object tracking algorithms.

Keywords: Object Detection, Object Tracking, Support Vector Machine.

1 Introduction

Object tracking in video is one of the highly challenging problems in various applications, such as video editing, video surveillance, video compression, video retrieval and etc. Some of the challenges that may happen during video tracking are occlusions with other objects, similar target appearances and inaccurate tracker responses. When the target object is known for some cases in video sequences, it is possible to collect the information to be used in the tracker. While for the other applications, the tracked object might be an arbitrary object that only can be specified in real time. In these cases, the object may change caused by object motion, illumination changing and occlusion with other objects. Hence, in this problem, the tracker must be able to build the appearance of the object in real time.

S.-M. Cheng and M.-Y. Day (Eds.): TAAI 2014, LNAI 8916, pp. 284–295, 2014.

Most recent object tracking algorithms [1], [2], [3] have used tracking-by-detection approaches to address these challenges. Tracking by detection approach treats the tracking problem as a detection task applied over time in video sequences. The methods first apply detection to the tracked object in the first frame and then obtain the detection responses to track the object during the video sequences. These methods maintain a classifier trained online to discriminate the target object from its background. The classifier is used to estimate object position by searching for the maximum classification score in a local region around the estimation position from the previous frame.

Structured output tracking with kernels (STRUCK) [1] provides an adaptive object tracking-by-detection approach with a kernelized structured output Support Vector Machine (SVM). With an online learning SVM, STRUCK perform object tracking which integrates learning and tracking, avoiding the need for update strategies in offline learning. While tracking-learning-detection (TLD) [2] proposes a long-term object tracking in a video by integrates the object detection task, learning and tracking. Each subtask in TLD is addressed by a single component and the component operate simultaneously.

However, many tracking-by-detection approaches fail to detect the right target object because sometimes it mixed with its background and some parts of other objects which leads to false detection for the features that not belonging to the object and missed classification in video sequences.

In this paper, we take different approach to track the object in the video by using the principle of structured output Support Vector Machine (SVM) [1]. Given the initial position of a target object in a frame of a video, we divide the bounding box into sub-blocks with predefined size. And then we extract the features from each sub-blocks and learn those features with structured output classifiers [12]. Given the radius size from the center of a sub-block, we define the search range which is the area inside the radius, excluding the initial bounding box area. Then, we divide those search area with the same size of the sub-blocks. Next, the features from all of the sub-blocks will be learned by using [12] method. And then we construct a region graph; the nodes are sub-blocks and the edges link any two adjacent sub-blocks that have 4-connected neighborhoods.

We compare our proposed method with [1] and [2] methods. From the experimental result, our method obtains better detection and tracking comparing to those two methods. Our work offers several advantages over existing object tracking schemes. With the sub-blocks as a unit, we still can detect the target object if some parts of the object are occlude with other objects.

The rest of this paper is organized as follows: section 1 presents introduction, section 2 explains our proposed methods to obtain efficient object video tracking by using structured output SVM. Section 3 will present experimental results while section 4 presents conclusions.

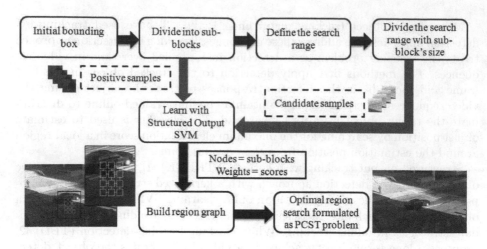

Fig. 1. Flowchart of our proposed structured output kernels

2   The Algorithms

In this section, we briefly describe the proposed object tracking method which employs structured output kernel function. The key ideas of our proposed method is the employment of the object detection with structured output kernels.

Given an initial bounding box, we divide the bounding box into sub-blocks with a predefined size. Next, we extract the features from each sub-block by using Haar-like features [8]. Then we learn all of those features with structured output Support Vector Machine (SVM). We adapt LaRank classifier [12] as structured output SVM method. And then, we define our search range to search the candidates samples based on the search radius r from the center position of each sub-block size. After that, we divide the search range with the same size as a sub-block. The positive samples for classifier are obtained from the initial bounding box in the first frame while the negative samples are obtained randomly in the search range, except for the positive sample area. And then, we build a region graph by using sub-blocks as nodes and scores from LaRank [12] classifier as weights for each node.

2.1   Structured Output SVM

Unlike regular SVM which consider only binary labels as the output prediction, structured output SVM can predict more complex object *e.g* images, sequences, strings, trees, lattices, or graphs. Structured output SVM uses structured learning which learns to predict outputs that are not simple binary labels. By using structured learning, we can modeling the relationship between the different output inside the output space, so we can learn classifier that makes better use of training data instead of using binary output. In the context of object tracking, the output space is the space of possible bounding boxes which can be parameterized by top, bottom, left, and right coordinates in the region. Those coordinates can take values between 0 and the frame size which can make the problem as structured regression.

2.2 Structured Learning for Object Localization

In this method, we learn a prediction function which estimates the object position in each frame instead of learning a classifier. First, we divide the initial bounding box from the first frame into the smaller box with specified size, called sub-blocks. The tracker will maintain the position of the object within a frame f_s where s is the number of frames. Given a set of input sub-block images $\{x_s^1, ..., x_s^n\} \subset X$ and their transformation position $\{y_s^1, ..., y_s^n\} \subset Y$, we learn a prediction function $p : X \to Y$. In this method, the output space is the space of all transformation Y instead of the binary labels ± 1. Next, the prediction function p is learned by using structured learning framework [13] according to:

$$p(x) = argmax_{y \in Y} d(x, y) \tag{1}$$

where $d(x, y)$ is a discriminant function that should give a maximum value to pairs (x, y) that are well matched. In our approach, a pair (x, y) is a labeled example where y is the preferred transformation of the target object.

In our approach, the discriminant function has the formulation:

$$d(x, y) = \langle w, \phi(x, y) \rangle , \tag{2}$$

where $\phi(x, y)$ maps the pair (x, y) into an appropriate feature space computed with the dot product. In the machine learning process, the feature mapping function ϕ is defined by a joint kernel function, formed as:

$$k(x, y, \bar{x}, \bar{y}) = \langle \phi(x, y), \phi(\bar{x}, \bar{y}) \rangle , \tag{3}$$

consider training patterns $x_1, ..., x_n \subset X$ and their transformation position $y_i, ..., y_n \subset Y$. The image kernels function use to compute statistics or features of the two sub-block images and then compare them. The overlapping sub-block regions will have the same common features and related statistics. By using kernel map, we make it straightforward to incorporate image features into structured output approach.

In this approach, we extract Haar-like features presented by Viola[8] to obtain features in each sub-block. A simple rectangular Haar-like feature can be defined as the difference of the sum of pixels of areas inside the rectangle, which can be at any position and scale within the original frame. The values from Haar-like features indicate the characteristics of a particular area inside the sub-blocks. Each feature type use to indicate the existence or absence of particular area characteristics in the sub-blocks, such as edges or changes in texture. We use 6 types of Haar-like features as shown in Fig. 2.

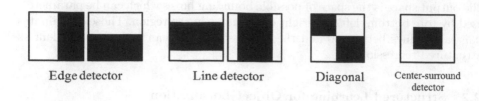

Edge detector   Line detector   Diagonal   Center-surround detector

Fig. 2. 6 types of Haar-like features

The advantages of using Haar-like features is when there is illumination change in the frame, the detector (black and white squares) of Haar-like features can easily separate and distinct the feature from the illumination changing.

After extracting the features, the objective is to learn the discriminant function $d(x, y)$ so that the scores $d(x_i, y)$ of the incorrect pairing are smaller than the score $d(x_i, y_i), y_i \neq y$ of the correct pairing.

To train the discriminant function d, we use the following minimization quadratic program of the support vector machine[14]:

$$min_w \frac{1}{2} \|w\|^2 + C \sum_{i=1}^{n} \xi_i$$

$$s.t.\ \xi_i \geq 0, \forall i \tag{4}$$

$$\langle w, \phi(x_i, y_i) \rangle - \langle w, \phi(x_i, y) \rangle \geq \Delta(y_i, y) - \xi_i$$

$$\forall_i, \forall y \neq y_i$$

where w is parameter vector, C is a constant that controls the trade-off between training error minimization and margin maximization, and ξ_i is the single slack variables for violations of the nonlinear constraints. This optimization aims to ensure that the score of each sub-block $d(x_i, y_i) > d(x_i, y)$ for $y \neq y_i$, by a margin depending on a loss function $\Delta(y_i, y)$.

The loss function denote by $\Delta(y_i, y)$ where y is a possible output and y_i is the true output. The loss function decrease as a possible output approaches the true output. The optimization is a convex and given appropriate definition of a joint kernel map $\Phi(x, y)$ and $\Delta(y_i, y)$ does not significantly differ from primal SVM.

2.3 Optimization Step

$$d(x, y) = \sum_{i, \bar{y}} \beta_i^{\bar{y}} \langle \Phi(x_i, \bar{y}), \Phi(x, y) \rangle, \tag{5}$$

where $\beta_i^{\bar{y}}$ is a support vector. The pair (x_i, y) denotes support vectors for which $\beta_i^y \neq 0$. And x_i included in at least one support vector as support patterns. For

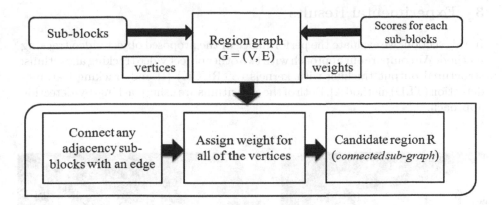

Fig. 3. Flowchart of region-graph algorithm

a given support pattern x_i, only the support vector (x_i, y_i) will have $\beta_i^{y_i} > 0$ and we refers this as positive support vectors, while any other support vectors $(x_i, y), y \neq y_i$, will have $\beta_i^{y_i} < 0$ and we refers this as negative support vectors.

The main step in this optimization step is a Sequential Minimal Optimization (SMO)-style step [16]. SMO is an algorithm that improves Lagrangian dual form with respect to a pair of coefficients β_i^{y+} and β_i^{y-}, where β_i^{y+} is positive support vector and β_i^{y-} is negative support vector. The coefficients must be modified by opposite amounts, $\beta_i^{y+} \leftarrow \beta_i^{y+} + \lambda, \beta_i^{y-} \leftarrow \beta_i^{y-} - \lambda$ because of the constraint $\sum_y \beta_i^y = 0$, leading to an one-dimensional maximization in λ [1].

The SMO step use to optimize the (i, y_+, y_-) in this online learning algorithm. Given the chosen i, y_+, y_-, we will define the most efficient search direction with the highest gradient. This gradient will represent a single coefficient of the dual form.

2.4 Budgeting Algorithm

The problem occurs when the number of support vector increase over time. Furthermore, when evaluating discriminant function $d(x, y)$ will take a high computational cost because it requires evaluating kernel function for each support vectors. This means that the storage costs grow linearly with the number of support vectors.

In this approach, we implement a budget maintenance adapted from [1] which choose a fixed budget so that the support vectors cannot exceed a specified limit. If a new support vector need to be added but the budget is already full, this method will choose an appropriate support vector that need to be kept and another support vectors that need to be removed.

3   Experimental Results

In this section, we evaluate the performance of the proposed object video tracking method. We compare our approach with two other object video tracking algorithms: structured output tracking with kernels (STRUCK) [1] and tracking-learning-detection (TLD) method [2]. Both of the algorithms are using tracking-by-detection approach.

(a)   (b)

(c)

Fig. 4. A snapshot of the test videos used in our experiments. (a) Crossing video. (b) Diving video. (c) Ironman video.

3.1   Experimental Design

We collect our test videos from TLD [2] and Kwon [18] databases for evaluation, as shown in Fig. 4. The sequences vary in length from dozens of frames to hundreds, contain diverse object types (rigid, articulated), have different scene settings (indoor/outdoor, static/moving camera, lightning conditions). Object occlusions also present in the test videos. The properties of our test videos are shown in Table 1. We use Crossing, Diving, and Ironman video as our testing data. We choose these 3 videos because each video has their own difficulties.

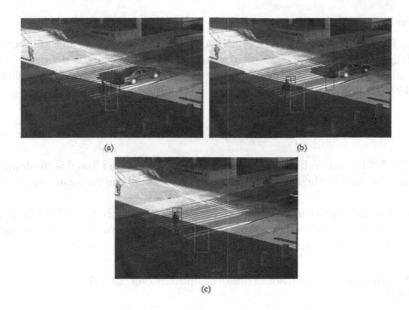

Fig. 5. Tracking results of Crossing sequence: red solid line represents our proposed method, green dot line represents TLD [2] and blue dashed line represents STRUCK [1] method. (a) Frame 49. (b) Frame 59. (c) Frame 81.

In the Crossing video, occlusion happens between crossing people and the car that passes by. While in the Diving video, the diver changes her movement that caused the target object change its shape. Also, the illumination change happens in Ironman video.

Table 1. Test Videos Properties

Name	Frames Number	Target Visible	Color	Resolution
Crossing	119	119	Yes	360x240
Diving	231	218	Yes	400x224
Ironman	165	165	Yes	720x304

For the experiments, we use 8 pixels sub-blocks size for Crossing video, 16 pixels for Diving video and 12 pixels for Ironman video. We use different minimum sub-blocks size for each video based on the best result from our experimental results for each video. We use 6 different types of Haar-like features arranged on a grid at 2 scales on a 4×4 grid, resulting in 192 features, with each features normalised to give a value in the range [-1,1]. We empploy Gaussian kernel with $\sigma = 0.5$. Fig. 5 shows the tracking result of the proposed method and the two exiting methods when dealing with challenging case.

3.2   Evaluation Metrics

Success Frame Numbers (SFN). Success frame numbers is the number of successfully tracked frames in a video sequence [19]. A success is defined if the overlap ratio of a tracked region and the ground truth is higher than a predefined threshold θ. Here we use $\theta = 0.5$.

$$SFN_\theta = \frac{1}{N} \sum_{i=1}^{N} \delta(O_i^{tracked} \geq \theta), \tag{6}$$

where $O_i^{tracked}$ is the overlap ratio of tracked region in frame i and θ is predefined threshold. The higher the successful number, the better the performance of the method.

The comparison between our proposed method, STRUCK [1] and TLD [2] in terms of SFN shown in Table 2. From the results, we know that our proposed method outperforms the other two approaches in the Diving video.

Table 2. Performance comparisons (ratio) of different object tracking approaches in terms of SFN

	STRUCK [1]	TLD [2]	Proposed Method
Crossing	**0.48**	0.42	0.38
Diving	0.7	0	**0.49**
Ironman	**0.6**	0.5	0.2

Accumulated Center Location Error (ACE). ACE use to measure the center location (CE_i) distance between the center location of the ground truth and tracker [20]. The formulation is as follows:

$$ACE = \frac{1}{N} \sum_{f_i} CE_i, \tag{7}$$

where N is the number of frames and f_i is the ith frame. The lower the center location error, the better the performance of the tracker.

The comparison between our proposed method, STRUCK [1] and TLD [2] in terms of ACE shown in Table 3. The average ACE from our proposed method is lower than the other two methods in the Crossing and Diving video. It means that our proposed method works better with the minimum error number.

Overlap Ratio. Overlap ratio is the percentage of overlapping area between ground truth and tracked region in frame [20]. *area* defines the total number of pixels which overlapping between ground truth and tracker. The equation shown in Eqn. 8.

$$O_i^{tracked} = \frac{area(R_{f_i}^{tracked} \cap R_{f_i}^{GT})}{area(R_{f_i}^{tracked} \cup R_{f_i}^{GT})}, \tag{8}$$

Table 3. Performance comparisons (pixels) of different object tracking approaches in terms of ACE

	STRUCK [1]	TLD [2]	Proposed Method
Crossing	51.51	16.52	**6.33477**
Diving	36.336	183.084	**14.01**
Ironman	**45.3682**	217.577	91.94

where $O_i^{tracked}$ is overlap ratio in i^{th} frame, $R_{f_i}^{tracked}$ is the bounding box area from tracking algorithms and $R_{f_i}^{GT}$ is the bounding box area from ground truth. The higher the overlap ratio, the better the performance of the video tracking approach.

The comparison between our proposed method, STRUCK [1] and TLD [2] in terms of overlapping ratio shown in Table 4. From the Table 4, we can conclude that our proposed method obtain the highest average percentage for both Crossing and Diving videos, while STRUCK [1] performs better in Ironman video.

Computational Time. We also compare our proposed method result with STRUCK [1] and TLD [2] by their computational time. The comparison shown in Table 5. From the Table 5, TLD [2] obtain the best result in all of video sequences, while our proposed method run slower than both STRUCK [1] and TLD [2].

Table 4. Performance comparisons (percentage) of different object tracking approaches in terms of overlap ratio

	STRUCK [1]	TLD [2]	Proposed Method
Crossing	49.03	28.68	**61.78**
Diving	45.38	40.77	**90.65**
Ironman	**20.90**	8.52	8.70

Table 5. Performance comparisons (seconds) different object tracking approaches in terms of computational time

	STRUCK [1]	TLD [2]	Proposed Method
Crossing	10.94	**9.09**	22.61
Diving	21.62	**17.3**	39.1
Ironman	21.99	**16.27**	39.6

3.3   Result

Our experiments aim to compare the results of the proposed approach with existing tracking-by-detection approaches. We prove that our proposed method can handle one of the main problems that usually occur during object tracking, that is, occlusion problem.

From Fig. 5, it can be observed that our proposed method is able to track the right object when the car passes by. STRUCK [1] fails to track the target object in frame 49 due to occlusion. And TLD [2] also fails to track the people in frame 59. Note that our proposed method always tracks the right target because we use sub-blocks to learn each samples and hence is able to identify the right object even when occlusion happens.

4   Conclusion

We presented a novel object detection and tracking method with structured output SVM. An adaptive tracking-by-detection based on structured output prediction had been perform to do the object tracking task. The experimental results verified that our proposed method outperforms the other two state-of-the-art tracking-by-detection approaches.

References

1. Hare, S., Saffari, A., Torr, P.H.S.: Struck: Structured Output Tracking with Kernels. In: IEEE International Conference on Computer Vision(ICCV), pp. 263–270. IEEE (2011)
2. Kalal, Z., Mikolajczyk, K., Matas, J.: Tracking-learning-detection. IEEE Transactions on Pattern Analysis and Machine Intelligence 34, 1409–1422 (2012)
3. Avidan, S.: Support Vector Tracking. IEEE Transactions on Pattern Analysis and Machine Intelligence 26, 1064–1072 (2004)
4. Vijayanarasimhan, S., Grauman, K.: Efficient Region Search for Object Detection. In: IEEE Conference on Computer Vision and Pattern Recognition (CVPR), pp. 1401–1408. IEEE (2011)
5. Lampert, C.H., Blaschko, M.B., Hofmann, T.: Beyond sliding windows: Object Localization by Efficient Subwindow Search. In: IEEE Conference on Computer Vision and Pattern Recognition (CVPR), pp. 1–8. IEEE (2008)
6. Lehmann, A., Leibe, B., Van Gool, L.: Feature-centric Efficient Subwindow Search. In: International Conference on Computer Vision (ICCV), pp. 940–947. IEEE (2009)
7. Yeh, T., Lee, J.J., Darrell, T.: Fast Concurrent Object Localization and Recognition. In: IEEE Conference on Computer Vision and Pattern Recognition (CVPR), pp. 280–287. IEEE (2009)
8. Viola, P., Jones, M.: Rapid Object Detection using a Boosted Cascade of Simple Features. In: IEEE Conference on Computer Vision and Pattern Recognition (CVPR), pp. 511–518. IEEE (2001)
9. Leibe, B., Leonardis, A., Schiele, B.: Combined Object Categorization and Segmentation with an Implicit Shape Model. In: Workshop on Statistical Learning in Computer Vision (ECCV), vol. 2, p. 7 (2004)
10. Gu, C., Lim, J.J., Arbeláez, P., Malik, J.: Recognition using Regions. In: IEEE Conference on Computer Vision and Pattern Recognition (CVPR), pp.1030–1037. IEEE (2009)
11. Murphy, K., Torralba, A., Eaton, D., Freeman, W.T.: Object detection and localization using local and global features. In: Ponce, J., Hebert, M., Schmid, C., Zisserman, A. (eds.) Toward Category-Level Object Recognition. LNCS, vol. 4170, pp. 382–400. Springer, Heidelberg (2006)

12. Bordes, A., Bottou, L., Gallinari, P., Weston, J.: Solving Multiclass Support Vector Machines with LaRank. In: International Conference on Machine Learning, pp. 89–96. ACM (2007)
13. Blaschko, M.B., Lampert, C.H.: Learning to localize objects with structured output regression. In: Forsyth, D., Torr, P., Zisserman, A. (eds.) ECCV 2008, Part I. LNCS, vol. 5302, pp. 2–15. Springer, Heidelberg (2008)
14. Tsochantaridis, I., Hofmann, T., Joachims, T., Altun, Y.: Support Vector Machine Learning for Interdependent and Structured Output Spaces. In: International Conference on Machine Learning, pp.104. ACM (2004)
15. Bordes, A., Usunier, N., Bottou, L.: Sequence labelling sVMs trained in one pass. In: Daelemans, W., Goethals, B., Morik, K. (eds.) ECML PKDD 2008, Part I. LNCS (LNAI), vol. 5211, pp. 146–161. Springer, Heidelberg (2008)
16. Platt, J.: Sequential Minimal Optimization: A Fast Algorithm for Training Support Vector Machines. MIT Press (1998)
17. Ljubić, I., Weiskircher, R., Pferschy, U., Klau, G.W., Mutzel, P., Fischetti, M.: An Algorithmic Framework for the Exact Solution of the Prize-Collecting Steiner Tree Problem. Mathematical Programming 105, 427–449 (2006)
18. Kwon, J., Lee, K.: Tracking of a Non-rigid Object Via Patch-Based Dynamic Appearance Modeling and Adaptive Basin Hopping Monte Carlo Sampling. In: IEEE Conference on Computer Vision and Pattern Recognition(CVPR), pp. 1208–1215. IEEE (2009)
19. Bashir, F., Porikli, F.: Performance Evaluation of Object Detection and Tracking Systems. In: IEEE Conference on Computer Vision and Pattern Recognition (CVPR). Citeseer (2006)
20. Wu, Y., Lim, J., Yang, M.: Online Object Tracking: A Benchmark

A Digital Stereo Microscope Platform for Microsurgery Training

James K. Rappel[1], Amitabha Lahiri[2], and Chee Leong Teo[1]

[1] Department of Mechanical Engineering, National University of Singapore, Singapore
{james.rappel,clteo}@nus.edu.sg
[2] Department of Hand and Reconstructive Microsurgery, National University Health System,
Singapore
amitaha_lahiri@nuhs.edu.sg

Abstract. We describe a software defined surgical microscope platform for developing AI applications in surgical training. The microscope has facility to merge and render multiple streams of live and/or stored video, and has the ability to enhance, annotate, and measure using a 3D position and orientation tracking forceps. A configuration mechanism controls the zoom, focus and disparity of the stereo view and stores surgeon and procedure specific configuration. The system tracks the surgical motion and analyses its quality in realtime. Several measures of quality of motion are described and can be used as a platform to develop AI applications in surgical training.

Keywords: AI Applications in Surgery, Surgery Training, Personalized Learning, Surgical Motion Analysis, Dexterous Motion Heuristics, Movement Classification.

1 Introduction

Microsurgical tasks are generally performed by viewing the tissue through an optical microscope. It is not an intelligent device and cannot analyze the surgical motions performed under its view. Hence the surgical movements cannot be practiced for improvement with realtime feedback. A digital stereo microscope, similar in function as an optical microscope, can analyze the surgical motion under its view, assess the quality of the motion and provide realtime feedback. It can be used to develop surgical training applications. The digital stereo microscope is a hand-eye collocated one where hand movements could be used both for surgical manipulation and for device control. We describe the appropriateness of this system design for learning and training dexterous manipulation such as microsurgery.

Firstly, due to this design, surgeons are able to use the dexterous hand and the tools held by them as the input mechanism to generate various kinds of movement. Human hand is known to have 27 degrees of freedom (DoF) [1] through the articulation of the 27 bones through its joints: 4 DoF in each finger with 3 DoF arising out of extension and flexion and one for abduction and adduction, amounting to a total of 20, one additional DoF for the thumb, 6 DoF for the rotation and translation of the wrist.

S.-M. Cheng and M.-Y. Day (Eds.): TAAI 2014, LNAI 8916, pp. 296–309, 2014.

This allows highly dexterous manipulations to be made at small scale of movement. The surgical manipulations use these degrees of freedom of the hand to produce smooth and precise movements. However, the increased degree of freedom also allows the same movement to be made in multiple ways. When there are multiple movement that depict the same motion profile, the preferred motion must be assessed. The system provides a means to capture the motion in fine details as well as allows to express the motion using the natural freedom of the hand through the use of the digital forceps.

Secondly, surgeons are able to achieve hand-eye coordination by placing hands along the line of sight of the field of view. It is the natural configuration in an unaided surgery and is a means of achieving better task performance [2-8].

Thirdly, merging multiple streams of video, both live and stored, to create surgical task contexts, is another advantage of the system. Finally, a number of functions are available to objectively assess aspects of the surgical motion. It can improve the surgeon in producing better surgical movements through realtime feedback. For producing specific types of motion, many surgical motion training systems can be designed.

In Fig.1, two surgical motion training targets which will be placed under an intelligent digital stereo microscope are shown. The training targets provide dexterous motion challenges very similar to the dexterity challenges encountered in surgery. The task targets may be oriented to present the complex anatomical orientations encountered in the surgery.

Fig. 1. Surgical motion training targets

Our study is unique in two aspects. This is the first study that constructed a hand-eye-colocated digital microscope to provide a surgery training platform. It is the first study where surgical motion elements, such as measurement noise, physiological tremor, and involuntary movements, are separated to study surgical motion performance.

The paper is organized as follows. In section 2, related work is discussed. Different existing methods of analyzing signals are discussed with ways of incorporating them into a training device. In section 3, the digital stereo microscope design and experimental setup to practice surgical movements are described. In section 4 the results of a new surgical motion learning experiment are described along with the conclusions.

2   Related Work

Surgical motion is considered a relevant predictor for analyzing surgical performance [9-17]. These studies [9-17] focus on parameters such as the economy of motion and patency. The problem with these studies is that they perform actual procedures and make assessment based on the economy of motion. They are disadvantageous due to (i) the subjective bias of the surgeons, (ii) the limited number of repetitions determined by the availability of the surgical cases and (iii) the lack of repeatability of the procedure.

Other surgical motion studies [18-21] decompose surgical motion into sub-tasks that can be independently evaluated. Existing analysis of surgical motion data is limited to the time of completion and number of movements. Some evaluations use error rate also as a measure. Without a means of assessing the quality of the movement, these measures cannot be trusted.

Another group of researchers have constructed Hidden Markov Model (HMM) [19, 22] using the surgical motion. Though this study can simulate motions based on the model, it does not help in training surgeons in using the surgical visual aids to produce better motion. HMM results are also difficult to explain to surgeons. Another recent attempt to classify and assess medical procedure training using virtual reality training systems is reported [30,31]. The motion based evaluation system is applied to classify the motion made on a virtual reality trainer of bone marrow extraction procedure.

Hence there are no suitable surgical training system to practice surgical motion with immediate feedback. There is a need for a system that can help create a standardized surgical motions and evaluate its quality. The evaluation must be deeper than the measurement of the time or the length of the movement.

Dexterous hand motion is a result of a cooperative controlled movement of a number of hand joints. The mechanical joint motions produce tremors [23-25] and its frequency is governed by the inertia and elasticity of the joint. If a method can isolate the signals corresponding to the tremors of these joints and the linear motion, then that method can be used to derive the basis data for computing the quality of motion.

Surgical motion represents a complex time series data denoting the working of a large number of human joints producing both desirable and undesirable motion. Capturing the motion through electromagnetic sensors may add instrument noise to the already complex data. The surgical motion will have involuntary motions [23, 27,28] such as physiological tremor in addition to the voluntary motion.

Though the range of frequencies of the components of surgical motion are known, they are also known to vary. Thus they are seen spread across the spectrum. A spectral decomposition method requires a model of the frequencies in the surgical motion. One such known frequency formulation [24] is given in (1)

$$d(t) = X \sin (\omega t) + 0.01 X \sin 10 (\omega t) \tag{1}$$

where d(t), the displacement, is composed of a 1 Hz oscillation of the wrist superimposed by a 10 Hz tremor. Using such models, the data may be approximated and the model can be fitted with the data by adding more signal components of tremor and noise.

An alternate approach is to extract the model of the motion from the data by identifying the oscillations (a range of frequencies) present in the data. An example is empirical mode decomposition. In Empirical Mode Decomposition [26] the temporal information is preserved while decomposing the signal into a number of lower frequency components. Unlike the Fourier and Wavelet methods, the original nature of the signal is maintained and each component can be easily be related to the original signal. This method can analyze surgical motion data to reveal the physical process of performing the surgical motion tasks.

In empirical mode decomposition [26] a time based signal D(t) is decomposed into a number of components Ij(t), known as IMFs (Intrinsic Mode Functions), which are individual oscillations of a scale. Individual oscillations are zero mean. By iteratively removing the individual oscillations, a monotonic signal tendency is observed at which point the decomposition stops. The residual signal that shows the monotonic signal tendency is called the trend part of the original signal.

Let D(t) be the displacement function of a surgical motion experiment which can be described as a discrete set of N points at N equally spaced times. Through Empirical Mode Decomposition [26], D(t) can be decomposed as shown in equation (2). $R_n(t)$ is the residual signal after extracting IMFs $I_j(t)$ in n iterations.

$$D(t) = R_n(t) + \sum I_j(t) \qquad \text{for } j = 1, \ldots, n \qquad (2)$$

By decomposing the complex motion data, we aim to identify physical processes such as oscillation of the measurement device, physiological tremor of the subject, dexterous movement by the subject, geometry of the path, etc. Since the isolated components (IMFs) are similar in nature to the original signal, it can be assessed using the number of movements present in it or the types of movement.

In Hotraphinyo et. al [29] a motion study of a microsurgical task is described, indicating the frequencies of motion components. Three types of involuntary motion were identified, tremor, jerk and drift in addition to the erroneous hand movement. However, it [29] does not decompose the motion data to physical processes, they are instead assessed using spectral decomposition. Further, a large sample study was not possible due to the need of consenting patients and surgeons to record surgical motion. Our study is aimed at removing these limitations.

Although the extraction of certain characteristic parameters such as frequency or velocity of surgical motion may be readily achieved, the quality of the movement is to be assessed.

3   Surgery Training System

In Fig. 2, the software architecture of the training system is given. The training system consists of four parts. The first component is a digital forceps that helps the surgeon to perform the movement. It uses a realtime magnetic position and orientation tracking system. The tracking system produces coordinate information at a speed of 240 Hz, which is fast enough to capture dexterous hand motions which are below 25 Hz. The digital forceps streams coordinate information.

The second component is a set of video sources which stream video frames at 30 Frames Per Second (30 fps). Multiple video sources including a pair of cameras capturing the live view of the hand motion to perform the surgical tasks are shown. It also has video input from the storage as well as the ability to store stereo video.

The third component is a foot-pedal control that adjusts the zoom and focus of the digital stereo microscope.

The fourth component is a mechanism to stream the statistics information about the surgical motion such as the number of movements made, the time taken, and the quality measure of the movements.

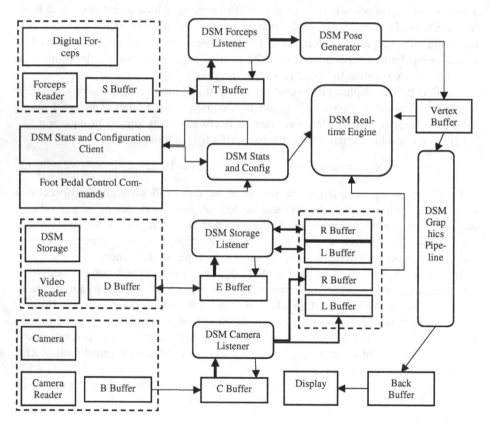

Fig. 2. Software Defined Stereo Microscope

These four components form a software defined surgical microscope. It is similar in function as an optical surgical microscope with the added facilities of programmability and ability to augment the scene. Due to the programmability, better applications can be made to train the surgeons using objective assessment.

For example, using the statistical measures, the ongoing training may be evaluated and fed-back to the training surgeon. Some of the important statistical measures are the statistics about the surgeon performing the training which aggregates the statistics of the training procedures the surgeon has done. For each training procedure, the measures of performance and quality computed from the motion data and the performance time can be maintained.

3.1 Experimental Setup

In Fig.3 (a), the experimental setup is shown with one of the task targets known as the microtrainer target.

(a) Surgeon using Microtrainer under Software Defined Digital Stereo Microscope

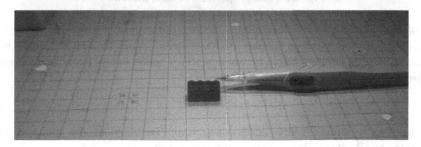

(b) Digital forceps and a micro block target

Fig. 3. Experimental setup

The experiment consists of placing the task targets (example task targets are shown in Fig.1) under the software defined microscope. Then a predefined surgical movement is made using the digital forceps.

The training surgeon uses the digital forceps shown in Fig.3(b) to trace, locate, place accurately and with less number of movements. The movement data is captured by the microscope system and is analyzed as described in section 3.2 and 3.3. The surgeon may visualize the movement profile with the quality markings and tries to make better movements. For each surgeon, we conducted 40 motion challenges. In the subsequent section, the data corresponding to one surgeon is used to explain the measures.

3.2   Motion Signal Characteristics

The frequency spectrum of the motion signal is shown in Fig. 4, the motion signal has two parts, the lower frequency (< 25 Hz) is a combination of voluntary motion signal and physiological tremor. Signal components above 25 Hz are instrument and electromagnetic noise. The noise may be filtered out through frequency based lowpass filter.

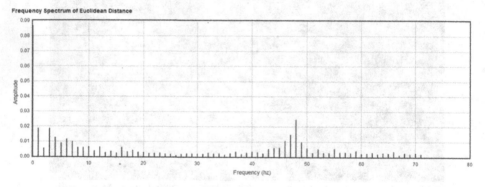

Fig. 4. Frequency spectrum of hand motion

Another characteristics of the motion is the size of the motion which is analyzed by segmenting the motion into a number of movements. A movement is defined as a sequence of spatial points wherein between any two points Pi and Pi+1, the following conditions hold.

$$|Pi, Pi+1| > \delta \tag{3}$$

Each movement represent one dexterous action. The size of the movement is represented by $(P_1, P_2, ... P_n)$ its path length defined as

$$L_{1,n} = |P_2 - P_1| + ... |P_{i+1} - P_i| + ... |P_n - P_{n-1}| \tag{4}$$

Using the size of the movement a histogram is computed and from the histogram the physiological process can be understood. As shown in Fig. 5, the histogram is multi-modal and can represent the physical processes. The small sized movements may be produced by the tremor or movement segmentation noise. The instrument and other types of noses may produce the smallest movement (less than 0.02mm) and the tremor may produce movement of 0.02mm – 0.03 mm. Voluntary movements will be coarser than this. However, surgeons make very fine movements while doing suturing. For example, a surgeon may tie 8 surgical knots while suturing a 1 mm diameter vessel which is approximately 0.5 mm apart. Hence it could be possible to make movements of fineness of 0.05mm by the surgeon.

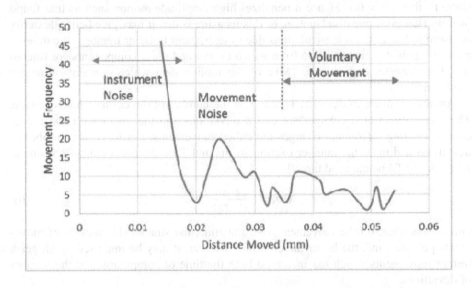

Fig. 5. Multimodal histogram of hand motion

A third way to characterize the signals is by decomposing the hand motion using EMD. The first two IMFs isolated represents the noise, the 3rd, fourth and fifth IMFs represents physiological tremor and the rest the remaining signal represents the voluntary motion.

3.3 Dexterity as Quality Measures

Dexterity as a measure of motion quality may be defined by using the signal characteristics in the frequency, spatial, and temporal domains.

If we count the oscillations that can account for the degree of control, we can determine the hand stability which is an indication of dexterity. The absolute magnitude of the oscillations are divided into oscillations of scale h units (of example, h = 0.01 mm). Oscillations are counted against the scale as follows.

Let N be the total number of peaks or troughs (oscillations) in the signal and n_i be the number of peaks or troughs having magnitude greater than (i * h) but less than or equal to $(i+1)*h$, and a n_0 be the number of peaks or troughs less than or equal to h, then dexterity Dx is defined as follows.

$$Dx = \frac{N}{n_0 + \sum_{i=1}^{b}(i+1)*n_i} \tag{5}$$

where the b is index corresponding to the maximum amplitude peak or trough. Typical value of h=0.01mm. It is assessing the homogeneity of the movement. The measure penalizes the high amplitude oscillations.

Let the signal be $h \sin(\omega t)$, then value of Dx $= 1$. Instead if the signal is $10 * h \sin(\omega t)$, then Dx $= 0.1$. Hence it penalizes high amplitude motion such as that found in Jerk. However, one disadvantage of this measure is that it may give better dexterity measure to low amplitude oscillations due to instrument noise or tremor. It can however, be applied to hand motion from which tremor and noise components are filtered out, for example, higher order IMFs of the motion data which contains voluntary motion and jerk.

Another measure of dexterity is based on the number of directional changes made. The minor directional changes are called deviations and the major path specific or error correcting directional changes are called movements. Let M be the number of deviations and m be the number of movements and T be the task completion time in seconds and Td be the dead time.

$$Dm = \frac{(M-m)}{(T-T_d)} \tag{6}$$

Dm is dependent on the movements per unit time, the smaller the number of movements per unit time, the better the control. However, it may be impacted by sluggish tremor movements which has increased both the time of completion and the number of deviations.

Another measure of dexterity D_l is obtained by computing the number of movements made per path length. The path length L is measured in mm.

$$D_l = \frac{M}{L} \tag{7}$$

In this case also, as the number of movements increase, the dexterity value decreases. However, here another factor, the length of the path being traversed is accounted. It promotes gradual movements. The deviations, which only change the direction of the movement is not considered. Hence it measures the smoothness of the movement by promoting smooth continuous movements in small steps of time.

In Fig.6, the dexterity indicators computed using the conventional parameters of the economy of motion are shown. The conventional parameters of the economy of motion are path length, time of completion and number of movements. Since D_m and D_l measure two aspects of the motion, their agreement is not expected. However, there is similarity in the dexterity change. The dexterity is computed for 40 motion experiments using dexterity targets.

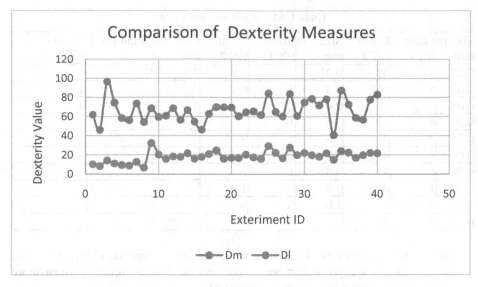

Fig. 6. Comparison of dexterity measures using economy of motion

Yet another measure of dexterity is obtained by using the histogram of displacements. The displacement histogram contains the movements in the multiple of h, the scale of the movement mentioned in equation (5). Let the movements be distributed into p buckets m1, m2, ..., mp with a separation of h between the buckets of movement amplitude. Here mi denotes the movement having dimension of (i*h). In Fig. 5, m0, m1, ..., m50 are shown. Peaks of the histogram denotes a process centered around it. In Fig. 5, we identify three peaks, one corresponding to very small movements such as instrument noise or segmentation noise, another corresponding to dexterous movements and another corresponding to the coarse movements.

One measure of dexterity that can be derived from the displacement histogram is the ratio of dexterous moved distance by non-dexterous moved distance. Let indices i= j ... k be dexterous movements and k+1 ... p be the coarse movements.

$$D_h = \frac{\sum_{i=j}^{k}(i*h)*m_i}{\sum_{i=k+1}^{p}(i*h)m_i} \tag{8}$$

For example, we partitioned movements into three scales, displacements (rounded up) into the buckets with h = 0.01 for a range from 0.01 to 0.1 and with h = 0.1 from buckets of size 0.1 to 1.0 and buckets with h = 1.0 for 1.0 to 5.0. All measurements are in mm. We took two of the 40 experiments of a subject and tabulated in Table 1.

In the table count indicates the number of movements (rounded) which had the same movement size indicated in the size column. Intuitively, the motion presented in EX 2 is better than the motion presented in EX 1 due to large number of fine movements and lack of very large movements. In the above dexterity measure if we fix the value of k to be at 1.0 mm, then the dexterity metric Dh will show better quality for measurements for EX 2. The value of k is dependent on the amount of precision needed.

Table 1. Movement size and count

Size in mm	Count EX 1	Count EX 2	Size in mm	Count EX 1	Count EX 2	Size in mm	Count EX 1	Count EX 2
0.01	9	32	0.2	4	10	2.0	0	0
0.02	9	16	0.3	1	6	3.0	2	0
0.03	4	10	0.4	0	3	4.0	2	0
0.04	4	14	0.5	1	5	5.0	0	0
0.05	4	5	0.6	1	2			
0.06	1	4	0.7	0	0			
0.07	0	4	0.8	1	0			
0.08	1	0	0.9	0	1			
0.09	0	2	1.0	0	5			
0.10	4	14						

Another measure may be derived by weighing the movements differently. The coarse movements are given less weightage and the fine movements given more weightage and the dexterity is defined similar to Dm.

$$D_k = \frac{\sum_{i=1}^{p} w_i m_i}{T - T_d} \tag{9}$$

Yet another measure can be derived by taking the ratio of the minimum distance to the displacement histogram defined distance.

$$D_r = \frac{L_c}{\sum_{i=1}^{p} (i*h) m_i} \tag{10}$$

Where Lc is the minimum path length. It may be the theoretical path length or the minimum path length by any of the valid experiments.

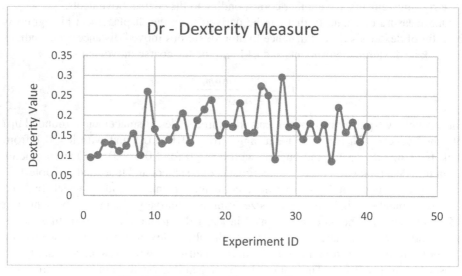

Fig. 7. Dexterity from histogram of movements

A representative dexterity measure is computed for the methods based on the histogram and is shown in Fig.7. In the case of Dr, the economy of path length is directly reflected. It is also a measure of accuracy as well as control.

4   Results and Discussion

The quality of motion has three components, the tremor content in the motion in comparison with the voluntary motion, the correctness of the motion or the lack of thereof and the smoothness of the motion. The tremor content may be assessed by using the motion produced by the tremor and by the voluntary motion. The correctness is analyzed by verifying the motion produced by the trainee and the intended motion.

The dexterity measures of the previous section considered many of these aspects. One method is combine the values obtained through the assessment by each of the methods and create a combined value of dexterity. However, the range of values of the dexterity measures are varied that a meaningful combination is difficult. Another approach is to assign grades or votes by each dexterity measure which can be combined.

A third approach is to combine the elements of the measures into a single measure. We present a single measure called the quality of the procedure which considers the number of movements and classify them as smooth movement or jerky movement.

The smoothness of other motion may be assessed by computing the Jerk (the rate of change of acceleration) in the segmented movements. A ratio of the movements where Jerk is present to that where Jerk is not present can indicate the smoothness of the movement.

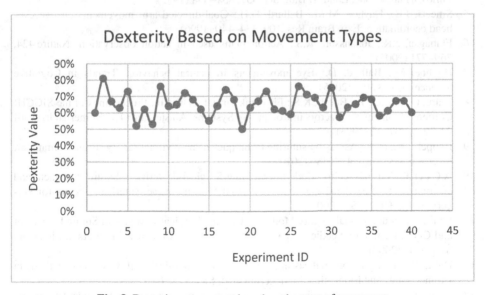

Fig. 8. Dexterity assessment based on the type of movement

In Fig.8, the dexterity assessment of the same motion data used in section 3 is presented. Here Dext(j) is the dexterity computed using movement classification based on jerk. By adhering to this method, users are provided with the realtime computation of the quality of the movement. At present movements are taken from the magnetic movement tracker.

Further work is to analyze the movements from the realtime video and compare the results of the movement quality obtained using the motion signal data from digital forceps with the motion extracted from the video. It will help create performing real suturing experiments under the training.

Acknowledgments. We acknowledge grants A*STAR ETPL HQ/S10-085COT0_06 and SPRING TI/TECS/POV/12/2 that enabled portions of this research. We also acknowledge the enthusiastic help from the staff of Robotics and Control Lab at NUS and Digital Surgicals Pte Ltd

References

1. Agur, A.M.R., Lee, M.J.: Grant'sAtlas ofAnatomy, 10th edn. Lippincott Williams and Wilkins (1999)
2. Desmurget, M., Pelisson, D., Rossetti, Y., Prablanc, C.: From eye to hand: planning goal directed movements. Neurosci. Bio. Behav. Rev. 22, 761–788 (1998)
3. Crawford, J.D., Medendorp, W.P., Marotta, J.J.: Spatialtransformations for eye-hand coordination. J. Neurophysiol. 92, 10–19 (2004)
4. Ballard, D.H., Hayhoe, M.M., Li, F.: Hand-eye coordination during sequential tasks. Philos. Trans. R Soc. Lond. B Biol. Sci. 337, 331–338 (1992)
5. Smeets, J.B., Hayhoe, M.M., Ballard, D.H.: Goal-directed arm movements change eye-head coordination. Exp. Brain Res. 109, 434–440 (1996)
6. Flanagan, J.R., Johansson, R.S.: Action plans used in action observation. Nature 424, 769–771 (2003)
7. Hayhoe, M., Ballard, D.: Eye movements in natural behavior. Trends in Cognitive Sciences 9, 188–194 (2005)
8. Ware, C., Arthur, K., Booth, K.S.: Fish tank virtual reality. In: Proceedings of the SIGCHI Conference on Human Factors in Computing Systems, Amsterdam, The Netherlands, April 24-29, pp. 37–42 (1993)
9. Rappel, J.K., et al.: Assessing suturing techniques using a virtual reality surgical simulator. Microsurgery 30(6), 479–486 (2010)
10. A.C., et al.: Virtual- reality Model for Grading Surgical-dexterity in Suture Placement and customization of needle shape. In: 59th Annual Meeting of the American Society for Surgery of the Hand, USA (2004)
11. Lahiri, A., et al.: Virtual- reality Model for Grading Surgical-dexterity in Suture Placement and Customization of Needle Shape. In: 7th NUH-NUS ASM New Frontiers in Medicine, Singapore (2003)
12. Datta, V., et al.: Motion analysis in the assessment of surgical skill. Computer Methods in Biomechanics and Biomedical Engineering 4(6), 515–523 (2001)
13. Datta, V., et al.: The use of electromagnetic motion tracking analysis to objectively measure open surgical skill in the laboratory-based model. Journal of the American College of Surgeons 193(5), 479–485 (2001)

14. Starkes, J.L., Payk, I., Hodges, N.J.: Developing a standardized test for the assessment of suturing skill in novice microsurgeons. Microsurgery 18(1), 19–22 (1998)
15. Macmillan, A.I., Cuschieri, A.: Assessment of innate ability and skills for endoscopic manipulations by the Advanced Dundee Endoscopic Psychomotor Tester: predictive and concurrent validity. The American Journal of Surgery 177(3), 274–277 (1999)
16. Egi, H., et al.: Objective assessment of endoscopic surgical skills by analyzing direction-dependent dexterity using the Hiroshima University Endoscopic Surgical Assessment Device (HUESAD). Surgery Today 38(8), 705–710 (2008)
17. Mason, J.D., et al.: Is motion analysis a valid tool for assessing laparoscopic skill? Surgical Endoscopy, 1–10 (2012)
18. Reiley, C.E., Hager, G.D.: Task versus subtask surgical skill evaluation of robotic minimally invasive surgery. In: Yang, G.-Z., Hawkes, D., Rueckert, D., Noble, A., Taylor, C. (eds.) MICCAI 2009, Part I. LNCS, vol. 5761, pp. 435–442. Springer, Heidelberg (2009)
19. Rosen, J., et al.: Task decomposition of laparoscopic surgery for objective evaluation of surgical residents' learning curve using hidden Markov model. Computer Aided Surgery 7(1), 49–61 (2002)
20. Pagador, J.B., et al.: Decomposition and analysis of laparoscopic suturing task using tool-motion analysis (TMA): improving the objective assessment. International Journal of Computer Assisted Radiology and Surgery 7(2), 305–313 (2012)
21. Cao, C., et al.: Hierarchical decomposition of laparoscopic procedures. Studies in Health Technology and Informatics, 83–89 (1999)
22. Chen, J., Yeasin, M., Sharma, R.: Visual modelling and evaluation of surgical skill. Pattern Analysis & Applications 6(1), 1–11 (2003)
23. Harwell, R.C., Ferguson, R.L.: Physiologic tremor and microsurgery. Microsurgery 4(3), 187–192 (1983)
24. Elble, R.J., Koller, W.C.: Tremor. Johns Hopkins University Press (1990)
25. Rappel, J.K., et al.: Tremor Profiling Using Digital Microsurgical Pre-Trainer. In: The Third Asian Pacific Conference on Biomechanics. The Japan Society of Mechanical Engineers, Japan (2007)
26. Huang, N.E., et al.: The empirical mode decomposition and the Hilbert spectrum for nonlinear and non-stationary time series analysis. Proceedings of the Royal Society of London 454, 903–995 (1998)
27. Schenker, P.S., et al.: Development of a telemanipulator for dexterity enhanced microsurgery. In: Proc. 2nd Intl. Symp. Med. Robot. Comput. Assist. Surg. (1995)
28. Riviere, C., Khosla, P.: Accuracy in positioning of handheld instruments. In: Proceedings of the 18th Annual International Conference of the IEEE Engineering in Medicine and Biology Society, Bridging Disciplines for Biomedicine. IEEE (1996)
29. Hotraphinyo, L.F., Riviere, C.N.: Three-dimensional accuracy assessment of eye surgeons. In: Proceedings of the 23rd Annual International Conference of the IEEE Engineering in Medicine and Biology Society. IEEE (2001)
30. Moraes, R.M., Machado, L.S.: Psychomotor Skills Assessment in Medical Training Based on Virtual Reality Using a Weighted Possibilistic Approach. Knowledge-Based Systems (in press, 2014)
31. De Moraes, R.M., dos Santos Machado, L.: A New Class of Assessment Methodologies in Medical Training Based on Combining Classifiers. In: 12th Safety, Health and Environment World Congress, San Paulo, Brazil, July 22-25 (2012)

Generating Comprehension Questions Using Paraphrase

Ya-Min Tseng[1], Yi-Ting Huang[2], Meng Chang Chen[1], and Yeali S. Sun[2]

[1] Institute of Information Science, Academia Sinica, Taipei, Taiwan
{tym,mcc}@iis.sinica.edu.tw
[2] Department of Information Management, National Taiwan University, Taipei, Taiwan
{d97725008,sunny}@ntu.edu.tw

Abstract. As online English learning environment becomes more and more ubiquitous, English as a Foreign Language (EFL) learners have more choices to learning English. There is thus increasing demand for automatic assessment tools that help self-motivated learners evaluate their understanding and comprehension. Existing question generation systems, however, focus on the sentence-to-question surface transformation and the questions could be simply answered by word matching, even without good comprehension. We propose a novel approach to generating more challenging choices for reading comprehension questions by combining paraphrase generation with question generation. In the final evaluation, although there is a slight decrease in the overall quality, our results outperform the baseline system in challenging score and have a significantly smaller percentage of statements that remain intact from the sources sentences.

Keywords: question generation, automatic assessment, reading comprehension, e-learning, multiple choice questions, paraphrase generation, discourse relation.

1   Introduction

Online learning has become a popular choice for English learners. Reading online news and watching talks, for example, are ways to learning English. There are all sorts of learning material on the Internet but there are only a limited number of human quiz creators to provide assessments based on online resources. Automatic assessment tools could help evaluate whether the readers comprehend the text well. Aware of the demand, several Question Generation (QG) systems have focused on the generation of questions for reading comprehension. These work, however, tend to generate simplistic questions with doubtful ability to assess comprehension. The same wording as the source sentences are applied to the questions, like the question *"what is often voted as the best treat in Taiwan?"* and its source *"bubble tea is often voted as the best treats in Taiwan."* Inevitably, such questions could be solved by searching for the same word spans in the article, even without good comprehension.

The over-simplicity problem might result from two common characteristics of existing QG systems. Firstly, the generating approaches have mostly focused on *wh*-questions or on question stems in the form of *cloze*. Answering these questions only requires a single piece of information, such as a location (*where*-question), a person

S.-M. Cheng and M.-Y. Day (Eds.): TAAI 2014, LNAI 8916, pp. 310–321, 2014.
© Springer International Publishing Switzerland 2014

(*who*-question) and time (*when*-question). On the other hand, due to the fact that in reading comprehension quizzes, the article is usually visible when the test takers attempt to answer the questions, it'd be hard for the automatically generated questions to reflect their comprehension rather than their test-taking skills. Most work concentrate on the surface transformation from declarative sentences to questions and barely discuss how different the resulting questions would look. While these questions are helpful in guiding the reading process and testing elementary English learners, the same might not be for more advanced ones. Self-motivated online learners tend to have higher English proficiency level, which enables them to learn independently without subscribing to any material and without human instructors.

> ... Thus, Western medicine focuses on the illness or the disease itself, while Chinese medicine focuses on keeping the body in balance and in harmony with nature ...
>
> Source Text

Which of the following statements is true?
  A. Chinese medicine focuses on keeping the body in balance and in harmony with nature.
  B. Due to the fact that Chinese medical specialty is focused on keeping the body in equilibrium and in line with nature, Western medicine concentrates on the very illness or the disease.
  C. Chinese medicine concentrates on the illness itself.

Fig. 1. Example question and choices

We approach the problem by developing generating approach for multiple-choice (non-) factual questions, as Fig. 1. The question form is selected because it's common in formal reading comprehension tests and it could be the container of different question types by casting each question into a statement with its answer. Fig. 1 (A) is transformed from the *what*-question that would be generated by many QG systems: "*what focuses on keeping the body in balance and in harmony with nature?*" along with its answer choice "*Chinese medicine*". We decode the task into generating true/false statements for these choices. By doing so, we could shift our focus from sentence-to-question transformation to increasing the difficulty of test choices. Our aim is to generate choices that test deeper knowledge and look different from the source sentences.

In this work, we present a new approach to generating more challenging choices for multiple choice questions. The novelty of this work lies in how we design choice generation and paraphrase generation towards the mutual goal and how to locate the best-quality choices among numerous variations, nice or erroneous. The Choice Generation System extracts and rewrites the sentences from the question generation aspect. We manually designed transformation rules, which use discourse relations as trigger, to bind up each generated statement with a specified testing purpose. The Paraphrase Generation System then moves on to enlarge the superficial difference by paraphrasing lexically, syntactically and referentially. We merged features from question generation and paraphrase generation to train the Acceptability Ranker, which determines any choice candidate as either acceptable or unacceptable. In the final evaluation, we conduct an experiment with the baseline system and show the effect of our approach on quality and on difficulty.

The remainder of this paper is organized as follows. Section 2 introduces closely related QG work and explains how our work differs. The generation and ranking of choice candidates are illustrated in Section 3. We do not reveal much implementation detail in this paper due to the page limit, yet any interested reader is referred to [21]. Section 4 gives the setup and the results of the experiments that evaluate our output statements. Finally, in Section 5, we conclude this paper and list possible future work.

2   Related Work

Question Generation (QG) is the task of automatically generating questions from some form of input [20]. When it comes to language learning assessment, automated question generation research are more on grammar and vocabulary. Little work have claimed themselves as aiming at reading comprehension assessment. Mostow and Jang [16] introduced DQGen, a system that automatically generates multiple-choice cloze questions to assess children's reading comprehension. They proposed to diagnose three types of comprehension failures by different types of distractors–grammatical, nonsensical and plausible distractors. In our work, we avoid generating choices that are ungrammatical or do not make sense because, to higher-level learners, they would appear to be obviously wrong choices even without the need to take a look at the article. Heilman [6] proposed a syntactic-based approach to generate factual questions, or wh-questions, from which teachers could select and revise useful ones for future use. In these years, many work (such as [17]) take advantage of domain ontology to create assessments. The generated questions, however, are not based on any input text and are more suitable to test domain-specific knowledge, like the quizzes in science classes.

Generating choices are, partially, equivalent to generating distractors. There is no answer generation in the past because words/phrases in the source sentences of the questions are directly used as answers. Existing distractor generators, as noted by Moser, Gütl and Liu [15], mainly consider single-word choices, or they generate multi-word or phrasal distractors by applying simple algorithms. Mitkov and Ha [14] select multi-word concepts that are similar to the answer from WordNet [13] as distractors and if this fails, phrases with the same head as the answer are selected from a corpus as substitutes. Moser et al. [15] extract key-phrases that are semantically close to the answer as distractors, using LSA for their similarity calculation. Afzal and Mitkov [1] generate distractors for biomedical domain based on distributional similarity. The similarity score is calculated between the answer named entity, which are possibly multi-word, and each candidate from a set of biomedical named entities. The higher scoring ones are more desirable distractors. Different from these approaches, we focus on generating sentential choices. While a small part of our generating approaches is similar to the secondary approach in [14], our approach to generate both answers and distractors via recombination of discourse segments and relations is novel.

Several research have noted the problem caused by the same wording between the generated questions and their source counterparts. Afzal and Mitkov [1] brought up the concern that generating approaches which concentrate on sentence-to-question transformation, are likely to result in questions that could only evaluate test takers' superficial memorization. They solve this problem by generating questions based on semantic relations which are extracted using information extraction methodologies. Bernhard, De Viron, Moriceau and Tannier [3] approached the problem by using two of the many paraphrase skills. They specify the question words and nominalize the verbs. E.g., from *"Where has the locomotive been invented?"* to *"In which country has the locomotive been invented?"* and *"When was Elizabeth II crowned?"* to *"When was the coronation of Elizabeth II?"*. On the other hand, Heilman and Smith [7] have developed sentence simplification for question generation based on syntactic rules. Although their work is intended to generate more concise questions, their simplification technique is also contributing to making surface difference. Our work is similar in intentions with most of these work, but paraphrase generation have never been systematically incorporated into these QG systems.

The Penn Discourse Treebank (PDTB) [18] is a large scale corpus based on some early work of discourse structure and is annotated with related information of discourse semantics. A discourse relation captures two pieces of information and the logical relationship between them. Prasad and Joshi [19] evaluated the feasibility of using discourse relations in the content selection of *why*-questions. They showed that the source of 71% of the questions in an independent *why* question answering data set could be found in the same PDTB subset with a marked causal discourse relation. Agarwal, Shah and Mannem [2] followed the proved idea and used discourse cues (e.g., *because, as a result*) as an indicator of question type to generate *why*-questions and other question types based on temporal, contrast, concession and instantiation relations. These work suggest the usefulness of discourse relations in QG. While they use discourse relations in satisfying the form of certain question types, our work take advantage of discourse relations in the generation of comprehension questions and the development of distractors.

3   Approach

In this section, we introduce our approach to generate more challenging choices, or statements, for multiple-choice reading comprehension questions. To generate superficially different statements, our intuition is to rewrite with the four basic actions: to rephrase, to reorder, to simplify and to combine. Most paraphrase generation systems, in practice, are inclined to rephrase more often than to simplify or to combine because they do not paraphrase recursively. We improve this by incorporating the structural paraphrases into the design of choice generation rules.

The overall system consists of two sub-systems and a ranker, as shown in Fig. 2. The arrows represent the flows of the generating process and ideally, all these flows should work to satisfy different demand of test choices. In the experiment of this work, only the flow that visits the three components in the order of left to right, from

Choice Generation System, Paraphrase Generation System to Acceptability Ranker, is implemented.

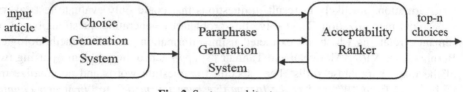

Fig. 2. System architecture

3.1   Choice Generation System

The Choice Generation System takes an article as input text and output a set of statements, each of which with a specific testing purpose. The testing purposes that are considered in this work are: understanding the cohesion of anaphora in the context, understanding the relationship (cause and effect, comparison, etc.) between details and identifying factual information that is explicitly stated in the passages. The overview of this system is given on the left of Fig. 3. In preprocessing, the information from the input article is extracted. The CoreNLP pipeline [11] splits the article into sentences and provides information on coreference chains, part-of-speech tags and syntactic trees. The PDTB-styled end-to-end discourse parser [10] recognizes intra- and inter-sentential discourse relations and the corresponding argument spans. Knowing the three basic elements (two arguments and the relation between them) allows the rules to rearrange them into new statements, with predetermined correctness. Since it's important not to produce vague statements, each pronoun, if not specified in the sentence, is replaced with the representative mention in the same coreference chain.

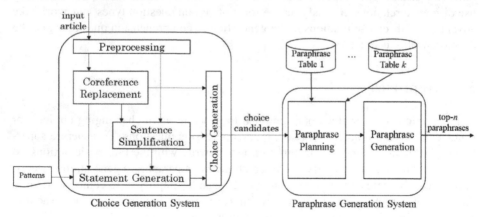

Fig. 3. Overview of the Choice Generation System and the Paraphrase Generation System

These clarified sentences are either sent to choice generation as choice candidates, which are intended to test the cohesion of anaphora, or enter the sentence simplification process. We utilize the sentence simplification work [7] that extracts simplified statements from complex sentences using a set of hand-crafted Tregex patterns. The simplified statements satisfy the testing purpose of identifying explicitly written fact.

The statement generation matches the source, clarified and simplified sentences with manually-defined rules. The discourse-based rules either recompose pairs of arguments with wrong discourse relations to form false statements or reorder the argument pairs and reunite with other discourse connectives in the same relations to create true statements. If the logical relation stays true, the generated statement is true and vice versa. In the experiment, the rules are applied only if the discourse relations that are involved are explicit because there is still room for improvement in the recognition of implicit discourse relations and because QG is more precision-favored. The relations we include in the transformation rules are: conjunction, cause, contrast, concession, condition and comparison. These allow us to provide more variety to the second testing purposes and to generate choices that test more than one piece of information. The SST (SuperSense Tag) -based rules transform a sentence by replacing a noun/verb phrase by another noun/verb phrase with the same SST for their head words. The generated statements should be plausible but false and should act as choices that assess learners' ability to identify explicitly written fact. A few sample rules are listed in Table 1. Rule #1 and #2 are discourse-based while #3 is SST-based. Fig. 1 (B) is the result of instantiating Rule #1 and Fig. 1 (C) is the statement generated by applying Rule #3. The head of the noun phrases *Chinese medicine* and *Western medicine* are categorized to the same SST (*B-noun.cognition*). The two choices have both been paraphrased whereas Fig.1 (A) has not, which has only undergone simplification and leaves the wording largely the same. The full set of rules can be found in [21].

Table 1. Sample rules

#	Rule	T/F
1	[Arg1] CONTRAST [Arg2] → [Arg2] CAUSE [Arg1]	False
2	[Arg1] CONJUNCTION [Arg2] CONTRAST [Arg3] → [Arg1] CONCESSION [Arg3]	True
3	Sentence={...NP_1...} & SST_{NP1}= SST_{NP2} → Sentence={...NP_2...}	False

3.2   Paraphrase Generation System

This system generates a ranked list of sentential paraphrases given an input sentence and a source article. It enables the overall system to produce lexically different statements and to avoid direct usage of text from the input article that would be easily answerable by word match. The architecture is given on the right of Fig. 3.

Paraphrases are 'sentences or phrases that convey approximately the same meaning using different words' [4]. Abiding by the definition, the correctness should remain unchanged for any true or false statement after paraphrasing. Research on paraphrasing is mainly divided into two lines, paraphrase extraction and paraphrase generation.

Paraphrase extraction focuses on approaches that automatically acquire paraphrases from corpora and paraphrase generation produces paraphrase for any input sentence.

Table 2. Paraphrase resources and likelihood

Alias	Resource	Paraphrase likelihood
PT-1	PPDB lexical paraphrase	$p(t\|s) \approx \sum_{e} p(t\|e)p(e\|s)$
PT-2	PPDB phrasal paraphrase	
PT-3	PPDB syntactic paraphrase	
PT-4	WordNet synonyms/entailments	e^1
PT-5	Inference rules for predicates	$score_{WT}(LHS \rightarrow RHS, w_x, w_y)$ $= \sqrt{sim(v_l^x, v_r^x, w_x) \cdot sim(v_l^y, v_r^y, w_y)}$
PT-6	Nominal Coreference	Representative mentions: e^1 Other mentions: $e^{0.8}$
PT-7	Self[1]	e^{-1}

Among the many paraphrase generation framework, we favor the idea proposed in [23] to combine multiple paraphrase resources, which allows us to flexibly introduce application-specific resources to the framework. We incorporate pairs of mentions extracted from the same coreference chain as paraphrases, which hasn't been exploited in existing paraphrase generation systems because they do not consider the article information. Besides coreference, resources like the ParaPhrase DataBase (PPDB) [5], WordNet and context-sensitive inference rules for predicates [12] are also included. These resources provide a diversity of paraphrases, from lexical, phrasal, syntactic to referential. For any input sentence, the paraphrase planning phase in Fig. 3 cuts the sentence into segments and transforms them into the search patterns of each resource. It outputs all possible paraphrases for all segments in the input sentence. In the next phase, to form a paraphrased sentence from all possible substitutes, we use a log-linear model [22] to score the combination:

$$p(t|s) = \sum_{k=1}^{K} \lambda_k \sum_{k_i} \ln \varphi_{PT_k}(\bar{s}_{k_i}, \bar{t}_{k_i}) + \lambda_{lm} \sum_{j=1}^{J} \ln p(t_j|t_{j-2}t_{j-1}) \qquad (1)$$

In Equation 1, s represents the source sentence and t is the target sentence. K is the total number of paraphrase tables and J is the unit of the J-gram language model. $\varphi_{PT_k}(\bar{s}_{k_i}, \bar{t}_{k_i})$ is the sum of the paraphrase likelihood scores of the substitutes for the i-th segment that are found in PT-k. The likelihood scores for each PT is defined in Table 2. The second part of the addition is the J-gram ($J = 3$) language model score of t and is retrieved via Microsoft web n-gram services[2]. λ_k and λ_{lm} are the parameters that represent the weights of the sub-scores. The calculation is reduced to the Viterbi algorithm and the top-scoring target sentences can be easily found.

---

[1] The self-table is created dynamically for each word in the input sentence. This allows words in the sentence to remain unchanged when there is no better substitute.

[2] http://weblm.research.microsoft.com/

3.3   Acceptability Ranker

Processed by the Choice Generation System and the Paraphrase Generation System, most source sentences are transformed into various statements with different testing purposes and with different appearances. Obviously, we don't need all these for the final application. A two-way classifier is trained to answer the question, *"can this statement be accepted as a choice?"* The probability scores provided by the classifier should help rank the choice candidates according to its acceptability in an assessment.

The features that the ranker is based on can be grouped into five types by function. We combine features commonly used in QG as well as those that are frequently concerned in paraphrase scoring. Surface features describe the appearance of the choice candidate from the view of grammaticality and length. Vagueness features include features that would tell the vagueness of the sentence. Grammar features [8] are part of the vagueness features because the information of part-of-speech tags and the grammatical structures may suggest how descriptive the sentence is. Transformation rule features capture the inherent accuracy of each transformation rule. Replacement features measure the quality of the replacement by considering the content and the context of the replacing phrase and the replaced phrase. QG challenging features suggest how challenging the choice candidate might be by features that summarize the category and the extent of paraphrasing. There are 90 features in total.

4   Experiment and Results

4.1   Parameter Estimations

The parameters in Equation 1 is estimated according to the settings in [23] and the optimization function in [22] with minor adjustment. The Acceptability Ranker is trained on the data that are partly rated by two human experts. The other part is rated by the workers on Amazon Mechanical Turk[3] (MTurk) service. The human experts worked individually and the ratings of any Turker should correlate with the others to at least a moderate degree on a batch basis. The raters were asked to rate the acceptability on a Likert scale rating, where the definition follows [9]. From 1 to 5, the acceptability score represents bad, unacceptable, borderline, acceptable and good, respectively. We binarize the rating to have scores that exceed 3.5 as acceptable and unacceptable otherwise. We also asked the raters to mark the choices as true or false, given the article.

In total, 10 articles, with 1065 related statements that are generated by our work, are annotated. 200 statements are randomly selected as the held-out test set while the rest are on the training set for logistic regression. The Acceptability Ranker that we trained in this work reflects an accuracy of 0.73 on the test set, as shown in Table 3. Since there is concern that the working quality of Turkers might not be as good as human experts, we also trained the Acceptability Ranker using only the data annotated by the human experts on the training set and the ones by the Turkers, respectively. The former subset hits a higher

---

[3] https://www.mturk.com/

accuracy of 0.7596 while the sub data set by Turkers reaches a significantly lower accuracy of 0.6875, suggesting that the work done by Turkers might be less consistent.

Table 3. Accuracy of the Acceptability Ranker

	HE+MTurk	HE	MTurk
Accuracy	0.73	0.7596	0.6875

HE: the data tagged by human experts
MTurk: the data tagged by Turkers

4.2   Experimental Settings

To show the overall performance, we evaluate the top-ranked statements from the view of question generation. The baseline system is proposed by Heilman and Smith [7], which is also intended to facilitate QG and outputs statements. Since the baseline is included in our system as the simplification component, the effect of adding other components could be shown.

Two articles, one from BBC news (22 sentences) and the other from GSAT English 2009 (15 sentences), are randomly selected. They represent different writing styles, one as news report and the other in a more formal way. They are processed by both the baseline and our system into factual statements. Two human experts, graduate students who are non-native English speakers but with high English proficiency, are asked to fulfill half of the rating work. A moderate degree of Pearson correlation coefficient is achieved. The evaluation metrics include *grammaticality* (1–5), *make-sense* (1–3), *challenging score* (1–3) and *overall quality* (1–5).

For each article, the baseline generated around 20-35 simplified statements while our system generated over 700 variations. All the statements from the baseline are evaluated. Since these statements cover all source sentences in the input, to make a fair comparison, the top-5 choice candidates for each source sentence are generated by our system for evaluation.

4.3   Experimental Results

If all transformations go well without errors, the transformation rules should determine whether the choice is true or false. A contingency table that summarizes the intended correctness and the actual correctness is shown in Table 4. The statistics are summed up based on the training and the testing data for the Acceptability Ranker. In consideration of the quality of work on MTurk, as Table 3 suggests, we only take the human-annotated data for evaluation in order to obtain more reliable results. Excluding the choice candidates that are unacceptable, 83% of the correctness labels remain identical as planned. For statements that are made to be true, 94% of them are successful. On the contrary, for statements that are designed to be distractors, a lower ratio of 75% is attained. True statements are more likely to maintain their correctness while false ones, or distractors, may be true when the transformation is based on weak discourse relations or on phrases with similar meaning.

Table 5 shows the evaluation results of the baseline and our system. The baseline system attains better overall quality. This matches what we predicted because our system integrates multiple components, each of which used to be an independent system and has distinctive errors, such as the simplification system, the paraphrase generation system and the question generation system. The errors that these systems bring in would definitely harm the overall quality as well as the grammaticality and the score of make-sense. Still, it's delightful to see that the decrease in these scores is slight and to have made the average difficulty of these choices higher. The challenging score is increased but not as much as we expected. This might be because the discourse-based rules are much less productive than the SST-based ones. The top-5 choices that we evaluated are overwhelmingly occupied the SST-based choices, which are on average not as difficult as those that involve discourse relations.

Table 4. Number of intended and actual TRUE/FALSE

	Actual TRUE	Actual FALSE	Total
Intended TRUE	257 (41%)	16 (3%)	273
Intended FALSE	90 (14%)	264 (42%)	354
Total	347	280	627

Table 5. Extrinsic evaluation results

	Grammaticality (1–5)	Make-sense (1–3)	Challenging score (1–3)	Overall quality (1–5)	Unchanged sentences
Baseline	4.86	2.5	1.2	3.76	38.10%
Our system	4.22	2.39	1.51	3.53	8.57%

The statistics also suggest that our system is generating statements with more variation. The percentage of unchanged sentences is 38.1% for the baseline system while only 8.57% of the sentences in our system output are identical to the source counterparts. Keeping a source sentence intact is sure to produce a grammatically perfect statement, which might be an easy test choice. On the contrary, making most of the source sentences changed should have largely affected the quality and the grammaticality but our Acceptability Ranker has successfully performed to maintain the good quality of the top-ranked choices.

5   Conclusion

In this paper, we presented a novel approach to generate statements for multiple-choice reading comprehension questions. By exploiting discourse relations, our system creates artificial statements that could test the knowledge of multiple spans of information. We introduced the concept of paraphrase when designing the rules, allowing them to perform paraphrasing actions. The Paraphrase Generation System includes paraphrase resources that are suitable to our system. Particularly, we added QG-specific resource, nominal coreference, to capture the article-wide coreferential relations. Finally, a two-way classifier, the Acceptability Ranker, was trained from an annotated data set generated by our system. We integrated useful features from both rankers for question generation and paraphrase generation. The experimental results suggest that our system are more capable of generating challenging test choices that would not be simply solved by matching exact word span and would be more likely to distinguish those who do not comprehend the reading article well from those who do.

In the future, we plan to investigate the possibility of using implicit discourse relations and incorporate entailment-based rules into our system. We believe that implicit discourse relations would test a higher level of comprehension than explicit ones because the former do not give obvious clues, like connectives. The idea of rewriting a statement while pertaining/changing its correctness conforms to rewriting a statement into another with/without an entailment relationship between them. Entailment is expected to increase the variety of the generated statements. Ultimately, we hope to develop directly applicable question generation system that benefits e-learning environment in the near future.

Acknowledgement. This research was partially supported by National Science Council of Taiwan under grant NSC100-2221-E-001-015-MY3.

References

1. Afzal, N., Mitkov, R.: Automatic generation of multiple choice questions using dependency-based semantic relations. Soft Computing 18, 1269–1281 (2014)
2. Agarwal, M., Shah, R., Mannem, P.: Automatic question generation using discourse cues. In: Proceedings of the 6th Workshop on Innovative Use of NLP for Building Educational Applications, pp. 1–9. Association for Computational Linguistics (2011)
3. Bernhard, D., De Viron, L., Moriceau, V., Tannier, X.: Question Generation for French: Collating Parsers and Paraphrasing Questions. Dialogue and Discourse 3(2), 43–74 (2012)
4. Bhagat, R., Hovy, E.: What is a paraphrase? Computational Linguistics 39(3), 463–472 (2013)
5. Ganitkevitch, J., Callison-Burch, C., Van Durme, B.: Ppdb: The paraphrase database. In: Proceedings of NAACL-HLT, pp. 758–764 (2013)
6. Heilman, M.: Automatic Factual Question Generation from Text. Ph.D. Dissertation, Carnegie Mellon University. CMU-LTI-11-004 (2011)
7. Heilman, M., Smith, N.A.: Extracting Simplified Statements for Factual Question Generation. In: Proceedings of QG 2010: The Third Workshop on Question Generation, pp. 11–20 (2010)
8. Heilman, M., Smith, N.A.: Good question! statistical ranking for question generation. In: NAACL-HLT, pp. 609–617 (2010)

9. Heilman, M., Smith, N.A.: Rating computer-generated questions with Mechanical Turk. In: Proceedings of the NAACL HLT 2010 Workshop on Creating Speech and Language Data with Amazon's Mechanical Turk, pp. 35–40 (2010)
10. Lin, Z., Ng, H.T., Kan, M.: A PDTB-styled end-to-end discourse parser. Comput. Res. Repository (2011)
11. Manning, C.D., Surdeanu, M., Bauer, J., Finkel, J., Bethard, S.J., McClosky, D.: The Stanford CoreNLP Natural Language Processing Toolkit. In: 52nd Annual Meeting of the Association for Computational Linguistics: System Demonstrations, pp. 55–60 (2014)
12. Melamud, O., Berant, J., Dagan, I., Goldberger, J., Szpektor, I.: A Two Level Model for Context Sensitive Inference Rules. In: Proceedings of the 51st Annual Meeting of the Association for Computational Linguistics, pp. 1331–1340 (2014)
13. Miller, A.G.: WordNet: A lexical database for English. Communications of the ACM 38(11), 39–41 (1995)
14. Mitkov, R., An, L.: Computer-aided generation of multiple-choice tests. In: Proceedings of the 1st Workshop on Building Educational Applications Using NLP, HLT-NAACL, pp. 17–22 (2003)
15. Moser, J., Gütl, C., Liu, W.: Refined Distractor Generation with LSA and Stylometry for Automated Multiple Choice Question Generation. In: Thielscher, M., Zhang, D. (eds.) AI 2012. LNCS, vol. 7691, pp. 95–106. Springer, Heidelberg (2012)
16. Mostow, J., Jang, H.: Generating diagnostic multiple choice comprehension cloze questions. In: Proceedings of the Seventh Workshop on Building Educational Applications Using NLP, pp. 136–146. Association for Computational Linguistics (2012)
17. Papasalouros, A., Kanaris, K., Kotis, K.: Automatic Generation of Multiple Choice Questions from Domain Ontologies. In: IADIS International Conference e-Learning, pp. 427–434. IADIS Press (2008)
18. Prasad, R., Dinesh, N., Lee, A., Miltsakaki, E., Robaldo, L., Joshi, A., Webber, B.: The Penn Discourse Treebank 2.0. In: Proceedings of the 6th LREC (2008)
19. Prasad, R., Joshi, A.: A Discourse-based Approach to Generating why-Questions from text. In: Proceedings of the Workshop on the Question Generation Shared Task and Evaluation Challenge (2008)
20. Rus, V., Graesser, A.C. (eds): Workshop Report: The Question Generation Task and Evaluation Challenge, Institute for Intelligent Systems, Memphis, TN (2009) ISBN: 978-0-615-27428-7
21. Tseng, Y.M.: Generating Reading Comprehension Questions using Paraphrase. Master's thesis (to be published), National Taiwan University, Taipei, Taiwan (2014)
22. Zhao, S.Q., Lan, X., Liu, T., Li, S.: Application-driven statistical paraphrase generation. In: Proceedings of the 47th Annual Meeting of the ACL and the 4th IJCNLP of the AFNLP, pp. 834–842 (2009)
23. Zhao, S.Q., Cheng, N., Zhou, M., Liu, T., Li, S.: Combining multiple resources to improve SMT-based paraphrasing model. In: Proceedings of ACL 2008: HLT, pp. 1021–1029 (2008)

A Pragmatic Approach to Summarize Association Rules in Business Analytics Projects

Swee Chuan Tan and Boon Hong Sim

SIM University, School of Business
461 Clementi Road, Singapore
jamestansc@unisim.edu.sg, jeffrey.swf@hotmail.com

Abstract. Association rule mining is an important data mining method primarily used for market basket analysis. However, the method usually generates a large number of association rules; and it is difficult to use domain-independent objective measures to help find pragmatically important rules. To address these issues, we present a general method that succinctly summarizes rules with common consequent(s). This consequent-based approach allows user to focus on evaluating a rule set based on the practical significance of consequent(s) in an application domain, which usually outweighs the importance of objective measures such as rule confidence. We provide a case study to demonstrate how the proposed method can be used in conjunction with a heuristic procedure to find important rules generated from large real-world data, leading to discovery of important business knowledge and insights.

1   Introduction

Association rule mining is a data mining method that discovers interesting and useful relationships hidden in data [1]. One common application of association rule mining is market basket analysis [11], where products that are usually purchased together in a supermarket can be identified. The relationships of products can then be studied and insight is then drawn for improving store layout and pricing strategies, or for designing promotional strategies such as cross-selling or product bundling.

Despite the usefulness of association rule mining, a common problem faced by end-users is that the method tends to generate too many association rules. When a large number of rules are generated, many of the rules are redundant because they convey the same amount of information, or are insignificant because they contain common knowledge about the business. In most cases, the number of redundant or trivial rules is a lot more than the number of essential rules, which makes the discovery of really interesting rules a challenge [3].

Another problem of using association rule mining is the need for users to specify minimum interestingness thresholds for discovering interesting association rules. Usually, a threshold is set arbitrarily. Using a threshold that is too low may generate too many association rules, which are difficult to interpret [4]. On the other hand, using a threshold that is too high may remove rare rules that could be important for discovering new information [10].

S.-M. Cheng and M.-Y. Day (Eds.): TAAI 2014, LNAI 8916, pp. 322–333, 2014.
© Springer International Publishing Switzerland 2014

Furthermore, most business users evaluate the usefulness of a rule by examining the practical significance of consequent(s), and the use of interestingness measure (such as support and confidence) is sometimes of secondary importance. This is logical because a rule with a significant consequent (e.g., the occurrence of a life-threatening disease) is more important than a rule with trivial consequent (e.g., the occurrence of minor cuts and bruises), even though the former rule may have lower interestingness values than the latter one. As far as we know, most previous studies in rule summarization have not taken this point into consideration.

The above observation motivates us to develop a new method called *Consequent-based Association Rules Summarization* (CARS). Previous scientific approaches for rule summarization, though theoretically interesting, are practically limited in reducing the number of rules. CARS is different. It is an applied approach designed for three pragmatic reasons. Firstly, CARS summarizes a large number of association rules into a few rule summaries, where each rule summary has the same consequent(s). This allows end-users to evaluate a set of rules based on consequent importance, an important angle for evaluating rules. Secondly, each rule summary ranks the antecedents that determine the consequent. Such information is useful for assessing the plausibility of the rules against business knowledge. Thirdly, each rule summary provides ranges of interestingness values to allow user to refine the search for rules of particular consequent(s). This is important because rules with different consequents may have different ranges of interestingness values. So CARS effectively compartmentalizes the search for rules of certain consequent(s).

The rest of this paper is organized as follows. Section 2 provides some preliminary information about association rule mining and discusses issues in association rule mining and review existing solutions to the issues. Section 3 describes the proposed method for summarizing association rules. Section 4 presents the results and demonstrates an application of CARS. Section 5 concludes this paper.

2   Related Work

This section first provides a brief introduction to association rule mining. Then, it discusses some common issues and solutions related to association mining solution.

2.1   The Association Rule Mining Process

Figure 1 shows the process of association rule mining. First, data is prepared and then read in by the association rule mining algorithm. Second, the algorithm parameter settings (such as the support and confidence thresholds) are defined and rules are generated from the input data. Third, the rules are (sometimes) sent to a post-processing stage to improve the presentation of rule mining results. This work focuses on improving the final stage.

2.2   Two Issues of Association Rule Mining

A longstanding issue of association rule mining is that the approach tends to generate excessively large number of rules. A common way to address this issue is to reduce the number of generated association rules. For example, one important early idea is to use multilevel organization and summarization of discovered rules to eliminate redundant rules [5]. Other early attempts include pruning association rules using the idea of *rule cover* and grouping similar association rules using clustering [13]. Such an approach processes the generated rules to create condensed rules that are easier to understand. Other proposals along this line of research explore the use of ontologies [7, 8] or domain knowledge [2] to prune or group discovered association rules.

Another direction of research focuses on generating non-redundant association rules. Some researchers use the concept of frequent closed itemsets to generate non-redundant rules [15], or use the notion of representative basis to identify minimum and unique association rules [6]. More recent proposals on generating non-redundant rules include the idea of using reliable basis to represent association rules [14]. These methods can effectively produce non-redundant rules that are a lot smaller than the rules generated from the traditional approach. However, the number of less-redundant rules generated is still high from a business end-user point of view.

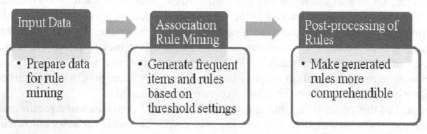

Fig. 1. Process of Association Rule Mining

The second issue of association rule mining is the difficulty in setting thresholds for interestingness metrics (e.g., support and confidence measures). Usually, improper threshold settings can result in generating either too few or too many rules, and in either case this impedes identification of interesting rules. To tackle this issue, some researchers (e.g., [12]) attempt to derive minimum support based on additional metrics such as lift or conviction measures, but this requires other user-specified input values. More recent work attempts to avoid user input by deriving the support threshold from the data alone [9]. However, different subsets of rules may need different thresholds and a single threshold value may not be able to extract all interesting rules.

Note that most of the aforementioned work focus on finding a small set of representative rules to *replace* redundant rules. Our work in this paper serves a different purpose---to provide a highly succinct summary of all the rules generated; and to provide a summary of the interestingness measures, so as to guide users in setting more appropriate interestingness thresholds. Hence, our proposed method focuses on the post-processing of rules *generated by any association rule mining methods*.

3 Proposed Method

The proposed Consequent-based Association Rules Summarization (CARS) method is simple. First, an association rule mining method with certain interestingness threshold settings is applied to a dataset. If the support-and-confidence framework is used, then its settings can abbreviated as $xAyC$, where x is the percentage of antecedent support threshold, and y is the percentage of confidence threshold. The rules generated are then grouped based by the consequent. Each group of rules that has the same consequent c forms a *Rule Summary* (*RS*), which consists of the following definitions:

- **Consequent Frequency:** Let $\mathbf{R_c} = \{r_1, r_2, ..., r_m\}$ be a set of rules with the same consequent c. That is, $\forall\ r \in \mathbf{R_c}: c \in r$. The number of occurrences of c in an *RS* is $|\mathbf{R_c}| = m$. We name $|\mathbf{R_c}|$ as *Consequent Frequency*.

- **Antecedent Frequency:** Let $\mathbf{R_a}$ be a set of rules in $\mathbf{R_c}$ (i.e., $\mathbf{R_a} \subseteq \mathbf{R_c}$), in which each rule of $\mathbf{R_a}$ contains antecedent a. That is, $\forall\ r \in \mathbf{R_a}: a \in r$. The number of times antecedent a appears in $\mathbf{R_c}$ is $|\mathbf{R_a}|$. We name $|\mathbf{R_a}|$ as Antecedent Frequency.

- **Interestingness Metric Range (*f_range*):** Let f be a function for measuring the interestingness of rules in an *RS*, then the range of f is $[f_{min}, f_{max}]$, where $f_{min} = \min(f(r_1), f(r_2), ..., f(r_m))$, and $f_{max} = \max(f(r_1), f(r_2), ..., f(r_m))$. The function f can be antecedent support, rule confidence, lift, etc.

With the abovementioned definitions, an *RS* has the following abstract representation:

$a_1 *|\mathbf{R_{a1}}|, a_2 *|\mathbf{R_{a2}}|, ..., a_n *|\mathbf{R_{an}}| => c*m$
with *f_range*: $[f_{min}, f_{max}]$

Supposed now a set of rules is generated from a dataset using $xAyC$, then rule summaries can be derived from each set of rules that have common consequent(s). Here we give an example of a rule summary from a set of two rules with the same consequent, with $x = 35\%$, and $y = 80\%$.

Example 1.

Rule 1: **A, B => C**, with antecedent support = 42%, and confidence = 90%.
Rule 2: **B => C**, with antecedent support = 45%, and confidence = 92%.

Using the CARS approach, these two rules can be summarized as:

A*1, B*2 => C*2
With *support range*: [42%, 45%], and *confidence range*: [90%, 92%].

We now describe four properties of a Rule Summary using this example.

Property 1: Consequent Frequency Indicates the Importance of a Rule Summary
Consequent Frequency indicates the importance of an *RS* as it denotes the number of rules that have been summarized in the *RS*. The higher the Consequent Frequency, the more important the *RS* is. In Example 1, the rule summary has a Consequent Frequency of 2.

Property 2: Antecedent Frequency Indicates Antecedent Importance within a Rule Summary
Antecdent Frequency indicates the relative importance of an antecedent as compared to other antecedents within the same *RS*. The higher the Antecedent Frequency, the more important the antecedent is. In Example 1, antecedent A is less important than B because it has a lower antecedent frequency compared to B.

Property 3: Upper Bound of Interestingness Metric in a Rule Summary
Let the interestingness metric range (i.e., *f_range*) of a rule summary be $[f_{min}, f_{max}]$. As long as the *other metrics' thresholds* are fixed, f_{max} is invariant when different values of f (i.e., support thresholds) are used. This implies that no association rules exist with an f value greater than f_{max}. Hence setting $f > f_{max}$ is meaningless because it will yield no rule.

Property 4: No Rule Exists in the Range of $[f, f_{min}]$ within a Rule Summary
Let the interestingness metric range (i.e., *f_range*) of a rule summary be $[f_{min}, f_{max}]$. As long as the *other metric thresholds* are fixed, there are no association rules in the range of $[f, f_{min}]$. This implies that there is no point in setting any new interestingness thresholds within the range of $[f, f_{min}]$ because it will not generate a different set of rules.

Here, we give an example of Property 3 using the support-and-confidence framework. Let the Antecedent Support Range of a rule summary be $[S_{min}, S_{max}]$. As long as the confidence threshold y is fixed, S_{max} is invariant when different values of x (i.e., support thresholds) are used. Property 3 implies that no association rules exist with a support greater than S_{max}. Hence setting x $> S_{max}$ is meaningless because it will yield no rule. In Example 1, with y being fixed at 80%, we know that setting $x > 45\%$ will not yield any rule for the rule summary with consequent C.

Similarly, Property 4 states that no association rules exist in the range of $[x, S_{min}]$. This implies that there is no point in setting any new support thresholds in the range of $[x, S_{min}]$ because it will not generate a different set of rules with consequent C. In Example 1, with y being fixed at 80%, we know that setting x in the range of [35%, 42%] will not change the rule summary with consequent C.

Note that Properties 3 and 4 are also applicable to rule confidence. If the end-user varies the confidence threshold while leaving the support threshold fixed, the same behavior can be expected about rule confidence.

4   Experimental Setup and Results

This section first presents the experimental data and setup, and then it discusses the usage and interpretations of rule summaries.

4.1   Experimental Setup

We used two sales transaction datasets for association rule mining. Each dataset consists of rows representing transactions and columns representing products. Purchased products are coded as 'True', and products not purchased are coded as 'False'. In our experiments, we use eight different sets of support and confidence thresholds for each dataset. Each setting is abbreviated as $xAyC$, where x is the percentage of antecedent support threshold, and y is the percentage of confidence threshold.

The first dataset is named "Online Purchase". It records 1000 over transactions of 17 anonymous products. We use this dataset to study the properties of rule summaries when different threshold settings are used.

The second dataset is named "*Sales Transaction*", it is a large real-world dataset that records 350 000 over transactions of 800 consumer electronics products in one year. We use this dataset to demonstrate how actionable insights can be derived from the rule summaries.

Since CARS is a general method that is not dependent on any specific association rule mining algorithms, we choose the most commonly used *Apriori* algorithm [1] for the experiments. This algorithm is available in the IBM SPSS Modeler® 14.1 data mining workbench, which is installed in a Pentium PC with Windows 7 Operating System. The algorithm was applied to the datasets using different support and confidence threshold settings. For each set of thresholds, the generated rules were summarized as consequent-based association rule summaries.

4.2   Interpreting and Tuning for Rule Summaries

To illustrate how CARS produces rule summaries, we examine two summaries derived from a set of five rules generated from the Online Purchase dataset using a support and confidence thresholds setting of 20A60C.

Table 1 shows that the first three rules having the same consequent (i.e., 'I') are condensed into Rule Summary 1 in Table 2. Similarly, Rules 4 and 5 having the same consequent (i.e., 'A') are condensed into Rule Summary 2.

In each rule summary, the count of occurrences for each item is shown by a number after the asterisk. For example, Rule Summary 1 has consequent item "I*3" meaning that the consequent item 'I' has occurred three times. Property 1 suggests that a more important rule summary has a higher consequent frequency. Hence Rule Summary 1 is more important than Rule Summary 2 because it has a higher consequent frequency.

In each rule summary, the count of occurrences for each antecedent item is reflected under the antecedent frequency. For example, in Rule Summary 1, items 'E', 'L', and 'M' all appear only once, so their antecedent frequencies are all one. If their frequencies were different, then the antecedents could be ranked, with antecedents having higher antecedent frequencies being considered more important.

With the confidence threshold fixed at 60%, Property 3 suggests that there is no point in setting an antecedent support threshold higher than 34.21%. This is because no rule exists in Rule Summary 1 for a support beyond 34.21%. Indeed, we found no rules generated for Rule Summary 1 when $x = 35\%$ in our experiments. Also, Property 4 suggests that no additional rule will be generated in Rule Summary 1 if we set an antecedent support threshold in the range of [20%, 24.36%]. In our experiments, we tried setting $x = 21\%$, $x = 22\%$, $x = 23\%$, $x = 24\%$ and found that the same set rules were generated, thus confirms the validity of Property 4.

With the antecedent support threshold fixed at 20%, Property 3 suggests that there is no point in setting confidence threshold higher than 68.77%. This is because no rule exists in Rule Summary 1 for a rule confidence beyond 68.77%. Also, Property 4 suggests that no additional rule will be generated in Rule Summary 1 if we set a confidence threshold in the range of [60%, 62.76%]. These properties were also validated in our experiments.

Table 1. Association rules generated from the Online Purchase dataset using 20A60C

Rule ID	Consequent	Antecedent	Support (%)	Confidence (%)
1	I	E	34.21	66.81
2	I	L	24.36	62.76
3	I	M	27.21	68.77
4	A	G	30.79	66.59
5	A	J	29.64	61.93

Table 2. Summaries derived from rules in Table 1

Rule Summary	Consequent	Antecedent	Support Range (%)	Confidence Range (%)
1	I*3	E*1, L*1, M*1	24.36 - 34.21	62.76 - 68.77
2	A*2	G*1, J*1	29.64 - 30.79	61.93 - 66.59

4.3   Properties of Rule Summaries

We now study the properties of Consequent-based Association Rule Summaries. Table 3 shows a set of rule summaries derived from rules generated from the Online Purchase dataset. The rules were generated using four different sets of support and confidence threshold settings.

Table 3 shows that, by fixing the confidence threshold at 60% and gradually decreasing the antecedent support threshold from 20% to 5%, the number of rules increases drastically. However, the number of rule summaries only increases marginally.

Although different threshold settings have been used, the most important rule summary tends to be the one with consequent 'I', which has the highest consequent frequency. This is followed by the summary with consequent 'A', and then the summary with consequent 'F', and so on. Such ranking information allows users to identify more important and interesting rules.

Similarly, the antecedents in individual rule summaries are ranked based on antecedent frequency. In the rule summary with consequent 'I' when 10A60C was set, antecedents 'E', 'M', and 'A' were the most important, this is followed by 'L' and 'Q', and lastly 'F' is the least important. Such ranking suggests affinity of the antecedents to the consequent within a rule summary.

Table 3. Rule Summaries for the Online Purchase dataset. Confidence threshold was fixed at 60%. Antecedent Support threshold was gradually reduced from 20% to 5%.

Threshold Setting (xAyC)	Consequent	Antecedent	Support Range (%)	Confidence Range (%)	Rule Reduction to Summary
20A60C	I*3	E*1, M*1, L*1	24.36 - 34.21	62.76 - 68.77	5 rules reduced to 2 summaries
	A*2	G*1, J*1	29.64 - 30.79	62.76 - 66.59	
15A60C	I*4	E*2, M*1, A*1, L*1	19.36 - 34.21	62.76 - 68.77	6 rules reduced to 2 summaries
	A*2	G*1, J*1	29.64 - 30.79	61.93 - 66.59	
10A60C	I*11	E*4, M*4, A*4, L*3, Q*3, F*1	10.64 - 34.21	60.71 - 69.61	19 rules reduced to 3 summaries
	A*6	G*3, J*3, Q*2, O*1	11.43 - 30.79	60.12 - 69.61	
	F*2	H*1, N*1, I*1	12.29 - 12.71	65.17 - 70.35	
5A60C	I*24	E*11, M*10, A*10, Q*8, L*6, F*3, B*2, C*2	5.00 - 34.21	60.71 - 89.19	61 rules reduced to 10 summaries
	A*17	G*8, J*6, Q*3, O*3, E*2, K*2, L*2, P*2, I*1, M*1, N*1	5.57 - 30.79	60.12 - 77.89	
	F*7	N*4, H*3, I*3, Q*2, A*1, B*1, L*1	5.71 - 12.71	60.00 - 84.09	
	G*5	A*2, K*2, J*1, M*1, O*1, P*1	5.64 - 9.86	68.52 - 100.00	
	J*2	A*1, G*1, M*1, O*1	6.93 - 7.71	60.19 - 62.89	
	K*2	P*2, G*1	6.14	65.12	
	E*1	A*1, I*1, L*1	7.86	60.00	
	L*1	F*1, H*1	8.64	61.16	
	N*1	F*1, J*1	5.86	84.15	
	Q*1	B*1, N*1	7.57	61.32	

Note that the ranking of rule summaries tends to remain the same even though there are changes in the antecedent threshold settings. Similarly, the antecedent ranking within each summary is also more-or-less retained despite changes of the antecedent support threshold settings. These observations suggest that the rule summaries tend to be consistent despite the changes in the antecedent support threshold settings.

Another interesting aspect is that, when the antecedent support threshold is reduced, the maximum support value of each rule summary remains unchanged. For example, the rule summary for consequent 'I' remains at 34.21%, despite the fact that different antecedent support thresholds were used. This validates Property 3.

When examining a rule summary, the range of its interestingness metric indicates the appropriateness of the minimum interestingness metric threshold. If a rule summary has a *narrow* interestingness metric range, it suggests that the threshold may be too high and should be adjusted down. If the interestingness metric range of a rule summary is too *wide*, it suggests that the threshold may be too low and should be adjusted up. For example, when the minimum antecedent support threshold is set at 5% in Table 3, the support ranges become quite wide and one might consider increasing the support threshold.

Notice that Table 3 also illustrates the effect of adjusting the interestingness thresholds. The effect of increasing the interestingness threshold will reduce consequent frequency, but narrow the range of interestingness metrics. On the other hand, decreasing the interestingness threshold will increase consequent frequency, but widen the range of interestingness metrics.

For the sake of completeness, we have also obtained summaries of rules generated from the Online Purchase dataset, with the antecedent support threshold fixed at 20% and confidence threshold reduced gradually from 60% to 55%, then 50% and 45%. We notice that the rule summaries tend to exhibit the same properties as those observed in Table 3. Due to the page limit for wiring this paper, we do not show the rule summaries here, but shall provide the details in a future publication.

4.4   A Case of Using CARS in a Business Analytics Project

Here, we illustrate how the proposed method can be used in conjunction with a heuristic procedure to help find interesting association rules in the *Sales Transaction* dataset. The procedure is as follows:

Step 1: Rule Generation). Given a dataset, define each attribute as *both* an input and output (i.e., an attribute can be antecedent in Rule i, and it can be consequent in Rule j, such that $i \neq j$). Use reasonably low interestingness thresholds to generate as many rules as possible for summarization.

Step 2: Rule Summary Evaluation). Summarize the rules using CARS. Sort the rule summaries based on the maximum confidence. Select rule summaries with consequents that are of *pragmatic importance* in the domain of application. Evaluate the impact of rule summaries using rule confidence and antecedent support ranges. Validate each interesting rule summary by examining the credibility of frequent antecedents in light of knowledge about the business domain.

Step 3: Result Refinement). Let the selected important consequents remain as both input and output, and set the rest of the attributes as inputs. If required, adjust (and readjust) the minimum support and confidence thresholds in light of rule summary properties, and re-execute Apriori until the results are satisfactory.

Analysis of Sales Transaction Dataset

We apply Apriori method on the *Sales Transaction* dataset using 5A20C. This produces 55 rules, which are then condensed as 25 rule summaries using CARS. Table 4 gives a quick overview of rule quality. In fact, all the rule summaries have low rule confidence and antecedent support values, suggesting that the 800 products are too specific such that most do not co-occur frequently. Hence, these products need to be meaningfully categorized so that there is sufficient number of frequent itemsets for rule generation.

Table 4. Some of the 25 Rule Summaries generated from the Sales Transaction data set. All the summaries indicate rules generated are of low support and low confidence.

Consequent	Antecedent	Support Range (%)	Confidence Range (%)
P101	P36*1, P131*1	2.4 - 2.5	20.0 - 20.1
P128	P57*1	2.3 - 2.3	20.4 - 20.4
...	...	...	...
P40	P101*1, P41*1, P84*1	2.4 - 2.4	20.7 - 20.7
P43	P39*1	2.5 - 2.6	20.1 - 20.3

We re-categorize the 800 products into 211 price-specific product categories. This results in 4222 rules being generated, which are then condensed as 23 rule summaries. Table 5 shows some typical rule summaries. The first summary with consequent "PMP-C1" has a rule confidence of up to 92.1%, suggesting that purchases of certain types of Portable Media Players (PMPs) are likely to lead to purchases of PMP-C1.

Table 5. Some typical examples of the 23 rule summaries generated after re-assigning the 800 products into 211 price-specific product categories. For simplicity, only the top few highly frequent antecedents are shown.

Consequent	Top Antecedent	Support Range (%)	Confidence Range (%)
PMP-C1	PMP-B1, PMP-A1, PMP-C2	5.0 - 14.5	20.5 - 92.1
PMP-C2	PMP-B1, PMP-C1, PMP-A2, PMP-D3	5.0 – 18.8	20.8 - 85.8
...	...	...	...
HW-49	PMP-B1, PMP-C1, PMP-A2, PMP-D3	5.0 – 9.7	20.0 - 21.7
PMP-D2	PMP-B1, PMP-A2, PMP-D3	5.0 – 6.2	20.1 - 21.1

Note that the last summary with consequent PMP-D2 is of low support and confidence. This rule summary will be deemed as least important if the consequent of purchasing any product results in similar profits. However, if PMP-D2 is a highly profitable product compared to PMP-C1, then the last rule summary may outweigh the first rule summary in practical context.

For simplicity of our subsequent analysis, we shall assume that all consequents are of equal importance. Under this assumption, we use 5A80C to generate 324 rules of higher confidence. These rules are summarized as four summaries shown in Table 6. These summaries suggest that there are five product categories that are of common interest to consumers, namely PMP-A1, PMP-B1, PMP-C1, PMP-C2, and PMP-D3. From the product database, we find that there are 46 PMPs under these five commonly purchased product categories. This information is important. For store layout, we know that there are about 200 different models of PMPs sold at the store, these 46 commonly purchased PMPs should be placed in the same area within the store. For product bundling, we should focus on formulating bundles based on these five PMP categories. Bundles of individual products may not yield the desired outcome because our rule mining results suggest that products are only commonly purchased at product category level, and not at individual products level.

Table 6. Summaries of 324 rules generated using 5A80C.

Consequent	Top Antecedent	Support Range (%)	Confidence Range (%)
PMP-C1	PMP-B1, PMP-A1, PMP-C2	5.0 - 8.5	84.8 - 92.1
PMP-C2	PMP-B1, PMP-C1, PMP-A2, PMP-D3	5.0 – 7.9	80.0 - 85.8
PMP-B1	PMP-C1, PMP-A1, PMP-C2	5.0 – 7.8	80.0 - 85.0
PMP-D3	PMP-C1, PMP-A1, PMP-C2	5.1 – 5.5	80.1 - 80.2

5   Concluding Remarks

This paper has presented a consequent-based approach to summarize association rules. The approach relaxes the notion of redundancy and combines rules with different antecedents and interestingness values into one summary with common consequent, and provides useful information such as antecedent ranking and range of interestingness metrics to help users in finding important rules. Using the case study on a real-world sales transaction dataset, we have also demonstrated how rule summaries can be used to find rules that lead to actionable insights.

The idea of focusing more on *consequent importance* and less on objective interestingness has two implications on the future research in association rule mining. Firstly, our study indicates that consequent importance should be factored into the design of practical association rule mining systems. We demonstrated that a consequent-based approach distills a set of 4222 rules into a final set of rule summaries that can help in product bundling or store layout improvement.

Secondly, this work suggests that while steady development of scientifically motivated rule mining methods is important, this process should be complemented by the development simple and practically useful rule mining systems to serve the impending need of the user community. The proposed method is one such example; it complements any existing association rule mining algorithms by producing useful summaries that help derive insights or aid discovery of interesting rules.

References

1. Agrawal, R., Imielinski, T., Swami, A.: Mining Associations Rules between Sets of Items in Large Databases. In: Proc. of the ACM Conference on Management of Data, pp. 207–216 (1993)
2. An, A., Khan, S., Huang, X.: Objective and subjective algorithms for grouping association rules. In: Proc of the Third IEEE International Conference on Data Mining, pp. 477–480 (2003)
3. Ashrafi, M.Z., Taniar, D., Smith, K.: A new approach of eliminating redundant association rules. In: Galindo, F., Takizawa, M., Traunmüller, R. (eds.) DEXA 2004. LNCS, vol. 3180, pp. 465–474. Springer, Heidelberg (2004)
4. Kotsiantis, S., Kanellopoulos, D.: Association Rules Mining: A Recent Overview. GESTS International Transactions on Computer Science and Engineering 32(1), 71–82 (2006)
5. Liu, B., Hu, M., Hsu, W.: Multi-level organization and summarization of the discovered rules. In: Proc. of the sixth ACM SIGKDD International Conference on Knowledge Discovery and Data Mining, pp. 208–217 (2000)
6. Luong, V.P.: The representative basis for association rules. In: Proc. of IEEE International Conference on Data Mining, pp. 639–640 (2001)
7. Mansingh, G., Osei-Bryson, K.-M., Reichgelt, H.: Using ontologies to facilitate post - processing of association rules by domain experts. Information Sciences 181(3), 419–434 (2001)
8. Marinica, C., Guillet, F., Briand, H.: Post-Processing of Discovered Association Rules Using Ontologies. In: Proc. of the IEEE International Conference on Data Mining Workshops, ICDMW 2008, pp. 126–133 (2008)
9. Sadhasivam, K.S.C., Angamuthu, T.: Mining rare itemset with automated support thresholds. Journal of Computer Science 7(3), 394–399 (2011)
10. Shaw, G., Xu, Y., Geva, S.: Eliminating Association Rules in Multi-level Datasets. In: Proc. of the 4th International Conference on Data Mining (DMIN 2008), Las Vegas, USA, pp. 313–319 (2008)
11. Tan, S.C., Lau, P.S.: Time Series Clustering: A Superior Alternative for Market Basket Analysis. In: Proc. of The First International Conference on Advanced Data and Information Engineering (2013)
12. Tseng, M.C., Lin, W.Y.: Efficient Mining of Generalized Association Rules with Non-uniform Minimum Support. Data & Knowledge Engineering 62(1), 41–64 (2007)
13. Toivonen, H., Klemetinen, M., Ronkainen, P., Hatonen, K., Mannila, H.: Pruning and grouping discovered association rules. In: Proc. of Mlnet Workshop on Statistics, Machine Learning, and Discovery in Databases, pp. 47–52 (1995)
14. Xu, Y., Li, Y., Shaw, G.: Reliable representations for association rules. Data & Knowledge Engineering 70(6), 555–575 (2011)
15. Zaki, M.J.: Generating Non-redundant Association Rules. In: Proc. of the 6th ACM Knowledge Discovery and Data Mining Conference (SIGKDD 2000), pp. 34–43 (2000)

Cross-Domain Opinion Word Identification with Query-By-Committee Active Learning

Yi-Lin Tsai[1], Richard Tzong-Han Tsai[2,*],
Chuang-Hua Chueh[3], and Sen-Chia Chang[3]

[1] Department of ISA, National Tsinghua University, Hsinchu, Taiwan
s102065514@m102.nthu.edu.tw
[2] Department of CSIE, National Central University, Chungli, Taiwan
thtsai@csie.ncu.edu.tw
[3] Industrial Technology Research Institute, Hsinchu, Taiwan
{chchueh,chang}@itri.org.tw

Abstract. Opinion word identification (OWI). is an important task for opinion mining. In OWI, it is necessary to find the exact positions of opinion word mentions. Supervised learning approaches can locate such mentions with high accuracy. To construct an OWI system for a new domain, it is necessary to annotate sufficient amounts of data to represent the new domain's characteristics. However, since annotating every new domain extensively is costly, how to best utilize existing annotated data is a very important challenge for mention-based OWI systems. In this work, we propose a cross-domain OWI system. The query by committee (QBC) active learning scheme is used to select controlled amounts of data in the new domain for manual annotation. This new annotated data is used to complement the existing annotated data of the original domain. We compile three annotated datasets, each for one of three different domains, and conduct domain adaptation experiments on all six domain pairs. Our experiments show that by adding only 1,000 newly annotated sentences from the new domain to the existing annotated data, our system can achieve nearly the same level of accuracy as a system trained on 10,000 annotated new-domain sentences. Our system with the QBC active learning scheme also outperforms the same system with a random selection scheme.

Keywords: opinion word identification, active learning, cross-domain.

1 Introduction

With the explosion of social media, blogs, and review sites, more and more customer opinions are available online. These are beneficial to both sellers interested in evaluating consumers' needs and shoppers looking for new products/services. Opinion word identification (OWI) is a fundamental task in opinion mining. According to output, OWI approaches can be categorized into two main types: list-based and mention-based.

---

* Corresponding author.

S.-M. Cheng and M.-Y. Day (Eds.): TAAI 2014, LNAI 8916, pp. 334–343, 2014.

List-based systems output a list of opinion words. Such systems are usually either propagation-based or co-occurrence-based. Propagation-based approaches have two main steps: sentiment seed collection and sentiment value propagation. In the first step, seeds with accurate sentiment values are collected. Usually, these seeds are manually annotated or collected from existing dictionaries. In the second step, an existing word/phrase/concept graph is used as the foundation. Sentiment values are propagated from seeds to the remaining parts of the foundation graph [3, 9]. Co-occurrence-based approaches employ co-occurrence statistics to estimate if an opinion word candidate corresponds to a given opinion target and vice versa [10, 6]. Both list-based approaches can construct opinion word dictionaries without human annotation.

List-based OWI, however, does not tell us much about the context in which opinion words are used—it simply outputs a list of all the opinion words in a body of text. To better understand opinion words in context, it is necessary to find the exact sentence positions where the words are mentioned. One common way of identifying the positions of opinion words in the output list is to match them back against the text. All matched occurrences in the text are then regarded as opinion mentions. The problem with this approach is that not all matched positions are actual opinion mentions. For example, the word "美味/delicious" would not necessarily represent an opinion in a review of a restaurant named "美味餐廳/Delicious Restaurant".

The mention-based approach is designed to identify and locate all opinion mentions in reviews. Mention-based OWI is usually formulated as a sequence labelling task in which tokens are either labelled as "opinion-word mention" or "other" [11]. The approach can achieve high accuracy, but because it requires large amounts of annotated data, construction of a mention-based OWI system for a new domain can be costly in terms of human effort. One way to reduce this cost is to adapt an existing system for use in a new domain. However, cross-domain OWI poses its own problems, as the original domain data may not be compatible with the new domain. Finding the optimal way to selectively annotate sufficient data from the new domain is a critical challenge in cross-domain OWI.

Active learning is a method employed in many NLP tasks to select new data. For example, it has performed well in named-entity recognition [8] and sentiment classification [5]. The objective of active learning is to use the least amount of annotated data to achieve the highest performance. Query by Committee (QBC) [7] is one of the most efficient active learning algorithms. The QBC approach asks every model (committee member) to vote on every query's (data instance's) label. Only the most uncertain instances (the most diversely labeled) are selected for manual annotation. In this study, we propose a new cross-domain opinion word extraction approach with QBC-based active learning. We adapt our system from one of three source domains to one of three target domains. Our system is tested on six source-target domain pairs in total. We review the related research in Section 2 and illustrate our approach in Section 3. In Section 4, we report our evaluation results. Our concluding remarks are given in Section 5.

2   Related Work

2.1   Cross-Domain Opinion Mining

Several studies have tackled the problem of cross-domain opinion mining. Aue and Gamon [1] compared four strategies for utilizing opinion-labeled data from one or more non-target domains and concluded that using non-targeted labeled data without an adaptation strategy is less effective than using unlabeled data from the target domain. Jakob and Gurevych [4] proposed a CRF-based approach to opinion target extraction in single and multiple domains. They used reviews from web-service, movie, automobile, and camera domains. They found that when the token string feature was removed, cross-domain extraction performance in terms of F-measure would approach the results of single-domain extraction.

Bollegala et al. [2] addressed the sentiment classification problem in different domains. They built a sentiment-sensitive thesaurus, using both labeled and unlabeled data from multiple source domains, and used it to find associations between words that express similar sentiments in different domains.

2.2   Opinion Mining with Active Learning

Active learning is used to reduce manual labeling of target domain data and enhance performance at the same time. Li et al. [5] proposed an active-learning-based selection strategy for cross-domain sentiment classification. They trained two classifiers, one on labeled source data and the other on labeled target data, and employed them to select informative samples. The two classifiers were then combined to make the final decision. We extend this approach and adapt it for OWI.

3   Our Approach

In our approach, we formulate OWI as a sequence labeling task and use conditional random fields (CRFs) to model this task. We use the CRF++ package.

Because Chinese words are not separated by spaces, we use the CKIP word segmentation tool[1] to segment all review sentences into individual words and tag each word's part of speech (POS).

3.1   Features

Contextual Part-of-Speech Features. Opinion words are generally adjectives, however, since not all adjectives are opinion words, we must consider the context of the target word (current token). Contextual part-of-speech features describe the POS's of the words surrounding the current token. The POS's of the words surrounding the target token are referred to as follows: pos_i is the POS of the word at position i relative to the target token pos_0. Our system uses a range of pos_{-3} to pos_3.

---

[1] http://ckipsvr.iis.sinica.edu.tw

Affix Features. Because of the characteristics of Chinese adjective morphology, the affix feature is important for opinion word extraction. For example, 難忘 (unforgettable), 難看 (unsightly), and 難吃 (unpalatable) all share the prefix character "難", which means "bad" here. It follows that new words with the "難" prefix may also be opinion words. We use two prefix features: "first character" and "first character to middle character", and two suffix features: "last character" and "middle character to last character".

Word Features. Given a target word w, the words in the context window, that is, w itself and words preceding or following w may be useful for determining if w is an opinion word. In our experience, a suitable window size is seven, i.e., the three preceding words, the current word, and the two following words.

Length Feature. In Chinese, if a word w's length ($|w|$) is longer than four characters in length, w tends to be a named entity, not an opinion word. Therefore, the length feature for w is designed as the follows:

$$\begin{cases} |w| & \text{if } |w| \leq 4 \\ 5 & \text{otherwise} \end{cases}$$

Near-Synonym-Cluster Feature. For this feature, we collect similar words from "Revised Ministry of Education Dictionary"[2] and group them into clusters. Some of the cluster examples are shown in Table 1. If a given word w appears in a cluster c_i, the value of w's near-synonym feature is c_i. Otherwise, the value of w's near-synonym feature is NULL.

Table 1. Cluster examples

Cluster	Words in Cluster
C_1	逐一,一一
C_2	別名,又名 ,別號,別稱
C_3	一瞬間,一剎那

Conjunction Features. To distinguish feature instances from the source domain and the target domain, we generate conjunction features by combining each aforementioned feature with a domain tag. For example, supposing a feature "word=華麗" (gorgeous) is found in the source domain, its corresponding conjunction feature is "word=華麗&source_domain".

---

[2] http://dict.revised.moe.edu.tw

3.2 QBC-Based Active Learning

Since the performance in cross-domain opinion extraction is not good enough (see Table 4 S setting), we use active learning to enhance accuracy. The main idea of active learning is to achieve high accuracy by using as few labeled instances as possible. In our case, we select few target domain instances by active learning, and use both source and target domain data for predicting the final result.

To learn the differences between two domains, we use M_T (the model trained from the target-domain instances) and M_C (the model trained from both the source- and the target-domain instances) to select target instances. Any sentences labeled differently by M_T and M_C are placed into our candidate pool. Then, we rank all sentences in the pool according to M_C uncertainty value (because M_C is more reliable than M_T). The lowest token confidence of a sentence, which is generated by the CRF model, is regarded as the sentence's uncertainty value.

At the beginning, we only have unlabeled target domain sentences (U_T) and labeled source-domain data (L_S). We use L_S to train the source-domain model M_S and use M_S to label U_T. The top 100 uncertain sentences in U_T are selected as the newly added data for manual annotation. These 100 sentences are added to the labeled target domain dataset L_T. L_T and L_S+L_T are then used to train two models M_T and M_C, respectively. Then we select the top 100 uncertain sentences with different labels for M_T and M_C for manual annotation. We repeat the step of updating L_T and U_T until the stop criteria are reached. Algorithm 1 and Figure 1 show the pseudo code and the flowchart of our QBC-based active learning, respectively.

Algorithm 1. The pseudo code of our QBC-based active learning

---

Input: Labeled source domain data L_S, Unlabeled target domain data U_T
Output: Labeled target domain data L_T
1 Initialize $L_T = \varnothing$;
2 Train the source model M_S with L_S;
3 Use M_S to select top 100 uncertain sentences from U_T as $\triangle L_T$;
4 Manually annotate $\triangle L_T$;
5 $L_T = L_T + \triangle L_T$, and $U_T = U_T - \triangle L_T$;
6 **while** *not reach stop criteria* **do**
7 | Train the combined model M_C with L_T and L_S;
8 | Train the target model M_T with L_T;
9 | Use both M_C and M_T to select top 100 uncertain sentences from U_T as $\triangle L_T$;
10 | Manually annotate $\triangle L_T$;
11 | $L_T = L_T + \triangle L_T$, and $U_T = U_T - \triangle L_T$;
12 **end**
13 **return** L_T;

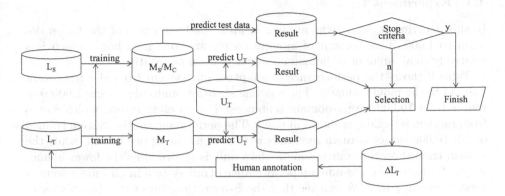

Fig. 1. Flowchart of our QBC-based active learning

Another issue in active learning is determining suitable stop criteria. Here we assume that the F-measure of the current combined model (M_C) is S_2, and the previous combined model's F-measure is S_1, when $S_2 - S_1$ is lower than a threshold t, the active learning process stops.

4   Experiments

4.1   Datasets

We compile three annotated datasets: 10,000 restaurant review sentences from iPeen.com.tw (denoted as D_R), 10,000 movie review sentences from atmovies.com.tw (denoted as D_M), and 10,000 hotel review sentences from agoda.com (denoted as D_H). All review sentences are written in Chinese and annotated by two experts.

We conduct domain adaptation experiments on all C_2^3 domain pairs. In each experiment, a dataset is chosen as the dataset of the source domain (denoted as D_S), and the other dataset is the dataset of the target domain (denoted as D_T). We use all of the 10,000 sentences from D_S for training and randomly select 3,000 sentences from D_T 30 times for testing. The remaining 7,000 D_T sentences are treated as the selection pool for active learning.

4.2   Evaluation Metrics

The results are given as F-measures and defined as $2PR/(P + R)$, where P denotes the precision of opinion word mentions and R denotes the recall of opinion word mentions. We sum the scores for all 30 tests, and calculate the averages for performance comparison. The results are reported as the mean precision ($\hat{P}$), recall ($\hat{R}$), and F-measure ($\hat{F}$) of thirty datasets.

4.3 Experiment 1

In this experiment, we fix the number of annotated sentences of the target domain to 1,000. This amount of annotation requires one man-hour, which is a relatively small amount of human effort for domain adaptation.

Table 2 shows the performance of adapting our system from the restaurant domain to the movie domain. The baseline strategy randomly selects 1,000 sentences from 10,000 target-domain sentences. The baseline result, which comes from random selection, is shown in row 1. The performance of the system trained on all 10,000 target domain sentences is treated as the upper bound, while the system trained on the source domain data only is regarded as the lower bound. Figure 2 shows the cross-domain performance of our system in all the six source-target domain pairs. We can see that the F-measure grows with the number of human-annotated sentences (A). The vertical axis corresponds to the F-measure and the horizontal axis corresponds to the number of manually annotated sentences in the target domain.

Table 2. Performance in different selection settings (Restaurant → Movie)

	$\hat{P}$	$\hat{R}$	$\hat{F}$	A
Random (baseline)	0.836	0.727	0.777	1,000
Proposed approach	0.852	0.784	0.816	1,000
Trained on all D_T sentences (Upper bound)	0.877	0.841	0.858	10,000
Trained on all D_S sentences (Lower bound)	0.723	0.554	0.627	0

In the beginning, performance improves greatly as more annotated data is added. However, after around 200 annotated sentences have been added, performance increase tapers off, though it still increases more than random selection. Unlike other domain pairs, the F-measures of our QBC-based system in movie → restaurant (Figure 2a) and movie → hotel (Figure 2f) increase sharply after 100 annotated sentences are added to the training set. To investigate the reason, we further analyze the overlapping ratio of every target-source domain pair. Table 3 shows the ratio of D_T tokens appearing in D_S. We can see that the domain pairs with the lowest two ratios are (movie, restaurant) and (movie, hotel). This explains why the CRF-based system achieves low F-measures when using only D_S, but after a few D_T sentences are added, its F-measures increase rapidly.

4.4 Experiment 2

In this experiment, we compare performance of configurations using source domain plus target-domain data to that of configurations using only target-domain data and only source-domain data. S denotes the system trained on the 10,000 D_S sentences, which is considered to be the lower bound. T denotes the system trained on the newly annotated D_T sentences only. The $S+T$ configuration is

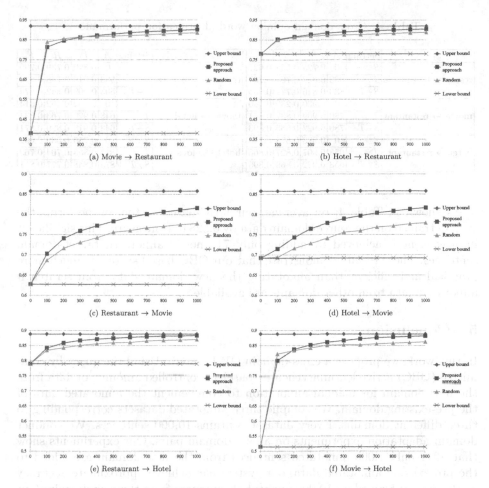

Fig. 2. Cross-domain performance in all the six source-target domain pairs

Table 3. The ratio of the tokens of the target-domain dataset (D_T) appearing in the source-domain dataset (D_S)

		Source		
		Restaurant	Movie	Hotel
	Restaurant	–	27.1%	35.8%
Target	Movie	32.6%	–	33.0%
	Hotel	33.5%	25.7%	–

our QBC-based method. The stop criteria threshold t is set to 0.003. $\hat{A}$ denotes the average number of human annotated sentences in thirty datasets. Table 4 shows the summarized results.

Table 4. Cross-domain opinion word identification performance

	Setting	A	P	R	F		Setting	A	P	R	F
restaurant → movie	S	0	0.723	0.554	0.627	restaurant → hotel	S	0	0.849	0.739	0.790
	T	833	0.832	0.700	0.760		T	503	0.919	0.748	0.824
	S+T	833	0.846	0.771	0.806		S+T	503	0.909	0.842	0.874
movie → restaurant	S	0	0.930	0.239	0.380	movie → hotel	S	0	0.952	0.352	0.514
	T	780	0.909	0.837	0.871		T	643	0.920	0.763	0.834
	S+T	780	0.922	0.865	0.893		S+T	643	0.918	0.829	0.871
hotel → restaurant	S	0	0.923	0.675	0.780	hotel → movie	S	0	0.755	0.639	0.692
	T	653	0.907	0.827	0.866		T	873	0.833	0.704	0.763
	S+T	653	0.922	0.869	0.895		S+T	873	0.848	0.777	0.811

As shown in Table 4, on average, our QBC-based system outperforms the system trained on the source-domain data by 0.228 in F-measure. This significant improvement is achieved by adding only 714 newly annotated target-domain sentences. These results demonstrate that our QBC-based system is much more practical and efficient than annotating the new domain data from scratch if annotated data from other domains are available.

5 Conclusion

In this work, we propose a cross-domain OWI system. Using the query by committee (QBC) active learning scheme, we select controlled amounts of data from the new domain for manual annotation to complement the annotated data of the pre-existing domain. We compile three annotated datasets corresponding to three different domains. Every dataset contains 10,000 sentences. We conduct domain adaptation experiments on all six domain pairs. Our experiments show that after only 1,000 annotated sentences from the new domain are added to the pre-existing annotated data, our system can achieve approximate accuracy as the system trained on 10,000 annotated sentences from the new domain. Our system with the QBC active learning scheme also outperforms the same system with random selection.

References

1. Aue, A., Gamon, M.: Customizing Sentiment Classifiers to New Domains: A Case Study. In: Proceedings of Recent Advances in Natural Language Processing (RANLP) (2005)
2. Bollegala, D., Weir, D., Carroll, J.: Using multiple sources to construct a sentiment sensitive thesaurus for cross-domain sentiment classification. In: Proceedings of the 49th Annual Meeting of the Association for Computational Linguistics: Human Language Technologies, HLT 2011, vol. 1, pp. 132–141. Association for Computational Linguistics, Stroudsburg (2011)
3. Cambria, E., Speer, R., Havasi, C., Hussain, A.: Senticnet: A publicly available semantic resource for opinion mining. In: AAAI Fall Symposium: Commonsense Knowledge, volume FS-10-02 of AAAI Technical Report. AAAI (2010)

4. Jakob, N., Gurevych, I.: Extracting opinion targets in a single- and cross-domain setting with conditional random fields. In: Proceedings of the 2010 Conference on Empirical Methods in Natural Language Processing, EMNLP 2010, pp. 1035–1045. Association for Computational Linguistics, Stroudsburg (2010)
5. Li, S., Xue, Y., Wang, Z., Zhou, G.: Active learning for cross-domain sentiment classification. In: Proceedings of the Twenty-Third International Joint Conference on Artificial Intelligence, IJCAI 2013, pp. 2127–2133. AAAI Press (2013)
6. Qiu, G., Liu, B., Bu, J., Chen, C.: Opinion word expansion and target extraction through double propagation. Comput. Linguist. 37(1), 9–27 (2011)
7. Seung, H.S., Opper, M., Sompolinsky, H.: Query by committee. In: Proceedings of the Fifth Annual Workshop on Computational Learning Theory, COLT 1992, pp. 287–294. ACM, New York (1992)
8. Shen, D., Zhang, J., Su, J., Zhou, G., Tan, C.-L.: Multi-criteria-based active learning for named entity recognition. In: Proceedings of the 42nd Annual Meeting on Association for Computational Linguistics, ACL 2004. Association for Computational Linguistics, Stroudsburg (2004)
9. Tsai, A.C.-R., Wu, C.-E., Tsai, R.T.-H., Hsu, J.Y.J.: Building a concept-level sentiment dictionary based on commonsense knowledge. IEEE Intelligent Systems 28(2), 22–30 (2013)
10. Wang, B., Wang, H.: Bootstrapping Both Product Features and Opinion Words from Chinese Customer Reviews with Cross-Inducing. In: Proceedings of the Third International Joint Conference on Natural Language Processing: Volume-I (2008), http://aclweb.org/anthology/I08-1038
11. Yang, B., Cardie, C.: Extracting opinion expressions with semi-markov conditional random fields. In: Proceedings of the 2012 Joint Conference on Empirical Methods in Natural Language Processing and Computational Natural Language Learning, EMNLP-CoNLL 2012, pp. 1335–1345. Association for Computational Linguistics, Stroudsburg (2012)

Classifying the TRIZ Contradiction Problem
of the Patents Based on Engineering Parameters

Chung-Kai Tseng, Chih-Heng Chung, and Bi-Ru Dai

National Taiwan University of Science and Technology,
#43, Sec.4, Keelung Rd., Taipei, 106, Taiwan, R.O.C
{M10015080,D9915015}@mail.ntust.edu.tw
brdai@csie.ntust.edu.tw

Abstract. TRIZ is a useful theory to solve the engineering contradiction problems. One of technological methods of TRIZ is Contradiction Matrix which is widely used for the solution of technical contradiction problems. For the TRIZ users, finding out some patent documents which had solved the same contradiction is helpful to solve the problems of this type of contradiction. Classifying patents contradiction based on the Engineering Parameters is more reasonable than the Inventive Principles, but all existing patent classification researches are unsuitable on patents contradiction classifying based on the Engineering Parameters directly. In this article, a new algorithm named MCIVC for classifying patents technical contradiction based on Engineering Parameters is proposed. This multi-layer classification algorithm adopts the associated rule-based approach combining the lazy learning. It does not only consider the semantic relationship among terms, but also consider the syntactic structure between words.

Keywords: patent classification, TRIZ, Contradiction Matrix, contradiction, multi-layer classification, associated rule-based approach, lazy learning.

1   Introduction

TRIZ, the Theory of Inventive Problem Solving proposed by Altshuller has become a more well-known and useful theory to solve the engineering contradiction problems. Altshuller addressed that only 1% of patents are genuine originations and the rest are based on known ideas and conceptions of the former plus novelty methods. He also recognized that the basics of innovation and new ideas were not in the brains of inventors, but in the published inventions [1,2,3]. He discovered that many problems arose because of technical contradiction between Engineering Parameters. The technical contradictions are solved by the Contradiction Matrix that utilizing 39 Engineering Parameters and 40 Inventive Principles [3].

Patents have already become very important knowledge source for product development, research, and innovation. Because of the tremendous amount of patents published in a short time, automatic patent classification becomes a very popular research issue of data mining. From the view of the Contradiction Matrix, most of contradiction occurs when there is a conflict existing between two Engineering Parameters. However, past

S.-M. Cheng and M.-Y. Day (Eds.): TAAI 2014, LNAI 8916, pp. 344–353, 2014.
© Springer International Publishing Switzerland 2014

researches are either lack of experiments or only classify patents according to Inventive Principles but not related to Engineering Parameters. In this paper, we focus on classifying the contradiction problem of the patents based on Engineering Parameters.

There are many challenges of classifying patents based on Engineering Parameters. First, the amount of data is very limited because that nearly all of the public domain databases or websites related to patent classification do not contain the information about TRIZ. The information of TRIZ can only be manually classified by experts. Second, the distribution of the conflicting Engineering Parameters of patents is imbalanced. Third, some Engineering Parameters have very similar concept and definition. Fourth, some Engineering Parameters related to the documents are not tagged because they do not cause the main conflict. This means the data are partially labeled or incomplete because there is no negative instance.

The contributions of this article are summarized as follows. First, this paper proposed an algorithm named Multi-layer Classification Including Verb Consideration (MCIVC) which is used for classifying patents based on Engineering Parameters. Second, it considers positive and negative words to improve the performance. Third, we proposed the algorithm Verb Including Split and Associate Termsets (VISAT) to find the relative candidate term sets automatically. The experimental results show that the MCIVC achieved good efficacy of classifying patent contradictions based on the Engineering Parameters.

The remainder of this paper is organized as follows. In Section 2, we discuss some patent analysis software and researches. In Section 3, we introduce the proposed framework of MCIVC and VISAT. Experimental evaluations and discussion are in Section 4. The conclusion will be described in Section 5.

2   Related Works

Our study focuses on classifying technical contradiction of patent documents based on conflicting Engineering Parameters. Some computer-aided innovation (CAI) software for TRIZ was proposed, such as InventionTool [4], Techoptimizer [5], Pro/Innovator [6], Creax [7] and Goldfire [8]. Most of this type of software only provides the corresponding Inventive Principles when contradictions of the problems are already defined. Except the software, the more related research issue is patent analysis. Some researches making efforts in estimating TRIZ level of invention of patents had been proposed [9,10]. This type of researches can be used to filter patents which never solved any technical contradiction. The algorithm proposed by Gaetano Cascini and Davide Russo [11] constructs the Subject-Action-Object model combining with the predefined specific patterns and the morphological patterns to extract useful information, but it cannot map the extracted features to the certain categories directly. The most relevant research issues with our research are the patent classification. There are many researches proposed for automatic patent classification [12,13,14,15,16,17], but most of them classify patents according to the technical fields, not the TRIZ information. Recently, there are some researches about classifying patent documents for

TRIZ users [18,19,20,21], but all these researches classify patents according to Inventive Principles and are not suitable for the conflicting Engineering Parameters.

3   Framework

In this section, we introduce how we classify technical contradictions of patents based on Engineering Parameters.

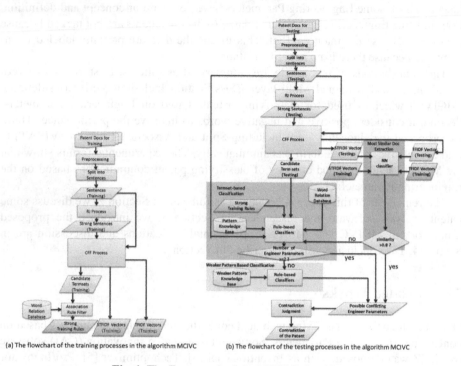

(a) The flowchart of the training processes in the algorithm MCIVC   (b) The flowchart of the testing processes in the algorithm MCIVC

Fig. 1. The Framework of the MCIVC algorithm

3.1   The Multi-layer Classification Framework

Fig. 1 shows the whole flowchart of our method named Multi-layer Classification Including Verb Consideration (MCIVC). All the training processes as shown in Fig. 1(a) are performed first, and then the outputs of the training processes will be taken as inputs of the testing processes as shown in Fig. 1(b). The outputs of the training processes include STFIDF Vectors, TFIDF Vectors and Strong Training Rules. STFIDF Vectors, TFIDF Vectors of training patents will be used in the purple concept block named Most Similar Doc Extraction, and Strong Training Rules will be used in the orange concept block named Termset-based Classification.

The algorithm includes four concept blocks. The first block contains four processes, including Preprocessing, Split into sentences, the Relationship Judgment

(RJ) Process and the Candidate Features Finding (CFF) Process. In the preprocessing step, we use Stemming [22] and TreeTagger [23] to process the input documents, and then it splits the documents into sentences. The Relationship Judgment step is used to extract some sentences which are more distinguished. Transitions, related, positive and negative words have stronger influence to judge the contradictions in patent documents. A sentence relates to at least one important word set is defined as strong sentence. We design an important algorithm named Verb Including Split and Associate Termsets (VISAT) which is included in the CFF Process to generate more meaningful termsets and to find candidate features from documents. We will give the detail of the CFF process and the VISAT algorithm in section 3.2.

All of the other blocks are mainly used to classify testing patent documents contradiction based on Engineering Parameters. As shown in Fig. 1, the Most Similar Document Extraction is the first layer of classification which extract the most similar training document. If there is such a training document which can be extracted, the classes belonged to the training document are assigned to the testing document.

The Termset-based Classification is the second layer of classification which is a rule-based classifier and tries to find out whether there are some training termset rules can match the termsets in the testing document. If there are some termset rules successfully match to the termsets in the testing document, the class labels in these rules are assigned to testing document.

The Weaker Pattern Based Classification is the third layer of classification is also a rule-based classifier. This classification is very similar to the second layer classification, but it only judges whether these patent documents belong to some very frequent classes by the sequential-termset rules and the one-word-termset rules.

After running through all above processes, possible conflicting Engineer Parameters are found out. The final process of MCIVC named Contradiction Judgment is performed to classify the type of technical Contradiction of testing patents.

This type of dataset has some challenging properties. The amount of data is very limited, the distribution is imbalanced, and the data are partially labeled or incomplete. These properties cause that the most common used method Bag-of-word cannot extract features discriminative enough, and some classification methods such as the SVM are not directly suitable for these datasets. Therefore we propose the VISAT algorithm to find more meaningful termset features and combine the VISAT with the knowledge base and the rule-based classifiers which consider the semantic relationship among terms to classify patents contradiction based on Engineering Parameters.

3.2   Candidate Features Finding Process (CFF Process) and the VISAT Algorithm

The process named Candidate Features Finding process (CFF process) is used for finding out candidate features. It generates two types of features, the TFIDF type vectors of set of sentences and the candidate termsets of set of each sentence. As shown in Fig. 2, the inputs of CFF process include strong sentences and all sentences included in training and in testing documents.

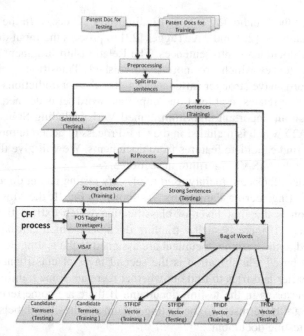

Fig. 2. The flowchart of the CFF process

The Processes for Generating TFIDF Type Features

For the inputs of the all sentences, the Bag-of-words process calculates TFIDF value of each word appeared in all sentences of the document, and then generates the TFIDF vector outputs for training and testing documents. For the inputs of the strong sentences, the sentences which the count of relating important set is equal or larger than one are extracted throughout the Bag-of-words process. The TFIDF value of each words appeared in extracted sentences of the document is calculated, and then the STFIDF vector outputs for training and testing documents are generated.

The Processes for Generating Termset Type Features

We proposed an algorithm named Verb Including Split and Associate Termsets (VISAT). It is a very important process included in CFF process, and we will illustrate this in detail later. We discovered that if the sentence relative to more important word sets, it is taken as more important sentence. Therefore, for training documents, only the sentences which the count of relating important set is larger than one in the strong sentences are needed to perform POS tagging to get their part-of-speech information. For testing documents, all sentences of testing documents are needed to perform POS tagging because the labels of Engineering Parameters of the document are unknown.

We use the VISAT algorithm to extract the candidate termsets in the CFF Process. According to our observation, the termsets containing two words are strong enough to represent the concept of the vast majority of Engineering Parameters, thus the VISAT algorithm only extracts the candidate termsets containing two words.

The Steps of the VISAT Algorithm
The VISAT algorithm includes four steps: (1) split sentence into several Split-PointSsegments (SPSs) and StringSegments (SSs), (2) reorganize some SPSs and SSs, (3) generate termsets in each segment itself and (4) generate termsets which combines two words belonging to two different segments.

In the first step, the VISAT algorithm takes the verb, the punctuation mark (,) and the conjunction (and, but) as split point to split each sentence, and then each sentence are split into several SplitPointSsegments (SPSs) and StringSegments (SSs). In Fig. 3, each segment of words tagged by the underline is StringSegment (SS) and each segment of words pointed by the arrow is SplitPointSsegment (SPS). Each number tagged below the underline is the index of SS, and each number tagged above the arrow is the index of SPS. There must be one SS after each SPS, even if some SS are empty set in the sentence.

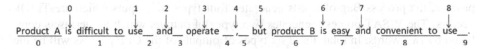

Fig. 3. An example of the first step of the VISAT algorithm to split sentence

In the second step, the VISAT algorithm reorganizes some SPSs and SSs. It checks each SPS containing the conjunction and the segments nearby the SPS to judge whether these segments should be reorganized. Fig. 4 shows an example.

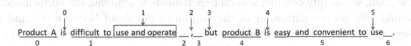

Fig. 4. An example of the second step of the VISAT algorithm to reorganize segments

In the third step, the VISAT algorithm generates termsets in each segment itself. From the view of the grammar and the structure of sentence, a complete sentence must have at least one verb and there are five types of the basic sentence structure. If the verb element is excluded, the remaining elements are the subject, the object and the complement. We take the subject and the object as the set of words which are combined together to represent the noun concept. The set of words in the complement concept should also be combined. The termsets should also be generated in each SPS which contains more than one word.

In the fourth step, the VISAT algorithm generates termsets which combine two words belonging to two different segments. It goes through every *SS* to check whether the words belonging to the SS which should be combined with the words belonging to other segments. There are four cases should be used to generate termsets with other segments as shown in Fig. 5.

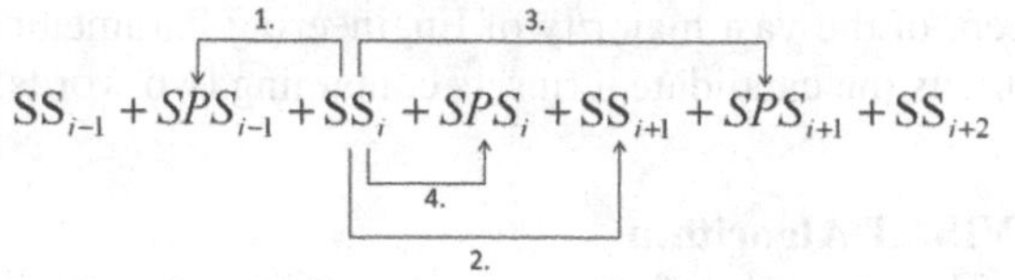

$$\text{SS}_{i-1} + S\dot{P}S_{i-1} + \text{SS}_i + S\dot{P}S_i + \text{SS}_{i+1} + S\dot{P}S_{i+1} + \text{SS}_{i+2}$$

Fig. 5. Four combination cases of the fourth step

As shown in Fig. 5, the case 1 is a standard process which is performed in any situation unless SPS_{i-1} does not exist. The case 2 is performed when SPS_i contains any verb to be (be Verb), or such as become, have, etc. The case 3 is performed when the segments meet all the conditions as we list below. First, SPS_i contains any verb which belongs to the verb to be (be Verb), or such as become, have, etc. Second, SS_{i+1} contains no noun or is an empty segment. Third, SPS_{i+1} contains the participle verb. The case 3 is checked for the passive voice. The case 4 is performed when the end word of SS_i is "to" or "of".

In summary, the VISAT algorithm can generate more meaningful termsets, because it considers the syntactic structure between words more in detail. In the CFF process, the process Bag-of-words generates four types of outputs which are TFIDF vectors. The VISAT process generates two types of outputs which are termsets combined by two words. In total, these six types of outputs of the CFF process will be the inputs for some classifications we proposed to judge the possible conflicting Engineering Parameters in later phase.

4   Performance

In this section, we mainly conduct several experiments to evaluate the performance of our method. We set the parameter of the similarity threshold between 0.7 and 0.8, according to our observation. There are totally 39 Engineering Parameters in the TRIZ theory originally, however some Engineering Parameters represent very similar concept, and we thus group some similar Engineering Parameters into some new classes as shown in Table 1.

The used training dataset includes only 115 patents collated manually by the researchers who were from the National Taiwan University Department of Mechanical Engineering. The distribution of the conflicting Engineering Parameters and the technical contradiction are imbalance. Most contradiction categories will only appear one time, thus we cannot classify these patent documents on the contradiction directly.

We conduct two experiments to evaluate and discuss the performance of our method. In our algorithm, the performance of final experiment results of MCIVC is highly relevant to the performance of the classification result of Possible Conflicting Engineer Parameters, thus we conduct the experiment to evaluate the performance from the point of view of multi-label classification problem in this intermediate phase. We also conduct another experiment and adopt different performance measurement to evaluate the final performance of MCIVC, where it is a single-label classification problem.

Table 1. Corresponding table of new class label and grouped Engineering Parameters

Class Label	Corresponding Engineering Parameters
40	**6**: Area of stationary object, **8**: Volume of stationary object
41	**19**: Use of energy by moving object, **20**: Use of energy by stationary object, **21**: Power, **22**: Loss of Energy
42	**13**: Stability of the object's composition, **27**: Reliability, **35**: Adaptability or versatility
43	**14**: Strength, **30**: External harm affects the object, **31**: Object-generated harmful factors
44	**9**: Speed, **25**: Loss of Time

Table 2. The performances of (a) intermediate phase and (b) final performance result

Algorithm	Precision	Recall	F1score	Algorithm	Accuracy
2gram	0.721739	0.660870	0.665217	2gram	0.652174
3gram-like	0.728841	0.717391	0.698302	3gram-like	0.643478
Sentence-based	0.660725	**0.791304**	0.692422	Sentence-based	0.600000
SentenceSegment	0.723913	0.747826	0.707536	SentenceSegment	0.591304
SPD_basic	0.709420	0.652174	0.660000	SPD_basic	0.643478
SPD_tree	0.728696	0.682609	0.681822	SPD_tree	0.617391
SPD_collapsed	0.728696	0.682609	0.681822	SPD_collapsed	0.617391
SPD_CCPropagated	0.743913	0.704348	0.698054	SPD_CCPropagated	0.626087
SPD_nonCollapsed	0.709420	0.652174	0.660000	SPD_nonCollapsed	0.643478
SPD_nonCollapsed Separated	0.709420	0.652174	0.660000	SPD_nonCollapsedSe parated	0.643478
SPD_Mix	0.743333	0.704348	0.697433	SPD_Mix	0.626087
MCIVC	**0.782464**	0.752174	**0.743520**	MCIVC	**0.695652**

(a)   (b)

There is no method which is designed for classifying patents contradiction based on Engineering Parameters in our survey until now, so we transform our comparing algorithms by using previous methods proposed by other researchers combining with the same knowledge base. In other words, all comparing algorithms use the same knowledge base we constructed after some observation and the same multi-layer classification we proposed, but use different algorithm to generate the candidate termsets for mapping to the rules in the knowledge base. All the experiments perform five-fold cross validation to obtain the average performance measurements. We choose the 2-gram algorithm [24,25], the 3-gram-like algorithm [24,25], the algorithm Sentence-based [21], the algorithm SentenceSegment [26] and the Stanford Parser as the comparisons, where all the algorithms which are named beginning with "SPD_" combine the base structure with Stanford Parser with different setting. At last, the algorithm we proposed named MCIVC.

The experiment results from the point of view of multi-label classification problem in intermediate phase are shown in Table 2(a). The average precision and the average F1-score are the best in our MCIVC algorithm. It means that our algorithm can generate meaningful termsets. Although the recall value of Sentence-based algorithm is a little higher than our MCIVC algorithm, its precision is much lower than other algorithms because it usually retrieves too many redundant classes.

The performance measurement we used to evaluate the final performance of MCIVC is the accuracy. The performance measurement should get scores only when all predicted Conflicting Engineer Parameters are exactly the same as all real Conflicting Engineer Parameters in the testing patent. The experiment results from the point of view of technical contradiction classification in final phase are shown in Table 2(b). The algorithm we proposed gets the highest accuracy. Therefore, we can conclude that our MCIVC algorithm performs better than other algorithms.

5   Conclusion

In this paper, we proposed a new algorithm named Multi-layer Classification Including Verb Consideration (MCIVC) for working on patent technical contradictions classifying based on Engineering Parameters. This multi-layer classification algorithm adopts the associated rule-based approach combining the lazy learning. We also designed the algorithm VISAT included in the MCIVC to generate meaningful termsets, it considers the syntactic structure between words in detail. The MCIVC algorithm does not only consider the syntactic structure between words, but also consider the semantic relationship among terms. Classifying patent technical contradictions based on Engineering Parameters is a useful and new issue. In fact, we have not found any research classifying patents contradictions based on Engineering Parameters in our survey. The experimental results showed that the MCIVC can achieve the good efficacy. Moreover, our algorithm which adopts the VISAT to generate candidate termsets performs better than comparing algorithms which adopt other methods to generate candidate termsets. In the future, we will consider whether there are some relationships among some special Engineering Parameters and try to utilize these relation-ships to improve the performance of the MCIVC algorithm.

References

1. Altshuller, G.S.: 40 principles: TRIZ keys to tech-nical innovation, translated and edited by Shulyak, L., Rodman, S., Technical Innovation Center, Worcester, MA (1997)
2. Altshuller, G.: The innovation algorithm: TRIZ, systematic innovation and technical creativity. Technical Innovation Center (1999)
3. Altshuller, G.S.: Creativity as an Exact Science: The Theory of the Solution of Inventive Problems. Gordon and Breach Science, New York (1984)
4. Computer aided innovation system: InventionTool 3.0, Chinese patent of software, 2006SR13729 (2006)
5. TechOptimizer (March 2009), http://www.invention-machine.com
6. Pro/Innovator (March 2009), http://www.iwint.com.cn/
7. CREAX INNOVATION SUITE 3.1 (March 2009),
   http://www.creaxinnovationsuite.com/
8. Goldfire (March 2009), http://gli.goldfire.com

9. Adams, C., Tate, D.: Computer-aided TRIZ ideality and level of invention estimation using natural language processing and machine learning. In: Tan, R., Cao, G., León, N. (eds.) Growth and Development of Computer-Aided Innovation. IFIP AICT, vol. 304, pp. 27–37. Springer, Heidelberg (2009)
10. Li, Z., Tate, D., Lane, C., Adams, C.: A framework for automatic TRIZ level of invention estimation of patents using natural language processing, knowledge-transfer and patent citation metrics. Computer-Aided Design 44(10), 987–1010 (2012)
11. Cascini, G., Russo, D.: Computer-aided analysis of patents and search for TRIZ contradictions. Int. J. Product Development 4(1/2) (2007)
12. Larkey, L.S.: Some issues in the automatic classification of US patents. In: AAAi-98 Working Notes (1998)
13. Larkey, L.S.: A patent search and classification systems. In: Fox, E.A., Rowe, N. (eds.) Proceedings of Fourth ACM Conference on Digital Libraries, DL 1999, pp. 179–187. ACM Press, New York (1999)
14. Gey, F.C., Buckland, M., Chen, C., Larson, R.: Entry vocabulary – a technology to enhance digital search. In: Proceedings of the First International Conference on Human Language Technology, pp. 91–95 (2001)
15. Fall, C.J., Torcsvari, A., Benzineb, K., Karetka, G.: Automated categorization in the international patent classification. ACM SI IR Forum, 37 (2003)
16. Sebastiani, F.: A Tutorial on Automated Text Categorisation. In: Amandi, A., Zunino, A. (eds.) Proceedings of the 1st Argentinean Symposium on Artificial Intelligence, ASAI, Buenos Aires, pp. 7–35 (1999)
17. Makarov, M.: The seventh edition of the IPC. World Patent Inform 2000;22:53 –8
18. Loh, H.T., He, C., Shen, L.X.: Automatic classification of patent documents for TRIZ users. World Patent Information 28, 6–13 (2006)
19. Liang, Y., Tan, R., Wang, C., Li, Z.: Computer-aided classification of patents oriented to TRIZ. In: IEEE International Conference on Industrial Engineering and Engineering Management, IEEM 2009, December 8-11, pp. 2389–2393 (2009)
20. He, C., Loh, H.T.: Grouping of TRIZ inventive principles to facilitate automatic patent classification. Expert System with Applications 34(3) (2007)
21. Cong, H., Loh, H.T.: Pattern-Oriented Associa-tive Rule-Based Patent Classification. Expert Systems with Applications 37(3), 2395–2404 (2010)
22. Porter, M.F.: An algorithm for suffix stripping. Program 14(3), 130–137 (1980)
23. Schmid, H.: Treetagger. In: TC project at the Institute for Computational Linguistics of the University of Stuttgart (1994)
24. Brown, P.F., Della Pietra, V.J., de Souza, P.V., Lai, J.C., Mercer, R.L.: Class-based n-gram models of natural language. Computational Linguistics 18, 467–479 (1992)
25. Cavnar, W.B., Trenkle, J.M.: N-gram-based text categorization. In: Proceedings of SDAIR-94, 3rd Annual Symposium on Document Analysis and Information Retrieval, Las Vegas, NV, pp. 161–175 (1994)
26. Liu, B., Hu, M., Cheng, J.: Opinion Observer: Analyzing and comparing opinions on the Web. In: WWW 2005 (2005)

A Robust Feature Matching Method for Robot Localization in a Dynamic Indoor Environment

Tsung-Yen Tsou and Shih-Hung Wu[*]

Department of Computer Science and Information Engineering,
Chaoyang University of Technology, Taichung City 41349, Taiwan (R.O.C)
p198910@yahoo.com.tw, shwu@cyut.edu.tw

Abstract. In this paper, we report how the feature matching method can be applied to deal with the indoor mobile robot localization problem. We assume that a robot equipped with a laser rangefinder can scan the environment in real time and get the geometry features, and then the robot can match these features with those collected in advance to find the possible locations. This approach would face two difficulties. Since there are locations with similar features, the robot have to move around and do the scan and match several times to make sure the right location. There is another difficult problem, the features might not be fix in real-world dynamic environment, e.g. people might be walking through, furniture might be shifted; therefore, a robust feature matching method is needed for dynamic environment. This paper describes an efficient method using omni-directional feature grouping to improve the feature matching method for robot localization. With the laser rangefinder, a robot finds the 360 degree coverage information. Omni-directional feature grouping has the advantage of dividing all the features of a hypothetical position through different directions to generate multiple sets of environmental features. The method can reduce the affection of moving objects in a dynamic environment. Experimental results show that our method improve the accuracy rate and has low average errors.

Keywords: Indoor localization, laser rangefinder, feature matching, robot navigation, dynamic indoor environment

1 Introduction

Indoor localization is an important issue for mobile robot research. There are many previous works focusing on the simultaneous localization and map building (SLAM) problem [1,2,3,4], [18], [22], which combine map building and localization as one problem. Unlike outdoor environment, where GPS can provide mobile robot reliable location information, GPS is not available in indoor environment. In order to deal with this difficulty, various sensors have been used in indoor localization, such as laser rangefinder, sonar, odometer, and camera.

There are two types of indoor localization problems. First one is the robot knows the initial location. This type is easier since robot must be in the neighborhood of the

---

[*] Corresponding author.

S.-M. Cheng and M.-Y. Day (Eds.): TAAI 2014, LNAI 8916, pp. 354–365, 2014.
© Springer International Publishing Switzerland 2014

initial location; a robot can update its new location with limited information from odometer and fine-tune the location with the help of a laser rangefinder. Second type is the robot does not know the initial location. This is a complicate problem since the robot might be in any possible location. This problem is sometimes called the global localization [6], [9], [13,14,15].

The global localization is matching the information gathered by the sensors on a robot with the information stored in a given map. Finding the best matched features leads to finding the most probable current location of the robot. Thus, it is necessary to have a pre-build map for global localization. The more information a map possesses, the higher accuracy a robot can achieve. For example, laser rangefinders are often used to scan the distance of each angel from a robot, and these distance values will be used to match with the stored values of each candidate point [9,10], [17], [21]. The information associated with all the candidate points is collect previously, which is a laborious task. Similarly, camera can be used as the sensor; it can be used to detect objects [11] or building topological maps with images [5], [12], [20]. Sensors are also used for map building, such as sonar and infrared sensor [7], inertia sensor [16], camera [19], and laser rangefinder [19], [23].

In previous works, the feature matching method on global localization works well for static environment [6], [9]. However, it does not work well in the real world dynamic environment, because the position of objects might be changed, or people might be walking around. To cope with the complicated dynamic environment, the feature matching method has to be refined to be able to recognize the moving objects. Recognize moving object can be done by camera and image processing method [3], [11]. However, photographing is not always agreeable in house because it may involve personal privacy.

In this paper, we use only the information provided by laser rangefinder. We improve the signature-rs method proposed in previous work [9] and propose a new multi-group feature matching scheme. We collect information from all possible 360° directions, and group them into several sets of information which only use 180° just as in previous work. Therefore, our method is robust since the moving object will affect only some of the information sets, not all of them. To reduce the cost of calculation, we also adopt the method in previous to group similar features. [8]

The paper is organized as the following. Section 2 introduces how the features are generated and our feature grouping method. Section 3 shows that feature matching with real-time localization can be improved with robot moving. The 4th section reports the experimental results and the comparison between static and dynamic environment. Section 5 is discussion and conclusion.

2   Feature Generation

2.1   Global Hypothetical Feature

In this paper, our assumption is that there is no additional tag for the robot in the environment. The robot use only the information gathered from the laser rangefinder to identify its own location. Since the compass is not very accurate in indoor environment, we also assume that the robot is without compass, i.e., the orientation is unknown.

An example map of a given environment is shown in Fig. 1. The hypothesis points are the possible location of the robots as shown in Fig. 2.

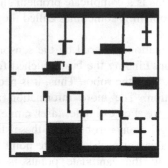

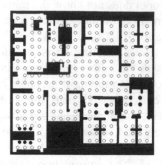

Fig. 1. Given map   **Fig. 2.** Hypothesis points

2.2   Real-Time Feature Generation

The robot with laser rangefinder can generate the features at real-time as shown in Fig. 3. We will resample the information and get a reasonable size of information vector, as shown in Fig. 4. Global hypothetical features are the $360°$ hypothetical feature points (HFP) information a robot might get in a given environment.

a

b

Fig. 3. a. Robot in an indoor envirionment. b. The information gathered by a laser rangefinder.

a
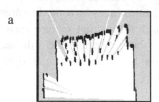
b

Fig. 4. a. the environment according to the information in Fig 3. b. local features of a robot.

2.3   Omni-directional Feature Grouping

In this paper, we divide the information gathered by the laser rangefinder into several groups, and repeat the feature matching for each group. We divide each of the hypothetical feature point (HFP) into 8 groups as shown in Fig. 5. Each of the group contains $180°$ length information gathered by the laser rangefinder.

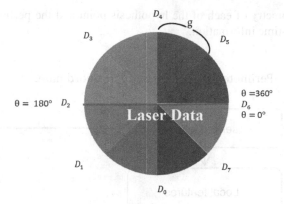

Fig. 5. Divide the information into 8 groups

3   Feature Matching and Move Tracking

The system flowchart is shown in Fig. 6. The robot use a laser rangefinder to gather local features. After grouping the features into 8 groups, our system performs the feature matching process. Our feature matching method is an enhanced version of the signature-rs method in a previous work [9]. The previous method contains three steps of matching to filter out impossible location candidates and to reduce the candidates that the system needs to do the feature matching. Our system applies the same steps to the 8 groups of features, and preserved the matched cases. If the number of matched cases excesses the threshold, the location is found. Otherwise, a move tracking method is necessary to guide the robot to move. The feature matching and move tracking are as follows.

3.1   Area Matching

For each given hypothetical feature point (HFP), the length of each feature is stored in the Feature Array (F_Array). Adding up the length in the F_Array can be a way to calculate the area (Area of Geometry) (1) ∘ The first feature matching is actually a comparison between the area of geometry of each of the hypothesis point and the area of geometry of the robot real-time information.

$$Area\ of\ Geometry = \sum F\_Array. \tag{1}$$

3.2   Perimeter Matching

The second feature is called the perimeter feature. We translate the information in the feature array (F_Array) as the location point on a plane, which is called depth coordinate (D_Coordinate). By connecting all the points in D_Coordinate, we get the perimeter (Perimeter of Geometry) (2). The second feature matching is comparing the perimeter of geometry of each of the hypothesis point and the perimeter of geometry of the robot real-time information.

$$\text{Perimeter of Geometry} = \sum \text{D\_Coordinate.} \qquad (2)$$

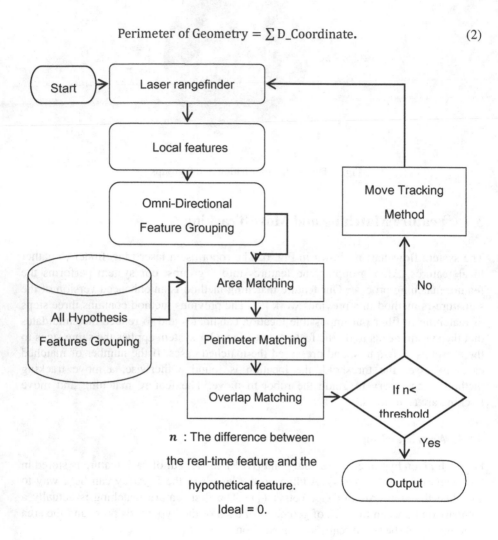

Fig. 6. System flowchart

3.3   Overlap Matching

The third feature is the overlap feature. To find which is the most possible direction of the robot (since the robot does not has a compass), the feature points will be rotated while matching. Since we have grouped the information of a laser rangefinder into d groups, the rotation range is defined as

$$\text{Rotation range} = \frac{360°}{d}. \tag{3}$$

The similarity is defined as the absolute value of the difference value of the length in RF_Array of each of the hypothesis point and the length in F_Array of the robot real-time information (4), where RF_Array is the rotation of F_Array of the hypothesis point.

$$\text{Similarity} = \sum_{i=0}^{T} |RF\_Array(i) - F\_Array(i)|. \tag{4}$$

T is the number of all the length information in the array.

3.4 Move Tracking Method

There are locations with similar or even identical information that the laser rangefinder will find. For example, the robot gets almost the same information at each corner. It is impossible to identify the location with feature matching. When there are several candidates need to be distinguished, the robot has to move and get new information.

The move tracking method will guide the robot to move to a safe position by commanding the robot move toward certain direction with certain distance. For example, as shown in Fig. 7, there are several possible candidate positions that the robot might be. The information that the laser rangefinder get, as shown in Fig. 8, can be represented as the histogram in Fig. 9. And we group every $20°$ as a sector; each sector has a character value which is defined by the smallest value, and the robot will find the sector with largest character value as new direction. Here we shoes $20°$ based on our experience, different angles are possible.

This approach helps the robot move to a safe place. Once the robot changes its position, it will gather new information and calculate new possible location. As shown in Fig. 10. Only points with consistent position will be preserved. Thus, we can delete impossible candidates and finally converge to one single location.

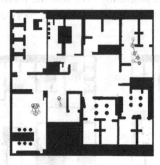

Fig. 7. The movement of robot

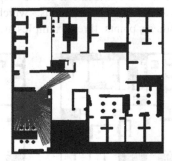

Fig. 8. The robot local information

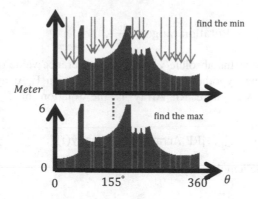

Fig. 9. Histogram of the laser rangefinder information, every 20°as a sector, the robot find the sector with largest value as new direction

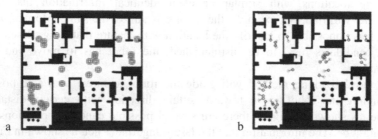

Fig. 10. (a) New hypothetical feature point(HFP). (b) Candidates.

4   Experiment

Consider a real world case; the input map will be like Fig. 2. The map shows a space with 18.5 meters long, 18.5 meters wide. The laser rangefinder is about 30 cm above the floor. Each of the following experiments is done in simulation 1000 times, each time a new robot location on the map is generated randomly. We test the method with several different resolutions, which is represented in the distance between two hypothesis points; three examples are shown in Fig. 11.

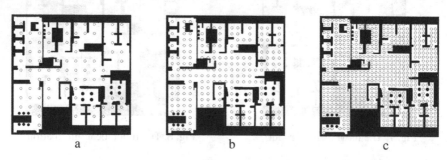

Fig. 11. Different resolution

Experiment 1 will test our method in a static environment. The termination criterion of our move tracking method is 15. That is, if the robot cannot converge to one location after moving 15 times, the algorithm will terminate and report fail.

4.1   Experiment 1: The Static Environment

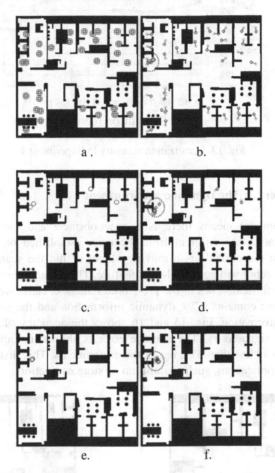

Fig. 12. Robot movement in the feature matching process

An example of move tracking method is shown in Fig. 12, from (a) to (f) where each movement will filter out some candidates and eventually converge to a correct point. Fig. 13 shows the average accuracy of finding correct location, out of 1000 tests, each test with a random position in the map. We can find that the accuracy is higher for a higher resolution (smaller distance between points).

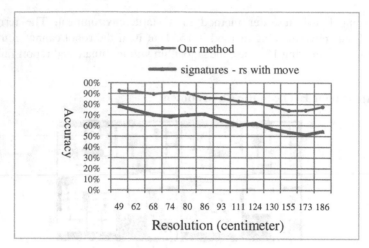

Fig. 13. Localization accurary in Experiment 1

4.2   Experiment 2: The Dynamic Environment

Dynamic environment means there is a new obstacle and the laser rangefinder scanning information are different from the prior established on the map, such as Fig. 14. Suppose the obstacle is a moving object within the scan area of the laser range-finder, the robot will get a real-time feature. The dynamic environment contains some dynamic information not in the pre-stored database. Here, we report 2 cases, in which the first one contains 2.7% dynamic information and the second one contains 22% dynamic information. Fig. 15 and 16 shows the accuracy of global location of our method and signature-rs. The average error is shown in Table 1. The average localization error is less than 37.2 cm in the experiments. This distance is acceptable for many robot applications, such as museum or store navigation.

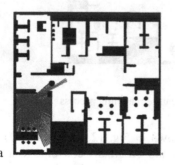
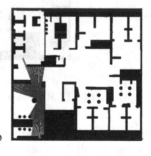

Fig. 14. a. An additional object appears at 434 cm. about 2.7% are affected. b. An additional object appears at 62 cm. about 22% are affected.

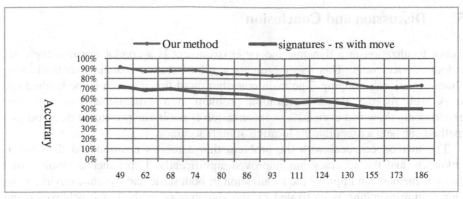

Fig. 15. Localization accurary in Experiment 2, with 2.7% dynamic information

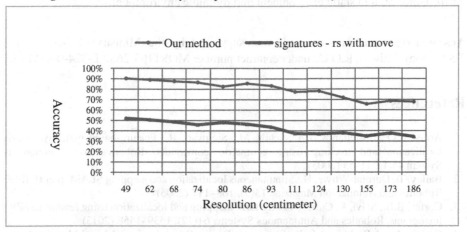

Fig. 16. Localization accurary in Experiment 2, with 22% dynamic information

Table 1. Average Error (cm) of Robot Localization in Dynamic Environments

Resolution	Distance of the obstacle object		Resolution	Distance of the obstacle object		Resolution	Distance of the obstacle object	
	434cm	62 cm		434cm	62cm		434cm	62cm
49cm	18.6	24.8	86cm	24.8	31	130cm	31	37.2
62cm	24.8	31	93cm	24.8	31	155cm	37.2	37.2
68cm	24.8	31	111cm	31	37.2	173cm	37.2	37.2
74cm	24.8	31	124cm	31	37.2	186cm	37.2	37.2
80cm	24.8	31						

5   Discussion and Conclusion

Robot localization in a dynamic indoor environment is a crucial research topic for indoor service robot. This paper presents a robust feature matching method using Omni-directional grouping. The main contribution of this research is the method can work well for the global localization problem in a dynamic environment. Our experiments show that even 22% of information is not in the pre-stored database; our method can help a robot find its location at high accuracy.

The method can deal with the problem that a robot's position and direction is unknown, and the accuracy has improved significantly. Experimental result shows that our method can improve the localization in both static and dynamic environment. Our feature matching is motivated by the signature-rs method, and achieves better performance both in static environment and dynamic environment.

Acknowledgement. This research was supported by the Ministry of Science and Technology, Taiwan, R.O.C., under contract number MOST103-2632-E-324-001-MY3.

References

1. Arras, K.O., Castellanos, J.A., Schilt, M., Siegwart, R.: Feature-based multi-hypothesis localization and tracking using geometric constraints. Robotics and Autonomous System 44(1), 41–53 (2003)
2. Bailey, T., Durrant-Whyte, H.: Simultaneous localization and mapping SLAM: part II. IEEE Robotics and Automation Magazine 13(3), 108–117 (2006)
3. Cortes, B.B., Salvi, J., Cufí, X.: Long-term mapping and localization using feature stability histograms. Robotics and Autonomous Systems 61(12), 1539–1558 (2013)
4. Corregedor, A.R., Meyer, J., Du Plessis, F.: Design Principles for 2D Local Mapping Using a Laser Rangefinder. In: IEEE Africon 2011 - The Falls Resort and Conference Centre, September 13-15, pp. 1–6 (2011)
5. Falomir, Z., Museros, L., Castelló, V., Gonzalez-Abril, L.: Qualitative distances and qualitative image descriptions for representing indoor scenes in robotics. Pattern Recognition Letters 34(7), 731–743 (2013)
6. Fox, D., Burgard, W., Thrun, S.: Markov Localization for Mobile Robots in Dynamic Environments. Journal of Artificial Intelligence Research 11, 391–427 (1999)
7. Hanzel, J., Kl'účik, M., Jurišica, L., Vitko, A.: Rangefinder models for mobile robots. Procedia Engineering 48, 189–198 (2012)
8. José, N., Tardós, J.D.: Data association in stochastic mapping using the joint compatibility test. IEEE Transactions on Robotics and Automation 17(6), 890–897 (2001)
9. Kar, A.: Linear-time robot localization and pose tracking using matching signatures. Robotics and Autonomous Systems 60(2), 296–308 (2012)
10. Lingemann, K., Nüchter, A., Hertzberg, J., Surmann, H.: High-speed laser localization for mobile robots. Robotics and Autonomous Systems 51(4), 275–296 (2005)
11. Li, Y., Li, S., Ge, Y.: A biologically inspired solution to simultaneous localization and consistent mapping in dynamic environments. Neurocomputing 104, 170–179 (2013)
12. Gerstmayr-Hillen, L., et al.: Dense topological maps and partial pose estimation for visual control of an autonomous cleaning robot. Robotics and Autonomous Systems 61(5), 497–516 (2013)

13. Luis, M., Garrido, S., Muñoz, M.L.: Evolutionary filter for robust mobile robot global localization. Robotics and Autonomous Systems 54(7), 590–600 (2006)
14. Martín, F., Moreno, L., Blanco, D., Muñoz, M.L.: Kullback–Leibler divergence-based global localization for mobile robots. Robotics and Autonomous Systems 62(2), 120–130 (2014)
15. Mirkhani, M., Forsati, R., Shahri, A.M., Moayedikia, A.: A novel efficient algorithm for mobile robot localization. Robotics and Autonomous Systems 61(9), 920–931 (2013)
16. Patrick, R., Angermann, M., Krach, B.: Simultaneous localization and mapping for pedestrians using only foot-mounted inertial sensors. In: Proceedings of the 11th International Conference on Ubiquitous Computing, pp. 93–96. ACM (2009)
17. Pinto, M., Sobreira, H., Paulo Moreira, A., Mendonça, H., Matos, A.: Self-localisation of indoor mobile robots using multi-hypotheses and a matching algorithm. Mechatronics 23(6), 727–737 (2013)
18. Sekmen, A., Challa, P.: Assessment of adaptive human–robot interactions. Knowledge-Based Systems 42, 49–59 (2013)
19. Siepmann, F., Ziegler, L., Kortkamp, M., Wachsmuth, S.: Deploying a modeling framework for reusable robot behavior to enable informed strategies for domestic service robots. Robotics and Autonomous Systems 62(5), 619–631 (2014)
20. Stephen, F., Pasula, H., Fox, D.: Voronoi Random Fields: Extracting Topological Structure of Indoor Environments via Place Labeling. IJCAI 7, 2109–2114 (2007)
21. Weiß, G., Wetzler, C., von Puttkamer, E.: Keeping Track of Position and Orientation of Moving Indoor Systems by Correlation of Range-Finder Scans. In: Proceedings of the IEEE/RSJ/GI International Conference on Intelligent Robots and Systems 94 Advanced Robotic Systems and the Real World, IROS 1994, pp. 595–601. IEEE (September 1994)
22. Durrant-Whyte, H., Bailey, T.: Simultaneous localization and mapping: part I. IEEE Robotics and Automation Magazine 13(2), 99–110 (2006)
23. Zhao, Y., Chen, X.: Prediction-based geometric feature extraction for 2D laser scanner. Robotics and Autonomous Systems 59(6), 402–409 (2011)

Multi-Stage Temporal Difference Learning for 2048

I-Chen Wu, Kun-Hao Yeh, Chao-Chin Liang, Chia-Chuan Chang, Han Chiang

Department of Computer Science, National Chiao Tung University, Hsinchu, Taiwan
{icwu,khyeh,chaochin,jimmy4834,passerby1023}@aigames.nctu.edu.tw

Abstract. Recently, Szubert and Jaskowski successfully used TD learning together with n-tuple networks for playing the game 2048. In this paper, we first improve their result by modifying the n-tuple networks. However, we observe a phenomenon that the programs based on TD learning still hardly reach large tiles, such as 32768-tiles (the tiles with value 32768). In this paper, we propose a new learning method, named multi-stage TD learning, to effectively improve the performance, especially for maximum scores and the reaching ratio of 32768-tiles. After incorporating shallow expectimax search, our 2048 program can reach 32768-tiles with probability 10.9%, and obtain the maximum score 605752 and the averaged score 328946. To the best of our knowledge, our program outperforms all the known 2048 programs up to date, except for the program developed by the programmers, nicknamed nneonneo and xificurk, which heavily relies on deep search heuristics tuned manually. The program can reach 32768-tiles with probability 32%, but ours runs about 100 times faster. Also interestingly, our new learning method can be easily applied to other 2048-like games, such as Threes. Our program for Threes outperforms all the known Threes programs up to date.

Keywords: Stochastic Puzzle Game, 2048, Threes!, Temporal Difference Learning, Expectimax.

1 Introduction

The puzzle game 2048 [7], a single-player stochastic game originated from 1024 [5] and Threes [6], has recently become very popular over the Internet. The author Gabriele Cirulli [11] claimed his estimation: the aggregated time of playing the game online by players during the first three weeks after released was over 3000 years. The game is intriguing and even addictive to human players, because the rule is simple but hard to win. Note that players win when reaching 2048-tiles, the tiles with the value 2048. For the same reason, the game also attracted many programmers to develop artificial intelligence (AI) programs to play it. In [17], the authors also thought that the game is an interesting testbed for studying AI methods.

Many methods was proposed to design AI programs in the past. Most commonly used methods were alpha-beta search [8][12], a traditional game search method for two-player games, and *expectimax search* [1], a common game search method for single-player stochastic games. Recently, Szubert and Jaskowski [17] proposed

S.-M. Cheng and M.-Y. Day (Eds.): TAAI 2014, LNAI 8916, pp. 366–378, 2014.
© Springer International Publishing Switzerland 2014

Temporal Difference (TD) learning together with *n-tuple networks* for the game. They successfully used it to reach a win rate (the ratio of reaching 2048-tiles) 97%, and obtain the averaged score 100,178 with maximum score 261,526. However, we observe a phenomenon: the TD learning method tends to maximize the average scores, but becomes less motivated to reach large tiles, such as 16384 or 32768.

In this paper, we first improve their result by modifying the n-tuple networks. However, we observe a phenomenon that the programs based on TD learning (together with n-tuple network still hardly reach 32768-tiles (the tiles with value 32768), even with the help of expectimax search.

Furthermore, we propose a new technique, named *multi-stage TD (MS-TD) learning*, to help reach large tiles more easily. In this learning method, we separate the training into multiple stages similar to those used in [4]. After incorporating shallow expectimax search, our 2048 program can reach 32768-tiles with probability 10.9%, and obtain the maximum score 605752, and the averaged score 328946.

To the best of our knowledge, our program outperforms all the known 2048 programs up to date, except for the one in [10], which heavily relies on deep search heuristics tuned manually. The program can reach 32768-tiles with probability 32%, but ours runs 300-1000 moves/second, about 100 times faster than theirs, 3-4 moves/second.

More interesting, our new learning method can be easily applied to other 2048-like games, such as Threes. Our program for Threes can reach 6144-tiles with probability 10%, which outperforms all the known Threes programs up to date and also won the champion in the 2048-bot tournament [18]. However, due to the limit of paper size, the research on Threes is omitted in this paper.

2 Background

This section reviews some backgrounds for this paper. First, introduce the rules of 2048. Second, we briefly review game tree search. Third, review TD learning, and discuss three different evaluation methods and n-tuple networks for 2048 proposed in [17].

2.1 Rules of 2048

The game 2048 is a single-player game that can be played on web pages and mobile devices with a 4x4 board, where each cell is either empty or placed with a tile labeled with a value which is a power of two. Let v-tile denote the tile with a value v. Initially, two tiles, 2- or 4-tiles, are placed on the board at random. In each turn, the player makes a move and then the game generates a new 2-tile with a probability of 9/10 or 4-tile with a probability of 1/10 on an empty cell chosen at random.

To make a move, the player chooses one of the four directions, up, down, left and right. Upon choosing a direction, all the tiles move in that direction as far as they can until they meet the border or there is already a different tile next to it. When sliding a tile, say v-tile, if the tile next to it is also a v-tile, then the two tiles will be merged into a larger tile, $2v$-tile. At the same time, the player gains $2v$ more points in the score. A move is legal if at least one tile can be moved.

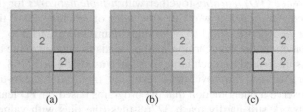

Fig. 1. Examples of 2048 boards

Consider an example, in which an initial board is shown in Fig. 1 (a). After making a move to right, the board becomes the one shown in Fig. 1 (b). Then, a new 2-tile is randomly generated as shown in Fig. 1 (c). The player can repeatedly make moves in this way.

A game ends when the player cannot make any legal move. The final score is the points accumulated during the game. The objective of the game is to accumulate as many points as possible. The game claims that the player wins when a 2048-tile is created, but still allow players to continue playing.

In a 2048-bot tournament held in [18], all the 2048-bot participants play 100 games. Their performances are graded by four factors, the win rates, the *largest tiles*, denoted by v_{max}-tiles, plus the reaching ratios of v_{max}-tiles, the average scores, and the maximum scores, in a formula described in [18].

2.2   Game Tree Search

A common game tree search algorithm used for 2048 bots is expectimax search [1]. Like most game tree search, the leaves are evaluated with values calculated by heuristic functions. An expectimax search tree contains two different nodes, max nodes and chance nodes. At a max node, its value is the highest value of its children nodes, if any. At a chance node, its value is the expected value of its children nodes, if any, each with a probability of instances.

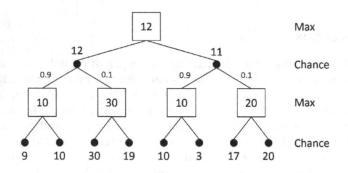

Fig. 2. An expectimax search tree

Consider the example shown in Fig. 2. For the left chance node of the root, its value is derived by calculating the expected value of its two children nodes: 0.9 * 10 + 0.1 * 30 = 12. For the right chance node of the root, its value is 11 which can be calculated in the same way. Thus, the root will choose the left and its value is 12.

Several features were used in heuristic functions for 2048-bot programs [10][21], and three of them are listed as follows. The first is the monotonicity of a board. Most high-ranked players might tend to play the game 2048 with tiles arranged decreasingly such as those described in [15]. The second is the number of empty tiles on board. The more empty tiles, the less likely for the game to end in a few steps. The third is the number of mergeable tiles, since it is a measure of the ability to create empty tiles by merging tiles of same values.

For game tree search, transposition table is a very important technique for speed-up. One common implementation is based on Z-hashing [23]. In Z-hashing, for each position, each possible tile is associated with a unique random number as a key. When looking up table, say 2048, the hash value is calculated by making an exclusive-or operation on 16 keys.

2.3   Temporal Difference (TD) Learning

Reinforcement learning is an important technique in training an agent to learn how to respond to the given environment [16]. *Markov decision process* (*MDP*) is a model commonly used in reinforcement learning, modeling the problems in which an agent interacts with the given environment through a sequence of actions according to the change of the state and the rewards, if any. In terms of MDP, an AI program for 2048-like game thus can be regarded as such an agent, which makes actions (legal moves) on board states and gets points as rewards.

Temporal difference (*TD*) *learning* [16][22], a kind of reinforcement learning, is a model-free method for adjusting state values from the subsequent evaluations. This method has been applied to computer games such as Backgammon [19], Checkers [13], Chess [2], Shogi [3], Go [14], Connect6 [22] and Chinese Chess [20]. TD learning has been demonstrated to improve world class game-playing programs in the two cases, TD-Gammon [19] and Chinook [14]. Since 2048-like games can be easily modeled as MDP, TD learning can be naturally applied to AI programs for 2048-like games.

In TD(0), the value function $V(s)$ is used to approximate the expected return of a state s. The error between states s_t and s_{t+1} is $\delta_t = r_{t+1} + V(s_{t+1}) - V(s_t)$, where r_{t+1} is the reward at turn $t+1$. The value of $V(s_t)$ in TD(0) is expected to be adjusted by the following value difference $\Delta V(s_t)$,

$$\Delta V(s_t) = \alpha \delta_t = \alpha\big(r_{t+1} + V(s_{t+1}) - V(s_t)\big) \tag{1}$$

where α is a step-size parameter to control the learning rate. For general TD(λ) (also see [22]), the value difference is

$$\Delta V(s_t) = \alpha\left((1-\lambda)\sum_{n=1}^{T-t-1}\lambda^{n-1}V(s_{t+n}) + \lambda^{T-t-1}V(s_T) - V(s_t)\right). \tag{2}$$

In this paper, only TD(0) is investigated.

In most applications, the evaluation function of states $V(s)$ can be viewed as a function of features, such as the monotonicity, the number of empty tiles, the number of mergeable tiles [10], mentioned in Subsection 2.2. Although the function was actually very complicated, it is usually modified into a linear combination of features [22] for TD learning, that is, $V(s) = \varphi(s) \cdot \theta$, where $\varphi(s)$ denotes a vector of feature occurrences in s, and θ denotes a vector of feature weights.

In order to correct the value $V(s_t)$ by the difference $\Delta V(s_t)$, we can adjust the feature weights θ by a difference $\Delta\theta$ based on $\nabla_\theta V(s_t)$, which is $\varphi(s_t)$ for linear TD(0) learning. Thus, the difference $\Delta\theta$ is

$$\Delta\theta = \Delta V(s_t)\varphi(s_t) = \alpha\delta_t\varphi(s_t) \tag{3}$$

TD Learning for 2048 In [17], Szubert and Jaskowaski proposed TD learning for 2048. A *transition* from turn t to $t+1$ is illustrated in Fig. 3 (below). They also proposed three kinds of methods of evaluating values for training and learning as follows.

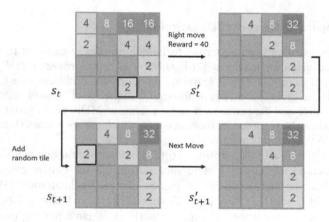

Fig. 3. Transition of board states

1. Evaluate actions. This method is to evaluate the function $Q(s, a)$, which stands for the expected values of taking an action a on a state s. For 2048, an action a is one of the four directions, up, down, left, and right. This is so-called *Q-learning*. In this case, the agent chooses a move with the highest expected score, as the following formula.

$$arg_a \max Q(s, a) \tag{4}$$

2. Evaluate states to play. This method is to evaluate the value function $V(s_t)$ on state s_t, the player to move. As shown in Fig. 3, this method evaluates $V(s_t)$ and $V(s_{t+1})$. The agent chooses a move with the highest expected score on s_t, as the following formula.

$$arg_a \max \left(R(s_t, a) + \sum_{s_{t+1}} P(s_t, a, s_{t+1})V(s_{t+1}) \right) \tag{5}$$

where $R(s_t, a)$ is the reward for action a on state s_t, and $P(s_t, a, s_{t+1})$ is the probability of turning into state s_{t+1} after taking action a on state s_t.

3. Evaluate states after an action. This method is to evaluate the value function $V(s'_t)$ on state s'_t, a state after an action, also called *after-states* in [17]. As shown in Fig. 3, this method evaluates $V(s'_t)$ and $V(s'_{t+1})$. The agent chooses a move with the highest expected score on s'_t, as the following formula.

$$arg_a max[R(s_t, a) + V(s'_t)]. \qquad (6)$$

In [17], their experiments showed that the third method clearly outperformed the other two. Therefore, in this paper, we only consider this method, evaluating after-states. For simplicity, states refers to after-states in the rest of this paper.

2.4   N-Tuple Network

In [17], they also proposed to use *N-tuple network* for TD learning of 2048. An n-tuple network consists of m n_i-tuples, where n_i is the size of the i-th tuple. As shown in Fig. 4, one 4-tuple covers four cells marked in red rectangular and one 6-tuple covers six cell marked in blue rectangular. Each tuple contributes a large number of features, each for one distinct occurrence of tiles on the covered cells. For example, the leftmost 4-tuple in Fig. 4 (a) includes 16^4 features, assuming that a cell has 16 occurrences, empty or 2-tile to 2^{15}-tile.

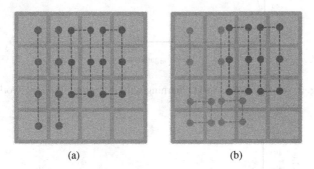

(a)   (b)

Fig. 4. (a) Tuples used in [17] and (b) tuples used in this paper

Based on TD learning, the expected score $V(s)$ is a linear summation of feature weights for all occurred features. For each tuple, since there is one and only one feature occurrence, we can simply use a lookup table to locate the feature weight. Thus, if the n-tuple network includes m different tuples, we need m lookups.

In [17], they used the tuples shown in Fig. 4 (a) as well as all of their rotated and mirrored tuples. All the rotated and mirrored tuples can share the same feature weights. Thus, the total number of features is roughly $2 \times 2^{16} + 2 \times 2^{24}$, about 32 million.

Their experiments showed that the tuples shown in Fig. 4 (a) outperformed all other n-tuple networks used in their experiments. The experimental results claimed in [17] include an average score of 100178 and a maximum score of 261526.

3   Our TD Learning Method for 2048

This paper designs our TD learning method for 2048 based on the method in [17]. In our method, we first change the n-tuple network in Subsection 3.1, and then propose MS-TD learning in Subsection 3.2. The experiments for MS-TD learning are described in Subsection 3.4 and some issues are discussed in Subsection 3.5.

3.1   New N-Tuple Network

In this paper, we use the tuples shown in Fig. 4 (b) as well as all of their rotated and mirrored tuples. In brief, we change 4-tuples (1x4 lines) to 6-tuples in a green knife shape as shown in Fig. 4 (a). Apparently, the new 6-tuples cover all the original 4-tuples. The number of features increases only by a factor of two or so.

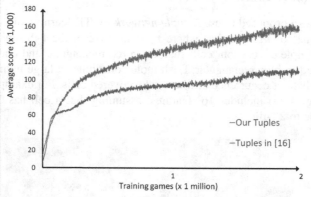

Fig. 5. Average scores in TD learning with different n-tuple networks

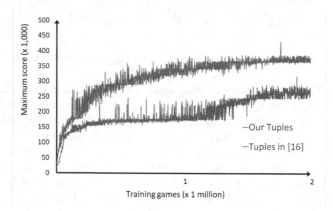

Fig. 6. Maximum scores in TD learning with different n-tuple networks

In our experiments, we further use a set of features representing large tiles, namely v-tiles, where $v \geq 2048$. These features are used to indicate difficulty due to large tiles. Our n-tuple network apparently outperforms the one used in [17] in terms of both average and maximum scores, as shown in Fig. 5 and Fig. 6 respectively. In these figures, the number of training games is up to 2 million and average/maximum scores in y axis are sampled every 1000 games. For simplicity of analysis, we use the n-tuple network in the rest of this paper.

3.2   MS-TD Learning

From above, TD learning is intrinsically to train and learn to obtain as high average (or expected) scores as possible, and the experiments also demonstrate this. However, TD learning does not necessarily lead to other criteria such as high maximum scores, high v_{max}, and the reaching ratios of v_{max}, though it does often.

From the experiences for 2048, we observed that it is hard to push to 32768-tiles or raise the reaching ratios of 32768-tiles from Fig. 6. However, for most players, earning the maximum scores and the largest tiles is a kind of achievement to players, and was also one of the criteria of the 2048-bot tournament [18].

In order to solve this issue, we propose *MS-TD learning* for 2048-like games. In this method, we divide the learning process into multiple stages. The technique of using multiple stages has been used to evaluate game states in [4] for Othello.

In our experiment, we divided the process into three stages with two important splitting times, marked as T_{16k} and T_{16+8k}, in games. T_{16k} denotes the first time when a 16384-tile is created on a board in a game, and T_{16+8k} denotes the first time when both 16384-tile and 8192-tile are created. The learning process with three stages is described as follows.

1. In the first stage, use TD learning to train the feature weights starting from the beginning, until the value function (expected score) is saturated. At the same time, collect all the boards at T_{16k} in the training games. Now, the set of trained feature weights are saved and called the *Stage-1 feature weights*.
2. In the second stage, use TD learning to train another set of feature weights starting from these collected boards in the first stage. At the same time, collect all the boards at T_{16+8k} in the training games. Again, the set of trained feature weights are saved and called the *Stage-2 feature weights*.
3. In the third stage, use TD learning to train another set of feature weights starting from these collected boards in the second stage. Again, the set of trained feature weights are saved and called the *Stage-3 feature weights*.

When playing games, we also divide it into three stages in the following way.
1. Before T_{16k}, use the Stage-1 feature weights to play.
2. After T_{16k} and before T_{16+8k}, use the Stage-2 feature weights to play.
3. After T_{16+8k}, use the Stage-3 feature weights to play.

The idea behind using more stages is to let learning be more accurate for all actions during the second or third stage, based on the following observation. The trained feature weights learned from the first stage (the same as the original TD learning) tend to perform well in the first stage, but may not in the rest of stages for the following reason. More large tiles in these stages increase the difficulty of playing the game, and therefore the feature weights cannot accurately reflect the expected scores with the difficulty. Thus, using another set of feature weights in the next stage makes it more likely for the feature weights to reflect the expected scores. In next subsection, the observation is justified in the experiments with significant improvements for 2048.

3.3   Experiments for MS-TD Learning

In the experiment for MS-TD learning, 5 million training games was run in each stage, and average and maximum scores are sampled every 1000 games.

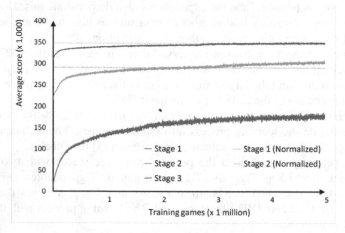

Fig. 7. Average scores in MS-TD learning

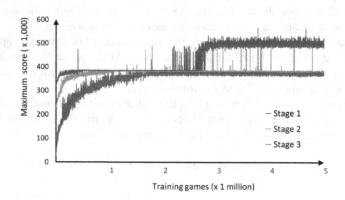

Fig. 8. Maximum scores in MS-TD learning

Fig. 7 shows the learning curves of average scores in the three stages. The learning curve of average scores in the first stage is marked in blue. However, the learning curves in the second and third stages need to be normalized for the purpose of comparisons, explained as follows. In the first stage, all the average scores includes those accumulated points before T_{16k}. In the second stage, if the average scores do not include those points before T_{16k}, then it is unfair for the second stage. However, if the average scores include those points before T_{16k}, it is unfair for the first stage since the average scores in the first stage include those failing to reach T_{16k} (the 16384-tile). For fair comparison, normalize the average scores in the first stage to a fixed value which is the average score of all the boards reaching T_{16k}. In addition, let the average scores in the second stage include those points before T_{16k}. Similarly, we also normalize average scores for the third stage in the same way.

In Fig. 7, the learning curve in the second stage, marked in orange, grows higher than the normalized of the first stage. This shows that the learning in the second stage does slightly improve over the first stage in terms of average scores. The learning curve in the third stage, marked in red, is nearly the same as the normalized of the second stage.

Fig. 8 shows the curves of maximum scores in the three stages. In this figure, the curve for the third stage does go up to 500,000 often, which actually indicate to reach 32,768-tiles. In contrast, the curves for the first and second stages rarely reach 32,768-tiles. This demonstrates that maximum scores can be significantly improved by using MS-TD learning.

3.4   Expectimax Search

Expectimax search fits after-states evaluation well. As described in Subsection 2.2, max nodes are the states, where players to move, and chance nodes are the after-states, where new tiles to be generated after moves. For TD learning, the learned after-state values can be used as the heuristic values of leaves. Thus, choosing the maximum after-state values can be viewed as expectimax search with depth one. Fig. 2 shows an example of expectimax search with depth 3. So, the depth for our expectimax search is an odd number. Then, we compare the performance results as follows.

Table 1. Result of 1000 games for TD learning

Depth Reaching ratio	1	3	5	7
2048	97.1%	99.9%	100.0%	100.0%
4096	88.9%	99.8%	100.0%	100.0%
8192	67.3%	96.9%	98.9%	98.5%
16384	18.1%	73.5%	80.7%	80.2%
32768	0.0%	0.0%	0.0%	0.0%
Maximum score	375464	385376	382912	382760
Average score	142727	282827	304631	302288

Table 2. Result of 1000 games for MS-TD learning

\Depth Reaching ratio\	1	3	5	7
2048	97.1%	99.9%	100.0%	100.0%
4096	88.9%	99.8%	100.0%	100.0%
8192	67.3%	96.9%	98.9%	98.5%
16384	18.1%	73.5%	80.7%	80.2%
32768	0.1%	9.4%	10.9%	4.6%
Maximum score	447456	536008	605752	581416
Average score	143473	310242	328946	313776

Table 1 shows the performance results of running 1000 games for the original TD learning in depths 1, 3, 5 and 7, respectively, while Table 2 shows those for MS-TD learning with three stages. Note that all the reaching ratios of all 16384-tiles and smaller tiles are the same, since both uses the same feature weights during the first stage. Besides, the comparisons between the two learning methods in the maximum scores and the average scores are shown in Fig. 9 and Fig. 10, respectively.

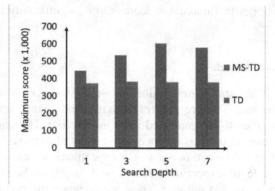

Fig. 9. Comparison of maximum scores

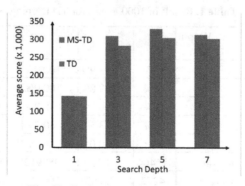

Fig. 10. Comparison of average scores

First, the results shows that the performance for MS-TD learning clearly outperforms that for the original TD learning. Especially, MS-TD learning significantly improves the maximum scores and the achieved ratios of 32768-tiles from 0% to 10.9%.

Second, the results also shows that the expectimax search in depth 5 performs the best, even better than the one with depth 7. The result shows that higher depths larger than 5 do not help much. Our observation is that the trained feature weights include noise which makes it less effective for deeper search.

From above, our 2048 program can reach 32768-tiles with probability 10.9%, the maximum score 605752, and the averaged score 328946. The program outperforms all the known 2048 programs up to date, except for the program in [10], which heavily relies on deep search heuristics tuned manually. Their program can reach 32768-tiles with probability 32%, but ours runs about 100 times faster.

3.5 Discussion

For MS-TD learning, an issue to discuss is what are the optimal number of stages and the splitting times. We did try several different kinds of stages by adding more splitting times. For example, add T_{8k}, the first time when a 8192-tile is created, and $T_{16+8+4k}$, the first time when all of 16384-tile, 8192-tile and 4096-tile are created. However, our experiments showed no better performance than the original three stages.

4   Conclusion

This paper proposes a new learning method, MS-TD (multi-stage TD) learning, which improves the performance effectively, especially for maximum scores and the reaching ratios of 32768-tiles. In our experiments, our 2048 program can reach 32768-tiles with probability 10.9%, the maximum score 605752, and the average score 328946. The program outperforms all the known 2048 programs up to date, except for the one in [10], which heavily relies on deep search heuristics tuned manually and runs about 100 times slower than ours.

Interestingly, MS-TD learning can be easily applied to other 2048-like games, such as Threes. Our program for Threes can reach 6144-tiles with probability 10%, which outperforms all the known Threes programs up to date and also won the champion in the 2048-bot tournament [18]. Furthermore, it is interesting and still open whether the method can be applied to other kinds of applications, such as non-deterministic two-player games, or even the planning applications, which can be separated into several stages.

Acknowledgement. The authors would like to thank Ministry of Science and Technology of the Republic of China (Taiwan) for financial support of this research under the contract numbers NSC 102-2221-E-009-069-MY2 and 102-2221-E-009-080-MY2, and the National Center for High-performance Computing (NCHC) for computer time and facilities.

References

[1] Ballard, B.W.: The *-Minimax Search Procedure for Trees Containing Chance Nodes. Artificial Intelligence 21, 327–350 (1983)

[2] Baxter, J., Tridgell, A., Weaver, L.: Learning to Play Chess Using Temporal Differences. Machine Learning 40(3), 243–263 (2000)

[3] Beal, D.F., Smith, M.C.: First Results from Using Temporal Difference Learning in Shogi. In: van den Herik, H.J., Iida, H. (eds.) CG 1998. LNCS, vol. 1558, pp. 113–125. Springer, Heidelberg (1999)

[4] Buro, M.: Experiments with Multi-ProbCut and a New High-Quality Evaluation Function for Othello. Games in AI Research, 77–96 (1997)

[5] Game 1024, http://1024game.org/

[6] Game Threes!, http://asherv.com/threes/

[7] Game 2048, http://gabrielecirulli.github.io/2048/

[8] Knuth, D.E., Moore, R.W.: An analysis of alpha-beta pruning. Artificial Intelligence 6, 293–326 (1975)

[9] Melko, E., Nagy, B.: Optimal Strategy in games with chance nodes. Acta Cybernetica 18(2), 171–192 (2007)

[10] Nneonneo and xificurk (nicknames), Improved algorithm reaching 32k tile, https://github.com/nneonneo/2048-ai/pull/27

[11] Overlan, M.: 2048 AI, http://ov3y.github.io/2048-AI/

[12] Pearl, J.: The solution for the branching factor of the alpha-beta pruning algorithm and its optimality. Communications of ACM 25(8), 559–564 (1982)

[13] Schaeffer, J., Hlynka, M., Jussila, V.: Temporal Difference Learning Applied to a High-Performance Game-Playing Program. In: Proceedings of the 17th International Joint Conference on Artificial Intelligence, pp. 529–534 (August 2001)

[14] Silver, D.: Reinforcement Learning and Simulation-Based Search in Computer Go, Ph.D. Dissertation, Dept. Comput. Sci., Univ. Alberta, Edmonton, AB, Canada (2009)

[15] StackOverflow.: What is the optimal algorithm for the game, 2048?, http://stackoverflow.com/questions/22342854/what-is-the-optimal-algorithm-for-the-game-2048/22674149#22674149

[16] Sutton, R.S., Barto, A.G.: Temporal-Difference Learning, An Introduction to Reinforcement Learning. MIT Press, Cambridge (1998)

[17] Szubert, M., Jaskowaski, W.: Temporal Difference Learning of N-tuple Networks for the Game 2048. In: IEEE CIG 2014 Conference (August 2014)

[18] Taiwan 2048-bot, http://2048-botcontest.twbbs.org/

[19] Tesauro, G.: TD-Gammon, a Self-Teaching Backgammon Program, Achieves Master-Level Play. Neural Computation 6, 215–219 (1994)

[20] Trinh, T., Bashi, A., Deshpande, N.: Temporal Difference Learning in Chinese Chess. In: Tasks and Methods in Applied Artificial Intelligence, pp. 612–618 (1998)

[21] Wu, K.C.: 2048-c, https://github.com/kcwu/2048-c/

[22] Wu, I.-C., Tsai, H.-T., Lin, H.-H., Lin, Y.-S., Chang, C.-M., Lin, P.-H.: Temporal Difference Learning for Connect6. In: van den Herik, H.J., Plaat, A. (eds.) ACG 2011. LNCS, vol. 7168, pp. 121–133. Springer, Heidelberg (2012)

[23] Zobrist, A.L.: A New Hashing Method With Application For Game Playing. Technical Report #88 (April 1970)

A Hybrid System for Temporal Relation Extraction from Discharge Summaries

Yueh-Lin Yang[1], Po-Ting Lai[2], and Richard Tzong-Han Tsai[3,*]

[1] Department of Computer Science and Engineering, Yuan Ze University,
Taoyuan, Taiwan
yuelin0324@gmail.com
[2] Department of Computer Science, National Tsing-Hua University, HsinChu, Taiwan
potinglai@gmail.com
[3] Department of Computer Science and Information Engineering, National Central
University, Taoyuan, Taiwan
thtsai@csie.ncu.edu.tw

Abstract. Automatically detecting temporal relations among dates/times and events mentioned in patient records has much potential to help medical staff in understanding disease progression and patients response to treatments. It can also facilitate evidence-based medicine (EBM) research. In this paper, we propose a hybrid temporal relation extraction approach which combines patient-record-specific rules and the Conditional Random Fields (CRFs) model to process patient records. We evaluate our approach on i2b2 dataset, and the results show our approach achieves an F-score of 61%.

Keywords: discharge summaries, conditional random fields, temporal relation extraction.

1 Introduction

Temporal information extraction (TIE), an important task in natural language processing (NLP), is the extraction of temporal relations among the events and dates/times found in plain text. TIE has been used for a variety of NLP applications in several domains. It is especially useful for processing patient records in the clinical domain. To improve TIE in the clinical domain, the Sixth Informatics for Integrating Biology and the Bedside (i2b2) NLP challenge [7] invites participants to develop TIE systems for processing patient records. The challenge released a dataset, which contains the TLINK, EVENT and TIMEX3 tags defined in TimeBank [4], and proposed three tracks: (1) EVENT/TIMEX3 track: recognize event and time expressions; (2) TLINK track: identify the temporal relations of the given EVENT and TIMEX3 tags; (3) End-to-End track: perform the above two tasks on raw discharge summaries. In this paper, we will focus on the TLINK track.

---

* Corresponding author.

S.-M. Cheng and M.-Y. Day (Eds.): TAAI 2014, LNAI 8916, pp. 379–386, 2014.

TLINK track systems usually use machine learning approaches such as Support Vector Machine (SVM) [6] and Maximum Entropy (ME) [1]. Some systems have used rule-based approaches [1]. Although generally rule-based approaches do not outperform machine learning [7], some linguistic rules can be especially useful in processing patient recordsfor example, a rule stating that an event in a patients hospital course section usually appears after the admission time and before the discharge time. In this paper, we explain an approach that combines linguistic rules and CRFs to carry out temporal information extraction.

2 Related Work

Chang et al. [1] proposed a hybrid method to identify TLink type. They combined a rule-based approach and an ME-based approach and developed an algorithm to integrate the results of the two approaches. Tang et.al. [8] divided the TLINK extraction task into three sub-tasks: 1. Identify TLinks between events and section time; 2. Identify TLinks between events/times within one sentence (sentence-internal TLinks); 3. Identify TLinks between events/times across sentences (cross-sentence TLinks). They built classifiers for each of the three categories of TLinks above. Then they applied event position information, bag-of-words, part-of-speech (POS) tags, dependency-related features, time-related features, event-related features, distance features and conjunction features. Their system, based on linear chain CRFs and the SVM model, achieved a F-score 69.32% in the TLINK-only track in the i2b2 2012 challenge.

3 Approaches

Our TLINK extraction approach includes a rule-based approach and a CRFs-based approach. The rule-based approach uses Tangs definition [8] to separate time-event and event-event pairs into three categories, including section-event, within-sentence, and cross-sentences pairs. According to the linguistic characteristics of these categories, our rule-based system assign TLink types to these pairs. Since some events/times are related to their surrounding event/times, we consider TLink extraction a sequence labeling problem and use the CRFs model to solve it.

3.1 Rule-Based Approach

We formulate TLink extraction as a relation-classification task. Given an event/time pair (i, j), which might be one of the event-event, time-event or section-event pairs, we need to determine the TLink type of this pair e.g., BEFORE, which means that i is before j. We use the predicate $TLink(i, j, tlink)$ to describe that i has the relation type $tlink$ for j, where $tlink \in$ {BEFORE, OVERLAP, AFTER, etc ...}. For example, $TLink(i, j, "AFTER")$ means that i occured after j.

Rule set 1: *Section-event Rules*

In patient records, we need to determine the TLink types between the events and identify the admission/discharge times. And we designed seven section-event rules (R.SE) to determine the TLink type of the section-event pair.

R.SE.1: $inHospitalCourseSection(s_i) \wedge inSentence(e_j, s_i)$
$\Rightarrow TLink(e_j, t_{admission}, "AFTER") \wedge TLink(e_j, t_{discharge}, "BEFORE")$

R.SE.2: $inClinicalHistorySection(s_i) \wedge inSentence(e_j, s_i)$
$\Rightarrow TLink(e_j, t_{admission}, "OVERLAP") \wedge TLink(e_j, t_{discharge}, "BEFORE")$

R.SE.3: $inAdmissionSection(s_i) \wedge inSentence(e_j, s_i)$
$\Rightarrow TLink(e_j, t_{admission}, "OVERLAP") \wedge TLink(e_j, t_{discharge}, "BEFORE")$

R.SE.4: $inDischargeSection(s_i) \wedge inSentence(e_j, s_i)$
$\Rightarrow TLink(e_j, t_{admission}, "AFTER") \wedge TLink(e_j, t_{discharge}, "OVERLAP")$

R.SE.5: $inOtherSection(s_i) \wedge inSentence(e_j, s_i)$
$\Rightarrow TLink(e_j, t_{admission}, "AFTER") \wedge TLink(e_j, t_{discharge}, "OVERLAP")$

R.SE.6: $inClinicalHistorySection(s_i) \wedge hasAdmissionKeyword(s_i)$
$\Rightarrow TLink(e_j, t_{admission}, "BEFORE") \wedge TLink(e_j, t_{discharge}, "BEFORE")$

R.SE.7: $inClinicalHistorySection(s_i) \wedge hasPastWord(s_i)$
$\Rightarrow TLink(e_j, t_{admission}, "BEFORE") \wedge TLink(e_j, t_{discharge}, "BEFORE")$

where s_i is the ith sentence, e_j is the jth event, $t_{admission}$ is the admission time, $inSentence(e_j, s_i)$ means the jth event is in the ith sentence, and $inHospitalCourseSection(s_i)$ means the s_i sentence is in hospital course section. The adminision keywords are "admission","admit" and "present". For instance, R.SE.1 means s_i is in hospital course section in the patient record and there is an event e_i in s_i. e_i will be $TLink(e_j, t_{admission}, "AFTER")$ and $TLink(e_j, t_{discharge}, "BEFORE")$.

Rule set 2: *Within-sentence Rules*

Events and times appearing in the same sentence are very likely to have the same TLink type. We developed five rules (R.WS) to classify their TLink types.

R.WS.1: $isEventType(e_i, "PROBLEM") \wedge$
$isEventType(e_j, "TREATMENT") \Rightarrow TLink(e_i, e_j, "AFTER")$

R.WS.2: $isEventType(e_i, "CLINICAL_DEPT") \wedge$
$isEventType(e_j, "TREATMENT") \Rightarrow TLink(e_i, e_j, "OVERLAP")$

R.WS.3: $isEventType(e_i, "PROBLEM") \wedge$
$isEventType(e_j, "TEST") \Rightarrow TLink(e_i, e_j, "BEFORE")$

R.WS.4: $isEventType(e_i, etype) \wedge$
$isEventType(e_j, etype) \Rightarrow TLink(e_i, e_j, "OVERLAP')$

R.WS.5: $inSentence(e, s_i) \wedge inSentence(t, s_i) \wedge$
$theNearestTime(e, t) \Rightarrow TLink(e, t, "OVERLAP")$

where $isEventType(e_i, "PROBLEM")$ means the e_i is the event type "PROBLEM", and $theNearestTime(e, t)$ means the time t is the nearest time to the event e.

Rule set 3: *Cross-sentence Rules*

Cross-sentence rules classify the TLink types of the event pairs which cross sentences. According to Tang et al. [8]'s observation, there are two main types of cross-sentence TLinks: (1) TLinks between main events in consecutive sentences, and (2) TLinks between events that are co-referenced. To resolve both cases, we designed three rules for consecutive sentences (R.CS) and one rule for co-referenced events (R.CR).

R.CS.1: $isEventType(e_i, \text{``}EVIDENTIAL\text{''}) \wedge isEventContain(e_i, \text{``report''})$
$\wedge\ isEventType(e_j, \text{``}PROBLEM\text{''}) \Rightarrow TLink(e_i, e_j.\text{``}AFTER')$

R.CS.2: $isEventType(e_i, \text{``}OCCURRENCE\text{''}) \wedge isEventContain(e_i, \text{``admission''}) \wedge isEventType(e_j, \text{``}TREATMENT\text{''}) \Rightarrow TLink(e_i, e_j, \text{``}AFTER\text{''})$

R.CS.3: $isEventType(e_i, etype) \wedge isEventType(e_j, etype)$
$\Rightarrow TLink(e_i, e_j, \text{``}OVERLAP\text{''})$

R.CR.1: $isCoreference(e_i, e_j)$
$\Rightarrow TLink(e_i, e_j, \text{``}OVERLAP\text{''})$

where; $isCoreference(e_i, e_j)$ means e_i and e_j have any word in common and are before/after one sentence with the same event type.

3.2   CRFs-Based approach

In the rule-based approach, once the event-time or event-event pair are matched by our rules, and they will be assigned the TLink types. The rules always assign the TLink type to each pair individually, and the dependency relation between the similar or near event/time are not considered. However, pairs are not wholly independent in following cases:

case i. Pair with the same time

case ii. Pair with the same event

We formulate the task of assigning TLink types to a series of pairs as a sequence labeling problem and solve it using CRFs. Pair with the same event/time in the same sentence are treated as a sequence in the order they appears in sentences. For example, if the order of the time and events in the sentence is $[e_1, t_1, e_2, e_3]$ and we will expand them into $\{(t_1, e_1), (t_1, e_2), (t_1, e_3)\}$; if the order of the events appear in the sentence is $[a, b, c, d]$ and we will expand them into $\{(a, b), (a, c), (a, d), (b, c), (b, d), (c, d)\}$

Conditional Random Fields

CRFs are undirected graphical models, in which each node represents a state that is trained to maximize a conditional probability [3]. A linear-chain CRF with parameters $\lambda = \{\lambda_1, \lambda_2, ...\}$ defines a conditional probability for a state sequence $y = y_1...y_n$ given a length-n input sequence $x = \{x_1, ..., x_n\}$ as follows:

$$p(y|x) = \frac{1}{Z(x)}\exp\sum_{c \in C} \sum_j \lambda_j h_j(y_c, x, c)$$
$$Z(x) = \sum_y \exp\sum_{c \in C} \sum_j \lambda_j h_j(y_c, x, c)$$

where $Z(x)$ is the normalization factor that ensures the probability of all state sequences sum to one, C is the set of all cliques in the target sentence, and c is any single clique. A clique is a fully connected subset of nodes. Note that $h_j(y_c, x, c)$ is usually a binary-valued feature function and λ_j is its weight. Large positive λ_j values indicate a preference for such an event, while large negative values make the event unlikely. The size of c determines which states h_j can refer to. If c contains only the current state, then h_j can only refer to the current state. However, if c contains the current and the previous states, then h_j can refer to all of them. We use the linear chain CRFs. Set C contains only current-state and current-and-previous state types. Given x, the conditional probability of y is equal to the exponential sum of $\lambda_j h_j$ in all cliques. The most probable label sequence for x,

$$y^* = argmax_y P_\lambda(y|x)$$

can be efficiently determined using the Viterbi algorithm [9]. The parameters can be estimated by maximizing the conditional probability of a set of label sequences, given each of their corresponding input sequences. The log-likelihood of a training set $\{(x^{(i)}, y^{(i)}) : i = 1, ..., M\}$ is written as: To optimize the parameters in CRFs, we use a quasi-Newton gradient-climber BFGS [5].

Features

We transform all rules used in the rule-based approach to CRF features. Feature set i corresponds to Rule set i.

Feature set 1: *Section-event Features*

The following are two examples of section-event features. The first feature is a unigram feature and refers to the pair y_i. The second one is a bigram feature and refers to y_i and y_{i-1}. For the admission and discharge times, we train different classifiers.

$$h_i(y_c, x, [i-1, i]) = \begin{cases} 1, & \text{if } R.SE.1(s_a, e_b, t_{admission}) \text{ and } y_i = B - AFTER \\ 0, & \text{otherwise} \end{cases}$$

$$h_i(y_c, x, [i-1, i]) = \begin{cases} 1, & \text{if } R.SE.1(s_a, e_b, t_{admission}) \text{ and } y_{i-1} = B - AFTER \\ & \text{and } y_i = I - AFTER \\ 0, & \text{otherwise} \end{cases}$$

Feature set 2: *Within-sentence Features*

The following are two examples of within-sentence features. The first refers to the pair y_i and the second refers to y_i and y_{i-1}:

$$h_i(y_c, x, [i-1, i]) = \begin{cases} 1, & \text{if } R.WS.1(e_a, e_b) \text{ and } y_i = B - AFTER \\ 0, & \text{otherwise} \end{cases}$$

$$h_i(y_c, x, [i-1, i]) = \begin{cases} 1, & \text{if } R.WS.1(e_a, e_b) \text{ and } y_{i-1} = B - AFTER \\ & \text{and } y_i = I - AFTER \\ 0, & \text{otherwise} \end{cases}$$

Feature set 3: *Cross-sentence Features*

The following are two examples of cross-sentence features. The first refers to the pair y_i and the second refers to y_i and y_{i-1}:

$$h_i(y_c, x, [i-1, i]) = \begin{cases} 1, & \text{if } R.CS.1(e_a, e_b) \text{ and } y_i = B - AFTER \\ 0, & \text{otherwise} \end{cases}$$

$$h_i(y_c, x, [i-1, i]) = \begin{cases} 1, & \text{if } R.CS.1(e_a, e_b) \text{ and } y_{i-1} = B - AFTER \\ & \text{and } y_i = I - AFTER \\ 0, & \text{otherwise} \end{cases}$$

4 Experiments

Dataset

We use the i2b2 2012 TLINK track dataset as our evaluation dataset. The dataset contains 190 patient history records in its training set and 120 patient history records in its test set.

Evaluation

The results are given as F-score and defined as $F = \frac{2 \times P \times R}{P+R}$, where P denotes the precision and R denotes the recall. The formulae for calculating P and R are as follows:

$P = \frac{\text{the number or correctly recognized TLink}}{\text{the number of recognized TLink}}$

$R = \frac{\text{the number or correctly recognized TLink}}{\text{the number of TLink}}$

Results

Table 1 shows the performance of our rule-based and CRFs-based approaches. The rule-based approach achieved an F-score 55% and the CRFs-based approach achieved an F-score 61%. Table 2 shows the performance of our CRFs-based approach on different relation pair categories. Our approach shows higher performance on event and time/section TLinks. It achieved an F-score of 80% for section-event pairs, which is the highest among all categories, and 67% for time-event pairs. Event-event pairs sometimes have no TLink; however, our approach fails to classify them into NULL. As a result, in the event-event category our system only achieved a precision of 33%. Our systems performance was worst in the coreference category (F-score 36%), likely because we have only one rule to classify coreference pairs.

Table 1. Performance of the rule-based and CRFs-based approaches on test set

Config.	Precision	Recall	F-score
Rule-based	0.66	0.47	0.55
CRFs-based	0.59	0.63	0.61

Table 2. Performance comparison of different temporal relation pair categories on test set

Relation Category	Precision	Recall	F-score
Event-sectime	0.88	0.73	0.80
Event-event	0.33	0.77	0.46
Event-time	0.62	0.75	0.67
Consecutive	0.68	0.46	0.55
Co-reference	0.32	0.42	0.36

5 Conclusion

We developed a hybrid TLink extraction system combining a rule-based approach and a CRFs-based approach to extract temporal relations in clinical records. In our rule-based approach, we define and apply a number of linguistic rules. Our CRFs-based approach divides the TLink extraction tasks into three sub-tasks and formulates them as sequence labeling problems. We use the above linguistic rules as features to solve these problems. We evaluate our system on the i2b2 2012 TLINK task dataset, and our results show that our approach achieves a F-score of 61%.

References

1. Chang, Y.-C., Dai, H.-J., Wu, J.C.-Y., Chen, J.-M., Tsai, R.T.-H., Hsu, W.-L.: TEMPTING system: A hybrid method of rule and machine learning for temporal relation extraction in patient discharge summaries. Journal of Biomedical Informatics 46(suppl.), S54–S60 (2013), 2012 i2b2 NLP Challenge on Temporal Relations in Clinical Data
2. Kovaevi, A., Dehghan, A., Filannino, M., Keane, J.A., Nenadic, G.: Combining rules and machine learning for extraction of temporal expressions and events from clinical narratives. Journal of the American Medical Informatics Association (2013)
3. Lafferty, J.D., McCallum, A., Pereira, F.C.N.: Conditional random fields: Probabilistic models for segmenting and labeling sequence data. In: Proceedings of the Eighteenth International Conference on Machine Learning, ICML 2001, pp. 282–289. Morgan Kaufmann Publishers Inc., San Francisco (2001)
4. Pustejovsky, J., Hanks, P., Sauri, R., See, A., Gaizauskas, R., Setzer, A., Radev, D., Sundheim, B., Day, D., Ferro, L., Lazo, M.: The TIMEBANK corpus. In: Proceedings of Corpus Linguistics 2003, Lancaster, pp. 647–656 (March 2003)

5. Sha, F., Pereira, F.: Shallow parsing with conditional random fields. In: Proceedings of the 2003 Conference of the North American Chapter of the Association for Computational Linguistics on Human Language Technology, NAACL 2003, pp. 134–141. Association for Computational Linguistics, Stroudsburg (2003)
6. Sohn, S., Wagholikar, K.B., Li, D., Jonnalagadda, S.R., Tao, C., Elayavilli, R.K., Liu, H.: Comprehensive temporal information detection from clinical text: medical events, time, and tlink identification. Journal of the American Medical Informatics Association 20(5), 836–842 (2013)
7. Sun, W., Rumshisky, A., Uzuner, O.: Evaluating temporal relations in clinical text: 2012 i2b2 challenge. Journal of the American Medical Informatics Association (2013), doi:10.1136/amiajnl-2013-001628
8. Tang, B., Wu, Y., Jiang, M., Chen, Y., Denny, J.C., Xu, H.: A hybrid system for temporal information extraction from clinical text. Journal of the American Medical Informatics Association 20(5), 828–835 (2013)
9. Viterbi, A.: Error bounds for convolutional codes and an asymptotically optimum decoding algorithm. IEEE Trans. Inf. Theor. 13(2), 260–269 (2006)

Tournament Selection Based Artificial Bee Colony Algorithm with Elitist Strategy[*]

Meng-Dan Zhang[1,2,3,4], Zhi-Hui Zhan[1,2,3,4,**], Jing-Jing Li[5], and Jun Zhang[1,2,3,4]

[1] Department of Computer Science, Sun Yat-sen University, China, 510275
[2] Key Lab. Machine Intelligence and Advanced Computing, Ministry of Education, China
[3] Engineering Research Center of Supercomputing Engineering Software, MOE, China
[4] Key Lab. Software Technology, Education Department of Guangdong Province, China
[5] School of Computer Science, South China Normal University, China
zhanzhh@mail.sysu.edu.cn

Abstract. Artificial bee colony (ABC) algorithm is a novel heuristic algorithm inspired from the intelligent behavior of honey bee swarm. ABC algorithm has a good performance on solving optimization problems of multivariable functions and has been applied in many fields. However, traditional ABC algorithm chooses solutions on the onlooker stage with roulette wheel selection (RWS) strategy which has several disadvantages. Firstly, RWS is suitable for maximization optimization problem. The fitness value has to be converted when solving minimization optimization problem. This makes RWS difficult to be generally used in real-world applications. Secondly, RWS has no any parameter that can control the selection pressure. Therefore, RWS is not easy to adapt to various optimization problems. This paper proposes a tournament selection based ABC (TSABC) algorithm to avoid these disadvantages of RWS based ABC. Moreover, this paper proposes an elitist strategy that can be applied to traditional ABC, TSABC, and any other ABC variants, so as to avoid the phenomenon that ABC algorithm may abandon the globally best solution in the scout stage. We compare the performance of traditional ABC and TSABC on a set of benchmark functions. The experiment results show that TSABC is more flexible and can be efficiently adapted to solve various optimization problems by controlling the selection pressure.

Keywords: Artificial bee colony (ABC) algorithm, roulette wheel selection, tournament selection, selection strategy, elitist strategy.

1 Introduction

With the development of optimization techniques, many heuristic algorithms play important roles in solving numeric and combinatorial optimization problems [1]-[3].

[*] This work was supported in part by the National High-Technology Research and Development Program (863 Program) of China No.2013AA01A212, in part by the National Natural Science Fundation of China (NSFC) with No. 61402545, the NSFC Key Program with No. 61332002, and the NSFC for Distinguished Young Scholars with No. 61125205.
[**] Corresponding author.

S.-M. Cheng and M.-Y. Day (Eds.): TAAI 2014, LNAI 8916, pp. 387–396, 2014.
© Springer International Publishing Switzerland 2014

Artificial Bee Colony (ABC) Algorithm is a novel swarm intelligence based algorithm introduced by Karaboga and Basturk to solve the optimization problem of multivariable functions [4]. Compared with Genetic Algorithm (GA) [5], Particle Swarm Optimization (PSO) [6] or some other population based algorithms, ABC algorithm has the faster convergence speed and the better ability to get out of a local optimal solution [4]. As a consequence, ABC algorithm attracts extensive attention and obtains rapid development in various fields.

Although ABC algorithm has good performances on optimization, there are still some insufficiencies in the selection strategy. In the onlooker bee stage of traditional ABC algorithm, an onlooker randomly chooses a food source with the probability value calculated from roulette wheel selection (RWS) strategy. However, compared with other selection strategies, RWS has two key disadvantages. Firstly, although RWS is a well-known random selection strategy according to the proportion of different components of a system, it is inconvenient when solving minimization problems because the fitness values have to be converted to make the smaller value has more probability to be chosen. Secondly, RWS has no adjustable parameters to adapt its selection pressure to different optimization problems. In order to improve the optimization ability of ABC algorithm, these two disadvantages should be avoided. In this paper, we propose to adopt tournament selection (TS) strategy in ABC to avoid the above two disadvantages. In the literatures, TS has been used in some optimization algorithms, such as Genetic Algorithm (GA), that shows good performance in population selection [7]. TS strategy can be applied easily in both minimization and maximization problems because it compares the fitness values to select better solutions. Moreover, TS strategy has a parameter λ (the proportion of solutions to be chosen) that can adjust selection pressure for various optimization problems. Therefore, the proposed TS based ABC (TSABC) algorithm can extend the generality of ABC algorithm. Another contribution of this paper is to design the elitist strategy to the standard ABC framework. Although ABC has been widely studied, it is strange that no literatures specifically claim that the ABC algorithm should not abandon the historically best solution that has found so far. On scout stage of ABC, the food source (solution) that cannot be improved for a certain generations will be abandoned. However, if the solution is the globally best one of the population, such abandon can make the ABC algorithm deteriorated. In order to avoid such bad influence on optimization, we propose the elitist strategy to ABC. This strategy uses an extensive archive to keep the historically best solution during the running. This solution is not in the ABC population, but is updated in every generation if the globally best solution of the population is better than this solution. Therefore, even though the scout stage may abandon the globally best solution of the population (e.g., it has not improved for a long time), the historically best solution won't be abandoned. This is only a slight change to the ABC framework. It not only has no negative influences on the performance, but also can be applied to any ABC variants, which can be considered as a standard component in the ABC algorithmic framework.

This paper aims to improve ABC algorithm with TS strategy and compare its performance with that with RWS. Also, the optimization ability of TSABC algorithm is analyzed under the change of control parameter values. The rest of the paper is structured as follows. Section 2 introduces ABC algorithm and its current development. The TSABC algorithm and the experimental results are presented in Section 3 and Section 4, respectively. Finally, conclusions are given in Section 5.

2   ABC Algorithm

2.1   Algorithm Framework

Inspired from the intelligent foraging behavior of honey bee swarm, ABC algorithm searches the optimal solutions with three groups of bees: employed bees, onlookers, and scouts. In the algorithm, one half of the colony consists of the employed bees, and the other half constitutes the onlookers. There is only one employed bee for each food source. Employed bees search available food sources and measure their nectar amounts, then change the food information with onlookers waiting on the dance area. The employed bee whose food source is exhausted will abandon the previous one and become a scout to search for a new food source.

In ABC algorithm, the position of a food source represents a possible solution to the optimization problem. The nectar amount is corresponded to the quality of the associated solution. In the initial phase, SN solutions are generated randomly, where SN denotes the size of population. And the number of employed bees or onlookers is equal to the number of solutions. Each solution is a D-dimensional vector. The initial solutions are randomly generated with the equation as follows:

$$x_{i,j} = x_{\min,j} + rand\,(0,1)\big(x_{\max,j} - x_{\min,j}\big)\qquad(1)$$

where $i = 1, 2, \ldots, SN$, $j = 1, 2, \ldots, D$, $x_{\min,j}$ and $x_{\max,j}$ are the lower and upper bounds of dimension j respectively.

After initialization, the population of the solutions is subjected to repeat cycles. An employed bee searches around the position in her memory to find a new food source and measure its nectar amount. Comparing the nectar amount of the new food source with that of the previous one, employed bee would memory the new position and forget the old one if the quality of the new position is better. Otherwise, employed bee keeps the information of the previous position. The employed bees produce a candidate food position from the old one as:

$$v_{i,j} = x_{i,j} + \phi_{i,j}\big(x_{i,j} - x_{k,j}\big)\qquad(2)$$

where $\phi_{i,j}$ is a random number between $[-1,1]$, $k \in \{1,2,\ldots,SN\}$ and $j \in \{1,2,\ldots,D\}$ are chosen randomly. Here k has to be different from i. If the value of $v_{i,j}$ exceeds the bound $[x_{\min,j}, x_{\max,j}]$, it can be set to an accept value. For instance, the value of the parameter exceeding can be set to its limit value.

On the dance area, an onlooker evaluates the nectar information taken by employed bees and chooses a food source with a probability related to its nectar amount. The probability p_i is calculated as follows:

$$p_i = \frac{fit_i}{\sum\limits_{n=1}^{SN} fit_n}\qquad(3)$$

where fit_i presents the fitness value of the solution i which is calculated by its employed bee and proportional to the nectar amount of the food source. It is observed that the position with better quality has more probability to be chosen. After choosing a food source, an onlooker searches the neighboring area of the source by Eq. (2) to generate a new candidate solution. Similar to the employed bee, if the new solution is better than the source, the source is replaced by the new solution. All the onlookers do similar work to explore new solutions for the sources.

In ABC algorithm, if a position cannot be improved through a predetermined number of cycles, which called *limit*, that food source has to be abandoned. Then the employed bee related to that position becomes a scout and searches a new food source randomly to replace the old one.

Above are the search processes of employed bees, onlookers, and scouts. The framework of ABC algorithm is described in Fig. 1.

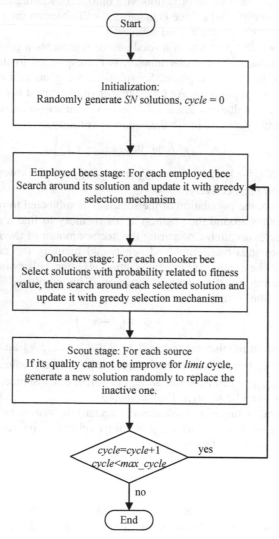

Fig. 1. Framework of ABC algorithm

2.2   Current Development of ABC

The ABC algorithm is introduced by Karaboga and Basturk in 2005. Because of its simplicity and ease of implementation, ABC algorithm has attracted more and more attentions. To make advances of ABC, many scholars do various researches from different aspects. One of the research trends is studying the search equation [8][9][10]. Inspired by PSO, Zhu and Kwong [8] proposed a gbest-guided ABC (GABC) algorithm which can incorporate the information of globally best solution into the solution search equation. Although improving the exploitation of the algorithm, GABC may cause an oscillation because of the guidance of two terms in the search equation. So on this basis, Gao et al. [9] presented a CABC algorithm which randomly chooses a solution instead of the current solution to compose the search equation. In CABC algorithm, the modified search equation can bring more information and produce an appropriate candidate solution to balance exploration and exploitation.

By now, ABC algorithm has been wildly applied to solve many problems. Karaboga [11] designed infinite impulse response (IIR) filters with ABC algorithm. Singh [12] applied ABC algorithm for the leaf-constrained minimum spanning tree (LCMST) problem. Rao et al. [13] used ABC algorithm to solve the distribution system loss minimization problem which showed that ABC has good performance in the quality of solution and computation efficiency. Furthermore, ABC algorithm has also been applied in many other fields, such as the lot-streaming flow shop scheduling problem [14], and training of neural network [15].

3   TSABC

In ABC algorithm, an onlooker selects one of the food sources after changing information with employed bees on dance area. This selection process influences the convergence speed and optimization ability of the algorithm. Low selection pressure (more solutions can be selected) may result in the ability to explore wide regions in the solution space to discover the global optimum, but is deficient in the rate of convergence. On the other hand, although high pressure (give more chance to better solutions) may perform well in convergence, it makes the search of solution restrained in a small region. Therefore, selection pressure should be properly adjusted under different optimization situations to keep the balance between exploration and exploitation. Traditional ABC algorithm is insufficient in adjusting selection pressure since RWS strategy has no parameter. TSABC uses TS strategy to select solutions on the onlooker stage. The process of TS is as follows:

Step.1 Determine the proportion of solutions to be chosen λ $(0 < \lambda < 1)$.

Step.2 Choose λSN solutions randomly, where SN is the number of food sources.

Step.3 Compare their fitness value and select the best one for an onlooker to generate a candidate solution and memory the one with better fitness value.

Step.4 Repeat step. 2 and step. 3 for SN times, where SN also presents the number of onlookers.

With the parameter λ, TSABC can adjust selection pressure flexibly under different optimization problems. On the other hand, RWS strategy has to be converted when solving minimum optimization problems. According to Eq. (3), the fitness value fit_i should be changed to its reciprocal or be switched within other functions which can make the solution with smaller value has more chances to be chosen. On the contrary, TS strategy is convenient and flexible for both minimum and maximum problems.

4   Experimental Studies

In order to evaluate the performance of TSABC algorithm, thirteen benchmark functions are used herein. These functions are described in Table 1. Each of them is 30-dimension function. $f_1(x)$ to $f_7(x)$ are unimodal functions while $f_8(x)$ to $f_9(x)$ are multimodal functions.

Table 1. Benchmark functions

Benchmark functions	Dimension	Domain	Min	Accepted value
$f_1(x)=\sum_{i=1}^{n}x_i^2$	30	[-100.100]	0	1.00E-06
$f_2(x)=\sum_{i=1}^{n}\|x_i\|+\prod_{i=1}^{n}\|x_i\|$	30	[-10,10]	0	1.00E-06
$f_3(x)=\sum_{i=1}^{n}\left(\sum_{j=1}^{i}x_j\right)^2$	30	[-100,100]	0	500
$f_4(x)=\max_i\{\|x_i\|,1\le i\le n\}$	30	[-100,100]	0	0.01
$f_5(x)=\sum_{i=1}^{n-1}\left[100\left(x_{i+1}-x_i^2\right)^2+\left(x_i-1\right)^2\right]$	30	[-30,30]	0	0.01
$f_6(x)=\sum_{i=1}^{n}\left(\lfloor x_i+0.5\rfloor\right)^2$	30	[-100,100]	0	0
$f_7(x)=\sum_{i=1}^{n}ix_i^4+random[0,1)$	30	[-1.28,1.28]	0	0.01
$f_8(x)=\sum_{i=1}^{n}-x_i\sin\left(\sqrt{\|x_i\|}\right)$	30	[-500,500]	-12569.5	-12569
$f_9(x)=\sum_{i=1}^{n}\left[x_i^2-10\cos\left(2\pi x_i\right)+10\right]$	30	[-5.12,5.12]	0	1.00E-06
$f_{10}(x)=-20\exp\left(-0.2\sqrt{\frac{1}{n}\sum_{i=1}^{n}x_i^2}\right)-\exp\left(\frac{1}{n}\sum_{i=1}^{n}\cos 2\pi x_i\right)+20+e$	30	[-32,32]	0	1.00E-06
$f_{11}(x)=\frac{1}{4000}\sum_{i=1}^{n}x_i^2-\prod_{i=1}^{n}\cos\left(\frac{x_i}{\sqrt{i}}\right)+1$	30	[-600,600]	0	1.00E-06
$f_{12}(x)=\frac{\pi}{n}\left\{10\sin^2\left(\pi y_i\right)+\sum_{i=1}^{n-1}(y_i-1)^2\left[1+10\sin^2\left(\pi y_{i+1}\right)\right]+(y_n-1)^2\right\}+\sum_{i=1}^{n}u(x_i,10,100,4)$ $y_i=1+\frac{1}{4}(x_i+1),u(x_i,a,k,m)=\begin{cases}k(x_i-a)^m,x_i>a,\\0,-a\le x_i\le a,\\k(-x_i-a)^m,x_i<-a.\end{cases}$	30	[-50,50]	0	1.00E-06
$f_{13}=0.1\left\{\sin^2\left(3\pi x_i\right)+\sum_{i=1}^{n-1}(x_i-1)^2\left[1+\sin^2\left(3\pi x_{i+1}\right)\right]+(x_n-1)^2\left[1+\sin^2\left(2\pi x_n\right)\right]\right\}+\sum_{i=1}^{n}u(x_i,5,100,4)$	30	[-50,50]	0	1.00E-06

To avoid interference from other influencing factors, all experiments were run for 300,000 function evaluations and each of them was repeated 30 times independently. The population size SN is 50, and the parameter *limit* is set as 1000. In addition, elitist strategy is applied in both ABC and TSABC algorithm. The experiments were divided into two parts. The first part is optimizing the benchmark functions by TSABC algorithm and comparing their optimal solutions under different values of parameter λ in the TS strategy. The other part is the optimizations of benchmark functions by traditional ABC algorithm and comparing them with the experiment results of TSABC algorithm.

In the experiment of TSABC algorithm, the proportion of solutions (λ) is set as 0.02, 0.1, 0.2, 0.4, 0.6, 0.8, and 0.9, respectively. The experiments are proceeded independently and the results are showed in Table 2 and Table 3, where the **bold** values is the minimum values in each function column, *avg* and *SD* present the average of fitness values and the standard deviation in 30 times respectively. It can be concluded from the experiment result that for different benchmark functions, the best results are obtained by TSABCs that use different values of λ. That is to say, different functions should be optimized with different selection pressure. In TSABC algorithm, we can control the selection pressure through determining different proportions of solutions (λ) in the TS strategy.

Table 2. Comparison among different value of parameter λ in tournament selection strategy with benchmark functions ($f_1(x) - f_7(x)$)

λ		$f_1(x)$	$f_2(x)$	$f_3(x)$	$f_4(x)$	$f_5(x)$	$f_6(x)$	$f_7(x)$
0.02	avg	**9.70E-47**	**2.15E-24**	4653.3	0.787244	0.0780279	0	0.0329599
	SD	**8.70E-47**	**9.70E-25**	943.819	0.118832	0.108088	0	0.00681458
0.1	avg	1.79E-37	9.57E-20	2136.7	0.102241	**0.0484923**	0	0.0172999
	SD	1.54E-37	3.73E-20	479.985	0.023434	0.0703702	0	0.00451125
0.2	avg	6.88E-34	5.97E-18	1302.43	0.0512829	0.0646095	0	0.0135199
	SD	7.01E-34	3.83E-18	412.324	0.00898793	0.142791	0	0.00400185
0.4	avg	3.06E-31	1.00E-16	666.061	0.0292305	0.0899865	0	0.00810017
	SD	4.92E-31	5.05E-17	219.095	0.00804453	0.206365	0	0.0026816
0.6	avg	3.32E-30	4.93E-16	452.737	0.0231311	0.0511788	0	0.00536595
	SD	2.76E-30	3.31E-16	194.462	**0.00465257**	**0.0677494**	0	0.00184911
0.8	avg	2.07E-29	1.30E-15	411.615	0.0230305	0.105486	0	0.0047305
	SD	1.57E-29	8.60E-16	172.012	0.00592132	0.164903	0	0.00180727
0.9	avg	9.71E-29	1.62E-15	**315.263**	**0.0223896**	0.182286	0	**0.00455137**
	SD	1.60E-28	5.77E-16	**143.722**	0.005066	0.243687	0	**0.00150967**

Table 3. Comparison among different values of parameter λ in tournament selection strategy with benchmark functions $(f_8(x) - f_{13}(x))$

λ		$f_8(x)$	$f_9(x)$	$f_{10}(x)$	$f_{11}(x)$	$f_{12}(x)$	$f_{13}(x)$
0.02	avg	-12569.5	0	**7.55E-15**	0	**1.57E-32**	**1.35E-32**
	SD	2.48E-12	0	**0**	0	**8.35E-48**	**5.57E-48**
0.1	avg	-12569.5	0	1.39E-14	0	1.57E-32	1.35E-32
	SD	**2.19E-12**	0	1.45E-15	0	8.35E-48	5.57E-48
0.2	avg	-12569.5	0	2.21E-14	0	1.57E-32	3.53E-32
	SD	2.34E-12	0	3.89E-15	0	8.35E-48	8.81E-32
0.4	avg	-12569.5	0	3.27E-14	0	1.79E-30	9.14E-29
	SD	2.55E-12	0	5.10E-15	0	6.58E-30	4.91E-28
0.6	avg	-12569.5	0	4.64E-14	0	2.67E-30	2.43E-28
	SD	2.68E-12	0	1.29E-14	0	1.15E-29	6.84E-28
0.8	avg	-12569.5	0	7.16E-14	0	1.61E-27	4.39E-25
	SD	3.04E-12	0	2.58E-14	0	5.76E-27	2.39E-24
0.9	avg	-12569.5	0	8.27E-14	0	6.48E-28	1.69E-24
	SD	2.74E-12	0	2.85E-14	0	1.97E-27	7.44E-24

In the comparative experiment of RWS and TS, the Eq. (3) has to be switched because the benchmark functions are all the minimum optimization problems. In this paper, the switch function is as follows:

$$f_i = \frac{1}{fit_i - OPT + 1}, \tag{4}$$

where fit_i is the fitness value of the solution i, and OPT presents the minimum value of the problem. In this work, the minimum value of the benchmark functions have already been given. If the minimum value is unknown, we can set the optimal value that has been found so far as OPT. Then the selection Eq. (3) becomes:

$$p_i = \frac{f_i}{\sum\limits_{n=1}^{SN} f_n}. \tag{5}$$

It can be seen that roulette wheel selection based ABC algorithm is inconvenient when solving minimum optimization problems since the switch function has to be designed under different situations. Within Eqs. (4) and (5), the optimizations of benchmark functions by ABC algorithm are showed in Table 4, which also displays the experiment results of TSABC algorithm with $\lambda = 0.05$.

According to the data in Table 4, we can notice that the optimization results by ABC are almost same with that of TSABC under $\lambda = 0.05$. That is to say, roulette wheel selection strategy and tournament selection with $\lambda = 0.05$ produce the same level of selection pressure. This selection pressure may have good performances in solving some optimization problems, but there are still many other problems which need less or more selection pressure to reach the optimal result. However, roulette wheel selection based ABC algorithm has no adjustable parameters to control it.

In this way, tournament selection based ABC algorithm has more adaptability for various optimization problems and can be applied easily in both minimum and maximum optimizations.

Table 4. Optimizations of ABC algorithm and TSABC algorithm with $\lambda = 0.05$

Function	Roulette wheel selection			Tournament selection (λ=0.05)		
	avg	SD	avgFES	avg	SD	avgFES
f_1	3.91E-43	5.08E-43	52376	1.06E-43	1.14E-43	59140
f_2	1.05E-23	4.64E-24	102296	6.39E-23	2.51E-23	89383
f_3	3254.14	929.843	-	3614.27	634.464	-
f_4	0.583742	0.169694	-	0.340325	0.0652423	-
f_5	0.0242212	0.028179	217184	0.0796629	0.150301	208400
f_6	0	0	11230	0	0	28800
f_7	0.0312633	0.00682426	-	0.0281961	0.00804064	278200
f_8	-12569.5	2.03E-12	103856	-12569.5	2.11E-12	122890
f_9	0	0	84203	0	0	104443
f_{10}	7.67E-15	6.49E-16	108773	1.00E-14	2.49E-15	104423
f_{11}	0.000246535	0.00135033	82875	0	0	72593
f_{12}	1.57E-32	8.35E-48	43533	1.57E-32	8.35E-48	49766
f_{13}	1.35E-32	5.57E-48	56303	1.35E-32	5.57E-48	57413

5   Conclusions

In this paper, we proposed a tournament selection based ABC (TSABC) algorithm and compared its performance with traditional ABC algorithm. Comparative experiments have been conducted on 13 benchmark functions. In the experiment, we applied elitist strategy to keep the historically optimal solution. This method can prevent the abandon of the best solution that has been found so far. The experimental results show that the TS strategy can be applied flexibly in both minimum and maximum optimization, and can adjust selection pressure for different optimization problems. Moreover, TSABC is easy for implementation for that TS strategy does not need to calculate the select probability of each solution.

References

[1] Pham, D.T., Karaboga, D.: Intelligent Optimisation Techniques. Springer, London (2000)

[2] Zhan, Z.H., Li, J., Cao, J., Zhang, J., Chung, H., Shi, Y.H.: Multiple populations for multiple objectives: A coevolutionary technique for solving multiobjective optimization problems. IEEE Trans. Cybern. 43(2), 445–463 (2013)

[3] Shen, M., Zhan, Z.H., Chen, W.N., Gong, Y.J., Zhang, J., Li, Y.: Bi-velocity discrete particle swarm optimization and its application to multicast routing problem in communication networks. IEEE Trans. Ind. Electron 61(12), 7141–7151 (2014)

[4] Karaboga, D., Basturk, B.: A powerful and efficient algorithm for numerical function optimization: artificial bee colony (ABC) algorithm. Journal of Global Optimization 39(3), 459–471 (2007)

[5] Ting, C.K., Lee, C.N., Chang, H.C., Wu, J.S.: Wireless heterogeneous transmitter placement using multiobjective variable-length genetic algorithm. IEEE Trans. Systems, Man, and Cybernetics–Part B: Cybernetics 39(4), 945–958 (2009)

[6] Li, Y.H., Zhan, Z.H., Lin, S., Zhang, J., Luo, X.N.: Competitive and cooperative particle swarm optimization with information sharing mechanism for global optimization problems. Information Sciences 239(1), 370–382 (2015)

[7] Zhang, C., Zhan, Z.H.: Comparisons of selection strategy in genetic algorithm. Computer Engineering and Design 30(23), 5471–5478 (2009)

[8] Zhu, G.P., Kwong, S.: Gbest-guided artificial bee colony algorithm for numerical function optimization. Applied Mathematics and Computing 217(7), 3166–3173 (2010)

[9] Gao, W.F., Liu, S.Y., Huang, L.L.: A novel artificial bee colony algorithm based on modified search equation and orthogonal learning. IEEE Transaction on Cybernetics 43(3) (June 2013)

[10] Banharnsakun, A., Achalakul, T., Sirinaovakul, B.: The best-so-far selection in artificial bee colony algorithm. Applied Soft Computing 11(2), 2888–2901 (2011)

[11] Karaboga, N.: A new design method based on artificial bee colony algorithm for digital IIR filters. Journal of The Franklin Institute 346(4), 328–348 (2009)

[12] Singh, A.: An Artificial bee colony algorithm for the leaf-constrained minimum spanning tree problem. Applied Soft Computing 9(2), 625–631 (2009)

[13] Rao, R.S., Narasimham, S., Ramalingaraju, M.: Optimization of distribution network configuration for loss reduction using artificial bee colony algorithm. In: Proc. International Conference on Advances in Mechanical Engineering, pp. 116–122 (2008)

[14] Pan, Q.K., Tasgetiren, M.F., Suganthan, P.N., Chua, T.J.: A discrete artificial bee colony algorithm for the lot-streaming flow shop scheduling problem. Information Sciences 181(12), 2455–2468 (2011)

[15] Karaboga, D., Akay, B., Ozturk, C.: Artificial bee colony (ABC) optimization algorithm for training feed-forward neural networks. In: Torra, V., Narukawa, Y., Yoshida, Y. (eds.) MDAI 2007. LNCS (LNAI), vol. 4617, pp. 318–329. Springer, Heidelberg (2007)

Author Index